COBRA II

COBRA II

THE INSIDE STORY OF THE
INVASION AND OCCUPATION OF IRAQ

Michael R. Gordon and
General Bernard E. Trainor

PANTHEON BOOKS   NEW YORK   2006

Library of Congress Cataloging-in-Publication Data
Gordon, Michael R., [date].
   Cobra II: the inside story of the invasion and occupation of Iraq / Michael R. Gordon and Bernard E. Trainor.
      p. cm.
Includes index.
ISBN 0-375-42262-5
   1. Iraq War, 2003– I. Title: Cobra two. II. Trainor, Bernard E., 1928– III. Title.

DS79.76.G67 2006
956.7044'3—dc22   2005051841

www.pantheonbooks.com

Printed in the United States of America
First Edition
2 4 6 8 9 7 5 3 1

To the courageous men and women of the armed forces

In July 1944, General George Patton led the Third Army breakout from Normandy to liberate France. It was called Operation Cobra. Almost sixty years later, another Third Army commander, Lieutenant General David McKiernan, sought to evoke the illustrious episode. He named the drive to Baghdad Cobra II.

Wars must vary with the nature of their motives and of the situation which gives rise to them. The first, the supreme, the most far-reaching act of judgment that the statesman and the commander have to make is to establish by that test the kind of war on which they are embarking; neither mistaking it for, nor trying to turn it into, something alien to its nature. This is the first of all strategic questions and the most comprehensive.

—*On War,* Carl von Clausewitz

Contents

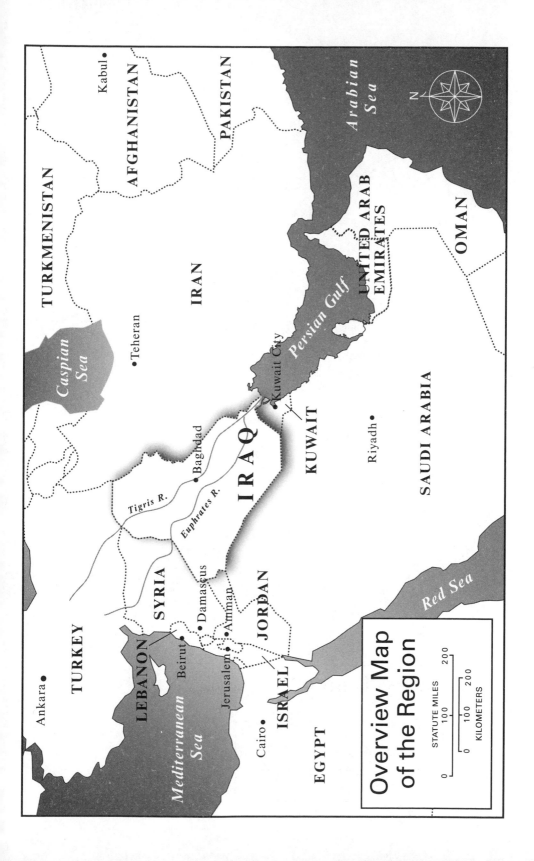

Overview Map
of the Region

TURKEY

SYRIA

IRAN

Kurdish-controlled Area

Mosul

Irbil

Kirkuk

Sulaymaniyah

Halabjah

Tigris R.

Euphrates R.

Tikrit

Samarra

Baqubah

N

Hit

Fallujah

Ramadi

BAGHDAD

Airport

Hwy. 6

Karbala

Numaniyah

Kut

Hillah

Hwy. 27

Diwaniyah

Tigris R.

Najaf

Hwy. 17

Amarah

Euphrates R.

Hwy. 8

Hwy. 1

Hwy. 7

Samawah

Qurnah

Nasiriyah

Tallil

Jalibah

Basrah

IRAQ

Safwan

Umm Qasr

Faw Peninsula

Kuwait City

KUWAIT

SAUDI ARABIA

Overview Map of Iraq

······ Kurdish region   Major oilfield   ═══ Major road   Marsh

STATUTE MILES
0   100   200

0   100   200
KILOMETERS

TURKEY

SYRIA

IRAN

■ Mosul

● Irbil

Tigris R.

● Sulaymaniyah

Kirkuk ●

Halabjah ●

Euphrates R.

Tikrit ●

Samarra

Baqubah ●

N

Hit ●

Fallujah

★ BAGHDAD

Ramadi ●

Airport ✈

Numaniyah ●

Karbala ●

Hillah ●

Kut ●

Diwaniyah ●

Najaf ●

Amarah ●

Hwy 8

Samawah ●

Nasiriyah ●

Qurnah ●

Tallil ●✈

Jalibah ●

Basrah

SAUDI ARABIA

I R A Q

Safwan

Umm Qasr ●

KUWAIT

Suspected WMD Facilities

STATUTE MILES

0   100   200

0   100   200

KILOMETERS

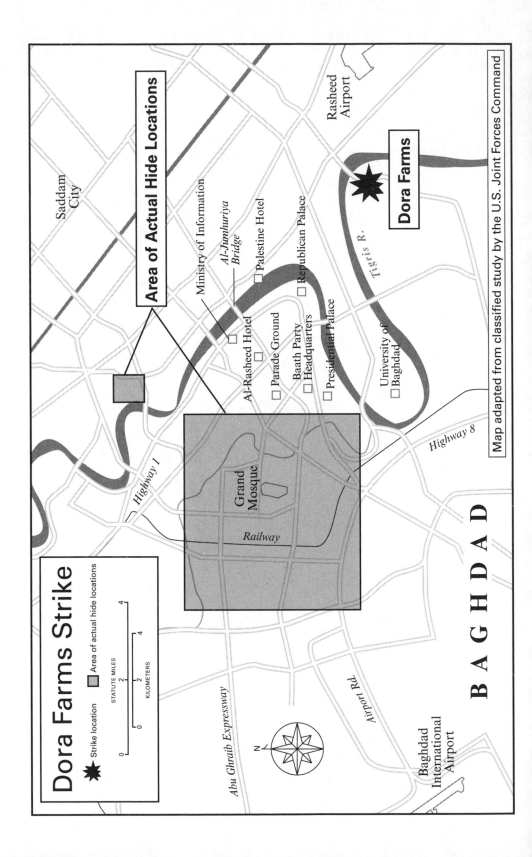

Dora Farms Strike

★ Strike location
▨ Area of actual hide locations

STATUTE MILES
0   2   4

KILOMETERS
0   2   4

Area of Actual Hide Locations

Saddam City

Ministry of Information

Al-Jamhuriya Bridge

☐ Palestine Hotel

☐ Republican Palace

☐ Al-Rasheed Hotel

☐ Parade Ground

Baath Party
☐ Headquarters

☐ Presidential Palace

University of
☐ Baghdad

Rasheed Airport

★ Dora Farms

Tigris R.

Highway 1

Grand Mosque

Railway

Highway 8

Abu Ghraib Expressway

Airport Rd.

Baghdad International Airport

N

B A G H D A D

Map adapted from classified study by the U.S. Joint Forces Command

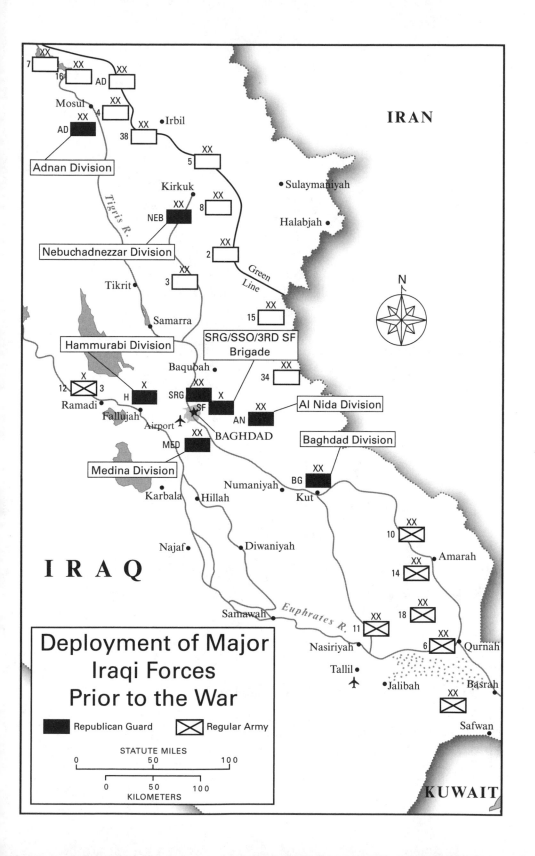

Deployment of Major Iraqi Forces Prior to the War

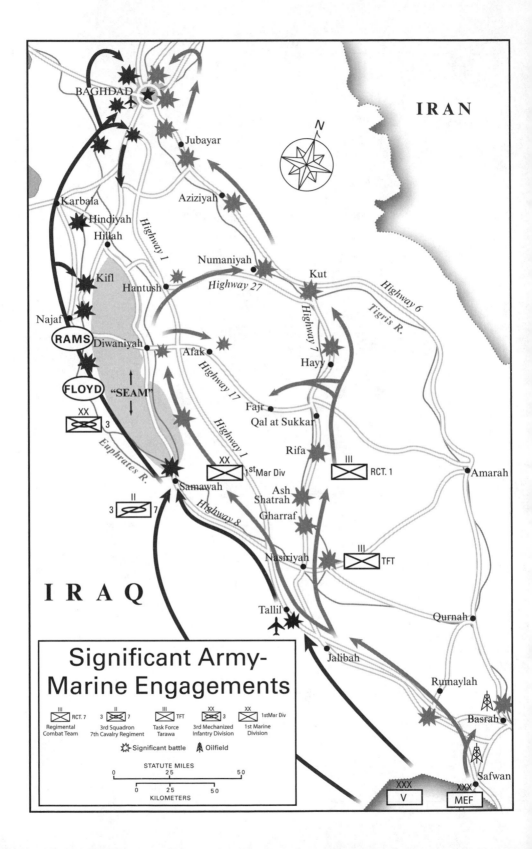

Significant Army-Marine Engagements

IRAN

IRAQ

BAGHDAD

Jubayar

Aziziyah

Karbala
Hindiyah
Hillah

Highway 1

Numaniyah

Kut

Highway 6

Tigris R.

Kifl
Hantush

Highway 27

Highway 7

Najaf
RAMS
Diwaniyah

Afak

Hayy

FLOYD
"SEAM"

Highway 17

Fajr
Qal at Sukkar

XX 3

Euphrates R.

Highway 1

Rifa

III RCT. 1

Amarah

XX 1st Mar Div

Samawah

Ash
Shatrah
Gharraf

3 II 7

Highway 8

Nasiriyah

III TFT

Tallil

Qurnah

Jalibah

Rumaylah

Basrah

Safwan

XXX V

XXX MEF

Significant Army-Marine Engagements

III RCT. 7	3 II 7	III TFT	XX 3	XX 1stMar Div
Regimental Combat Team	3rd Squadron 7th Cavalry Regiment	Task Force Tarawa	3rd Mechanized Infantry Division	1st Marine Division

Significant battle   Oilfield

STATUTE MILES
0   25   50

0   25   50
KILOMETERS

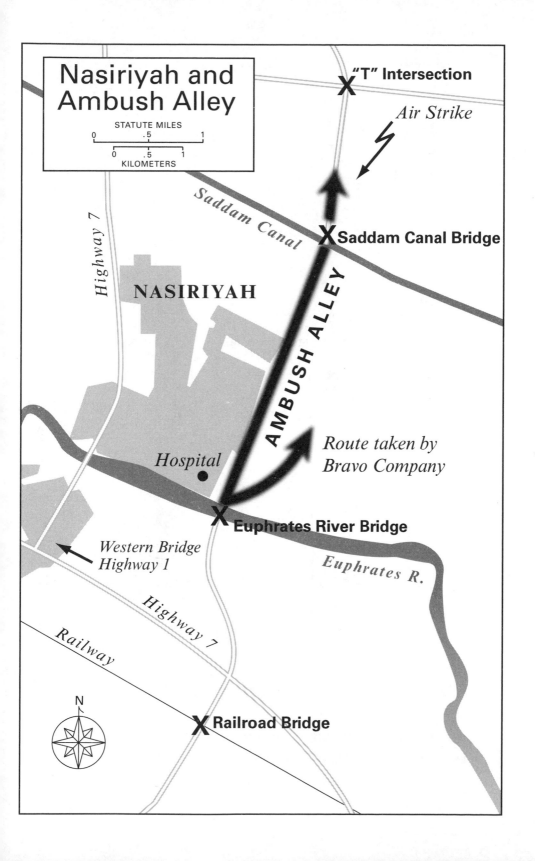

Nasiriyah and Ambush Alley

STATUTE MILES
0   .5   1

KILOMETERS
0   .5   1

"T" Intersection

Air Strike

Saddam Canal Bridge

Saddam Canal

NASIRIYAH

AMBUSH ALLEY

*Route taken by
Bravo Company*

Hospital ●

Euphrates River Bridge

*Western Bridge
Highway 1*

Euphrates R.

Highway 7

Highway 7

Railway

N

X Railroad Bridge

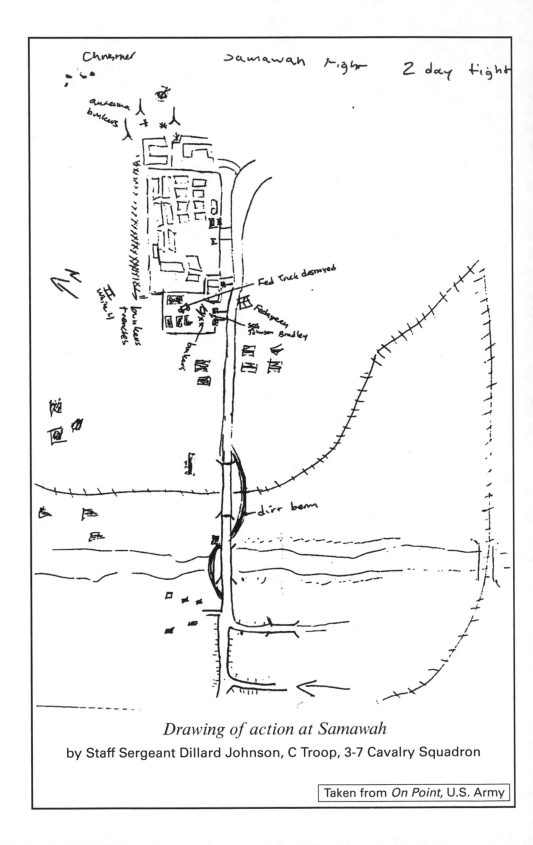

Drawing of action at Samawah
by Staff Sergeant Dillard Johnson, C Troop, 3-7 Cavalry Squadron

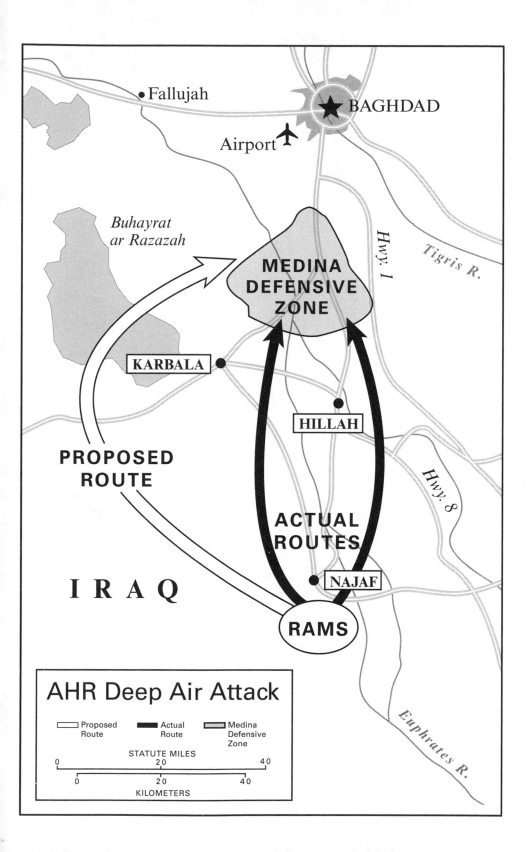

Fallujah

★ BAGHDAD

Airport ✈

Buhayrat ar Razazah

MEDINA DEFENSIVE ZONE

Hwy. 1

Tigris R.

KARBALA

HILLAH

PROPOSED ROUTE

Hwy. 8

ACTUAL ROUTES

I R A Q

NAJAF

RAMS

Euphrates R.

AHR Deep Air Attack

☐ Proposed Route   ▬ Actual Route   ▨ Medina Defensive Zone

STATUTE MILES

0   20   40

0   20   40

KILOMETERS

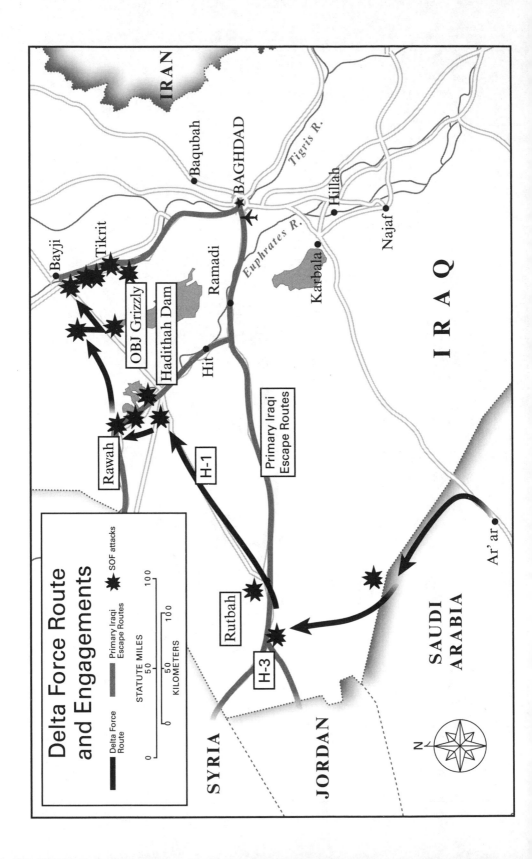

Delta Force Route and Engagements

Legend:
- Delta Force Route
- Primary Iraqi Escape Routes
- ✶ SOF attacks

STATUTE MILES
0   50   100

KILOMETERS
0   50   100

IRAN

Baqubah

BAGHDAD

Tigris R.

Hillah

Najaf

I R A Q

Karbala

Euphrates R.

Bayji

Tikrit

OBJ Grizzly

Hadithah Dam

Ramadi

Rawah

Hit

H-1

Primary Iraqi Escape Routes

SYRIA

JORDAN

Rutbah

H-3

SAUDI ARABIA

Ar' ar

N

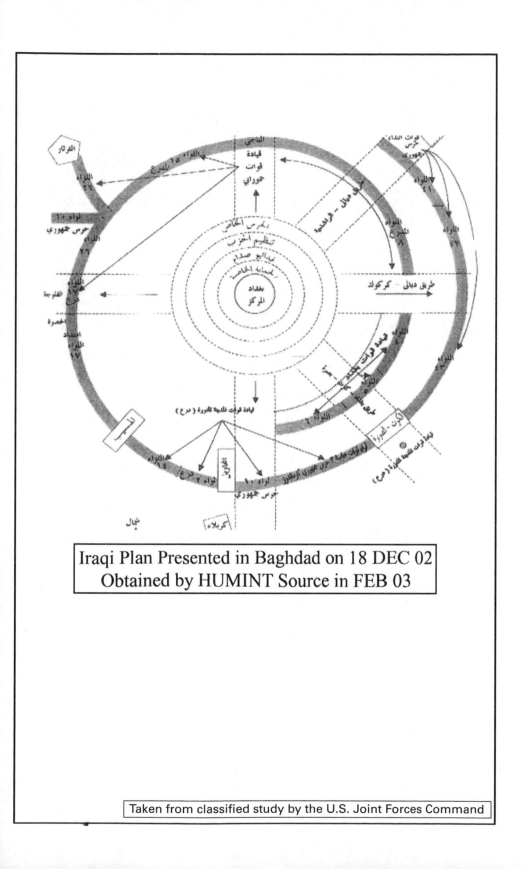

Iraqi Plan Presented in Baghdad on 18 DEC 02
Obtained by HUMINT Source in FEB 03

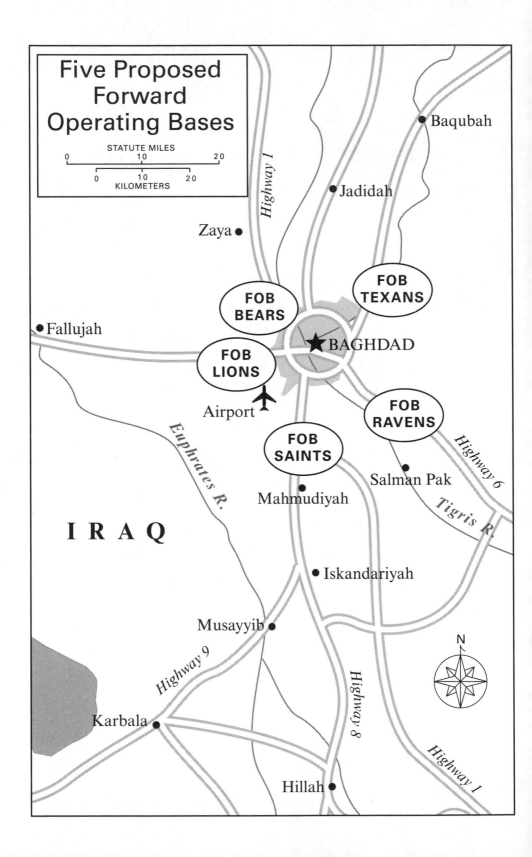

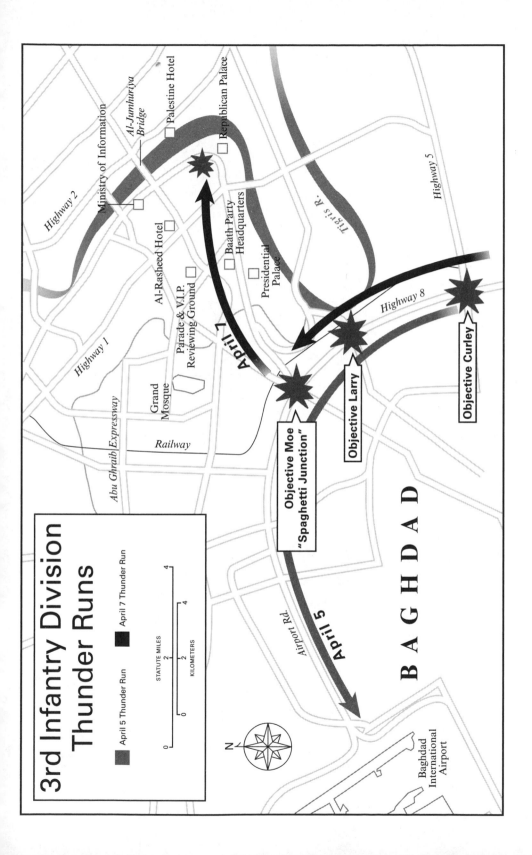

3rd Infantry Division Thunder Runs

▮ April 5 Thunder Run   **▮** April 7 Thunder Run

STATUTE MILES
0   2   4

KILOMETERS
0   2   4

N

Highway 2

Ministry of Information

Al-Jumhuriya Bridge

Palestine Hotel

Republican Palace

Al-Rasheed Hotel

Baath Party Headquarters

Presidential Palace

Tigris R.

Highway 5

April 7

Highway 1

Parade & V.I.P. Reviewing Ground

Highway 8

Objective Curley

Objective Larry

Abu Ghraib Expressway

Grand Mosque

Railway

Objective Moe "Spaghetti Junction"

Airport Rd.

April 5

B A G H D A D

Baghdad International Airport

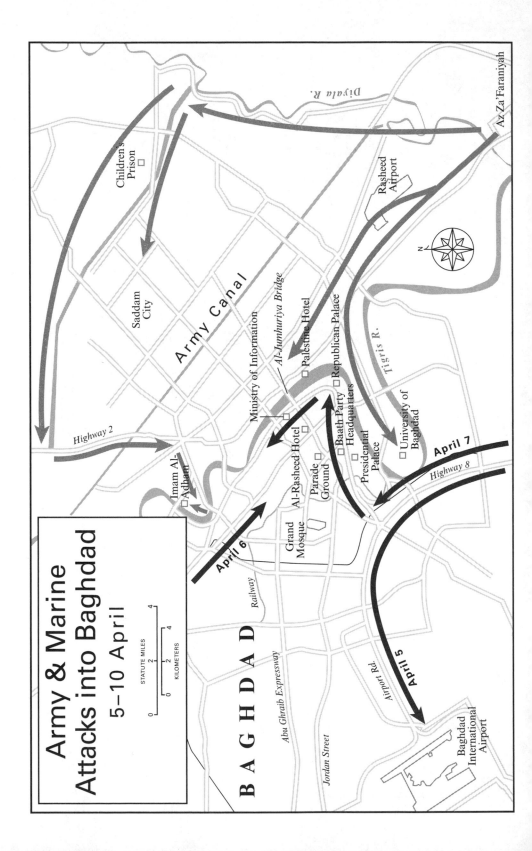

Army & Marine
Attacks into Baghdad
5–10 April

STATUTE MILES
0 2 4

KILOMETERS
0 2 4

BAGHDAD

Diyala R.

Az Za'Faraniyah

Children's Prison

Rasheed Airport

Saddam City

Army Canal

Al-Jumhuriya Bridge

Ministry of Information

Palestine Hotel

Republican Palace

Tigris R.

Highway 2

Baath Party Headquarters

University of Baghdad

April 7

Imam Al-Adham

Al-Rasheed Hotel

Parade Ground

Presidential Palace

Highway 8

Grand Mosque

April 6

Railway

April 5

Abu Ghraib Expressway

Jordan Street

Airport Rd.

Baghdad International Airport

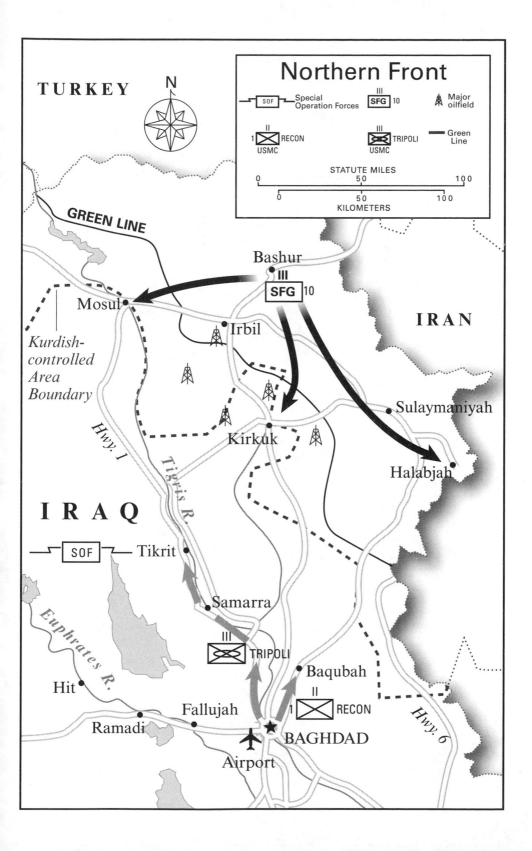

Northern Front

- Special Operation Forces
- SFG 10
- Major oilfield
- RECON USMC
- TRIPOLI USMC
- Green Line

STATUTE MILES
0 — 50 — 100

KILOMETERS
0 — 50 — 100

TURKEY

N

GREEN LINE

Bashur

SFG 10

Mosul

Irbil

IRAN

Kurdish-
controlled
Area
Boundary

Sulaymaniyah

Kirkuk

Halabjah

IRAQ

Hwy. 1

Tigris R.

SOF — Tikrit

Samarra

TRIPOLI

Euphrates R.

Baqubah

1 RECON

Hit

Fallujah

Hwy. 6

Ramadi

Airport

BAGHDAD

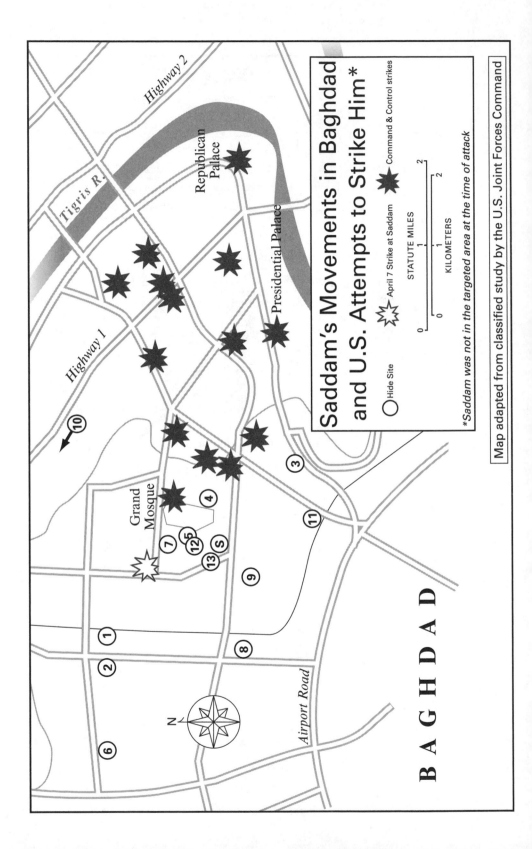

Saddam's Movements in Baghdad
and U.S. Attempts to Strike Him*

○ Hide Site

✴ April 7 Strike at Saddam

✴ Command & Control strikes

STATUTE MILES
0   1   2

KILOMETERS
0   1   2

*Saddam was not in the targeted area at the time of attack

Map adapted from classified study by the U.S. Joint Forces Command

B A G H D A D

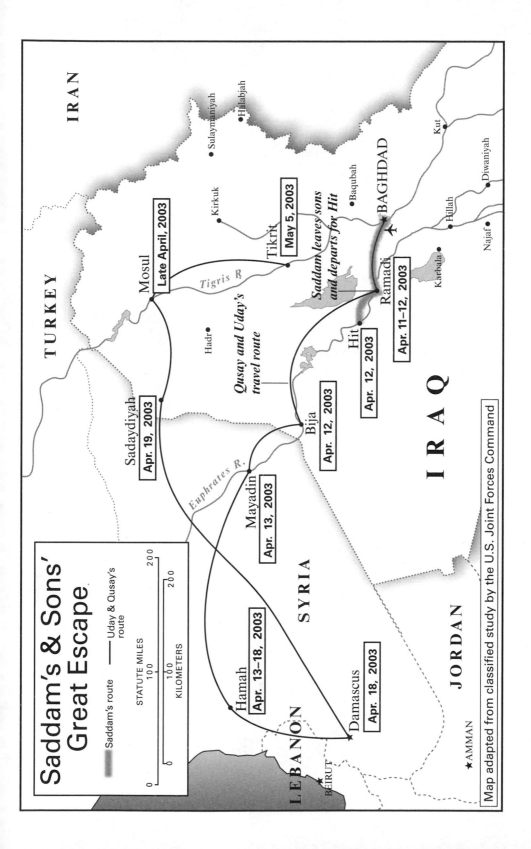

Saddam's & Sons'
Great Escape

Saddam's route
Uday & Qusay's route

STATUTE MILES
0   100   200

KILOMETERS
0   100   200

Map adapted from classified study by the U.S. Joint Forces Command

TURKEY

IRAN

SYRIA

IRAQ

JORDAN

LEBANON

Mosul

Sadaydiyah
Apr. 19, 2003

Hamah
Apr. 13–18, 2003

Damascus
Apr. 18, 2003

Mayadin
Apr. 13, 2003

Bija
Apr. 12, 2003

Euphrates R.

Tigris R.

Hadr

Kirkuk

Tikrit

Late April, 2003

May 5, 2003

Sulaymaniyah

Halabijah

*Saddam leaves sons
and departs for Hit*

Hit
Apr. 12, 2003

Ramadi
Apr. 11–12, 2003

Baqubah

BAGHDAD

Kut

Diwaniyah

Hillah

Karbala

Najaf

*Qusay and Uday's
travel route*

BEIRUT

AMMAN

Foreword

We wrote this book to provide an inside look at how a military campaign that was so successful in toppling Saddam Hussein's regime set the conditions for the insurgency that followed. The Iraq War was a war of choice, not necessity. It was also one of the most covered but least understood episodes in recent history. The development of the U.S. military plan was shrouded in secrecy. The debates among the generals were conducted behind closed doors. Saddam's deliberations with his war council were unknown. Many of the key battles are only dimly understood.

For three years, we have done exhaustive research on all these fronts. Our mission was not to offer up a slice of the war, to cover the action of a single unit, or to concentrate exclusively on the decision-making in Washington. Instead, we sought to prepare a contemporary history of the entire conflict with all of its complexity, to relate the planning behind closed doors, the bloodletting on the battlefield, and the parallels among disparate battles, and to provide a comprehensive account and rationale of the foreign policy strategy, generalship, and fighting.

We assembled the history from the ground up. We were able to learn about the development of the American plan by reviewing the contemporaneous and unpublished notes of participants and through repeated interviews with senior officials, generals, and their staffs. The research took us to Iraq, the White House, the Defense Department, the Central Command, the State Department, and military headquarters from the Persian Gulf to Texas, North Carolina, Kansas, Georgia, Nevada, and California.

We were able to reconstruct the key battles by interviewing hundreds of participants of all ranks, amassing previously undisclosed and, in some cases, still classified accounts of the clashes, canvassing military archives for written and oral histories, and visiting most of the major battlefields in Iraq, including Kifl, Samawah, Objective Floyd, Tallil, Objective Rams, Hindiyah, the Euphrates River crossing at Peach, Baghdad, Mosul, and Fallujah. The process of embedding provided Michael Gordon extraordinary access over a period of almost five months to a variety of military commands and units. From the allied land war command, the V Corps headquarters, the 3rd Infantry Division, and the 101st Airborne Division, we had access when many of the key decisions about the war were made and postwar policies set. In addition to the conventional fights, we were able to document in detail the engagements of the Delta Force.

We reconstructed decisions by Saddam and his war council through access to a still classified report, "Iraqi Perspectives," by the U.S. Joint Forces Command. The extensive briefing, which had been given to the president, is the product of years of research and is based on Iraqi documents and interrogations with senior regime officials and military commanders. The secret study outlines how the Iraqi war strategy was devised, Saddam's perception of the American plan as it unfolded, the Iraqi leader's thinking on weapons of mass destruction, his meetings with his high command, his whereabouts during U.S. bombing strikes, and even the actual escape routes he and his sons took from Baghdad.

Accessing the internal records of each side has enabled us to chronicle the misperceptions that each adversary had of the other and how they interacted to produce an outcome that neither side intended. Our research has yielded a new and more comprehensive record of how the war was actually planned and fought. Guided by Donald Rumsfeld and executed by Tommy Franks, the American-led campaign was a fulfillment of the defense secretary's vision of military transformation, calling for the use of precision weapons and the latest reconnaissance and command and control systems to rapidly defeat the foe. By and large, the strategy worked—only to leave American forces facing a new and more dangerous phase of the conflict. There were indications from the first days of the invasion of the insurgency and guerrilla tactics to come, but they were ignored at the highest levels in Washington and at the Central Command.

The Iraq War is a story of hubris and heroism, of high-technology wizardry and cultural ignorance. The bitter insurgency American and British forces confront today was not preordained. There were lost opportunities, military and political, along the way. The commanders and troops who fought the war explained them to us. A journey through the war's hidden history demonstrates why American and allied forces are still at risk in a war the president declared all but won on May 1, 2003.

COBRA II

Snowflakes from the Secretary

In late 2001, Secretary of Defense Donald H. Rumsfeld summoned the senior military leadership to his office on the E-ring of the Pentagon. It had been an extraordinarily eventful period for the administration of George W. Bush. Kabul had recently fallen. U.S. commandos and Pashtun commanders in southern Afghanistan were on the hunt for Osama bin Laden. In Bonn, Germany, the United States and diplomats from allied nations were prepared to anoint a new group of Afghan leaders.

During his short tenure at the Pentagon, Rumsfeld had established himself as an indomitable bureaucratic presence. It was a commonplace among the Bush team that the military needed stronger civilian oversight, and Rumsfeld exercised control with the iron determination of a former corporate executive. He had a restless mind and was given to boast that he was genetically impatient.

When he arrived at the Pentagon, Rumsfeld made clear that his goal was nothing less than to remake the U.S. military to fashion a leaner and more lethal force. Notepads were strewn throughout his outsized office. When the defense secretary had an idea he scribbled it down. Four-star generals and high-ranking aides were accustomed to receiving snowflakes: terse memos that captured his latest brainstorm or query and that landed with a thud.

Rusmsfeld had been receiving his daily CIA briefing shortly before the American Airlines plane plowed into the building on September 11. Afterward, he had staked out a clear position on how the Bush team should respond. The United States should take the fight to the Taliban and Al Qaeda camps in Afghanistan, but it would not end there. The Pentagon needed to take an even more forceful step that would let its enemies know that the United States was now involved in a global war against the terrorists and the renegade states that helped them. The U.S. needed to land a series of blows well beyond Afghanistan. The question was where and when to strike.

The defense secretary's meeting had been called to ponder the war plan for another potential adversary. General Richard B. Myers, the pliable chairman of the Joint Chiefs of Staff (JCS) who was picked by Rumsfeld because of his reputation as a team player, was there. So was Peter Pace, the ambitious vice chairman who was already being talked about as an officer who might follow in Myers's footsteps. Greg Newbold, the three-star general who served as chief operations deputy for the JCS, had the main assignment for the session. He was to outline Central Command's OPLAN 1003-98, the military's contingency plan in the event of a war with Iraq.

Newbold was armed with a pile of slides as the generals and Rumsfeld sat around a conference table. As Newbold outlined the plan, which called for as many as 500,000 troops, it was clear that Rumsfeld was growing increasingly irritated. For Rumsfeld, the plan required too many troops and supplies and took far too long to execute. It was, Rumsfeld declared, the product of old thinking and the embodiment of everything that was wrong with the military.

Myers asked Rumsfeld how many troops he thought might be needed. The defense secretary said in exasperation that he did not see why more than 125,000 troops would be required and even that was probably too many. Rumsfeld's reaction was dutifully passed to the United States Central Command.[1]

"My regret is that at the time I did not say, 'Mr. Secretary, if you try to put a number on a mission like this you may cause enormous mistakes,' " Newbold later recalled. "Give the military the task, give the military what you would like to see them do, and then let them come up with it. I was the junior military guy in the room, but I regret not saying it."[2]

The 1003 plan was ripe for review and was based on the assumption that it would be Iraq that would start the fight. Nonetheless, the plan, which had been regularly exercised in war games, reflected long-standing military principles about the force levels that were needed to defeat Iraq, control a population of more than 24 million, and secure a nation the size of California with porous borders. Rumsfeld's numbers, in contrast, seemed to be pulled out of thin air. He had dismissed one of the military's long-standing plans and suggested his own force level without any of the generals raising a cautionary flag.

General Tommy Franks, the CENTCOM commander, would draw up the new plan, but Rumsfeld would poke, prod, and question the military at every turn. Defense Department civilians would move into Franks's planning cells to monitor his work, and the general would be summoned to Washington repeatedly to present his evolving plan and receive new guidance from his civilian master. The JCS chairman and his staff would be little more than onlookers. Two momentous signals had been sent at Newbold's briefing. Iraq would be the next phase in the Bush administration's self-declared "global war on terror" and the defense secretary would insist on an entirely new kind of Iraq war plan.

When he was running for president, George W. Bush had signaled that he wanted to overhaul the U.S. military. His father's earlier victory in the Persian Gulf, Bush said in a 1999 speech at the Citadel, was an impressive accomplishment, but also one that had taken six months of planning, amassing of military forces and supplies, and preparation. That was too long for the sole remaining superpower to project its power throughout the world. Bush pledged to develop lighter, more mobile, and more lethal forces.

Nor did Bush see the need for the sort of lengthy peacekeeping operations or difficult nation-building missions that the administration of Bill Clinton had undertaken in the Balkans. The purpose of the military, Bush argued, was to fight and win the nation's wars, not to linger to bring stability to newly ordained states. A strong secretary of defense would be appointed and he would have a broad mandate to develop a new military structure. Generals and admirals who supported the new program would be promoted. Billions of dollars in new spending would be channeled for the research and development of missile defense and other high-technology military systems.[3]

The speech was drafted by some of the so-called Vulcans, the cluster of conservative former national security officials who had formed the nucleus of a shadow government during the Clinton years and would later find a place at the top of the new administration. The idea of using advanced reconnaissance systems, command and control networks, and precision weapons to strip away the fog of war and strike the enemy with devastating effect had attracted a small, but influential, group of adherents, and the Vulcans were among them. It was supposed to be nothing less than a revolution in military affairs that would reduce the requirement for large land armies, and with Bush's election some of the self-proclaimed revolutionaries would be in charge.

Once in office, Bush made good on the pledge to support a powerful defense secretary, settling on Rumsfeld, a choice that was strongly endorsed by Vice President Dick Cheney, who sensed that his former mentor would not only have a strong hand at the tiller but would serve as an ally in policy debates.

At sixty-eight, Rumsfeld was full of energy and brimming with confidence. He had been a wrestler in college, a combative and solitary sport, run with the bulls in Spain, followed his father into the Navy, been NATO ambassador, won a seat in Congress, earned a small fortune as the CEO of a pharmaceutical company, and run two government commissions: one on ballistic missile threats from Third World countries and the other on space policy. Rumsfeld was both the youngest and the oldest person to serve as defense secretary, having served as the Pentagon chief under President Gerald Ford. He had not been among the drafters of the Citadel speech, but he wholly supported the theme.

As Rumsfeld prepared to take on his responsibilities at the Pentagon he met with William S. Cohen, the Maine Republican who served as Bill Clinton's secretary of defense. Cohen, who had traveled widely in the post, advised Rumsfeld to go to Wehrkunde, the premier European security conference, which was held annually in Munich over a February weekend. Rumsfeld, he said, needed to get to know the European allies, as otherwise there would not be another opportunity to do so until a NATO meeting the following June. Rumsfeld resisted the idea, arguing that he could not afford to loosen his grip on the Pentagon even for a weekend. Rumsfeld eventually relented and went to Munich, delivered a speech on missile defense, pronounced allied unease about the project to be utterly incomprehensible, and rushed back. The episode was telling: Rumsfeld's principal battleground was the Pentagon, his concern over relations with the allies was secondary, and he was uneasy leaving others in charge even for a day.

At the Defense Department, Rumsfeld was quick to demonstrate and solidify his authority. Each month, the defense secretary was required to approve sensitive reconnaissance operations. The missions were listed in a top secret binder, and once when an action officer came in to get Rumsfeld's okay he noted in passing that the State Department had already reviewed the list and had not seen any problems. The innocent comment was like waving a red flag before a bull. Rumsfeld refused to sign, saying he would need to study the binder first. For several days, there was a mysterious lull in reconnaissance operations as the new defense secretary made clear that the building he was trying to bend to his will could not take him for granted. There were small changes that sent a message as well. The elaborate honor ceremonies for visiting dignitaries were declared to be an unnecessary frill and cut back.[4]

As Rumsfeld saw it, the biggest obstacles to his authority and vision were institutional. All of the Joint Chiefs of Staff—the leaders of the Army, Navy, Air Force, and Marines, who were presided over by a chairman selected by the president—were holdovers from the Clinton administration. Soon after arriving at the Pentagon, Rumsfeld met with General Hugh Shelton, the chairman of the Joint Chiefs of Staff, a former Special Operations Forces commander and an imposing physical presence. Shelton sought to assure Rumsfeld that there was no such thing as Clinton generals and admirals. Shelton and the chiefs would be loyal to the new administration. Rumsfeld, however, was concerned that the JCS and its staff had emerged as a rival source of power. The new defense secretary complained that the Joint Staff was too large and recommended that it be reduced by dispensing with Shelton's office of legislative affairs and his office of public affairs. Shelton stood his ground, arguing that the JCS chairman, by law, was the principal military adviser to the president and the National Security Council as well as the secretary of defense and that he needed a staff to support those responsibilities. Besides, Shelton argued, the civilian staff that reported to the defense secretary was even larger.

At one point, Shelton received a tip from a friendly member of the defense secretary's staff that Rumsfeld planned to fire Scott Fry, the Navy admiral who served as the director of the Joint Staff, which supported the chairman, and who never clicked with the new defense secretary. Shelton burst into Rumsfeld's office unannounced and said he would resign if Fry was replaced. Rumsfeld would then have two vacancies on his hands. Rumsfeld, who had made no secret of his disdain for Fry, insisted he had no such plan. The episode spoke volumes about the strains between the new civilian leadership and the military during the early months of Rumsfeld's tenure. Shelton was determined to defend the prerogatives of his office and its independence. Rumsfeld approached defense like a businessman who saw himself on the top of a steep pyramid.[5]

In his quest to remake the armed forces, Rumsfeld did not hesitate to go outside the military and tap a network of formal and informal advisers. Rumsfeld was fascinated by the views of Andrew Marshall, the seventy-nine-year-old head of the Defense Department Office of Net Assessment, a sort of Pentagon think tank, who saw satellites, information systems, long-range precision weapons, and advanced military technology as a way to check the rise of China. Marshall had not been an influential figure during the Clinton administration, and Cohen had proposed moving Marshall's office across the Potomac River and installing him at the National Defense University. Cohen relented following protests from Marshall's high-level friends, including Rumsfeld, who wrote Cohen a letter describing Marshall as a national treasure.[6]

At the Pentagon, Rumsfeld's program was dubbed "transformation," and it soon acquired the aura of an official ideology. The secretary was enamored of missile defense and space weapons, the issues he had worked on during his years out of office. He was also skeptical about the Army leadership, which he considered to be too old-fashioned, wedded to heavy forces, and too slow to change. Bush's Citadel speech had spoken of developing land forces that were more mobile and easier to deploy. Further, even with the hefty budget increases the new administration was projecting, there was not enough money to fund all the programs on the Pentagon wish list. With 476,000 troops, Army personnel costs were a major claimant on the budget—and, for the proponents of transformation, a sponge that soaked up much of the funding that could be used for space-based radars and other new systems they hoped would replace the cumbersome "legacy" systems of the Cold War.[7]

With Rumsfeld at the helm, some long-standing critics of the Army leadership felt that they had an ally at the top. Douglas A. Macgregor, an iconoclastic Army colonel who believed his service had too much of a Cold War focus, was one of them. When Macgregor ran into Steve Cambone, Rumsfeld's closest and most loyal aide, Cambone jested that Rumsfeld thought the Army's problems could be solved by lining up fifty of its generals in the Pentagon and gunning them down.[8]

General Eric Shinseki, the Army chief of staff, and Tom White, the secretary of the Army, sometimes felt as if they were a bureaucratic target and were not amused. Shelton, for his part, felt that Rumsfeld was not so much a visionary as parochial. Rumsfeld, the JCS chief told associates, had been a Navy fighter pilot, seemed partial to the Navy and the Marines, and was biased against the Army because it had mechanized forces and had taken on Balkan peacekeeping missions that the Bush administration considered to be a distraction.

With transformation in the air, a lively debate developed over which forces were most needed and the sort of wars the U.S. should prepare to fight. In the wake of the Gulf War, Dick Cheney had ordained that the United States should be able to fight two major wars in far-flung regions. The worry was that if the United States was tied down in one conflict a foe in another crisis zone might try to take advantage unless the U.S. had available forces that could be drawn on for the fight. It was not a hypothetical problem, but a real concern. When the United States was leading the coalition to retake Kuwait it had to keep a wary eye on North Korea.[9]

The problem with the two-war concept for Rumsfeld was that it required a large ground force. The Pentagon needed to have four Army corps, as well as the transport ships and planes to take them, nearly simultaneously, to distant battlefields. During a much ballyhooed review, it was decided that the requirement should be substantially watered down. Under a new doctrine, if adversaries attacked in two separate regions the goal would be to hold the line in both. The president would then pick the one the United States would "decisively win" while continuing to contain the other.[10]

As the two-war doctrine was being amended, the secretary and his aides turned their attention to trimming the forces. Shortly before September 11, Rumsfeld had presided over a meeting at which Cambone laid out several options, including one to reduce the Army by as much as two divisions, a proposal that drew vociferous and ultimately successful protests from the Army leaders, who argued that the service was already stretched thin.[11]

On September 10, Rumsfeld held a town meeting at the Pentagon to let officials know that he felt the main threat to a more efficient and innovative defense structure was internal. "The topic today is an adversary that poses a threat, a serious threat, to the security of the United States of America," Rumsfeld began. "From a single capital, it attempts to impose its demands across time zones, continents, oceans and beyond. With brutal consistency, it stifles free thought and crushes new ideas. It disrupts the defense of the United States and places the lives of men and women in uniform at risk. . . . You may think I'm describing one of the last decrepit dictators of the world. But their day, too, is almost past, and they cannot match the strength and size of this adversary. The adversary's closer to home. It's the Pentagon bureaucracy."[12]

The next day, the Pentagon and the World Trade Center were attacked. The proposals to cut the Army receded into the background and Rumsfeld turned his restive intellect to the administration's new war on terrorism.

Strategizing with his top aides, Rumsfeld was not satisfied with the idea of pounding the Taliban. Striking back at the Afghan regime was a given, but it was not necessary that the operation be the nation's only mission or even its top priority. The Bush administration needed to demonstrate that the United States had the will to take the fight beyond Afghanistan as well as the guile to hit enemies when and where they did not expect it. First and foremost, it needed to head off future attacks by preventing terrorists from acquiring biological, chemical, or even nuclear arms from the United States's enemies.

"The idea was, of course, to go after Al Qaeda," said Douglas Feith, the undersecretary of defense for policy and a member of Rumsfeld's inner circle. "But punishment was not the issue. . . . Rumsfeld understood that the problem is not dealing with one organization in one place. It would not be solved by fighting Al Qaeda inside Afghanistan. It was a bigger problem. His mind ran immediately to the extra danger of the nexus of terrorism and WMD [weapons of mass destruction]. We were not going to solve this problem by focusing narrowly on the perpetrators of 9/11. Rumsfeld wanted some way to organize the military action so that it signaled that the global conflict would not be over if we struck one good blow in Afghanistan."[13]

Many of the secretary's musings were later included in a memorandum that Feith drafted on the limited value of hitting targets in Afghanistan. The independent commission that investigated the 9/11 attack cast the memo as a series of proposals by Feith, but in fact many of the notions had come from Rumsfeld himself.[14] Before 9/11, Rumsfeld had not been obsessed with Iraq. After 9/11, Iraq was elevated as a potential military front.

For the first eight months of their term in office, the Bush administration's approach to Iraq was more of an attitude than a plan. Many of the administration's top echelon had been in office during the Persian Gulf War and their intuitions for how to respond to Saddam were shaped by that experience.

When the 1991 Persian Gulf War drew to a close, the administration of George H. W. Bush thought it might soon see the last of Saddam Hussein.

Although the removal of the Iraqi leader had not been an explicit goal of the Desert Storm campaign, U.S. air war commanders had directed strikes against virtually every location where they thought the Iraqi leader might be located and targeted the security forces, communications network, and Baath Party organizations that American intelligence believed he relied on to stay in power. The last target that was bombed in the Desert Storm operation had been the massive edifice that served as the Baath Party headquarters in Baghdad, a parting shot that expressed contempt for Saddam's ruling apparatus. The mission of the U.S.-led coalition, however, had been to evict Iraqi forces from Kuwait and to deprive Saddam of the ability to threaten his southern neighbor again by destroying the Republican Guard divisions that had rolled into the tiny Gulf state and later taken up positions south of the Euphrates. A Western and Arab coalition had been raised on this premise. Eliminating Saddam, however, had not been essential but was seen as a potential bonus.

When the Iraqis were ejected from Kuwait in the 100-hour war, President George H. W. Bush calculated that Saddam might be overthrown by humiliated and disgruntled Iraqi generals.[15] But Saddam proved to be a far more durable figure than the Americans expected. His network of security operatives and internal police was vast. His powerful Tikriti clan enjoyed the trappings of power. His sheer ruthlessness was a potent weapon. Beyond that, enough of his Republican Guard forces, including the critically important corps headquarters, had escaped during the Gulf conflict to help him contend with a spontaneous rebellion in the Shiite-dominated south and resistance in the Kurdish north. Saddam put down the uprisings with extraordinary brutality.[16]

The messy aftermath of a seemingly decisive war created a dilemma for Washington: whether to pocket its victory and turn its back on the anti-Saddam rebels or support the resistance and risk being drawn into Iraq's internal strife. General Colin L. Powell, the pragmatic chairman of the Joint Chiefs, was satisfied with the endgame. Shaped by his Vietnam experience, the four-star general had become the foremost advocate of a doctrine that called for using overwhelming force and then making a clean break. He was wary of civilians whom he thought were too quick to send forces in harm's way and was anxious to avoid a potential quagmire. For Paul Wolfowitz, who served as the chief policy official in Cheney's Pentagon, the victory had been tarnished: U.S. forces had stood on the sidelines while anti-Saddam rebels were ruthlessly suppressed by Saddam's troops. He had been intrigued by suggestions from the Saudis that it might be wise to stir up trouble for Saddam by covertly arming the Iraqi Shiites and was concerned that Iraq would remain a danger.[17]

The dominant view, however, was summed up by Brent Scowcroft, Bush's national security adviser. While the administration was concerned about the repression of the Shiites, it was anxious to avoid any steps that would deepen the United States's involvement on the ground or risk the breakup of a nation that had served as a buffer against the expansion of Iranian power. Asked why the United States did not ally itself with the Shiite rebels after the war, Scowcroft summed up the policy in a word: "geopolitics."[18]

The Bush administration settled on a policy of economic sanctions, military containment, and regular United Nations inspections to dismantle Saddam's programs to develop nuclear, biological, and chemical arms. It was a strategy for a slow, steady squeeze, not deeper involvement. A no-fly zone was decreed over northern Iraq, effectively making Kurdistan an autonomous enclave. Six months later, as the Iraqis kept up their air raids against the Shiites, a no-fly zone was belatedly established over southern Iraq as well.

The Clinton years marked a curious role reversal in which the Democrats continued the containment policy of their predecessor while Republicans began to snipe at the strategy President Bush had originally put in place. By the late 1990s, there was growing debate over what to do with Iraq.

After meeting with Iraqi exiles, Wayne Downing, the former head of the Special Operations Command, drafted a plan, which he modestly entitled "An Alternative Strategy for Iraq." The idea was to grab a piece of southern Iraq, establish a provisional government in "liberated" Iraq, protect it with airpower, use the enclave to launch intelligence and commando operations into the nonliberated sectors, call on the Iraqi public to rise up, and gradually expand the zone until it included the entire country. The Iraqi Liberation Army could number as many as 10,000 and would be assembled in a year.[19] The general strategy, which harked back to the proposals for arming the Shiites at the end of the Gulf War, was endorsed in an open letter to President Clinton from a list of conservatives that read like a who's who of the George W. Bush administration, including Rumsfeld, Wolfowitz, John Bolton, Zalmay Khalilzad, Richard Armitage, and Robert Zoellick. In 1998, the Republican-led Congress passed the Iraq Liberation Act giving the executive branch the authority to dispense up to $97 million worth of military equipment and weapons to the potential insurgent army.[20] Eager to protect his right flank, Clinton signed it, though he had no intention of arming Iraqi insurgents and starting a proxy war.

With Saddam often at loggerheads with the United Nations weapons inspectors and the Republicans baying for the overthrow of his regime, the Clinton administration ordered a major air attack. To catch the Iraqis off guard and prevent them from moving their presumed caches of prohibited weapons, the plan was to outfox the Iraqi leader by striking just hours after U.N. inspectors were withdrawn from Iraq. The operation was consequently named Desert Fox. Only later was it pointed out that the Pentagon had inadvertently invoked the nickname of the World War II Nazi general Erwin Rommel. During the four-day blitz in December 1998, 415 cruise missiles were launched while American and British planes dropped more than 600 bombs. The Pentagon later estimated that it had killed 1,400 members of Iraq's Republican Guard and set back Saddam's supposed weapons program two years.[21]

Soon after the debate over the chads and ballots was settled by the Supreme Court in 2000 and George W. Bush was finally proclaimed the victor, Cohen received a call from the new vice-president-elect. Though he had defended the original decision to end the 1991 ground war at 100 hours, withdraw U.S. troops, and avoid the snare of potential occupation duties in Iraq, Cheney had come to believe that the containment strategy he had helped put in place was faltering. The web of economic sanctions seemed to be fraying and Cheney was convinced that Saddam was still a threat. He was the only senior member of the old team whose views on how to deal with Iraq had fundamentally changed. Now, Cheney wanted the Pentagon to arrange a security briefing for the president-elect. As Cohen recalled, Cheney made it clear that he did not want an eighty days around the world kind of approach. The session should focus principally on Iraq.[22]

On December 19, a month before Bush was inaugurated, he went to the White House to meet with the outgoing president. The two men posed for pictures and were conspicuously gracious to each other.

"I'm here to listen, and if the president is kind enough to offer some advice I will take it in," Bush said.

"My only advice to anybody in this is to get a good team and do what you think is right," Clinton added.

Once the two men were behind closed doors. Clinton told Bush that he had read his campaign statements carefully and his impression was that his two priorities were national missile defense and Iraq. Bush said this was correct. Clinton proposed a different set of priorities, which included Al Qaeda, Middle East diplomacy, North Korea, the nuclear competition in South Asia, and, only then, Iraq. Bush did not respond.[23]

The Clinton administration left office believing that Saddam was a manageable nuisance. Most of the new Bush team read the situation differently. The new team did not have a preconceived plan on how to deal with Saddam's regime or a timetable for action, but there was an assumption on the part of the new president, his vice president, and most of his national security team that something had to be done.

For all that, the first six months of the Bush presidency seemed to be focused on everything but Iraq. The new administration scrapped the antiballistic missile treaty and endured a mini-crisis with China over the collision of a Chinese fighter with a U.S. Navy reconnaissance plane. The new defense secretary brusquely pursued his transformation agenda at the Pentagon and Bush fretted about finding a way to extract the U.S. military from its nation-building efforts in the Balkans. During a July swing through Kosovo, Bush leaned over to Brigadier General William David, the commander of U.S. forces there, and expressing his disdain for peacekeeping said, "We've got to get you out of here."[24]

When the administration did focus on Iraq, its initial deliberations were inconclusive. One of the first high-level meetings on Iraq policy came on June 1 when Bush's national security adviser, Condoleezza Rice, chaired a meeting of the Principals Committee, a panel that included the vice president, defense secretary, CIA director, and secretary of state. Four options were on the table: continuing the current containment strategy, continuing containment while actively supporting Saddam's opponents, setting up a safe haven for insurgents in southern Iraq, and planning a U.S. invasion. No policy was set and administration officials continued to pursue their separate agendas.

At the State Department, Colin Powell led the effort to narrow and tighten economic sanctions. The new secretary of state's first instinct was to constrain Saddam through diplomatic efforts with allies and leave force as a last resort. At the Pentagon, Wolfowitz's view of Saddam had only darkened over time. The new deputy defense secretary saw Saddam as unchastened by his Gulf War defeat and a supporter of terrorism.

After he received his new Defense Department post, Wolfowitz sought to enlist the Joint Staff's support to develop a strategy for aiding an anti-Saddam resistance. Saddam had drained the southern marshes in Iraq to deprive Shiite rebels of a sanctuary, so Wolfowitz wondered if the dams could be bombed to re-create them. The Pentagon lawyers challenged whether such a strike would be consistent with the rules of war. Wolfowitz's view was that it would be more humane than leaving the Shiites to Saddam's mercy. Wolfowitz also wanted to know what it would take to arm and train Iraqi insurgents. At the White House, Zalmay Khalilzad, the National Security Council aide for the Middle East who had worked under Wolfowitz in the Cheney Pentagon, drafted papers that argued that supporting the Iraqi resistance in exile could lead to fissures in the regime.[25]

As for Rumsfeld, he was working on a new strategy for enforcing the no-fly zones as a means of weakening the regime. If the Iraqis fired at U.S. or British planes, the allies would deliver a disproportionate response. Instead of going after air defenses, the U.S. would begin to whittle away at the weapons and capabilities that Saddam used to stay in power. It would be a way of keeping Saddam in check and adding a muscular element to the administration policy. One potential target was the concentrations of tank transporters the Iraqi military relied on to move Republican Guard T-72 tanks around the country.[26]

Newbold had been in London briefing the plan to the British, who patrolled the Iraqi skies with the Americans, on September 11, 2001, when the news broke about the terrorist attacks in New York and Washington. When he returned and talked to Feith he was surprised to find that the Rumsfeld aide had other things on his mind besides Afghanistan. "The environment was one of extreme tension," Newbold recalled. "We truly thought another attack might be imminent and that Al Qaeda was the cause of this Pearl Harbor–style attack. You could still smell the smoke in the corridors. In the middle of this I assured Feith that we were working hard on Afghanistan. Feith told me, 'Why are you working on Afghanistan? You ought to be working on Iraq.' "[27]

Newbold, from his perch as the senior Joint Staff operations officer, later told some of his fellow officers that he considered the focus on Iraq to be a strategic blunder and a distraction from the real war on terror, but he was not in charge. Feith later denied making the comment and insisted that he was expressing the thinking Rumsfeld and his aides had been doing about taking the war on terrorism beyond Afghanistan and giving it a global dimension.

On September 15, Bush summoned his top aides to a two-day war council at the president's mountain retreat at Camp David to decide how to respond to the 9/11 attacks. The administration's top security hands were there. CIA director George Tenet presented his plan for operations inside Afghanistan. Shelton, the JCS chairman, briefed a preliminary plan for military intervention in Afghanistan, including the significant use of ground troops, and also outlined additional bombing options. Powell explained his proposal to present the Taliban with an ultimatum to hand over bin Laden and to enforce the demand with a U.S.-led coalition.

The briefing papers that Rumsfeld and Wolfowitz took with them included three sets of potential targets: the Taliban, Al Qaeda, and Iraq. The papers asserted that only two of them—Al Qaeda and Iraq—were strategic threats to the United States. That day, Saddam had issued an open letter to the American people in which he declared that the United States was getting a taste of the pain it had inflicted on the Arab world. The Iraqi leader did not take responsibility for 9/11. While some State Department officials saw it as bluster, Wolfowitz saw Saddam's words as a threat.[28]

Rumsfeld encouraged Wolfowitz to raise Iraq at the meeting. After Rumsfeld posed the question of what should be done about Saddam, Wolfowitz, who was sitting in a back row, pressed the case for confronting Iraq during the first round of the administration's new war on terror.

Powell pushed back. Afghanistan needed to be the main focus, he argued. Taking on Iraq would make it hard, if not impossible, to assemble a coalition. Rumsfeld countered that a coalition that was not willing to stand with the United States was one that was not worth having.

At the end of the day, Wolfowitz found himself in a discussion with the president over coffee near a fireplace. Vice President Cheney and I. Lewis Libby, known to everyone as "Scooter," Cheney's chief of staff, stood nearby. Bush remarked that the military options he had seen for Iraq were not that imaginative. Wolfowitz offered an option of his own. A large fraction of Iraq's oil was within forty miles of the Kuwait border. Most of southern Iraq was made up of Shiites who were deeply hostile to Saddam Hussein. The region included Basra, the second largest city in Iraq. The U.S. military could grab a foothold in southern Iraq, set up an enclave that would roughly parallel the sanctuary the Kurds enjoyed in northern Iraq, and gain a stranglehold on the Iraqi economy. The enclave could be used to arm insurgents and prepare for a push to Baghdad. It was a variation of the enclave plan that Wolfowitz and other conservatives had promoted during their years out of office. Bush listened and the argument appeared to register.[29]

At the end of the Camp David meetings, Bush spoke privately with Shelton, who was in his final month as the JCS chairman. The president asked Shelton to tell him if he was making a mistake by focusing on Al Qaeda instead of Saddam. Shelton reassured the president that he had made the correct call. Attacking Iraq out of the blue and apparently without clear provocation, Shelton argued, would upset the Middle East and hamper the coalition-building effort. Nor, he added, was there any reason to think that Iraq was linked to the September 11 attacks.

"That's what I think," Bush told Shelton. "We will get this guy but at a time and place of our choosing," Bush added, referring to Saddam.

With an Afghan operation fast approaching, Shelton's biggest worry was not Iraq but his concern that Rumsfeld's new principles of transformation would be applied in Afghanistan too enthusiastically by an overzealous defense secretary. Five days before he retired at the end of September 2001, Shelton ran into Dell Dailey, the two-star head of the Joint Special Operations Command, in the White House parking lot. The Afghan war plan depended heavily on Special Operations Forces, and Shelton warned Dailey that the military had to resist Rumsfeld's instinct to pare the Afghan force to a minimum. The defense secretary was prepared to send fewer forces than even the White House was willing to dispatch, Shelton argued. Dailey needed to hold firm. There was no need to take shortcuts that would risk unnecessary casualties. Lives and the success of his mission hung in the balance.[30]

The president decided to keep the focus on Al Qaeda and eliminating its sanctuary in Afghanistan, reaffirming the counsel of the vast majority of his advisers. But Bush had signaled that Iraq was still on his mind. On Sunday, September 16, Bush called Condoleezza Rice. He wanted the focus to be on Afghanistan but also wanted plans drawn up in case it turned out that Iraq was somehow implicated in the 9/11 attacks. The next day, the president convened a meeting of his National Security Council during which there was some discussion of what might follow an Afghan campaign. Bush reaffirmed his decision that contingency plans should be drawn up to deal with Iraq, including a plan to seize Iraq's oilfields.[31]

After Rumsfeld was selected as defense secretary, Richard N. Perle secured an influential position for himself as chairman of the Defense Policy Board, an advisory panel that counseled Rumsfeld on military and defense planning issues. The move gave Perle the latitude to express his own, characteristically strong opinions and pursue his agenda while having an inside track.

On September 19, Perle convened the panel for two days of meetings, which largely concentrated on Iraq. Washington was still in a state of shock from the terrorist attack and security was extraordinarily tight. The board members gathered at a Washington hotel, boarded minibuses, and were whisked across the 14th Street Bridge to the Pentagon with a police escort. They convened in Rumsfeld's conference room to hear from the visiting speakers: Professor Bernard Lewis, the emeritus Princeton University professor who was among the conservatives who had long advocated arming and backing Iraqi insurgents, and Ahmed Chalabi, the director for the Iraqi National Congress, the umbrella organization of anti-Saddam exiles.

Lewis set the tone. Iraq needed to be liberated, and Middle East nations would respect the use of force. Chalabi spoke next. The CIA considered him a scoundrel who, it charged, bilked the Petra Bank in Jordan out of millions and was little more than a poseur as a London-based guerrilla fighter. The State Department thought he was a master manipulator with little constituency inside Iraq. But Perle, Wolfowitz, and aides in Cheney's office saw him as a talented and dedicated organizer who had made more than his share of enemies with his single-minded focus on stirring a rebellion in Iraq.

Chalabi argued that Saddam acted like an occupying power. He was surrounded by bodyguards and fearful of assassins and coup plotters. The north was virtually out of his control. The south was isolated. Saddam's armored forces were desperately in need of maintenance and lacked fuel. Officers were not being paid. True, his army had tanks and helicopters and WMD, but Saddam could be toppled by Iraqi insurgents with U.S. airpower. The uprising would turn Iraq into a good, stable, modern, pro-Western free market country. The Iraqi military forces would help stabilize the country afterward. Ordinarily, Chalabi was not permitted to move around the Pentagon without an escort, but that day he and Francis Brooke, his public affairs adviser, were given passes that allowed them to walk the corridors on their own, and after Chalabi's presentation they went like a couple of tourists to see the damaged, smoke-filled wing.

Rumsfeld showed up toward the end of the session and made a broader point. Yes, it was important to topple the Taliban as quickly as the U.S. could, but that would not be enough. The United States needed to do more to demonstrate that there were serious consequences for mounting an attack on the U.S. and to show it would not suffer unsavory governments that were affiliated with terrorists. There was no flowery talk of inculcating democracy in the heart of the Middle East. Rumsfeld was advocating a demonstration of American power. It was a reprise of the brainstorming session the defense secretary had carried out with Feith and his aides soon after the 9/11 attacks. Rumsfeld had not proclaimed Iraq to be the next target, but he had made it clear that he felt there needed to be a Phase 2.[32]

Washington's new interest in Iraq was soon apparent to the military's war planners in the field. Lieutenant Colonel Thomas Reilly was at Fort McPherson when he heard a snowflake was coming down from the Defense Department. Fort McPherson was the home of the Third Army, an Atlanta-based headquarters that would serve as the major command for land warfare in the event of a conflagration in Central Asia, the Horn of Africa, or the Middle East.

When the query arrived, Reilly and his team of five planners were summoned to a windowless room in the bowels of the Third Army headquarters that was reserved for the most sensitive communications. Lieutenant General Paul T. Mikolashek, the Third Army commander, pulled the message off a classified fax machine and passed it around. The Third Army planners had seventy-two hours to sketch a plan to seize and hold Iraq's southern oilfields. The operation, indeed the very existence of planning effort, would be classified at the highest level: Polo Step.

The snowflake had arrived on September 13, two days before the Camp David war council. Rumsfeld's Pentagon was one step ahead of the president. By the time Bush ordered that a contingency plan for Iraq be drawn up the effort was already quietly under way.

Closeting himself with his team of planners, Reilly sketched out the strategy to seize a chunk of southern Iraq. The U.S. military would control everything from the port city of Umm Qasr and the southern Shiite city of Basra to Nasiriyah along the Euphrates River. That would give the U.S. control of the Rumaylah oilfields and cut Saddam off from his only seaport.

The mission of preparing the invasion of southern Iraq was assigned to V Corps, the Army's main fighting force in Europe. In October, the Third Army staff gathered more than 1,000 slides of background material on terrain, Iraqi forces, and other vital data and sent them over the military's classified e-mail system to the V Corps planners in Heidelberg, Germany. The cover slide showed a picture of a flying duck striking a Saddam Hussein–like figure with a frying pan. Underneath was written: "Operation Schwack Iraq." The official code name was more patriotic: Vigilant Guardian.

In Heidelberg, Lieutenant Colonel James Danna, the chief V Corps war planner, was cranking up the work on Vigilant Guardian. In addition to the background material, Reilly sent him a five-page paper to guide the planning. The V Corps would be under the operational control of CENTCOM on Iraq, and it should be ready to attack as early as January or February 2002. There was no talk of going to Baghdad; the mission was described as establishing an enclave in southern Iraq.

Danna fleshed out and expanded the plan. To control the southern Iraqi oilfields, he envisioned a substantial security zone, one that extended north of the Euphrates. A security zone of that size would keep any U.S. forces that arrived in Kuwait out of the range of Iraq's short-range missiles. The lodgment would also give the United States a base for further attacks deeper into Iraq: the V Corps would operate within 75 miles of Baghdad. The Army could fly UAVs (unmanned aerial vehicles) in and over Baghdad, dispatch attack helicopters, or strike targets to their north with ATACMS surface-to-surface missiles. In the meantime, the American forces could sell oil and import food to the presumably grateful residents of southern Iraq.

Danna and his planners figured that the risk was manageable. Iraq's Republican Guard was barred from driving south of the 32nd parallel. If the Iraqis dispatched forces south to attack the Americans they would be destroyed by airpower.

The U.S. would need two divisions, the requisite artillery, Patriot anti-missile batteries, logistics, and fuel. With the combat service support the invasion force could amount to 75,000 to 100,000 troops and would take thirty to forty-five days to deploy from "go." Once the force was assembled in Kuwait, Danna figured that establishing a lodgment in southern Iraq would take four days.[33]

When Wolfowitz and other conservatives advocated arming and equipping the Iraqi resistance, they estimated that a rebel force of fewer than 10,000, supported by U.S. airpower, could establish and protect an enclave in southern Iraq. They could stir up a rebellion across the country. But now, Army planners were projecting an industrial strength operation.

To further develop the strategy, Lieutenant General William Scott Wallace and his V Corps planners donned civilian clothes and caught a commercial flight to Kuwait the next month to meet with Mikolashek, who had moved his headquarters there to oversee the Afghan campaign. Mikolashek was concerned by the V Corps plan, which took forces beyond the Euphrates so they could launch attacks near Baghdad and favored something more conservative.

Lieutenant Colonel Charles Eassa was among Danna's team of planners. His father was a Lebanese Christian who had immigrated to the United States, made a career for himself at the Carrier air-conditioning company, and later represented the firm in the Middle East. One of his father's major projects was overseeing the installation of an air-conditioning system in the Republican Palace, a citadel on the Tigris that Saddam Hussein later expanded and adorned with four helmeted figures that bore a striking likeness to himself. Eassa had never been to Baghdad, but now it looked like he might one day make the trip.[34]

Vigilant Guardian turned out to be little more than a contingency plan, but it energized Third Army headquarters, as well as the Army's V Corps, which would later be the Army corps that would carry out the main attack. It also reflected many of the assumptions that would guide the planning effort: an opponent whose military was weakened by more than a decade of sanctions and a welcoming Iraqi population in the south. When it came time to drawing up an invasion strategy for Iraq, however, Rumsfeld intended to control the process.

On November 21, Newbold called Victor "Gene" Renuart, an Air Force two-star general who served as Franks's chief operations officer, and gave him a quick heads-up: CENTCOM would receive an order to develop a new estimate of how many forces would be needed to invade Iraq and remove Saddam from power. Five days later, Rumsfeld flew to Tampa to meet with Franks. Later that day, at a joint press conference with Franks, Rumsfeld was asked if pursuing terrorist groups in Somalia would be the next phase in the war on terror. Rumsfeld parried the question, but the defense secretary was actually thinking much bigger.

Rumsfeld met alone with Franks. But before he engaged with the CENTCOM commander, he had drafted a set of talking points with the assistance of Wolfowitz and Feith. A review of the document provides a sense of Rumsfeld's guidance for drafting a new war plan. There were indications, Rumsfeld maintained, that Saddam's hold on power was brittle. So the key was to identify the vulnerabilities that could be exploited to heighten Saddam's paranoia and strip away his supporters. The talking points listed the main objectives, describing them as "slices." They included the northern and southern oilfields, Saddam's presumed stocks of WMD, Iraq's missile sites and air defenses, and the Republican Guard.

The campaign, the talking points note, should be marked by surprise, speed, shock, and risk, as well as actions that, Rumsfeld wrote, would add to the momentum for regime change. It would be important to start the military action before moving all the forces in place for the worst case. The decapitation of the Iraqi government could occur early. It would be important to cut off communications as well as any orders to "sleepers," terrorists who might be positioned around the world.

Rumsfeld's document also said it would be necessary to deploy Special Operations Forces in the north to work with the Kurds, protect a provisional government, seize the western desert, and cut off Baghdad. Steps had to be taken to deter Saddam from lashing out at the Kurds and to respond if he ignored the warnings. Rumsfeld's talking points further stressed the need for a "declaratory policy" to warn Saddam of the consequences of using chemical and biological weapons.

Rumsfeld's talking points further indicated that he wanted Franks to produce a "rough concept," not a finished plan for execution. And he stressed the need for tight deadlines. The secretary wanted to iterate a plan, develop it through constant interaction with the military instead of waiting for a finished product. Rumsfeld's talking points also indicated that he offered to have the services contribute staff if Franks was shorthanded because of Afghanistan. The planners could work at the Pentagon or at CENTCOM's headquarters in Tampa. Clearly, Rumsfeld was not about to let the war in Afghanistan get in the way of a new war with Iraq.

Rumsfeld also wanted to think ahead. The Bush administration had gotten lucky in Afghanistan, Rumsfeld noted, when it found Hamid Karzai and arranged for him to run the country. But this time the administration could not afford to muddle through. Along with a new war plan it would need a political solution for postwar Iraq.[35]

After his meeting with Rumsfeld was over, Franks related much of the guidance to his trusted officers. Aides to Rumsfeld described the defense secretary's approach as "an exercise in suasion." Rumsfeld never directed Franks on how to write the plan. But he would plant ideas, send concepts and papers his way, and ask questions to shape the plan. There is a saying in Washington that you can get a lot done if you do not want credit for it. Rumsfeld took the notion a step further. It was better that he not receive credit. Rumsfeld understood that there was political value in being able to stand at the Pentagon podium and say that the Bush administration was implementing the military's plan.

In the case of Afghanistan, the Pentagon had to throw together a strategy on the fly. With Iraq, the administration had the luxury of time. It could challenge old assumptions and develop a bold new plan.

CHAPTER 2

The Generated Start

At CENTCOM, Tommy Franks got to work. Franks had been through Afghanistan with Rumsfeld and found the defense secretary so overbearing that he had hinted he might resign. Since then, the two men had backed off a bit.

The domineering former CEO and the general from Texas made an unlikely pair. Franks was a former artillery officer and a muddy-boots general. He was earthy—his critics called him vulgar—lacing his talk with profanity and sometimes seeming to play the role of an old parade ground master sergeant. The troops seemed to eat it up. The reviews among the officers were mixed.

Franks had attended high school in Texas with First Lady Laura Bush, joined the Army, served in Vietnam, and then returned to finish his college education and later earn an MBA with the encouragement of his wife, to whom he was utterly devoted and whom, as CENTCOM commander, he often took on his travels. (His seat on the plane had four stars. Hers had four hearts.) Rising through the ranks of the Army, Franks became the head of the Third Army under Anthony Zinni, the Marine general who led CENTCOM during the Clinton years. Zinni considered Franks to be a loyal and diligent subordinate and recommended him as his successor.[1]

Franks often reveled in his down-to-earth, no-nonsense manner. In his zeal to reform the Pentagon, Rumsfeld later decided that the heads of the commanders were misnamed. For as long as anyone could remember they had been called CINCs, which stood for commander-in-chief of a unified command. Insisting that only the president could be the commander-in-chief, Rumsfeld drew up an edict that the CINCs should henceforth be known as "combatant commanders." When Franks's staff asked him what he thought about the new title as he was flying around the Middle East he responded: "I don't give a rat's ass." To Franks, this Rumsfeld obsession was a waste of time.

Nobody could confuse Franks with an intellectual. His favorite way to pass time was to watch movies on a portable DVD player he took on his long plane trips. When he visited a base he often went to the PX and bought the latest DVDs. One of his favorite movies was *The Nutty Professor*. Nonetheless, Franks considered himself an innovator, and had fashioned a unique idiom that was part military theory, part country. Franks liked to talk about "strategic exposure" and "functional componency."

Like Rumsfeld, he believed that the war in Afghanistan had demonstrated some of the principles of transformation—the utility of a small number of forces and the ability of technology and surprise to substitute for mass. Like many of his generation, he had no fondness for Clinton-style nation-building. Franks had been to Vietnam and Korea, but unlike many Army officers had never served in Bosnia or Kosovo, where Army officers got firsthand experience on what it took to prevent ethnic fighting and build new governing institutions. Nor had CENTCOM tried its hand at nation-building since the confused mission in Somalia.

Franks was disciplined and ambitious. He seemed to get up at 4:00 a.m. regardless of whether he was in Tampa or traveling through the Middle East. When he was on the road he would review the message traffic by dawn and go through his e-mails, exercise at 5:00, and come back to work at 6:00 and start grilling his aides for details. By 7:00 a.m. he would be ready to engage the officials in Washington.[2]

Newt Gingrich, the former House Speaker and Pentagon defense adviser who interacted with both Franks and Rumsfeld, described their relationship as fraught with creative tension. Franks understood that Rumsfeld would throw ideas at him and would grill him about any and every aspect of his plan. Rumsfeld knew that there was a line beyond which Franks could not be pushed. Franks later described the constant back and forth between them as an "iterative process." Gingrich had a more apt description: it was "constant negotiation."[3]

When it came to Iraq, Franks was not starting with a blank slate. General Binford Peay, the commander of the 101st Airborne during the Gulf War, had been appointed to run CENTCOM in 1994. He had been particularly concerned about a "Basra breakout," the possibility that Saddam would mass five divisions in the southern part of Iraq and rush them into Kuwait before the Americans could respond. If war came, the United States would defend Saudi Arabia, again fight to reclaim Kuwait, and then press north into Iraq.[4]

Anthony Zinni, a blunt-spoken barrel-chested Marine, followed Peay and updated his plan. It was the Desert Fox bombing campaign, however, that led Zinni to do some rethinking on Iraq, including what it would take to secure the country if Saddam's regime collapsed. After the four days of Desert Fox's air strikes, intelligence trickled in from the Polish mission in Baghdad, which functioned as the eyes and ears of the Americans, and from Arab nations that the air strikes had shaken the regime much more than Washington had initially realized. Saddam and his top aides were said to have been unhappy that his military establishment was caught flat-footed. The Jordanians and Kuwaitis, in particular, were concerned that Saddam's days might be numbered and that Iraq might implode if he was toppled, leading to chaos on their frontier. Zinni was also concerned that Iraq could shatter and he then would be called on to restore order and keep the nation from fragmenting along ethnic lines. Containing Saddam was not the problem. It was filling a potential power vacuum that worried him. Zinni was not eager to invade Iraq and thought the idea of arming anti-Saddam insurgents was lunacy, but if the Iraqis did the job themselves he had to be ready.[5]

With an eye on a potential Iraqi collapse, Zinni developed the plan further. CENTCOM's OPLAN 1003-98 called for three corps, some 380,000 troops in all. Under the plan, the XVIII Airborne Corps would secure northern Iraq. The V Corps or another heavy corps would occupy the potentially volatile Sunni Triangle. A Marine Expeditionary Force would have the south. Their job would not only be to dispatch Saddam's Republican Guard but stop Iranian- and Syrian-sponsored groups from sneaking into the country to stir up trouble, maintain law and order, and, in general, prevent chaos. The goal would be to "freeze things in place." If the full complement of support troops were sent, the force would be well over 400,000. As for the Iraqi army, CENTCOM was already dropping leaflets urging the troops not to fight if there was another clash with the United States and assuring them the American authorities would take care of them afterward.[6]

Nobody knew how long United States forces would need to be in Iraq, so CENTCOM's war planners wrote that the occupation would last as long as ten years.

There was a gaping hole in the occupation annex of the plan. CENTCOM would have the responsibility of general security. But there was no plan for the political administration, restoration of basic services, training of police, or reconstruction of Iraq. Zinni organized a secret war game in June 1999, dubbed Desert Crossing, to explore what might be needed. The State Department and other civilian agencies sent representatives, but they later insisted they had no mandate to plan for the occupation of Iraq. The civilian complement to the plan was never completed: Clinton officials had their hands full with Arab-Israel peace negotiations and talks with North Korea, and there was little appetite to prepare for the occupation of Iraq.

Franks was well versed in Zinni's 1003-98 and shared his deep suspicion of any plan to sponsor a rebellion. While Zinni ran CENTCOM, Franks headed the Third Army, the command that was earmarked for duty in the event of a major conflict in the Middle East. Franks had taken on his assignment with enthusiasm, drawn up force requirements, tested the 1003 plan in computerized war games, spent considerable time in Kuwait, and worked on plans for a new headquarters that would command all of the allied ground forces in the event of war. If the U.S. had gone to war with Iraq during Zinni's tenure, Franks would have been his land forces commander.

"If I had to point to one person who was deeply involved in 1003-98 it was Tommy Franks," Zinni recalled. "He was the major contributor to the force levels and the planning and everything else. He was more involved in it than just about anybody else. That was his life. He and his planning staff seemed to be committed to the plan."[7]

When it came time to retire from his post in the summer of 2000, Zinni was convinced he had frustrated Iraq's effort to develop nuclear, biological, and chemical arms and reduced Saddam to a secondary threat, one that could be contained through U.N. sanctions, the enforcement of no-fly zones over northern and southern Iraq, and occasional bombing.

Zinni recommended Franks as his successor. In Franks, Zinni saw a loyal subordinate who would bring a measure of continuity to CENTCOM and who had never voiced anything but enthusiasm for Zinni's concept for what would be needed to win a war with Iraq and secure the peace.

. . .

After fielding Rumsfeld's thoughts on force levels, slicing up the regime, and engineering a post-Saddam political order, Franks passed the input to Renuart and his planning team in Tampa, who were holed up in the back half of Trailer 13, which was crammed full of desks and computers and located in a fenced-off portion of the CENTCOM parking lot. The arrangement kept the planners separate from the rest of the CENTCOM bureaucracy. Some of the brainstorming sessions were so disputatious that the planners began to refer to the trailer sarcastically as the Love Shack.

Rumsfeld was looking for a quick response, and Franks provided his preliminary thinking on December 4 in a video conference from Tampa. The goal at this point was not to produce a full-fledged plan, but to provide a commander's concept of how the war would be waged and a commander's estimate of how many forces might be required.

Franks's estimates depended mightily on how much cooperation the United States would receive from its allies, including Arab states. The numbers varied depending on whether CENTCOM would receive "robust" or "reduced" allied support or whether it would mount a "unilateral" attack. Those arrangements would depend greatly on what Franks called his "declaratory policy," a reference to the diplomacy that needed to be conducted to secure basing rights and to come up with the appropriate casus belli. Since it was possible that the Bush administration might attack with little coalition support, Franks used the unilateral numbers in his presentations to Rumsfeld. This force was the largest and took the most time to deploy, especially since the assumption was that all the equipment would flow through a single port in Kuwait. The numbers were based on what it would take to defeat the Republican Guard and demolish Saddam's regime. As Franks saw it, that was the first order of business. Settling a plan to secure Iraq after the regime was ousted was an issue to be dealt with later.

Based on these assumptions. Franks and his team of planners had shaved the numbers in 1003-98 to some 385,000, essentially the minimum number of troops that Zinni had concluded were necessary to occupy Iraq. But when Franks presented them on December 4 it became clear that that was not what Rumsfeld expected. He was not looking to just trim numbers, but to change the paradigm.

When CENTCOM conferred by video conference with Rumsfeld a week later he was able to present more of his thinking. Rumsfeld had offered his thoughts on how to slice the regime. Drawing on Rumsfeld's slices, the CENTCOM planners had created a matrix, which Franks dubbed his grand strategy.

The slices were listed on a horizontal axis and included leadership, internal security, Iraq's presumed WMD sites, Saddam's Republican Guard, his Regular Army, territory, infrastructure, civilian society, and the commercial sector. Those were the things the planners wanted to be able to affect or influence. The vertical axis listed the "lines of operation." These were military capabilities that could be brought to bear on the slices, such as airpower, Special Operations Forces, conventional ground forces, information operations, and civil-military operations. The chart showed which capabilities could influence which slices, using, at Franks's suggestion, drawings of tiny starbursts.

The matrix suggested that Franks was prepared to reexamine the very foundations of the CENTCOM strategy for Iraq and was prepared to incorporate some of the defense secretary's concepts into the plan. As for the numbers, Franks had managed to shrink the ground force to 300,000 by fiddling with the assumptions. The attack would use Kuwait as a springboard, did not involve allies, and entailed a troop deployment that could last 120 days. Like the reference to Rumsfeld's slices, those planning factors were still up for grabs, but Franks had demonstrated that he was trying to meet Rumsfeld partway.

The plan was moving in Rumsfeld's direction, but the defense secretary indicated that he was still not satisfied. He wanted the force level to be smaller and thought the four-month period to deploy the forces too long. It would constrain the president's diplomatic flexibility and send a message that he had decided to go to war. CENTCOM needed to find a way to compress the deployment.

By the time Franks presented the plan to Rumsfeld in Washington on December 19 he had managed to shrink the force some more and shorten the timelines. An initial invasion force of 145,000 would be deployed over ninety days. The war would begin at that point while reinforcements would continue to flow until the force reached 275,000 or so. As for the war itself, the plan projected that the major attack would take 45 days. Another 90 days were allocated for completing the destruction of Saddam's regime, meaning the war could last as long as 135 days. At that point, the United States would transition into reconstruction.[8]

Rumsfeld thought the plan had improved, but lay down yet another marker that it still needed to be smaller and faster. He indicated that Franks might be asked soon to show his thinking to the president. After laying out the plan, Franks left for Afghanistan for the installation of Hamid Karzai as the Afghan president. In Tampa, the planners continued to crank away. The sense of urgency was high. The president was interested in being briefed on an executable plan.

In the Love Shack, Lieutenant Colonel John Agoglia, one of CENTCOM's main planners, speculated about the Bush administration's new war on terror and their new target: Iraq. What was Al Qaeda up to?, he noted in his diary. Did the terrorist group have a grand strategy? Were they trying to bait the U.S. to strike in Iraq or elsewhere in the region and prompt the United States to overextend its forces? "We got to be careful," Agoglia confided to himself. "They may be thinking more long-term than we are."[9]

The next week was not an easy period for Franks. The United States and its Afghan allies had Osama bin Laden on the run, but the Al Qaeda leader was holed up with his disciples in the mountains of Tora Bora and there was every chance he would get away. Franks wanted the Pakistanis and the Afghan mujahidin that the CIA had recruited and paid to serve as U.S. allies to "hold hands" and jointly seal the Afghan-Pakistani border. But the Pakistani forces were not effective and the mujahidin were ill-motivated and corrupt. The Afghan war had turned into a manhunt and the U.S. did not seem to have the right search party.

Unhappy with the way Tora Bora was going, Franks voiced to his staff dissatisfaction with Lieutenant General Paul Mikolashek, his successor at Third Army, who was overseeing the land war in Afghanistan from Camp Doha, Kuwait. "Either he produces or I take it over," Franks barked. It was an empty threat, but an accurate reflection of the frustration CENTCOM was having in bringing the Afghan war to a successful close and finding the elusive Al Qaeda leader.[10]

As Franks returned to Tampa he learned that he was scheduled to go to Crawford, Texas, to present his thinking on Iraq to the president at his ranch on December 28. Rumsfeld would not be there, but like other cabinet members would join the meeting in a video conference. It was a command performance and one of the most important sessions of Franks's career. Bush had been unhappy that Franks had not had an effective plan on the shelf to deal with the Al Qaeda camps in Afghanistan after the 9/11 attack, but had grown more comfortable with the campaign as the war went on. Now Franks would be giving an accounting of an unfinished war and submitting a concept for a new one.

Franks's two-year term as CENTCOM commander was due to expire in the middle of 2002 and would need to be extended if he was to preside over the Iraq operation. The president and his men would not only be evaluating the Iraqi war plans, but taking the measure of the man who might command the invasion. For Franks, winning the confidence of the president was vital. As a young captain in 1971 Franks had written a poem. "Grant me," Franks had written,

> One opportunity to influence the course of history
> The foresight to anticipate that opportunity
> The conviction to plan for it
> The fortitude to implement the plan.[11]

The chance he had dreamed of thirty years earlier now seemed within his grasp.

Franks flew to Texas in CENTCOM's Gulfstream jet along with Victor "Gene" Renuart, the cerebral Air Force major general whom Franks had called on to head the planning effort. After being greeted by the president, Franks was led to a room in Bush's Crawford house that was impervious to eavesdropping and outfitted with video systems for classified discussion with the president's far-flung cabinet. Cheney would be participating from his Wyoming vacation home and Rumsfeld was tuning in from his retreat in New Mexico. Powell, George Tenet, Rice, and Andy Card, the president's chief of staff, would be tuning in from the White House situation room.

Franks gave an update on Afghanistan and talked about his trip to attend Karzai's swearing in. He did not confide his misgivings over Mikolashek and the way the battle had gone at Tora Bora. That would stay within the CENTCOM family. Franks might berate his subordinates but he would express nothing but confidence to the commander-in-chief.

Then Franks laid out his commander's estimate on Iraq. He began by saying that the existing plan was old-think. He said that his biggest worry was Saddam's WMD. Much would depend on how much cooperation the United States was able to elicit from its allies.

As Franks presented the plan it became clear that Rumsfeld was more concerned about the number of forces than the president. As Franks was briefing regarding the 275,000-strong force, Rumsfeld intervened over the video teleconference. "Mr. President," Rumsfeld said. "We are still working through the number. The number Tom is giving you is soft." Rumsfeld had made a big show about allowing Franks to go to Crawford unescorted, but he did not hesitate to call the shots.[12]

Secretary of State Powell, the former JCS chairman under Bush senior, had concerns about the number of troops. He cautioned Franks to be sure that he had enough forces, including logistics personnel. Powell's view of what was required was very different from Rumsfeld's. As the top diplomat, Powell had to be careful not to intrude on Franks's prerogatives as a commander, but he was signaling Franks to be certain he had all the muscle that might be required. Condoleezza Rice was worried about how CENTCOM would respond if WMD were used, how to stop Scud missles from being fired at Israel, and the role of coalition partners.

The president was engaged. Bush said that it looked as if Franks was developing a plan that could be executed. He was beginning to see that it was something the United States could do. But Bush indicated that he was still nervous about the long lead time to deploy forces and wanted some way to compress it.

After the meeting, the president and Franks jumped into a pickup truck and Bush gave the general a tour of the ranch. He apparently passed muster with the president. They stopped at the house and Laura Bush invited Franks and Renuart to stay for lunch. Franks begged off. He needed to get back to Tampa and get back to work. There would be several weeks before the next command performance in Washington, but there was an enormous amount still to do.

To assist the command in its work, the planning staff in the CENTCOM parking lot was expanded to include two officials from Doug Feith's office. Rumsfeld had offered to contribute staff to the planning effort, and Franks had made a gesture toward accommodating the secretary by opening his planning team to two officials: Abram Shulsky, a policy official who had gone to graduate school at the University of Chicago with Wolfowitz, and Bill Bruner, an Air Force colonel who had served in the Black Hole, the offensive air war planning cell in Riyadh during the Gulf War, and later did a stint as an aide to Gingrich. It was highly unusual for CENTCOM's war planning team to include Rumsfeld aides, but this was not to be a usual war. Renuart figured that there was some value in having aides who provided an understanding of what the Defense Department wanted but some CENTCOM officials had a less flattering description: "Feith spies."[13]

· · ·

At the Pentagon, Rumsfeld and his advisers saw that the plan was at a formative stage and that this was the time to shape it. Newt Gingrich was one of them. The former House Republican leader had long been a military history buff, traveled in conservative circles, and had Rumsfeld's ear. Gingrich had been appointed by Rumsfeld to the Defense Policy Board, the advisory panel, which was headed by Perle. He was a wholehearted supporter of toppling Saddam, and as a proponent of Rumsfeld's military transformation he was equally interested in how the military went about it.

Gingrich had been introduced to Doug Macgregor by Art Cebrowski, a retired Navy admiral who had been tasked by Rumsfeld with coming up with ideas for the military's transformation. Macgregor had served in the 2nd Armored Cavalry Regiment during the Gulf War and fought in the battle of 73 Easting, one of the major tank engagements with the Republican Guard. He had earned a doctorate in international relations from the University of Virginia and had held a variety of important command assignments at NATO and in the Army. He was the rare breed of officer with strong views about the need to overhaul the Army. He thought many of the service generals were more bureaucrats than warriors and was not shy about publicly expressing his view. After the Gulf War, he had written a provocative book, *Breaking the Phalanx,* which argued for a reshaped Army built around mobile armored brigades. In later writings, he argued that the Army, properly restructured, could attack Baghdad with 50,000 troops and win within two weeks.

In 2001, Macgregor was transferred to the Pentagon and assigned to work on Shinseki's plan to reform the Army. His views were radically different from the Army chief of staff's and he saw the move as a way for the Army leadership to keep him in line. If that was the intent, Macgregor was having none of it.

As the Pentagon's focus shifted to Iraq, Macgregor received a call from Gingrich, who told him that Rumsfeld was frustrated with the military's suggestion that hundreds of thousands of troops would be needed to defeat and occupy Iraq. The defense secretary, Gingrich told Macgregor, was concerned that his generals did not want to fight. Gingrich asked Macgregor to draft a briefing, which the former lawmaker could quietly slip to Rumsfeld. For Macgregor, it was a golden opportunity to do an end run around the Army hierarchy and promote his views to the Pentagon official who mattered most.

Macgregor put together a briefing, which he delivered to Gingrich's house in McLean, Virginia, on New Year's Eve. The paper called for a "Rapid, decisive strike to the center," which in the case of Iraq meant Baghdad. Macgregor advised assembling an armor-heavy force of 342 tanks and 400 Bradley Fighting Vehicles, which would be divided into three battle groups of 5,500 soldiers. The force would rush to Baghdad, avoiding contact as much as possible with Iraqi army forces, who Macgregor thought were ill motivated and who could be used later to police the country. After the capital was taken, 15,000 light infantry soldiers and additional reinforcements would be flown in to maintain order. Macgregor argued that the value of small, more lethal formations had been demonstrated in Afghanistan and that a "paradigm shift" was needed to put them into effect in Iraq as well. After he received the paper, Rumsfeld had it sent to Franks as an example of the creative thinking the CENTCOM commander should consider.[14]

The next thing Macgregor knew he had an invitation to Tampa to meet with the CENTCOM commander himself. Franks knew better than to anger Rumsfeld by rebuffing the officer, but the staff was not shy. In one of Macgregor's initial meetings he discussed his thinking with Mike Fitzgerald, an Army colonel and one of Franks's chief war planners. Fitzgerald was concerned that Macgregor was giving short shrift to logistics and noted that an artillery unit had run out of gas in the 1991 Gulf War. Macgregor said that artillery would not be needed in the upcoming fight, which prompted Fitzgerald, who started out as an artilleryman, to get up in disgust and walk out.

Saturday, January 12, was set aside for Macgregor's meeting with Franks. Franks's office was decorated with country music paraphernalia, NFL football helmets, and a carpet from Afghanistan. Colonel Michael Hayes, a Franks aide, cautioned Macgregor in advance not to get upset if the general used a lot of profanity. The CENTCOM chief was waiting for him along with his top staff.

Franks began the session with a long monologue. Throughout the sessions Franks referred to Rumsfeld, somewhat sarcastically, as "his nibs," a derisive British term that Macgregor believed expressed some of the frustration he was having with the constant questions from Rumsfeld. Then Franks turned to Macgregor and asked him to outline his case.

Macgregor presented his plan, which he said would enable U.S. forces to reach Baghdad and take out the regime in ninety-six hours. As a feint, he proposed stationing Army helicopters on an aircraft carrier and launching them into southern Iraq. Mike "Rifle" DeLong, the three-star Marine general who served as Franks's deputy, was skeptical. He thought the small force might be vulnerable to Iraqi WMD. Macgregor argued that the forces would be more vulnerable if the U.S. engaged in a lengthy buildup. If the U.S. forces moved fast they would catch the Iraqis flat-footed.

Macgregor also suggested that the light infantry forces might be secretly based in Oman and could be whisked to Baghdad to keep order. Franks mused that the light infantry might also be based in Afghanistan. Macgregor could not imagine Iran giving permission for the U.S. to overfly its territory on the way to battlefields in Iraq, but withheld comment.

Franks summed up his response to Macgregor's presentation in a staccato burst of phrases: "Attack from a cold start. I agree. Straight at Baghdad. I agree. Small and fast. I agree. Simultaneous air and ground. Probably, but not sure yet."[15]

On the way out, Franks handed Macgregor a coin commemorating CENTCOM, a common military token. Hayes said Franks would call if he wanted more help, which he never did. Macgregor concluded that Franks had simply given him a polite reception in order to mollify Rumsfeld and had no intention of implementing his advice. After returning to Washington, Macgregor wrote a memo detailing the meeting. Gingrich sent copies to eleven key participants, including Cheney's office. Macgregor was not inclined to temper his view and continued to channel his advice through Gingrich and Jamie Durnan, a Defense official who was a friend of Andy Card, Bush's closest adviser.

In Tampa, Renuart headed up the effort to explain to the Pentagon why CENTCOM considered Macgregor's ideas extreme. CENTCOM was prepared to attack with fewer forces, but nothing as light as Macgregor proposed. It was not, however, the end to the suggestions from Washington.

Rumsfeld sent a note to Franks in December suggesting that the CENTCOM commander and his planners review *Shock and Awe,* a study co-authored by Harlan K. Ullman and James P. Wade, the latter a defense intellectual and former Pentagon official. The tome argued that salvos of precision weapons could be used to paralyze the enemy's command and control and thus achieve "rapid dominance" on the battlefield. Along with a summary of a report on the subject, Wade forwarded an endorsement of the idea by Charles Horner, the air component commander during the Persian Gulf War. This suggestion was easier for Franks to finesse. As with Rumsfeld's slices, Franks appropriated the term "shock and awe" but not the details.[16]

On January 29, the president devoted much of his State of the Union address to security issues and proclaimed Iraq, Iran, and North Korea to be part of an "axis of evil." Bush declared that WMD in the hands of rogue states was an unacceptable threat and warned that he would not wait while dangers gathered. It was the first hint of what CENTCOM already knew: Iraq would be the next phase in the White House campaign against terror.[17]

Three days later, Franks flew to Washington to present Rumsfeld with the latest version of the plan. It was no longer called the commander's estimate but dubbed the Generated Start, an allusion to the idea that the United States would rapidly generate the air and ground forces to topple Saddam. Under the plan, the White House was to give CENTCOM thirty days' notice that it had decided to attack so that the command could begin gearing up the forces. Then Franks would take sixty days to deploy the air and ground force.

The attack would kick off with three divisions but ultimately build to five and two-thirds divisions, or some 275,000 troops. As CENTCOM envisioned the attack, the Marines would attack in the east, seize the oilfields, the bridges at Nasiriyah, and control the corridor up to Kut and along the Iranian border. The planners recalled the failed Shiite uprising after the 1991 war and Saddam's subsequent crackdown. They felt the Marines would have to control the east to prevent a recurrence. The Army, meanwhile, would move on Baghdad to the west. Special Operations Forces would work with the Kurds in the north and would prowl western Iraq to suppress Scuds, with the help of the Air Force.

As the CENTCOM planners saw it, there would be a number of innovations. The attack would begin while the last of the reinforcements were still streaming to Kuwait. That would reduce the time to prepare and enable the U.S. to catch the Iraqis by surprise. The United States would attack before waiting for all of the divisions to deploy, unlike during the Gulf War. Another innovation was that there might be a near simultaneous ground and air attack against the regime. The United States would be taking advantage of what the Iraqis had come to expect from the Americans. After a decade or more of confrontation they would anticipate a preliminary air campaign.[18]

Rumsfeld still thought the plan took too long. He told Franks he needed to try to compress the deployment phase from sixty to thirty days, a shift that would require beginning with far fewer troops. At CENTCOM, the planners were striving for a compromise, a plan that would be smaller than Zinni's 1003 but far larger than anything Macgregor had in mind. Rumsfeld, however, was still not satisfied and was keeping up the pressure.

CHAPTER 3

Smaller Is Beautiful

On March 3, 2002, Franks had yet another meeting with the president. CENTCOM had continued to refine the Generated Start, but there were a number of matters that Franks could not settle. A "coalition of the willing" depended on some allied support. To carry out the most effective plan possible, Franks needed access to foreign bases and the right to fly over other nations' territories.

Another imperative added urgency. In early February, Rumsfeld had asked Franks if he could carry out the attack in the spring of 2002. That suggestion had hit the CENTCOM planners like a thunderbolt. Rumsfeld seemed to think the Afghan and Iraq wars might be a one-two punch in the Bush administration's war on terror. Whenever the United States attacked, CENTCOM needed to have a springboard for its invasion.[1]

To help line up prospective allies, Bush decided to dispatch a senior official, and there was quick agreement that it should be Dick Cheney. As a former defense secretary, Cheney had the contacts in the region and as vice president he spoke with authority. Foreign governments understood that in talking with Cheney they would not be hearing only the view of one faction within the government but getting the authoritative view from the White House. Three days later, Franks met with Cheney to explain, country by country, the cooperation he needed to carry out the war plan.

Cheney was, by common consent, the most powerful vice president in history. He had been picked by Bush for his experience and had used it to bring Rumsfeld on board as defense secretary to shape the new government. Within the administration, Cheney's alliance with Rumsfeld allowed him to set the terms of the policy debate. While Rumsfeld would often be vocal in National Security Council meetings, Cheney saved his advice for his one-on-one meetings with the president. Cheney's sense of discipline and penchant for secrecy were legendary. Bush could announce a policy without it being obvious that he was endorsing Cheney's line.

Cheney's staff functioned like a mini-NSC. A fair number of Cheney's team had backgrounds in defense from Cheney's days at the Pentagon and they interacted easily with Rumsfeld's team. Wolfowitz kept a photo on his wall that symbolized the bond. It showed Wolfowitz flanked by Rumsfeld on one side and Cheney on the other. The caption read: "Who is the best defense secretary?"

This arrangement was enormously frustrating to Colin Powell, who often found himself the odd man out in determining the nation's foreign policy and trying to reopen issues that Cheney and Rumsfeld had all but decided between them. Powell's relationship with Cheney, while cordial, was never warm. In the lead-up to the Gulf War, Cheney had been decidedly more hawkish than Powell about the need to evict Iraqi troops from Kuwait and had presented an alternative war plan to the White House without consulting the JCS chairman. Powell noted in his memoir that during their years in the Pentagon they never spent a social hour together.

Later, after the fall of Baghdad, as Bush was completing his first term in office and Powell was preparing to leave the State Department, he told the president in a private meeting that the national security decision-making process was broken. Even so, Powell was not sure his point had registered. Bush had picked Cheney and Rumsfeld for a number of reasons and their tough-minded approach to the exercise of power was one of them. It was a troika. The president would preside, the vice president would guide, and the defense secretary would implement.[2]

The vice president also had decidedly firm views on Iraq. Cheney was the only senior official from the administration of Bush senior whose views on Iraq had changed markedly. Cheney had defended the decision to end the ground war at 100 hours, withdraw the troops, and avoid the snare of potential occupation duties in Iraq in 1991. But in so doing, Cheney had calculated that Saddam would be overthrown by humiliated and disgruntled Iraqi generals. He even placed a friendly wager that Saddam would fall within a year or two.[3] But in his years out of office Cheney came to believe that the containment strategy he had helped put in place was faltering, that the web of economic sanctions was fraying, and that Saddam was a growing menace. As vice president, he was now advising a more aggressive president.

The message Cheney intended to deliver to potential allies was clear and direct. If there was any question about what threat the U.S. would focus on after Afghanistan, Cheney had the answer: it was Iraq. Saddam's presumed weapons programs were an unacceptable menace, one that Washington did not intend to live with any longer. If it came to war, this time the United States would finish the job of removing Saddam. Cheney did not intend to get involved in detailed negotiations on the trip, but he would lay the basis for lower-level consultations to come. During Cheney's whirlwind journey, he would visit twelve countries in ten days.

The nations selected for Cheney's visit included most of those the United States would need to use to organize an attack on Iraq: Saudi Arabia, Qatar, Bahrain, Oman, Kuwait, Jordan, Turkey, the United Arab Emirates, Egypt, and Israel. The only Arab nation in the region he would not visit was Syria, which had contributed troops for the Desert Storm campaign but under Bashar al-Assad was now seen as part of the problem by Pentagon officials, who suspected that Syria had its own WMD programs and cited Damascus's support for Hezbollah, the anti-Israel terrorist group. The Bush team, in fact, hoped that toppling Saddam would throw enough of a scare into Syria that it would temper its support for Hezbollah and stay in line.

On the way over to the Middle East, Cheney would also stop in London. The coalition of the willing that the Bush administration hoped to assemble needed a European member or two. Britain, virtually alone among European nations, had both the military means and the close ties to the United States that would enable it to make a major contribution to a potential invasion force. In fact, the senior British military representative at CENTCOM had already quietly let it be known to Franks's command that if the United States planned to lead an invasion against Saddam, Britain would consider contributing a division for the effort.

Still, CENTCOM's wish list was extensive and it was far from clear that even Cheney could pave the way for the requests. There was no problem with Kuwait, which would be the main launching pad for an invasion. Kuwait's only worry was that the United States might somehow not finish the job of getting rid of Saddam. But some of the other nations, like Saudi Arabia, Jordan, and Turkey, would be more difficult to engage.

During Cheney's visits, the Gulf States signaled that they were prepared to be the most cooperative. The high point of Cheney's trip was Qatar, which had long sought a closer association with the United States military. The Qataris had built the Al Udeid Air Base at a cost of $1 billion at a time when they did not have an air force. Al Udeid was used by the U.S. during the war in Afghanistan, but its existence had been an official secret. The first U.S. casualty of the Afghan war was an airman who was crushed by a truck on a darkened runway at Al Udeid, an event that was acknowledged at the time as occurring "somewhere in southwest Asia." When Cheney arrived at the base with a small group of reporters in tow, Al Udeid was officially unveiled. Qatar was also prepared to let CENTCOM establish a forward headquarters on its territory.

In Bahrain, a spokesman accorded Cheney the highest honor, referring to him as the "deputy president." The United States Navy had its Middle East headquarters in Bahrain and was proud of the fact that the American naval relationship with the small Gulf state predated the opening of the U.S. embassy.

Saudi Arabia was a far more complicated case. The Saudis had allowed the United States and other allied forces to deploy hundreds of thousands of troops on its territory for the Gulf War, but had adopted a less visible form of cooperation with Washington since then, fearful that too close an identification with the United States would stir up Islamic fundamentalists at home. Cheney had experienced a taste of that in the aftermath of the Gulf War when he was defense secretary. Cheney had sought to arrange for the U.S. Army to store a division's worth of equipment at King Khalid Military City so the United States would be better poised to rush troops to the region if there was a future crisis, only to be turned down. Since then, the United States had flown air patrols over southern Iraq (but not bombing missions) from Saudi territory and had managed the air war in Afghanistan from a multimillion-dollar command center at Prince Sultan Air Base outside Riyadh. CENTCOM wanted a lot from Saudi Arabia. Most important, it wanted to continue to use the Prince Sultan command center. It wanted to base aircraft in Saudi Arabia and to carry out attacks from Saudi territory. It wanted fuel for its aircraft. It wanted to launch Special Operations missions into Iraq from Ar'ar in western Saudi territory. It also wanted to disembark ground forces at the Saudi port of Al Jubayl in the northeast part of the country to relieve the dependence on Kuwait's port. Cheney's visit would be the beginning of a long conversation.

Jordan was also tricky. CENTCOM wanted to explore a western front: mounting attacks from Jordan with conventional as well as Special Operations Forces. King Abdullah of Jordan, which has a large Palestinian population, was uneasy about the requests.

As for Turkey, General James Jones, the Marine commandant and fu-

ture NATO commander, had pushed the idea of a northern front as had
Mikolashek and some CENTCOM staff. The idea appealed to Franks.
The United States could come at Baghdad from two directions: heading
north from Kuwait and south from Turkey. Along with a near simultaneous air and ground war the invasion would be Franks's version of "shock
and awe." Contingency plans for a Turkish front—clumsily code-named
Pilgrim—were drawn up, but the White House would be asking a lot from
the Turks.

Turkey was a NATO member and the Turks had been helpful on
Afghanistan: Ankara approved within an hour the American request to
fly over Turkish territory and had agreed to lead the small peacekeeping
contingent in Kabul. But Turkey's stand on Iraq was different. Turkey had
allowed the United States to conduct air strikes from its bases during the
Persian Gulf War, but it had not been an easy decision. The economic
consequences of the Gulf War, as Turkey tabulated them, had been severe
and American assistance in the aftermath of the war had fallen short of
what the Turks had expected. The Turkish public was also overwhelm-
ingly against another war with Iraq, no small consideration, as Turkey
was the only Islamic democracy in the region. Beyond that, the Turks
feared that a war would facilitate the breakup of Iraq and lead to the establishment of an independent Kurdish state, which would fan secession-
ist tendencies among Turkish Kurds.

Cheney indicated in advance that he wanted to meet with the chief of
the Turkish general staff, Huseyin Kivrikoglu, as well as Turkish prime
minister Bülent Ecevit. The request to meet with the Turkish military
bothered the government, which bridled at the suggestion that the Turkish generals called the shots. In the end Cheney got the meeting, which
was held at the Ankara airport.

Cheney made clear to the Turks that the Americans would involve
them fully in the war planning for Iraq. The U.S. would disclose its plans
to them and look to them for advice. The Turks repeated their concerns,
including the imperative of ensuring the territorial integrity of Iraq and
their fears that an attack on Iraq would hurt the Turkish economy. Both
sides left feeling they had influenced the other. Cheney had demonstrated
how serious the administration was about confronting Saddam and expressed the U.S.'s desire to treat the Turks as full partners, while the Turks
had voiced their concerns. Ecevit moved to reassure his public that war
was not imminent. Cheney, the Turkish leader said on March 19, had
underlined that "there will not be an operation against Iraq in the near
future."

During his trip, Cheney stopped in Yemen and met with President Ali Abdullah Saleh at the Sanna airport. The Bush administration did not need Yemen for a war with Iraq; the subject was fighting terrorism. Saleh, who had close ties with Saddam, told Cheney that Saddam did not want to go to war but would use chemical weapons if attacked. Cheney did not blink. If Saddam used chemical weapons, then the Americans would deal with it.

One of Cheney's stops along the way was the USS *John C. Stennis,* an aircraft carrier in the Arabian Sea. Wearing a white helmet bearing the initials "VP," Mr. Cheney told the sailors, "Our next objective is to prevent terrorists, and regimes that sponsor terror, from threatening America or our friends and allies with weapons of mass destruction. Wherever threats are forming against the civilized world, we will respond and respond decisively."[4]

It was a public version of the argument Rumsfeld and his aides had made in the days after the September 11 attacks and which Bush had articulated in his January State of the Union speech. There would be a second phase in the administration's war on terror and Iraq could well be it.

At CENTCOM, the report card from Cheney's trip showed that the U.S. was making headway in winning support, but that there was more work to do. Kuwait, Qatar, the United Arab Emirates, and Bahrain were deemed to be supportive. Jordan would probably help, but it needed to be done covertly. Egypt would quietly provide limited support in the form of providing access through the Suez Canal and possibly more. The Saudi position was still unclear, and Turkey remained a big question mark. The Bush administration wanted to assemble a coalition of the willing, but some key allies were not yet all that willing. CENTCOM in the words of one ranking officer was "a little unfulfilled. There was no strong feeling that we had gotten anything yet."[5]

On March 21, Franks convened a meeting at the U.S. air base in Ramstein, Germany, with his component commanders: his ground, air, sea, and Special Operations deputies who would run the war. It was a convenient location to hold the session but there was more than a measure of irony in the decision to hold a war council right under the nose of the antiwar Germans. To maintain security, the officers were told to wear civilian clothes.

When Franks arrived he warmly greeted Scott Wallace, the V Corps commander, who had been working on Iraq since he was tasked with fleshing out the Vigilant Guardian plan in the fall of 2001, and Mike Hagee, the commander of the Marine Expeditionary Force, which would have an important role in the invasion. But Franks was somewhat distant toward Mikolashek, the commander he had complained about when U.S. forces were trying to corral bin Laden at Tora Bora.[6]

The first day was devoted to Afghanistan, but the second day was all about Iraq. Franks gave his "Burglar in the House" speech, which was becoming a standard part of his repertoire. The component commanders needed to take the meeting with deadly seriousness. This was not a pro forma planning exercise. Otherwise, they might find themselves confronting a burglar with a fly swatter. Franks knew the administration was deadly serious about Iraq, and was looking for a way to convey that to his subordinates without talking out of school.

Then Franks laid out his vision as embodied in the Generated Start plan. Franks said he was convinced that Saddam could not deal with more than one crisis at a time. So Franks would present him with multiple crises. The ground forces would attack on multiple axes and close on Baghdad as quickly as possible. Franks said he envisioned a near simultaneous air and ground attack to create "shock and awe," the term he had appropriated from Rumsfeld, who had lifted it from the Wade and Ullman tract. To get ready, Franks said that the Global Hawk reconnaissance drone and other surveillance platforms could be shifted to Iraq, which meant diverting assets from Afghanistan.

There were, however, some notable differences among Franks's subordinates about how to attack. T. Michael "Buzz" Moseley, the air war commander, said that he needed a minimum of ten to fourteen days, perhaps even more, to pummel Iraq's surface-to-air missile sites, airfields, radars, command and control facilities, and leadership targets in Baghdad before the ground forces crossed into Iraq. U.S. and British warplanes had been patrolling northern and southern Iraq for more than a decade but hundreds of surface-to-air missiles were clustered in central Iraq, including the Baghdad area, which the U.S. Air Force had taken to calling the "Super MEZ," or missile engagement zone. Moseley argued that he needed to establish air superiority first to support the ground forces as they pushed north. He was puzzled about why any commander would not want to make ample use of U.S. airpower before sending the troops into harm's way. The United States and its allies had bombed the Iraqis for five weeks before carrying out the 100-hour ground war in 1991.

Mikolashek had a diametrically different view. He wanted the Marines and Army to kick off the war. Mikolashek needed to seize the Rumaylah oilfields, among other tasks, and he wanted to catch the Iraqi ground forces unaware. The air and ground commanders were in competition to come up with ways to achieve surprise. Each saw a military advantage in going first.

Franks had problems with both. He did not buy Moseley's argument for such a long air campaign. A war game carried out by Franks's planners had recommended that the air and ground attacks begin within twenty-four to sixty hours of each other. But Franks was not happy with Mikolashek either. He thought that the land plan took too long to get to Baghdad. Franks wanted to get to the Iraqi capital fast. As the discussion unfolded, Franks wanted to know how quickly the ground forces could roll toward Baghdad. Wallace looked at Lieutenant Colonel Jim Danna, the chief V Corps war planner who had spent the past few months laboring over Vigilant Guardian before switching to the Generated Start. Danna said 18 miles per hour, which was a pretty good rate for mechanized forces.[7]

After meeting with his commanders, Franks returned to Tampa to further develop the Generated Start. The next step was to present the latest iteration of the plan in Washington, including to the Joint Chiefs. Upon his return from Ramstein, Franks instructed his planners to put together the brief.

The planners in the Love Shack had been answering one Rumsfeld question after another and the unusual collaboration with the representatives from Doug Feith's office, Abe Shulsky and Bill Bruner, had not survived the strain. After Franks endured a particularly difficult grilling from Rumsfeld the planners suspected that Feith's aides were feeding tough questions to Washington in advance. Dealing with Rumsfeld was hard enough without the boys from Feith's office tipping the secretary to their every move. The two Defense aides were told they would not be welcome if they were going to function as moles for the Pentagon, and they stopped working in the trailer. The planners had differences among themselves and saw no need to broadcast them to Washington. CENTCOM continued to work with the two officials, who showed up at the classified conferences at Scott Air Force Base in Illinois on troop deployment planning. But they were no longer part of the planning team.

With Rumsfeld pressing for a smaller force there was debate among the senior officers as to how to respond. Mike DeLong, Franks's deputy commander, thought that the briefing should show just the three divisions that were needed to begin the invasion and not the entire five and two-thirds divisions that would eventually be deployed under the plan. That was what he thought Rumsfeld wanted.

The planners were not happy with this request from their superior officer. If the briefing simply showed the number of troops that were needed to start the fight there was a risk that Rumsfeld would conclude that this was all that was needed for the entire war. Beyond that, the planners believed it was important to mobilize the entire five and two-thirds divisions in order to achieve surprise. If the United States let it be known that it was preparing more than five divisions for the war but attacked when only three of the divisions were in Kuwait there was a good chance that CENTCOM might catch the Iraqis off guard. Saddam would be waiting for the United States to assemble a large invasion force only to discover that CENTCOM had begun the war.

When it came time for the planners to preview the briefing with Franks they left in the slide that showed the deployment of all five and two-thirds divisions. After some debate among his subordinates, Franks opted for the larger plan. As Franks explained the logic to his commanders, "We cannot hide that we are coming, but we can make him think we are coming in six months, not three months." CENTCOM was in a tug-of-war with Rumsfeld over the size of the invasion force but on this occasion Franks stuck to his guns.[8]

Unlike the Ramstein meeting, there would not be a lot of glad-handing when Franks went to see the chiefs on March 29. The retirement of Shelton as chairman in September 2001 had removed an Army officer who was dubious about the extravagant claims made by the advocates of transformation. Rumsfeld chose Richard Myers, an Air Force general who once headed the Space Command and had been the vice chairman, as the successor. Myers once jested during a Pentagon briefing for the press that he and Rumsfeld shared a "mind meld," but there were those who had a less charitable view. After hearing Rumsfeld testify on troop levels around the world, Senator John McCain, the Arizona Republican, said cuttingly there was no need to hear from Myers as well since he knew the chairman was incapable of expressing an independent view.[9]

Still, Franks worked for Rumsfeld and only barely tolerated the JCS. When Cheney was defense secretary he had interacted with Powell. He had largely left it up to the JCS chief to deal with General H. Norman

Schwarzkopf, the Desert Storm commander. Zinni had briefed his Desert Fox plan to bomb Iraq's suspected WMD sites to the JCS and the chiefs had even voted on it. But Franks tended to view the chiefs as meddlesome military bureaucrats. Their role was to give advice to the defense secretary and the president and to train and equip forces under Title 10 of the Goldwater-Nichols Act to reform defense so that war-fighters like Franks could take on the nation's foes. In a reference to this landmark legislation, which reinforced the power of the theater commanders, Franks had even denounced the chiefs as "Title Ten Motherfuckers" after a fall meeting on Afghanistan.[10]

Some of the chiefs were not happy with Franks either. After the USS *Cole* was attacked in Yemen in 2000 and the Congress began to question the Pentagon about its effort to protect the fleet, there was muttering among the chiefs that Franks, who was the theater commander, had spent the time traveling about the Middle East and had allowed Vern Clark, the chief of naval operations, and Zinni, who was then retired, to take all the blame. "The absence of the combatant commander was noticeable," said one of the former chiefs. "You could not find Tom Franks."

As the head of their respective services, the chiefs naturally felt they had something to offer. Eric Shinseki, who had lost part of a foot in Vietnam, had run operations in Bosnia. John Jumper, the Air Force chief, had been the head of Air Force operations in Europe during the Kosovo campaign, and Jim Jones had led the initial relief effort in Iraqi Kurdistan after the Gulf War. When Shinseki had heard an early version in January, he had wondered whether the leaner invasion strategy CENTCOM was putting together adequately provided for the considerable logistical demands of pushing to Baghdad. Jumper recalled that Franks's disdain for the chiefs was palpable. "He would come in there all tight-jawed about having to explain to the chiefs what his plan was and would bristle when we offered our experience with him," Jumper said. "He resented the input."[11]

When Franks met with the JCS on March 29, none of the questions posed by the chiefs were showstoppers. Rumsfeld was the key decision-maker in the Pentagon.

The JCS made an indirect contribution. While Franks was working to shorten the plan to suit Rumsfeld, the JCS staff was trying to figure out how to hedge against other threats. They conducted a war game dubbed Prominent Hammer and concluded that if the Generated Start plan was implemented, the U.S. would need to take steps to deter the North Koreans from taking advantage of the U.S. focus on Iraq. B-52s and later B-2s were moved to Guam and planes were shifted to South Korea.

Little more than a week later, Franks met with Bush for yet another session on Iraq. Franks was anticipating an air campaign of four days. He would begin the war when the ground force reached 180,000 and end up with upward of 250,000. As he had at Crawford, Bush worried about the time it would take to deploy the forces, a development that the White House feared could fuel unrest in the Arab world. Franks agreed to see what he could do.

Under pressure to speed up the deployment, Franks had worked to compress the Generated Start, but the changes were on the margins. There was just so much one could do to trim the time it took to move men and matériel from the United States to the Persian Gulf. The political imperative to shorten the deployment time was at war with the physics. The best Franks could do was to suggest that it might be possible to shave the deployment period from sixty to forty-five days. That assumed that the administration would spend some $700 million in "prep actions," preparatory steps like enlarging airfields, building fuel stocks, moving equipment to Kuwait that was secretly stored elsewhere in the region, and upgrading the communications suite for the land war command.

As the planning moved ahead, CENTCOM had three main problems. How to deploy tens of thousands of troops and hundreds of airplanes to the Middle East without tipping its hand to the Iraqis, how to respond if Baghdad recklessly struck first, and how to put off the suggestion from Rumsfeld that they might need to fight a war before the summer of 2002.

The first problem was resolved by Gene Renuart and Buzz Moseley, who proposed a "Spike Plan" to keep the Iraqis off balance. There would be more aggressive patrols of the no-fly zones in southern and northern Iraq while airplanes and aircraft carriers would move in and out of the region. When the actual preparations for war were made it would be unclear to the Iraqis if the U.S. was saber-rattling or it was the real thing. The Spike Plan was a way to desensitize Saddam and, for that matter, the region about what was to unfold.[12]

The solution to the second problem was also in hand. CENTCOM had a long-standing plan, code-named Desert Badger, to carry out a walloping series of air strikes in the event that Saddam managed to down an American pilot. Elaborating on that concept, Franks's planners devised an escalating series of air strikes, which would be carried out by planes already in the region and others rushed over from the United States. If Saddam provoked Washington, CENTCOM could invoke the Red plan (seven days of air strikes), move on to the White plan (eleven more days of air strikes), and then invoke the Blue plan (twenty additional days of bombing). Franks was not enthusiastic about the idea of only pounding Iraq from the air. That seemed like a throwback to the old Clinton-era strategy and was unlikely to seal the fate of Saddam's regime. Franks put the point more colorfully in a meeting with his commanders: "Blue is like peeing on yourself in a dark suit. It feels good, but nobody notices."[13]

In addition to giving Franks additional options on Iraq, however, it was a way to assure an impatient Rumsfeld that there were steps that could be taken immediately in the event things heated up with Iraq. With CENTCOM primed to strike fast, some of Rumsfeld's aides began to float the idea of provoking Iraq to take action, which would provide Washington with an indisputable casus belli and avoid lengthy rounds of diplomacy, including at the United Nations. If the United States put a lot of Special Forces into Iraqi Kurdistan it might prompt the Iraqis to attack. The Kurds might take a beating initially but it would provide the United States with a clear-cut rationale for war. "The idea of provoking Saddam into action did come up in discussions with the OSD [Office of the Secretary of Defense] staff," one CENTCOM planner recalled. For their part, the CENTCOM planners would have nothing of it. If the United States went to war it would not be the result of a trick: there would need to be a clear policy rationale.[14]

The third problem was a bigger worry. Rumsfeld had raised the possibility of an early war, an invasion that could be carried out in the spring or summer of 2002. After the defense secretary made the point, Franks's planners began a series of top secret sessions in February at the Transportation Command headquarters at Scott Air Force Base to arrange the flow of troops, weapons, and war matériel that would be needed for fighting in April or May. But for CENTCOM, fighting before the summer was a bridge too far.

CENTCOM toted up the risks and included them in the slides it briefed in Washington. If the U.S. had to attack early, the military in Kuwait would not have time to adequately prepare the infrastructure or deploy more than a portion of the projected invasion force. CENTCOM would be forced to attack toward Baghdad sequentially, sending an initial force and then follow-up units, instead of mounting simultaneous attacks from multiple directions. U.S. casualties, thus, would be higher. In short, the invasion could be mounted quickly but it would take longer and be messier.

No Washington politician was about to mount an attack that had the potential for high casualties in the face of clear warnings from the field commander that he would be taking significant and unnecessary risks— and all before the November congressional elections. By May, the idea of an early war was all but dead.

Saturday, May 11, 2002, had been set aside for a major review of the planning by the president at his Camp David retreat. The president was not just getting a briefing, but offering advice. It was important, Bush instructed, to portray the invasion as the liberation of Iraq. Messages should be prepared stressing that American forces were moving to free the Iraqis and were not interested in being occupiers.

Franks had an important contribution, too. For months, he had sought to shave the deployment times in the Generated Start and bring them to an irreducible minimum. That, however, had not been enough to satisfy Rumsfeld. Now, Franks had an alternative plan to present: the Running Start. If the Generated Start took too long, CENTCOM could invoke the Red, White, and Blue air strike plans and use them, in effect, as a bridge to a land war. The U.S. could start bombing almost immediately and pummel the Iraqis until the ground forces were in place.

Under the Running Start, the air war would take forty-five days. The ground attack would start as soon as twenty-five days after the air strikes began, in which case the United States would be attacking with as little as a 2,000-man Marine Expeditionary Unit and two Army brigades. Alternatively, CENTCOM could begin the ground war at the forty-five-day mark, which meant that it would be attacking with a complete Army division and complete Marine division.

The Running Start provided something that Rumsfeld had insisted on from the beginning: the avoidance of a long, Powell-style buildup. Instead of taking two months to deploy forces, the U.S. would begin with a near instantaneous attack. That would also go a long way to meeting Bush's concern about an overly long deployment time, which could complicate diplomacy, roil the Middle East, and put the United States's Arab allies under pressure for months before the war got under way. But the Running Start was more of a traditional operation in another respect: as in the Gulf War, there would be a several-week air campaign before the land war. And by attacking before most of the forces were in place there was also the risk that it would drag the war out.

Still, Franks was not withdrawing the Generated Start. That remained on the table. He was simply adding another option, previewing a dramatically new concept with a promise to flesh out the details over the ensuing weeks.

The president did not commit himself to either variant. The Camp David war council produced a series of additional questions. What if the Iraqis hunkered down in Baghdad? How could CENTCOM keep Israel, which had threatened retaliation if struck by Iraqi missiles, out of the fight? Was CENTCOM prepared if and when Saddam unleashed WMD? How would CENTCOM respond if Saddam fled the country?

Of all the queries, avoiding a grueling fight in the streets of Baghdad was the toughest problem. Nobody doubted that the military would trounce the Republican Guard and Saddam's other forces on the march north. But there was palpable concern in the White House that Saddam might order Republican Guard units into the capital to try to turn it into a Mesopotamian Stalingrad. To preclude this scenario, Franks and his planners developed the "Inside-Out Plan." Moseley's warplanes would strike command and control targets in Baghdad at the start to make it hard for Saddam to control his forces, and they would strike the Republican Guard right away to pin them down. Any Republican Guard units that sought to drive to Baghdad would be pounded on the move. In the 1991 Gulf War, the Republican Guard had not been an early target. The war planners had been more concerned with hitting Saddam's command posts in Baghdad and only later got around to striking the Iraqi forces in the field. But the goal this time was regime change and that meant the Medina and its sister Republican Guard divisions would be at the top of the target list.[15]

In late May, Bush sought to repair ties with Europe and promised a deliberate response to the terrorist threat, one that would not be purely military and would enlist the help of the U.S. allies. In a May 23 press conference in Berlin, Bush asserted that Iraq's WMD programs were a serious threat but that he had not prepared an invasion strategy. "I told the Chancellor that I have no war plans on my desk, which is the truth, and that we've got to use all means at our disposal to deal with Saddam Hussein." The president made a similar comment in Paris three days later.[16]

Franks went further. In late May, a radio reporter asked him how many troops he would need for an invasion of Iraq. "That's a great question and one for which I don't have an answer because my boss has not yet asked me to put together a plan to do that," Franks said. "They have not asked me for those kinds of numbers. And I guess I would tell you, if there comes a time when my boss asks me that, then I'd rather provide those sorts of assessments to him. But thanks for the question."[17]

The president's statement was true in only the most literal but trivial sense. Bush had ordered the development of a new CENTCOM war plan, repeatedly met with Franks to hear its details, offered his own views on the schedule for deploying troops and on the military's effort to couch the invasion as a liberation, and sent his vice president halfway around the world to secure allies for the war. And as for Franks, even the cleverest hair-splitting could not reconcile his remarks with the activity at CENTCOM during the previous six months.

On June 19, Franks had yet another war planning meeting with the president to brief the finished version of the Generated Start and promised to do more work on Running Start. By June there was not one war plan. There were two: the Generated Start, which gave the military ninety days to prepare to attack, and the Running Start, which was just what the name advertised. Bush made no decision on which one to adopt. When Franks met again with his land, war, and sea commanders in Ramstein on June 27 and 28, he told them to focus on the Running Start. The administration had given every sign that it was impatient and CENTCOM could not afford to be caught short.[18]

While CENTCOM was laboring over its parallel war plan, the Joint Staff conducted a classified study to assess the new principles of war. General Pete Pace, the vice chairman of the Joint Chiefs of Staff, launched a classified study entitled "Operational Availability," which was directed by Marine General James "Hoss" Cartwright.

Cartwright used Iraq, among other war scenarios. The study reflected the new bureaucratic realities within the Pentagon as much as the breakthroughs in technology and the results were shared with CENTCOM. The study reaffirmed Rumsfeld's intuition that speed had an intrinsic value. If the United States struck fast in a war, it could win with substantially less force and less in the way of logistics. The study also challenged the notion that specific units should have a geographical focus. Each division needed to be flexible enough to take on an array of global missions.[19]

For years, conservatives had seen the Powell doctrine of overwhelming force as an impediment to action and an inhibition against the exercise of American power. If the United States had to engage in a six-month buildup every time it confronted a potential adversary it would rarely act. Rumsfeld and his deputies had argued that there was military utility in getting into the fight quickly and avoiding the sort of massive logistical buildup that Powell had overseen in the Persian Gulf War.

The Army leadership, however, believed that war could not be fought on the cheap, notwithstanding technical advances. In their view numbers and weight of fire counted. It was a view dating to Ulysses S. Grant's formula for success in the Civil War and an ingrained part of Army culture that had served it well in earlier wars. While supporting modernization, the military, in general, took a test-before-buying approach.

But this was not good enough for Rumsfeld, who characterized it as "legacy thinking" and out of step with the times. Heartened by the small-force stunning victory in Afghanistan, the rapid defeat of Iraq on his terms would break the spine of Army resistance to his transformation goal once and for all. With the "Operational Availability" study, the Joint Staff was signing off on the concept. With the help of technology and more astute military planning, the Pentagon could have it both ways: a U.S. intervention could be speedy *and* lethal. The study reflected Rumsfeld's belief that a revolution in military affairs as espoused by Andy Marshall and other defense intellectuals had indeed taken place. As the result of technological advances in electronics and computerization, warfare was being elevated to a new level.

There was one area that the "Operational Availability" study did not address: the military requirements for stabilizing a vanquished nation after a war. In postwar situations, speed does not substitute for mass. It takes a lot of troops to control a nation of some 24 million, which was the population estimate for Iraq. Stability operations are a labor-intensive task. Concerns about securing Iraq after Saddam was gone, in fact, informed Zinni's 1003-98 plan and its minimal requirement for a force level of 380,000.[20]

The results of the study were conveyed to CENTCOM, where they added to the pressure to come up with a smaller invasion force. Not everybody was comfortable with the push for small formations.

In July, Prime Minister Tony Blair's cabinet met to discuss their likely alliance with the Americans. Geoff Hoon, the British defense minister, reported that the most likely time for a U.S.-led invasion was January, but noted that CENTCOM, drawing on Moseley's desensitization plan, had also begun "spikes of activity." Still, the British had some serious military and political questions about the Americans. Sir Richard Dearlove, the director of MI6, the British foreign intelligence service, reported that his visit to Washington had convinced him that the administration's decision to invade Iraq was inevitable but that there seemed to be little deliberation among the Americans of what to do after Saddam was toppled.

There were a number of military options for the British. The smallest was to offer the United States access to British bases, such as the Indian Ocean island of Diego Garcia and on Cyprus in the Eastern Mediterranean, as well as dispatching three Special Forces squadrons to the fray. An expanded option would contribute British warplanes and ships. The most substantial option would add as many as 40,000 British troops, who would open a front from Turkey and tie down the Iraqi divisions in the north.

Sir Michael Boyce, the head of the British Defence Staff, described the two plans Franks had put before the White House. The Americans, he told Blair, were considering the Generated Start, which involved a slow buildup of 250,000 troops, a seventy-two-hour air campaign, and then a push to Baghdad from the south. The second option was the Running Start, which would entail a continuous air campaign and could be kicked off with ground forces already in the region, perhaps as few as 18,000 troops.

The Running Start, Boyce reported, was "a hazardous option." Boyce was not convinced that the United States had a workable military strategy. He was not sure how the U.S. would respond if Saddam used WMD or if street fighting raged in the streets of Baghdad. The British military, Boyce noted, still had a lot of questions.

While British officers were worried about the state of the U.S. planning, the civilians in Blair's cabinet were more assured. It was a faith-based confidence grounded on the assurance that Bush would not stake his presidency on a war with Iraq unless he knew what he was doing. Surely, argued Jack Straw, the British foreign secretary, the United States would not take the momentous step of invading and occupying Iraq unless it was persuaded that it had a winning plan.[21]

CHAPTER 4

The Other Side of the Hill

In Baghdad, Saddam Hussein had his own idea of how best to defend his regime. The Iraqi leader's top priority was protecting his government against potential coups and internal threats, such as a Shiite rebellion. Iran, an adversary with whom he had fought a bloody eight-year war, was next on the list of danger. Fighting a ground war with the Americans was a distant third. For all of the war talk and preparations in Washington, his real worries were closer at hand.

Saddam's attitude toward the Americans was clear when he met with his ministers after the September 11 attack on the United States. The cabinet was worried that the Bush administration would lash out at its enemies and that Iraq would be one of them. It recommended a statement of condolence to head off new troubles with Washington. Saddam rejected the idea. If Iraqi ministers wanted to convey their sympathies, they could do so quietly and informally to select U.S. officials, but there would be no formal expression of commiseration. The United States, Saddam told Tariq Aziz, his deputy prime minister, was getting its just deserts, a position the Iraqi leader later expressed in an open letter to the American people. Saddam was not looking for a war with the United States and he was not expecting one either.

Saddam's formative military crisis was not his lopsided defeat in the 1991 Persian Gulf War, but the sudden Shiite uprising in the south that followed. His regime had experienced enormous problems deploying loyal troops to the troubled locations with enough speed and firepower to put down the insurgency. By March 1991 his regime was so worried about losing its grip that it ordered helicopters to drop bombs full of Sarin nerve gas on Shiite rebels in Karbala and Najaf. It was a rash step given that the

U.S. forces that had evicted the Iraqis from Kuwait were still sitting on Iraqi territory south of the Euphrates. It was Saddam's good fortune that the bombs malfunctioned and that the episode was not publicly confirmed until after the fall of Baghdad twelve years later.[1]

Still, the assault testified to the anxieties of Saddam's inner circle. The regime was concerned, first and foremost, with the threat from within. It was a fundamental worry that colored all of the military's planning and which did not become clear to U.S. intelligence until after the regime fell, when they conducted top secret interrogations of Saddam and his top aides.

With his extraordinary requirement for security and the powers of an absolute leader to enforce obedience, Saddam's key decisions and those of his aides and top military officers remained veiled during the buildup to the war. But they were documented after the collapse of Saddam's regime as part of a classified effort by the U.S. military to reconstruct Iraqi decision-making through the fall of Baghdad and the flight of Saddam and his sons.

Posing as military historians, interrogators working on behalf of the U.S. Joint Forces Command interviewed fifteen of the top fifty-five regime officials, some of whom were questioned in the "special confinement facility" for high-ranking Iraqi prisoners at the Baghdad airport, while others were interrogated at the Abu Ghraib prison. Still others were debriefed in safe houses around Baghdad and at lavish lunches designed to loosen their tongues. The senior Iraqi officials questioned included Saddam's personal secretary, a Republican Guard corps commander, division commanders, Saddam's minister of defense, and Ali Hassan al-Majeed, Saddam's cousin, who was known as "Chemical Ali" for his role in supervising the chemical weapons attacks on the Kurds, among many others. More than 450 other interrogations by the CIA and other intelligence organizations were also accessed for the assessment, as were almost 600 captured Iraqi documents.

Overseen by the U.S. Joint Forces Command, the study, "Iraqi Perspectives," was presented to President Bush two years after the war began but has never been publicly released. Along with the work done by the CIA-sponsored Iraq Survey Group, which examined Iraq's WMD efforts or lack thereof, the study provides an unvarnished view of how the Iraqi leadership managed its military establishment, sized up its foes, and prepared for war. It is, in effect, the secret history of how Saddam and his generals waged the war.[2]

Saddam viewed himself as a modern-day Nebuchadnezzar. The entire country, in fact, was subjected to a colossal cult of personality. Saddam's picture was everywhere, as were his agents. The airport was known as the Saddam International Airport. The capital's most imposing and garish war memorial consisted of massive crossed sabers that created a triumphal arch, which rose out of a bed of 5,000 Iranian helmets. The German company that erected the monument was given a photograph of Saddam's forearms. The hands that grasped the swords were modeled on those of the nation's absolute leader. When workers began to reconstruct the palace of King Nebuchadnezzar II they used many of the original bricks but added others that bore the marking "made in the era of Saddam Hussein, protector of Iraq, who rebuilt civilization and rebuilt Babylon."[3]

Saddam ruled with the aid of two of his sons: Qusay, a somber figure who never served in the military but who nonetheless was given authority over the Republican Guard, the Special Republican Guard forces in Baghdad, and the internal police, and who appeared to be Saddam's anointed successor, and Uday, a notorious and cruel playboy, who oversaw the Saddam Fedayeen paramilitary forces, ran the youth magazine, and presided over Iraq's Olympic sports teams, where his motivational techniques included beating losing athletes.

Saddam's increasing reliance on family members and extensive precautions to foil potential assassins and coup plotters made the Iraqi leader only sporadically accessible to many senior Iraqi officials. An assassination attempt on Uday, in 1996, which left his gold Porsche riddled with bullets and a bullet lodged near his spine, made Saddam even more reclusive.

Convinced that the high-tech American intelligence services could pinpoint his whereabouts through his phone calls, the Iraqi leader refused to use the telephone; his senior advisers told their U.S. interrogators after the fall of Baghdad that they could recall only two occasions when he used a telephone since 1990. Despite United Nations sanctions, Saddam ordered the construction of vast marble palaces in and around Baghdad—some 7,000 workers were involved—establishing so many official residences that he was able to vary his sleeping quarters day to day and still live in luxury. Government meetings became a traveling road show. Ministers would be summoned to a session, driven in limousines with darkened windows to a location none of them knew in advance.

Even when Saddam met individually with his most senior officials a body-guard was always present.[4]

As a consummate survivor, Saddam had conducted an important review of Iraq's military strategy in 1995, though the deliberations were unknown to U.S. intelligence at the time. Four years after Iraq's defeat in the Gulf War, Iraq's military strategy was still rudimentary. Border guards or an equivalent would man the first line of defense. The Regular Army would be arrayed in depth behind them, with Saddam's Republican Guard, the most loyal and best-equipped units in the army, held in operational reserve for decisive battle—and to guard against a coup by the Regular Army. The strategy had worked against the Iranians but had failed miserably against the U.S.-led coalition during the Gulf War.

The generals at the conference divided threats into three categories: international, regional, and internal. Fearing another defeat at the hands of the Americans, some of Saddam's generals urged that Iraq employ a Russian-style defense in depth. The idea was to learn from the strategy Russia employed against Napoleon and Hitler. Baghdad would be like Moscow, a power center that could be reached only by pushing deep into the heart of the homeland. The Iraqi tribes would be like the Russian partisans. The desert sands would be like the Russian snows. Territory could be traded for time. Iraqi forces and local tribes would "chew" on the invaders as they advanced; armored formations, including the Republican Guard, would play a more modest role. They were good at fighting a regional power like Iran but were easy pickings for U.S. warplanes. "If we build mechanized brigades in large scale, so long as they control the air, they will just fly in and destroy the mechanized force," said a ranking Iraqi general, alluding to the Americans.

While the idea of bleeding the enemy until it collided with a more formidable defense in the rear seemed logical to the generals, the notion of arming the tribes for a people's war did not sit well with Saddam. There was always a chance that he himself could end up as the target of the people's war. The conference signaled the end of realistic planning. Rejecting the generals' criticism of relying so heavily on armored forces, Saddam pointed to all the military men in the room, and said, "If what this officer told you is correct, you'd all be dead, because we'd have lost. You would have been locked in an American prison or killed on the battlefield. Since we didn't lose, why would we exchange a winning concept for a foreign concept that's not applicable here?" The official mythology of the Gulf War held that Saddam's Republican Guard had stopped the U.S.-led forces at the Euphrates and prevented them from going to Baghdad. Saddam repeated the argument so often that some officers concluded that he actually believed it.

At the Pentagon there was a cult of the new. The existing war plans that derived from the experience of the Gulf War were put aside even when they had proved successful, if unimaginative to Rumsfeld. Rumsfeld was not looking to salvage what he could from CENTCOM's 1003-98 plan: he wanted to rethink the plan from scratch, in keeping with his transformation policy. In Baghdad, however, old plans were enshrined and lauded by the regime even though some of Saddam's more astute professionals were looking to revise them. It had a stultifying effect on Iraqi military planning.[5]

Even the most capable subordinates could challenge the official wisdom at their peril. "It was not allowed to raise your hand above anyone around you; it was dangerous," Tariq Aziz told his interrogators after the war. "If a military leader disappeared we did not know how it happened, but he was probably dealt with by the security services." After Saddam decreed the old strategy to be a success, a senior air force officer who had up to that time been reporting and bemoaning the functional demise of his service suddenly began reporting a 40 percent increase in capabilities. "It was at this time that everyone started lying," one captured Republican Guard general later told his U.S. interrogators. "Since that time all military planning was directed by Saddam and a select few. It was much like Hitler and his generals after 1944."

Although never having served as a soldier, Saddam was not shy to give advice or relieve commanders he did not like. He once issued orders during the Iran-Iraq War based on a dream, Saddam's personal secretary confided to his U.S. interrogator. During the Gulf War Saddam insisted that the battle at Khafji be pressed as the "Mother of All Battles" even though the Iraqi forces were being decimated. In the late 1990s he stopped making regular visits to units, but he never stopped telling the military how to do things. Saddam played a role in drafting the Republican Guard manual, urging snipers to climb palm trees to get a better shot at their foes.[6]

A further problem for the regime was that its own military was a potential threat. Regular Army units, whose ranks were often filled with

Shiites and whose loyalty to the regime was not beyond question, were stationed far from the capital, along the "Green Line" that marked the boundary with autonomous Kurdistan and along the Iranian border. Even the Republican Guard was not allowed inside the capital.

Baghdad was to be defended by the loyal Baathist Special Republican Guard, and its officers were prohibited from interacting with their counterparts in other Republican Guard divisions for fear that even they might foment a coup. Division commanders could not make any decisions without approval from the Republican Guard chief of staff in Baghdad, a trusted Saddam loyalist. In fact, the strictures against contacting, let alone coordinating with, neighboring units were so severe that the commander of the I Republican Guard Corps developed a new use for his reconnaissance units: scouting the location and strength of nearby Iraqi divisions.

Saddam's demand for absolute loyalty took its toll on the officer corps. Iraq was not short of competent professional officers, but within a regime that was wary of fresh thinking and lived in a world of politically correct assumptions, they were at a severe disadvantage. Republican Guard and other senior officers were often chosen on the basis of family ties and loyalty, not competence. Saddam himself had to approve the appointment of any officer to the rank of lieutenant general or above.

One of the most admired officers in the Iraqi officer corps was Lieutenant General Sultan Hashim Ahmad al-Tai, the defense minister. Junior generals had looked to him to speak up as the most knowledgeable about warfare. Once ensconced in his post, however, he hewed unswervingly to the party line. Ahmad told his U.S. interrogators that he had little authority despite his august title and reported to Qusay.

"I effectively became an assistant to Qusay only collecting and passing information," he said. "Qusay knew nothing, his understanding on general things was like a civilian." Challenging Saddam or his sons on military issues, Ahmad acknowledged after the war, was unwise. "Only his relatives would dare to present him with even mildly opposing views," he told his interrogators.[7]

The advice of Majeed, Saddam's cousin who organized the poison gas attacks against the Kurds, was especially highly regarded by the Iraqi leader. In contrast, Lieutenant General Raad Majid al-Hamdani, the commander of the II Republican Guard Corps and one of Iraq's most proficient officers, was ridiculed for "thinking like an American" by Saddam because of Hamdani's interest in military history. Hamdani sought to protect himself against suspicions from on high by making sure that he invited all the regime's spies, including the ones he was not supposed to know about, to his important planning meetings. As a result of Saddam's policies, "the clever men learned not to involve themselves in any decision-making," he told his questioners.[8]

Blood ties and associations with Saddam's relatives in Tikrit conferred authority more than practical military experience. The commander of the Al Nida Republican Guard division, Saddam's second cousin, enjoyed considerable authority, while the commander of the Baghdad Republican Guard infantry division had no more power than a captain in the U.S. Army.

The elevation of loyalty over competence led Saddam to make an especially dubious appointment. He made Brigadier General Barzan abd al-Ghafur Sulayman Majid al-Tikriti the commander of the Special Republican Guard forces responsible for the defense of Baghdad. The officer had no field experience, failed staff college, was a known drunk, and was generally held in low regard by his fellow officers. When General Ahmad, the defense minister, was queried by interrogators about the commander's skills he laughed out loud. Ahmad said there were three reasons the officer was chosen for such an important post: he was a close cousin of Saddam; he was not clever enough to put a coup together on his own; and he was scared to participate in anyone else's "good ideas."[9]

Even so, the Special Republican Guard commander was closely monitored by Qusay. Questioned by American officials after the war, he confided that he was not happy about receiving an appointment that subjected him to constant surveillance and scrutiny. It was, he added, the most dangerous job in Iraq. So great was the pressure that the officer said he considered suicide when he learned the job was his. "They watched you go to the bathroom. They listened to everything you said and bugged everything," he told interrogators.[10]

While the army languished, development of militia and paramilitary forces for internal security took on great importance. Saddam set up a parallel military structure for that mission. There were already Al Quds in every governorate, but this volunteer militia was deemed ineffective. In 1994 the Fedayeen was formed under Uday Hussein. They grew and proliferated. These paramilitary cadres were trained in basic small arms skills and the protection of Baath Party headquarters and other key sites, which was one of the missions that the Iraqi military failed to carry out in the uprising of 1991.

With preservation of the regime the top priority, a Baath Emergency Plan was drawn up. Not a homeland defense plan, in effect, it was a counterinsurgency plan to stop the sort of uprisings that the Shiites had mounted after the Gulf War. The idea was for the Fedayeen and other militia to contain any uprising long enough for Republican Guard units to arrive and crush the opposition. It was assumed that local Baathists would be cut off for a period of time and would have to survive on their own until the army or Republican Guard arrived to rescue them.

Each village, town, and city would become a small semi-independent citadel. Fedayeen units would put down local revolts, drawing on caches of light weapons like AK-47s, machine guns, mortars, and RPGs (rocket-propelled grenades), which would be kept under close guard by the Baathists. Despite requests for heavy weapons, none were allotted because of Saddam's fear that they might fall into the hands of rebels.

Though their primary role was to squelch internal threats, if an invasion occurred, the paramilitaries were expected to defend each town and bloody the invaders. The military did not have a plan to carry on an insurgency if Baghdad fell, according to senior Iraqi leaders. As one former general put it, "There were some things you just didn't talk about, because of morale." General Ahmad, the defense minister, said the army was not trained to fight both a conventional foe and a guerrilla war. "We're not a two-for-one force," he said.[11]

Saddam's Baath Emergency Plan was a profound evolution in Iraq's security forces, but the stockpiling of weapons and ammunition was not detected by spy satellites, and the U.S. intelligence community missed the significance of the Fedayeen organization. It was a striking omission given the visibility of the Fedayeen in Iraqi towns and cities and the vital importance of the Fedayeen to the regime, but understandable given the CIA's dearth of human sources and overreliance on satellite and other forms of reconnaissance.

With its focus on internal and regional threats, Saddam overlooked the war clouds gathering in Washington. There were abundant indications in Washington that the Bush administration had Iraq in its sights. The president had cited Iraq in his "axis of evil" speech in January. On June 1,

2002, Bush made a comprehensive effort to delineate a rationale for a war to the graduating class at West Point. If an adversary provided weapons of mass destruction to a terrorist group, the U.S. might be attacked but might not ever know who sponsored the blow. Deterrence—essentially, the threat of devastating retaliation—would not forestall the attack, since the source of the weapons of mass destruction might never be known. The only way to guard against the threat would be to eliminate the weapons of mass destruction at their source. Nor would the United States wait too long before it acted. The president noted that the traditional notion of preemption held that a nation would be justified in striking first if an adversary began to make discernible war preparations and began to move its ships, ready its planes, or mobilize its troops. But that, Bush argued, would not work in the post-9/11 world. If the United States waited for threats to materialize, Bush said, it would have waited too long. It was not so much a doctrine of preemptive as preventive war.[12]

The development of the preemption strategy had an instructive history. When Cheney was defense secretary his aides prepared the "Defense Planning Guidance," a classified document that was intended to guide military planning. Cheney's policy team at the time was headed by Paul Wolfowitz, Zalmay Khalilzad, the NSC aide who later became the United States's ambassador to Iraq, and Scooter Libby, who became the vice president's chief of staff.

Khalilzad did an early strategy draft and it read like a neoconservative tract. Khalilzad's paper argued that the United States should be prepared to use force preemptively to prevent the spread of nuclear weapons, declared that the goal of American policy should be to maintain United States military primacy, and argued that military coalitions should not necessarily be based on formal alliances but rather on ad hoc assemblies of nations, a practice that meant Washington would not necessarily be bound by the view of its allies. The draft set off a furor when it was leaked. It had emanated from the most conservative wing of the government and George H. W. Bush's White House quickly disavowed it. Cheney later issued a more politically acceptable draft that watered down and omitted the most controversial points.[13]

When it came to military planning, Rumsfeld had promoted a new agenda, but the foreign policy doctrine that was being presented was a case in which an old doctrine that had been considered beyond the pale in 1992 was being revived by aides who were now at the core of a conservative administration. Presented by Bush at West Point, the doctrine was further polished by Condoleezza Rice, the president's national security adviser, as part of the United States National Security Strategy, which was released with fanfare and put on the White House Web site.[14]

In theory, the preemption doctrine could apply to a range of current and aspiring weapons powers. North Korea, which had the most advanced WMD of the countries cited in Bush's "axis of evil" speech, was believed to have nuclear weapons and had Seoul within artillery range. Iran's WMD programs were deemed more advanced than Iraq's and Iran had a history of supporting Hezbollah and the Palestinians. But it is a large and populous nation, still in the process of modernization, and has strong political and economic ties to Europe. Iraq had the least developed weapons programs of the three. But it was an outcast, in violation of U.N. resolutions and the cease-fire arrangements that had ended the Gulf War, and had a military severely deteriorated by more than a decade of sanctions.

For the Bush administration, Iraq was an inviting target for preemption not because it was an immediate threat but because it was thought to be a prospective menace that was incapable of successfully defending itself against a U.S. invasion. For an administration that was determined to change the strategic equation in the Middle East and make Saddam an object lesson to other proliferators, Iraq was not a danger to avoid but a strategic opportunity. On July 19, Bush gave a rousing patriotic speech to the 10th Mountain Division at Fort Drum, New York. A soldier yelled out, "Let's get Saddam." The president cracked a smile.[15]

Even in the face of Bush's preemption doctrine, the Iraq regime continued to plan for other threats. Since 1989, the military had been conducting a war game code-named Golden Falcon, which revolved around Iran. It was Iran that had lobbed missiles at Baghdad in the 1988 "War of the Cities," and Iran that had joined Iraq in using poison gas during their bitter war. Iran had a larger population, an active military industrial complex, and was not subject to debilitating U.N. sanctions. Iraq's National Security Committee, the organization that coordinated the work of the nation's many intelligence services, advised Saddam's regime after 9/11 that Iran was and would remain Iraq's principal external threat. "What did we think was going to happen with the coalition invasion? We were more interested in Turkey and Iran," the director of Iraq's military intelligence told U.S. officials after the fall of Baghdad.[16]

Saddam's concern with Iran, however, had enormous implications for his relations with Washington. While Iraq had disposed of its stocks of chemical and biological weapons during the 1990s, Saddam had never dispelled the mystery of whether he might have a hidden cache of WMD.

His declarations to the U.N. of what stocks he had possessed and how he had disposed of them were old and full of holes. Nor would Saddam allow his weapons scientists to leave the country.

His political strategy was to keep Tehran in check by maintaining some measure of ambiguity over Iraq's WMD, what Hamdani dubbed "deterrence by doubt." While a decade of sparring with United Nations inspectors over the fate of his past weapons programs meant that Iraq faced economic sanctions, Saddam saw value in not letting the world know that his officials had disposed of his chemical and biological arsenal.

From the Iraqi leader's perspective, WMD had helped in fending off Iran's human wave attacks during their war: by one count Iraq had used no fewer than 101,000 chemical rounds and bombs against the Iranian ground forces. With that experience in mind, Saddam never lost his interest in missile programs, which he insisted incorrectly should not be considered to be a type of WMD, although Iraq was forbidden to develop medium- and long-range missiles by the U.N. The appearance of possessing weapons of mass destruction was all the more important for Saddam given the shoddiness of Iraq's army. For Saddam, the most important counter against Iran was not his troops but his Military Industrial Committee, which was in charge of missiles and other weapons programs.

Saddam also believed, wrongly, that it was the threat of chemical weapons that had prompted the United States not to march on Baghdad during the Gulf War. He was also persuaded that they deterred uprisings at home. In the 1991 attack against the Shiites, twelve to thirty-two Sarin bombs were dropped from Mi-8 helicopters, according to the Iraq Survey Group. (The Iraqis decided not to use mustard gas for fear it would be detected by the U.S.-led coalition.) The R-400 bombs did not function properly, prompting the Iraqi military to drop 200 bombs filled with tear gas instead. The Kurds were less fortunate; an estimated 5,000 were killed in the Halabjah attack in 1988.[17]

Viewed from Baghdad, the U.S. demand that Iraq make clear beyond a shadow of a doubt that it had abandoned its weapons of mass destruction undermined Saddam's efforts to deter Iran and frighten into submission the Shiites and other potential rebellious groups.

While Saddam believed that revealing the absence of WMD was risky, he discounted the danger of alarming the United States. According to his associates, he did not consider the United States a natural adversary. He saw no reason why the Americans would want to invade Iraq. And he believed the Americans had no stomach for a bloody war.

His attitude toward the United States was influenced by the 1987

episode in which an Iraqi F-1 plane had misidentified an American warship as an Iranian ship and blasted it with two Exocet missiles. Saddam,
U.S. officials were told after the war, was surprised when he received a dé-
marche instead of a bombardment. He was also aware that after a few casualties in Lebanon and Somalia, the Americans had retreated with their
tails between their legs. In 1991, the Americans had fulfilled their limited
aim of liberating Kuwait and elected not to press on to Baghdad. Saddam
saw that not as forbearance, but as an aversion to casualties. In Somalia,
the United States had disengaged after suffering eighteen dead in the
streets of Mogadishu. In Kosovo, the U.S. had relied on a seventy-eight-
day air war and prided itself that it had won without a single combat
casualty.

Even after the four-day air strikes the Clinton administration unleashed in 1998 in its Desert Fox campaign, Iraq did not fear challenging
Washington. After the raids, Saddam pressed the Revolutionary Command Council to adopt a secret resolution severing all forms of cooperation with the United Nations.[18] The weapons inspectors were not invited
back. By the end of President Clinton's tenure, Saddam was trying to re-
dress the affront to his sovereignty by shooting down one of the American
and British aircraft that were patrolling the northern and southern swaths
of his country.

Nor were the election of George W. Bush and the return of much of the
team that had overseen the Desert Storm campaign cause for undue
alarm. Despite a one-sided drubbing at the hands of the American-led
coalition, repeated allied bombing raids, and the fact that Washington
held him responsible for a failed plot to assassinate former president
George H. W. Bush, the Iraqi leader was still defiant, chafing at the insult
to his sovereignty by the American and British air patrols, persuaded that
there was little the Americans could do to defeat him. The United States
could lob bombs and cruise missiles at Iraq, but he did not believe the
United States would invade the country without a coalition, such as it had
in 1991, and nobody seemed to be lining up to join Bush's crusade. As one
of the senior Iraqi officials pointed out, "No one is as good at absorbing
U.S. precision munitions as Iraq. So if that's all the Americans have got,
it's not a threat to our national survival."[19]

On the first two days of August 2002, Tommy Franks held a meeting with
his top commanders in Tampa to discuss the latest iteration of the war
plan, which called for much more than using precision-guided bombs.

The CENTCOM commander cautioned them that they needed to be ready to attack virtually on a moment's notice. Nobody knew how and when the invasion would start, but CENTCOM would be on alert from that day on.

The briefing slides for the meeting outlined the basic principles of Franks's plan. The commander's intent, Franks's strategic goal, was also clear: allied forces "will effect the elimination of the Iraqi regime by pressuring Iraqi centers of gravity in order to create crises to which the regime cannot respond.

"The end state for this operation is regime change," the slides continued. "Success is defined as regime leadership and power base destroyed; WMD capability destroyed or controlled; territorial integrity intact; ability to threaten neighbors eliminated; an acceptable provisional/permanent government in place."

The plan was still in a state of flux. It was clear that Rumsfeld was unhappy with the Generated Start and inclined toward a plan that offered the Pentagon a way to begin the war with the smallest buildup time and fewest number of troops. The theory behind the Running Start was that even a modicum of force would keep the Iraqis off balance while additional U.S. troops streamed to the region. If Saddam's regime was sufficiently fragile, the Running Start might be enough to spark a coup or uprising that would end the war before it really got started. That was known to some around CENTCOM as the "balloon theory": if the regime was as delicate as a balloon it could be destroyed with a simple pinprick.[20]

Even as they developed the Running Start, however, Franks's planners were aware there were some serious drawbacks, which were noted at the meeting. The Running Start gave CENTCOM less time to nail down the final basing arrangements in the region. By starting the war with a fraction of the overall force that was needed to knock the Iraqi military on its heels, it could prolong the war. That, in turn, would give the Iraqis more time to react and give them more opportunity to "induce mass U.S. casualties." CENTCOM might lose momentum and support from Arab nations and Turkey might waver if the conflict dragged on. Some of the planners put it more quaintly. The balloon might turn out to be a bowling ball. For nine months, the administration had been struggling to choose between the Generated Start, which Rumsfeld did not like, and the Running Start, which made many of the planners uneasy.

Struggling to find some middle ground, the planners developed still another plan, which was dubbed the Hybrid. The plan took advantage of some of the preparations that had already been made in Kuwait to move forces to that country more quickly. Under the Hybrid, the president would give CENTCOM five days to quietly mobilize. For the next eleven days, CENTCOM would flow troops, aircraft, and other war matériel to the region. At that point, a sixteen-day air campaign would start. By the time the air campaign ended, some 20,000 Army and Marine troops would be in Kuwait and CENTCOM would start the ground war. The invasion would start while tens of thousands of reinforcements continued to flow to Kuwait and would last up to 125 days. Those numbers had been bandied about so much at CENTCOM that among the war planners the Hybrid was also known as the 5-11-16-125 Plan.

The first order of business in the ground attack would be to seize the southern oilfields, the bridges the forces would need to move north, and the port of Umm Qasr, which would facilitate the delivery of humanitarian aid. Reflecting suggestions from Rumsfeld's aides, there was an option to grab Basra International Airport by airborne assault, a measure that seemed to be a vestige of the old plan to establish an enclave in southern Iraq. Neither the Army nor the Marines had much enthusiasm for the mission and the Air Force had little use for the airfield. CENTCOM slides said that the airfield could be seized "to demonstrate coalition resolve."

As for what would happen after the regime was toppled, Franks told his commanders that his assumption was that Colin Powell's State Department would have the lead for the rebuilding of Iraq's political institutions and infrastructure. With regard to CENTCOM forces, after the fall of Baghdad, there would be an initial two- to three-month "stabilization" phase and then an eighteen- to twenty-four-month "recovery" phase during which the bulk of the invasion force would be removed. The intention was to make "maximum use of Iraqi resources," including the Iraqi military and Iraqi police, to maintain control. They would gradually take over from the Americans. The plan also postulated a final twelve- to eighteen-month transition period.[21]

A big worry for Franks was that the Iraqis might strike before the Bush administration could mount its preemptive war. CENTCOM's intelligence shop outlined a range of steps that Iraq might take: from attacking into Kuwait to flooding the Mesopotamian Valley, igniting its oilfields, going after the Kurds, or enacting some version of a scorched-earth policy. And of course there were always WMD to worry about.

Franks could hedge against the possibility of an Iraqi attack by shifting planes to the region under the Spike Plan. Beyond that, CENTCOM would try to quietly beef up its small presence in Kuwait by deploying artillery, Special Forces, and AH-64 attack helicopters. Other steps would involve moving Global Hawk, a reconnaissance drone, and Special Operating Forces from Afghanistan, where they were still involved in fighting remnants of the Taliban and tracking down Al Qaeda operatives.

By and large, though, it was the United States that was on the offensive. The patrols of the southern no-fly zones provided a way to steal a march on the Iraqis. In July, Moseley authorized a series of air strikes under a secret plan dubbed Southern Focus. Allied warplanes had routinely launched bombing raids if they were fired on by Iraqi antiaircraft artillery or attacked by surface-to-air missiles or painted by air defense radars during their patrols. Under Southern Focus, Moseley expanded the list of targets. It was a way of compensating for the possibility that the air commanders might have little time to set the stage for a ground assault.

There was a circularity to the operations that worked entirely to Moseley's advantage. As U.S. warplanes began to strike a broader array of targets the Iraqis began to fire more on allied patrols, which in turn provided Moseley with an opportunity to carry out still more raids. As the Southern Focus campaign unfolded, Moseley used Iraqi antiaircraft fire at planes patrolling over northern Iraq as a rationale to strike targets several days later in the south. "We became a little more aggressive based on them shooting more at us, which allowed us to respond more," Moseley recalled after the war.

In all, the United States dropped 606 bombs on 391 targets under the plan. One major target was the network of fiber optic cables that transmitted military communications between Baghdad and Basra and Baghdad and Nasiriyah. The cables themselves were buried underground and impossible to locate. So the air war commanders focused on the "cable repeater stations," which relayed the signals.[22]

The Americans also carried out a punishing raid at the air defense command center at H-3, an airfield in western Iraq 240 miles from Baghdad. That center had to be neutralized if Special Operations Forces and allied warplanes were to operate in the western reaches of Iraq at the start of the war and take out of action any surface-to-surface missiles within range of Israel. Moseley also authorized the use of Predator drones, which gathered intelligence, used lasers to pinpoint targets for other planes, and in one notable episode took on an Iraqi plane. After being threatened by Iraqi planes, a Predator drone was secretly outfitted with a Stinger air defense missile and sought to lure the Iraqi fighters within fir-

ing range. The Iraqis got the best of the exchange, however, and downed
the Predator, marking the first dogfight between a fighter and a flying
drone.[23]

Franks cautioned that the air strikes should not be too obtrusive.
Rumsfeld had issued clear guidance to "stay below the CNN line," Franks
reported. Even so, CENTCOM, for all intents and purposes, was waging
a quiet little war. When the real war came, Franks quipped to his commanders, CENTCOM would blast Saddam's yacht. Franks said that
Moseley or Vice Admiral Tim Keating, the senior naval commander in
the region, should hold a crud tournament to see who got to "whack the
boat."[24]

The British, who had a more punctilious attitude toward international
law, declined to participate in the Southern Focus operation on the
grounds that the United Nations resolutions that were used to justify the
patrols of the no-fly zones did not authorize bombing to smooth the way
for an invasion.[25]

Franks briefed the Hybrid Plan in Washington to the president. It was a
hit at the White House. After a long odyssey, the administration thought
it had settled on a plan.

Powell, however, continued to have concerns, especially about the part
of the mission that Franks assumed would be led by the State Department: administering and rebuilding postwar Iraq. Powell had been un-
comfortable with Franks's planning ever since the late December 2001
meeting at Crawford. To Powell, CENTCOM had spent an inordinate
amount of attention on cutting the time for deployment and less on how
to fight in Baghdad and deal with the realities of Iraq once U.S. forces got
there. CENTCOM's briefings often seemed more about transporting
troops than anything else, Powell told associates. The Hybrid force still
seemed too small to Powell to control supply lines and dominate the terrain.

Rich Armitage, the deputy secretary of state and a Powell confidant,
had yet another worry. Audacity is worth a great deal in warfare, Armitage acknowledged, but what would happen if the United States began
the attack and the Iraqis attacked the one port and one airfield in Kuwait
with chemical weapons? The administration would not be able to get the
reinforcements into the fight and would be stuck battling the Iraqis with
little more than a division's worth of troops. "We had an extraordinarily
high-risk strategy," Armitage recalled.

On the evening of August 5, Powell had a long dinner with Bush and Condoleezza Rice at the White House residence. Powell told the president that he had been receiving briefings about the war plan, but had not heard enough on what the aftermath might look like. When the United States took out the Iraqi military it would be striking a blow at the institution that held the country together. When the army cracked, the Iraqi government structure would crack and Bush would be the proud owner of 24 million people. It would take time to put a new Iraqi government in place and in the meantime the United States would be the government. It would be a multiyear commitment, which would tie up 40 percent of the U.S. Army for years. It would, Powell said, suck the oxygen out of everything else the administration wanted to do. Powell was later said to have invoked the Pottery Barn rule: if you break it you own it. But the message was more blunt: it *will* break and you *will* own it.

If Bush was determined to go ahead, Powell stressed, he would have to go to the United Nations and get some diplomatic cover. If Bush obtained U.N. support there was a chance that Saddam would allow weapons inspectors to return and disarm. If it did not get solved diplomatically and force was necessary, the United States would have allies to share the burden.

There was a potential catch and Powell told Bush it was important to be aware of it. If Saddam elected to comply with the U.N. demands and gave up his suspected WMD programs, the United States would have to take yes for an answer and give up its policy of regime change. Bush would have to accept that possibility before turning to the U.N.

In directing Bush to the United Nations, Powell was challenging Cheney, who had taken the position that the U.S. already had a casus belli: Saddam's refusal to cooperate with U.N. weapons inspections as required by the cease-fire arrangements that ended the Gulf War. Cheney and Powell had made a team during the Gulf War, but even then they had had their differences, including how to deal with Iraq. Cheney thought that diplomatic wrangling at the U.N. would make it harder to take military action, though in the end he supported Bush's decision to bring the issue to the organization.

In this debate, Powell had a critical ally. Britain had made it clear that a U.N. ultimatum was a requirement for its participation in the invasion. Bush gritted his teeth, accepted the small prospect that Saddam might comply with all of the U.N. demands and live to rule another day, and decided to seek the backing of the United Nations Security Council. At the same time, Bush was prepared to attack once Washington had concluded he failed—even if the other members of the Security Council disagreed.

When word of Powell's intervention with the president seeped out, some commentators concluded that the secretary of state had been opposed to going to war against Saddam. Close aides to Powell say his position was less categorical. Powell preferred a solution through the U.N. if possible, but he was not averse to confronting Saddam militarily if diplomatic efforts to ensure Iraq had disarmed failed.

"Powell and I did not object to the prospect of taking out Saddam Hussein, but we had real questions about the timing," Armitage recalled. "Neither the secretary nor I can tell when the president made his mind up to go. The secretary thought he had the president in a good place. A good place meant we would consolidate Afghanistan, work vigorously with the allies to get as many people on board, and then go. The thinking I had in mind was January 2005—win the election and then that would be a good time to begin the attack."[26]

At the Pentagon, Rumsfeld's aides were determined not to let Saddam wriggle off the hook or to delay the day of reckoning. Greg Newbold said he was told by Feith: "In crafting a strategy for Iraq we cannot accept surrender." Feith denied making this comment. At CENTCOM, the decision to go to the U.N. was warmly received. Nobody knew how long the U.N. diplomacy would go on, but it would not be quick. Renuart figured that CENTCOM had won another two to three months to prepare for the war.[27]

In mid-August 2002, top Bush administration officials drafted a top secret document for the president to sign, laying out the goal of the war. Blandly titled "Iraq: Goals, Objectives and Strategy," the document outlined the broad goals for a military operation. It asserted that a free Iraq would eliminate the threat of WMD, the means of delivering the weapons, and prevent Saddam from breaking out of containment. The broader goals of the operation were to eliminate the Iraqi threat to its neighbors, liberate the Iraqi people from tyranny, and prevent Baghdad from supporting terrorists. The United States, the document boldly noted, would help the Iraqis "build a society based on moderation, pluralism and democracy."

The military campaign, the document noted, would be designed to minimize the chance of a WMD attack against the U.S., its forces, and friends. The U.S. would take steps to deter Iran and Syria from helping Iraq, and also would minimize the disruption of the international oil market. The U.S. would use "all instruments of national power" to free Iraq, working with a coalition if possible and acting alone if necessary.

The United States would work with Iraqi opposition groups to demonstrate that the military attack was a liberation and not an invasion and they would have a role in building "a pluralistic and democratic Iraq" that would have a new constitution, adhere to international law, and respect the rights of all Iraqis, including women. Iraqis would have freedom of speech and worship. After the fall of Baghdad, the U.S. would demonstrate that it was prepared to play a sustained role, along with other nations, in the reconstruction of Iraq and the reform of its bureaucracy and security institutions."[28]

The goals for the Iraq operation were far-reaching, indeed. The aim was not just to topple a dictator. While many observers viewed an intervention in Iraq with anxiety, the White House approached it as a strategic opportunity. The U.S. would implant democracy in a nation that had never known it and begin to redraw the political map of the region. The United States would finally do away with its long-standing worries over Saddam's weapons programs. And although the document did not say so, it would be a demonstration of American power for Syria and other wayward regimes.

The foreign policy stakes were high. On the face of it, it would also be a daunting exercise in nation-building. Yet in keeping with the Bush administration's antipathy toward Clinton-style nation-building, the Bush team intended to carry out this project by relying heavily on Iraqi institutions like the military and the police to maintain order. The Hybrid Plan, which provided only half the troops that Zinni had envisioned for precisely this task, made that clear.

On August 21, Rumsfeld visited Bush at his Crawford ranch to discuss a range of military issues. In a brief appearance before the press afterward, the president complained that the media seemed to be focusing on the possibility of military action in Iraq. There was, he said, too much "churning" about the subject. Rumsfeld agreed. There seemed to be some kind of media "frenzy." All the activity at CENTCOM, Bush said, merely involved contingency planning and no decision to go to war had been made. Eight days later, Bush signed the classified statement of objectives for the Iraq mission.[29]

In early September, as Bush prepared to go to the United Nations, Franks got ready to brief the president on the Hybrid Plan one more time. To prepare their commander for the meeting, Franks's staff put together a top secret "POTUS Talking Paper." It was military-speak for a presentation for the President of the United States. The strategic objectives of the campaign, the paper noted, was not only to produce regime change in

Iraq but to "convince or compel other countries to cease support to terrorists and to deny them WMD." A successful campaign would not only
change Iraq but let other adversaries know they should watch their step.

The paper noted that Franks would prevent Saddam from employing a
"Fortress Baghdad" strategy by bombing the regime's command and control centers, attacking the Republican Guard and the heavy-equipment
transporters they needed to move their tanks, using Special Operations
Forces to work with anti-Saddam groups, and encouraging Iraqi forces to
surrender or defect.

Once Saddam was removed from power there would be a "post-
hostilities" phase that might last for one year or more, the talking points
said. CENTCOM would support the U.S. civilian institutions that worked
with the Iraqis. A maximum of Iraqi resources would be used to speed the
nation's recovery. The Iraqi military and security forces would be reestab-
lished to defend the borders and provide for internal security.

Basing arrangements, however, were still unsettled, as was the Turkish
approval of a northern front. When Franks met with Bush and the National Security Council on September 6 to go over the planning, Rice alluded to the basing issues. It was late in the day for diplomacy with the
allies, she said.[30]

Franks politely agreed. "Yes, we need to catch up," he said with some
understatement.

Having recently approved the goals for the operation, Bush came to the
point. "Can we win this thing?" Bush asked.

"Absolutely," Franks said.

"Can we get rid of Saddam?" Bush asked again.

"Yes, sir," Franks replied.

CHAPTER 5

Back to the Future

As the United States headed toward war, the Army decided to make a change at the top. With Franks's blessing, a new general was brought in to run the land command. Taciturn and unflappable, Lieutenant General David McKiernan had long been one of Eric Shinseki's most trusted officers. He had run the VII Corps Tactical Command Post during the Gulf War and spent time in Sarajevo when NATO stepped in to stop the killing in Bosnia. McKiernan was in command of the 1st Cavalry Division during the September 11 attacks but shortly after moved to the Pentagon, where he became the Army's chief operations officer.

McKiernan had been read into Tommy Franks's ever-changing war plan at an early date. Wearing civilian clothes and telling his staff that he was going to Germany to visit his wife's relatives he had even made a quick trip to review the planning with Scott Wallace, the V Corps commander, and his staff. While Franks had a strained relationship with Paul Mikolashek dating back to the Afghan war, he respected McKiernan. With the invasion of Iraq imminent, the Army and Franks wanted its top officers in place. McKiernan was in, Mikolashek was out.

In September, McKiernan moved into his headquarters, which was housed in a series of sheet metal warehouses north of Kuwait City and just down the road from Entertainment City, an aging Kuwaiti amusement park. This was Camp Doha, and movement in or out of the fenced-off and secured compound was so tightly regulated that some soldiers jested it was a minimum-security prison. When McKiernan arrived, much of the military infrastructure in Kuwait was still a work in progress. An amphitheater-sized command center at Camp Doha, filled with comput-

ers and wall-size screens for video displays and graphics was under construction. McKiernan's main worry, however, was not to upgrade his
command post; it was the Hybrid war plan itself.

Over the past year, the strategy for the war had mutated from the Generated Start to the Running Start to the Hybrid, which had been developed by CENTCOM, sanctioned by Franks, and sold to the White
House. It was, in effect, a somewhat more elaborate version of the Running Start, one that took advantage of the small deployments and im-
provements to the military infrastructure that had been quietly put in
place. When McKiernan arrived at Camp Doha, Colonel Kevin Benson,
the chief planning officer for the command, had filled him in on the latest
iteration. In some respects, the Hybrid seemed to be the very model of
joint warfare. In the first phase of the war, the Marines would command
the initial invasion force, comprising two brigades of the Army's 3rd Infantry Division and a Marine Expeditionary Brigade. The Army brigades
would secure Iraq's southern oilfields even as the Marines grabbed the
port of Umm Qasr. The troops would push north to the Euphrates and
seize the critical Highway 1 bridge outside of Nasiriyah. All of the United
States's objectives in the southern tier of the country would thereby be secured. After moving up to the Euphrates, the forces would wait for Wallace's V Corps headquarters and additional Army units to arrive in Kuwait
and then drive deeper into Iraq. During the next stage, all Army forces
would shift to Wallace's V Corps, and the Army and Marines would proceed along separate axes toward Baghdad, while the British and the U.S.
Army's 4th Infantry Division attacked south from Turkey.

The Hybrid satisfied the yearning in Rumsfeld's Pentagon for a lean
force that could attack without a long buildup. For those Rumsfeld aides
who were convinced that the regime would crack as soon as the Americans put boots on the ground, the handful of units CENTCOM would
use to kick off the war was force enough. But McKiernan noted two
major flaws in the plan. The Hybrid would enable CENTCOM to attack
quickly but could drag the war out. Wallace's planners estimated that it
would take up to forty-five days for the deployment of the V Corps headquarters and reinforcing units in Iraq. Unless Saddam's regime cracked at
the start of the war, the Hybrid, in effect, would be akin to sprinting
around a track and stopping to catch your breath before resuming the
race. There was also the complication of introducing a new three-star
headquarters in the middle of a shooting war. In essence, McKiernan
thought the plan was short on combat power at the start, could lead to an

extended pause in the ground fight, and was unnecessarily complex. The plan that Franks had put forth with considerable pride and that had dazzled the president and his aides was sorely deficient as far as McKiernan was concerned—no small matter, as he was the officer who was to oversee the ground attack.

One year after the military was told to get ready to invade Iraq the strategy was still not finalized and the planning for the postwar phase had barely begun. About the only thing that was fixed was the code name of the land campaign: Cobra II. Lieutenant Colonel Evan Heulfer, one of Benson's planners and an officer with a flair for military history, had proposed it, alluding to the code name of the first large-scale Third Army operation in World War II led by George Patton, the Normandy breakout. McKiernan quickly adopted Cobra II.

On October 9, Franks convened a video conference with his commanders to address some uncertainties in the war plan. The president wanted to be assured that CENTCOM would be able to take the Iraqi capital without engaging in bitter house-to-house fighting. Franks already had CENTCOM's Inside-Out Plan whereby warplanes would pin down the Republican Guard, preventing it from withdrawing into the capital. But the ground forces still lacked a plan for capturing the city after arriving at the approaches to Baghdad. "POTUS is unfulfilled," Franks said, using the military acronym for president of the United States. Baghdad "is the president's strategic exposure." Bush also wanted to be certain that CENTCOM knew how to cope with Saddam's caches and expected use of WMD. McKiernan and his team agreed that work needed to be done on both fronts. Still, McKiernan believed, Washington seemed to be missing the forest for the trees. Washington should have been worrying about the Hybrid Plan itself.[1]

Nonetheless, McKiernan and his deputies went about setting up his headquarters, determined to deal with the problems they could solve. For CENTCOM, McKiernan's headquarters was something of a doctrinal innovation. During the Persian Gulf War, there had been no single ground force commander. The Army had fought its war, the Marines theirs, leaving it to Schwarzkopf to harmonize the whole thing. The approach had been out of step with the military's practice of unity of command.

This time, there would be one land war commander who would preside over all ground forces, including allied troops, and who would report to Franks. In the acronym-happy military, McKiernan would be the CFLCC commander: the head of the Coalition Forces Land Component Command. Anthony Zinni had espoused the concept of a single commander when he was the CENTCOM commander, and Mikolashek had officially stood up the command during the Afghan campaign. But that war had been largely fought by an Afghan-based opposition group, CIA paramilitary units, Special Forces, local warlords, and a relatively small deployment of Marines. The Iraq War would be the real test.

McKiernan staffed the new headquarters with up-and-coming officers he knew from previous assignments. J. D. Thurman, an Oklahoma native who had previously commanded the Army's National Training Center in California and who had a grip like a vise, would be the chief operations officer. Brigadier General James "Spider" Marks, a third-generation West Point graduate who ran the Army's Intelligence School at Fort Huachuca, Arizona, would be the senior intelligence officer. Major General Chris Christianson was the logistician. William Webster, a two-star Army general who had been based at CENTCOM and got along with the thin-skinned Franks, was McKiernan's deputy. Most of the officers had served with McKiernan in previous operations, and knew each other well. He also brought in the command sergeant major from his days commanding the 1st Cavalry Division. Command Sergeant Major John Sparks was McKiernan's closest friend and confidant.

But for all the talk of joint warfare, McKiernan's headquarters was dominated by Army officers. The lone Marine near the top of the organizational chart was Major General Robert "Rusty" Blackman, who had been educated at Cornell University and who served as McKiernan's chief of staff. To smooth relations with Buzz Moseley and facilitate interaction with the air war commanders, Major General Daniel Leaf was brought in later to be part of the team. Leaf had been the commander of an Air Force wing at Italy's Aviano Air Base during the Kosovo campaign and despite his amiable manner drank his coffee from a cup molded like a human skull. Benson, who had served as Franks's chief planning officer at the Third Army, was to do the same for McKiernan.

One of the most important members of the staff was not an active duty officer but a civilian contractor who, clad in khaki pants and a button-down shirt, seemed to accompany McKiernan everywhere: Terry Moran, a retired lieutenant colonel, was brought in at McKiernan's request to serve as his strategist. As a CENTCOM planner in the mid-1990s and later as a war planner on the Army staff, he knew the Iraq war plan soup to nuts. Moran had spent two years doing security assistance work in Riyadh and had done a stint at the CIA. He was well connected to a number of key organizations in the shadowy intelligence community, and as McKiernan's adviser he was more influential than some of the command's senior officers. He was one of a handful of people who knew about Franks's war planning at its earliest stage.

As McKiernan worked on Cobra II, Franks visited the White House on October 31 for yet another briefing on the war plan. After his session with the president, Franks passed along some additional guidance to his commanders. If Saddam mounted a preemptive attack against the Kurds—a dire scenario of which the CIA had warned—the game would be on. The president also wanted an effective information campaign in place to publicize Iraq's transgressions. When U.S. forces uncovered Saddam's stockpiles of WMD, Bush wanted CENTCOM to get the word out. Franks instructed that specially trained public affairs camera crews should be prepared to document discoveries for immediate release to the media. The administration was not only convinced that Iraq had WMD but was planning its discovery as a photo op.[2]

To tackle the fear that Saddam would turn his capital into Fortress Baghdad, McKiernan turned to Scott Wallace, who would be leading the main attack on the Iraqi capital. McKiernan planned to bypass Iraq's southern cities on the way to Baghdad so as to avoid being entangled in unnecessary street fighting. But, as the locus of power of Saddam's regime—what the generals called Iraq's "center of gravity"—the capital had to be taken one way or another. The Army had lost eighteen soldiers in the streets of Mogadishu, Somalia: Baghdad was a city of some six million, defended by the Special Republican Guard and paramilitary forces under the iron fist of a dictator who was deemed to possess weapons of mass destruction.

Together with his planners, Wallace crafted a strategy to use the converging Army and Marine forces to establish a cordon around the city, cutting off major roads to prevent senior Iraqi officials from escaping with their WMD. The military would then ring the city with forward operating bases code-named after NFL football teams. Saddam International Airport would be the first to be established; the others would be manned by task forces that would be built around Army or Marine regiments. Each task force would mount raids into the capital, using M1 tanks, infantry, attack helicopters, and warplanes, striking at key power centers before withdrawing. Instead of fighting block by block in a nightmarish Arabian Stalingrad, the U.S. would pick apart Saddam's defenses with, as it were, a series of rapier thrusts. All the while, U.S. psychological operations teams would be broadcasting messages on television and radio, and by loudspeaker and leaflets, urging the Iraqis to surrender. Combat camera teams would, one version of the plan noted, relay "images of success to international audience." Camps would be set up for Iraqi citizens fleeing the battle, and a logistics base for nongovernmental relief organizations would be established southwest of the city to stockpile humanitarian aid. McKiernan supported this plan and briefed Franks, who in turn endorsed and proposed it to the White House.[3]

As for seizing and controlling the dissemination of WMD, this was altogether more complicated than it seemed. For all of the Bush administration's many calamitous warnings about Saddam's potential use of WMD, much work had yet to be done to develop an effective military plan to cope with the presumed caches of biological and chemical weapons. The troops were equipped with bulky protective masks, suits, gloves, and boots, which they would wear when they crossed into Iraq. They were also inoculated for anthrax and smallpox. Much of the war plan had been designed according to scant intelligence about the disposition of Saddam's presumed WMD arsenal.

How to secure the caches of WMD was a complex assignment that illustrated how little concrete information U.S. intelligence had actually generated about Iraq's supposed chemical and biological weapons. Because Iraq had not been an imminent flashpoint, did not have nuclear weapons, and, in the view of the intelligence agencies, lacked the means to launch a direct attack on the United States, Iraq had long been considered by the CIA a "Tier 2" country—a secondary priority for the overstretched U.S. intelligence network. Much of the intelligence that had been gathered since the Gulf War was in fact geared simply to facilitating the U.S. and British air patrols over southern and northern Iraq. Although the U.S. had an abundance of technical data on Iraq's air defense systems and the fiber optic network that linked them, it did not have an effective network of intelligence operatives and spies in Baghdad and the south. There was a big difference between citing circumstantial evidence that Iraq had weapons of mass destruction and pinpointing the sites where they were deployed or hidden. For all the accusations, the U.S. did not have a single smoking gun.[4]

The limits of U.S. intelligence soon became apparent as Spider Marks worked on the war plan. By culling through the intelligence, Marks was able to identify 946 sites on the WMSL, the weapons of mass destruction master site list. Each had a target folder containing whatever information had been gathered, human intelligence reports, blueprints, and imagery, some of which were years old. But there was no prioritization as to which sites needed to be secured first to preserve evidence of Saddam's WMD program and prevent his stockpiles from falling into the hands of terrorists—the Bush administration's stated purpose for going to war. The Hybrid invasion force would not be able to seize control of all 946— certainly not in the opening days and weeks of the attack.

Marks communicated the problem to McKiernan in November. The general was not amused to learn that his already overstretched force would need to take on yet another crucial, labor-intensive task. Marks asked for guidance from CENTCOM and the Defense Intelligence Agency as to which sites were most critical, which needed to be secured at the outset. He never got a clear answer. Working with his own team of analysts, he narrowed the list of high priority sites to some 130. "The good news is we took the initiative and ran with it and no one stopped us," Marks recalled. "It just seemed like this was something that should have been granularly ripped apart long before we rolled in. That's what was most amazing to me. The nation had been looking at and studying the WMD issue. It was the raison d'être for war and nobody pored or labored over the details of the list where this stuff was supposed to be stored or developed. My routine question was who cares about this besides us? Without prioritization from our many bosses, we just did it ourselves and never received any help doing it nor did we receive scrutiny or challenge with the priority we set."[5]

Still, even 130 sites were more than the land forces could properly address in the opening days of the war. With no guidance from above, Marks and Thurman set the priorities as reasonably as they could: the first suspected WMD sites to be visited would be those along the invasion route to the capital and those in and around Baghdad. In the absence of solid intelligence from Washington, proximity seemed to be as good a criterion as any. McKiernan reviewed and approved their detailed work.

What is more, while reading the war plan, Marks and Benson discovered that the command was also responsible for confirming the very presence of WMD. In CENTCOM's yearlong planning no technical intelligence team had been assigned to the mission. More important, the Kuwaitis, who had already agreed to provide the U.S. military with fuel, make a third of their territory available to the U.S. ground forces, and hand over a part of their airport to the 82nd Airborne, had drawn the line at the American request that samples of Iraqi WMD be brought to Kuwait for analysis. The Kuwaitis were happy to facilitate the U.S. invasion but made it clear that they would not allow Iraqi refugees, prisoners of war, or WMD into their country.

Improvising a solution, the land command picked the unlikely 75th Field Artillery Brigade headquarters, located at Fort Sill, Oklahoma, for the mission. The artillery unit had been slated to support Major General Ray Odierno's 4th Infantry Division drive south from Turkey. But McKiernan's planners were not persuaded it was needed and had recommended leaving it out of the attack as a way of reducing the number of U.S. troops that would flow through Turkey and of making the idea of a northern front somewhat more palatable to Ankara. Instead of lobbing shells at the Iraqis, the brigade headquarters would be seeded with intelligence analysts and a wide range of technical experts and equipment, and converted into a WMD exploitation team. The 75th Exploitation Task Force, as the new unit was called, was not formally given its assignment until Christmas Day: it would have only about a month to get ready, rehearse, deploy, and integrate intelligence and technical experts it had never met before.

This irregular fix aside, there was a profound and irreconcilable tension between Rumsfeld's push to enact his principles of transformation by beginning the attack with a lean force and the administration's rationale for the war, disarming Iraq and preventing WMD from falling into the wrong hands. As long as Saddam was in power there was every reason to think his suspected WMD sites would be under the control of his security organizations. The allied air and ground attacks were designed to shatter Iraq's command and control and destroy the regime's most loyal troops, inspiring "shock and awe." In the process, the United States might well break the chain of custody of WMD, risking an unintended consequence: the possible dispersal of chemical or biological weapons.

Securing the WMD required sealing the country's borders and quickly seizing control of the many suspected sites before they were raided by profiteers, terrorists, and regime officials determined to carry on the fight. The Hybrid force was too small to do any of this. The United States would be bombing for sixteen days before ground forces even crossed the border and after that it would take weeks more for the main force to arrive. In the months after the war, the Bush administration was criticized for exaggerating Iraq's WMD potential, but if the administration's assessment had been correct it might have been confronted with the very threat it claimed it was seeking to avoid.

As McKiernan and Marks pondered the WMD issue, the land command received new guidance from CENTCOM. Franks wanted McKiernan and his team to work on a plan for "early regime collapse." The White House wanted to move virtually unopposed in the event that Saddam suddenly lost his hold on power as the allies crossed the border. It was imperative to stabilize the country and ensure that the successor regime was to Washington's liking. Franks had broached the idea at the early August meeting with his commanders, but now it was being pressed with considerably more emphasis by Washington. If Saddam's regime was ready to crack, CENTCOM needed to be ready. In November, CENTCOM's planners called Benson and relayed the need for an "early regime collapse plan" so insistently that he wondered whether the United States was in possession of hot, new intelligence suggesting that Saddam's regime was indeed on its last legs. Benson rushed into Marks's windowless office at Camp Doha and asked if Saddam's forces were already surrendering, whether U.S. intelligence had been seeing white flags raised. Marks was puzzled. As McKiernan's chief intelligence officer, Marks had access to all the classified data on Iraq and enjoyed excellent relations with the CIA. There was no human intelligence from operatives in Iraq or signal intelligence from intercepted communications that indicated Saddam's hold on power was weak, supporting the early collapse scenario. "Early collapse?" Marks wrote in a November 30 entry in his log. "No Humint. No Sigint." Marks figured that Rumsfeld or his aides had sent yet another snowflake to Franks and that CENTCOM was rushing to appease its civilian masters. Benson concurred: "I never saw any intelligence that would let anyone say this was right," he recalled after the war. "Our feeling was that somebody in Washington must know something we do not know."[6]

Still, the command had to plan for the contingency, however slight, of Saddam's imminent collapse. The plan envisioned that Task Force 20, the Special Operations Forces that were to be secretly based at Ar'ar, Saudi Arabia, would attack by helicopter to secure Saddam International Airport. Paratroopers from the 82nd Airborne would assault the next night to reinforce TF 20 while Major General Buford "Buff" Blount's 3rd Infantry Division raced north. McKiernan had eight vans of specially configured equipment that could be flown to the airport in C-17s and used to set up a command post. He even went to Fort Bragg, North Carolina, to coordinate the planning among the Special Operations Forces, the 82nd Airborne, and his command. But even if there was a coup the plan could be risky. The airport was defended by SAM batteries, antiaircraft artillery, and shoulder-fired missiles. The Army Concepts Analysis Agency performed a war game and determined that between two and five aircraft would be lost to ground fire.

To determine if and when Saddam had lost his grip on power, Lieutenant Colonel Frank Jones, one of Benson's planners, developed a list of potential indicators, including the death or flight of key Iraqi players, a decrease in communications among the senior Iraqi leadership, public displays of defiance, the presence of demonstrators in the streets, and the like. If it looked like the early collapse plan needed to be activated, Franks would make the call. McKiernan's command also developed a variant, which became known as "early, early regime collapse," essentially a scenario in which Saddam fled or lost power before a shot was fired.

It was reasonable to have a contingency plan in case the regime turned out to be a house of cards, but the pressure to develop such a plan said more about expectations in Washington than reality in Iraq. McKiernan was convinced that he had too few forces to fight his way to Baghdad; Washington appeared to think that Saddam was teetering. Evan Heulfer, the planner who came up with the name for the land war plan, summed up the situation with skepticism by repeating the military's then common refrain: what if the balloon everybody in Washington was talking about turned out to be a bowling ball?

Toward the end of November, McKiernan's command conducted an exercise—dubbed Lucky Warrior—to evaluate in a definitive manner the Hybrid, or as it was also known, the 5-11-16-125 Plan. Fred Franks, the retired general who led the VII Corps during the Gulf War and who had been McKiernan's commander at the time and a mentor since, was invited to observe the exercise and was briefed on the plan on November 22. When he was alone with McKiernan, he was so convinced of the plan's flaws as to pose a simple question: "Is this your plan?" The query from his mentor reinforced McKiernan's determination to push for a new plan.[7]

As McKiernan worried about the plan, Franks focused on getting more allies on board to fight the war, including Arab governments in the region. Franks was accustomed to such diplomatic missions. To cement arrangements, he planned a quick trip to the Middle East. Before he left he met with the president and with Rumsfeld. Bush gave some general advice: he wanted to have as much muscle in the region as possible but did not want to see it atrophy. When Franks stopped in Bahrain—the Middle East headquarters of the U.S. Navy—he projected absolute confidence. "Bush is a man with an iron will," Franks declared in a private meeting with Bahrain's defense minister, General Shaikh Khalifa bin Ahmed al-Khalifa. "I go where they send me but I win where I go." Either Saddam Hussein gave up his WMD or the U.S. would take them. The U.S. could not risk WMD falling into the hands of terrorists.

Franks assured the minister that United States intelligence had been in touch with Iraqi officers. "Every day in Iraq people contact us," Franks said. "Some want to surrender entire units." The Bahrainis would be protected, Franks assured the minister. He promised to dispatch Patriot anti-missile batteries to the Gulf state to guard against an Iraqi missile attack. During the conversation, the minister told Franks that an acquaintance of his was a military adviser to Saddam Hussein. He wanted to know if the United States could find a way to get him out before the war. Franks seized the request as an opportunity to use the minister as a conduit to warn the Iraqi military not to use their WMD arsenal. "Generals like the one you named should keep their fingers off the trigger. If they use these weapons they will become like Saddam Hussein in our eyes." The Bahrainis worried that Iran might become a problem and flex its muscle. Franks replied that Iran was under control, alluding to discussions that Zalmay Khalilzad, the White House aide, had secretly had with the Iranians. They had even privately agreed to having American planes stray through their airspace, Franks added.

That same day, Franks went to Saudi Arabia to see Prince Khalid bin Sultan al-Saud, the deputy defense minister. Khalid had been Schwarz-kopf's counterpart during the Gulf War. He had attended Sandhurst, the British military academy, and Auburn University. But now Iraq was not knocking at his door; it was the Americans who were talking about up-setting the uneasy status quo and the Saudi deputy defense minister was tense. "Our requests will be painful," Franks told him. "We just want to let you know that if we have the war we want it to be short. The contribution of our friends will determine the length of the war." The Saudis had to be handled carefully. There was a lot CENTCOM wanted from them, and it would probably not get everything. The U.S. wanted to use the combat center at Prince Sultan Air Base to run the air war and wanted access to Prince Sultan and other bases for its air refueling tankers, AWACS, and other planes. The United States wanted to base Special Forces at Ar'ar to mount attacks in western Iraq. Beyond that, CENTCOM hoped to use the Saudi port of Al Jubayl to unload troops that would be needed for the invasion, taking some pressure off Kuwait's lone port.

Khalid said he hoped the Iraqi people would get rid of Saddam themselves. Franks suggested that this was wishful thinking and that Saudi cooperation would be essential to get the job done. "The more power that is brought against the center of the threat the shorter the threat will be there," Franks said. Khalid replied: "From a friend to a friend: don't put us in a hot spot." He added that the Saudis were willing to set up a liaison office in a trailer at CENTCOM headquarters in Tampa—within the "coalition village" there. This would be a first for them, though the liaison office would be established in the context of the Afghan war, not the war in Iraq. Franks said, "I will treat them as my sons."

Yet the Saudis were anxious to avoid too public an association with the Americans and sought to rush them out of town. After the meeting, Franks's entourage drove to the airport. Franks got on his plane. The Saudis were in such a hurry to say goodbye that they yanked away the steps to the plane before the rest of his motorcade arrived, leaving Brigadier General Elbert Perkins, a CENTCOM aide, and Jim Wilkinson, the press spokesman, temporarily stranded until the stairs were returned so they could get on board.

As he traveled through the region, Franks received a call from the leader of Yemen, Ali Abdullah Saleh. Saleh's son had been learning to fly aircraft in Florida, had inadvertently wandered near a nuclear plant, and had been arrested. Saleh wanted Franks's help in releasing his son and also dropped a not-too-subtle hint that he would like more U.S. aid. The Yemenis were making their airport available to CENTCOM for its war on terror and that was pushing up their insurance rates. Then Saleh asked if White House Deputy Chief of Staff Karl Rove thought Bush's statements on the Middle East conflict were helping Bush politically.[8]

In the United States, the CENTCOM planners, like McKiernan himself, had been rethinking the war plan, not withstanding the fact that the Hybrid had already received plaudits from the White House. The Hybrid had been devised to address Rumsfeld's insistence that CENTCOM be able to begin the attack quickly and without a large troop buildup. But now that the Bush administration had gone to the United Nations in pursuit of a resolution authorizing military action, and, since the diplomatic discussions were dragging on, there was no need for a plan to begin the war with little notice. There was time to send more forces to Kuwait to get ready.

One weakness in the Hybrid noted by the CENTCOM planners was this: if Saddam's regime was quickly defeated, CENTCOM would need to manage the chaos in Iraq, and the plan did not give them much to work with. John Agoglia prepared an analysis for Franks that underscored the problem. Ten days into the ground war CENTCOM would have only ten brigades to secure all of Iraq under the Hybrid. Under the Generated Start, CENTCOM would have fifteen brigades to take control ten days into the fight. If CENTCOM had more forces to begin the attack, it would be in a better position to deal with the aftermath.

In a November 8 meeting with his planners, Franks had touted the value of speed and surprise. "I believe it is probable that just driving a division and a MEB into Iraq will cause it to implode," Franks had said, referring to the 3rd Infantry Division and the Marine Expeditionary Brigade that were beginning to assemble in Kuwait. But when he heard his planners' analysis Franks was sympathetic to their case for more forces.

After a meeting with Franks, Agoglia called Terry Moran, McKiernan's adviser. Agoglia relayed Franks's attitude on additional troops. If McKiernan was serious about winning support for a new Cobra II plan, this was the moment to strike. There would be a two-day session involving Franks and his air, land, and sea commanders on December 7 and 8, a get-together that was dubbed a Rock Drill, an allusion to the days when commanders sketched out their war plans with rocks and sticks in the dirt instead of with PowerPoint. Shortly afterward, CENTCOM would enact a major war game, Internal Look, to test its command and control systems and rehearse its invasion plan.

Though the Internal Look exercise was a perennial training event for CENTCOM, this time it was unique. In the past, the war game had always been carried out at CENTCOM's headquarters in Tampa. Raytheon had constructed, at a cost of $58 million, a mobile command post that would be flown from Florida to the As Sayliyah base in Qatar for use by Franks and a 600-member staff. As Sayliyah, a 262-acre installation, conveniently had lots of extra room. Hundreds of U.S. M1 tanks and Bradley Fighting Vehicles had been stored there in climate-controlled warehouses, but had since been moved to Kuwait. Internal Look, in effect, was also a way of setting up Franks's forward headquarters in the guise of an exercise and getting it ready for war. Rumsfeld himself planned to attend. The Rock Drill and Internal Look would be pivotal events, offering McKiernan perhaps his last chance to press for a revision of the war plan.

Before making his case to Franks, McKiernan met on December 5 with Wallace, the corps commander, and his Marine counterpart, Lieutenant General James Conway, who had succeeded Mike Hagee as the commander of the corps-size 1st Marine Expeditionary Force. McKiernan outlined his worries about the Hybrid and explained the new plan he intended to propose. If the United States began the war with too small a ground force, sure enough it would burst out of the starting blocks but lose momentum just as quickly. McKiernan wanted a more adequate number of forces deployed before the war, namely the entire 3rd Infantry Division, the Army's 11th Attack Helicopter Regiment, as well as a CH-47 helicopter battalion. He also wanted the 5th and 7th Marine Regimental Combat teams to fill out Major General Jim Mattis's 1st Marine Division, and a large complement of the 3rd Marine Air Wing. Additional units, including the 3rd Armored Cavalry Regiment, the 101st Airborne, the 1st Armored Division, and the 1st Cavalry Division, could arrive after the attack was under way and would be fed into the fight to build up combat power for the eventual confrontation with the Republican Guard and the seizing of Baghdad. The units arriving after the fray had begun would also provide the foundation for securing Iraq after Saddam's regime was destroyed. Moreover, McKiernan had a different concept of how to fight. He wanted to begin the war with two three-star headquarters under his immediate command—instead of establishing Wallace's V Corps and Conway's MEF headquarters after the invasion had started. There would be two simultaneous and coordinated attacks under two separate headquarters, which reported to McKiernan, from the very start. The Marines would take the oilfields and maneuver in the east as the supporting attack. The Army would rapidly penetrate in the west and move on Baghdad as the main effort.

In the back and forth between Rumsfeld and CENTCOM, the war planning had been accordion-like. It had begun with a small force under the Vigilant Guardian plan—from a 4,000-strong brigade to as many as 70,000, depending on who was shaping the plan. It had expanded to the Generated Start, which would have begun the invasion with a force of 145,000 and grown to 275,000. Then it had shrunk to the Running Start, which envisioned kicking off the war with as few as 18,000 troops. The Hybrid was essentially a larger variation of the Running Start.

McKiernan briefed Franks and laid out his concerns about the possible loss of momentum as the invasion force waited in southern Iraq for reinforcements. He summed up the problem in a slide: "Dilemma: Cannot exploit with Operational Maneuver early." In addition to recommending additional forces, McKiernan also proposed that Franks do away with a sixteen-day air campaign, an important feature of the Hybrid Plan. "A-day," when the air campaign was to begin, and "G-day," when the land was to kick off, needed to be close together.[9]

In the Rock Drill discussion among the commanders, the recommendation to curtail the air campaign drew protests from Moseley, the air component commander, who insisted he needed time to reduce the Iraqi air defenses and strike other targets before the land war got under way. Franks seemed persuaded by McKiernan's main argument, but he did not have the final say. That would be Rumsfeld's prerogative. Although the ground plan was undecided, Franks outlined his thinking to his commanders on the rest of the invasion, which was chronicled in notes taken by participants. The war, Franks said, would not begin until Special Operations Forces, protected by Moseley's warplanes, were in position in western Iraq and able to prevent Iraq from lobbing Scud missiles at Israel. Then there would be a near simultaneous air and ground attack. The aim was to throw the Iraqis off balance, as they would likely expect an extended bombing campaign before the ground war, as in the Persian Gulf War and Kosovo.

Franks gave guidance on the air war. Command facilities and communications centers—Franks termed them "media" targets—needed to be struck or neutralized quickly by electronic jamming within the first twenty-four to forty-eight hours. Buzz Moseley would have to isolate the Iraqi leaders. Air strikes would be used to prevent the movement of the Republican Guard into Baghdad, in keeping with the Inside-Out Plan that had been briefed in Washington. Franks also indicated that he would not hesitate to propose attacks that put civilians at risk if high-priority targets were identified. "High collateral damage targeting will occur," he said. Franks wanted to dispel the notion that Baghdad could be a sanctuary for the regime. It was vital to shock the regime and to do so as rapidly as possible. Under existing procedures, however, any attack that was estimated to result in the death of thirty or more civilians had to be approved by Rumsfeld.

Franks made clear that he intended to press his commanders and his forces hard. "No one knows the pressure I will put on you to get to Baghdad. You will assume risk. Assume limited LOC protection," he added, referring to the lines of communication or supply lines. The CENTCOM commander told his officers that he was prepared to take significant risks to attack "high-payoff sites." "This is Omar's compound applied to Iraq," Franks said, alluding to the Ranger raid near Kandahar directed against the Taliban leader in the early part of the war in Afghanistan.

Franks did not think much of the Iraqi military. After taking out their command and control the Iraqis would not have the capability to fight in a concerted fashion. "Platoon and company size fights of the Republican Guard and Regular Army will not exist. They will aggregate but probably not fight." Franks was confident that U.S. forces would get to Baghdad quickly. "We will have soldiers on the ground in Baghdad at C plus 38," "C-day" being when the deployment of troops to Kuwait would begin, Franks said, insisting that U.S. forces would get to the capital in eleven days. "It may be a platoon but we will be there."

The commanders then turned their attention to the prospects for a northern front. With the political decision to go to war still unmade in London, a British officer acknowledged that the British were falling behind in their military preparations. Lieutenant General John Abizaid, Franks's deputy, said the big problem was not the state of British preparation but the Turks. If it was not possible to get U.S. and British forces into Turkey in time, Abizaid said, CENTCOM might want to consider using the northern front as a deception.

Franks noted that if Saddam's regime collapsed soon after the war began there would be pressure from Washington to stop sending additional troops. Franks raised the issue of whether CENTCOM should change the mix of forces that would be sent if the regime was toppled, sending units more geared to dealing with civil affairs than combat operations. Abizaid said that if Saddam was quickly ousted from power it might affect what sort of coalition would help occupy Iraq in the postwar period. It might be easier for nations to contribute forces for an occupation, he reasoned, if it did not follow a bloody war.[10]

Franks added that all of CENTCOM's assumptions should be scrutinized by CIA psychologists and trusted Iraqi defectors. They should "red team" the briefing slides.

Gary Luck, the XVIII Airborne commander in the Gulf War and Franks's former commander in Korea, who had been installed at

CENTCOM as a mentor and adviser to Franks, raised the possibility that Saddam might use his WMD to frustrate the assault on Baghdad and the military's plan to encircle the capital with operating bases. "Saddam is probably going to leave behind a CW [chemical warfare] or a BW [biological warfare] weapon for remote detonation, and it is probably going to be at BIAP [Baghdad International Airport], don't you think?" he said. CENTCOM was so confident of victory that it had already renamed the airport.

On December 8, the generals continued their discussion of the plan, including the insertion of Special Operations Forces in western Iraq to stop the Iraqis from firing Scuds. Gary Harrell, the brigadier general who oversaw Special Operations Forces, made the case for getting the commandos in early. There would be, he argued, a "deterrent effect" if the U.S. had Special Operations Forces in Iraq. It would dissuade Saddam from attacking Israel. But Franks did not want to trigger the war prematurely. Four days before A-day, Franks mused, might be too early. "The nation is committed to disarmament, not war," Franks responded, "but we must be ready."

Recalling his trip to Saudi Arabia, Franks noted that the Saudis were resisting the U.S. request to use the port of Al Jubayl in the northeast part of the Saudi kingdom to bring in U.S. troops for the war. Franks stressed flexibility in the deployment of forces. We need a "chunky TPFDL," he said, referring to the Time-Phased Force and Deployment List (or "Tip-Fiddle"), which spelled out the units to be sent to war. Franks wanted a way to identify required units on the military's computerized list the better to move forces forward if needed.

CENTCOM and the Bush administration assumed that there would be thousands of homeless and hungry Iraqi refugees. Franks said that his commanders must also be prepared to provide humanitarian aid. "Humanitarian assistance is a moveable feast looking for a location. I want everyone crossing the LD to have a humanitarian ration in their hands," Franks said—LD being military-speak for line of departure. The details of humanitarian assistance "belong to some in the inter-agency community. There is too much waiting on the word. We are going to force the word."

Abizaid repeated that he was still worried about how CENTCOM would control and administer Iraq after Baghdad fell, a subject that had received relatively little discussion in Washington. He said that CENTCOM should gather up any information on local police forces or other security institutions that could be preserved.

With the Rock Drill over, the time was ripe for Internal Look. The U.S. military had acquired a new tool for waging war: video conferencing. In the new age of digital communications, Franks and his top commanders would run the war in Iraq from literally four different countries. Franks would oversee the theater of war from Qatar. Air Force Lieutenant General Buzz Moseley would run the air campaign from his state-of-the-art command center at Prince Sultan Air Base outside Riyadh. Vice Admiral Tim Keating would oversee the maritime action from his command post in Bahrain. McKiernan would operate out of Kuwait.

During the prosecution of the war, Franks or his top deputies would conduct two regularly scheduled video conferences a day. Separate video conferences would be arranged as needed with the White House, Pentagon, or other military headquarters. The commanders and their legion of staff officers would spend several hours each day in, or preparing for, meetings. The system was a blessing as well as a curse. Communications among the top commanders was easier than ever before, but more time was consumed by meetings and intrusions from Washington.

Internal Look would put the system to the test. The war game examined several aspects of the invasion, including the initial push by the Army and Marines from Kuwait to the Euphrates and the convergence of U.S. troops on Baghdad. It provided some useful data: Iraqi defenses were so formidable it would be difficult to carry out an airborne operation at the Baghdad airport, and the Marines were put on notice that they might need to rush to Kirkuk in northern Iraq later in the campaign to control the oilfields there. An event of this prominence in governmental circles attracted some American visitors of stature. Senators Joseph Biden and Chuck Hagel were in the region on a fact-finding mission and, along with the U.S. ambassador to Kuwait, briefly attended the classified war game. Though they played no part in the military chain of command, lawmakers controlled the purse strings and could influence public attitude toward the upcoming war. So Franks and his commanders went to great lengths to make them feel welcome. Biden had a concern on his mind: the biggest worry in Washington beyond the White House and the Pentagon was the lack of clarity about the postwar plan. "Phase IV worries America," Biden said, referring to the official designation of the postcombat phase of the war.[11]

When Rumsfeld arrived to confer with Franks on December 12, the two men held a joint press conference for the media that were already beginning to assemble in Qatar. Franks declared that Internal Look would advance Rumsfeld's program of transforming the military. "You know, the doctrines that existed for our armed forces several years ago really don't apply to the first war of the twenty-first century," Franks said.[12] Once he was behind closed doors, Rumsfeld delved into the planning.

With Franks sitting by his side, Rumsfeld heard McKiernan's pitch to put aside the Hybrid Plan in favor of Cobra II, which presumed a larger force. Rumsfeld did not provide a definitive response, but offered other advice. The defense secretary suggested recruiting Arab nations to do peacekeeping duty in Iraq after Saddam was toppled. Even if only a few participated and performed largely humanitarian functions, the presence of Arab soldiers in postwar Iraq, Rumsfeld said, would help calm the "Arab street."

Rumsfeld inquired about Saddam's fortified bunkers and advised CENTCOM to avoid overdependence on the German decontamination units that had been deployed in Kuwait to clean up after a WMD attack. It was unclear whether the German government would order their withdrawal before the war. If the units remained, Rumsfeld suggested, they should be assigned to assist Kuwaiti civilians, not U.S. forces, so they would not seem to be a part of the American war effort. That would make their mission that much easier for the German government to accept.

Franks ended Internal Look by telling his commanders that he expected them to work together; he did not want to encounter the sort of friction and bickering between the Army and Air Force that had cropped up during the unsuccessful Operation Anaconda in Afghanistan, which left the services blaming each other for its failure. "We are going to fight joint, I want you and Buzz Moseley to eat with the same fork," Franks told McKiernan. "The childish behavior we saw in Afghanistan will not be repeated. There is a long road in front of us, but we have the best team in history. Welcome to history. This ain't no Kosovo. This is a real big deal because of you."[13]

By the end of December, word had come down that Rumsfeld had accepted the basic outline of McKiernan's Cobra II plan. Here was a critical decision. The war planning had gone on for more than a year, and now had come almost full circle. The Running Start and its spin-off, the Hybrid, were dead. McKiernan's plan was closest to Franks's Generated Start, which had drawn stern objections from Rumsfeld almost a year earlier. Precious time had been spent that might have been devoted to the more daunting problem of how to cope with Iraq after Saddam's fall. Still, it was not a certainty that McKiernan would end up getting all the reinforcements and combat support troops he wanted. Regarding force levels, Rumsfeld would be ever vigilant and fully intended to keep tight control. Rumsfeld's visit to Internal Look had been a breakthrough for McKiernan, but some battles with the defense secretary still lay ahead.

The adoption of Cobra II aside, Franks continued to refer to the plan as the Hybrid, or, alternatively, the 5-11-16-125 Plan, even though it now bore only a faint resemblance to that plan. There would be neither a mere eleven-day deployment before the attack began nor a prolonged sixteeen-day air campaign. The force level, headquarters, and schemes of maneuver had been radically revised in line with McKiernan's recommendations. But Franks had already won White House approval for the 5-11-16-125 Plan and he could avoid reopening planning issues while moving forward with Cobra II.

In his memoir, *American Soldier,* Franks wrote that CENTCOM went to war with the Hybrid Plan, making no mention of the objections from his land force commander nor of the fact that he essentially adopted a plan promoted by his subordinate. Neither Franks nor Rumsfeld were the architects of Cobra II. But Franks and other officials would provide their airbrushed version of history to some leading authors. The CENTCOM commander's motivation was perhaps understandable. Despite Franks's boast at his joint press conference with Rumsfeld in Qatar, CENTCOM'S Cobra II plan was not about to make existing military doctrines obsolete. Cobra II did not represent the radical revolution in warfare promised by Rumsfeld's doctrine of transformation.[14]

CHAPTER 6

'Round and 'Round We Go

After McKiernan's Cobra II strategy had been approved in principle by Rumsfeld and Franks in December, McKiernan pressed for the forces required to execute the plan. Under Cobra II, as with the Hybrid, the attack was to start before all the forces had arrived in the region. McKiernan had two concerns: not only getting the forces in place that he needed to begin the attack but ensuring that the flow of the rest of the Cobra II force was uninterrupted so as not to lose momentum and be short of combat power at a critical stage of the fight.

McKiernan had reason to be worried. Rumsfeld's relentless scrutiny of troop requests was well known among the generals. Before McKiernan had even pitched his Cobra II plan, Franks had submitted a request for some of the forces and arms that would be needed to start the invasion, which an irreverent CENTCOM staff member had dubbed the "Mother of All Deployment Orders." The MODEP request, as it was known by the acronym-loving military, was received by the Pentagon on November 26. It remained stuck there for a month or so until the deployment orders were issued on Christmas Day.[1]

Rumsfeld and his field commanders looked at troop requests through opposite ends of the telescope. The defense secretary approached these requisitions with the ruthless efficiency of a businessman for whom excess inventory was to be avoided at all cost. During his years as a corporate executive in Chicago, Rumsfeld had talked to Gus Pagonis, the Army general who supervised the vast amount of supplies transported to Saudi Arabia for the Persian Gulf War. Rumsfeld regularly told Pentagon officials that the United States had sent more forces and supplies than were needed, and the Iraqi military was weaker than it had been in 1991. For Rumsfeld, too large a buildup was not only a waste of effort and a violation of the new way to wage war but a drag on the deployment phase, making it more difficult to secure the cooperation of Arab nations in the endeavor.

Rumsfeld's tightfistedness aside, McKiernan still needed to be sure he had sufficient forces and logistical capability to initiate and sustain the invasion. When units were needed to support the march to Baghdad, they had to be already in Kuwait and prepared to move north—not on a ship still en route to the Persian Gulf. The only reserve McKiernan would have on hand when the war began would be a brigade of the 82nd Airborne Division. The last thing the American generals wanted to hear during combat was that the check was in the mail. A lot of the "check" covered the cost of fuel, ammunition, medical supplies, maintenance units, and trucks to sustain the offensive. There was a saying in the military: amateurs talk about strategy, professionals talk about logistics.

The military had a computerized system for deploying forces that would have precluded the tug-of-war between CENTCOM and the defense secretary over troop numbers. The TPFDL automatically determined not only which logistical and auxiliary units should be sent to support the combat forces earmarked for the war plan, but also the order in which they should be sent. It was far from perfect, requiring ungodly hours to assemble; it sometimes included surplus units, but it was the only system the military had.

The TPFDL was particularly important for the Army. More than the other services, the Army depended on the carefully coordinated deployment of weapons and matériel by the military's Transportation Command. Most of what the Marines needed to fight in the Persian Gulf was already stocked in maritime prepositioning ships, huge floating warehouses kept during peacetime at Diego Garcia, the island in the Indian Ocean that belongs to the British. The Navy and Air Force had the means to bring to the region much of what they themselves needed. But most of the Army's armor, artillery, helicopters, and other equipment had to be transported from the United States and Europe. Moreover, the Army had responsibilities the other services did not have, including operating the port and airfield in Kuwait and managing logistics for the entire military theater. The deployment of the units that handled these tasks had to be carefully sequenced so that they arrived in time to support the rest of the force, and the TPFDL was the system that was used to do so.

At the December Rock Drill, McKiernan had let Franks know that he wanted the Pentagon to flow the entire TPFDL associated with Cobra II, with the understanding that only a portion of the force would be in place on G-day to launch the attack. Regardless of what happened in the early days of the invasion, McKiernan wanted a commitment by the Pentagon to send all of the units designated by the TPFDL to hedge against the unexpected and meet the demands of securing postwar Iraq.

Nonetheless, Rumsfeld regarded the TPFDL as a wasteful anachronism that took decision-making out of his hands. Rumsfeld did not trust the generals to send the minimum force necessary to win and secure the peace, and he wanted to be able to cut off the flow of reinforcements and support units if they were deemed unnecessary once the war was under way. Without reliance on the TPFDL, Rumsfeld would be the arbiter of which units were to be sent.

As with Franks's Mother of all Deployment Orders, the initial indications suggested that getting the forces from Rumsfeld would be a hard sell. According to McKiernan's planners, the initial complement of forces that were to be deployed for Cobra II was 86,000 troops, including 17,000 reservists, many of whom were critical for operating the port and airfields, driving the trucks, setting up the communications, and putting in place the logistics needed by the ground forces for the invasion. But in a mid-December video conference, Colonel Mike Fitzgerald, a lead CENTCOM planner, passed along some guidance from the Pentagon. CENTCOM had been in touch with the Joint Staff, and word had come from Peter Pace's office that the troop request was too large. As Fitzgerald explained to Kevin Benson, there was no cap on the number of forces that McKiernan could ask for; there was, however, a threshold. CENTCOM did not want to approach Rumsfeld with a request that he was sure to reject. It did not want to preempt the possibility of getting the forces it wanted.

In early January, Benson received an e-mail from Fitzgerald, who was in Washington working on a brief that Franks was to give to Bush on January 9. Rumsfeld "had a cow" regarding the size of the Army forces on the troop request list, Fitzgerald noted, and wanted to know if a British division could be substituted for a U.S. division. Instead of deferring to his generals on matters of war planning, Rumsfeld was poring through the deployment requests and insisting that CENTCOM explain why it needed all the additional forces.[2]

The feedback following Franks's meeting with Bush was no more reassuring. Mike DeLong, the three-star Marine general who served as Franks's deputy, reported that CENTCOM needed to be ready to attack as early as February 15. But instead of concentrating on how to get forces to the Persian Gulf in time, Rumsfeld and Wolfowitz wanted Franks to identify points at which the president could stop the flow of reinforcements midstream. If the regime collapsed quickly, units should be "off-ramped" in the jargon of the Pentagon. DeLong added that Rumsfeld wanted to reduce the number of troops that would be used to secure Iraq after the fall of Saddam's regime as quickly as possible.

To McKiernan and his staff, it seemed as if the Pentagon was giving with one hand and taking with the other. McKiernan did not want to off-ramp any of the forces he was asking for. Even if the Iraqi regime immediately collapsed, he wanted the forces for the postwar period. To ensure that there were no delays in receiving reinforcements once the attack had begun, McKiernan sought to develop a plan that would give the land command assurance that reinforcements would be available if needed, while bowing to Rumsfeld's mandate. Equipment for U.S. units like the 101st Airborne Division or the 3rd Armored Cavalry Regiment would be positioned on ships that would loiter in the Arabian Sea. If CENTCOM won quickly and order was quickly imposed on the country the equipment could be sent home. If not, soldiers would be flown to Kuwait and assigned their equipment as it was unloaded from the ships. Franks agreed with the scheme, but the plan did not receive a positive reception from Rumsfeld's Pentagon and was dropped.[3]

By the end of January, McKiernan was getting increasingly anxious that, though he would have enough forces to start the war, he would not have sufficient reinforcements to continue the attack. In a message to Franks, McKiernan wrote that he was not trying to build a Rolex watch, simply trying to carry out the mission as efficiently as possible. The initial forces Franks had approved would enable the U.S. military to get to the Euphrates and beyond. But McKiernan would need additional forces to advance to Baghdad—the prime objective—and seize the capital. If the Pentagon was reluctant to deploy the additional units right away, McKiernan wrote, he would settle for the 3rd Armored Cavalry Regiment, a unit well suited to protecting vulnerable supply lines, and additional V Corps combat service support. The 101st could be put on alert and sent later. McKiernan would not be getting everything he wanted—just enough to make the plan work.

Franks agreed with McKiernan's general argument, but decided that the 101st should be deployed ahead of the 3rd Cavalry Regiment. Franks favored the longer operational reach of the 101st, which had hundreds of helicopters, arguing that the sudden collapse of Saddam's regime was more likely than Kursk, an allusion to the World War II tank battle between the Russians and the Germans. The logic of Franks's position was that protecting supply lines would be less important than flying to the Baghdad airport or to the north in a post-Saddam Iraq.

For the generals, Rumsfeld's tenacious insistence on oversight was becoming as much of a hindrance as the difficulty of transporting troops and matériel halfway around the world to Kuwait. McKiernan was not the only frustrated general. When senior Army officials sought to alert reserve units before the Christmas holiday that they might be called up early in the new year, Rumsfeld had balked. It was the first time that a defense secretary had managed the deployment process with such scrutiny. Rumsfeld was not only deciding which units should ultimately be sent to Kuwait but also when the units should be alerted for possible deployment, which was traditionally an Army prerogative.

In the field, the second-guessing in Washington was enormously disruptive. The decision to delay activation of many of the reservists and to jettison the TPFDL delayed the establishment of the Theater Support Command, which was to manage the logistics for the ground forces, and played havoc with the deployments. The reservists who would run the port and airfield were not fully in place as the troops and equipment started to flow in, nor were many of the military police. To get the command up and running, J. D. Thurman, the two-star general who served as McKiernan's operations deputy, had to go down the list of individual reserve units, name by name, and insist they be deployed. "Because we didn't use a TPFDL, I think we were inefficient in flowing forces over here," Thurman recalled. "It was very hard to get forces over here. There was reluctance to mobilize reserve components prior to Christmas. That happened to be the forces that we needed to set the stance for the logistics in the theater."[4]

Tom Reilly, the lieutenant colonel who had helped draft the Vigilant Guardian plan and who later worked in McKiernan's headquarters, told Army historians after the war that the civilians at the Pentagon simply did not understand how dependent the military was on reservists, especially for logistics.

"Typical questions that we got were: why are you asking for so many reserve component forces?" Reilly recalled. "To me, that was clear evidence that OSD did not understand the makeup of the military forces of the United States, for example, the Army. We often joked that we would like to be able to invite Mr. Rumsfeld down here and say to him, 'Mr. Secretary, meet Isaac Newton. We live in a Newtonian world. We cannot change the size of the ocean or the distance between CONUS [continental United States] and Iraq. With no maintenance problems it takes twenty-one days to sail from Beaumont, Texas, to the port of Ash Shu'ayba, Kuwait.' Some say that the secretary of defense is not supposed to worry about those details, and that it is the Joint Staff that is supposed to inform him about those issues and how they impact on the desires of the senior civilian officials. If that is the case then it appears that the Joint Staff failed to do its job."[5]

After the fall of Baghdad, an independent commission chaired by former Defense Secretary James R. Schlesinger concluded that the decision to do away with the TPFDL had played a role in the Abu Ghraib prison scandal. Without that system, military police units had been deployed pell-mell. Units had arrived without their equipment and often in no clear sequence. There had been less opportunity to train the units, and commanders found themselves in charge of units with which they were unfamiliar. "The flow of equipment and personnel was not coordinated," the report noted. "The unit could neither train at its stateside mobilization site without its equipment nor upon arrival overseas, as two or three weeks could go by before joining with its equipment. . . . MP brigade commander did not know who would be deployed next."[6]

In early February, Newt Gingrich paid a visit to Kuwait and met with McKiernan's staff. The former House Speaker had been a big booster of military transformation and had passed Doug Macgregor's invasion plan to Rumsfeld a year earlier. But Gingrich thought some of Rumsfeld's aides had exaggerated lessons learned in Afghanistan. A more mobile and lethal military was all to the good, but some on Rumsfeld's team were prone to take a good thing too far. In particular, they overemphasized the utility of the Special Operations Forces, overstated the fragility of Saddam's regime, and undervalued the advantage conferred by armored units. Macgregor himself had advocated attacking with a very small force—but an armored force. "There is a mind-set of arrogance compounded by what they saw in Afghanistan that has led people to think that 3 JDAMs [Joint Direct Attack Munition, a satellite-guided bomb] and five guys on horseback equal a RG [Republican Guard] division," Gingrich said. But Iraq was not Afghanistan. It was, Gingrich added, a totally different "target set."

Gingrich was also taken aback by the constant interventions by Rumsfeld and his staff. The defense secretary was not proffering new war-waging concepts for Franks to build on. He was micromanaging the deployment process. Gingrich had talked to General John Handy, the head of the military's Transportation Command, and had been given an earful on how the transportation plans had been severely disrupted. "I am going to go back and press Don to quit screwing around with tactical-level decisions," Gingrich told McKiernan's planners. "The worst they can do is take my designated parking space away."[7]

For more than a year, deliberations between Franks and Rumsfeld had focused in the main on what was needed for Phase III, the major combat operations that would take American forces to Baghdad. Shinseki had offered his view on the invasion planning. While McKiernan was pressing his troop requests, Bush had called the Joint Chiefs to a January 30 meeting at the White House to hear what they had to say about the war plan. Myers, Rumsfeld's appointee as JCS chairman, was happy with the plan. Vern Clarke, the chief of naval operations, and John Jumper, the Air Force chief of staff, praised it. Shinseki, the Army chief, gave a more qualified assessment. Shinseki said that he would have liked to have more forces in place before kicking off the attack, and Turkey's agreement to open a northern front. He also cautioned that the logistics would be crucial and it would be important to keep reinforcements flowing, a reference to the tightfisted allocation of forces that was frustrating his former operations officer McKiernan. With these caveats, Shinseki advised that the plan was executable and that Franks had the situation in hand.[8] Two weeks later, while visiting Kuwait, Shinseki was blunter to McKiernan's staff in a meeting at Camp Doha. You had to be on a highway before you could get off, Shinseki argued. It was premature to talk about off-ramps when the Army did not have all of its pieces on the move. Nor did Shinseki approve of Rumsfeld's decision to discard the TPFDL. Many in the military saw the TPFDL as a holdover from the Cold War in need of revision. The planners at CENTCOM and the Transportation Command had been working on the TPFDL for war in Iraq for more than a year.

In late February, Steve Hawkins, a brigadier general from the Army Corps of Engineers who had been assigned by the Joint Staff to work on postwar planning issues, dropped by the Pentagon to provide an update to Shinseki. Shinseki asked him how many troops he thought were needed to secure Iraq after Saddam was toppled. Hawkins said that no fewer than 350,000 coalition forces would do, and CENTCOM might need as

many as half a million. There was a huge array of tasks. The U.S. and its
allies needed to control major population centers, protect the country's
infrastructure, control its borders, and provide postwar support. Shinseki, who had commanded the U.S. peacekeeping forces in Bosnia, was
not surprised by the figure and told Hawkins that his estimates were in
keeping with those provided by his own staff. It was a professional conversation between two generals and Hawkins did not see anything remotely controversial about it. Amassing that large a force would require
deploying all of the units called for by McKiernan's Cobra II plan and
drawing on large numbers of allied forces as well, but Hawkins assumed
that was just the price of carrying out regime change and building the
new Iraq that the administration kept talking about.[9]

On February 25, Shinseki and his fellow chiefs went before the Senate
Armed Services Committee, which was probing the preparations for
the all but certain war. During the proceedings, Carl Levin, a Michigan
Democrat, asked Shinseki how many troops would be needed to control
Iraq after Saddam was ousted. Shinseki noted that he was not in the chain
of command, but matter-of-factly said that it would take several hundred
thousand. The lawmakers did not ask any follow-up questions. Shinseki's
comments, however, suggested that the invasion and occupation of Iraq
might be a more demanding undertaking than the administration had indicated and generated headlines.[10]

Tom White, the civilian secretary of the army, was at his well-
appointed apartment on the Georgetown waterfront when he received an
early morning phone call the next day from Paul Wolfowitz. White, a retired Army brigadier general, who had worked for Colin Powell, made a
small fortune at Enron, and become an active supporter of George Bush,
had volunteered for the job of army secretary, wanting to be part of the
Republican effort to infuse new money into the Pentagon and beef up
American defense. But he had a contentious relationship with Rumsfeld
over the future and size of the Army. Rumsfeld wanted his civilian secre-
taries to promote his own military vision, but as a former Army officer
White felt a personal and intellectual kinship with Shinseki and believed
the secretary of defense did not know what it took to put boots on the
ground to fight land campaigns.

On Rumsfeld's instruction, Wolfowitz complained that Shinseki had
spoken out of turn and was off base. Shinseki was not the commander of

the operation, and service chiefs should not be offering their independent view on the war plans. White argued that Shinseki had simply done what Congress had asked him to do: provide his professional assessment. That day, Rumsfeld told reporters that it was ludicrous to think that it would take more forces to secure the peace than win the war. But White dug in his heels. Shinseki never pressed the issue with his fellow chiefs, nor did he mention that his estimate had corresponded to those provided by one of the military's postwar planners.[11]

For all of the controversy, Shinseki's numbers were similar to those generated by CENTCOM. Franks had projected that, while CENTCOM would begin the attack with a portion of its invasion force, it would have 250,000 troops in Iraq by the time Saddam was defeated and the United States began to stabilize Iraq. There was, however, a subtle but significant difference between Franks, on the one hand, and Shinseki and White on the other. As Rumsfeld had indicated, he hoped to off-ramp some of the force if the Iraqi military's resistance crumbled, and he wanted to reduce the occupying force as quickly as possible. Franks himself had acquiesced in Rumsfeld's position and told his planners that if there was little war damage and the invasion was over quickly fewer troops would be needed for Phase IV. Mike Fitzgerald, Franks's chief planner, also passed this guidance on to McKiernan and his staff: if the fight ended quickly, there would be tremendous pressure from Rumsfeld's office to stop the force flow.

Even before Shinseki made headlines with his troop estimate, a Marine officer on the NSC staff, Major Jeff Kojac, had prepared on his own initiative a briefing to draw attention to the need for adequate postwar forces, bearing the anodyne title "Force Security in Seven Recent Stability Operations." Military aides did not have the power and authority to make policy recommendations, but they could frame an issue by collecting facts, and on this issue the facts were more in line with Shinseki's testimony than anything that was coming from Rumsfeld or his top civilian aides.

The briefing made the point that however many forces might be required to defeat the foe, maintaining security afterward was determined by an entirely different set of calculations, including the population of the occupied nation, its geographic size and terrain, and degree of urbanization. There was no single troop-to-population ratio that governed all cases. For example, if the United States wanted to maintain the same ratio of troops to population that it had in Kosovo, where there were 40,000 peacekeepers and two million citizens, it would have to station 480,000 troops in Iraq. If Bosnia was used as a benchmark, 364,000 troops would be needed. These figures were well in the range cited by Shinseki. But if the Bush administration used Afghanistan as a template, then only 13,900 would be required. The implicit question was whether Iraq would be more like the Balkans or Afghanistan.

The NSC briefing made clear that in one key respect Iraq had more in common with the Balkans than Afghanistan: three-quarters of Iraq's population lived in urban areas; in Bosnia and Kosovo, city dwellers comprised half of the population, while in Afghanistan they made up only 18 percent. This difference was significant because, as the briefing stated, it generally took more troops to control heavily urbanized areas. The briefing was delivered to Rice; the deputy national security adviser, Stephen J. Hadley; and Eric Edelman, Scooter Libby's chief deputy and Doug Feith's eventual successor at the Pentagon. When the briefing was given, Hadley seemed to take comfort in the Afghan parallel. At the White House, the briefing never prompted any second-guessing of Rumsfeld's position. As far as the White House was concerned, the briefing largely spelled out how the Clinton administration and foreign governments had carried out nation-building and peacekeeping operations in the past. Afghanistan had been the Bush administration's first foreign intervention and it was charting a new course.[12]

At McKiernan's headquarters, there was a gnawing worry that the land command could find itself short of the forces it needed for the postwar phase of the campaign. For even if the Pentagon flowed all the troops for Cobra II that McKiernan had asked for, he would not have enough forces to seal Iraq's borders, impose order throughout the country, protect the nation's infrastructure, and carry out myriad other tasks to stabilize the new Iraq. He would have his hands full just securing Baghdad and southern and northern Iraq. Western Iraq—including Anbar Province, where Sunni Fallujah and Ramadi were located, and which stretched to the Syrian border—would be an "economy of force" operation. With few forces to spare, no more than an armored cavalry regiment would initially be deployed in the vast province abutting an unfriendly country and including large Sunni cities. While McKiernan hoped that thousands of fresh allied forces would be available, no major contributions had yet been promised. The only substantial allied force on hand at the start of the war would be the British, and they planned to control Basra and a swath of southern territory.

McKiernan and CENTCOM, however, were counting on another source of manpower: the Iraqi military. During Desert Storm, while Iraqis had surrendered in droves, there had been no instance of an entire division or brigade joining the United States's cause. This time, the CIA figured, would be different. Entire units might come over to the U.S. side with their equipment and structure intact. The military's name for this was "capitulation." Wholesale capitulation and not just battlefield desertions was an important assumption of the invasion planning. Leaflets and messages for broadcast were prepared, calling on the Iraqi forces to arrange their vehicles in a predetermined pattern, turn their gun turrets to the rear, and step away from their vehicles. Military lawyers drew up Articles of Capitulation, which the Iraqi commanders would be called on to sign.[13]

The capitulation instructions were not to be disseminated until the eve of the war. CENTCOM was concerned that, if it provided them earlier, Saddam's intelligence agents might arrange fake ones. But considerable efforts were made to soften up the enemy psychologically. In one five-day period in late November and early December, U.S. aircraft dropped some 6,000 leaflets near Kut while Commando Solo, a Special Operations aircraft, flew along the Kuwaiti border broadcasting messages advising Iraqi commanders not to fight. There were years of psychological operations to build on. Even during Zinni's tenure at CENTCOM, U.S. planes had dropped leaflets telling Iraqi troops that if war with the United States broke out and they refused to fight they would be taken care of afterward.[14]

At CENTCOM, the plan was to use members of the Iraqi Regular Army who had capitulated to control the country's borders and take on other tasks that the overstretched allied troops would be faced with after the war. Saddam's Republican Guard forces and his intelligence apparatus would of course be disbanded, but Regular Army units that were prepared to help the victors would be embraced. Rarely has a military plan depended on such a bold assumption. The Bush administration was not only confident that it would quickly defeat the Iraqi military but also counted on Iraqi forces to work under American supervision and even to help police the occupation.

At the Pentagon, Wolfowitz and his aides had taken the idea of enlisting Iraqi assistance a step further. Dusting off his proposal, made during his years out of office, to arm and equip Iraqi insurgents, Wolfowitz's initial goal was to raise an indigenous opposition army. As first imagined the plan was bold: there would be thousands of Iraqi freedom fighters who would battle Saddam's forces alongside U.S. and allied troops. Abizaid, who had served on the Joint Staff before moving to CENTCOM as Franks's deputy, supported Wolfowitz's concept. Like Wolfowitz, Abizaid wanted to put an Iraqi face on the invasion force.

Most of the administration was skeptical, if not opposed, to Wolfowitz's plan. Outside of the Pentagon, only Steve Hadley supported it. The CIA, which was given the mission to train a small, covert Iraqi force, was not enthusiastic about the establishment of an overt, Pentagon-trained unit and was deeply suspicious of Chalabi's potential influence among such troops. The State Department suspected that Wolfowitz's hidden agenda was to establish a Chalabi army. Franks thought that an Iraqi force would just get in the way and gave no weight to the benefits such a unit might provide in terms of local knowledge and language.

The plan was scaled back and worked hard by William J. Luti, a senior aide to Doug Feith who later became the top NSC staff official on defense, and Chris Straub, an Arabic-speaking former Special Forces officer. Iraqi freedom fighters would now serve as scouts, advisers, and experts on civil affairs. They could also hold secure supply lines and assume command of defecting units. The fighters would be trained in self-defense and armed with 9-millimeter pistols. Their role would be to help the U.S. forces understand Iraq and assure the Iraqis that they were not being occupied by an infidel army.

In December 2002, Luti met in London with representatives from a dozen Iraqi organizations in exile at the European headquarters of the U.S. Navy. He asked them to submit names of potential fighters. The Iraqis would be trained by Dave Barno, a U.S. Army two-star general, at Tazar, an air base in Hungary. To facilitate recruitment in the United States, a gathering point was established at Fort Bliss, Texas. To equip the force the Pentagon would draw on the $97 million worth of equipment it was authorized to provide under the Iraq Liberation Act that Clinton had signed.

Even this more modest project ran afoul. Hungary did not want potential mercenaries to flock to Tazar. It insisted that the Iraqi freedom fighters arrive in uniform and be issued identity cards after undergoing medical examinations. Potential recruits had to be vetted by U.S. intelligence to ensure they were not Iraqi or Iranian spies. Some of the Iraqi opposition groups had their own militias and were reluctant to put them under the control of the United States. Franks remained unenthusiastic, to say the least.[15] After a briefing from Luti on his pet project, Franks turned to Feith in a Pentagon corridor, letting him know where he stood: "I don't have time for this fucking bullshit," Franks exclaimed. Rumsfeld was not pushing the idea hard and Franks was not shy about taking on the defense secretary's subordinates.

By February, the pool of applicants was so small that Wolfowitz and his aides decided the United States needed to appeal to Iraqi exiles hiding out in Iran and northern Iraq. As the United States had no formal diplomatic relations with Iran this was no small task. Wolfowitz asked Franks to arrange for a transit point in the Persian Gulf where 3,000 Iraqi exiles could be brought from Iran, 300 at a time, and then flown to Hungary for training. But the plan was never implemented; time had run out. Of the 6,000 names submitted by Iraqi opposition groups, only 622 were vetted by the United States. More than 500 invitations were sent out, but only 95 showed up for training at Tazar. Of these, 73 completed the four-week training program, an embarrassingly meager result for the millions of dollars spent and such prodigious work. They were sent primarily to a civil affairs unit that supported the Army, Marines, and McKiernan's command. The Defense officials blamed bureaucratic obstacles and lack of enthusiasm on the part of CENTCOM. White House officials and CENTCOM said that the fiasco showed that Feith and his team were better at drafting conservative policy manifestos than instituting programs.[16]

Wolfowitz and his aides suffered another setback when the White House rejected their proposal for the establishment of a provisional Iraqi government. While Wolfowitz favored forming a government in exile, the State Department thought it would give Iraqi opposition leaders like Ahmed Chalabi too much power, as State officials thought Iraqi "internals" had to play a major role. Unlike his Defense Department deputies, Rumsfeld also saw a downside in speedily handing over power to an exile-dominated Iraqi government. Rumsfeld "wanted total freedom of action," a senior official recalled. "He wanted to ensure he could root out Saddamism, terrorism, and get at WMD. He was concerned that an Iraqi entity could be in the way." While Rumsfeld and Wolfowitz were both hawks on Iraq, there were subtle and important differences between the two.

In February, Khalilzad, the White House's ambassador to the Iraqi resistance, met with representatives of the Iraqi opposition groups in Ankara, Turkey, to deliver the administration's message: after Saddam was deposed, the United States would be running the country for up to a year. The Iraqis would have an advisory role. There could be local elections and eventually national elections. Kanan Makiya, an Iraqi human rights activist who lived in exile in the United States and who had written a damning indictment of Saddam's abuses, was outraged by Khalilzad's hard line. Makiya drafted an op-ed piece affirming his views and sent it to Cheney's office, which asked that he not publish it for twenty-four hours. But no change of policy was forthcoming. When Khalilzad visited northern Iraq a week later he warned the opposition leaders that if they declared a provisional government he would walk out of the meeting. The U.S. prevailed.[17]

With few if any Iraqi freedom fighters in the offing, Rumsfeld suggested another source for fielding additional forces: Muslim nations might be approached to guard religious sites in Iraq. The defense secretary had first suggested using Arab troops during Internal Look. In February, Mike Fitzgerald pressed the matter in a message to McKiernan's command, noting that a snowflake about it had come down from Rumsfeld. During the Gulf War, the U.S.-led coalition had included an Egyptian and even a Syrian division. The Egyptians had even been officially charged with "liberating" Kuwait City. After U.S. Marines had chased Iraqi forces from the area, the Egyptians arrived, marching in parade formation. But now the mission was not to evict an invader; it was regime change. And there was uncertainty as to whether troops from neighboring Arab states would be welcomed by the Iraqis. No Arab nation had so far contributed forces to the imminent invasion, and soliciting Arab aid for the postwar phase seemed highly problematic. McKiernan's command could draw up a plan for using Arab troops but his planners doubted there would ever be a need for it.

After receiving Fitzgerald's note, Colonel Benson responded that most of the Muslim nations that theoretically might contribute forces were Sunni. Having Sunnis guard the Shiite holy sites in Shiite-dominated cities like Najaf and Karbala, Benson wrote back sarcastically, would be like having Fitzgerald and Benson go to Belfast to guard the Orange Day parade.[18]

. . .

As the generals and the Pentagon played tug-of-war over U.S. forces, the United States sought to keep the Iraqis off balance by carrying out a highly classified deception plan. The idea was to fool Saddam on how many forces CENTCOM planned on using to start the invasion and where they would attack. Under the still secret scheme, a U.S. military officer contacted an Iraqi operative and offered to sell the Iraqis information about the war plan. The officer met with his Iraqi contact in Morocco and accepted substantial payments for the documents.

To make the information appear credible, U.S. officials had modified actual CENTCOM documents. The doctored plans indicated that the war would not begin until a large invasion force was in place, a force much larger than the one McKiernan planned to initiate Cobra II. They also specified a series of airborne operations in and around Tikrit, so as to induce the Iraqis to shift the Hammurabi Republican Guard Division north from its positions just west of Baghdad. That would prevent Saddam from reinforcing the Medina Division south of Baghdad.

To reinforce the ruse, scripts, which vaguely alluded to airborne operations in the north, were prepared, and McKiernan and officers from the 82nd Airborne and 1st Cavalry Division were instructed to read them in telephone conversations that Washington assumed would be tapped by either the Iraqis or foreign intelligence services friendly toward them.[19]

In a parallel effort, the CIA made phone calls to Iraqi commanders warning them not to use WMD and advising them to switch sides. The callers were fluent in Arabic and even spoke with an Iraqi accent. Most of the Iraqi commanders, however, concluded that Saddam was testing their loyalty; many switched their phones off or changed their numbers, which later made it harder for them to exercise command and control during the war.[20]

There were signs that the Iraqis were puzzled by what the Americans were up to. On February 27, an Iraqi MiG-25 zoomed to the Saudi border at an altitude of 70,000 feet and then raced back. Pentagon officials hinted darkly that the Iraqis might be testing their ability to carry out a desperate WMD attack. Senior U.S. Air Force officials later concluded that the flight had been a reconnaissance mission. The Iraqis had been surprised by Schwarzkopf's "left hook" in the Gulf War and were now trying to ascertain whether a U.S. invasion force was again lurking in the western Saudi desert.

. . .

With the war fast approaching, Franks prepared for a final swing through the Middle East to seal the secret arrangements on the use of Arab bases. Before setting out on his trip, he had held a meeting on January 16 in Tampa with his commanders to review the state of the military preparations. "We are at a crease in history," Franks explained. "I sum it up in two words: fast and final. If we fought this on an attritional basis we would be like Alexander the Great and Eisenhower requiring a 3:1 advantage. We bring a 1:6 force ratio. How can I stand up to you and the President and Tony Blair and say this? Precision for sure, experience and acceptance of risk—we are there. Staying with reality we are the most flexible and adaptable and experienced force available."[21]

In the opening days of the war, Franks planned a devastating series of air strikes—scheduled to take place five days before the ground war, though they could be shifted a few days either way. "The regime has not figured out what we are doing," he said confidently. Four hundred thirty-seven targets were designated for the first four days alone, 330 of which were in Baghdad. Most would be hit multiple times. Of the 437 targets, 22 were "high CD"—meaning that by the Air Force's reckoning, there was a possibility of more than 30 civilian casualties, what the Air Force called "collateral damage." The estimates of civilian casualties were derived using a software program nicknamed "bug splat," which projected destruction from an air strike. Nonetheless, Franks wanted all of them to be struck as a signal to the regime that the gloves were off. "The recommendation to the President is to hit all twenty-two," he said. "We need to get the head in under the tent."

Franks then turned to the outstanding basing issues. In addition to solidifying arrangements to base U.S. forces and aircraft, enough fuel and munitions needed to be on hand to support potential allies like France, which CENTCOM still hoped would join the coalition.

Despite months of diplomacy, some of the arrangements were less than ideal. The U.S. had wanted to put 14,000 troops in Jordan but had to settle for 5,000. Franks noted that King Abdullah was under tremendous pressure from his largely Palestinian population not to allow U.S. troops on Jordanian soil. Anxious to keep the U.S. presence in his country to a minimum, Abdullah had made a suggestion unlikely for an Arab leader; as to where the U.S. might station some of its aircraft, "the King of Jordan's idea is to use Israeli bases," Franks said.

"I promised the King of Jordan we would take care of them and we have not. It is not the legal purview of the President's advisers to do it. We need to fill Jordan's tanks," Franks added. "He is trying to balance his population with our force. We need to support him with what he needs. He is getting F-16s, has to pay overtime and maintain an oil reserve. He is nervous and cranky and sending love notes to me and can't wait to see me. We will get him everything he needs to keep stability in Jordan."

As for Egypt, the government was officially opposed to the war. Unofficially, it planned to give U.S. warships access to the Suez Canal and accepted that the United States would fire cruise missiles from the Red Sea. Franks wanted more. The U.S., he said, could base refueling tankers at the Cairo West airfield. "Let me put pressure on the Egyptians now," Franks said, as he turned to Moseley, his air war commander. "I want to get Mubarak more pregnant. Give me the entire package so I can run it through."

Turkey was the big concern for Franks. McKiernan considered Turkey to be critical. Before the meeting, he had sent Franks a message arguing that an attack from the north would compel Saddam's regime to divide its attention and resources, easing the arrival of U.S. units in the south through one airport and one seaport. Beyond that, northern Iraq was a potential tinderbox. Without a northern option, it would take longer to get U.S. forces into the north to safeguard the oilfields near Kirkuk and prevent ethnic fighting between the Kurds and Arabs, McKiernan thought. If it took spending a "national blue chip" to get the Turks on board, it would be worth it, he argued. The minimum force for the northern mission, McKiernan believed, was about 35,000. Franks agreed. The issue was undecided and Franks wanted it settled. "We are going to turn it up until they realize what is at stake is the next two generations of Turks," Franks said. "Spend the money and put the ships in place. We want to drive the system crazy. Identify who says 'no' and take care of him. Throw my name around. Set conditions for a compressed timeline. We do not want to be the source of 'no.' "

Franks's trip to Kuwait went well. The Kuwaitis rolled out the red carpet for him. The Kuwaitis told Franks that Saddam had built man-made lakes to hide his WMD and that weapons were hidden in the Haditha Dam. They asked for a week's notice of the war so they could move their emir to safety. "If we do this my intent is to surprise Saddam Hussein, not to surprise my friends," Franks said graciously.

Franks was less diplomatic when he stopped by the Marine headquarters at Camp Commando in Kuwait. Franks reported that he told Bush that forces would be in place to launch an attack by February 15. If the president wanted to attack earlier, Franks wanted to be ready. Seeking to fire up the Marines, Franks declared that CENTCOM was prepared to fight with or without the Turkish option. Franks was blunt about how he would feel about Turkey if it refused and lapsed into a string of profanities: "Fuck Turkey. Fuck their families. Fuck their dogs."[22]

In Egypt, Franks met with the Egyptian defense minister at the airport. The Egyptians asked Franks what the likelihood of war was. Franks responded that he was 90 to 95 percent sure there would be a war. "This man [Saddam] is crazy and is not going to leave," he said. "My greater worry is not Saddam Hussein. The problem is Turkey, the Kurds, and the Kirkuk oilfields."

Turkey, in fact, was being worked on at the highest levels. To win the Turks over, the Bush administration offered billions in grants and had quietly shown the Turks the war plan. It had also agreed that 20,000 Turkish troops might be allowed to cross into northern Iraq and take up positions near the border. The concession would enable the Turks to prevent refugees and infiltrators from the PKK Kurdish separatist group from crossing into Turkey. Turkish troops would also be empowered to restore order in the oil-rich region of Kirkuk should U.S. commanders determine that Ankara's help was needed.

At NATO headquarters, the United States pulled out all the stops to encourage the Turks to cooperate. One of Ankara's major worries was that a U.S. attack from the north would prompt the Iraqis to lash out by firing Scud missiles or even using WMD. Spurred by Washington, the Turks asked for protection under the NATO charter, which provided that the alliance would rally to the aid of one of its members if it was attacked. Specifically, the Turks wanted NATO to send Patriot antimissile systems, decontamination units to protect against chemical or biological attack, and AWACS planes.

Eager to reassure the Turks that NATO would be in their corner, the United States urged the alliance to back Turkey. France, Germany, Belgium, and Luxembourg balked. The looming war was highly unpopular in Europe and these governments did not want NATO involved, even indirectly. With strong support from George Robertson, the NATO secretary general and former British defense minister, the United States and Britain pressed for a vote. Luxembourg dropped its objections to show solidarity for an alliance member. The Germans made it clear they would not stand in the way of enforcement of the provision. The United States sidestepped the French by moving the issue to the Defense Planning Committee. This body had been created after Charles de Gaulle evicted NATO from Paris in 1966 and France dropped out of the alliance's military command, though it continued to participate in political discussions. The committee had not recently been the venue for major policy decisions but for the Bush administration it had a major advantage: France was not a member. That left Belgium as the lone holdout. On the weekend of February 15, Nicholas Burns, the U.S. ambassador to NATO, met with Belgium's representative to deliver a stunning message. Throughout its history, NATO had operated on the basis of consensus. It was one of the bedrock principles that the alliance had honored.

Burns now explained to Belgium, in no uncertain terms, that whether it continued to block NATO's assistance of Turkey or not, the alliance would comply with the Turkish request. Robertson's staff had determined that there was some fine print that allowed NATO's military commander to deploy military assets in case of a crisis. The authority had never been used but Robertson was prepared to invoke it if Belgium held fast. Belgium would be blamed for dividing the alliance, even as its stance would have no effect. Belgian officials were dumbfounded that the United States was ready to push the matter that far.

On Sunday, February 15, at 11:45 p.m., Belgium reluctantly withdrew its objections. The U.S. had threatened to abandon consensus to achieve the appearance of consensus. To win Turkish support for the war, NATO had been pushed to the brink, but had survived intact. The United States and Britain justified their pressure tactics by arguing that the failure of NATO to support the Turks would have risked the demise of the organization as an effective alliance. Three days after Belgium acquiesced, Robertson arrived at the White House for a meeting with Bush in the Oval Office. Bush led his team in a standing ovation. "All hail the conquering hero," Bush said. Bitter feelings among European powers, however, would linger and would come back to haunt the United States when it sought to marshal allied assistance for Iraqi authorities after the fall of Saddam.[23]

·   ·   ·

In late February, Franks went to London to meet with the United States's only significant military ally, the British. After more than a year of planning, CENTCOM would now be giving the British a status report. The northern front was a key item on the agenda. "Where are we?" asked British Defence Staff head Sir Michael Boyce at the February 25 session. Franks said that he was in the process of building the air bridge and that this would take three days. Boyce asked if continuing Turkish indecision would force a delay. Franks said no. "At the end of the day we win," he told Boyce. "With the Turks we win. Without the Turks we win." Franks proceeded to discuss the role that France and Germany were playing unwittingly. Their opposition to the war, Franks said, had confused Saddam and led him to think the war might not start soon. Franks allowed that he might take advantage of that by being conspicuously present in Washington when the war started. "There is opportunity for strategic surprise," he claimed.

Addressing the air strikes on Baghdad, Franks indicated that Washington faced a dilemma: if the U.S. attacked as many targets as it intended, it could knock out Iraqi command and control and shock the enemy. But the more bombs the U.S. dropped, the greater the potential for backlash in the Arab world. Or as Franks put it to Boyce, "The operation is longer the less kinetic we put into Baghdad; the more kinetic the strategic exposure goes up." Franks said that twenty-five targets involved enough collateral damage risk as to give him "heartburn."

Franks brought up the possibility of an airborne operation to take control of the Baghdad airport. The quicker the U.S. moved on Baghdad the more difficult it would be for the Iraqis to retreat into the capital and try to engage the U.S. in street fighting. Franks wanted to "reduce Fortress Baghdad possibilities." The CENTCOM commander also told the British that CENTCOM had learned through intelligence channels that the Iraqi chief engineer for the southern oilfields had been replaced by a Baghdad official. The Americans saw this as an ominous sign.

Franks and Boyce talked briefly about what to do if Saddam were to flee Iraq. Franks said the Bush administration planned to send American forces in anyway to secure WMD, provide humanitarian assistance, and address civil affairs. Stating the official British position, Boyce noted that the sooner Iraq was turned over to the United Nations the better. Boyce asked about the possibility of civil war. Franks discounted that scenario, asserting that the Iranian-backed Badr Corps would remain in place and Iraq's western tribes would be cautious. It had been an intense and exhausting trip. On the way back to Tampa, Franks watched *Dirty Harry* on his DVD player to relax.[24]

On March 1—less than three weeks before the start of the war—the Turkish parliament rejected a measure that would have permitted the establishment of a northern front. Parliament had failed to secure a majority of lawmakers in attendance, even though the final tally had been 264 in favor, 251 opposed. There had been 19 abstentions.[25] Turkey's refusal to facilitate the war complicated American strategy. During the Gulf War, the United States had launched air strikes and search-and-rescue operations from Turkish bases. But air operations for the new war, including the right to fly over Turkish territory, had been part and parcel of the measure just voted down by the Turkish parliament. Unless the Turks relented, the U.S. would not be able to fire Tomahawk cruise missiles into northern Iraq from the Mediterranean, or launch air strikes from aircraft carriers in the Mediterranean or B-52 runs by bombers based in Britain.

In Washington, the Bush team debated how to respond. The tanks and equipment for Ray Odierno's 4th Infantry Division were already on ships in MODLOC, military-speak for "modified location": they were circling off the coast of Turkey waiting for the Turks to come around. Scooter Libby, the vice president's chief of staff, was so frustrated by the turn of events that he advocated a hard line with Ankara: screw the Turks. Pull the 4th ID (Infantry Division) out of the Mediterranean. The Turks would be giving up billions in U.S. aid. Washington should stand back and let the financial markets take their toll on the Turkish economy.

White House aides were surprised by the vigor of Libby's reaction. He was usually self-contained.[26]

At the State Department, Colin Powell had always been skeptical that the Turks would agree to have American troops stationed in their country in the first place. But he also thought that the plan for a northern front was more difficult to carry out than CENTCOM seemed to realize. A northern front, Franks had argued, would pin down Iraqi divisions in the north. Powell thought the value of so doing was overrated. If Iraqi divisions started moving south, Powell figured, they would be excellent targets for U.S. airpower. Keeping the 4th Infantry Division in the Mediterranean would make the invasion force in the south smaller and might please Rumsfeld, but it was not Powell's idea of a war well run.

Powell believed it was time to face the political music and send the 4th Infantry Division to Kuwait to attack from the south.

In early February, McKiernan himself had petitioned Franks to do precisely what Powell was now suggesting. Concerned as he was that he
would not have the promised forces on hand when he needed them—
given Rumsfeld's hyper-scrutiny of all requests for reinforcements and
abandonment of the TPFDL—McKiernan had proposed that, if Odierno
could not fight his way south from Turkey, his division should be part of
the attack north. The V Corps would thereby have more troops to smash
the Republican Guard defense around Baghdad and attack into the north.
And if the Turks were to belatedly approve a northern front, smaller,
later-arriving units could be moved through Turkey.

But Franks was adamant that positioning Odierno's division in the
north would keep the Iraqis off balance. When the war began, this was a
division that McKiernan would initially have to do without. After Baghdad fell, Franks touted his stratagem as an effective part of his deception
campaign, but McKiernan believed it had deprived him of forces he urgently needed to proceed to Baghdad and beyond. "We wanted more
combat power on the ground. The decision was made way late to move
the 4th ID south," Thurman recalled in the summer of 2003. "We've still
got people getting shot at up there and dying up there right now. We've
got to clean that up. You clean that up with combat power on the
ground."[27]

With few allies on board and the 4th Division still at sea—and only a
trickle of Iraqi freedom fighters—even some of Rumsfeld's aides became
uneasy about the war plan, seemingly concurring with McKiernan.
Joseph Collins, a retired Army colonel and former military assistant to
Wolfowitz from 1989 to 1991, headed the Defense Department's office
that dealt with postwar issues. He had never accepted Rumsfeld's theory
that the war might be won with a modest number of troops. In a March
memo to Feith, titled "Rear Area Forces Gap," Collins reported on a recent visit to Qatar and Kuwait, where he had met with CENTCOM officials and McKiernan's staff.

With limited forces, CENTCOM would have few troops to spare for
keeping supply lines open and order in the rear, as lead units advanced
toward Baghdad. "In our force posture, there is a dynamic tension between the need to keep a small, united force moving forward rapidly, and
the degree to which you can 'drop off' forces to handle potential problems
in the rear. A clear decision has been made to accept risk in the rear and to

move forward as fast as possible," Collins wrote. "As one planner noted, however, it sure would be nice to have a few additional divisions available on 'go day' for ground force. Note: If 4th ID ends up landing in Kuwait, this problem could be somewhat ameliorated. Also, as mentioned in first report, all want carabinieri or gendarme or guardia civil troops for rear area use, during and after combat."

Collins never received a reply. By this point, the invasion plan was set and ready to go.[28]

CHAPTER 7

The Red Line

In December 2002, Saddam Hussein convened a series of meetings with his Revolutionary Command Council, Baath Party aides, and top military commanders to make a surprising announcement. Iraq, Saddam declared, did not possess WMD. Iraq's military establishment was, by design, highly secretive and compartmentalized. Only Saddam, his sons, and a handful of trusted aides knew the whole story. Iraq's generals had long assumed that Saddam controlled a hidden cache of chemical or biological agents despite the United Nations demands that Iraq disarm. To make sure that regime officials and generals believed the admission, Saddam called on several select officials to confirm his disclosure.[1]

Iraq's defense minister, Sultan Hashim Ahmad al-Tai, told U.S. interrogators after the fall of Baghdad that many of the generals were stunned by the news. Iraq had relied on chemical weapons to fend off the Iranians during their long war with Tehran. Saddam had propagated the notion that Iraq's arsenal of chemical and biological weapons had enabled him to deter U.S. forces from marching on Baghdad after the 1991 Persian Gulf War. The Iraqis had also used the threat of WMD to keep the Shiites in line. The disclosure that the cupboard was bare, Tariq Aziz, Saddam's deputy prime minister, later told U.S. officials, sent morale plummeting.[2]

Saddam had an important reason to deliver the unwelcome news. The Iraqi leader was hoping to influence the contentious debate at the United Nations or at least encourage enough votes to block the Security Council from authorizing a military attack against Iraq. And if war was to come, his generals needed to know they could not rely on WMD to defeat the invaders. After a decade of obstreperous relations with U.N. weapons inspectors, Saddam was determined to deprive the Bush administration of a casus belli.

In January 2003, Saddam directed his top aides to grant United Nations inspectors the access they wanted. There would be no efforts to keep presidential compounds or other government sites off limits. That would simply play into the hands of Washington. Even the Republican Guard was ordered to make their records available to the U.N. monitors. The U.N. inspectors would be able to go where they liked and would, Saddam predicted, issue a report that Iraq was cooperating with the world organization.

To ensure that Iraq would receive a clean bill of health, Saddam's aides mounted a crash effort to scrub the country so that the U.N. inspectors did not discover any vestiges of old WMD, no small concern in a nation that had once amassed a considerable arsenal of chemical weapons, biological agents, and Scud missiles, and was not now a model of governmental organization. On January 25, Hussam Amin, the director of Iraq's National Monitoring Directorate, which was officially charged with implementing the U.N. disarmament resolutions, delivered a stern warning to Republican Guard military commanders: they needed to ensure that there were no traces of WMD in their units or bases. If any was uncovered it was to be turned over to Amin immediately. Saddam would hold them responsible if they did not comply with this order. The caution set off a flurry of activity as the units hurried to sanitize their areas.[3]

Still, Saddam was playing a risky game. The Iraqi leader stopped short of providing the United Nations with airtight proof that he did not have a hidden cache of WMD. Iraq's declarations to the U.N. covering what WMD stocks it had possessed and how Iraq had disposed of them were old, full of holes, and would remain that way. Nor would Saddam allow his weapons scientists to leave the country, which would have enabled them to be interviewed by the U.N., where they would be beyond the regime's control. The goal was to cooperate with the inspectors while preserving a measure of ambiguity about the ultimate disposition of Iraq's WMD—the "deterrence by doubt" strategy discussed by Lieutenant General Raad Majid al-Hamdani, the II Republican Guard corps commander.

According to Hamdani, Saddam was determined to avoid the appearance that he was weak and told his inner circle that the "better part of war was deceiving." Saddam's strategy, in effect, was to cooperate with the letter but not the spirit of the U.N. demands. It was a difficult balancing act.[4]

As he directed the political strategy Saddam also shaped the military one in case his efforts to sway the U.N. failed. At a December 18, 2002, gathering of senior military officers, Lieutenant General Sayf al-Din al-Rawi, the chief of staff of the Republican Guard, announced that there had been an important strategic development. Saddam had approved a new plan to concentrate on the defense of the Iraqi capital: Baghdad would be protected by concentric defense lines that would ring the city. To the generals, the plan was a bolt out of the blue and an unwelcome one at that. The scheme reflected Saddam's desire to protect his regime at all costs. An impenetrable Red Zone would be established around the capital and the Republican Guard would defend it to the death. Camouflage and fortifications would provide protection from air attack. While Republican Guard troops would be positioned close to the capital to seal off the approaches to Baghdad, only the Special Republican Guard would be allowed inside the capital, a measure to guard against a coup. All of the Republican Guard forces would answer to Qusay. Defending Iraqi territory against an outside invader was subordinated to protecting the regime. The plan was unimaginative and developed without any regard for terrain, Iraqi military capabilities, or those of a potential invader. In order to establish a solid positional defense, the plan sacrificed maneuverability and wrote off much of the south.

The idea of a ring defense was first discussed by Iraqi officials in the 1990s as a way to make the most of the military's limited forces and control the flow of people in and out of Baghdad, but had soon faded. Now it was being revived by a small knot of top officials that included Saddam, Qusay, Saddam's heir apparent, and two of the Iraqi leader's inner circle, Rawi and Izzat Ibrahim al-Duri, a top Saddam aide and vice chairman of the Revolutionary Command Council.

Hamdani recalled after the war that he had warned Qusay that the plan was "full of bad assumptions and lacked any basis in facts." The general, however, was a lone voice. No other commander dared to challenge the plan. "The other commanders were afraid to speak clearly where they had a conflict with the original ring plan," Hamdani said. "Our academies teach the ideas of debate and discussion but for the last ten years or so our reality has been tribal. In a tribal situation you do not question things." Qusay, for his part, put an end to all discussion. Saddam's word was absolute. "Qusay said that the plan was already approved by Saddam and it was you who would now make it work," Hamdani recalled. Questioning the maximum leader was risky and Saddam was not one to test his theories with his military high command.[5]

Saddam had his own ideas as to how a U.S. attack might work. If the war came, the Iraqi leadership assumed, it would be a replay of the Gulf War. There would be a long bombing campaign, a setback to be sure but not a knockout blow for a nation that endured forty-three days of bombing in 1991 and which had been repeatedly bombed ever since.

There might be a shallow thrust into southern Iraq, a temporary occupation, and then withdrawal. A major assault on Baghdad would not be part of the U.S. plan. As Ibrahim Ahmad abd al-Sattar Muhammad al-Tikriti, the chief of staff of the Iraqi armed forces, later told his U.S. interrogators, "No Iraqi leaders had believed coalition forces would ever reach Baghdad."

Tariq Aziz later told his interrogators that Saddam "thought they would not fight a ground war because it would be too costly to the Americans. He was overconfident." A worst-case scenario envisioned by some senior Iraqi officials was a lengthy series of air strikes and the establishment of a Shiite-controlled enclave in the south that would resemble the Kurdish enclave in the north. As long as Saddam's regime held the Kirkuk oilfields in the north, even the loss of southern Iraq and its oil was not seen as a development that would upend the regime. "Two or three months before the war, Saddam Hussein addressed a group of 150 officers," the director of Iraqi military intelligence told U.S. interrogators. "Saddam and his inner circle thought the war would last a few days and then it would be over. They thought that there would be a few air strikes and maybe some operations in the south, then it would be over."[6]

It was not its military technology or training that would enable Iraq to hold off the Americans. It was the nation's will and the toughness of his soldiers. To motivate his officers, Saddam told them they were involved in a spiritual struggle. "Saddam told us that God wanted to insult Americans in Iraq by giving his strongest ability to one of his weakest creatures," Hamdani recalled. "This was the reason the USSR did not defeat the U.S. in the Cold War. It was because the USSR was trying to be strong like America to defeat America. But if a weak nation can defeat a strong nation then this is a miracle." So convinced was Saddam that he would prevail that, in Baghdad, the paintings and faux antique French furniture were removed from the Abu Ghraib North Palace and other presidential residences and taken to a nondescript building near the Tigris. Each item was carefully catalogued and had a note attached specifying the precise floor, room, and location from which it had been taken. The regime knew that Saddam's palaces would be American bombing targets and planned to safeguard the items until the regime had weathered the storm.[7]

The regime also made plans to deal with the scenario that worried it the most: a repeat of the 1991 Shiite rebellion, which had taken advantage of an American attack to seize control of the cities and towns in the south. To guard against another revolt, Saddam ordered that Iraq be divided into sectors and put his most trusted relatives and aides in charge of them. Ali Hassan al-Majeed, Saddam's cousin—Chemical Ali—was put in control of the Shiite-dominated south. Izzat Ibrahim al-Duri, Saddam's right-hand man and vice chairman of the Revolutionary Command Council, would oversee the north. Saddam's son Qusay would control the center. Each possessed complete authority over his sector, including Republican Guard units stationed there.

Even as the Iraqi general staff focused on defending the nation with the Republican Guard and Regular Army divisions, Saddam and his sons focused on preventing a Shiite uprising by deploying the Fedayeen. Saddam did not want to distribute ammunition too soon for fear that restive tribes might confiscate it and use it to grab control of the region. With the prospect of an American bombing campaign, however, in early March the regime ordered that ammunition be dispersed throughout the country, including to the Fedayeen. Iraq had also trained foreign fighters over the years as a gesture of support for the Palestinian and other Arab causes, and in March it summoned some of the fighters back. Documents retrieved by American intelligence after the war show that the Iraqi Ministry of Defense coordinated border crossings with Syria and provided billeting, pay, and allowances and armaments for the influx of Syrians, Palestinians, and other fighters.

Majeed, whose advice Saddam valued, told Saddam that if the Americans tried to take over the cities and towns there, they would run into enormous problems, but not of the kind U.S. intelligence had predicted. U.S. intelligence had warned ominously that Saddam might adopt a scorched-earth policy and order the destruction of Iraq's oilfields or dams, but this was never part of his plan. Destroying dams or bridges would have made it harder to put down an uprising. Reflooding the southern marshes would inhibit forces moving south, as would dropping the bridges—actions that would also have provided cover to the rebellious tribes and rebels in the south. Saddam was adamant about maintaining the country's infrastructure.

At CENTCOM'S headquarters in Qatar, U.S. intelligence officers received a hot tip from one of the unlikeliest of sources. Two German agents in Baghdad had obtained Saddam's latest plan for defending the capital. Chancellor Gerhard Schröder had rankled the Bush administration during his successful campaign for reelection by deriding American plans to topple Saddam Hussein and declaring that his country would not participate in the war. Bush had responded by declining to congratulate Schröder on his election victory, while Rumsfeld and Rice complained that U.S-German relations had been poisoned.[8]

But the German government had cooperated to a limited extent with the U.S. military's war preparations. In Germany, German troops helped guard U.S. bases, freeing up more of Scott Wallace's V Corps to deploy for the war. The German soldiers at McKiernan's Camp Doha who operated equipment that was designed to detect and clean up a potential chemical or biological weapons attack were another example. The mission, known euphemistically as "consequence management," was described as purely defensive, but this was an artificial distinction, since any Iraqi attack on Kuwait would likely be a response to the U.S. invasion plan. Moreover, Germany had given the Turkish military Patriot antimissile interceptors, a move intended to protect the Turks against an Iraqi missile attack, but which the Bush administration hoped would make Ankara more receptive to the idea of opening a northern front. In the Red Sea and the Gulf of Aden, German ships guarded the sea lanes on behalf of Franks's CENTCOM. The operation was to deter an attack by Al Qaeda or other terrorist groups, but, in effect, the Germans were safeguarding the waterways the United States was using to build up its forces in the Persian Gulf. "That is not our mission, really, but it does certainly have this effect," Rear Admiral Rolf Schmitz said in an interview on the *Brandenburg,* a spick-and-span warship that was a model of efficiency. "We are stabilizing the area, and that probably is an advantage for your [American] forces as well," he added.[9] At the Pentagon, the Joint Staff noted that Germany was in an odd category. It was quietly contributing to the U.S. effort, but opposed to the war.

The German decision to provide the Americans with Saddam's secret plan for protecting his capital was not a defensive precaution but an act that facilitated CENTCOM's U.S.-led invasion to topple Saddam's regime. The world's intelligence organizations and militaries were after all bound together by a web of arrangements that transcended politics. The German agents—who continued to work actively for their government and would eventually take refuge in the French embassy during the war[10]—passed the plan up their chain of command. In February 2003, a German liaison officer in Qatar slipped a copy to U.S. officials, illustrating in detail Saddam's concentric defensive lines around his capital.

In Washington, U.S. intelligence studied the Baghdad defense plan and arrived at a disturbing conclusion. In planning the ring defense, the Iraqis had dubbed one of the circles the Red Line. It was the final barrier to be defended at all costs and a throwback to defensive tactics the Iraqi military had learned generations ago when their officers had attended the British military academy at Sandhurst. The CIA and military intelligence, however, had a darker interpretation: approaching the Red Line would trigger the use of chemical weapons against the Army and Marines.[11] The dominant view within the U.S. intelligence agencies was that Saddam's WMD would be withheld in the early phases of the fight so as not to anger world opinion—which the Iraqis assumed would shift heavily in their favor and make it hard for the Bush team to prosecute its war. U.S. intelligence, however, concluded that the Iraqis were prepared to use poison gas or germ weapons, if necessary, as U.S. forces closed in on the capital.

Iraq's WMD programs had been a major worry for the United States ever since the end of the Persian Gulf War. For most of the 1990s, Iraq and the United Nations were involved in a tug-of-war over Iraq's reluctance and sometimes outright refusal to grant access to suspected weapons sites. When he assumed his new post as the chief U.N. weapons inspector in 1997, Richard Butler, an Australian arms control expert, told Anthony Zinni that whether the Americans liked it or not he was prepared to give the Iraqis a clean bill of health if they complied with the terms of U.N. inspections. When Zinni saw Butler again a few months later the U.N. inspector seemed frustrated beyond endurance. "He was the angriest, most pissed off man in the world. He hated Tariq Aziz and his silk suits and his cigars and the suffering of the people and the lies and the deception," Zinni recalled. "It was clear to the inspectors, I think, that even if you could not find smoking guns that Saddam had the framework to restart a program."[12]

The CIA had become so used to relying on the U.N. for reporting on WMD that it was accustomed to doing without spies in Iraq's weapons program. Its window on Iraq was shut in 1998 when Saddam stopped co-operating with the inspectors. The U.N. monitors were recalled and the Clinton administration ordered the four-day Desert Fox bombing raids that were intended to pulverize much of Saddam's weapons infrastructure. In spite of the bombardment, Saddam defiantly refused to readmit the weapons inspectors. Without U.N. monitors, the CIA was forced to develop its assessments based on satellite photographs, the occasional defector, and extrapolation from past experience. As the quality of its information on Iraq declined, its fears grew. Toward the end of the Clinton administration, U.S. intelligence agencies began to issue a stream of disturbing reports.

In February 1999, they concluded that the Desert Fox raids had failed to damage most of Iraq's suspected chemical warfare facilities. Iraq, the intelligence agencies inferred, still retained stockpiles of poison gas and had the capability to quickly resume the production of chemical weapons. Later that year, U.S. intelligence predicted ominously that the Iraqis were expanding their germ warfare program as well. The CIA's fears were heightened when German intelligence gained access to an Iraqi defector—code-named Curve Ball—who reported a nefarious scheme: biological weapons labs had been installed in trucks and rail cars so they could be moved around the country to elude detection. In December 2000, the CIA and other intelligence agencies produced a National Intelligence Estimate entitled "Iraq: Steadily Pursuing WMD Capabilities," a document intended to be a comprehensive and authoritative account of what the best and the brightest among the U.S. intelligence community had been able to establish about their past and potential future adversary.

The estimate concluded that Iraq had stockpiled up to 100 tons of mustard gas and Sarin nerve agents, had stepped up its efforts to buy industrial equipment for military purposes, and had expanded its civilian chemical industry to support a clandestine weapons program. Regarding germ warfare, the report asserted that Iraq had the potential to produce as much as several hundred tons of unconcentrated biological agents per year. Relying on Curve Ball's allegations, the estimate said there was intelligence that Iraq might have mobile germ warfare factories. Although this had not been corroborated, the National Intelligence Estimate declared that it was consistent with evidence gathered by U.N. monitors. As for nuclear weapons, the intelligence agencies reported that Saddam had the scientists he needed to resume his quest for a nuclear bomb, but Iraq did not appear to have reconstituted its nuclear weapons program. Despite a budget of some $40 billion a year, U.S. intelligence had little direct knowledge about Saddam's weapons program. In 2001, the CIA had just four sources in Iraq and none had access to information about Saddam's WMD.[13]

As the Bush administration took office, the view of most of its top officials was that, if anything, the intelligence agencies might have understated the threat posed by Saddam. Cheney had never forgotten how U.S. intelligence had underestimated the Iraqis before the Gulf War. After the conflict, intelligence experts had been surprised to learn that Iraq had a hidden nuclear program and might have been only a year or two away from fielding a nuclear bomb when it invaded Kuwait.[14] The vice president visited the CIA half a dozen times for updates on Iraq's weapons programs, agency officials later reported, and was generally in "the receive mode." With absolute conviction that the Iraqi leader was secretly pursuing his old ambitions, the Bush team never asked that a new intelligence estimate be produced on Iraq's WMD.[15]

The dismantling of Saddam's cache, however, was only part of the rationale for confronting Iraq. The administration's case also turned on establishing a link between Iraq and terrorists determined to attack the United States. In making his argument for preemption in his June 2002 West Point speech and later in his official strategy document, Bush argued that deterrence—the threat of devastating retaliation that had kept the peace throughout the standoff with the Soviets during the Cold War—no longer could guarantee the peace. States like Iraq might supply terrorists with chemical, biological, or one day even nuclear arms. The United States could be the target of another 9/11-like attack but never learn who had sponsored it. There would be nobody to threaten with retaliation because the culprit would not be known. The only way to ensure the nation's safety was to neutralize WMD at their potential source—a nation hostile to America like Iraq.

The worrisome reports from the CIA on WMD largely tracked suspicions about the Iraqi leader held by Cheney and Rumsfeld. But the agency parted company with them insofar as it declined to draw a clear link between Iraq and Al Qaeda. The agency's regional analysis took the view that a secular, authoritative regime like Saddam's would not form an alliance with a fundamentalist group like Al Qaeda. The agency's experts also discounted reports that Mohammed Atta, who planned the 9/11 attacks, had met in Prague with a head of Iraqi intelligence. In June 2002, the CIA distributed a classified report, "Iraq and Al-Qaida: Interpreting a Murky Relationship." The report noted that Saddam and bin Laden regarded each other warily, but did not exclude the possibility that there might be "limited offers of cooperation." Even that heavily qualified conclusion was controversial within the agency. The CIA ombudsman for politicization received a confidential complaint that the conclusion went too far.

At the Pentagon, Rumsfeld's aides did not think the report had gone far enough. They thought there might be an Iraqi connection to the 9/11 assault and even to the letters full of anthrax that had mysteriously been sent to the Congress and White House and others. Like Cheney, Wolfowitz thought the CIA was far from perfect and was given to understating threats to U.S. security. Wolfowitz had been a member of a panel Rumsfeld chaired in the late 1990s that faulted the CIA for underestimating the potential of Third World nations to develop ocean-spanning ballistic missiles. Three decades earlier, he had served on Team B, a panel of largely conservative analysts that criticized the U.S. for downplaying the Soviet threat; it had concluded that Moscow believed it could fight and win a nuclear war.

Feith assigned two reserve military officers to pore over the intelligence and determine if the CIA was understating its case. In a briefing of Rumsfeld, the reservists laid out their conclusions. The intelligence agencies had wrongly discounted the possibility that Iraq and Al Qaeda might be working together. The reservists reaffirmed as fact the Atta meeting in Prague that the CIA was insisting had never happened. After the session, Wolfowitz sent a note to Feith noting that Rumsfeld had been impressed. The team later repeated their conclusions at the CIA and to Steve Hadley and Scooter Libby. Libby's interest was piqued: he wanted more information on Atta's travels.[16]

Paul Pillar, the national intelligence officer for the Near East and South Asia at the time, was not persuaded. "After 9/11, the administration was trying to hitch Iraq to the wagon of terror," he later recalled. "With regard to this issue, the analysts that followed it saw nothing more than incidental contact: the two sides feeling each other out. There was a major disconnect between the public case and the judgment of the intelligence community." John McLaughlin, the deputy CIA director, told his colleagues that he was constantly battling Cheney's and Rumsfeld's staffs over the issue.[17]

With a vote on the war coming up in Congress, Senator Bob Graham, the Florida Democrat who served as vice chairman of the Senate Intelligence Committee, pressed for a fresh National Intelligence Estimate (NIE) on Iraq's suspected WMD programs. Graham wanted the assessment by October 1. Like college students pulling an all-nighter to complete a term paper, the intelligence experts had one month or so to complete a task that ordinarily might have taken six—a massive undertaking given the technical complexity of some of the issues and the disagreements among the analysts themselves.

During the debate over the Persian Gulf War there had been a hard-fought and surprisingly close vote on George H. W. Bush's decision to liberate Kuwait. Most of the Democratic Party had opposed military action, including its principal military expert, Senator Sam Nunn of Georgia. One of a few who did not was Senator Albert Gore Jr. of Tennessee, who would go on to become vice president in the next administration. The lesson was not lost on the Democrats. There was a political cost in opposing military action against Saddam. But the Republicans had learned a few lessons, too. The vote over the 1991 Desert Storm campaign had been held in January, two months after the congressional elections. This time, the vote to authorize the president to go to war was scheduled to occur just weeks before the elections. Given the steady drumbeat of incriminating allegations on Iraqi WMD, any congressman who voted against the war risked alienating his constituency. The NIE ordered by Graham was crucial to the vote.

When the classified assessment was finally submitted, the conclusions about Iraq's WMD went a step further than those in the December 2000 report. Much of the evidence on chemical and biological weapons was similar to that of the earlier estimate but the caveats were omitted. The new report asserted flatly that Iraq was producing poison gas and possessed chemical and biological weapons. The 100 metric tons of chemical agents that were cited in the December 2000 report had grown to as much as 500 metric tons. The study also asserted that Iraq's program to make germ weapons was bigger than ever. In an important departure from the 2000 report, the estimate noted that Iraq was moving to reconstitute its nuclear weapons program. There was, the estimate noted, a split decision on an important issue: whether Iraq was importing aluminum tubes to make centrifuges to enrich uranium. The CIA, supported by the Defense Intelligence Agency and experts at the National Ground Intelligence Center, believed the tubes were for nuclear purposes. The Energy Department challenged this conclusion though it acquiesced in the broader assertion that Iraq was trying to revive its nuclear weapons program based on other evidence—such as Iraqi efforts to import special magnets. Only the State Department's Bureau of Intelligence and Research challenged the nuclear case in its entirety and its dissent was registered in a footnote in the document. The estimate also warned that Iraq's oil sales had increased its ability to covertly finance its weapons program. Acknowledging that much was still not known, the estimate stated that this was a result of Saddam's vigorous determination to hide his activities. In other words, the message was: it could be worse than we think.

The conclusion on Iraq's link to Al Qaeda–like terrorists was decidedly less alarming. Drawing on the analysis of the CIA's latest report on Iraq's links to terrorist groups, the estimate noted that Iraq would be fearful of attacking the United States with biological or chemical arms, as that would provide Washington with a clear rationale for making war against Baghdad. The only situation in which Saddam might take the "extreme step" of assisting an Islamic terrorist group like Al Qaeda in attacking the United States would be one in which Saddam had been cornered and felt the United States was on the verge of upending his regime. In essence, the document implied that not only was preemption unnecessary in the case of Iraq but could backfire and bring about the very disaster it was intended to avert: the provision of WMD by Saddam to terrorists who sought to destroy America.[18]

After receiving the NIE, the Democrats pressed the CIA on the section on Iraq's tenuous links to Al Qaeda terrorists. After considerable importuning, segments of the analysis, along with an exchange in a closed session of the Intelligence Committee, were provided in an October 8 letter from John McLaughlin, the deputy director of the CIA. As the declassified fragments were distributed on Capitol Hill, word spread that there was a new intelligence analysis that contradicted the White House case. George Tenet, the CIA director, rushed to quell the debate, insisting in an interview with Alison Mitchell, the congressional reporter for the *New York Times,* that there was nothing in the document that was inconsistent with the president's case. It was an unusually public role for the director of Central Intelligence, who was supposed to stay above the partisan fray; Tenet was in the odd position of downplaying the conclusions of his own analysts. After the fall of Baghdad, critics of the war complained vociferously about the quality of American intelligence on Iraq's weapons programs. There was indeed much to criticize. But for those who read the NIE carefully the document had already poked a gaping hole in the White House's case for war.[19]

With the congressional vote around the corner, Bush delivered a speech in Cincinnati that laid out the particulars—but not the caveats—of the estimate. Ignoring dissenting views from the State Department, the president flatly asserted that Iraq was pursuing nuclear arms and even drones that could be used to attack the United States from ships at sea—an allegation that Air Force intelligence had challenged in a footnote of the classified version of the NIE. Bush pointedly warned Iraqi generals that they would be prosecuted for war crimes if they carried out Saddam's orders to undertake "cruel and desperate measures," an allusion to intelligence that Saddam was planning to take preemptive action against the Kurds and was sure to use WMD.

On the afternoon of October 10, the House of Representatives voted, 296 to 133, to authorize the president to use military force against Iraq; the Senate followed shortly after midnight, passing the measure by a vote of 77 to 23. Virtually all of the Democratic members with presidential ambitions voted for the measure, including Senator Hillary Rodham Clinton and Senator John Kerry, who declared he had received personal assurances from Colin Powell that force would be the last resort. The Democrats were trying to walk a fine line by insisting they were not voting for war but for diplomacy backed up by the threat of force.[20]

The day of the vote the administration began to brief select lawmakers in private on disturbing nuclear developments in another part of the world. Six days earlier in Pyongyang, Kang Sok Ju, the vice foreign minister of North Korea and one of the most important officials in the country, had delivered a fifty-minute harangue—in which he confirmed American allegations that North Korea had a covert program to develop nuclear weapons from highly enriched uranium—to a group of high U.S. officials led by James Kelly, an assistant secretary of state. It was a stunning admission and established that North Korea, like Iran, was far ahead of Iraq in developing WMD.[21]

Instead of publicly disclosing the threat posed by North Korea, the White House initially kept the news under wraps. The Bush administration, determined as it was to topple Saddam, was not about to be diverted. North Korea was already presumed to have one or two nuclear weapons. In addition to its nuclear potential, its artillery was deployed close to the DMZ and could wreck Seoul before Pyongyang was defeated. There were no good military options there. Nor had the administration settled on a durable diplomatic strategy for dealing with a recalcitrant North Korea.

The story about North Korea's admission finally broke on October 16 after an enterprising reporter from *USA Today* dug up the development, forcing the administration's hand. At the State Department, Jack Pritchard, the State Department's ambassador for talks with Pyongyang and a retired Army colonel whose son was serving in the 3rd Infantry Division, quickly surmised the administration's strategy. The president had made it clear that he did not intend to have a crisis over North Korea's nuclear program. In contrast to Iraq, the issue would be handled diplomatically. "The message was there is nothing that North Korea can do to cause a crisis," Pritchard recalled.[22]

The Bush administration was convinced it had military options in Iraq that it simply did not have vis-à-vis North Korea: Iraq did not have the most advanced weapons programs among the countries of Bush's "axis of evil," the strongest association with terrorists, or a track record of disseminating WMD. But Iraq's truculent relationship with Washington, its failure to honor its obligations to the United Nations for more than a decade, the relative weakness of its conventional forces, and the fact that it had yet to cross the nuclear threshold defined its singularity: Iraq was a hostile but vulnerable adversary that had run afoul of its U.N. obligations. By the administration's calculations, of the "axis of evil," Iraq was a prime candidate for regime change. September 11 had opened in the United States a political window for action, and Iraq's vulnerabilities now opened a strategic window.[23]

In February 2003, the administration prepared to make its case for war against Iraq to the United Nations Security Council. Colin Powell had pressed the president to take the Iraq issue to the United Nations. Bush instructed Powell to present U.S. intelligence data on Iraq's WMD programs to the council. Some of the secretary of state's aides were not enthusiastic about their boss's new assignment. During the Cuban Missile Crisis, President John F. Kennedy had relied on his U.N. ambassador, Adlai Stevenson, to make the United States's case before the international body. Powell had a reputation for being cautious about using force and had credibility among the allies. He understood the logic of the task at hand. "Who else can they send?" Powell confided to Larry Wilkerson, the retired Army colonel who served as Powell's chief of staff. "Is Condi going to go?"[24]

Powell's was not mission impossible. While Mohamed ElBaradei, the director general of the International Atomic Energy Agency, was challenging the nuclear case, Hans Blix, the chief U.N. monitor, had been loudly complaining about the holes in Iraq's story about its weapons program. Blix warned that the deficiencies were so grave as to suggest that Saddam did not grasp the gravity of the situation. Iraq, Blix told the Security Council on January 27, did not seem to have accepted "the disarmament which was demanded of it and which it needs to carry out to win the confidence of the world and to live in peace."[25]

Powell had had his doubts about the Bush administration's statements about Iraq's weapons program. When he was pushing for tougher sanctions against Saddam in February 2001 Powell insisted that Iraq had "not developed any significant capability with respect to weapons of mass destruction." In November 2002 he wondered aloud to Wilkerson what would happen if the United States scoured Iraq from one end to another but found nothing. Wilkerson replied that experts at the U.S. weapons labs had told him that Iraq's WMD might well be hard to find. Some of it might be moved to Syria. There were probably no chemical stockpiles and the nuclear program consisted of little more than scientists and their software. Saddam, Wilkerson said, was biding his time, waiting for the sanctions to be lifted so he could crank up his program again.

At the U.N., Powell would need to make the strongest case possible. The nuclear argument, the White House said, was not yet sufficiently persuasive and the account of Iraq's biological and chemical program needed to be more vivid. The CIA sent more information in, drawing on the work of its Bureau of Weapons Intelligence, Nonproliferation and Arms Control, a unit that included a then unknown undercover CIA operative named Valerie Plame. The Red Line defense around Baghdad was highlighted; clearly the Iraqis would not have a Red Line for launching WMD unless they had WMD, the agency argued. Scooter Libby drew up a bill of particulars on Iraq's supposed links with Al Qaeda. The White House initially wanted Powell to deliver a three-day presentation to the Security Council, a notion that he rejected as utterly impractical. Powell, however, did not want to go the U.N. with a handout. He was determined to meet with the experts at the CIA to ensure he had a solid case.

For the better part of a week, Powell huddled with Tenet, McLaughlin, and Robert Walpole, the national intelligence officer for strategic programs. Walpole had been criticized by congressional Republicans during the 1990s for failing to foresee advances in the North Korean missile program, a charge that led the lawmakers to establish a commission headed by Rumsfeld to look into the matter. For years, the intelligence agencies had been assailed for failing to anticipate threats, from nuclear tests by India and Pakistan to the Al Qaeda attacks on the United States. There was a powerful incentive to make sure that they were not caught short again. During their meetings with Powell, McLaughlin and Walpole argued strenuously that the aluminum tubes that had been intercepted on their way to Iraq were manufactured to a tolerance that made them suited for nuclear purposes. Walpole also presented data that the Iraqis had paid top dollar, more than they should have if the material was for their rocket program, as the State Department had suggested.

The State Department's intelligence bureau vetted drafts of Powell's speech and noted that thirty-eight claims were "weak" or "unsubstantiated." Twenty-eight were removed from the text. Powell rejected his own agency's assessment of the tubes and opted for the CIA's claim, which the president had already repeatedly publicized. He also included the CIA's assertion that Iraq had dispersed rocket launchers with biological warheads despite a warning from State Department experts that the charge was highly dubious. But it should also be noted that Powell stayed clear of the charge that Iraq had sought to buy uranium in Niger, Africa, an allegation that had surfaced in Bush's State of the Union address in January. "We went to the agency for five or six grueling days," Wilkerson recalled two years later. "It is safe to say that he changed his mind. He was convinced by what the agency and members of the IC [intelligence community] were able to present to him."

Wilkerson was persuaded as well. He would later recall that there was wide agreement among government experts that Iraq had chemical arms and was working on germ weapons. As for the tubes, Wilkerson said he was no longer sure what to think. There had been several shipments and State Department objections might not have applied to all of them. Even French intelligence, Wilkerson asserted, thought there was some merit in the CIA's argument on the tubes. After the war Wilkerson complained that Cheney and Rumsfeld had made so many foreign policy decisions between themselves that they functioned like a virtual "cabal." But Powell's case on Iraq's WMD to the United Nations had come largely from the CIA; not even Wilkerson claimed that it was Cheney's or Rumsfeld's handiwork.[26]

As was the case with the NIE, the vast majority of Powell's assertions were not based on information from defectors. Two important charges were, however: the allegation that Iraq had mobile germ warfare laboratories and the charge that Iraq had taught Al Qaeda operatives how to make poison gas or germ weapons. Two days before Powell's speech, a Defense Department official who was seconded to the CIA was reading a draft and was surprised to see that the secretary of state planned to cite the mobile germ warfare laboratories as fact. Alone among U.S. officials, this man had met Curve Ball. The defector had been hungover and his account seemed fishy. The Defense Department official fired off an e-mail to the Iraq Task Force at the CIA warning that Curve Ball's account was not reliable enough to be used as a source for one of the most riveting allegations in Powell's address. "Let's keep in mind the fact that this war's going to happen regardless of what Curve Ball said or didn't say, and that the Powers that Be probably aren't terribly interested in whether Curve Ball knows what he's talking about." The director of the task force responded in an e-mail: "In the interest of Truth, we owe somebody a sentence or two of warning, if you honestly have reservations."[27]

Powell made his presentation to the Security Council on February 5, 2003. The most compelling evidence was the photographs and signals intelligence that indicated the Iraqis were rushing to sanitize suspected weapons sites. Their cleanup efforts to ensure that their sites did not contain any vestiges of Iraq's old WMD programs had been photographed by U.S. satellites and their communications intercepted. Saddam's efforts to comply with the U.N. inspections had been misinterpreted as yet another sign that he was out to deceive the inspectors. The secretary of state also cited reports from a captured Al Qaeda fighter that the terrorist group was being trained by Iraqis on how to make chemical and biological weapons. It was not until almost three years later that it would be disclosed that the Defense Intelligence Agency had warned in February 2002 that the prime source for Iraq's supposed training of Al Qaeda operations was likely a fabricator.[28]

Looking back on the intelligence reports, Pillar noted that there had been a subtle but significant tendency by analysts to give the White House what it wanted. "It was certainly clear fairly early in 2002 to just about anyone working in intelligence on Iraq issues that we were going to war, that the decision had essentially been made. For any analyst, favorable attention to policymakers is a benchmark of success. There was a natural bias in favor of intelligence production that supported, rather than undermined, policies already set," he said.[29]

In Baghdad, some of Saddam's aides were puzzled by the United States's charges that Iraq had WMD. The military had made no preparations for the use of chemical or biological weapons. No regime security officers had informed military commanders that convoys of chemical weapons had been shipped. No meeting had been held to make sure that friendly and enemy positions had been pinpointed. Nor had the military rehearsed tactical operations using chemical weapons since 1991. The II Republican Guard Corps had chemical defense battalions—equipment they could use to protect themselves if attacked with chemical weapons—but those stayed in their barracks. Hamdani, the corps commander, knew his forces did not possess chemical or germ weapons and was confident that the United States military would not use them.[30] 'Abd-al-Tawab 'Abdallah al-Mullah Huwaysh, who oversaw Iraq's military industry, had no idea what America was talking about; he was not aware of Iraq's possessing any WMD and he was in a position to know a great deal. But the charges leveled by Washington had been so unqualified and persistent that he started to wonder whether Saddam might not control a secret cache after all. "I knew a lot, but wondered why Bush believed that we had these weapons," he told his interrogators after the war.[31]

Saddam believed that Powell had failed to win the U.N. debate over the authorization of military action. He took comfort in the fact that the Security Council was split and the regional powers and most of America's allies opposed a war. Besides, he had come clean and destroyed all vestiges of WMD, the only casus belli Bush had. Saddam was so convinced that the United States would not prevail in the political debate that he denied a request by his military commanders that Iraq begin to sow mines in the Persian Gulf. Saddam did not want to give the United States any excuse to start the war.

At CENTCOM, the military was so persuaded that Iraq had and would use chemical or biological weapons that Buzz Moseley was drawing up plans to strike suspected WMD sites. The Army and Marines ordered their troops to wear chemical protective gear when they invaded and to undergo inoculations for anthrax and smallpox. The classified operations order for Scott Wallace's V Corps asserted that it was unlikely that Iraq would make early use of WMD, reasoning that Saddam would have an incentive to hide his possession of chemical and germ weapons in the initial stages of the conflict. But the order added ominously that Saddam would launch a chemical and germ attack to "inflict maximum U.S. casualties" as American forces approached Baghdad.[32]

The Marines provided a similar assessment in their own classified operations order, noting that "Iraq will likely employ chemical and biologi-

cal weapons once the survival of the regime is threatened." The order
added that the Iraqis might use chemical weapons when the Marines
sought to cross the Euphrates River or defend the Rumaylah oilfields. If
the Iraqis did not use their WMD arsenal in these battles, they certainly
would to try to stop the Marines from crossing the Tigris.[33] As they
moved north, Jim Mattis's 1st Marine Division planned to stay well outside of artillery range as it approached Kut: U.S. intelligence had reported
that the Baghdad infantry division there was equipped with chemical
weapons. One major concern for Mattis was the possibility that toxic
gases from oilfield fires might trigger the sensors the Marines relied on to
determine the presence of chemical or biological weapons, generating so
many false alarms that the detection system would be all but useless. The
solution was to purchase 175 pigeons from the Kuwaitis to use as a "sen-
tinel species." (The original plan called for using chickens but the hens
could not endure the cold desert nights or vanished at the hands of
Marines who were determined to supplement their bland diet of military
rations.)

U.S. intelligence analysts had grossly misinterpreted Saddam's new defensive strategy, assuming that the ring plan that had so dismayed the
Iraqi generals in December was a scheme to unleash chemical and possibly biological weapons against U.S. troops as they closed in on the Iraqi
capital. But while U.S. intelligence was busy worrying about the ring plan,
Saddam's Republican Guard, and his unconventional weapons, it dismissed as minor the role of the Fedayeen and entirely missed the fact that
tons of arms caches were distributed in March and stored in schools and
mosques in southern cities and towns. The supply of weapons had been
so abundant that they were even being stashed in bathrooms, according
to one Iraqi commander.

The CIA did not have the same long-standing relationships in Iraq as it
had in Afghanistan, where it had armed and funded the mujahidin resistance in the 1980s. But as the Iraq War approached, it began to dole out
funds liberally to build new ties. Throughout the winter of 2002–2003,
CIA agents had been operating in southern Iraq and were convinced that
the U.S. forces would not face determined resistance but would actually
receive active cooperation.

Months before the war, the CIA reported that "tribal elements" opposed to Saddam might seize the critical Highway 1 bridge over the

Euphrates and some of the key oil facilities in the Rumaylah oilfields and turn them over to the Americans. The most upbeat assessment was provided by a team who met with McKiernan and his aides at Camp Doha in early 2003. The CIA was so sure that American soldiers would be greeted warmly when they pushed into southern Iraq that a CIA operative suggested sneaking hundreds of small American flags into the country for grateful Iraqis to wave at their liberators. The agency would capture the spectacle on film and beam it throughout the Arab world. It would be the ultimate information operation. Iraqi forces would not interfere. McKiernan objected. To avoid being perceived as an occupying army, American forces had been instructed not to brandish the American flag. The idea was dropped, but the CIA's optimism remained.

The agency believed that many of the towns were "ours," said Rusty Blackman, the two-star Marine general who served as McKiernan's chief of staff. "At first, it was going to be U.S. flags," he said, "and then it was going to be Iraqi flags. The flags are probably still sitting in a bag somewhere. One of the towns where they said we would be welcomed was Nasiriyah, where Marines faced some of the toughest fighting in the war."[34]

CHAPTER 8

A Little Postwar Planning

Franks had told his commanders in early August 2002 that the State Department would take the lead in planning for the leap into the unknown that would follow the ouster of Saddam Hussein. But even as the Internal Look war game had ended, it was apparent that Franks's assumption was no longer valid. By late December, the White House initiated a government-wide plan to provide the Iraqi people with food and relief supplies until they were back on their feet after the war. For his part, McKiernan, figuring that he might very well end up as the temporary custodian of the country, had begun to sketch out his own plan. Phase IV, as the postwar phase was designated, though, was still a muddle and incomplete. What was missing was a comprehensive blueprint to administer and restore Iraq after Saddam was deposed and identification of the U.S. organizations that would be installed in Baghdad to carry it out.

The problem of governing post-Saddam Iraq had been underscored well before Bush was elected. During the Clinton years, Tony Zinni had been concerned about the absence of an effective plan to administer and restore the country if the regime collapsed or war broke out during his term as the CENTCOM commander. Not only had he developed an invasion plan that called for a minimum of 380,000 troops to control the country, Zinni had organized the war game Desert Crossing, intended to integrate the civilian agencies—from the Agency for International Development to the Treasury Department—that would help to govern the country.

As there was little interest in forcing regime change in Iraq during the Clinton years, Desert Crossing did not get very far. Zinni's effort was preliminary and focused more on solving short-term humanitarian problems than on designing a new U.S.-led organization to run the country after the war and before the installation of a new Iraqi government. Franks had done little to pick up where his predecessor left off. Zinni and Franks, in fact, never talked from the day Zinni relinquished command of CENTCOM in 2000. When Zinni had later called Mike DeLong, Franks's Tampa-based deputy and fellow Marine, to ask if the command was trying to build on Desert Crossing, DeLong indicated that he had never heard of it.[1]

The CENTCOM commander had been focused on developing one invasion plan after another, while responding to an endless stream of questions from Rumsfeld on the strategy and minimum force necessary to get to Baghdad. Unlike many of his subordinates, Franks had no experience in Bosnia or Kosovo and was inclined to think of nation-consolidating efforts as an afterthought. To be sure, Franks appointed a tiny cell of planners working on ways to get humanitarian assistance to the Iraqis. But he seemed content to leave the lion's share of the Phase IV planning to others in the government.

Major Ray Eiriz of CENTCOM, who had worked on plans to cope with up to 1.1 million refugees, acknowledged that postwar planning did not receive much attention at Franks's command. "From an operational perspective our main focus was on the first three phases and Phase IV is something we were planning but there were many intangibles and we didn't focus as much time on it as we should have," he told Army historians after the war. "CENTCOM never wanted to have military administration and the Joint Staff and OSD [Office of the Secretary of Defense] had not decided what it would look like."[2]

John Agoglia said that the CENTCOM planners had been told early on that others in the government would assume the principal responsibilities for Phase IV—the command's dry designation for the vicissitudes of postwar Iraq. But for months the planners could never locate the officials who were supposedly preparing for Iraq's future. "We knew there was a void in our ability to deal with Phase IV, the post-hostilities piece, unless we clearly had an interagency link," he told military historians. "We kept on getting told that 'oh yeah, it's coming.' We're asking for policy on who is going to be in charge? How do we interact with them?"

It was not until August, he said, when the Joint Staff instructed CENTCOM that it would have to support the administration of the country. By then, the planners were consumed with planning the war and preparing Franks for his meetings with the president and top administration officials. CENTCOM's team had been told to get cracking on Phase IV, but at a difficult time. "The ability to focus on it was very difficult at the command perspective," added Agoglia. "You had a lot of energy focused on the tactical piece, again Phase I through III. There wasn't a whole lot of intellectual energy being focused on Phase IV."[3]

With Franks and Rumsfeld dominating the strategizing, the Joint Chiefs of Staff had been pushed to the margins of the war planning. But, in the fall of 2002, the Joint Staff did dwell on the sore lack of military planning for postwar Iraq. The issue was bigger than CENTCOM seemed to appreciate. Every time U.S. forces were sent to a trouble spot they seemed to stay longer than policymakers had anticipated. Whatever happened, it seemed clear that the Pentagon would be dealing with Iraq in one way or another for years to come. The message was driven home when the Joint Staff conducted its own classified war game: Prominent Hammer II. One of their recommendations, issuing from the exercise, had been to design and staff a new military headquarters that would be responsible for Iraq after Saddam and his Baathists were swept out of power. It was a simple and overdue suggestion, and yet like much of Phase IV it had yet to be addressed.

By October, the Joint Staff had drafted a plan. To manage postwar Iraq, the headquarters would be overseen by a three-star general and staffed by experts drawn from throughout the U.S. government in twenty-one areas, including public health, banking, transportation, and oil. As Iraq gradually returned to stability, the headquarters would coordinate its efforts with a newly appointed U.S. ambassador in Baghdad. Eventually, the military headquarters would be replaced by a "high civilian commissioner" or an interim Iraqi government.[4]

As the Joint Staff saw it, there was much to be gained by forming the headquarters in advance. While Franks was preoccupied with the looming invasion, the new headquarters would deal with the myriad issues that were bound to crop up after Saddam was ousted—from planning the rehabilitation of the Iraqi army to repairing and upgrading Iraq's electrical grid and its decaying economic infrastructure. Once the war was over, the headquarters would relieve Franks of the burden of overseeing Iraq—no small benefit, as CENTCOM would be busy dealing with Afghanistan and other hot spots in the administration's war on terror. Rear Admiral Carlton B. Jewett, the deputy director for political military affairs of the

Joint Staff, had tactfully highlighted the issue in an August 14 memorandum: "The CENTCOM plan is committed to assisting such an effort but is not resourced to military administration," Jewett wrote.

John Abizaid, who served at the time as the director of the Joint Staff and would later become Franks's deputy, had offered a variant of the Joint Staff plan. Abizaid believed that postwar planning should be assigned to an Army corps not tied up with the invasion, which would be brought into Iraq to administer the country after Saddam was toppled. He suggested the Army's III Corps, based at Fort Hood, Texas, as a candidate for the mission, but his plan never gained traction.[5]

While the Joint Staff plan for a new headquarters looked good on paper, Rumsfeld had yet to be persuaded. After he was briefed, he decreed several important changes. The Defense Department would take the lead in all postwar efforts. References to the State Department disappeared from the organizational chart. As for the new headquarters, Rumsfeld also decreed that there would be two entities: a civilian administrator to oversee the reconstruction and governance of the country and a U.S. military commander responsible for security and retraining the Iraqi military. Each would report to CENTCOM and, ultimately, to Rumsfeld himself.

After receiving the amended version of the plan on October 16, Dick Myers, the JCS chairman, offered his thoughts on Rumsfeld's insistence that his department have primary responsibility for the postwar effort: "This is SecDef desire. We agree," Myers wrote. "This is very good work. POTUS/Dr. Rice agreed that DOD lead initially was OK." Bush and Condoleezza Rice had tentatively endorsed Rumsfeld's plan.[6] The Bush administration had arrived at a crucial juncture. The State Department had led postwar efforts in the Balkans and Afghanistan. As Rumsfeld would have it in Iraq, the Defense Department would have direct authority for the administration and rebuilding of an occupied country for the first time since World War II. With a budget approaching $400 billion, the Pentagon had the resources but not the experience for the work it was undertaking.

After the Pentagon established its primacy in postwar Iraq, the Phase IV planning effort slowed to a crawl. Rumsfeld did not seem anxious about the lack of momentum. His assumption was that he and his department would not be organizing a massive nation-building program, but facilitating Iraqi efforts to secure and reconstruct their own country, using their oil exports to finance whatever was needed. Doug Feith, the top Defense Department policy official, described Rumsfeld's approach as "enabling." It was intended to reduce the U.S. burden in postwar Iraq and facilitate the quick departure of the bulk of U.S. forces.

At the White House, there was intuitive support for the "enabling" strategy, which would allow the United States to dispose of its foe, quickly withdraw many, if not most, of its troops, and avoid the decade-long commitment Clinton had initiated in the Balkans.

During the 2000 presidential election campaign, Condoleezza Rice, who was already serving as Bush's national security adviser, had created a stir by criticizing the open-ended U.S. peacekeeping mission in the Balkans, and promising a new division of labor in which the armed forces would stick to war-fighting while other nations tended to the peace. The outcry from European capitals led the administration to temper its position, but Bush had never lost his skepticism about peacekeeping in the Balkans.

Now the White House would elaborate on this stance—but with one important change. Instead of handing over much of the responsibility for administration, reconstruction, and peacekeeping to allies, of whom the administration had precious few, the White House was proposing that the Iraqis would do much of the work themselves. "The concept was that we would defeat the army, but the institutions would hold, everything from ministries to police forces," Rice recalled in an interview after the war. "You would be able to bring new leadership but we were going to keep the body in place."[7]

For the Joint Staff, however, the projected reliance on the Iraqis did not obviate the need to set up the U.S. organizations that were to oversee the occupation. Since mid-October, there had been no additional guidance or input from the civilians on Rumsfeld's staff on how to turn their plan into reality, prompting one senior officer on the Joint Staff to propose a new nickname for Rumsfeld's policy team: "the black hole."[8] By December, Myers, who had endorsed Rumsfeld's scheme, had become concerned. With the war fast approaching, Rumsfeld's plan for two headquarters was dusted off. Myers's staff began to develop plans for the military-led organization that would secure postwar Iraq. The Joint Staff would leave it to Rumsfeld and the White House to define the parallel civilian administration. These kinds of decisions, as the military liked to say, were beyond its pay grade.

As a first step, Lieutenant General George Casey, the chief planning officer for the Joint Staff, summoned Brigadier General Steve Hawkins to Washington. As the commander of the Great Lakes and Ohio Division of the Army Corps of Engineers, Hawkins had not been thinking deeply about Iraq. His organization had an annual budget of $1.5 billion and its main concern was preventing floods in the Midwest. Still, Hawkins, who had known Casey since their days together in Bosnia, was up for a challenge. When Hawkins arrived at the Pentagon on December 18, Casey briefed him on his new assignment. He would form a new organization called Joint Task Force 4. JTF-4 would not run Iraq during the postwar period. Rather, it would help design and provide the nucleus of the follow-on headquarters that would be called CJTF-I, or Combined Joint Task Force–Iraq. The chiefs ordered that JTF-4 be at full strength and hard at work by February 1, and in early January 2003 Rumsfeld signed an order officially establishing it. Meanwhile, the chiefs asked Franks to provide, by the end of January, a detailed postwar plan for the follow-on headquarters. As a stopgap, Casey approached McKiernan, asking for his thoughts on dealing with post-Saddam Iraq.

For such a formidable task, Hawkins was given very modest resources. He had no budget of his own. His staff would be supplied from the Joint Forces Command, headquartered at Norfolk, Virginia, which was designing and war-gaming new military ideas as part of Rumsfeld's program of military transformation. JFCOM, as it was known, was run by Rumsfeld's former military assistant, Admiral Edmund Giambastiani, a cerebral officer who was close to the defense secretary and would later be promoted by Rumsfeld to serve as vice chairman of the JCS. An innovation Giambastiani had been nurturing was something called a standing joint task force, essentially a well-oiled military staff that would train regularly and could be dispatched on a moment's notice to help commanders plan operations anywhere. It was the military planners' equivalent of a SWAT team, and the idea had been tested in a war game, Millennium Challenge. When Hawkins went to Norfolk, however, he was disappointed to discover that the task force was more a concept than a real capability. Some members of the task force were civilian contractors, who were not about to deploy to Iraq, and many officers assigned to the task force were not available for reassignment. Hawkins ended up recruiting a fifty-eight-person staff of uneven quality that had never worked together, trained in a crash program by the Millennium Challenge task force.

His reception at CENTCOM's main headquarters at MacDill Air

Force Base in Tampa, Florida, was no more encouraging. Hawkins later characterized his greeting in Tampa as "who are you and why are you really here." To Hawkins, CENTCOM was suffering from the "not invented here" syndrome and rebuffing help for a mission it was ill prepared to plan or carry out itself. CENTCOM officials, for their part, found Hawkins overbearing and did not think they were being offered much of an asset: a fledgling and untested task force with no budget of its own.

Eager to get going on his task despite his mounting problems, Hawkins headed down to a trade fair at the base to scrounge up office supplies. He went from booth to booth, appropriating pads, pens, and staplers—not an auspicious start for an organization charged with smoothing the path to a new Iraq. By the end of January, Hawkins had managed to get himself and his team on a flight to Kuwait, figuring he should set up shop at Camp Doha where McKiernan's headquarters was located. When the plane stopped to refuel in Qatar, Hawkins was summoned to CENTCOM's forward headquarters at As Sayliyah to meet with John Abizaid, who by then had been appointed to serve as one of Franks's two senior deputies. Abizaid stressed the importance of Hawkins's effort and then sent him on his way.[9]

At Doha, McKiernan was initially uncertain about what to do with Hawkins and his small team. Fully expecting that he might end up, at least temporarily, as the military commander in post-Saddam Iraq, McKiernan had not only begun to plan for the war's aftermath but had already put an officer in charge of the effort: Major General Albert Whitley, the senior British representative at McKiernan's headquarters. Whitley was an exuberant pipe-smoking officer who had worked with McKiernan in Bosnia. An engineer by training, he had already been given the title of deputy commander for post-hostility coordination and control. Working with Kevin Benson, McKiernan's chief planner, the general had produced a Phase IV plan, Eclipse II, named after the post–World War II plan for Germany. McKiernan had told his staff that they could expect to be in Iraq for as long as six months to support either a civilian administrator or an incoming transitional military headquarters that would work with an interim Iraqi government. When McKiernan sought to subordinate Hawkins and his staff to Whitley and his already established planning team there was some initial unpleasantness, as Hawkins insisted that he reported only to Abizaid. CENTCOM settled the issue:

McKiernan was the chief land war commander and the new task force would be under his jurisdiction.[10]

McKiernan's Eclipse plan laid down the main precepts that he thought should guide the postwar effort. It instructed that coalition forces would "control as we go," and there would be a "rolling transition" to what the military called stability operations. That is, southern Iraq would be secured and postwar efforts could begin there even as combat forces were still fighting near Baghdad. After the collapse of the regime, U.S. forces would rely on the Iraq military, the Iraqi police and existing legal system, provincial governments, and Iraqi ministries to maintain order and administer the country. An Iraqi consultative council would be established to help govern Iraq until an independent Iraqi government was established. During the first sixty days of fighting, coalition forces would "secure key infrastructure," "support the maintenance of public order and safety," "support the restoration of critical utilities/basic services," " 'empower' selected Iraqi officials," and "begin reintegration of the Iraqi military." U.S. forces would fan out through Iraq, having been assigned particular sectors to control. They would eventually be replaced in the main by allied forces, which thus far had not volunteered for the mission.[11]

But the plan left many questions unanswered and was informed by untested assumptions: that Iraqi institutions would remain more or less intact and that other U.S. governmental organizations would be prepared and funded to restore Iraq's infrastructure. And while it looked like McKiernan would be in charge for the first few weeks or months of the occupation, neither Washington nor CENTCOM had yet decided which general or which command would oversee the military forces in Iraq after that. Colonel Jim Rabon, the chief of staff of JTF-4, later complained that the Eclipse plan was "PowerPoint deep."[12]

Lieutenant Colonel Steven Peterson, one of Marks's planners, identified another problem with Eclipse II, one that went to the core of the CENTCOM plan and the effort to apply the principles of transformation in Saddam Hussein's Iraq. To encourage the collapse of Saddam's regime and speed the push to Baghdad, the air and ground campaign was designed to destroy the regime's command and control—the "shock and awe" promised by Franks. Yet, some command and control was essential, for the postwar plan assumed that McKiernan would use Iraqi Regular Army forces, police, and institutions to help maintain order. There was little in the way of a U.S. reserve should the Iraqis not be up to the task or

could not be controlled. This contradiction and its potential to undermine U.S. postwar efforts were noted by Peterson in a classified assessment he prepared before the war.

"Over a month before the war began, the Phase IV planning group
concluded that the campaign would produce conditions at odds with
meeting strategic objectives," Peterson later wrote in an unpublished
paper that he submitted to the National War College, course work that
became the talk of military war colleges but was never noted by the
media. "They realized that the joint campaign was specifically designed
to break all control mechanisms of the regime and there would be a period following regime collapse in which we would face the greatest danger
to our strategic objectives. This assessment described the risk of an influx
of terrorists to Iraq, the rise of criminal activity, the probable actions of
former regime members, and the loss of control of WMD that was believed to exist."

To hedge against the risk that a newly liberated Iraq could spin out of
control and that WMD would go missing, Peterson and his fellow planners stressed the need to seal the borders, identify infrastructure that
needed to be protected, and gather Iraqi troops and resources to quickly
reestablish control of the country. But Peterson understood all too well
that McKiernan had only a limited number of forces and was struggling
to persuade Washington to send the reinforcements, military police, and
support he believed were needed. Not even Peterson thought there were a
lot of extra troops to take on the missions he foresaw for Phase IV. Zinni
had based his old 1003 plan on the assumption that it took more troops to
secure the peace than to upend Saddam's regime, and the rejection of that
assumption had led to a dilemma. "No officer in the headquarters was
prepared to argue for actions that would siphon resources from the war
fighting effort, when the fighting had not yet begun," Peterson wrote.
"The war was not yet started, let alone finished, when these issues were
being raised. Only a fool would propose hurting the war fighting effort to
address post-war conditions that might or might not occur."

Peterson's paper spoke volumes about the incessant pressure to fight
the war with as few troops as possible, the military's unease about the
outcome and its unwillingness to take a firm stand on troop requirements
for a phase of the conflict that was replete with uncertainty. The military's reluctance to address this, Peterson concluded, was one of biggest
mistakes of the war.[13]

·   ·   ·

As the military was struggling to develop its plans for securing postwar Iraq, Rumsfeld's aides finally returned to the unfinished business of establishing the civilian administration with which it was to work. While Rumsfeld had decided in October that such an organization should be established, there had been no follow-up to formalize it. It would take a presidential order to do so. On January 4, Doug Feith contacted Steve Hadley, the deputy national security adviser, to restate the Pentagon's position. The Afghanistan reconstruction, Feith insisted, had been mishandled by the State Department and hampered by the division of authority between Foggy Bottom and the Pentagon. This time, the new civilian administration in Iraq should report to the Defense Department. By overseeing the civilian administrators as well as the military commander in Iraq, Feith argued, Rumsfeld would ensure unity of command.

In another administration, the president's national security adviser staff might have assumed the primary role for overseeing the postwar planning. But Condoleezza Rice had never aspired to be a domineering adviser in the mold of Henry Kissinger or Zbigniew Brzezinski. Brent Scowcroft, the adviser to George H. W. Bush, had been her mentor when she served as an aide on the NSC staff and his low-key approach was more her style. Rice was close to the president and had helped to frame his preemption doctrine. But as the president's adviser on national security she was more coordinator than maestro and not one to knock heads to get something done. Rice had been the provost at Stanford University during the Clinton administration. A conservative in her early forties at the time, she had managed a liberal campus and distinguished academics. But in Washington Rice was dealing with Cheney, Rumsfeld, and Powell, officials with long experience in Washington, considerable skills in the use of power, each of whom had at one time or another considered a run for the presidency.

A career attorney, Hadley was Rice's loyal second-in-command, and was no more suited to play the role of enforcer than she. With tortoise-shell glasses and gray features, Hadley did not focus on grand strategy, but worked long hours as a behind-the-scenes bureaucratic lever-puller keeping the machinery of the NSC running. Outside the door to Rice's office hung a large photograph of her piano performance with cello virtuoso Yo-Yo Ma at the Kennedy Center. Inside her office, a painting from the Harlem Renaissance was displayed along with NFL football helmets, a testimony to her passion for sports. Hadley's office was essentially bare other than a bird's-eye picture of late-nineteenth-century Washington. Hadley was not eager to challenge Rumsfeld. He had served under Wolfowitz at the Pentagon when Cheney was defense secretary. Although a dyed-in-the-wool conservative, he was not a Rumsfeld disciple, but the Pentagon had been his training ground in government.

In short, the National Security Council was a system that assumed senior officials would cooperate and share information with their counterparts and which rarely cracked down when they did not. Rumsfeld fully understood the weakness of the NSC system and took advantage of it. In briefing his war plans at the White House, Rumsfeld would routinely retrieve the slides and take them back to the Defense Department. He once instructed Frank Miller, the senior defense aide on the NSC staff, who had been entrusted with the deepest secrets of nuclear targeting during his prior years at the Pentagon, not to take notes. In Washington, information was power, and Rumsfeld did his best to control the flow.

As the war planning dragged on, the NSC staff was forced to wage something of a guerrilla war to counter Rumsfeld's fetish for control. Miller dispatched military aides on the NSC staff to the Pentagon so they could quietly and surreptitiously secure the background information the White House needed from their Joint Staff colleagues. Marine Colonel Tom Greenwood, who worked for Miller, said: "I would put on my uniform and go to the Pentagon as though I was visiting friends. I'd then pick up the material we were looking for and spirit it back to the White House." If Rumsfeld found out it could be the end of a career. Rice also quietly sent Miller to brief Powell and Richard Armitage, the deputy secretary of state and Colin Powell's confidant, to ensure that they were kept in the loop. These tactics were odd given Rice's and Hadley's nominal roles as the chief stewards of the national security apparatus who presided over the interagency process, but they revealed much about the real power structure within the administration. Rice was not the only senior official who had the ear of the president. Cheney and Rumsfeld did as well, and they called most of the shots.[14]

There was no objection, however, to Miller's taking on broad planning responsibilities to facilitate the war. In August, Rice had put him in charge of the Executive Steering Group, an interdepartmental committee that included officials from throughout the government, whose mission was to oversee some of the preparations for the war and, in theory, the peace that was to follow. Much of Miller's time was initially consumed with seeking access to overseas bases, as well as the right to fly over foreign territory and in checking on the thirty-three construction projects that needed to be completed so that Franks's invasion force would have the runways, ports, and other infrastructure it needed.

In November, Miller had asked Elliott Abrams, a senior aide for humanitarian assistance, and Robin Cleveland, a top budget official, to prepare a plan to avert a potential humanitarian crisis in Iraq, which the White House feared might occur during the war itself or in the months that followed. The plan that emerged called for such measures as stockpiling relief supplies in bordering countries. One vexing problem that preoccupied the administration for months was finding a way to maneuver around the legal requirement that no goods be brought into Iraq without a license from the Treasury Department. Intended as a tool to enforce economic sanctions against Saddam, the measure, literally interpreted, precluded volunteer organizations from providing relief to needy Iraqis as the American forces began to roll in. The Bush administration was not worried about how to square "regime change" with international law, but in a capital full of lawyers and bureaucrats the United States's own regulations could very well become a problem.

Rumsfeld was happy to let the rest of the government focus on the humanitarian task ahead as long as the Defense Department had the lead in the postwar mission. Rumsfeld's proposal to oversee the mission was endorsed in a meeting of senior officials in the White House Situation Room. It was agreed that Hadley would draft a directive for the president to sign formalizing Rumsfeld's move.

Surprisingly, neither Powell nor Armitage objected. Though there was a bit of grumbling at the State Department, the secretary of state and his deputy took the position that the Pentagon had the money and resources for the postwar mission and therefore was entitled to run it. In August, Powell had warned the president that if the U.S. invaded Iraq the government structure would break and the administration would effectively own it. If Rumsfeld wanted to be the man in charge of the messy aftermath, that was fine with his rival at the State Department.

Jay Garner was in New York on business on January 9 when he received a call from Douglas Feith. The retired three-star general had been trained as an air defense officer, but had been involved in overseeing the relief efforts in Kurdistan after the 1991 Persian Gulf War, had a lucrative position in the defense industry, and had served on a panel on space policy that Rumsfeld had chaired during the Clinton years. Feith wanted to know if Garner would head a new civilian postwar planning office and eventually take it to Iraq. The organization would oversee the early phase of the occupation and Garner would eventually be succeeded by a more prominent political appointee, such as a Republican former state governor. Garner consulted with his wife and business associates and concluded he could allot only four months to the job. On January 20, Bush signed National Security Presidential Directive 24, formalizing Rumsfeld's authority for postwar Iraq.[15]

Garner had been called into the game late. He was able to draw on the work done by Frank Miller and his colleagues on the NSC staff, but he had been assigned massive responsibilities. The directive made clear that he was to draft plans to deliver food and other emergency assistance, reestablish the provision of electricity and other basic services, reshape the Iraqi military and safeguard Iraq's infrastructure, and dismantle the newly uncovered stashes of WMD. The directive also instructed Garner to coordinate his efforts with the United Nations, nongovernment relief organizations, and Iraqi exiles.

Garner began recruiting a senior staff and set up shop in a suite of offices at the Pentagon. The nucleus was composed of Ron Adams and Jerry Bates, two retired generals Garner had recruited, as well as Colonel Thomas Baltazar and Colonel Paul Hughes, a brainy Army officer who had been at the National Defense University. Soon Carl Strock, a major general with the Army Corps of Engineers, joined the team. Having been left out of the early planning on Afghanistan where the corps's capabilities had immediate relevant use, particularly in areas like road building, Strock had taken the initiative and offered his services. Strock and his civilian deputy went looking for the small Garner team at the Pentagon.

Garner thought the corps should be involved in construction, though some other issues did not play to the corps's strengths. One task the corps was to undertake was the repair of Iraq's electrical grid. The experience of the corps, however, was in managing hydroelectric plants in the United States, not in running a grid powered by oil-fueled power plants in the Third World. Strock received intelligence from the Joint Warfare Analysis Center, focused on the likely damage that would be caused by U.S. bombing and the fighting to get to Baghdad. "Our whole focus on our reconstruction effort was really not to go in and fix this country, but to fix what we broke," Strock recalled. "And we sort of made the assumption that the country was functioning beforehand. I had a dramatic underestimation of the condition of the Iraqi infrastructure, which turned out to be one of our biggest problems, and not the war damage."[16]

. . .

Having grabbed responsibility for postwar Iraq, Rumsfeld proceeded publicly to outline his vision. On February 14, he and Tommy Franks flew to New York for a black-tie gala on the *Intrepid,* a World War II aircraft carrier that was anchored in the Hudson River and turned into a military museum. Founded by a real estate developer, the museum was hosting the event to honor the armed forces, but the evening was actually devoted to the team that was about to take the nation to war. Rumsfeld would be given the Intrepid Freedom Award in the hangar bay. Franks would do the honors of presenting it.

After praising the CENTCOM commander, Rumsfeld launched into a speech entitled "Beyond Nation-Building," which boldly outlined the Bush administration's vision of how to administer trouble spots once the shooting had stopped. As Bush and Rice had done during the presidential campaign, Rumsfeld depicted the Balkans as a model of how a postwar policy could go wrong. The Clinton administration's intervention in Kosovo, he declared, and the lengthy deployment of U.S. and allied peacekeeping forces there, had led to a "culture of dependency" that had made it hard for the Kosovars to stand on their own feet. Afghanistan, in contrast, was an example of getting it right. The Bush administration had resisted the temptation to mount a major nation-building effort or deploy a large peacekeeping force; instead, it was helping the Afghans build their own country.

"Some ask what lessons our experience in Afghanistan might offer for the possibility of a post-Saddam Iraq," Rumsfeld said, using his favorite rhetorical technique of posing and then answering his own question. Restoring Iraq, Rumsfeld said, might be easier than Afghanistan in several respects. Iraq was rich in oil and the Bush administration had more time to prepare the postwar plan for Iraq. "The effort in Afghanistan had to be planned and executed in a matter of weeks after September 11," Rumsfeld said. "With Iraq, by contrast, there has been time to prepare." Then, he added: "We have set up a Post War Planning Office to think through problems and coordinate the efforts of coalition countries and U.S. government agencies. General Franks in an interagency process has been working hard on this for many months."[17] In truth, Garner's postwar planning office was just opening shop and Franks had been so consumed with planning the invasion that Myers and the Joint Staff had felt compelled to intervene with Rumsfeld himself to prepare for the occupation.

Though the particulars of his speech were misleading, Rumsfeld had given a surprisingly blunt and public explanation of the "enabling" philosophy of nation-building that he and Rice had trumpeted. In short, the war seemed like a win-win situation. The United States could oust a dictator, usher in a new era in Iraq, shift the balance of power in the Middle East in the United States's favor, all without America's committing itself to the lengthy, costly, and arduous peacekeeping and nation-building, which the Clinton administration had undertaken in Bosnia and Kosovo. The new policy would be best for both sides, Americans and Iraqis, or so the theory went.

Not everyone was as sanguine about the postwar scenario. Joe Collins, the Pentagon official who dealt with peacekeeping operations, was anxious about what might unfold. Collins was very much a supporter of the president, but he feared that the occupation might be much more burdensome than the White House anticipated. With the lean force the U.S. was sending, it would be hard to safeguard the vulnerable supply lines, he feared. Administering the peace could be more costly and problematic as well. Collins shared his worries with Elliott Abrams. The invasion, he fretted, might be the Bush administration's political undoing. "The way I do the math, Bush will be a one-term president," Collins said. "That's not the way Karl Rove sees it," Abrams quipped. The White House's political maestro had famously drafted a memo that predicted that the war could be a boon to the president's reelection effort, which, to the embarrassment of the White House, had leaked.[18]

On February 20, Garner convened two days of closed-door meetings in a packed amphitheater at Fort McNair, the stately home of the National Defense University, abutting the Potomac River in Washington. The assembly included most of the players in the government's postwar game, including the Pentagon, State Department, CENTCOM, the vice president's office, and McKiernan's command at Camp Doha. Garner's Rock Drill was intended as an opportunity for each agency to pitch its ideas about how to proceed, but there was, as yet, no master strategy. "There is a misconception that we were rehearsing a plan," recalled Colonel Hughes. "There was no plan."[19]

As the session began, Garner outlined some of the basics. Garner's Post War Planning Office would fill a gap in Iraq temporarily, but another entity would take over before the reins of power were handed to the

Iraqis. The office would divide Iraq into three areas: north, center, and south. Garner's office would pay salaries to keep the Iraqi government functioning. It planned to have enough money for 600,000 public sector employees, but recognized that there were 1,400,000 more and at least 300,000 in the army. Additional funds would have to be tapped. Like McKiernan and Abizaid, Garner was short of personnel for the tasks he was assigned and counted on using the Iraqi army. While McKiernan needed the Iraqi troops to help with security, Garner initially wanted them as a cheap source of labor before retraining them to serve in a newly created Iraqi military. Pentagon contractors—MPRI, an organization made up largely of retired military officers, and RONCO, a Washington-based consulting firm, would do the retraining at several centers Iraq.

After Garner described the big picture, George Ward, a top deputy, delved into particular issues. Garner's postwar planning operation would be going to Iraq with a number of fundamental assumptions, many of which reflected work by Abrams's committee. A big one was that McKiernan would establish a secure environment after Saddam was toppled so that Garner's team could provide humanitarian assistance. Another was that homeless civilians and refugees would be a major and immediate problem. It was also assumed that the program under the auspices of the United Nations by which Iraq had sold oil to import food would be disrupted. The United States estimated that without the program many Iraqis would have food for only six weeks. Providing shelter to the thousands of displaced Iraqis and feeding them were the big worries. That the war would produce thousands of "displaced civilians" reflected Washington's experience in the 1991 Gulf War when Saddam turned his wrath on the Kurds and drove hundreds of thousands into the northern mountains of Iraqi Kurdistan. There were intelligence projections that Saddam might seek to hamper the coalition by creating a humanitarian crisis.

To deal with the potential threat, Ward sketched out a plan: to employ 40,000 Iraqi officials who had administered the food distribution system under Saddam's oil for food arrangements. To make sure they did not flee their posts, Garner might issue a proclamation imploring them to stay. The State Department would send four disaster assistance teams, which would work in Iraq for ninety days. There was no discussion of de-Baathification of the Iraqi civil bureaucracy.

There would have to be steps taken to clear the minefields to protect refugees, particularly on the border with Iran. An initial $130 million was needed for humanitarian assistance, enough for several weeks. Also needed was passage of a new U.N. resolution giving the United States the authority to export Iraq's oil, the proceeds going to assist the Iraqi people. But clearly the U.S. government would have to provide additional funds.

As the session wore on, the emphasis was more on urgent disaster relief than on long-term reconstruction. Even so, rehabilitating Iraq was a formidable and costly task. The cost of reconstruction was put at $1 billion a year for three years—in retrospect, a fraction of the more than $20 billion that was later authorized. Still, it was unclear which governments or agencies would foot the bill. There were millions in the U.N. escrow account, derived from the oil for food program, but every U.S. agency that had a plan to rehabilitate Iraq seemed to assume that it could tap into the funds. Garner was concerned that the escrow account was way oversubscribed.[20] Nor had it been decided how much of Iraq's reconstruction would be Washington's concern. Would the administration be responsible for a complete reconstruction of the country or just patching things up? As the meetings wore on, Hughes wrote a note to himself that Garner's group had to get administration guidance on what level of efficiency was to be achieved in housing, health care, and military infrastructure.

Security was another unsettled issue. Albert Whitley, McKiernan's deputy for postwar issues, tried to inject some realism into the discussion of the postwar planning by drawing on his experience in the Balkans. The British officer said that the coalition would probably suffer three to five casualties a week after the fall of Baghdad and the casualties would not only be among the troops fighting. This was just the cost of doing business in that part of the world. Nor would coalition military be able to accompany civilians on all their missions. That was simply unrealistic, but quick-reaction forces would be poised to spring to their aid if civilians were attacked. Whitley's talk about casualties unnerved some of the civilians, and some State Department aides said that they could not participate under those circumstances. The State Department disaster relief teams did not want to venture into areas of Iraq that were still contested by Saddam's supporters. In the military lexicon, the areas needed to be "permissive." Ron Adams, one of the retired generals recruited by Garner to run his organization, told Whitley after the session that he should not have provided such a stark view of security risks after the fall of the regime, as that would scare everyone off.

Not all of the security problems fell on the military's shoulders. Dick Mayer, a former policeman who earned a law degree at night and worked for the Justice Department, identified another potential difficulty. Mayer had honed his skills in post-conflict reconstruction while serving in the Balkans and Haiti. He was the deputy director of an obscure program known as the International Criminal Investigative Training Assistance Program, which made him one of the government's few genuine experts on what it took to establish law and order in a post-conflict environment. Mayer proposed a plan calling for some 5,000 international police advisers to be rushed to Iraq to fill the law enforcement vacuum after the collapse of Saddam's government. It was vital to establish an immediate security presence so that the population would retain confidence in their liberators. The advisers would train the Iraqis in modern police tactics, weed out the committed Baathists, and help maintain order. Mayer estimated that the program would cost $600–700 million. But at the Rock Drill he provided an estimate of what it would take to jump-start the larger effort: $38 million and, more important, five to six weeks of advance preparation. When Mayer mentioned the $38 million there was an audible gasp from some of the Defense Department officials, who considered it an extravagant and unnecessary expenditure and seemed to bridle at the suggestion that the United States would be responsible for enforcing the law in Iraq. When the State Department's Bureau of International Narcotics and Law Enforcement later refined the estimate for the overall program it rose to close to $1 billion.

Rear Admiral James A. Robb, the chief planning officer at CENTCOM, outlined his command's views, which were heavily influenced by Abizaid. It would be best that the organization responsible for administering occupied Iraq not be a U.S. headquarters, he argued. Abizaid did not want Americans to be perceived as the occupying authority; he wanted international cover. As for the Iraqis, Robb emphasized the importance of establishing an Iraqi consultative council early on. There should be a blacklist, not widespread de-Baathification. His views were noted, but by and large, these matters were not Garner's to decide.[21]

The day after the Rock Drill, Garner gathered his top aides for a postwar council. Garner had a series of upcoming meetings with Rumsfeld and Rice, and he had a list of outstanding issues. Security in postwar Iraq was a troublesome matter, and Garner wanted to see CENTCOM's Phase IV plans to stabilize the country. The coalition forces that Garner assumed would be sent to help keep order after the war needed to arrive as quickly as possible. Garner was also worried about the security of

Iraq's presumed WMD sites. CENTCOM, he said, seemed to be double-counting: assuming that the forces that would be needed to guard the sites would also be available to carry out the battle with Saddam's forces. With so many suspected sites there did not seem to be enough troops to go around. It was the same issue that Spider Marks had identified months earlier, but which had never been resolved. Garner thought that hiring private guards to protect the sites might be the answer.

Hughes and Colonel Tom Gross, who constituted Garner's secretariat, prepared a briefing of other major outstanding issues that Garner would deliver at the Pentagon and the White House in the hope that this would elicit government-wide support: the need to monitor and have arrangements for the selective opening of Saddam's borders and provision to decontaminate and treat Iraqi civilians and international aid workers should Saddam use his WMD. Garner also wanted the authority to screen Iraqis and appoint and hire those who passed his test. A nagging worry was a possible breakdown of some of Iraq's essential services—water, power, health. Any gap in providing such services, the briefing warned, "might be interpreted by the international community as a failure of the USG [U.S. government]." The briefing recommended approaching Iraq's neighbors, Syria, Turkey, Saudi Arabia, Kuwait, and Iran, and coaxing them to help. Beyond that, there was the Rock Drill's unresolved reconstruction issue: would the U.S. only fix war damage or modernize the country? "With no policy decision on restoration levels, the U.S. is faced with open-ended financial requirements," the briefing noted.[22]

That same day Garner's team arranged a video conference with McKiernan, who was at his Camp Doha headquarters. It was a chance for the military and civilian officials who were planning for the postwar period to put their heads together. Whitley, who participated in the session and was famous for his candor, delivered a discouraging assessment of the state of the administration's preparations. The U.S. agencies were not ready, had no real understanding of what Iraq was like, and did not yet have a coherent plan, he told McKiernan. There was no clear demarcation between what would be run by the civilians and what the generals would control. The funding for the multibillion-dollar undertaking in Iraq was still up in the air, and it was ludicrous to expect that it would all come from the U.N. There would need to be another United Nations resolution to deal with postwar Iraq. Garner's team needed maps and logistical support. Fuel would have to be made available and another Rock Drill should be scheduled to examine plans to distribute water, food, and fuel,

Whitley said. The message was that if the military was hoping that the civilians had Phase IV under control it would be sorely disappointed.

As the video conference proceeded, McKiernan and Jerry Bates, who sat in for Garner at the session, dealt with an important divergence between their plans. Garner had planned to start his humanitarian operation in Basra, a Shiite-dominated city in southern Iraq, to get the kinks out of his plan before heading to the more challenging Sunni-controlled north. This was logical but had been decided without any knowledge of the war plan. McKiernan explained that he had no intention of sending troops into Basra until Baghdad was taken. For the military, occupying and securing Basra at the start of the war was an unnecessary diversion. Garner would have to adjust accordingly.[23]

While everyone had agreed that the early establishment of public order was essential and Mayer had flagged the issue at the Rock Drill, no decision had yet been made on how many U.S. law enforcement personnel to send and what role they would play. Mayer had not been the only one to identify the potential for disorder. When Jalal Talabani and other Iraqi opposition leaders had gone to Washington to confer with Rumsfeld and Cheney in August 2002, he had warned about the potential for looting. There were many poor people in Baghdad, he cautioned, and they were likely to take the law into their own hands. The concerns had been duly noted by the administration.[24] But when Garner took Mayer's plan to the White House, he was told it was not going to go anywhere. The Bush administration had decided that it did not want American police to enforce the law in Iraq. As Rumsfeld's *Intrepid* speech had indicated, this was something best left to the Iraqis themselves.

The administration eventually decided that 1,500 advisers would be sent to train the Iraqi police force. Of these, 500 were to be recruited from European countries; the rest would be Americans. But with little prospect of recruiting advisers from foreign countries and limited funds, a decision was made to hire a private contractor to line up 150 potential advisers. Fifty experts would go to Iraq first to conduct a fact-finding mission. None would directly enforce the law. Puzzled by this decision, Mayer later cornered Garner and asked for an explanation of why nothing was being done. Carrying out an assessment before sending international police officers raised the risk that if the Iraqi police did not go back to work immediately after the war ended, there would be a breakdown of law and order before the United States was in a position to help. "We'll know what we're going to do when we get there," Garner replied.

As dismayed as Mayer was, Greenwood, the Marine aide on the NSC, was also frustrated. So was David Kay, the security expert who would later lead the CIA effort to investigate the mystery of Iraq's missing weapons of mass destruction and who joined Garner's team as Mayer's boss. When Kay arrived Mayer laid out the administration's plan for law enforcement. The situation was dismal. The need for police was being ignored. Kay resigned the next day, determined to distance himself from a venture that he concluded was headed for trouble. "I told Jay that it was headed for disaster," Kay disclosed. "There was a reluctance to divert resources to post-conflict maintenance of law and order and when you don't you get organized crime and political chaos."[25]

On February 28, Robert Perito, an expert on peacekeeping operations at the United States Institute for Peace, a government-financed research center, was invited to the Pentagon to outline his recommendations to Richard Perle's Defense Policy Board. Perito, who had extensive experience in the Balkans, believed that the U.S. needed to establish a civilian constabulary to help maintain order in trouble spots and had first outlined his views to Perle at his home in September. At the Pentagon, Perito said that in Iraq the U.S. would not be able to rely on local authorities. The Iraqi police would be unavailable, intimidated, or unprepared. Nor did it look like NATO or the OSCE, the Organization for Security and Co-operation in Europe, which contributed police and legal experts in Bosnia and Kosovo, would have an interest in Iraq. Relying on U.S. military forces was also not the answer since they are trained to concentrate mass and firepower to destroy the enemy. It would be vital to have international police on the ground to stop any rioting or disorder before it got out of hand. Police needed to be recruited, trained, and ready to go. Perito urged the Pentagon to establish a "stability force" for Iraq that would include a civilian constabulary and legal experts, some 2,500 personnel in all. "The fact that we may be within weeks of a decision by the president to intervene in Iraq should not deter us," Perito said. "Experience in the Balkans, East Timor, and Afghanistan shows that a coalition force will have to deal with high levels of violence for the first two years of the mission." Perito was thanked for his contribution. He never heard from the Pentagon again.[26]

Garner planned to start moving his team to the region in March so as to be in position to roll into Iraq when Saddam was defeated. Garner had already taken two State Department officials on board: Tom Warrick, who oversaw the department's "Future of Iraq Study," a series of briefings

President George W. Bush reviews the progress of the war with his war council on April 2, 2003. LEFT TO RIGHT: Chairman of the Joint Chiefs of Staff Richard Myers, President Bush, Vice President Dick Cheney, White House Chief of Staff Andrew Card, Defense Secretary Donald Rumsfeld, then National Security Adviser Condoleezza Rice, and Deputy Defense Secretary Paul Wolfowitz. (WHITE HOUSE PHOTOGRAPH BY ERIC DRAPER)

Cheney visits Jeddah and meets with Saudi Arabia's Crown Prince Abdullah on March 16, 2002. Saudi Arabia's support for the war was essential. (WHITE HOUSE PHOTOGRAPH BY DAVID BOHRER)

General Myers was known for being a team player, but the Joint Chiefs had little influence over the war planning. CENTCOM commander Tommy Franks resented their advice and preferred to deal directly with Donald Rumsfeld. (DEPARTMENT OF DEFENSE PHOTOGRAPH BY STAFF SERGEANT D. MYLES CULLEN, USAF)

Tommy Franks and Donald Rumsfeld at CENTCOM's forward headquarters in Qatar on December 12, 2002. Before he was made CENTCOM commander, Franks worked on a plan that called for no fewer than 380,000 troops to defeat Saddam and secure postwar Iraq. After becoming the head of CENTCOM, Franks embraced Rumsfeld's view that a much smaller force could do the job. (NAVY PHOTOGRAPHER GARY P. BONACCORSO)

Lieutenant General David McKiernan oversaw the allied land war from the coalition's headquarters at Camp Doha, Kuwait. (SERGEANT 1ST CLASS DAVID DISMUKES/CFLCC PUBLIC AFFAIRS)

McKiernan (CENTER) meets in Iraq with Marine Lieutenant General James Conway (LEFT) on April 4, 2003. Unflappable under pressure, McKiernan commanded all of the allied land forces. (SERGEANT 1ST CLASS DAVID DISMUKES/CFLCC PUBLIC AFFAIRS)

Lieutenant General John Abizaid (CENTER), Tommy Franks's deputy commander, warned that U.S. forces would be an antibody in Iraqi society. (U.S. ARMY CENTER FOR ARMY LESSONS LEARNED)

Lieutenant General William Scott Wallace (LEFT), the commander of the Army's V Corps, talks with Major General David Petraeus, the commander of the 101st Airborne Division. Wallace stirred Franks's ire by acknowledging that the U.S. forces had not anticipated such determined attacks by the Fedayeen. (JAMES BARKER/U.S. ARMY PHOTOGRAPH)

Air Force Lieutenant General Michael T. "Buzz" Moseley (SECOND FROM RIGHT) and Tommy Franks (SECOND FROM LEFT) participate in a video conference with the White House. They are joined by Group Captain Geoff Brown from Australia (FAR LEFT) and Air Vice Marshall Glenn Troy from Britain (FAR RIGHT). Moseley commanded the the air war from a state-of-the-art operations center in Saudi Arabia. (NAVY PHOTOGRAPHER GARY P. BONACCORSO)

A towering presence, Lieutenant General James Conway (LEFT) commanded the Marine Expeditionary Force. Colonel Steve Hummer, the commander of RCT-7, is on the right. (USMC PHOTOGRAPH BY SERGEANT JOSEPH R. CHENELLY)

Major General Buford "Buff" Blount III (STANDING), the soft-spoken commander of the 3rd Infantry Division, was one of the military's most aggressive commanders. (WARREN ZINN/*Army Times*)

This sandstorm produced such an eerie glow that the Marines described it as "orange crush." (USMC PHOTOGRAPH BY LANCE CORPORAL ANDREW P. ROUFS)

A Marine from the 15th Marine Expeditionary Unit charges forward on March 23, 2003, near Zubayr, Iraq. (DEPARTMENT OF DEFENSE PHOTOGRAPH BY LANCE CORPORAL BRIAN L. WICKLIFFE, USMC)

Major General James Mattis (RIGHT), commander of the 1st Marine Division, confers with James Conway. Mattis was one of the Marines' most hard-charging commanders. His call sign was "chaos." (USMC PHOTOGRAPH BY SERGEANT JOSEPH R. CHENELLY)

To get to Baghdad, the 3rd Infantry Division had to proceed through this narrow cut in the escarpment north of Najaf. (U.S. ARMY PHOTOGRAPH)

A destroyed T-72, a remnant of the Medina Division, on the outskirts of Baghdad (DAVE PERKINS)

Lieutenant Colonel Terry Ferrell (LEFT), the commander of the 3-7 Cavalry, was told to expect a parade in Samawah. Instead, he found himself in an unexpected fight with Saddam's Fedayeen. Ferrell's soldiers later fought a fierce battle to isolate Najaf, and they protected the western flank during the 3rd Infantry Division's attack on Baghdad. (WARREN ZINN/*Army Times*)

based on seminars about many aspects of running Iraq after Saddam was gone, involving U.S. experts and Iraqi exiles, and Megan O'Sullivan, who was working in the department's Office of Policy Planning. Powell proposed to add several more—all told, seven ambassadorial-level officials, three of whom were Arabists. Rumsfeld rejected all of them, arguing that fresh ideas and new blood were needed. The Pentagon had not grabbed control of the postwar effort to hand its portfolio over to the State Department.

After Powell threatened to withdraw all State Department participation in the enterprise, Rumsfeld relented but Warrick was now out. Warrick had been involved in a bitter feud with the Defense Department for some time over which agency would shape the future of Iraq. The dispute had even spilled over into the Iraqi community in the United States. The State Department was working with one group of Iraqis; Wolfowitz was recruiting another. Some Iraqis felt that if they worked with the Defense group they might find themselves cut off from Warrick's effort. Rumsfeld told Powell that the decision to block Warrick was made at a higher level, hinting that it came from Cheney's office.

The decision typified the ill will between the State and Defense departments, but was not in itself a crippling blow. After the war, it was commonly held that failure to rely on the "Future of Iraq Study" had deprived Garner and his team of a vital blueprint at a critical moment. The more than 1,000-page study was the product of seventeen working groups and was of uneven quality. It offered a useful way to bring Iraqi exiles together to discuss the problems of a new Iraq and proposed some good ideas but it was far short of a viable plan.

Kay, who read the study, summed it up: "It was unimplementable. It was a series of essays to describe what the future could be. It was not a plan to hand to a task force and say 'go implement.' If it had been carried out it would not have made a difference."[27] Hughes agreed. "There is a real lack of planning capacity at the Department of State, hence, just about any study gets labeled a plan," he said. "While it produced some useful background information it had no chance of really influencing the post-Saddam phase of the war." Even so, the study was eventually conveyed to the U.S. officials who administered Iraq.[28]

By March 2003, the Pentagon's authority over postwar Iraq was complete. It would keep order, oversee the first efforts at reconstruction, and help build Iraq's new political institutions. But there were some glaring weaknesses in its grand scheme. The establishment of JTF-4 could not hide the fact that the military had sufficient forces to topple the regime but not to seal the borders or deal with the disorder that followed. Garner's team would spend weeks more amassing its staff. While it was preparing to assist refugees and distribute humanitarian assistance, it had neither the funds nor personnel for major nation-building tasks or for engineering a new political order in Iraq. McKiernan and Garner headed parallel efforts that were only loosely coordinated. Tommy Franks had decided that Garner should report to McKiernan, but it was far from clear how this would work in practice. Garner had his own relationship with Rumsfeld. When Garner's team got to Kuwait they moved into the Hilton hotel by the shore miles away from the jam-packed Camp Doha. As the clock ticked down toward the war, they did not share even a common headquarters.

In Washington, Bush and his team had begun to focus on the postwar phase, but with little of the attention and energy devoted for sixteen months to the invasion plan. On March 5, Franks made his final presentation to the president and his National Security Council before the war. Bush asked what the commander's plans were for Phase IV. Franks replied blithely that the military would have "lord mayors" in every major Iraqi city and town, the general's way of alluding to his plans to have the invading forces temporarily administer the population centers. Frank's response seemed to satisfy Bush and there was little follow-up.

On March 10, barely a week before the commencement of the war, President Bush and his top aides met in the Situation Room of the White House to go over the basic game plan for postwar Iraq. It was time for the Bush team to review the broad guidance that would be given to the Pentagon for execution. Frank Miller, the top defense aide on the NSC, had overseen and would give the presentation, which the staff referred to as "mega-brief four." From the start, the Bush administration was committed to a program of de-Baathification. Those who ran Saddam's Iraq would not work for the U.S., Miller explained. The Baath Party had 1.5 million associate members and supporters, but only 1 or 2 percent, perhaps 25,000 in all, were active. They constituted the party elite, who would be removed from their government posts and barred from any role in the new state. While there might be exceptions, the burden of proof would be on the high-level Baathists, who would need to demonstrate they were prepared to build a new order.

Miller told the NSC that the de-Baathification process would make room for new faces. The bureaucracy was currently heavily Sunni, and as Baathists were expelled the new authorities would bring in Shiites, Kurds, and other minorities to participate in politics and government. The CIA and Pentagon would vet Iraqis for government posts; as for lower-level Baathists, membership in the party would be considered a negative, but not determining, factor.

To deal with war crimes, a Truth and Reconciliation Commission, modeled on tribunals in South Africa and Eastern Europe, would be established. The U.S. reserved the right to prosecute Iraqis for war crimes and atrocities against U.S. personnel committed even during the Gulf War in 1991, and Washington might impose capital punishment. The Truth and Reconciliation Commission would gather evidence, write a contemporary history, publicize transcripts of hearings, identify villains, and grant amnesty to those who cooperate. All victims would be given the opportunity to tell their stories. The new Iraqi authorities would deal with war crimes against Iraqis, as well as war crimes against Kuwait and Iran, so practicing the rule of law.

On police, Miller told the president that, according to the CIA, the Iraqi police appeared to have extensive professional training and were not closely tied to the Saddam Hussein regime. The U.S. would send only a limited number of experts and no U.S. personnel would be deployed in an operational capacity in the police, justice, or prison systems.

The briefing noted that "successful establishment of the rule of law in the immediate post-conflict environment is critical to ensuring stability, allowing for relief and reconstruction activities, rapidly rebuilding Iraqi society," but added that "long-term US interest would be served best by empowering Iraqis and developing indigenous capacity to perform law enforcement and justice functions."

Regarding Iraq's foreign affairs, Saddam's former officials could have no role in representing the country nor should they be able to contest the authority of the new government. Iraq's U.N. seat would be vacant pending the appointment of a new ambassador. The Ministry of Foreign Affairs would be overhauled. New representatives would be sent to OPEC and to the Organization of the Islamic Conference.

Miller had also drafted plans for the Iraqi military, but Rumsfeld had insisted that this was the prerogative of the Pentagon. So the NSC slides were identified with the Defense Department logo and presented to Bush two days later. In line with the recommendations from CENTCOM and

Garner to use Iraqi forces, Feith presented a plan to "reshape the Iraqi military." Feith said that three to five Iraqi divisions would form the nucleus of the new military. The force needed to be apolitical and representative of Iraq's ethnic composition, and the Kurdish Peshmerga militia might be an element of the new military.

The Iraqi force would initially be used as a "national reconstruction force." Feith issued a stark warning about the perils of completely dismantling the Iraqi military. It would be dangerous, Feith's presentation noted, to "immediately demobilize 250,000 to 300,000 personnel putting them on street." It was a central point and nobody disagreed.

Saddam's intelligence apparatus, Republican Guard, and pro-regime tribes, however, would need to be disarmed and demobilized. These personnel and former soldiers who did not find a place in the new army would need to be integrated into civilian society.

Differentiating the administration's plan from nation-building efforts in the Balkans, Feith's briefing noted that the military training program in Bosnia took seven years and cost the United States and its allies $500 million. The rebuilding of the Iraqi military, Feith suggested, would be easier and cheaper, and the training should be funded by the new Iraqi government itself. It would not be necessary to provide weapons and equipment. If Iraqi funding was inadequate, coalition funding might be required, and much of that would likely come from allies.

There would be a civilian-led Defense Ministry and a counterterrorism unit. The many intelligence organizations would be consolidated into a single agency. As the purpose of the military would be to deal with foreign threats, domestic security would be the province of the Interior Ministry.[29]

The White House was outlining its principles for governing the new Iraq only days before the war. The plan approved by the president heavily relied on existing Iraqi police and military forces to guarantee security post-Saddam. There was no discussion of a fallback plan.

There would be no ceding of control of the postwar Iraq to the United Nations or to an international administration, as had been done in the Balkans. When British officials came to the White House for a discussion on postwar planning they had suggested a prominent role for the United Nations—to give the occupation a sense of international legitimacy and facilitate the securing of allied aid. The administration's response was that it would welcome whatever aid the U.N. wanted to provide, but Washington would make it clear that it would be calling the shots. "Where has the U.N. been successful?" Robin Cleveland asked pointedly. Elliott Abrams joined the chorus of criticism: "Any organization where Libya could chair the human rights commission has severe problems," he interjected.

In the Persian Gulf, some of the generals who were to assume responsibility for Iraq had a different view. While Miller was working on his brief to the president, Joe Collins, the Defense Department deputy for postwar issues, traveled with a delegation to the Gulf States to assess the war planning. Abizaid, Collins reported to his Pentagon colleagues, appeared to be more concerned than Washington about how the U.S.-led effort would unfold. "We are an antibody in their society," Abizaid said in the closed-door meeting. "The key thing is to internationalize the problem. We really need the U.N. stamp of approval. It would be crazy to keep the U.S. government in charge for too long."[30]

CHAPTER 9

Dora Farms

On March 14, 2003, Tommy Franks summoned his Army, Navy, Marine, Air Force, and Special Operations commanders to his Qatar headquarters for a final huddle before the allied attack. As the officers entered the CENTCOM command center the lights were brought low, and Russell Crowe appeared on the screen as Marcus Aurelius's favorite general, preparing to smash a rebellious Germanic tribe, who were resisting the expansion of the Roman Empire. The Roman legions magnanimously gave the barbarians one final chance to surrender only to see their offer spurned. With their superior weaponry and daring military tactics, the Romans readied themselves for battle. The clip ended with the general's cry: "On my signal, unleash hell." Franks was trying to infuse his commanders with a warrior spirit by showing the opening scenes of *Gladiator*, but the event seemed jarringly over the top to some of the British officers.[1]

The signal for mounting the allied assault to unseat Saddam was fast approaching. "D-day," in fact, was scheduled to begin on the evening of March 19. Special Operations helicopters and Air Force planes would attack the thirty-one Iraqi observation posts along the Saudi and Jordanian border. Then Dell Dailey's commandos at Ar'ar, Saudi Arabia, and Gary Harrell's Special Forces in Jordan would begin their evening infiltration of western Iraq, as allied planes provided air cover. Special Operations forces in Kuwait would also cross the border that evening to monitor the crucial Highway 1 bridge, dams, and the southern cities, along with the Southern Iraq Liaison Element, CENTCOM's euphemism for the CIA.

Two days later—on March 21, at exactly 9:00 p.m.—the major fireworks would begin with CENTCOM's version of "shock and awe." Tomahawk cruise missiles, F-117 stealth fighters, and B-2 bombers would begin to strike targets in and around Baghdad. Jim Conway's Marines and Scott Wallace's V Corps would begin to cross into Iraq on March 22 at 6:00 a.m., a nearly simultaneous air and ground attack that was intended to surprise the Iraqi generals, who would be expecting a weeks-long allied bombing campaign.

If it all went according to plan there would be mass capitulations by the Iraqi military in and around key southern cities like Nasiriyah, where the CIA reported that the Iraqi 11th Infantry Division and 51st Mechanized Division were poorly motivated and on the verge of switching sides. The advancing allied units would carry the Articles of Capitulation for the surrendering Iraqis to sign.

The military timetable was synchronized with the ultimatum President Bush was to issue on March 17, following his Azores meeting with British Prime Minister Tony Blair, Spanish Prime Minister José María Aznar, and Portuguese Prime Minister José Manuel Barroso—that Saddam and his two sons were to leave Iraq within forty-eight hours. The Special Forces and CIA infiltrations would take place the night before the ultimatum expired, giving CENTCOM a stealthy head start, but the Baghdad air strikes that were to kick off the main invasion would begin almost two days after time ran out. Even if Saddam yielded, which few if any U.S. officials expected, allied forces would cross into Iraq anyway to stabilize the country and ensure the emplacement of a pro-Western regime. If Saddam refused, like the barbarian tribe in *Gladiator,* the invasion would begin. For Iraqi soldiers who stood and fought, CENTCOM would "unleash hell."

As D-day approached there were no signs that Saddam was interested in going anywhere. On the contrary, the Iraqis were making hasty preparations for war. On the day Bush issued his ultimatum, the Iraqis began to block access to Shatt-al-Arab, flushing from the waterway the small dhows that carried goods for trade to and from Iraq, and threatening to sink them if they refused to leave. The runways at Saddam International Airport on the outskirts of Baghdad were blocked by trucks and defended by antiaircraft guns. The Iraqis had dug hundreds of trenches, filled them with oil, and set some aflame, in an attempt to interfere with American reconnaissance. The Iraqi army was observing radio silence.

Now that it was finally clear to Saddam that war was all but unavoidable, the Iraqi leader held his own meeting with generals and top aides to issue his final instructions. Saddam told his military "to hold the coalition for eight days and leave the rest to him," recalled 'Abdallah al-Mullah Huwaysh, the minister of military industrialization. The mysterious order came as a relief to some of Saddam's military officers. Despite Saddam's earlier revelations that Iraq was bereft of WMD, they concluded that Saddam must have a secret supply of prohibited weapons after all and that the defense of Iraq would not depend entirely on their overmatched, ill-motivated troops.[2]

At the windowless warehouse that served as McKiernan's main intelligence center in Kuwait, Chief Warrant Officer Henry Crowder saw a worrisome sign: images from a Predator drone indicated that seven oil wells in the south were on fire, with flames as high as 100 feet. Crowder had been concentrating on Iraq's southern oilfields for months, mapping the 1,074 oil wells and the all-important gas oil separation plants, pumping stations, and a control center that were vital for processing the crude.[3]

Securing Iraq's infrastructure was one of CENTCOM's top priorities. The Pentagon had promised that the reconstruction of Iraq would be "self-financing," and the preservation of Iraq's oil wealth was the best-prepared and -resourced component of Washington's postwar plan. The United States had received intelligence from sources in Iraq's Oil Ministry that Saddam had no intention of laying waste to the Rumaylah oilfield, the main source of income for a regime that expected to prevail in its test of will with the Bush administration. But some of the CIA contacts had reported that teams of operatives from Iraq's intelligence services had been moving around the area and demolitions were reported to be stored nearby.

Crowder's job was not to divine Iraq's ultimate intentions but to scrutinize the wells, and he was convinced that the Iraqis had rigged some of the wells with explosives. A telltale sign, he informed superiors, was the presence of small flares, which the Iraqis had placed in the oilfields weeks before. Crowder reported that the flares enabled the Iraqis to simulate the burn-off of natural gas from a working well, while temporarily shutting it down to attach explosives and demolition charges. Now Crowder alerted senior intelligence officers that the long anticipated oilfield fires had begun. His alert raced up the chain of command, from Spider Marks and McKiernan to Franks and on to Washington.

That was not the only problem. The Iraqis had two offshore oil terminals, Kaaot and Mabot, from which a group of U.N. oil inspectors had been evacuated. Some of them, secretly working for U.S. intelligence, had reported that Iraqis had recently arrived with mysterious boxes, wires hanging from them. If the Iraqis blew up the platforms, there would be a massive oil spill, spoiling the Persian Gulf and interfering with allied naval operations. CENTCOM had to find a way to prevent any sabotage and rescue the U.S. agents.[4]

Spider Marks, McKiernan's chief intelligence officer, later concluded that the oil well fires were a tactical move that was intended to obscure the battlefield, and not the enactment of a scorched-earth policy. Only a tiny fraction of the wells were on fire—seven—and only thirteen were later discovered to be rigged. Reports of railcars full of explosives being sent south were never validated. The northern oilfields near Kirkuk were not rigged at all. As for the Mabot, Navy SEALs later recovered RPGs, AK-47s, blasting caps, about 200 pounds of explosives, and an Iraqi demolitions expert. The Iraqis, however, had made no attempt to rig any of the explosives. The intelligence that Iraq planned to destroy its oilfields was in fact worst-case intelligence. Interrogations of senior Iraqi officials and officers after the fall of Baghdad also revealed no plan to destroy Iraq's oilfields or infrastructure. On the contrary, Saddam and his closest aides had calculated that the U.S. attack would be temporary and would stop short of Baghdad.

There was, however, no way for the United States to know that. Determined to head off a possible scorched-earth policy that would deprive the new Iraq of its major source of revenue, Franks wanted to advance the attack. The timing of the assault was critical and extremely sensitive. There were no command-wide video conferences on this issue. The matter was to be handled with encrypted phone calls and personal visits. Franks asked McKiernan if the land attack could begin forty-eight hours early. The Marines would take the oilfields, and Navy SEALs would take care of the offshore terminals and the nearby oil installations on the Faw Peninsula. Army troops would begin their thrust to Baghdad. After checking with Jim Conway and Scott Wallace, McKiernan determined that the attack could be moved up twenty-four hours with an acceptable degree of risk.[5] Franks then flew to Saudi Arabia to consult with Moseley, who argued, however, that it would be hard to advance A-day by even twenty-four hours. The air battle was tightly choreographed and depended on American planes coming from all over the world—the United States, Diego Garcia, the United Kingdom. There were too many moving pieces to change the plan now.

Franks agreed to leave the air campaign on its previous schedule. The

Special Operations infiltrations would take place that evening as scheduled. The main land attack would be moved up by a day and would start on the evening of March 20. The air strikes would begin as planned on the evening of March 21. G-day had been moved ahead of A-day. In the lead-up to the war, Colonel Kevin Benson, McKiernan's chief planner, had argued that the best way to catch the Iraqis off guard would be to launch the ground attack before beginning the air campaign. Events and the inflexibility of the air campaign had combined to produce a strategic innovation.

The war had a dynamic of its own now. There was an escalation of moves and countermoves, as CENTCOM and the Iraqis tried to gauge each other's intentions. With the invasion fast approaching, the White House had arranged for a classified video conference between President Bush and his senior commanders. That day, Bush had officially notified Congress that he was prepared to use force, citing Iraq's alleged support for terrorists and its suspected caches of WMD. The video conference was one last opportunity for the commander-in-chief to talk directly to the generals and admirals who would take the nation to war—and for the White House to document that the invasion plan had the support of the military. One by one, the president asked the air, land, naval, and special operations commanders if they had everything they needed. Cheney, Rumsfeld, Rice, and Powell were with the president as he made his final check. The tug-of-war over the TPFDL and combat service support was left unmentioned. With war just days away, each commander expressed confidence that he could do the job. McKiernan was succinct: "Mr. President, there are 140,000 soldiers and Marines trained, prepared, and ready here in the desert of Kuwait. We are prepared to execute our mission to remove Saddam Hussein from power."[6]

That evening, a Pentagon aide passed a message to a senior military public affairs officer in the Gulf from Torie Clarke, the Pentagon spokesperson. POTUS, the president of the United States, wanted the military to facilitate three types of news reports: of Iraqis celebrating the arrival of the victorious American troops, of allied shipments of humanitarian assistance to the Iraqi population, and of the newly discovered arsenals of WMD. The White House seemed secure in its cause and confident of victory. Bush was convinced that grateful Iraqis and disclosed WMD would provide the White House with the ultimate photo op.[7]

The administration's allies in Washington were calm and confident. In a conference call with a Wall Street firm, Richard Perle predicted a quick war and an easy occupation. "There is no plan for an extended occupation in Iraq," Perle assured the investors. "The size of the force to maintain order will be much smaller than people believe."

The Iraqis, Perle said, would greet the Americans as liberators, and government functions would be turned over as quickly as possible. As for the Iraqi army, secret police, and intelligence services, "there will be a process akin to de-Nazification after World War II, in which we will attempt to identify and root out people who cannot be allowed to remain in authority."

The president's decision to invade would soon be vindicated. "There is no question that we will find weapons of mass destruction."[8]

Late that evening, the officers in Moseley's air-war command learned that the conflict was approaching faster than they had expected. The command had devised a plan to keep a B-52 with conventional cruise missiles on call in case an opportunity emerged to strike at Saddam and his top lieutenants. When Colonel Mace Carpenter, Moseley's chief of strategy, asked his boss if the plane needed to be ready that night, he was told that Franks had given explicit instructions that there were to be no significant air strikes for two more days.

To confirm, Carpenter checked on the intelligence from Washington. Franks's guidance, they learned, had been dramatically overtaken by events. It looked like the Air Force would have a Baghdad mission after all. At 10:00 p.m., Carpenter informed Moseley that that there was, in fact, a requirement to launch a mission, and it needed to be done in just six hours.[9]

The CIA was 99.9 percent sure that it had located Saddam and both of his sons, Moseley told his staff. The three were said to be meeting at Dora Farms, a compound outside Baghdad often frequented by Saddam and his family. CENTCOM was accustomed to receiving all sorts of tips regarding the whereabouts of the Iraqi leader, but this one was extraordinarily specific. Bush's forty-eight-hour ultimatum was due to expire at 4:00 a.m. Dora Farms would be a tempting target for the White House— too tempting to pass up.

Cruise missiles, which, in addition to the Air Force, the Navy flotilla in the Persian Gulf had in abundance, could level the buildings of the compound. But there appeared to be more to the site. Gene Renuart, the Air

Force major general who served as Tommy Franks's chief operations officer, had studied the satellite photos of the site and was convinced that he
had detected the telltale signs of an underground command post: sod that
seemed to be laid in a man-made pattern, as if to cover a buried object.
There was no way that cruise missiles could take out an underground
sanctuary. A squadron of F-117 Stealth Fighters, however, had been deployed at Al Udeid in Qatar, where it was being readied for its starring
role in the A-day attack; its ordnance included bunker-busting bombs. Of
the allied aircraft, the Stealth Fighters had the best chance to carry out the
sneak attack. Instead of waiting for two days Moseley would have to
strike in a matter of hours.

Moseley began to sketch out a plan. There was a name for the type of
attack Moseley was preparing: the Air Force called it a TST, or time sensitive target. Since the Persian Gulf War, the Air Force had worked hard to
compress the period it took to locate, target, and strike an "emerging target." Moseley had a cell of TST planners in his command center: officers
whose shoulder patch featured the Grim Reaper with his scythe. Now
Moseley and his planners had the most important emerging target of
them all in their sights.

To pull off the mission, the planes would have to fly into the teeth of
the Iraqi defenses. The Baghdad "Super MEZ" was heavily protected,
chock-full of surface-to-air missile sites and antiaircraft artillery. Thanks
to air strikes carried out under Southern Focus, Iraq's air defenses had
taken a real shellacking in the south. But there had been no effort to
weaken the air defenses in and around Baghdad. The stealthy F-117s were
hard to detect on radar, but they were not invulnerable, and certainly not
invisible. An F-117 had been shot down in the Kosovo war, and Air Force
intelligence suspected that the Iraqis and the Serbs might have compared
notes on their American adversary. Sensitive to the F-117 being put in
harm's way, Moseley had ordered that the result of the top secret inquiry
into the shoot-down of the F-117 be briefed to key officers in his command, including the British.

Moseley was determined to give the F-117s as much protection as possible. Marine and Navy EA-6B electronic warfare aircraft would fly north
into Iraq to jam Iraqi radars. F-16CJs, equipped with HARM antiradiation missiles, would accompany the F-117s part of the way to strike
Iraqi air defense radars that sought to illuminate the F-117s. Moseley figured there was a chance that F-117s might just catch the Iraqis off balance. For several nights, he had been putting hundreds of aircraft aloft to

get the Iraqis accustomed to the presence of a vast air armada and mask the preparations for an imminent attack. With all the air activity, and the orbits allied planes would be flying over western Iraq—as the Special Forces infiltrated—the Iraqis might not notice the two F-117s shooting north toward their capital until it was too late. But timing was a problem: the sun would rise in Baghdad at 5:35. Painted black, the F-117s were designed for night operations and were clearly visible in daytime. They would have to get in and out before it got light.

Shortly after 3:00 a.m., Moseley received a call from Dick Myers, the chairman of the Joint Chiefs of Staff and a fellow Air Force general. Myers wanted to know whether Moseley had a plan to deal with Dora Farms. Moseley outlined the plan to Myers, but Myers did not have the last word. That would come from President Bush.

Bush had been meeting with Cheney, Rumsfeld, Rice, and Tenet, who had delivered the intelligence on Saddam's suspected whereabouts. Striking now was a gamble. If Saddam was not at Dora Farms, the United States, in effect, would be serving notice that a major air and ground attack would soon be under way. The president saw himself as a bold and decisive leader, and it was a risk he was prepared to take. Thirty minutes later, Myers called from the Oval Office. It was the moment of decision.

"The president has one question," Myers said. "Can you get the pilots back?"

"I can get them to the target," Moseley replied. "I don't know if I can get them back."

Myers relayed Moseley's assessment to Bush and then relayed the president's response. "Strike," Myers said.

Moseley had a question: "Are you going to call the CINC or do you want me to?" Franks was aware of the focus on Dora Farms, but the White House decision-making was moving so fast that there had not been time to include him in the final deliberations. Now that the decision to start the war had been made somebody needed to tell the CENTCOM commander. It was left to Moseley to pass the word to his boss.[10]

At Franks's headquarters in Qatar, there was a sense of expectation. McKiernan had made preparations to fly a mobile command post to the Baghdad International Airport in C-17 transport planes if the regime collapsed quickly. That contingency included well-rehearsed plans for Dell Dailey's special operators to initially secure the airport, reinforced by a brigade from the 82nd Airborne Division, heavy-rigged to jump with equipment right onto the runway. Renuart told the staff to make sure the plans were in order. If Saddam was killed and his regime toppled, the commanders wanted to establish a presence in the capital right away. It looked like CENTCOM might end the war with one blow before it had really begun.

At Al Udeid, Lieutenant Colonel Matt McKeon was in a mad scramble to prepare for the mission. The squadron had received advance warning the day before that CENTCOM was tracking some "high-value targets." But the squadron had not been told what the targets were. All they knew was that a bunker might be involved. They had no idea the F-117s would be called into action so soon until an earnest aide rushed into the Al Udeid chow hall at 1:30 a.m. with news of a possible mission. Al Udeid was teeming with aircraft. The sprawling base, built by the Qataris at enormous expense, was now home to U.S. F-15Es, British Tornados, Australian F-18s, and even Navy planes that wanted to avoid the long return flights to their carriers. There were more than 5,000 military personnel and more than 100 fighters on the ramp, but tonight the starring role would be played by two F-117s from McKeon's Black Sheep Squadron.

McKeon had a new weapon to bring to the fight, though no one in the squadron had actually dropped this latest addition to the F-117's arsenal. During the 1991 war, the F-117s had relied on laser-guided bombs, which required the pilot to keep his laser on the target and worked well as long as there were no clouds or humidity to interfere. But this time the F-117s had the EGBU-27. The 2,000-pound bunker-busting bomb steered itself toward its target using an advanced guidance system, which relied on updates from satellites. If the weather was clear, the pilot would use the system to guide the weapon toward the target and shine a laser on the precise point where the bomb was to land. If clouds rolled in and it was not possible to use the laser, the pilot could rely solely on the guidance system. Either way, the system was highly accurate. It was a quantum improvement that gave the Stealth Fighters all-weather capability in the upcoming war.

Two of the new bombs had been loaded onto an F-117 just hours prior to the order to strike so that the squadron pilots could rehearse the process of loading the target coordinates in the weapon and determining how the bomb interacted with the control system in the plane. To use the weapon most effectively on heavily defended and fortified targets, each F-117 pilot needed to drop two bombs at once. That way they would not have to double back to restrike the target or send in additional planes to finish the job. The tactic had been devised just a month before by Lieutenant Colonel Charlie Langlais, an F-117 pilot who had been dispatched to Moseley's command center to help plan the air war. Before Langlais's tactic could be used, weapons testers in the United States needed to conduct an actual drop to verify that the bombs would not collide when dropped simultaneously, an event that could blast the aircraft out of the sky or, at a minimum, frustrate the entire mission. After repeated delays, the first and only test had finally occurred earlier that day. McKeon had learned of the results in a terse e-mail: "Go for it. Paperwork to follow."

When McKeon called Major Sam Hinote, the squadron's liaison officer at Moseley's headquarters, to get more information on the operation, Hinote told him that Moseley was on the line with the White House. "This thing is going to happen, get 'em airborne quick," Hinote said.

During the Gulf War, the F-117 commanders had been given twelve hours to brief the pilots, program the targeting data into the plane's computer, and otherwise get their pilots ready for their mission. Now, the squadron was being asked to execute a risky mission in a fraction of the time from a cold start. The flurry of activity on the F-117 parking ramp looked more like an aircraft carrier deck in the heat of battle than the methodical preparation the Stealth squadrons had been accustomed to.

Racing the clock, McKeon ordered a full-court press. Maintenance crews rushed to top off the planes with fuel, check the radar absorbent material, and deliver an additional set of bombs from the weapons storehouse across the base, a process that would take at least forty minutes. On the operations side, Major Don Cornwell and others, who worked in the squadron's mission planning cell, pulled together the targeting and other data the pilots needed; the squadron was still waiting to receive the coordinates for the bunker.

McKeon picked two of his most experienced pilots to fly the mission: Lieutenant Colonel Dave Toomey, the squadron's director of operations, and Major Mark Hoehn. Both were combat veterans who were told to collect their gear and get to the jets ASAP. The information they needed to conduct the mission would be run out to their planes. McKeon dispatched Major Steven Ankerstar to the operations center for the F-15E wing, which oversaw all of the aircraft operations at Al Udeid. If the Black Sheep were to start the war that night, the operations center needed to be brought into the loop.

All of a sudden, the can-do mission seemed to be mission impossible. When Ankerstar outlined the plan to Colonel Daryl Roberson, the chief operations deputy for the wing at Al Udeid, the colonel questioned whether it could be carried out expeditiously. Baghdad was one hour ahead of the time at Al Udeid, and to avoid being silhouetted in the dawn sky and becoming easy pickings for the Iraqi air defenses, the pilots were told they had to strike their target by 5:30 a.m.

Further complicating the picture, the most direct route cut through Saudi Arabia, and nobody had cleared that flight pattern with the Saudis. Two Marine EA-6B jamming aircraft that were to accompany the F-117s into Iraq were to take off from Prince Sultan Air Base near Riyadh, as was the aerial refueling tanker that was to support the F-117s and the two F-16CJ planes that were to blast any Iraqi air defense radars that threatened the mission. But while the Saudis were happy to allow the Americans to run the air war from the command center at Prince Sultan and to dispatch aircraft that would facilitate the strike, they drew the line at launching bomb droppers from their territory. It was a specious distinction, but one that the Americans were bound to honor. The F-117s would have to fly around Saudi Arabia, which would lengthen the flight time by twenty minutes. After adding a fudge factor, Ankerstar reported that the attack would have to be delayed by forty minutes.

The adjustment would not be as simple as it sounded. The F-117 strikes were carefully synchronized with the Navy's cruise missile strike. The initial response from Moseley's command center was that the Navy strike could not be held back; the F-117 mission would have to be canceled. Finally, the word came down that the F-117 attack would in fact be delayed by forty-five minutes. The Stealth Fighters were to drop their bombs at 5:30. A massive salvo of cruise missiles would follow five minutes later. To meet the schedule, the attacking F-117s, Ram 1 and Ram 2, would receive the final go-ahead in flight.

An officer was sent to the control tower at Al Udeid to tell the Qataris that two aircraft would be taking off. They would not be squawking electronic Identify Friend or Foe signals, would be taxiing and flying with their lights off, and would not need any help from Qatar's air traffic controllers. There was a momentary hitch when one Qatari, who did not get the word, queried the F-117s and a pilot responded, but by 3:38 Qatari time the pilots were aloft.

Brigadier General Eric Rosborg, the F-15 wing commander who was in charge of allied aircraft at Al Udeid, had been working the day shift and was sleeping in his quarters, unaware of the frenzied final planning, when an aide woke him up and told him two aircraft had just taken off on a surprise mission to strike Saddam. "From here?" he asked incredulously.[11]

Toomey and Hoehn flew north, maneuvered their black jets to take gas from the tanker, and then streaked toward Baghdad in a race with the dawn. As the pilots approached the capital, an indicator light in Toomey's plane warned that the satellite guidance system for one of the new EGBU-27 bombs had gone dead. Toomey pulled out the manual, rebooted the computerized guidance system, and hoped for the best. Stealth operations left no opportunity for communications to a fellow pilot or to the home base in Qatar. Toomey and Hoehn were on their own.[12]

At its command center in Bahrain the Navy rushed to hold up its end of the mission. Vice Admiral Tim Keating had spent the day touring the three battle groups in the Persian Gulf and keeping up morale. Holding up a folder for top secret documents, Keating told the sailors that he had the classified plans that would have allied jets and missiles hurtling toward Iraq to unseat Saddam. The tension on the ships was palpable. Only Keating knew the folder was empty. The former aviator was engaging in a little theatrics to keep spirits high and convey the reality of a fast approaching war.

Keating had returned to find out that American intelligence thought it had located "Rocket One," Navy jargon for Saddam. He had then ordered up a salvo of forty-five Tomahawk land attack missiles. It was an enormous barrage—each TLAM, as the Navy called them, carried a 1,000-pound warhead, guaranteed to pulverize every structure in the vicinity. What Keating did not factor in was the seemingly inexplicable possibility that someone in the Navy's worldwide communications network would use this moment to take the extremely high frequency system down for routine maintenance. EHF was the most efficient way for Navy headquarters to transmit the targeting data that had to be loaded into the missiles. Keating had no choice but to go to the Inmarsat satellite backup system, which was a far slower way of sending the information. The targeting data was passed in time to launch thirty-nine of the forty-five missiles that had been planned. Some of the missiles, however, would arrive several minutes late.[13] Once the missiles were under way there was no recalling them. The decapitation strike was on. The Stealth Fighters and the Tomahawks would deliver a one-two punch. At Prince Sultan, Moseley was confident. "We're about to send him some bundles of love," he told his staff.

Back at Al Udeid, McKeon and his officers waited to see if they had struck their mark. Fox News had a crew in Baghdad and the officers at the wing operations center at Al Udeid monitored the broadcast for any clues about the success of the impending attack. About five minutes before the F-117s were to drop their bombs, Ankerstar was startled to see that the streetlights in Baghdad were turned off. A wave of anxiety swept through the operations center: had the Iraqis begun to black out the capital? If the Iraqis had detected the attack, they would fill the air with antiaircraft artillery, fire their surface-to-air missiles, and hope for a lucky hit. Finally, it occurred to Ankerstar that there was another explanation: the sun was coming up and the streetlights were timed to go off at dawn.[14]

As the officers counted down to the strike, Fox News went to a commercial break. By the time the broadcast resumed the strike had occurred, the TLAMs had come in, and Iraqi air defense units were firing wildly into the air. While the squadron waited for Toomey and Hoehn, a report trickled in that an F-117 had been hit and was diverting to a base in Kuwait. A contingency plan to land in Kuwait in the event of low fuel had been misperceived as a mishap. It was another case of what the military called rumint: rumor and garbled communications masquerading as intelligence.

Hoehn was the first one back. He flew over the base before landing. Toomey landed about twenty minutes later. Rosborg and hundreds of pilots, mechanics, and bomb loaders came out to greet them, some carrying cameras. The F-117 area was normally off limits to other personnel, but this was an exception. People were celebrating as if the United States had just won the war. The pilots were asked if they had finished off Saddam. Toomey and Hoehn were instant heroes. They could not say for sure if they had gotten Saddam, but reconnaissance photos showed that they had dropped four bombs precisely on target.

At the air war command center in Saudi Arabia, Moseley was ecstatic that the F-117s had carried out their mission and returned safely. The F-117 pilots had not talked on the radio in flight, following procedure for flying undetected into enemy territory. The first clue that Moseley received that everything had gone as expected came when the black jets returned to the refueling tankers. "Bitchin', dudes, bitchin'," Moseley exclaimed. Vice Admiral David C. Nichols, Moseley's chief deputy, quipped that A-day had just gone from 770 sorties to 2. It looked like the Air Force might have won the war.

Forty-five minutes after the attack, Bush addressed the nation from the Oval Office. "On my orders, coalition forces have begun striking targets of military importance to undermine Saddam Hussein's ability to wage war," the president said. "Now that the conflict has begun, the only way to limit its duration is to apply decisive force."[15]

Several hours later Saddam Hussein appeared on television very much alive, wearing an army uniform and a beret and fulminating against the American attack. Saddam spoke for seven minutes, wore glasses, and read from a notepad. It was not clear to the United States whether the address was live or taped or whether Saddam had used a double. Among the reports filtering back to CENTCOM was one that Saddam had been badly injured and pulled from the wreckage, his face covered with an oxygen mask.

After the fall of Baghdad, U.S. forces examined the Dora Farms site. There was no underground bunker and no evidence that Saddam Hussein had been there. Ram 1 and Ram 2 had bombed an empty field. The suggestion that a surgically adjusted look-alike had delivered the address also turned out to be lore. There was a simpler explanation for the glasses. Abd Hameed, Saddam's personal secretary, who was apprehended after the collapse of the regime, told U.S interrogators the Iraqi side of the story: the Iraqi leader had not been to Dora Farms since 1995 and was nowhere near the site on the night of the attack. After the strike, Saddam showed up at Hameed's home, which was equipped with a satellite dish for receiving international news broadcasts. Saddam and Hameed then went together to a safe house near the upscale Al-Mansur neighborhood in Baghdad. Saddam, Hameed explained, wrote his speech by hand and ordered that it be videotaped. Usually, Saddam's speeches were printed in large text so he could easily read them. But no printer was available, so Saddam put on his glasses to read his small handwriting. The tape was then sent to Muhammad Said al-Sahaf at the Ministry of Information to be edited and broadcast.[16] There was no doubt that the F-117s had performed exemplarily, but they had been sent in harm's way to bomb a target that did not exist.

As the war was waged, allied planes would carry out strikes against other time sensitive targets, including Chemical Ali. But not one of the top 200 figures in the regime was killed by an air strike. The United States's reconnaissance, communications, and precision weapons gave it the capability to strike enemy leaders, and to strike quickly. But such attacks would be only as good as the intelligence they were based on, and as the opening night of the war demonstrated, that intelligence was often not reliable.

. . .

At Franks's headquarters, CENTCOM felt that, if nothing else, it had grabbed the initiative and rocked the Iraqi regime on its heels. Soon the regime struck back. Shortly after 1:00 p.m., a Seersucker missile came streaking from Iraq's Faw Peninsula. The Chinese-made weapon was a sea-skimming antiship cruise missile, which carried a massive 1,000-pound warhead and was the bane of navies around the world. Flying at 100 feet, the missile clipped the northern edge of the Persian Gulf, crossed into Kuwait, and landed at the doorstep of Camp Commando, the head-quarters in northern Kuwait for the Marine Expeditionary Force that Lieutenant General James Conway was preparing to lead into Iraq. The shock wave from the massive explosion kicked up a cloud of sand. Marines grabbed their gas masks and put on their chemical-protective MOPP suits, fearing that they might be under a chemical or biological at-tack. There were no U.S. casualties, but the Iraqis had sent their own sig-nal. They had mounted their own decapitation attack. It was the first time that a modern cruise missile had been used against a land target, and the missile had flown so low to the ground that it avoided detection.

That same day the Iraqis launched an Ababil-100 surface-to-surface missile at Thunder Road, the assembly area for the 101st Airborne Divi-sion in northern Kuwait, and one at McKiernan's headquarters at Camp Doha, the site from which the allies were to run the land war. The missiles were intercepted and destroyed by Patriots. The episode at Camp Doha was what the military liked to call with some irony a "significant emo-tional event." Powerful loudspeakers, dubbed "giant voice," broadcast: "Lightning, Lightning, Lightning"—the code name for an incoming mis-sile attack. Patriot missiles roared overhead. Huge explosions shook the camp and debris from the Patriots and Iraqi missiles fell on the metal roofs of the warehouses. McKiernan and his staff took to conducting their meetings in chemical protective suits and gas masks.

The Americans had anticipated that the Iraqis would turn to their ar-senal of surface-to-surface missiles. In the Persian Gulf War, the Iraqis had lobbed Scud missiles at Saudi Arabia and Israel. The missiles were not very accurate, but they did not need to be to punish the Saudis for hosting the Americans or to put pressure on Israel to enter the war. A Scud missile that landed in Khobar, Saudi Arabia, killed twenty-eight American troops and wounded ninety-eight, which made it the largest single U.S. casualty toll of the Gulf War. The U.S. had learned the hard way that Scud missile firings could not be stopped by airpower and Patriot missiles alone. British and American Special Operations Forces had eventually been sent into the fight. Still, there was not a single confirmed case of a Scud missile launcher being destroyed during the war.

CENTCOM planned to do better this time, by infiltrating Iraq with Special Operations Forces so they could direct American air strikes against any and every suspected missile launcher in the west. For months, in fact, the commandos and pilots had secretly trained together at Nellis Air Force Base. But this time the Iraqis were not hiding missiles in the western desert or even using Scuds. The Iraqis had two new systems: the Ababil-100, which was a solid-fueled missile, and the Al-Samoud, a liquid-fueled rocket. Both were mobile and the Iraqis had hidden them in and around Basra and north along Highway 6. The region was filled with palm groves and buildings, excellent terrain for hiding mobile missiles.

Much of the Iraqi army was also stacked up along Highway 6, making it virtually off limits for the lightly armed special forces teams. The Ababil-100s and Al-Samouds were short-range missiles, but they could reach most of Kuwait from their sanctuaries in southeastern Iraq. Pressing Seersuckers into service was a new twist. The Iraqis were confident they had enough cover not to have to wait until nightfall to fire, as they had in the Gulf War. They were firing their missiles during the day. And they clearly had good intelligence on the whereabouts of their foe. It was easy enough for Iraq's agents to get the precise coordinates of the principal American assembly areas and bases. Any GPS device, even the Thuraya satellite telephones that were commonly used in the Middle East, would do. Instead of lobbing missiles at cities, as they had done during previous conflicts, the Iraqis were targeting military installations and command centers, some of which had only recently been established.

Moseley had F-16s up, looking for the Iraqi missile launchers, but they were notoriously difficult to find. CENTCOM had planned to combine its air and ground forces to suppress the Iraqi missiles but now it would have to rely on airpower alone—all over again. There was no quick fix for the Iraqi missile threat.

At his headquarters at Camp Doha, the burden for holding the line fell on Brigadier General Howard Bromberg, the head of the 32nd Army Air and Missile Defense Command. The coalition had stationed forty-nine Patriot batteries throughout the region, and Bromberg controlled most of them. The Camp Doha base and other critical facilities in Kuwait were defended by the PAC-3, the most modern of the Patriot systems. It used an advanced seeker to intercept and destroy the warhead on an enemy missile by smashing into it. Other nations had to make do with the PAC-2, still a major improvement over the Patriots used in the Gulf War. Some of the PAC-2s were equipped with "guidance enhanced missiles," which had an exploding warhead and homed in on the front end of the enemy missile, destroying or deflecting it. (Israel was also defended by U.S. PAC-2 batteries, which were deployed under the guise of a military exercise. The batteries, which supplemented Israel's Arrow antimissile system, were not directly under Bromberg's command. Major General Chuck Simpson, a U.S. Air Force officer, was based in Israel and briefed Israeli Prime Minister Ariel Sharon on CENTCOM's war plan on March 10. The briefing, Patriot batteries, and Scud-hunting missions planned for western Iraq were part of the Bush administration's strategy to keep Israel out of the war.)[17]

For early warning, Bromberg drew on an elaborate surveillance network. An Aegis guided missile destroyer, the USS *Higgins,* which had a powerful phased array radar, had been moved into the Persian Gulf. Cobra Judy, a sea-based system that had been used during the Cold War to monitor Soviet ICBM tests, had also been quietly moved to the Gulf. Defense Support Program satellites that detected the plume from ballistic missile launches were linked to the system as well. Bromberg arranged for an early warning message to be sent out, including on beepers that had been given to top Kuwaiti officials and to the American ambassador.

The early warning network had its troubles. The Cobra Judy and Aegis radars proved to be so powerful that they interfered with other military radar and electronic systems, as well as simple cell phone calls, and had to move farther from shore. The Ababils and Al-Samouds were slower and did not break up in flight, as did the Scuds, making them easier targets. The burn time of the Ababils and Al-Samouds was too short to register on U.S. spy satellites. None of the reconnaissance systems detected the sea-skimming Seersuckers, which the U.S. had not anticipated would be fired at land targets. But the Patriots proved their ability to neutralize Iraq's short-range missiles.[18]

The first day of the war had been a draw. The two sides had mounted decapitation strikes and exchanged punches, but none of them had landed. The big question was how the Iraqis would respond once the land war was under way. As the land forces prepared to lurch forward, McKiernan issued a classified proclamation to rouse the troops for battle and as-

sure them of the righteousness of the cause. There was no longer any alternative to force, McKiernan wrote. Saddam had refused to cooperate
with the United States or abandon his weapons programs. The land forces
would fight to remove him from power and help welcoming Iraqis. But
there had been one encouraging sign for the Americans. On March 19,
Jim Conway, the Marine commander, had seen a picture of an Iraqi formation that was taken by a Pioneer drone. The vehicles were lined up in
formation. Marine intelligence analysts thought this could mean that the
Iraqis were getting ready to capitulate. Conway held up the photo in a
video phone call with McKiernan. It seemed to be what CENTCOM was
looking for. The next day would tell.

CHAPTER 10

The Opening Gambit

When McKiernan finalized the plans to move up the ground attack, he had scheduled the invasion to begin at dawn on March 21. The land war commander wanted to keep the "friction" of war to a minimum. Attacking into Iraq was complicated enough without having to maneuver around the Iraqi oil infrastructure and through unfamiliar terrain at night. Though the lead reconnaissance units would cross over the border in darkness, the main attack, McKiernan's order noted, would be BMNT—beginning morning nautical twilight.

The vital mission of securing the Rumaylah oilfield went to Jim Mattis, who led the 1st Marine Division. A lifelong bachelor who wore glasses and prided himself on his knowledge of military history, Mattis had a reputation as a sort of warrior monk. Jim Conway, the commander of the 1st Marine Expeditionary Force, Mattis's direct superior and a former football player, towered above the short and wiry two-star general, but no Marine officer was more impatient or aggressive. Mattis had made his mark in Afghanistan when he led a Marine task force based on ships in the Arabian Sea 400 miles to Khandahar; he was determined to shine in Iraq as well. When the salty-tongued Mattis learned that the Running Start iteration of the invasion plan had given the mission of seizing the southern oilfields to the Army's 3rd Infantry Division, he muttered at one planning session that he felt like a towel boy at a whorehouse.

As McKiernan's Cobra II plan had developed, there was no danger that the Marines would miss out on the action. Mattis's division was to seize the Rumaylah oilfields, roll north across the Euphrates, protect the V Corps's right flank, and, ultimately, drive toward the Iraqi capital. From

McKiernan's perspective, the Army's V Corps was still the main attack force, but Mattis planned to get to Baghdad and to get there fast.

For a service that had long been tethered to the sea, Mattis's mission was an ambitious undertaking. Mattis would be leading more than 20,000 Marines and 5,000 vehicles over desert, half-paved roads, and through a fertile crescent replete with palm groves, marshes, and canals. The 1st Marine Division had a long and illustrious history dating back to Guadalcanal and the difficult days in the South Pacific during the Second World War. Its logo was a blue diamond, which featured the numeral 1 and the Southern Cross; its radio call sign for its field headquarters was "Blue Diamond." Now Mattis planned to add another chapter to the service's saga: the division's attack north would be the longest Marine land operation since First Lieutenant Presley Neville O'Bannon led a force of Marines and other troops 600 miles across the Libyan desert to attack a fortress at Derna, Tripoli, in 1805.

Mattis referred to the first phase of his operation as the "opening gambit." The goal was to defeat or accept the capitulation of enemy forces in and around the Rumaylah oilfields, while securing intact the five gas oil separation plants and the pumping station near Zubayr, which the Marines had nicknamed the "Crown Jewel." To accomplish their mission, the Marines did not need to secure the almost 1,100 wells in the Rumaylah field, but they did need to control the infrastructure that was vital for processing and transporting Iraq's crude. The mission required a delicate balance of restraint, firepower, and maneuvering—all the more so since the Iraqis had moved troops and artillery near some of the oil works. The British 1st Armored Division, also under Conway's command, would then relieve the Marines in the Rumaylah field and isolate Basra, Iraq's second-largest city, which would enable Mattis to resume his march north. While Blue Diamond was attacking into Iraq, British Royal Marines would seize the oil infrastructure on the Faw Peninsula.

As he pushed north, Mattis was intensely eager to get to Baghdad. For months, Mattis and his officers had tried to think of all the angles. To choreograph the assault, the division bought 6,000 multicolored Lego blocks, representing every unit and vehicle in the division, and laid them out in a parking lot at Camp Pendleton. Mattis and his officers had brainstormed with the colored blocks, done numberless sand table exercises and computer simulations, and calibrated the logistics. To understand the terrain and the difficulties of maneuvering in Iraq, Mattis had studied intelligence from JSTARS surveillance planes, reconnaissance photos, and *The Siege,* a history of the British division that sought to march on Kut in World War I, but which ended up surrendering there. The book was required reading for senior Marine officers.

To keep up the pace with the ever-lengthening supply lines, Mattis ordered his planners to go "logistic lite." The regiments would have to operate at times with less than the customary three days' supply of food, fuel, and ammunition, and would bring along only the bare essentials. There would be no cots, no sleeping bags, and each Marine would have just one extra charcoal-lined MOPP suit to protect against chemical or germ weapons. It was decreed that there would be one funnel for every four Marines to ensure that they did not spill any water when filling their canteens and CamelBaks (water bladders), and the Marines were warned in advance that they should eat every ounce of their MRE field rations, as there might be days when they received only one. Units were outfitted with fuel test kits, as the division planned to use as much fuel as it could capture. Fuel bladders were hung on M1 tanks and gypsy-racks bolted to Humvees to expand their cargo capacity. Vehicles had to be scrupulously maintained, since it was doubtful that the division would quickly receive the parts it would need to fix them on the move. Logistical support units were considered combat units and were expected to defend themselves.

Once it crossed into Iraq, the division planned to conserve artillery rounds by relying more on the firepower provided by the 340 combat aircraft in Major General James Amos's Third Marine Air Wing. Blue Diamond, Mattis boasted, would be the most "air-centric" division in Marine history. C-130s of the Air Wing would also be a major source of resupply en route. The standard battle formation for a Marine division is to carry out the attack with two regiments, holding one in reserve. Ignoring the manual, Mattis planned to attack with all three of his regiments and use Marine air support as a reserve.

To deal with the risk of enemy agents infiltrating his division once it had crossed into Iraq—U.S. intelligence had reported, inaccurately, that Iraqi Special Forces had obtained U.S. military uniforms and planned to sneak in among U.S. formations—Mattis ordered his Marines to grow mustaches while still in Kuwait, though some were too young to do so. Mattis knew that mustaches were de rigueur in the Iraqi military—after the fashion of their leader. Iraqi agents would assume that they would fit right in. But before crossing into the country, Mattis planned to order his troops to shave off their facial hair, which would facilitate the unmasking of any Iraqi agents trying to infiltrate his division.[1]

With the war around the corner, the division's officers rushed to complete the seemingly endless list of last-minute preparations, which included scrounging up extra doses of doxycycline, the antibiotic of choice to combat anthrax, and freeing the 30,000 respirators, vital for coping with the noxious oil fumes and threat of poison gas, that were somehow still stuck in Kuwaiti customs.

But the most serious issue facing him, Mattis felt, was the quality of U.S. intelligence about Iraqi forces—not so much about where Iraqi units were, but who the enemy commanders were, where they had studied, what their previous military experience had been, and what decisions they had made on the battlefield. Mattis had ordered a select few of his officers to pull together everything they could get their hands on from intelligence channels, but they had come up with precious little. In the twelve years since the Gulf War, the United States had conducted regular air patrols over southern and northern Iraq and regularly bombed the country. The U.S. emphasis on high-tech satellite and other reconnaissance systems and the dearth of reliable agents within the country had left a gaping hole in the area that Mattis believed mattered most.

"In trying to map out the opposition's reactions we were largely relegated to OSINT [open source intelligence] sources and rank speculation based on our own perceptions of the battlefield to make our assessments," Mattis wrote in an internal report to Conway after the war. "There was no available intelligence on the opposition commanders' personalities, education, decision-making styles or previous experience. Lacking this information we were left to guess what we would do in their place. This met with predictable results."[2]

After a steady stream of CIA reports about possible surrenders, Jim Conway believed there was an excellent chance many of the units in the south would not fight. "We were led to believe that a major portion of some of those divisions would capitulate," Conway recalled after the war. On the outside chance that he could get the Iraqi 51st Mechanized Division facing the Marines across the border to capitulate, Mattis sent a message to its commander through the CIA, asking him to meet at the border and arrange for the surrender of his forces or face destruction. There was no response.

The Marines would take no chances. U.S. intelligence was also reporting that Chemical Ali had taken up position in the south and had received authorization to use chemical weapons. Gas masks dangling by their sides, the Marines planned to cross into Iraq ready to fight in bulky chemical suits.[3] Blue Diamond knew the "opening gambit" backward and forward and was ready to go. Mattis had his own radio call, which reflected the confusion he hoped to engender in the enemy ranks: "Chaos."

Major Ron Spears, the intelligence officer for Regimental Combat Team 7, was monitoring the latest data on the enemy on the day of the attack when he was summoned by Colonel Steve Hummer, his commanding officer. Hummer wanted to know what Spears had on Iraqi T-72 tanks. Like a good intelligence analyst, Spears had been going over the intelligence on southern Iraq with a fine-tooth comb. Iraq's 51st Mechanized Division was defending opposite the Marines with units along Highway 8 and Highway 31. A brigade from Iraq's 18th Infantry Division had moved into the south Rumaylah oilfields, supported by several batteries of artillery. Iraq's 6th Armored Division, which had more than 100 older T-54 and T-55 tanks, defended the approaches to Basra. And the 11th Infantry Division was dispersed along the marshes to the east of Nasiriyah. The weather had been poor for several days, which made reconnaissance difficult, but none of these units had T-72s in their inventory.

"Walk with me," Hummer said as he led Spears outside, where a half-dozen small trucks with M240G machine guns were parked—the sort of "technical vehicles" the CIA paramilitary forces favored. A CIA operative was there, along with a former Iraqi army colonel, one of the agency's contacts. The Iraqi gave up some details. A brigade or two of T-72 tanks, as many as 180, had secretly taken up positions near the border. The T-72s were from the Medina Division and had been brought by train to Zubayr and then driven through the farmland at night to avoid detection. One brigade of T-72s was arrayed along Highway 31 between the Safwan cloverleaf and Umm Qasr, a route the Marines would be taking on their push north.

The new intelligence on Iraqi tanks stood in sharp contrast to the reassuring assessment the CIA had previously provided the division. The CIA had briefed Mattis and his officers that there was a good chance Iraqi forces in and around the Rumaylah field would actually cooperate in securing the GOSPs—the gas oil separation plants. The agency said it had already paid $80,000 to the Iraqi engineers at the facilities and was negotiating with an important Iraqi brigade commander. Now the agency was warning that Saddam was craftier than the Americans had anticipated and was laying an armor trap to outflank one of their key divisions. Hummer asked the CIA official if the Iraqi officer could be trusted, and was told that the Iraqi had never been wrong. The intelligence threw the carefully rehearsed Marine plan into a cocked hat. The Marines seemed to have thought about every risk except the possibility that Republican Guard T-72s could be waiting to pounce as soon as they crossed the border.

With the attack just hours away, the new piece of intelligence was kicked up to Mattis, who arrived within thirty minutes in his command helicopter to size up for himself the CIA's source. When he got there, Mattis was told that the Iraqi had definitive confirmation: he had made a cell phone call to a friend in southern Iraq who claimed to have seen the Iraqi T-72s firsthand and even recounted how the tank crews ran for cover when allied planes swooped by. Jim Amos, the Third Air Wing commander, was convinced the report was bogus, especially after he sent a Harrier equipped with a special LITENING targeting pod along Highway 1 and it came up dry. Although skeptical, Mattis concluded that he would not take any chances. The opening gambit would have to be overhauled in a hurry to take into account the possible existence of the T-72s.

Under Mattis's original plan, Hummer's Regimental Combat Team 7, his eastern flank unit, was to mount the main attack at dawn on March 21 from just south of Safwan. Joe Dunford's RCT-5, to the left of the Marine zone of action, was to capture the western portion of the Rumaylah oilfields and block the main east–west routes between Basra and Nasiriyah, a move that would thwart a potential counterattack by the Iraqi 51st and 6th armored divisions. But with T-72 tanks apparently waiting to slam into the flank of RCT-7, Mattis reversed the sequence and timing, deciding that Dunford's RCT-5 would be the first regiment to cross into Iraq. It would secure the GOSPs and pin down the brigade of T-72s. Hummer's RCT-7 would then follow, outflanking and destroying the enemy. Mattis told Hummer, "If they're there, your job is to kill them all." "I did not want to have them just retreat and have to fight them all over again," he recalled after the war.[4]

Mattis called Dunford at 5:00 p.m. and asked how soon he could attack. After checking with his staff, Dunford, a tough Boston Irishman, responded that he could launch his regiment in four hours. Mattis then recommended stepping up the already accelerated attack to Conway, who obtained McKiernan's approval. Dunford's attack time was moved up by seven and a half hours. It would not be a daytime attack. Dunford's regiment would be striking at 8:30 p.m. through the defunct DMZ after a thirty-minute artillery preparation.

While the division was grappling with the new intelligence, Captain Dave Banning led his tank company to the border. Crossing the Kuwaiti-Iraqi border would be no small task. The United States not only had to eliminate the Iraqi border outposts and observation points but also had to contend with the multimillion-dollar fortifications the Kuwaitis had established after the Persian Gulf War to keep the Iraqis from invading again. The Kuwaiti defenses included a 1,600-volt electrified fence hemmed on each side by deep antitank ditches and tall sand berms.

The Kuwaitis were loath to see American forces plow over their investment. After considerable discussion with McKiernan's staff, the Kuwaitis had arranged for contractors to take down thirty-six sections of the fence so that the Army, Marines, and British forces could advance into Iraq. As the contractor began the work, there was sporadic Iraqi mortar fire. The Marines' 11th Artillery Regiment fired at one Iraqi mortar position across the border. Banning's Alpha Company was dispatched to the border area to provide extra security.

As night fell, the driver of Banning's M1 asked for his night vision screen, which would enable him to see the enemy in the dark. With the occasional shelling and gunfire, Banning thought better of ordering his loader to get out of the tank and hand the screen to the driver through the hatch. So Banning turned his turret to the rear, a move that enabled the loader to pass the device into the driver's compartment.

The next thing he knew his M1 was rocked by a huge blast. A Hellfire missile from a Marine Cobra helicopter, maneuvering along the border, had struck the left skirt of his M1. A close call, this was the first friendly fire episode of the war and an example of the miscues created by unconfirmed intelligence. The Marines still had not spotted any Iraqi T-72s but had attacked one of their own. Banning was lucky: The Cobra was armed not with the tank-smashing version of the Hellfire but with the blast fragmentation variant, now being fired at Iraqi observation posts and troops near the border. In the fog of war, the crew of the Cobra had seen a tank north of the electrified fence with its barrel pointing south, and attacked it. Banning, however, felt their blunder was inexcusable. The M1 tank had thermal panels identifying it as friendly.[5]

· · ·

Before Dunford began his attack north, the Marines had to take care of Jabal Sanam, a massive high point in southern Iraq. The mound was near Safwan, where General Schwarzkopf and Iraqi generals had negotiated the cease-fire agreement that ended the 1991 Persian Gulf War. Many of the young Marines, influenced by the battle of Iwo Jima in World War II and by tours of duty in the Western Pacific, took to calling it Mount Suribachi. Jabal Sanam dominated the surrounding desert and provided excellent observation of the border region for Iraqi spotters. Along with the many Iraqi guard posts dotting the northern side of the now abandoned U.N. demilitarized zone between Kuwait and Iraq, it gave Iraqi military observers the perfect perch to monitor Marine war preparations near the border.

The plan for seizing Jabal Sanam specified that Marine F/A-18 Hornets would pound the hill with JDAM satellite-guided bombs, while Marine Harriers dropped MK77s, cigar-shaped bombs filled with napalm. Cobra helicopter gunships would also join the attack. Then a twenty-two-man force reconnaissance team would be helilifted to the site to take care of anyone still alive, and then would use the observation post to chart enemy positions. With the acceleration of Dunford's attack, the Jabal Sanam mission was put on a fast track, too.

At Joe Foss field, a dirt airstrip in northern Kuwait, Lieutenant Colonel Darrell Thacker, the helicopter mission commander, had spent the day jumping in and out of his MOPP chemical protective suit as the Iraqis lobbed missiles at the allied formations. At 5:30 p.m. he learned that his mission would start in an hour. The Marine reconnaissance team would be inserted at 6:40.

As evening fell, the choppers headed for the mount, where they hovered, waiting for the F/A-18s to strike. Lieutenant Colonel Matt "Jams" Shilhadeh, the commander of the F/A-18 squadron, had run into a series of communications glitches but managed to start his attack at 6:44. Looking through his infrared targeting system, Shilhadeh watched as his first two bombs pulverized two buildings. His third bomb crashed through its target but failed to explode. All told, the Hornets had managed to drop fourteen of fifteen planned bombs. In their haste to attack the hill, the napalm-dropping mission was canceled. But the Cobras attacked and destroyed a vehicle that was trying to flee north.

After the pounding, the CH-46s tried to land the reconnaissance team. But the dust kicked up by the explosions and the whirling blades of the choppers was thick and fierce. The choppers could not approach close enough to enable the Marines to slide down by rope. After several attempts, the mission was aborted. The Americans did not own the mountain, but neither did the Iraqis. Jabal Sanam was now a cratered and desolate no-man's-land.[6]

Outfitted in their MOPP chemical protective suits, Dunford's Marines began to roll north. All the color-coded lanes through the border fortifications were open, save Red 2, which had been mined by the Iraqis, and Orange 4 and 5, which had been abandoned by the Kuwaiti contractors after the Cobra had blasted Banning's M1. Fred Padilla's battalion was the first to move through the eastern breach site. In the days leading up to the invasion, Padilla had seen the glow from the GOSPs from afar and been worried that the assault might come too late. Every day the attack was delayed would be a day when the Iraqis could lay new mines and torch the oilfields. Now his battalion—mounted in AAVs, Humvees, and trucks, and supported by a platoon of tanks—had gotten a go, hours ahead of the original attack order. Padilla's was the first American unit to cross the line into Iraq.

Driving up Shoe Road—a service road for the oilfields—Padilla found it hard to navigate. "We were in a wedge formation, but it was so dusty and dark we could hardly see. And our NVGs [night vision goggles] didn't help. Before long we were all mixed up," he recalled. Padilla had one of the few Blue Force Tracker devices that, using coordinates transmitted to a satellite, pinpointed the location of friendly units; he positioned his Humvee at the front of the battalion. "Things eventually sorted themselves out, but it was not an auspicious beginning," he added.

Padilla pushed his Alpha Company toward a quarry and quickly destroyed two Iraqi tanks. Padilla was pleasantly surprised by the spotty Iraqi infantry resistance and lack of artillery or mortar fire. Thirty minutes of artillery prep had had its effect. By daylight Padilla had secured his area and the three critical gas oil separation plants and pumping station assigned to him. British and American engineers quickly determined that none of the plants was rigged to self-destruct.[7]

Lieutenant Colonel Sam Mundy's battalion followed on Padilla's heels, swinging around its sister battalion to seize the next set of GOSPs. By then, the Iraqis had recovered from their initial shock and were responding with artillery and small arms fire. They also lit fire trenches in the oilfields. Dust and smoke interfered with helicopter gunship support, but the battalion swept its area and seized the plants without a casualty.

Ten hours later, Lieutenant Colonel Dan O'Donohue's infantry battalion and the 2nd Tank Battalion, under Lieutenant Colonel Mike Oehl, raced through their western breach site. They sped unimpeded twenty-five miles north toward Highway 8 and Highway 1, capturing the last of the western Rumaylah GOSPs before taking up blocking positions facing Zubayr and Basra. The Iraqi 51st Division and the phantom T-72 tank brigade were isolated. RCT-5 mopped up and collected Iraqi prisoners trying to flee westward, including senior officers from the 51st. But the battalion's day was just beginning.

Captain Blair Sokol's Alpha Company, in Padilla's battalion, was assigned to take Pumping Station 2, a 1,800-yard-square compound, which was surrounded by high sand walls and antiaircraft artillery. When the company was 1,000 yards from the site, Sokol called for artillery, and Marines fired DPICM, one of the most feared antipersonnel munitions, which emitted a shower of deadly bomblets. When the battalion came upon an Iraqi mortar position that had been hit by DPICM shells, it found the grisly proof of the weapon's effectiveness: a red film and body parts.

The results at Pumping Station 2 were just as devastating. The Marines arrived to find a dozen or so bodies, as well as some wounded Iraqis. As Lieutenant Therral "Shane" Childers's platoon scoured the site, Corporal Brenton Groce tripped a mine, setting off a blast that broke his ankles and splattered him with shrapnel. A Medevac was called. It was the battalion's first's WIA (wounded in action) but, to the relief of the company, not as serious as it could have been.

Childers, a Gulf War veteran, was one of the battalion's most exemplary Marines. He had been drawn to the service when his father was posted in Tehran as a Seabee during the shah's reign: he was captivated by the spit and polish of the embassy's Marine guards. Childers had enlisted after graduating from high school in Mississippi, and then entered a special program at the Citadel so he could earn his officer's commission. He was a rare breed: a "mustang," an enlisted man who had gone on to become an officer. With Pumping Station 2 under control, Childers ordered his platoon to mount their AAVs so they could clear some nearby bunkers.

As they gathered at the tracks, a tan Toyota pickup truck began to approach Childers's platoon. The Marines were not sure how to respond. They had been primed to take on Iraqi T-72s , T-55s, and Soviet-designed armored personnel carriers called BMPs—not a lone civilian vehicle. The truck picked up speed until it was bouncing across the desert at seventy miles per hour. As it flew by the platoon, civilian-clad Iraqis in the cab and bed of the truck raised AK-47s and sprayed the Marines with automatic weapons fire. Most of the bullets ricocheted off an AAV, but one bullet struck Childers just below his flak jacket. As the truck raced away, the platoon trained its weapons on it, riddling it with bullets until it came to a standstill.

Childers seemed stunned that he had been hit in a drive-by shooting. A Medevac was already on the way to pick up Groce, but now a call went out that it was needed urgently. Meanwhile, a Navy corpsman attached to the platoon furiously began to attend to Childers, who was laid on the ramp of a track. The corpsman performed mouth-to-mouth resuscitation and tried to keep Childers from losing consciousness.

Padilla was on his way to the site when he heard about the shooting over his tactical radio. As he approached the pumping station, he learned that the Medevac request had been downgraded from urgent to routine, a telltale sign that the platoon had lost its commander. When he arrived, Padilla received a report from the Navy corpsman. Tears were streaming down his cheeks, and he had blood up to his elbows. There was nothing they could do. The round had struck Childers's liver and exited his back, setting off massive internal bleeding. Padilla said that there would be time to mourn Childers later, but this was just the start of the war and there was plenty of fighting ahead. When the day's toll was tallied, the Marines determined that Childers had been the first allied soldier killed as a result of enemy action in the war.[8]

After sixteen hours of desultory fighting, Joe Dunford's initial mission had been accomplished: the Iraqis east of his zone were hemmed in; the critical western GOSPs and pumping stations had been seized intact; and a couple of hundred Iraqis had been killed, captured, or disarmed. Dunford's regiment was preparing to be relieved by the Royal Irish Brigade, which had an attachment of Gurkhas. While some Iraqis fought, many fled the onslaught, but there were no mass surrenders. The climactic battle with the T-72s had not occurred; the feared tanks had not been found.

With Marine aircraft and Cobra gunships desperately searching for Iraqi armor north of Safwan, Steve Hummer's RCT-7 plunged across the Kuwait border at daylight. In anticipation of the clash with the T-72 brigade, Hummer, who was on the right of the division, had first call on the Marines' artillery. Hummer led with the 1st Tank Battalion, led by

Lieutenant Colonel Jim Chartier, and Lieutenant Colonel Bryan McCoy's 3rd Battalion, 4th Marines who were mounted in AAVs. Chartier's and McCoy's Marines advanced without opposition. The route was littered with abandoned weapons, equipment, and military clothing. Despondent Iraqi soldiers were fleeing west individually or in small groups. There was no fight in them. Upon reaching Highway 8, the battalion turned east and, after some skirmishing with Iraqi infantrymen, reached the bridge leading to Basra at dusk. There the battalions halted for the night, exchanging fire with Iraqis who were holding the span. To the south, RCT-7's other two advancing battalions also found the detritus of a defeated army as they moved on Zubayr.

Zubayr, a dusty town ten miles southwest of Basra, was adjacent to the Crown Jewel, the single most important control and pumping station for the Rumaylah oilfields. Fourteen percent of all the world's oil was controlled by the station, which received oil from the Rumaylah fields and pumped it to Iraq's offshore oil export terminals. Its sabotage or destruction by the Iraqis would be crippling. The Shuabaya barracks nearby was reported to be the headquarters for one of the brigades of the 51st Division. There were also numerous reports of substantial Iraqi defenses and reinforcements. If there was to be a serious fight, it looked like it would be here.

Lieutenant Colonel Chris Conlin, the commander of 1st Battalion, 7th Marine Regiment, had the mission of seizing the oil complex. He attacked and, to his surprise, the Crown Jewel fell to him undamaged and without a fight. The resident Iraqi managers of the complex were still on the job. They reported that some Iraqi intelligence officers had visited the facility with the aim of sabotaging it, but insisted that they had chased them away. As Marines fanned through the station, Conlin received a distressing report. Some of the machinery there appeared to have been seriously damaged. It seemed that Conlin's regiments might have arrived too late to prevent sabotage. When the Marines talked to oil workers about their discovery, the Iraqis assured them that everything was in order. The badly damaged machinery simply reflected Iraq's oil infrastructure in its normal state of disrepair. It was an eye-opening experience for Conlin and a portent of what the United States would later encounter in Baghdad. The Rumaylah field had been secured, but Iraq's infrastructure was far shabbier than Washington seemed to realize. Protecting the infrastructure was just a first step; there would be major rehabilitation work ahead.[9]

. . .

The Marines' initial success was reported up the chain of command. At Camp Doha, McKiernan was told that the Marines had not only defeated their foe but had also captured the commanding general of the Iraqi 51st Division, the highest-ranking Iraqi officer to surrender so far. McKiernan was eager to put out the news. The Iraqis were not capitulating en masse as the CIA and CENTCOM had hoped, but at least there were some indications that senior Iraqi officers were prepared to submit to the Americans. For a world starved for news about the early days of the invasion, the development produced headlines. Several days later, a new intelligence report trickled in. It turned out that the presumed commander of the 51st was just a junior officer exaggerating his status to receive better treatment from his captors.[10]

After Conlin had taken the Crown Jewel, he rejoined RCT-7 on the march north. But the Iraqi paramilitary Fedayeen quickly occupied Zubayr and treated the British who followed the Marines to a hail of rocket and machine gun fire whenever they approached the town. Major General Robin Brims commanded a formidable British force. Brims's division included 7 Armoured Brigade, the famous Desert Rats who fought in North Africa during World War II, 16 Air Assault Brigade, and 3 Commando Brigade, among others. The British quickly took control of bridges over the Shatra, isolating Basrah. They soon isolated Zubayr as well.

The British also had a parallel mission on the Faw Peninsula, one that was launched while the Marines were moving into the Rumaylah fields. After the timing of the land attack was moved up, British and Australian ships had begun to bombard enemy positions on Al Faw; British artillery, emplaced on Kuwait's Bubiyan Island, had also lobbed shells. Royal Marines were lifted to the peninsula without incident, securing the key facilities and four large pipelines that fed the offshore platforms. The most symbolic expression of the American and British partnership, and the most collaborative operation of the war, was the plan to airlift British Royal Marines to Al Faw. An initial force of Royal Marines from 40 Commando were to be flown to the peninsula from British ships, but 550 more from a sister unit, 42 Commando, would go to the peninsula courtesy of the U.S. Marine Corps.

The British mission was to secure not only the oil infrastructure but also Umm Qasr, Iraq's only deep-water port, which CENTCOM needed to bring in relief supplies. U.S. Navy SEALs were to grab the offshore platforms and the pipelines that fed them in the opening minutes of the war. After that it would largely be a British show. To the satisfaction of the British, the 15th Marine Expeditionary Unit, some 2,000 Marines, were temporarily put under British command, which both strengthened the Royal Marines and helped to soothe political sensitivities in England. The British land forces reported to Conway's Marine Expeditionary Force, but at least some U.S. Marines would be commanded by a British officer.

There was a lot at stake for both sides. The British would be taking advantage of the Marines' superior night-flying technology and greater lift capacity to insert 42 Commando north of the town of Al Faw—something the British commanders deemed vital to protect the flank of the vulnerable British toehold on the peninsula. For the Marines, the mission would be an important demonstration of their air assault techniques. The Marines had planned to airlift Task Force X-Ray—troops, weapons, and vehicles—during the Persian Gulf War, only to cancel the operation because of concerns about Iraqi antiaircraft artillery and bad weather. Now they would be mounting the largest air assault since the Vietnam War. It was a chance to make history, and an opportunity to strengthen the close cooperation between American and British forces.

The Marine flight commander and the British mission commander would be in a Huey command and control chopper. Cobras would provide an escort. Because of the large number of Royal Marines, the American pilots planned to make two trips. All in all, the attack involved fourteen CH-53s, fourteen CH-46s, twelve AH-1Ws, four UH-1Ns, and a pair of F/A-18s. The Cobras would clear the landing zones. Then the CH-46s and CH-53s would lift the British troops. The mission would be canceled if it was discovered that the Iraqis had contaminated the landing areas with chemical weapons or if visibility dropped below two miles. The Iraqis took some steps to strengthen their defense in the areas. In response to CENTCOM's deception campaign—some of the phony documents passed indicated that the 101st Airborne was to attack near Basra—the Iraqi regime ordered two brigades to move toward the Faw Peninsula. The actual number of Iraqi forces that actually moved, though, was probably not more than several battalions. The Marines felt well prepared. They had rehearsed the mission with the British, had reviewed photos of the peninsula, and even inspected soil samples gathered by U.S. intelligence.

On a good, clear night, the Marine pilots would have proceeded without any problems and exploited their night vision goggles. But some had recently seen how the weather could interfere with the Marines' best-laid plans. A few weeks before, a sandstorm had forced one of the unit's helicopters to land in the middle of the Kuwait desert and settle down for the night near an Army base. The Marines formed a hasty security perimeter and waited until morning to fly to their base.

At 2:50 a.m. the Marines began to take off, the Cobras leading the way. At first visibility was two miles but, as the choppers headed east, it began to worsen. Oil fires the Iraqis had set to obscure the battlefield were having their desired effect. Wind was carrying smoke over the flight route and there was no way to maneuver around it. The Marines were flying at an altitude of 225 feet and having trouble finding the horizon.

Lieutenant Colonel Jerome E. Driscoll, the assault flight leader, was about halfway through the route in his helicopter Dash 1 and approaching Bubiyan Island when he heard a radio transmission from a fellow pilot. "Power, power, power, pull up," yelled Dash 4. Driscoll saw a flash out of the corner of his eye. "Dash 3 is down," Dash 4 reported. Driscoll passed the word to Lieutenant Colonel James Braden, the Marine flight commander. Braden's first thought was that Dash 3 had landed because of a malfunction. Driscoll corrected him, making it clear that Dash 3 had crashed: the disoriented crew had flown into the ground at 3:37 a.m. Braden aborted the mission.[11]

The Marine choppers began to make their way back at 300 feet, doing their best not to collide with helicopters still en route. This was the end of the Marine helicopter squadron's collaboration with the British, as its chief role was to support RCT-5 in evacuating casualties, among other missions in the upcoming days. The Marine pilots had no more time for the Al Faw mission. The British would have to transport the Royal Marines themselves.

The Marines' decision to abort the mission did not go down well with the British ground commander, Lieutenant Colonel Buster Howes, who led 42 Commando. In the crash of Dash 3, his unit had already suffered casualties—eight Royal Marines and their four-member American aircrew. Howe was worried that his entire mission had been put in jeopardy.

The Marines had left the initial complement of Royal Marines without reinforcements for nine hours. Fortunately, Iraqi resistance on the peninsula turned out to be light.

It was the first day of the war and already there was a rift between the allies. Compounding the ill will was confusion about who should secure the crash site. The bodies remained in the wreckage for twelve hours before they were pulled out by a Marine logistical unit and a British team. The morning after the crash Jim Conway made a radio call to his Marine and British officers. Major General Robin Brims noted that the British were considering using an amphibious landing craft to get their commandos to Red Beach. Amos was irritated. "I don't know what the deal is with the Brits. If they want to do a lift, that's fine with me. I suspect it's one of those national things that I hate. In other words, they seem to be saying 'You killed one of our helicopters and some of our Royal Marines, and we're not giving you a second chance'. . . . We'll get beyond that."[12]

Between Dunford's and Steve Hummer's regiments, the key oil works in the Rumaylah fields had been seized intact in less than two days. The Iraqi 51st Division and 6th Armored Division had been mauled and ceased to exist as organized forces. Dowdy's RCT-1 was already on the approach to Nasiriyah, the Marines' next objective. The phantom brigade of T-72s had never materialized. The only Marine killed by the enemy had died at the hands of a bunch of Iraqis in civilian dress riding in a pickup truck.

Still, Wallace's V Corps and Conway's Marines had a long way to go before reaching Baghdad. "There were a couple of days after the seizure of the GOSPs where we saw nothing but happy, waving civilians," recalled Major Craig Wonson of Dunford's RCT-5. "But when we skirted south of Nasiriyah and saw CAS [close air support] aircraft making their attack runs and watching the smoke rise up from the city, we knew there was a big fight and knew that things would be picking up for us very soon."[13]

CHAPTER 11

Objective Liberty

Standing in the hatch of his M113 command track, Major General Buff Blount swatted Captain Erik Berdy on the back of his helmet. It was time, the commander of the 3rd Infantry Division explained, for Berdy to contact "Bob," the nom de guerre of a CIA operative, and find out what the agency had managed to put together in southern Iraq.[1]

While Mattis was securing Iraq's southern oilfields, Blount was setting the stage for the push to Baghdad that was to follow. A Mississippi native from a long line of military officers, Blount had been trained as an armor officer. He had spent four years as an adviser to the Saudi National Guard program, an assignment that had convinced him that it was possible for armored vehicles to move swiftly through the desert.

During his years in Saudi Arabia, Blount had given some thought to how best to invade Iraq if he were ever given the opportunity. Start fast and never stop was how to do it. Blount had a plan to lead his division to the Iraqi capital in seventy-two hours should Saddam's regime collapse. Even if Saddam's Republican Guard resisted, Blount was confident he could prevail. Blount's 3rd Infantry Division had spent months training in the Kuwaiti desert and was at its peak. He was convinced there was no way Saddam's army could stop him.

Although he was of a different service and tradition, Blount had more in common with the Marine Mattis than with some of his Army superiors. The two generals seemed to be cut from the same cloth. When CENTCOM was considering the Running Start war plan, Blount's planners had worked closely with their Marine counterparts, who welcomed them with open arms. (Blount's division would have begun the attack under the command of the I Marine Expeditionary Force.) But Blount and his staff did not always see eye-to-eye with the V Corps, the Army command to which they now reported and which they considered unduly cautious.

Before he took the fight to the Republican Guard, however, Blount had to attend to some other important business. His division had to seize the Highway 1 bridge, which was vital for the Marine push north, and grab the sprawling Tallil air base southwest of Nasiriyah, which U.S. commanders hoped to use as a logistics hub and airfield. Both were key pieces of real estate that the U.S. military planned to use to spring north. While Blount expected tough fighting when he closed in on Baghdad, the CIA had told him he would be pushing on an open door in the Shiite-dominated south. Since the Shiites had risen up against Saddam after the Gulf War and the agency considered southern Iraq to be full of potential allies who would be inclined to join a common cause against Saddam if the Bush administration proved it was determined to march on Baghdad.

In the weeks before the invasion, "Bob" and a team of fellow CIA operatives had produced encouraging reports about the willingness of allies to help Blount's division after it crossed the border. Anti-Saddam tribes were planning to seize the Highway 1 bridge and turn it over to U.S. forces when they moved into the area. The 11th Iraqi Division was also likely to capitulate. The CIA hoped to deliver the division's chief of staff, who would arrange the surrender. To facilitate a linkup, the agency had outfitted Berdy with a Thuraya satellite phone so one of "Bob's" agents could call him as the division approached the Tallil air base. McKiernan had rejected the CIA plan to distribute U.S. flags in southern Iraq, but the agency's operatives had nonetheless briefed the idea to Blount.

As the 3rd Infantry Division crossed the border and moved north it was not clear where or whether an Iraqi capitulation would occur. The division's push had provided little indication of serious resistance. After 458 artillery rounds and Apache helicopter attacks, the strings of Iraqi border outposts were little more than piles of debris. Still, the division had a few anxiety-inducing moments. One Apache conducting reconnaissance of the outposts had to make a precautionary landing across the border when it was hit by small arms fire, but it was able to take off again. Then scouts reported that a company's worth of T-72 tanks had taken up fighting positions. Scott Rutter's 2-7 Infantry Battalion quickly attacked the presumed Iraqi armored unit, only to discover that it had been firing away at dilapidated T-55 tanks abandoned across the battlefield after the

1991 Persian Gulf War. The rusty armor had absorbed the sun's heat during the day and appeared as threatening hot spots on the battalion's thermal sights.

Blount was not sure what kind of reception his troops would receive after crossing the border. He knew his troops were ready and eager to get the fight started, but he also sought to prepare them for the possibility that the CIA's assessment might be right. For an Army unit that was about to invade enemy territory, the rules of engagement that were passed down the chain of command were unusually restrictive. Iraqis slinging weapons were not to be considered necessarily hostile; they might be Iraqi soldiers waiting to join forces with the Americans.

"The ROE was very strict then," recalled Captain Doug Phillipone, the commander of B Company for 1-15 Infantry. "The CG [commanding general] had given us a speech about how there were going to be parades for us here, and we were really expecting them to surrender. The ROE was even if you see weapons, we're giving them the opportunity to surrender first. Initially, I'd say we were very trigger-shy. We didn't want to shoot until they were positively identified as enemy and they were even almost firing at us."[2]

With no call from "Bob's" agent, Blount instructed Berdy to call "Bob" himself, but no one answered. After weeks of discussions about how the CIA might abet the division attack and the likelihood of mass Iraqi surrenders, "Bob" had vanished without a trace. The division, it seemed, would not know the Iraqis' intentions until it approached its first objectives.

Colonel Dan Allyn, the commander of the 3rd Brigade Combat Team, would be one of the first to know. A former Army Ranger who had parachuted into Panama during the invasion to topple Manuel Noriega, Allyn had served with Wayne Downing's Special Operations Forces during the 1991 Gulf War. Allyn's brigade had been exercising at the Udairi Range in Kuwait since March 2002, and, arguably, had spent more time in the desert than any other divisional unit.[3]

Blount had advised Allyn that if enemy resistance evaporated he should be prepared to detour to Nasiriyah and march through the city to demonstrate solidarity with the newly liberated Iraqis. Allyn did not want his soldiers to become complacent, so he kept the CIA's promise of a parade to himself and his team of senior officers. Still, he was determined to give any well-motivated Iraqis a chance to surrender. Allyn was concerned that some Iraqi troops might make a halfhearted attempt to fight to placate their officers before giving up.

Allyn sent his Brigade Reconnaissance Troop ahead to scout the route to Tallil. After thirty minutes, they ran into a group of Iraqis in civilian dress who had arrived in Toyota pickup trucks to lay a hasty minefield about nine miles south of the Iraqi air base. The Americans made short work of their foe, shooting several and capturing five, who were discovered to be carrying large wads of Iraqi dinars. Allyn was not sure what to make of the unorthodox Iraqi tactics. Given the unrelenting flow of upbeat intelligence assessments, he surmised that these unfortunate Iraqis had been given the impossible mission of stopping the American juggernaut. Perhaps they were outfitted in civilian dress because they planned to desert at the first possible moment, as many of Noriega's forces had done during the Panama invasion.

By afternoon, the lead elements of Allyn's force had driven 75 miles, to a stretch of desert just south of the air base. The brigade commander planned to pause long enough to bring up the rest of his combat forces and logistics, and to refuel before moving to take the Highway 1 bridge and the air base. The brigade would not move on those objectives until late that evening. A phone call from Brigadier General Lloyd Austin, Blount's deputy, altered that carefully rehearsed plan. With no reports from "Bob" or any other CIA operative, the division would be putting the brigade's attack in fast-forward. Blount did not want to give the Iraqis a chance to blow up the bridge. Allyn was to get forces up to the Highway 1 bridge and move on Tallil as fast as possible.[4]

Lieutenant Colonel J. R. Sanderson, an officer from Waynesville, North Carolina, was given the mission of taking the bridge. Sanderson played at being a simple country boy, but he was widely read in military history. Sanderson had led a Bradley infantry company past the Tallil air base and into the Iraqi oilfields during the Gulf War, and taught tactics at the Armor School. A master of tank warfare, he commanded 2-69, an armor battalion and the most potent force assigned to Allyn's brigade.

Sanderson's battalion had been one of the first major Army units to cross into Iraq, and his initial problem had not been the enemy but logistics. Despite the Kuwaiti efforts to take down sections of their extensive border obstacle belts and electrified fence, some of the lanes were too rough for wheeled vehicles. Sanderson moved all of his combat vehicles through two lanes, but his fuel tankers, ammunition trucks, headquarters company, and mine-rolling equipment had become bogged down and were lagging way behind. While his executive officer and headquarters command worked all night to push and pull the vehicles through the lanes, Sanderson would have to manage with what he had. "The bridge was the prize—it was our reason for existence and defined our collective purpose," Sanderson later recalled. "Regardless of what happened to our flanks or rear it was incumbent upon the battalion to seize the bridge."

As Sanderson prepared to resume the march north he approached the CIA operatives traveling with his battalion. The CIA officers were still hopeful that the Iraqi tribes they had enlisted would take the Highway 1 bridge, but were unsure whether the tribes actually controlled the span. Their vagueness led to a tense exchange between the battalion commander and the intelligence operatives. Despite the optimistic chatter about capitulation, Sanderson was not about to give the enemy an opportunity to shoot at his soldiers first. If his tank battalion moved on the bridge, weapon control status would be "red direct three"—troops would be free to shoot at anything on the bridge. This was going to be a night attack and his battalion would be using thermal sights. The CIA needed to say now if it planned to secure the bridge; otherwise, Sanderson warned, anyone on the span was going to die.

After a few minutes of fussing, the CIA officers acknowledged that they could provide no assurance. As Sanderson's battalion prepared to advance up Highway 1, it came under Iraqi artillery fire. Within minutes, Lieutenant Colonel Doug Harding unleashed a barrage of lethal counterfire. This was the first significant artillery duel of the war. The Americans got the better of the exchange, suppressing Iraqi fire for the time being.

The battalion moved forward four companies abreast until the terrain forced it to proceed in a single column. Sanderson's biggest worry was having to stop to clear Iraqi minefields before breaking through obstacles in the way. Surprisingly, the battalion encountered neither mines nor barriers. But the situation at the bridge remained unclear.[5]

Sanderson radioed the Apache helicopters overhead. With no input from the CIA or a Special Forces team inserted two days earlier to monitor the span, any information about it would have to come from the division's choppers.

After shooting up the Iraqi observation posts along the border, the division's choppers had flown to the deserted Iraqi air base at Jalibah to set up operations. On the basis of intelligence briefings prior to the war, Colonel Curtis Potts, the commander of Blount's aviation brigade, expected the Special Forces team and its Iraqi allies to be on the bridge before Sanderson's arrival. As Potts approached the span in his command and control helicopter, he sought to call the SOF team that was supposed to be there, using its code name: Serpent 6. As with Blount's call to "Bob," there was no answer.

In the wake of the CIA's poor showing in the opening days of the war, Army and Marine field commanders' faith in the agency was shaken. The White House had been mesmerized by the performance of the CIA and Special Forces in Afghanistan. It expected much from them in Cobra II. But Iraq was not Afghanistan. Having been in Afghanistan, working with the Mujahidin throughout the Soviet occupation, the CIA and its operatives were fully knowledgeable about the country and its main players. In Iraq, however, no identifiable insurgency existed, and the CIA had few contacts in the ruthlessly controlled regime of Saddam Hussein. CIA expertise and Special Forces skills were not as easily transferable from Afghanistan to Iraq, as Franks and others thought. Clandestine teams were now largely operating in terra incognita.

When the Apaches arrived on the scene, they blasted three Iraqi BMPs just north of the bridge with Hellfire missiles, and then attacked a group of Iraqis that appeared to be setting up an antitank ambush south of the bridge. The Iraqis responded with SA-7 shoulder-fired surface-to-air missiles and ground fire, but missed.

Sanderson's troops reached the span soon after and rushed to clear the buildings on each side. That night, Sanderson got out of his tank, walked across the bridge, and ordered his ordnance teams to ensure that it had not been rigged with explosives. By midnight he had radioed Allyn with the news that Objective Clay, the code name for the bridge, had been seized, and that a team of combat engineers had determined it was clear and could bear the weight of heavy armor—vital information for the Marines, who planned to use it to send combat regiments north. There had been one casualty: a soldier hit by sniper fire.

By first light a tank company had established a bridgehead on the far side and Sanderson's battalion had cleared a zone that was 4 miles deep on each side. That same day a Patriot antimissile battery arrived—the first time that a Patriot battery had moved into enemy territory with an attacking U.S. force. The bridge was vital to the American war plan, more vital than the Iraqis seemed to realize, and the United States was determined to preserve it.

Only later would it become clear what had happened to the SOF team. Having infiltrated before G-day, it had found no tribal allies but had been embroiled in a running gun battle with Iraqi forces. Surprisingly, the SOF team had been woefully out of sync with the brigade plan. The commandos had taken up positions near the span before 11:00 a.m. on March 21, having assumed that Allyn's brigade would not be far behind, only to discover that they had been the victim of an enormous planning snafu: the special forces were on local time, while Blount's division was on Zulu, military-speak for Greenwich Mean Time—a three-hour difference. In dire need of assistance, the team had contacted the SOF's liaison officer in Allyn's brigade, only to be told that the brigade had its hands full with other battles. An internal team report later faulted the SOF's own commanders for failing to meet with Blount or his chief officers to carefully coordinate the seizure of the bridge. The oversight had led to a "near disaster."

The role of special forces would be much touted after the war, but at the Highway 1 bridge they were more a danger to themselves than to the Iraqis. "We had a very confused picture of what the SF were capable of doing," Allyn recalled later. "We knew more about what the Marines were doing than the SF elements." More important, the hoped-for, near-real-time intelligence on enemy activity at the bridge had not been forthcoming. Reports had ranged from no sign of enemy presence to the bridge is rigged to blow.[6]

While Sanderson was taking the bridge, the rest of Allyn's forces moved on Tallil, code-named Objective Firebird. The base was surrounded by a series of berms and fences and was replete with hardened aircraft shelters, which the U.S. had bombed during the Gulf War. To the east was a garrison for the 11th Iraqi Infantry Division. The job there was to seize the air base and neutralize a reported thirty to thirty-five T-55s at the garrison, which, if bypassed, could be used by the Iraqis to attack the Army's supply lines.

It was clear there would be some Iraqi resistance. Allyn's artillery had been forced to stop on its way to Tallil after U.S. forces came under artillery fire. With the assistance of Q36 and Q37 counterfire radars, U.S. guns had fired back for an hour. Under Scott Wallace's plan, the Iraqi artillery and armor in and around Nasiriyah were to be pounded the night before by two battalions of Apache attack helicopters from Colonel William Wolf's 11th Attack Helicopter Regiment. The regiment was the largest helicopter task force in the Army, and many of its Apaches were equipped with the Longbow missile and targeting system, which gave the Apache a "fire and forget" capability. Instead of directing a laser at a target until the missile struck, an Apache pilot would be able to fire at an Iraqi tank and immediately turn his attention to other targets.

The regiment had practiced the Nasiriyah raid extensively, including in Poland, using a training area that had once been occupied by Soviet forces. Under the regiment's plan, Apaches from 6-6 squadron would attack north of the city while Apaches from 2-6 squadron would attack to the southeast. CH-47s would fly north of the border and set up a refueling base; Black Hawk search-and-rescue helicopters would dash there to be in position in case an Apache was shot down and the crew needed to be recovered. Wolf would command the entire operation from his command and control Black Hawk.

When the Apaches began to take off, however, the regiment ran into problems. The Apaches were able to navigate using their FLIR, which generates images by sensing the heat or infrared energy of objects. But Black Hawk and CH-47 pilots flew using night vision goggles, and the dust kicked up by 3rd ID and other obscurants made it impossible for them to navigate. Determining that the mission was too risky, Lieutenant Colonel Michael J. Barbee, the 6-6 commander, aborted it. Like the Marine helicopters that were supposed to fly British commandos to the Faw Peninsula, the Apaches were "RTB'ed," returned to base, because of poor visibility. Barbee's was a frustrating and morale-dampening decision for a regiment that had dreamed of replicating the dramatic episodes of the 101st Airborne during the Persian Gulf War.[7]

Using an artillery smokescreen to obscure the Tallil air base, the 1-30 Infantry Battalion easily took its objective. The Americans captured more than 100 prisoners, Iraqi army soldiers and air force personnel, who appeared to have no idea that they were on the U.S. invasion route. Among those captured was General Saiyf Nasser, the Tallil base and air defense commander for southern Iraq. His Thuraya satellite phone was seized; its computer memory contained a valuable list of phone numbers, including that of the Iraqi defense minister.

. . .

For its part, the 1-15 Infantry Battalion moved on the Iraqi 11th division garrison adjacent to Nasiriyah, with artillery and air strikes by A-10s. In a military first, Doug Harding's artillery battalion destroyed an Iraqi T-55 by firing twelve rounds of SADARM, an advanced artillery shell that released an antitank killing munition that homed in on enemy armor. By early morning much of the fighting had died down. Many of the Iraqi soldiers and officers surrendered; some of them helped the Americans locate weapons caches the following day. This was not the wholesale capitulation of Iraqi units that CENTCOM had foreseen, but it seemed as if some Iraqis were prepared to cooperate after it became clear to them that they had been defeated.

At 5:00 a.m. the next day, scouts at a blocking position on the road to Nasiriyah came under fire from a series of trenches and warehouses on the outskirts of the city. An Army psychological operations team blared surrender appeals, but the enemy fighters were having none of it. Captain Dave Waldron, the commander of B Company, 1-64 Armor, who headed the forces in this sector, checked with some prisoners the Army had caught the previous night to find out who was firing at his forces. The Iraqis told him that none of the troops from their division were still in the vicinity. Instead, U.S. forces would do well to watch out for the Saddam Fedayeen. Waldron soon found out what they meant.

Specialist Williams, a scout at the blocking position, was in his armored Humvee returning fire at the enemy when his .50 caliber machine gun jammed. He began to scream. Sergeant Terrance Grant, who was in the vehicle with Williams, thought the gun had blown up in Williams's face and tugged on his leg.

"What's wrong?" Grant asked.

"I'm paralyzed," Williams said, as he slid down in the turret.

Like Marine Lieutenant Shane Childers, Williams was wearing body armor, but the bullet had struck just below it. Like Childers, he had been shot by a fighter who was not part of any recognizable Iraqi unit. Unlike Childers, he survived.

"He got shot from the flank," said Lieutenant Colonel John Charlton, the 1-15 Infantry Battalion commander. "We suspect Fedayeen. It's kind of hard to tell. They weren't wearing uniforms. Some had partial uniforms, others were wearing the black. . . . I think we faced primarily paramilitary forces."

The engineers moved their M113 armored personnel carrier up to provide cover as Williams's comrades pulled him behind the vehicle and the medic began treating him. The engineers fired at the enemy until they ran out of ammunition. Stung by the wounding of Williams, his soldiers lashed back. Tanks and artillery blasted away. A-10s leveled the buildings where enemy fire must have come from. "We shot an immediate suppression," recalled Lieutenant Colonel Doug Harding, the commander of 1-10 Field Artillery Battalion. "When a U.S. soldier is shot the brigade needed to unleash hell on them." But there was no way of telling if they had killed Williams's shooter.

The Iraqis were not deterred. They lobbed artillery rounds that landed about half a mile from the forward U.S. positions. Harding determined that some of the shells had come from a clearing within Nasiriyah. Harding checked with Allyn and was told he was free to return fire. He shot back. In addition to Harding's artillery fire, an adjoining battalion of Multiple Launch Rocket Systems (MLRS) fired a barrage of deadly bomblets. Colonel Tom Torrance, who commanded the division's artillery, quickly intervened to stop any further MLRS missions. Torrance had no intention of shelling targets in Iraqi cities, especially towns like Nasiriyah, which the CIA, again, had said would welcome the Americans. Blount, for his part, was sufficiently concerned about the episode that he later arrived to check out the situation for himself. After being briefed, the general left without saying a word.

Torrance later concluded that the MLRS assault on Nasiriyah had been a mistake and accepted blame. The division's Q37 radar, which was used to pinpoint the source of enemy fire, had identified two artillery positions: one to the west of the city and one in a clearing in Nasiriyah itself. In the heat of battle Torrance had gotten them confused. Mistake or not, Harding felt the attack was justified: there was no sense, he reasoned, in waiting for the enemy to adjust his fire before shooting back. It was fine to show restraint and give the Iraqis a chance to capitulate, but the enemy was not following the CIA script.[8]

"The ROE was very tight," Harding recalled, alluding to Blount's visit. "We went into this fight assuming we weren't going to fire anything. Now we're receiving incoming artillery. We'd always been told that we'd never be second-guessed. I really wasn't. He just wanted to see what was going on. Later on in the fight, we ended up having to shoot into cities more often because that's where [Saddam had] put his artillery."[9]

Later that day, American scouts near Tallil had another encounter with the Fedayeen. Lloyd Austin, the assistant division commander who was monitoring the brigade's progress from his command vehicle, called to relay a report about "some suspicious-looking characters." Staff Sergeant Jamie Villafane of 1-30 Infantry took several Humvees, a Bradley, and a tank to investigate. As Villafane crested the bridge, an antitank missile crashed through the windshield of his Humvee, wounding him in the arm and blowing him out of the vehicle. Sergeant Nicholas Swartz, who was riding in the truck directly behind Villafane, thought that nobody in the Humvee could have survived the explosion, but jumped out to help when he saw that Villafane and two other soldiers were still alive. Seconds later, his own truck exploded. The Americans had driven into an ambush and were taking fire from fighters armed with machine guns, RPGs, and antitank missiles.

Villafane threw a smoke grenade to provide some cover while an M1 tank fired a round under the bridge. With his 9mm pistol he managed to capture four stunned Iraqis and haul his wounded gunner out of the battle zone. Despite the intensity of the fire, Juan Rodriguez, a scout platoon sergeant, felt the soldiers were lucky in one respect: the antitank missiles had gone in one side of the Humvee and out the other.

Meanwhile, Major Jim Desjardin, the operations officer for 1-30 Infantry, rushed to the scene of the fighting, had some of the wounded moved into his Bradley, and called for a Medevac chopper before rejoining the fight. Colonel Potts sent a few Apaches as an escort to the Medevac. Hardly intimidated, the Iraqis started firing antitank missiles at the choppers as they closed in. As the Apaches fired back with their 30mm cannons, a large truck drove up to the scene. Ripping away the canvas top, fighters in civilian clothes began spraying machine gun fire at the Apaches. The Apaches destroyed the truck, but the episode was telling. The Iraqis were using guerrilla tactics; they were not marshaled in conventional formations. They were trying to ambush the U.S. convoys as they headed north. And they were not surrendering but fighting tenaciously. The Apache crews made it back to Jalibah shaken by their experience, having fired three Hellfires, two rockets, and 500 rounds of 30mm cannon.[10]

"So it was a long day," Desjardin said later. "The first day that I had seen the enemy and realized we were fighting a different force. They weren't in uniform. They were civilian individuals that were running around with weapons, people dressed as civilians that were engaging our forces from that site."[11]

While the Army and Marines were attacking in the south, the air war command was winding up for its big punch. The decision to secure the oilfields early had inadvertently led to a strategic innovation. Contrary to Iraqi expectations, the ground forces had attacked before the main air strike was to take place.

Franks, however, was still committed to a big A-day strike, part of the campaign that, as he promised the president, would produce "shock and awe." By any measure, the air war plan was ambitious. Moseley, in effect, had to wage several wars at once. He was to strike at Saddam's regime and simultaneously prevent Iraq from firing Scud missiles at Israel or Arab states friendly to the United States. Moseley also needed to carry out air strikes on behalf of the Kurds and special forces in northern Iraq and, as part of CENTCOM's information campaign, beam surrender appeals into and drop leaflets on Iraq.

Supporting McKiernan's ground forces as they moved north was also key. Most of his strikes would be carried out on behalf of the allied land forces. Moseley was proud of the efforts to support the Army and Marines. Jim Roche, the Air Force secretary, and John Jumper, the Air Force chief of staff, had done their part to facilitate cooperation with the ground forces. As Roche later recalled, the Air Force had transferred its "air-heads," the most zealous advocates of victory through airpower, to other commands before the war.

In sharp contrast to the Gulf War, much of Iraq's infrastructure was now off limits. As a general rule, the United States would not strike power plants, the electrical grid, or oil refineries. Bridges would be struck sparingly. The United States had promised to help rebuild Iraq after the war and did not want to create more work for itself than was necessary. Nonetheless, the regime was to be hit, and hit hard.

Moseley and his deputies had worked for a year to develop a plan to unhinge the regime. In January, Moseley's chief of strategy, Colonel Mace Carpenter, invited a group of experts to Shaw Air Force Base in South Carolina for a brainstorming session. The best and brightest included Major General Dave Deptula, who had helped prosecute the air campaign during the Gulf War, and Kenneth Pollack, a former CIA analyst and Brookings Institution scholar who had written a book advocating military intervention as the only way to end Saddam's WMD programs. One of the main lessons that emerged from the session was that upending the regime required more than going after the leader himself. The United States had to strike the Special Republican Guard and security forces that Saddam relied on to stay in power.[12]

Drawing on their ideas, the strategy for unleashing no fewer than 1,565 weapons on targets in Baghdad over the first four days was finalized.

Twenty-two communications links and command centers were high CD, the collateral damage from the strike expected to exceed thirty innocents. The Al-Rasheed Hotel and the Baghdad Media Center were among the high CD targets. In a final twist, the first day's attacks had initially been scheduled for midday, when more of the regime's leadership would be at work. This would maximize the killing power of the raids and achieve "shock and awe."

In the final weeks before the war, however, the Bush administration had had second thoughts when confronted with one of the paradoxes of its "shock and awe" program. Even in an age of precision warfare, stunning the enemy with massive air strikes added substantially to the risk of unintended death and destruction. Convinced it would quickly win, the administration decided to pull some of its punches. In late February, Moseley learned that Bush, who would be following the progress of the war as intently as he had the planning, had expressed concern about striking the Al-Rasheed Hotel, the location of key communications cables and the information ministry. So in the weeks leading up to the war, all twenty-two of the high CD targets were temporarily pulled from the attack plan, and the A-day strikes were shifted from day to night.

Soon after the Dora Farms strike there were new concerns. With Washington persuaded that Saddam might have perished in that strike but as yet with no official Iraq surrender, the word was passed in Moseley's command center that there was no need to destroy more of the Iraqi infrastructure than was absolutely necessary.

Captain Michael Downs, who worked for the Guidance, Apportionment, and Targeting team that picked the targets, was instructed to adjust the plan. The order was given without the knowledge of Mace Carpenter and his Strategy Division. Downs removed more than a quarter of the 2,000 strikes from the list only to learn at midday that there had been some confusion. Rear Admiral Dave Nichols, Moseley's top deputy, made clear in no uncertain terms that the aimpoints were to be put back on the list. With just hours to go before the planes took off, Downs rushed to restore the original list and arrange for the word to get to the aircrews. But he was under no illusions that all the strikes had been restored. An air war was a complicated ballet, and aircraft were flying from Britain, Diego Garcia, the United States, and the Persian Gulf. It was not an easy thing to pull together at the last minute.[13]

Moseley expected the A-day attacks to deliver a crippling body blow to the enemy. For two days, allied planes had been operating freely over western Iraq as special forces looked for Iraq's supposed supply of Scud missiles. Now CENTCOM would go after the regime. B-2 Stealth Bombers would be flying from Whiteman Air Force Base in Missouri and from the British island of Diego Garcia in the Indian Ocean, while B-52s would be taking off from Fairford, England. Cruise missiles would be launched from ships in the Persian Gulf and the Mediterranean. The stars of the affair, the F-117 Stealth Fighters that had attacked Dora Farms, would again take off from Al Udeid.

The strike on Baghdad was set to begin at 9:00 p.m. on March 21. As the clock wound down, Franks convened a satellite video conference with his commanders. CENTCOM, he said, was on schedule, but entering a vulnerable period. U.S. forces needed to maintain and even increase their momentum to keep the enemy off balance and maintain the initiative. "Shock will be introduced at 2100," Franks announced. "You're all doing great."[14]

There would be three near simultaneous waves of strikes. TLAM cruise missiles would go first. The Iraqis were expected to respond with wild antiaircraft fire. When the Iraqis had exhausted themselves, the F-117s would come in. For the early part of the war, F-117s would attack, six to eight aircraft at a time. But for opening night the number had been expanded to nine. Next, B-2s would inflict their punishment. The air war commanders had taken Franks's injunction to heart. They would keep the heat on.

After the Dora Farms raid, the F-117 pilots were eager to get back into the thick of things. This time, the attacks had not been thrown together at the last moment; they had been laboriously scripted. But as the F-117s flew north, they soon ran into a problem that Moseley had been facing for a while: a shortage of bases for his aircraft refueling tankers. Now, the chickens came home to roost. Only three of the F-117s would reach a tanker and refuel in time for the final push to Baghdad. The other six arrived at their respective rendezvous but with insufficient boom time for all of them to refuel in order to get to Baghdad as planned. The vaunted F-117 strike on Baghdad was now down to three planes, piloted by McKeon, Ankerstar, and Captain Brent Blake.

As the F-117s flew north, the sprawling city of Baghdad appeared in the distance, partially covered by clouds and obscured by the gray haze resulting from the preceding cruise missile strike. Despite the cruise missile attack minutes before, the Iraqis were still frantically shooting skyward as the F-117s arrived on target. Antiaircraft artillery filled the skies over Baghdad. Surface-to-air missiles were popping off at random intervals.

Ankerstar approached along the Iranian border and at 9:17 dropped the first bomb on a communications center north of Baghdad, which was three minutes' flight time from the city. The goal was to sever communications with the Iraqi army units in the north. His second target was a four-way intersection in Baghdad, which ran over a supposed tunnel system. He was to put a GBU-27 earth-penetrating bomb right on it. McKeon and Blake quickly followed with their strikes.

McKeon's first target was the Baath Party headquarters, a massive domed building the size of a city block that was believed to house an important command center. As the 2,000-pound bomb penetrated the roof, the dome collapsed. His second target was the same communications center Ankerstar had attacked minutes before. Blake was also successful in his attack on a regime target in the heart of Baghdad. All three jets quickly slipped away and were back at Al Udeid two hours later.

The refueling problem faced by the F-117s was a major snafu that had blunted the striking power of the United States Air Force on the opening night of the war, but the episode was never disclosed by the service. Nor was that the only time the tanker refueling issue would raise its head. The very next night, three of eight jets were forced to land at Al Jaber in Kuwait on their way back from Iraq after the tanker they approached turned out to have a refueling system compatible only with Navy planes. By the third day of the war, however, tanker issues no longer hampered the F-117s, and the Black Sheep Squadron was back on track.[15]

Back at Camp Doha, McKiernan and his staff scrambled to make sense of the first few days of the war. The capture of General Saiyf Nasser, the commander of the southern air defense sector, at Tallil air base, and, more important, of his Thuraya telephone, constituted a potential breakthrough. The numbers in the phone's memory could be exploited to locate top regime and military leaders. The list of numbers and names programmed in the phone were later added to the U.S. intelligence database. The phone was initially overlooked, however. Marks, McKiernan's intelligence officer, had to order a subordinate to go fetch the telephone after it had been inadvertently left behind.

McKiernan was satisfied with the progress the Army and Marines had made. The oil wells had been secured, as had Tallil and the Highway 1 bridge west of Nasiriyah. But the Iraqis had yet to capitulate en masse, as the CIA kept insisting they would. Indeed, there had been a few engagements with organized, conventional forces. Many of the enemy in civilian clothes encountered were determined fighters employing guerrilla tactics. The Marines and the Army were troubled by the misleading intelligence, but it was still the early days of the war.

CHAPTER 12

Everyone Loves a Parade

While Dan Allyn was fighting in Tallil, Lieutenant Colonel Terry Ferrell was rumbling toward Samawah. The 3-7 Cavalry, a storied unit established in 1866, had played a big role in settling the American West, including at General Custer's last stand at Little Bighorn. In the Iraq War, the squadron was organized for fast-paced armored thrusts. It was equipped with M1 tanks, Bradley Fighting Vehicles, 155mm artillery, and Kiowa Warrior helicopters. It had no infantry and was not designed for urban warfare.

Ferrell's mission was to conduct reconnaissance and protect the right flank of the 3rd Infantry Division as it raced toward the Karbala Gap and on to Baghdad. His first task was to streak to Samawah and secure two bridges over the man-made canals south of the town. If there was any resistance there, the squadron was to contain it. The rest of the 3rd ID and most of the Army's logistics would then head west and, eventually, north without being molested. The squadron, in effect, would be holding the door open so the V Corps could skirt Iraqi defenses in its drive to Baghdad, west of the Euphrates.

Once most of the 3rd ID had passed Samawah, 3-7 Cavalry's second task was to carry out a giant feint designed to fool the Iraqis about the direction of the Army advance. As a practical matter this meant that the squadron was to move through Samawah, cross the Euphrates River, and head north on Highways 8 and 1 toward the Medina Republican Guard Division until it approached the outskirts of Baghdad.

The squadron would hold the Medina by the nose so that Blount's division could envelop it from the west through the Karbala Gap and smash into it from behind. If the Iraqis used chemical weapons to block the V Corps advance through the gap, the squadron would have opened up another potential avenue of advance. Either way, by Scott Wallace's plan, the 3-7 Cav would be the only Army unit on the east side of the Euphrates in the early part of the war, and the only one to challenge the Republican Guard head-on.

It was an audacious mission, but Ferrell was told he would have lots of help. The Medina would be worked over by allied warplanes and Army Apache helicopters before the squadron engaged it. The squadron would have aircraft stacked overhead and on call wherever it went on the battlefield, as well as first call on supporting fire from the V Corps Multiple Launch Rocket Systems. To further strengthen the squadron, Wallace had ordered that it have its own battery of artillery. Throughout the planning phase, the focus was on the Republican Guard Medina Division. The Baathist irregulars, who had already caused minor problems for the Army and Marines, had not been seriously factored in.

The push through Samawah was to be the easy part, with little to no enemy resistance expected. A week before the war, Blount had briefed Ferrell on what to anticipate. The 3-7 Cav needed to be prepared to go in soft, the general explained, as there were indications that the Iraqi military would not put up a fight and would capitulate. American forces should not assume that every Iraqi who carried a weapon was a foe. A U.S. Special Forces team would sneak into Samawah before the squadron got there to make contact with the locals and encourage them to take up arms against the regime. The Iraqis might be holding little American flags, courtesy of the OGA—"other government agencies," the thinly disguised designation for the CIA. Like Allyn in Nasiriyah, Ferrell should be prepared to shake hands with town elders and even conduct a parade through the streets of the city. It would demonstrate that the Americans were working hand in glove with the Iraqi public and that Saddam had lost control of the southern part of his country.

The assessment coming through the intelligence channels was that there was a fifty-fifty chance that the Iraqi army would give itself up and the Shiites would seize control of the southern cities, which gave Blount some hope there would not be tough resistance. According to the intelligence, Samawah was defended by no more than a brigade of militia equipped with rifles and pistols and maybe RPGs, but they had little training and were not expected to put up much of a fight.

Some officers worried that the Samawah mission could be trickier than

Blount anticipated. Bill Weber, the 3rd ID assistant division commander for support and a former cavalry officer who had fought his way through southern Iraq during the Persian Gulf War, was one of them. Two days after Blount's visit to the squadron, Weber climbed on top of a Humvee and talked to the squadron through a set of loudspeakers. "There'll be people who will tell you that you will see Iraqis waving flags and that you will greet them and shake their hand," Weber said. "But I have been in the city before, and I tell you they are going to fight. We'll fight first and talk about it later."[1]

As Ferrell drove north, the immediate problem was not the enemy but the terrain. The dunes and fissures seemed like the surface of the moon. A cold drizzle turned the dust that was whipped up by his soldiers' advance into mud. The night was so dark that the squadron's scouts began tossing chem lights out of their Bradleys to mark the trail. Even so, two Fox vehicles—armored vehicles specially configured to detect the presence of nuclear, biological, or chemical weapons materials—slammed into each other, blowing several of their tires. During the day and a half of travel, fatigue was a constant worry. Every time the formation ground to a halt, NCOs ran down the length of the convoy, banging on the doors to stir the soldiers.

There were so many accidents in the division's push north that Lloyd Austin, the assistant division commander for maneuver, got on the radio and ordered the troops to turn on their headlights. Ferrell decided that, despite the order, the vehicles at the head of his march should continue the drive with their lights blacked out. His Crazy Troop was less than twenty miles from hitting the highway to Samawah, and turning on the lights was a risk he did not want to take.

As the squadron approached the outskirts of the town, the troops saw 1-64, the lead battalion from Colonel Dave Perkins's 2nd Brigade Combat Team, parked in a depression off to the side. Stripped down to their T-shirts, the soldiers were sleeping on top of their tanks and Bradley Fighting Vehicles, or on cots under mosquito nets. Perkins had wanted to get his armor deep into Iraq as quickly as possible and had taken a direct route toward Samawah through forbidding terrain. The thought was that the sudden arrival of Perkins's M1s and Bradleys in the Euphrates River Valley might be such a shock to the Iraqis that it might even precipitate the collapse of Saddam's government. Saddam's loyalists would wake up to see that the better part of a U.S. mechanized brigade was well inside Iraq, with a straight shot to Baghdad. It would be proof positive, if any was needed, that the Americans had the will and means to march on the capital. It was also a sign to Saddam's many opponents that the moment of their liberation was finally at hand. The soldiers from 1-64, however, were exhausted after their 160-mile march from Kuwait and were waiting for a rendezvous with their logistics trains. But their presence was a curious and comforting sight for the troops in Ferrell's squadron: how bad could the fighting be if there was time for a nap? When it came to Samawah, however, 3-7 Cav would wake everybody up.[2]

Sergeant First Class Anthony Broadhead, an outgoing soldier who possessed enormous confidence, was leading a team of mechanized vehicles that approached the canal bridges just south of the town. A platoon sergeant with the squadron's Crazy Troop, Broadhead was paired with Dillard Johnson, Crazy Troop's senior scout. Another tank and two more Bradleys—one of the squadron's hunter-killer teams—was right behind them.

It was supposed to be an easy bridge to take and the rules of engagement had been adjusted accordingly. As with the Highway 1 bridge west of Nasiriyah, an SOF team had been inserted into Iraq before G-day to make sure the bridges were intact and to make contact with friendly locals. Broadhead and Johnson were looking to link up with the SOF team and find out if their welcome had been arranged as expected. The soldiers were not anticipating any problems, but as a precaution Broadhead's M1 was in the lead, with Johnson's more vulnerable Bradley just behind. "We had got the whole brief that As Samawah was the good guys, and they're not gonna fight," recalled Johnson. "Our rules of engagement said that, 'You will see guys standing with rifles on their shoulders, and you'll see guys in uniforms with weapons, and they are waiting for you to overthrow their officers.' "

When Broadhead was about 2,000 yards from the canal bridges, he caught a glimpse of the SOF team: it was racing toward him in a trucklike vehicle with a large American flag flying from the rear for identification. The truck went flying past him without stopping. Whatever was going on near the bridges, the team seemed eager to flee the scene. Broadhead then saw a group of Iraqis standing at the far side of the first bridge. "I've got dismounts on the bridge," Broadhead called out.

When his team was about 500 yards from the bridge, Broadhead stood up in his tank and started waving. The Iraqis fired at the Americans with

AK-47s and machine guns, and soon after, an RPG was fired from a bunker. Broadhead dropped back down and started firing back with his own .50 caliber and the tank's coaxial machine gun. He then asked for permission to fire back with his main tank gun. "Permission to engage with a HEAT [High Explosive Anti-Tank] round?" he asked Captain Jeff McCoy, the Crazy Troop commander.

After receiving the go-ahead, Broadhead pumped a tank round into a guard post. The structure was painted brown but made of tin. Broadhead's 120mm high explosive round had blown a hole in one wall and gone through another, exploding behind it. Johnson joined the fight, opening up with his 25mm chain gun. When a group of Iraqis raced into what appeared to be another concrete bunker, Johnson trained his 25mm on it. Several Iraqis seemed to have been killed or wounded, but a group of them jumped into a truck and raced away. The Americans wondered if the fire had done the trick. Maybe the Iraqis had put up token resistance under pressure from their officers and would soon give up.

"We let 'em drive off," Johnson recalled. "We figured, 'Hey, those guys are part of the surrendering guys.' Once again our rules of engagement are if they're not shooting at you, you can't shoot at them." Moving to the far side of the bridge, Broadhead and Johnson made sure that it was not wired with explosives. The other M1 and two Bradleys in the mechanized team waited on the near side of the bridge.

Moving north, Broadhead and Johnson came face-to-face with a Toyota pickup truck occupied by a man, woman, and a group of children. In the distance was an Iraqi army truck and the soldiers in it appeared to be firing. Shooing away the civilians, Broadhead and Johnson took off in pursuit, following the army truck until it made a hard left into a large walled compound.

The Americans immediately began taking fire from a guard shack in front of the enclosure. By now, Broadhead and Johnson were beyond asking for permission to return fire. Broadhead dispatched the guardhouse with a tank round. The Iraqi army truck continued to race to the far side of the stockade. Eager to get off a shot, an Iraqi launched an RPG from the back of the truck, emitting a back-blast that knocked some of his comrades out of the vehicle. Johnson's Bradley fired back with its 25mm gun; the truck burst into flames, and Iraqis spilled out onto the ground.

The skirmish quickly escalated into a full-scale melee. Iraqis clambered out of bunkers to challenge the Americans. As Broadhead directed his M1 to the right of Johnson's Bradley, a hundred or more fighters began to shoot over a wall. Broadhead sprayed them with machine gun fire and maneuvered his tank around the barrier only to find that he had ventured into an adjoining military complex. It was later shown to be replete with a firing range, a first aid station, and a chamber for practicing how to put on chemical protective gear to endure poison gas attacks. Broadhead's M1 blew through a metal gate and starting pumping HEAT rounds into buildings while he blasted away with his machine gun. Grossly outnumbered and involved in a nasty fight, Broadhead would later say: "The ROE was a little shaky at this time." The Iraqis began to set up several mortars to lash back at the American intruders. Broadhead tried to suppress them with his machine gun but the enemy kept crawling back to the mortar pits for yet another shot. Finally, Broadhead silenced them with his main tank gun.[3]

While Broadhead was waging a one-tank battle, Johnson and his crew were fighting their own. Johnson's Bradley had knocked over a flagpole in the compound. Johnson jumped off his vehicle and grabbed the Iraqi flag—the squadron had its first war trophy. The firefight was fierce. Johnson's M240 machine gun was destroyed by small arms fire. The Iraqis were firing RPGs from a range so close that they did not fly far enough for their warheads to activate. Like rocket-propelled spears, the RPGs were bouncing off the Bradley. Johnson fired back with his M4 carbine and even his 9mm pistol, while his gunner fought with a second M240 that had been mounted on the back of the vehicle.

As the firing began to ebb, Johnson felt a sharp blow that knocked him into the vehicle. Johnson thought that he might be mortally wounded. He was wearing a flak jacket, but did not have the armor plates to insert in it. The squadron did not have enough to go around and only support personnel, traveling in thin-skinned vehicles, had them for added protection. When he regained his senses, Johnson found out that he was bruised and sore but otherwise all right. An estimated 150 or more dead Iraqis were scattered around his small battlefield. And his section had captured several prisoners, including some who were wounded.

Johnson and a crew member were tending to the wounded prisoners when it became clear that the break in the fighting was just a lull before another battle. Eight trucks and SUVs full of fighters dressed in black came down the road and stopped. Initially, they concentrated on the one tank and two Bradleys—the hunter-killer team—which had come forward and taken up positions on the north side of the bridge. Johnson's gunner opened up with the 25mm and Johnson fired his M203 grenade launcher, turning one vehicle into a mass of flames. Johnson called Broadhead and told him that he needed support and that Broadhead should leave the compound and help him. "I've got prisoners up around me, I need you to come back and support me so we can get these prisoners up out of here," Johnson said.

When Broadhead left the complex, Iraqi fighters and RPG teams ran out of their houses, shooting at the tank's vulnerable rear engine compartment. Johnson tried to cover the tank's rear. The Americans had sought to avoid firing into civilian homes, but the enemy was in some of the buildings. The rest of the hunter-killer team, meanwhile, started to provide covering fire, sending tank rounds and other ordnance into homes on both sides of the street. Johnson continued to round up prisoners, grabbing two in the best-looking uniforms, hoping that they might be of high rank and good interrogation subjects.

An enemy mortar round put an end to that, landing among the prisoners and killing thirteen of them. Signaling with his hand, Johnson directed the others to run away. It was time to mount up and take off. Johnson climbed up in the turret to grab his mike to let his commanders know they were moving on. The mortars kept landing. One struck a palm tree next to the Bradley and exploded, knocking Johnson and his observer into the cargo compartment of their vehicle. The shrapnel from the blast destroyed their duffel bags, water cans, the remaining M240 machine gun, Johnson's night vision goggles, and just about everything else that was exposed on the upper deck of the vehicle. Johnson suffered a burst eardrum and shrapnel wounds to his legs and arms; his observer received shrapnel wounds to his hands. The mortar barrage began to intensify.

Johnson no longer had a working machine gun and was out of radio contact with his commanders: the radio antenna had taken a hit, too. He had run through all of his HE ammunition and was firing armor-piercing rounds, which were great for attacking Iraqi tanks but traveled so fast they would go right through the trucks without disabling them, much less blowing them up. To his relief, all of the American vehicles were ordered to return south. Broadhead's tank took off and Johnson followed to protect its rear. On the way back, Johnson's Bradley hit a mortar crater and veered off the road and down a steep slope. It took some doing, but he was eventually able to maneuver the Bradley back onto the road.[4]

Ferrell had positioned his command vehicle just south of the town and was monitoring the reports about the escalating brawl in Samawah. In addition to Broadhead and Johnson, all of Crazy Troop was engaged, and the squadron's Kiowa Warrior helicopters had flown north to check on the bridge over the Euphrates in northern Samawah to make sure it was still intact. Once it had secured the canal bridges south of the city and handed them over to Dan Allyn's 3rd Brigade, the squadron planned to cross the Euphrates River bridge, head north on Route 8, and conduct the V Corps feint. Ferrell had so much trouble making radio contact with his air troop commanders that he took to communicating with them via satellite phone; they had only one, which they rotated among themselves.

Captain Thomas Hussey and Chief Warrant Officer 2 Jeff Pudil from Demon Troop, one of the squadron's two Kiowa Warrior units, were flying one of the lead aircraft into Samawah when they started taking fire from RPGs and air defense guns. They started firing back with rockets. As the fight intensified, Chief Warrant Officer 3 Dave Whalen and Chief Warrant Officer 4 Randy Godfrey, piloting another Kiowa, thought it would be safer to fly over the river, avoiding fire from buildings beneath them. They flew low between the riverbanks. As they rose to monitor the fighting, they came under attack from nearby palm groves. Determining that the bridge was still intact, the Kiowa pilots looked for muzzle flashes coming from houses below, and began firing whenever they saw them. One of the choppers was hit by small arms but was not badly damaged and fought on.

As Eagle Troop entered the fray, an RPG streaked by, narrowly missing one of his Kiowas. The air troops had removed their aircraft doors to increase the pilot's ability to observe enemy fire. The RPG had come so close that Chief Warrant Officer Mitch Carver could feel the heat of the glowing orange round as it flew by. To avoid the fire, some of the helicopters tried "under the wire" flying—piloting their aircraft under power lines, hugging the ground. This quickly became the necessary survival tactic for all the KWs.[5]

With his squadron under attack on the ground and in the air, Ferrell tried to get word to Blount, who was operating out of his assault command post at Tallil air base and was out of range of radio contact. Ferrell again used his satellite TacSat, finally getting the division tactical command post to answer. Ferrell had not seen any of the American flags that the CIA had told Blount it planned to distribute, but he had seen plenty of Iraqi fire. "This is Saber 6," Ferrell said. "There's not a goddamn flag anywhere in sight, but there are artillery rounds and small arms going off all around us."

A little later, Blount called. Ferrell said he had troops in contact. The Iraqis were using civilian pickup trucks with weapons mounted on them. They were using mortars. Ferrell didn't have a full picture, but he was sure that his squadron was not fighting a conventional foe. The squadron had encountered individuals dressed in black shirts and pants, fighting with small arms and RPGs, and using women and children as shields to move in and out of buildings. "There's no tanks, there's no BMPs, there's no uniforms. This is not anything we planned to fight. I mean they're running around in black pajamas," Ferrell recalled. This was the last contact he had with Blount for several hours.[6]

Ferrell began to think about how to confront the unexpected threat. If the squadron were to go north on Highway 8 it would need to fight its way through the town and over the Euphrates River bridge. Crazy Troop sent three tanks and two Bradleys back to retake the far side of the bridge. But as the vehicles entered the town they came under mortar fire. As they sought to pull back, one of the Bradleys drove into a mortar crater, spun around, and went off the road, hanging by its tracks on the edge of a ravine. Enemy combatants began to swarm and move in on the Bradley, which was not in a position to fire back. Johnson drove his Bradley back into the city and dropped the ramp so the crew of the stricken vehicle could get in. A tank and a Bradley came up to help, but it would be hours before Crazy Troop recovered the disabled vehicle.

As the squadron prepared to head back into town, an Iraqi missile flew into the sky, crossed the canal, leveled off at approximately 300 feet, and landed behind Crazy Troop. The soldiers could not tell if the Iraqis had fired a surface-to-air missile at a Kiowa or a surface-to-surface missile at the American invasion force. Ferrell immediately reported the missile to Blount's headquarters. Word came back that the V Corps artillery would take out the enemy missile site with an ATACMS surface-to-surface missile. The 3-7 Cavalry squadron had been promised support, and now it would come. The Army had two types of ATACMS, one that carried a massive unitary round and another that fired thousands of tiny bomblets. Both were lethal.

Jeff McCoy, the Crazy Troop commander, ordered his soldiers to stay out of the city and withdraw to the near side of the first bridge, maintaining control of the crossing site. The squadron wanted to avoid any chance of friendly fire. They waited for an hour. Nothing happened. After three hours, the squadron heard that the ATACMS strike had been called off. Firing an American missile into the heart of an Iraqi city without observers and on a mobile target was not a risk the senior commanders wanted to take. This was an understandable decision, but the delay played into the enemy's hands. The United States had given their foe three hours to reposition their forces and prepare for another attack. Ferrell ordered Crazy Troop back into the city, with Demon Troop providing overwatch of their move from the air.

The Iraqis put the time that had been given them to good use. Several dozen fighters reoccupied the buildings near the canal bridge that Broadhead and Johnson had attacked at the start of the fight. Others moved back into the military compound. They continued to fire mortars and rockets. The squadron watched from afar as the enemy brought reinforcements in by ambulance and herded women and children—human shields—into houses. For the Americans, the rules of engagement were still an inhibition.

"They were using an ambulance to pull up, drop new soldiers, and pick up the dead guys and leave," Broadhead recalled. "So they did this all day long. Sergeant McCollough wanted to kill the ambulance and I'm like no, we can't do that. As long as they're not firing, even if they're transporting new soldiers to the battlefield, they got the Red Crescent on it, they're picking up dead bodies, then they're dropping off new guys—if they're live guys you can shoot them, but not while they're in the ambulance." The squadron also had to be mindful of civilians. It did not want to hinder those leaving the combat area. But on occasion a vehicle would speed by U.S. positions and return. The soldiers were convinced that some civilians were helping the enemy adjust its mortar fire.

That night Ferrell's command post received an urgent call from the Special Operations team working for the squadron. The team had pulled out but were in touch with the CIA, which still had contacts in the town, including one with a cell phone. They gave Ferrell a ten-digit grid of a Baath Party headquarters that the enemy was said to be using as a base. They reported that Chemical Ali might be there, and the building was reported to be near a school that the Iraqis had turned into an armory. They wanted Ferrell to call in an air strike on the Baath Party building.

Ferrell dispatched Demon Troop to look into the potential target but was not prepared to attack. It had become increasingly clear to Ferrell that there was a lot about Samawah that he did not know. He had not anticipated that the Saddam Fedayeen would turn the town into a stronghold, and he had not known that the CIA had operatives in the city. At one point, one of the squadron's Kiowas saw a vehicle that looked like one of the Fedayeen trucks driving out of the city and fired several rockets at it. Though the rockets missed, they prompted the vehicle's occupants to put a thermal panel on the roof of the truck—a device used by U.S. military units and intelligence operatives to identify forces as friendly. The Kiowa noticed what was happening just as it was closing in on the truck and held its fire, reporting the incident to Ferrell.

The request by the Special Operations team to bomb the Baath Party headquarters where Chemical Ali was supposed to be hiding led to a squabble between Ferrell and the SOF team leader about who was in charge of Samawah. The leader insisted that he was the senior officer on the ground, had had a contact living in the town for ten months, and wanted the building leveled. Ferrell was as clear. He was in charge, and his orders did not call for blowing up buildings in the center of an Iraqi city. After meeting with the Special Forces and CIA operatives, Ferrell called up to division and spoke to Austin, Blount's top deputy. Ferrell requested permission to attack the building, citing the SOF and CIA reports. Austin told Ferrell that he would get back to the squadron within an hour, and that he needed to get clearance from McKiernan's headquarters.

Meanwhile, Ferrell ordered Crazy Troop's tanks and Bradleys to fight from their positions around the edge of the city. Ferrell had learned the hard way that it could take hours to clear a missile or air strike and knew that putting his own operations on hold would give the enemy an edge. McCoy sent four tanks and six Bradleys to assault the military compound again. As the vehicles approached the main gate, RPGs started flying. The Americans responded by spraying the compound with machine gun fire and its tank guns. Most of the enemy fled, but not all. Some of the most determined fighters, dressed in camouflage jackets, white shirts, and pants, stayed.

Broadhead saw one fighter dart from building to building. His gunner shot .50 caliber armor-piercing rounds into the building the fighter had entered. In less than a minute, the fighter threw out his gun and jacket and surrendered, emerging with a large, red bloodstain. Broadhead reported that he had a wounded prisoner, provided the coordinates, and moved up, hunting for any remaining fighters. He shot one and then noticed a blood trail that led into a building. Broadhead, Specialist Michael Sullivan, and several other soldiers then went into the compound and started to clear it room by room. When they found the blood trail, Broadhead pointed his pistol around a corner leading to a room and fired four or five rounds. Sullivan did the same. When they stepped into the room, they found an

Iraqi sitting on a pile of ammunition, his AK-47 in one hand, a magazine in the other, trying to reload it. Broadhead shot him twice in the chest. The Iraqi slumped to the floor. He had already taken rounds in the rear, thigh, and calf.

The compound was filled with ammunition: rifles, 60mm mortars, mortar tubes, and bayonets. Broadhead—who had been under orders to blow up an antenna complex in the compound—took some of the weapons, grabbed a load of documents, and threw an incendiary grenade into the room to explode the remaining ammo and weapons. He got back in his vehicle with the wounded POW. As the grenade set the building aflame he fired HEAT rounds inside to ensure that the weapons were destroyed. Then Broadhead, Sullivan, and the rest pulled back to the bridge to drop off the injured prisoner. Ferrell gave Crazy Troop new orders to hand over security of the crossing sites to Apache Troop and expand operations. All Crazy Troop forces were required to continue the fight around the city.

Six hours after he sought permission to attack the Baath Party headquarters, Ferrell finally got the go-ahead. An F-16 was on station. The plan was to bring in two Kiowas so they could identify, or "paint," the building with laser designators. The F-16 would use the laser to identify the building it was to target, which would minimize the risk of civilian casualties in the bombing of a building in the center of town.

Captain Darin Griffen, Demon Troop commander, would lase the building. His Kiowa kept popping up and down as he tried to evade enemy fire, preventing him from getting a lock on the building with the laser. So the squadron came up with a surefire way to mark the structure: the helicopter fired a Hellfire missile at the building. Then the F-16 dropped three satellite-guided JDAM bombs. Two hit the building; the third landed between the party headquarters and a school. "When we hit the Baath Party headquarters, everything in that schoolhouse lit up," Ferrell recalled. "Anything and everything that had a weapon came out the door and they were shooting. Charlie and Demon troops engaged and that's where we killed an estimate of about a hundred-plus. They were coming out pretty heavily, just streaming out of this building."[7]

Colonel Will Grimsley, the commander of the 1st Brigade Combat Team, could tell that Ferrell had his hands full in Samawah. Under the 3rd ID plan, Grimsley had passed through Dan Allyn's 3rd BCT near the Highway 1 bridge and was heading west on two parallel routes: Route 8 along the Euphrates River and Route 28, which was several miles to the south along an elevated dike. With Grimsley's units were Blount in his assault Command Post (CP) on Route 28, and Austin in the jump CP on Route 8. Trouble loomed ahead. The brigade's reconnaissance troop had been ambushed on Route 8, twelve miles west of Samawah. Two scouts had been wounded—one a platoon sergeant—by paramilitary forces. The troop arranged to pass the brigade's first wounded back to Scott Rutter, whose 2-7 Infantry Battalion was part of Grimsley's formation and next in line.

As Rutter's battalion approached Kindr, a small town on the way to Samawah, his soldiers came upon a group of Iraqis pointing and yelling, all to no effect as there was no interpreter in Rutter's unit. Minutes later, it became clear what they were shouting about. As First Lieutenant Stephen Gleason moved forward an RPG or larger-caliber round buzzed over the hood of his up-armored Humvee. Some of the Iraqis in the south were cooperating after all, as the CIA had promised, at least in towns like Kindr, where the Fedayeen had not established a dominant presence. But without interpreters, the Americans were unable to take advantage of the little collaboration they were receiving.

Rutter left a company behind to guard the route through the town and pressed on. As the company settled in for a long night, all of the town's lights suddenly went out. Fighters had infiltrated the town. Not appreciating the night vision capability of the U.S. forces, they had shut off the electricity to provide themselves with a cover of darkness. Uncertain as to whether the ROE allowed them to shoot the Iraqis as they retrieved arms from the battlefield, the U.S. soldiers withheld their fire.

As he headed toward Samawah, Rutter ordered some of his infantry to secure a foothold on the city's southern outskirts. But Captain Jimmy Lee's tank company missed a turn and ended up in the heart of the city. Rutter frantically ordered his tank company to turn around. He had visions of Black Hawk Down in Somalia: an American unit cut off and surrounded in an enemy-controlled city. Grimsley, who was west of Samawah and out of radio contact with Rutter, knew something was amiss when he checked Blue Force Tracker: there were blue icons in the heart of Samawah. He sent Rutter an e-mail message asking what the hell Jimmy Lee was doing there. Rutter's terse reply was that he was in heavy contact, understood the order, and had to go.

As RPGs and fire from small arms pinged off their armor, Lee was glad his men were traveling in M1s and Bradleys. After it was certain that 3-7

Cavalry was nowhere nearby, the tank company was authorized to fire on threatening crowds of Iraqis, and began to push through the narrow streets and alleys until it had bulled its way back out of the town. It had been a close call, but the unit had averted casualties because of its armor and training—and luck.[8]

After two days, the sporadic fighting in Samawah had turned into a major battle. Unable to control the town, the U.S. troops also had their hands full stopping Iraqi fighters in the town from attacking the roads leading to it. The shooting was so persistent that Austin reported to Blount that movement on the route had come to a halt. Blount was concerned about a bottleneck developing on Route 8. In a radio call to Ferrell, he complained that U.S. forces driving past the south of the town were taking fire, and he wanted to know why 3-7 Cav couldn't do something about it. Meanwhile, Blount sought to adjust by ordering the division to avoid Route 8 near the Euphrates until the Iraqi attack ceased and channeling his forces onto Highway 28, farther south. But this solution only created another problem: positioning all the units on one road slowed the division's westward advance.

"He ripped me a new ass, because the route was not secured," Ferrell recalled. "I figured I was going to get fired before long. I said, 'Look, I've reported all damn day that we're in contact and that this city's not secure, not once have I said it was secure.' I said the crossing sites were secure. We own them, they were intact, you can get across them, but you're going to be in contact when you skirt this city, there's no way out of it, because the dirt trail and the hardball [unsurfaced road] were within range of their weapons systems. So I could have put the whole goddamn division on line and there'd still have been someone able to fire on the passing columns."[9]

To deal with the unexpected fighting in Samawah and along Route 8, Blount gave a new order to Allyn, who had taken the Highway 1 bridge and Tallil. After turning the Highway 1 bridge over to the Marines, he was to divert the 1-15 Infantry Battalion, which had been intended to support the division's push to Baghdad, to reinforce Ferrell's squadron at Samawah. Allyn himself was to head to Samawah and take charge of the fight. By securing the division's routes west, he would eventually free Ferrell's squadron to conduct its feint north through the city.[10]

Leaving the 1-30 Infantry Battalion behind to secure Tallil and the eastern portion of the division's supply lines, Allyn moved west along

Highway 28. As he bypassed stalled convoys, Allyn saw that Highway 28 was free of enemy fire, but heavily congested. Much of the division appeared to be snarled in a massive traffic jam. When he arrived at Samawah, he huddled with Lieutenant Colonel John Charlton, the commander of 1-15, and Ferrell in the captured Iraqi military compound to assess the situation. As the officers talked, the Iraqis unleashed an artillery barrage directly on the 1-15 column. The battalion was still en route to the southern sector of Samawah and had part of its formation exposed on an elevated dike. After days of only sometimes accurate Iraqi mortar fire, the U.S. troops did not have much respect for Iraqi artillery. But now the Iraqis were firing large caliber artillery, and the congestion along the route had presented them with an inviting target. One round landed just a few yards from First Sergeant Roger Burt, seriously wounding him. The shell had come so close that many soldiers initially assumed Burt had to be dead.

Allyn quickly sized up the situation. There was no way for Ferrell's squadron to drive through Samawah and conduct the feint that Scott Wallace had ordered, unless the 3rd BCT secured the city and guarded the bridge across the Euphrates. But that would require a brigade to isolate the entire town, all but abandoning other missions. Nor did Allyn think the cavalry squadron's logistics for the feint north were up to the task under the circumstances. By now the squadron was low on fuel and ammunition. Allyn's soldiers had given Ferrell some fuel, but it would take a day or more for more fuel and ammo to arrive.

Allyn called Austin and reported that the V Corps needed to reconsider its plan. Conducting a feint through an enemy stronghold would be challenging enough, but keeping the supply lines secure would exceed Allyn's combat power. After conferring with Blount, Austin said that Ferrell was to bypass Samawah and find another crossing point farther to the west. For now Allyn's brigade would contain the Fedayeen in Samawah and stop them from harassing the Army columns to the south—vital support for the division's passage westward, and the rapid buildup of combat power needed for the final drive to Baghdad. Hundreds of fuel tankers, ammo trucks, and other vehicles still had to move south of the town. Beefing up Allyn's forces, Blount sent the 2-70 Armored Battalion to help establish a cordon around Samawah. As for venturing into the town to pacify the city, another unit could take that on later.

To keep the Iraqi fighters off balance, Allyn carried out a series of limited attacks on the city. His intent was to keep the Fedayeen focused only on defending Samawah itself and not outlying regions, by creating the impression that he was probing the Iraqi defenses as a prelude to attacking the city. This, Allyn calculated, would stop the Fedayeen from venturing beyond the city limits to threaten the Army's supply lines in the south. Two battalions were now involved in isolating Samawah, cutting into the combat power the division would otherwise have used to drive north.

As he settled in outside the town, Allyn's soldiers brought him an Iraqi captain who'd been taken prisoner. The Iraqi was sure that the U.S. troops meant to execute him, and began to hug and kiss them when he discovered his life was not in jeopardy. But the picture he painted was troubling. Several hundred Saddam loyalists had recently arrived in Samawah and had taken over the town. School had been canceled and the fighters had moved into the schools and occupied the mosques. Iraqi soldiers who failed to demonstrate sufficient determination were being executed. Townspeople were being pressed into service against the U.S. troops. If the Americans really wanted to win, the Iraqi captain said, they needed to blast all the schools and mosques in the city. That was not an option for the U.S. forces, but neither was driving through Samawah. The plan to screen the flank of the 3rd ID with a cavalry unit and to use it to deceive the Iraqi Medina Division with a feint up Highway 8 was in shambles, the work of an enemy who was not supposed to exist.[11]

After his firefight in Samawah, Ferrell's cavalry squadron was ordered to move west. But Ferrell and Pete Bayer, the 3rd Infantry Division operations officer, had gotten their signals crossed on how the squadron should get there.

With the squadron out of tactical radio range, Bayer transmitted the coordinates in a brief text message on Blue Force Tracker, which noted that the route was clear. Bayer intended to direct the squadron along the same route the division had taken to Rams, one that was relatively free of the enemy. But when he plotted the coordinates, Ferrell mistakenly thought he was talking about a parallel road along the Euphrates, code-named Appaloosa, which was clear of the columns of Army vehicles that were threatening to turn the blitz to Baghdad into a rush-hour traffic jam. It was the sort of communications breakdown that illustrated the cobwebs that gathered when officers pushed themselves for days without rest. In the swirl of confusion, Bayer and Ferrell would not discover the problem for hours.

Ferrell felt good about the route when he started out on the afternoon of March 25. He put Apache Troop, which was led by Captain Clay Lyle, in the lead. By 9:00 p.m., the squadron was about four miles shy of Fay-sailiyah, a small town along the river. As if somebody hit a button, the squadron suddenly started taking fire from the woods to the left and riverbank to the right. Ferrell's troops were caught in a perfect infantry school L-shaped ambush. This was not the benign route Ferrell had expected, and he was not in the best position to respond. Not only was he moving in column, but the weather had grounded the squadron's Kiowa Warriors, and many of the enemy fighters were too close to be engaged by the squadron's artillery.

Ferrell was in a jam. As bad as the ambush was, he figured it would only get worse when the squadron rolled through Faysailiyah and the enemy fighters were able to fire from rooftops and alleyways. Ferrell told Lyle to find a detour around the town. In the meantime, he kept the column creeping along at five miles per hour. While Lyle's scouts searched for a bypass, Ferrell ordered his Paladin artillery batteries to fire on the Iraqi mortar positions on the eastern side along the Euphrates. Ferrell would need the Air Force to take care of the enemy to the west. The 3-7 Cavalry had been promised continuous air support before it crossed into Iraq. Now it was time to put that promise to the test.

Ferrell radioed Technical Sergeant Mike Keehan, his Air Force forward air controller, who was in an M113 behind Ferrell in the column. Keehan reported there were A-10s on station. Ferrell said the A-10s should lay waste to the fighters on the west side of the road and provided a grid. Seconds later, Ferrell heard someone banging on the side of the truck. Keehan had jumped out of his vehicle and was pounding on the side of Ferrell's command vehicle, desperately trying to get his attention. "Sir, I need your name, your rank, and your social security number," Keehan exclaimed.

The bombs would be falling so close to the squadron that there was a substantial risk of a friendly fire incident. The Air Force, he said, would not attack unless Ferrell took personal responsibility for the bombing raid. An irritated Ferrell gave him the information, and as an afterthought he said that the Air Force should keep his personal information on file: the way things were going, they would need it again. The A-10s came in a flight of two, using everything from cannon to rockets. After one pass, the field to the west was on fire. Ferrell told his artillery to cease fire and had the A-10s do the same on the other side.[12]

By now, Apache's scouts had found a potential bypass that went down a twisting dirt trail and passed over a small bridge that spanned a canal. Lyle was not certain that the bridge would support his vehicle, but the engineers thought it might hold. One by one, the vehicles started to cross. Two of the scouts' Bradleys made it over the bridge, as did three of the tanks. As the fourth tank moved on the bridge, however, it finally gave way. Lyle passed the bad news to Ferrell. First Lieutenant Matthew Garrett and Sergeant First Class Paul Wheatley were on the other side of the canal with five vehicles, cut off from the rest of the squadron. An M1 tank had gone straight through the bridge and fallen fifteen feet into the canal. The situation was potentially desperate, only the V Corps and the division did not know about it. With all the communications difficulties, Ferrell would have to solve this problem on his own.

Ferrell tried to deal with the stress by resorting to an old habit. Officers were discouraged from smoking, but Ferrell lit a cigarette. There was only one option: reverse course on the bypass and then go through Faysailiyah after all. If the Iraqis were seeking to lure the Americans into an ambush they would now have their chance. Bravo Troop, which was at the end of the column, would now be in the lead.

The M1 had survived the fall into the canal but there was no way to recover it. The soldiers stripped the sensitive items off the tank—radios, maps, night vision gear, anything the enemy could use—and jumped into other vehicles. As one of the fuel trucks tried to do a U-turn, however, it slipped off the narrow road and also landed in the canal. The front end of the vehicle was buried so deep in mud that soldiers had to cut away the cab of the truck, wrap a chain around the drivers, and pull them out one by one, a process that broke one of the drivers' hands.

More vehicles were lost. As Bravo Troop turned around, Captain Gary O'Sullivan's tank skidded off the side of the road and fell on its side. One of the wingman's Bradleys threw a track as it was turning and dropped into a canal. O'Sullivan was agitated by the setback and seemed to lose control of the troops; Ferrell was thankful there was a strong executive officer who could take charge.

Leaving its stricken vehicles and crews behind to temporarily fend for themselves, Ferrell's squadron fought its way through Faysailiyah only to encounter a new threat on the other end: enemy fighters paddling across the Euphrates in wooden boats. The squadron began to take them out, and Ferrell sent a text message to Charlie Troop, which was just preparing to leave Samawah: Captain Jeff McCoy was told to stay off Route Appaloosa and take the parallel road west. The message was never received.

Exhausted by the ordeal, Ferrell tried to call the division for help. He could not get headquarters on the TacSat or HF radio. Finally, he got Pete

Bayer, the 3rd Infantry Division operations officer, at 4:30 in the morning on his satellite telephone. Bayer said there was nothing he could do. The Apaches were not flying because of the weather and a heightened appreciation of the threat to the choppers. The MLRS artillery could not reach at that range. No other forces were nearby to help out. Bayer told Ferrell that he sounded like he had a handle on the situation and that he could not do anything more than talk to him.

Ferrell called once more for the A-10s. The planes made two passes and saturated the riverbanks. The planes dropped 500-pound bombs and strafed with their cannons. The concussions from the explosions were so powerful that some of the soldiers could feel the hot wind and were pushed back in their turrets. As dawn approached, Ferrell was depleted. Five of his vehicles were cut off in enemy territory and struggling to regroup. Others were lost at the canal. The soldiers had had to deal with everything from snipers in a mosque to fighters in boats. Charlie Troop was unknowingly headed through the gauntlet of fire and there was no way to warn them.[13]

When the sun rose, an Iraqi ran out with a white flag. The soldiers did not know if this was a ruse or a genuine appeal. At the start of the war they had held their fire when they saw Iraqi troops, figuring every combatant was a potential ally. But after three days of firefights against an enemy in civilian dress they were beginning to view every Iraqi as potential Fedayeen. This Iraqi was desperately seeking help. Several civilians had been killed in his house, which had been near an enemy mortar position. Others were wounded, including a small child, who was crying for his father. The medic quickly treated the wounded and loaded them on civilian Iraqi ambulances that showed up at the scene. Ferrell needed to keep moving. The Iraqis would have to take care of the civilians who had been caught in the crossfire.

At 6:15 a.m., Ferrell successfully contacted Blount's headquarters. After a nightlong ordeal he was off schedule. Lloyd Austin, the deputy commander of the 3rd Infantry Division, came on the radio and had three direct questions: "Now where are you at? Where are you supposed to be at? Why are you on that road?" The 3rd Infantry Division commanders still did not realize that Ferrell's squadron had spent the night on the wrong road in a vicious firefight.

Ferrell filled him in. He reported that he had fought two battalions of dismounts, equipped with technical vehicles, RPGs, 30mm cannons, and mortars. After a fifty-mile march, the squadron had lost two Humvees, two tanks, a fuel truck, and a Bradley. Wheatley and Garrett had narrowly escaped being another friendly fire statistic when Charlie Troop canceled an urgent request for an air strike after learning that the "enemy" was the cutoff Bradleys and tanks. Ferrell still needed to find a way to bring them back. Surprisingly, no soldiers had yet been killed.

Austin said that based on what the squadron went through it would be ordered to Rams, where it could rest and regroup before it took on its next mission on the following day. Ferrell started planning his next steps and sent a team to recover one of his tanks. It had been a nonstop ordeal and his soldiers desperately needed a break. Then Austin called back. "Hey, Saber," Austin said, using Ferrell's call sign. Ferrell thought when Blount's deputy called him by his code name it was usually because he had something to tell him that he did not want to hear. With the constant attacks by the Fedayeen, there would be a new mission for the squadron near Najaf. "Saber, I need you to go ahead and execute today. I need you to execute as soon as you can."[14]

CHAPTER 13

Task Force Tarawa

On the evening of March 22 Brigadier General Rich Natonski set up his command post near the Jalibah airfield, twelve miles from Nasiriyah. The Marines' "opening gambit" had gone well. As the commander of the 2nd Marine Expeditionary Brigade out of Camp Lejeune, North Carolina, Natonski was to set the stage for the next phase of the Marine attack.

Natonski had two tasks. The first was to race north and take control of the Highway 1 bridge that had been seized on the first day of the war by Dan Allyn's soldiers. Once the Army had transferred the bridge to the Marines, Jim Mattis would use it to send two of his regimental combat teams north on the route toward Baghdad. The second and more challenging mission had not been given to Natonski's task force until that evening. Natonski's Marines would also be capturing two bridges in the eastern sector of Nasiriyah. That would open the door for the third regiment in Mattis's division—Joe Dowdy's Regimental Combat Team 1—to drive north up Highway 7 toward Kut. Both routes were vital to Blue Diamond. By using two avenues of attack, Mattis calculated that he could reduce the bottleneck at the Highway 1 bridge and keep the division moving. And by driving up Highway 7 toward Kut, Dowdy's regiment would be able to pin down the Baghdad Infantry Division, which, according to U.S. intelligence, was deployed in and around the city and was armed with chemical artillery shells.

Natonski's brigade was not part of Mattis's 1st Division and not the obvious choice for its assignment. Natonski had had to push hard for the Nasiriyah mission. In the initial planning phase of the war, it looked as if his brigade would be little more than occupiers: they were to secure the

Rumaylah oilfields and provide rear-guard security for much of the south after Mattis's division had passed through. Fittingly enough, early on, Natonski's unit had been called Task Force South. But no sooner did Natonski's Marines embark for Kuwait than their mission was changed.

After the Turks slammed the door on a British assault from the north, Major General Robin Brims's 1st U.K. Division had been given responsibility for securing southern Iraq after the "opening gambit." Natonski's Marines would have a new charge: facilitating Mattis's attack north. They would also have a new designation: Task Force Tarawa, which Natonski had settled on in honor of a bloody World War II battle fought by Marines from Camp Lejeune. Natonski hoped that his Iraqi campaign would add to the glory of the Marines.

The Marine strategy roughly paralleled the one the Army's V Corps had devised for its attack north. Just as Terry Ferrell's 3-7 Cavalry Squadron was supposed to conduct a feint to distract the Medina Division, Mattis hoped to use Dowdy's regiment to do much the same with the main Republican Guard unit that threatened his march to the Iraqi capital. After holding the Baghdad Division in place, RCT-1 would join its brother regiments for the final assault on the Iraqi capital. Natonski had no time to discuss the fine points of the strategy when Colonel Ron Bailey, the commander of his 2nd Regimental Combat Team, came to his Jalibah headquarters that night. "We got the bridges," Natonski stated, referring to the Nasiriyah spans—a mission he had had his eye on as a way to play a more visible and important role in the war.

Mattis, for one, thought that bringing Task Force Tarawa into Nasiriyah would be a recipe for confusion, as it meant he would be passing a regiment through a unit that was not under his command. Nor did Mattis think that Nasiriyah would be benign. He found it hard to believe that the city would be given up without a fight, no matter what the intelligence said. Nasiriyah had recently been visited by Chemical Ali, Saddam's cousin and strongman for southern Iraq. Mattis, hard-charging general that he was, thought that the best way to guarantee success was for Jim Conway to give Blue Diamond the entire Nasiriyah mission up front. At Camp Doha in Kuwait, Dave McKiernan had his doubts about the wisdom of venturing into Nasiriyah at all. He thought the city should be bypassed, like others in the south. Even so, McKiernan was not about to dictate tactics to Conway.

. . .

In his Jalibah headquarters on the evening of March 22, Natonski told Bailey that he needed to gain control of the Highway 1 bridge by 12:30 a.m. and to begin the attack to seize the two bridges in Nasiriyah three and half hours later. Bailey was surprised and decidedly less enthusiastic than Natonski about the timing of the mission. He was worried about getting it all done as planned. Methodically, Bailey had planned on securing the Highway 1 bridge during daylight hours and then preparing for the Nasiriyah task. Now, things were moving precipitately even as one of his battalions was at the Highway 1 bridge, separated from the rest of the regiment by twenty miles.

Bailey asked for intelligence on Nasiriyah. Lieutenant Colonel Joseph Apodaca, Natonski's intelligence officer, had little to offer. Apodaca was a counterinsurgency specialist who once did a tour at the CIA. He had received CIA reports that the commander of the Iraqi 11th Division in Nasiriyah was ready to surrender and that Iraqi intelligence and paramilitary units in the city would break and run for fear of retribution by the local population—very much along the lines of what "Bob" and other CIA operatives had said to Buff Blount.[1] But Apodaca had also heard about the Fedayeen's ambush of Dan Allyn's soldiers near Tallil. He did not have much to work with. The Marines had a limited number of reconnaissance drones, which had been allocated to the units that Conway's staff thought would see most of the fighting: Mattis's 1st Marine Division and the British. Task Force Tarawa had no UAVs to reconnoiter what lay ahead. Thus, Apodaca was going on early intel and whatever updates he could get on the move.[2]

Anxious as ever about Task Force Tarawa's Nasiriyah operation, Bailey told Natonski that he needed some "push-back": his tank company and AAVs needed to refuel, and his Marines needed some rest. Natonski, who was under pressure from his superiors to carry out the mission as quickly as possible, was not sympathetic. The Marines would have to move on adrenaline. Bailey should not expect anything more than small arms fire, the general explained.[3] There had been an underlying tension between Bailey's and Natonski's staffs for a while and, with the urgency of the new mission, it came to the fore. Major Andy Kennedy, Bailey's operations officer, was displeased with the rush to take the bridges. Kennedy argued with Colonel Ron Johnson, Natonski's operations officer, about the mission and muttered profanities as he walked away. But Bailey was outranked; the decision had been made.

Overseeing the handoff of the Highway 1 bridge was challenging enough. Bailey dispatched his Light Armored Reconnaissance company—fast-moving light armored vehicles (LAV)—to the bridge. He also sent the truck-mounted 3rd Battalion of RCT-2, commanded by Lieutenant Colonel Paul Brent Donahoe. As Bailey himself drove to the western bridge, he got stuck in traffic. Army convoys were moving on both sides of a divided highway. Refuelers were doing sixty miles per hour. It was, Kennedy would later recall, "the most insane Mr. Toad's Wild Ride you could possibly imagine." As the Marines raced to get to the Highway 1 bridge, one Humvee in Donahoe's regiment smashed into the back of an Army ambulance that had come to a stop. The exhausted Marine driver, a sergeant, was half asleep, and an Army commander had temporarily positioned his vehicles across the highway so that other units would not push ahead of him. The Marine sergeant died in the collision.[4]

When Bailey finally arrived at the bridge, he was met by Lieutenant Colonel James Reilly, commanding officer of the First Force Reconnaissance Company, which had been sent ahead by Natonski's command to scope out the situation. With just two platoons and a Special Forces team, Reilly's small unit had been the first Marine force on the scene. The accident had delayed Donahoe's battalion, so Bailey asked Reilly to remain in place until 3/2 arrived. Reilly had picked up precious little information on the enemy from the 3rd Infantry Division soldiers who'd handed over the bridge and departed. Mounted in four interim fast attack vehicles (IFAVs), "Dune Buggies," Reilly and twelve of his men went on reconnaissance north of the bridge on Highway 1, and then back along Highway 8 toward Nasiriyah.

At dawn, on the Nasiriyah leg, Reilly triggered an Iraqi ambush on the outskirts of the city. Though he was heavily outgunned and outnumbered, the Iraqi fire was so inaccurate—Reilly called it, politically incorrectly, "The Raghead Spray"—that his men suffered no casualties before Reilly disengaged. He radioed news of the contact to Task Force Tarawa and provided a fuller account of the action after he returned to Tarawa's command post in the morning. It was an early indication that Nasiriyah was not as quiet as it was supposed to be.[5]

As Bailey returned south after checking on the Highway 1 bridge handoff, he gave his full attention to planning the attack for securing the Nasiriyah bridges. Bailey intended to proceed cautiously, step by step. He would begin the attack at 7:00 a.m. by clearing both sides of the road leading to Nasiriyah with Lieutenant Colonel Rick Grabowski's 1st Battalion, 2nd Marines. He would then bring up his supporting artillery. Bailey would also refuel his tanks and get them in place so they could provide covering fire. Grabowski's battalion would take up defensive positions south of the city, and, when the order was given, move in to capture the bridges. Since Bailey had spent the night on the move, he had had no time to download any new electronic orders that might have been sent to his SMART-T, a satellite communications system. In the months leading up to the war, Conway and his senior officers at the Marine Expeditionary Force had never convened all of the commanders to go over the plan for Nasiriyah. Bailey figured that he could do the job his way and on his time. "All I received orally was 'we got the bridges,' " Bailey recalled after the war. "I never received an order to get the bridges at this time."[6]

Jim Conway's command had its own set of expectations. The command anticipated that the Nasiriyah bridges would be available for use by 10:00 a.m. on March 23. And Mattis had always planned to move quickly—his push north would be delayed only if Task Force Tarawa was slow in doing its job.[7] While Bailey himself did not receive a formal order from Natonski's command, or a schedule for taking the bridges, his deputy, Andy Kennedy, did. But even so, Bailey was prepared to back off the schedule that had been imposed on him if the fighting got tough. The thinking, Kennedy later explained, was that "if there was resistance over there we would probably not do that mission, just because we did not want to get involved in a slugfest in an urban area."[8]

Bailey ordered Grabowski to clear the route from Jalibah to the southern outskirts of Nasiriyah. At 5:30 a.m. the battalion embarked in its AAVs. A tank company from the Marine Corps Reserve—led by Major Bill Peeples, a city planner from Avon, Indiana—was in the lead. The rest of the battalion was in a typical Marine Corps tactical formation, "two up, one back," an inverted triangle well suited for movement into an unknown situation. But the marshy terrain could not support armored vehicles on the flanks, and the battalion was forced to stick to the road and move in a column.

As Grabowski approached the town, the battalion began to take intermittent artillery, mortar, and machine gun fire. He dismounted his infantry from their AAVs and methodically began clearing possible ambush sites along the way. Grabowski was perplexed. He had been told that there would be no resistance in Nasiriyah, and he wanted to exercise restraint. But his battalion was being fired on. He didn't know who was behind it—a few hotheads or a hostile population.

Grabowski had been told by Kennedy to advance to a specific location and hold. As he approached his limit of advance, Grabowski asked and received permission to move up another mile, so that Lieutenant Colonel Glenn Starnes's artillery battalion could find suitable terrain for its guns. "I had no idea we were going for the bridges at that point," Grabowski recalled. "I was thinking we were going to set up a defense south of the city."[9]

In the lead, Peeples was also puzzled by the unexpected, sporadic attacks against the battalion. At first he thought the mortars might be friendly fire—some Marine unit, he figured, was dropping 81s on them. But when the small arms fire started, he realized he was facing his first enemy contact of the war. Peeples's company was not at its strongest. His unit had shrunk from fourteen to twelve tanks after two of his M1s had broken down. He responded to the attack with machine gun and tank fire, but that ran afoul of the guidance the unit had been given to avoid using main tank guns unless the enemy attacked with a like weapons system. So he ordered his company to go "weapons tight" with the main guns and use .50 caliber and coax.

Then Peeples saw what appeared to be a truck driving south on Route 7, heading toward his tank. "I looked up and said, 'What is that?' I was getting ready to fire when it turned about and headed back north." There was no reason for the tanks to chase the truck. As Peeples tried to make sense of what was happening, several Humvees drove south into the tanks' lines. Peeples was again startled: he had not known there were any friendlies ahead of him. Suddenly, a frightened Army captain pulled up, jumped out of his Humvee, drew his pistol, and crouched behind the door. The officer told Peeples that there were still wounded Army soldiers in the city. A surprised Peeples got back in his tank and radioed the battalion: he was moving forward to try to help U.S. forces ahead of him. U.S. soldiers were in the truck that he had almost fired on.[10]

Grabowski did not know what to make of Peeples's report. In early planning discussions, it had been decided that a 3rd Infantry Division unit would take up position just south of Nasiriyah and remain, like the unit at the Highway 1 bridge, until it was relieved by the Marines. Grabowski wondered if the old plan had been activated. So did Rob Fulford, the chief operations officer of the 2nd Battalion, 8th Marines, which rounded out Bailey's regiment. But the old plan had been abandoned even before the Army division crossed into Iraq. No Army units were supposed to be in front of the Marines.

The mystery would later be solved. The Army captain who had told Peeples about wounded Americans in Nasiriyah was Troy King, the commander of the 507th, a Patriot maintenance company that had been trying to catch up with the Patriot antimissile units speeding north to protect the Army advance from Iraqi missile strikes. The company had gotten lost, blundered into Nasiriyah, and crossed the Euphrates River bridge—and then another spanning the Saddam Canal—without interference. Realizing that it was on the wrong route, the company had turned around only to come under fire.

As King's column sought to retrace its steps and flee south, it had missed a turn leading to the bridge over the Saddam Canal, forcing it to make another U-turn under fire. Fleeing south, the convoy had splintered into several groups. Many soldiers had been unable to return fire, as their weapons were poorly maintained. King, at the front of the convoy, had made it out of town, but many of his soldiers had been left behind—some wounded, some dead, and some taken prisoner. Of thirty-three soldiers in the column, eleven were killed. Seven were captured, including Private Jessica Lynch, who had been in the back of a Humvee that crashed into an Army truck. She had been knocked unconscious without firing her weapon. The remainder of the company made it to safety, although several of them were wounded.

For the Americans, the episode illustrated the hazards of going to war with vulnerable supply lines and no clear front lines. It was also a telling demonstration of how ill prepared some Army logistics units were for combat. The 507th was accustomed to performing its duties only in the rear and had failed its first combat test.[11]

As Peeples moved toward Nasiriyah, he used a system called "bounding overwatch," in which one company provided fire support as the others leapfrogged north. But he immediately ran into a problem: the ground was wet and soft. When his 3rd Platoon got off the road, it began to sink. Here was an omen of what was in store, but no one knew it at the time.

The Iraqis were close to a railroad overpass on the outskirts of town, in and atop buildings. Peeples pushed forward with three tanks and found a group of ten Army survivors from the 507th, four wounded, hunkered down in a ditch behind their destroyed trucks and Humvees, taking intermittent fire from four different locations. Three tanks maneuvered the best they could to put themselves between the survivors and the Iraqis, spraying suppressive fire with their main guns and machine guns. Peeples sent a "troops in contact" alert to the rear. He had no air cover and needed support. "All of a sudden the floodgates opened up and we had lots of air going in," Peeples recalled. Two AAVs from Bravo Company also arrived to evacuate the wounded.

Unaware that Bailey's RCT-2 was already under orders to take the bridges, Grabowski ordered the tanks to the rear to refuel. He wanted to top off the tanks while he had the chance and did not want Peeples to get too decisively engaged with the enemy at that time. The battalion commander was still operating on the assumption that his immediate mission was to hold south of the city and wait for instructions. The refueling point was a five-mile drive south. Peeples was not happy about breaking away from the fight; he was eager to refuel his tanks and get back to the front. When he arrived at the refueling station, Peeples found only a single truck with a broken pump. It contained a mere 1,400 gallons—only a little more than 100 gallons per tank. To pump the fuel into the M1s, supply personnel had to rely on the force of gravity. It would take fifteen minutes or so to refuel each.[12]

Shortly before noon, an impatient Natonski choppered in to confer with Bailey. Natonski had wanted the assault on the bridges to begin no later than 7:00 a.m. The general felt Bailey was moving too slowly and asked him if Grabowski was being aggressive enough. Bailey said Grabowski was doing fine. As far as Bailey was concerned, everything was going according to plan—his own, which called for systematically clearing the road, consolidating just south of the railroad bridge, bringing up the artillery, refueling, and moving another battalion up behind Grabowski before advancing on the bridges. Bailey thought Natonski should have understood that he could not fulfill his mission more quickly. He had told him the night before that he was low on tank fuel. Unsatisfied with what he was hearing, Natonski decided to talk to Grabowski himself. Bailey figured he'd better tag along. When Natonski and Bailey arrived at Grabowski's position, the general asked for an update. The battalion commander proceeded to explain that his Marines were clearing houses along the route to Nasiriyah. Bailey was satisfied with this, but Natonski's jaw tightened and the general shook his head.

Natonski led Grabowski to the side of the road so the two officers could be alone. "Ricky, I need you to fucking get up there and seize the bridges by 1500 today," Natonski said. "I don't need you clearing houses. You can bypass and 2/8 will follow up." Natonski pointed up the road to the city and added: "There is nothing up there that can stop you." Grabowski had armor and mechanized infantry, and it was time to put them to use.

The tension between Bailey's and Natonski's staffs had put the battalion in a difficult situation. Bailey and Kennedy were determined not to rush into the fray and were working off their own schedule. From the start, Conway and Natonski had assumed a different timetable. After the battle Starnes, the artillery commander, and Grabowski asked for an explanation of the confusion. How was it that they had been kept in the dark about the generals' orders? Kennedy made a belated and somewhat startling confession in a message, one that was never disclosed and which stayed within the Marine family.

"Gentlemen, why did we not pass the timeline for seizing the bridges?" Kennedy wrote in an e-mail. "I'm not sure. I thought I passed we would attack them after we gathered ourselves at the 20 northing. I may not have done so. I wanted to see what the situation was in the area before we went to attack the bridges (all concerned about level of violence and urban suck etc.). . . . My intentions were to not go in half cocked but to assess the situation. The orders we'd received were sufficiently annoying that I did not want to execute them as briefed and so I asked Col. B about why and when. He got me to shut up by telling me we need not attack until we were ready. In the rush of events that night I have no idea why I did not mention the fact that MEB [headquarters] wanted us to attack the bridges. I thought I passed this."[13]

On the morning of the twenty-third it was clear to Grabowski that, regardless of what Bailey or Kennedy may have had in mind, the commanding general of Task Force Tarawa wanted him to take the bridges, and take them fast. Grabowski considered all that had to be done to carry out the attack. Peeples's tanks were supposed to support the assault, but they were refueling. As there was not enough time to refuel all of Peeples's tanks, he ordered them back. Grabowski would have to reconstitute his armor piecemeal with whatever tanks he could muster and move out. As Grabowski's mind raced, and with Natonski still at his side, Major Dave Sosa, the battalion's operations officer, pulled up. He said reports from the 507th indicated there were more American soldiers in the city. Leaning on a Humvee, Natonski began rubbing his head. "Ricky, you have got to see if you can find those guys," Natonski said. "They'd do it for us."

At the refueling point, Peeples got the word that the attack was under way, and he needed to rush back to the front. Three tanks had already been refueled and were soon attached to one of Grabowski's companies—Bravo—to add to its punch. Peeples stopped refueling his own tank midstream and headed off. He did not get very far before his M1 broke down. He called ahead and asked his soldiers to send him another. The new tank did not have a commander's radio; Peeples would have to find another way to communicate with his company—or whatever portion managed to get into the fight.[14]

Natonski returned to his command post at Jalibah and phoned Conway, the MEF commander, to tell him about the wayward Army unit. Still impatient at the pace of the attack so far, Natonski was back at Bailey's position thirty minutes later, more determined than ever to speed things up. By now, Colonel Joe Dowdy's RCT-1, one of Mattis's regiments, was approaching Nasiriyah and planning to drive through the town. Task Force Tarawa's delay in taking the bridges threatened to hold up the Marine attack on Kut and frustrate Mattis's strategy.

Short of tanks and with his methodical plan in disarray, Bailey received help from an unlikely source. Lieutenant Colonel Eddie Ray, the commander of a Light Armored Reconnaissance battalion from Dowdy's unit, had been watching the attack unfold and proposed to join the action. He was eager to get into the fray. Ray was something of a legend. He was a former football player for the Washington Huskies, and had been awarded the Navy Cross—the Navy's highest award for bravery—in the Gulf War for repelling an Iraqi assault, out of the Burqan oilfield, on the division commander's command post. Ray, whose call sign was Barbarian 6, offered an LAR company, which Bailey was more than happy to receive, as his own was still at the Highway 1 bridge. Ray's offer was quickly communicated to Grabowski by John O'Rourke, the regimental executive officer: an LAR company was headed Grabowski's way. If Grabowski did not take the bridges quickly, O'Rourke advised, it would pass through his lines and carry out the mission itself. O'Rourke asked Grabowski to repeat the message to make sure he understood it. Grabowski was taken aback by his request but read the order back. He was outraged that an

LAR company might be dispatched to do a job for which he had prepared for weeks.

Grabowski got on the radio with his company commanders and relayed his frustration. "It will be a cold day in hell before I allow regiment to send an LAR company to assume our mission, especially when Barbarian 6 has had no time to plan or prep for this task! Now press hard for those damn bridges . . . 6 Out!" More important, Ray, who had a difficult relationship with Dowdy, his commander, had not run his offer of assistance by him. When Dowdy, who had no intention of diminishing his combat power, heard about Ray's offer, he quickly vetoed it. The episode served only to compound the growing confusion. Grabowski took Ray's offer as a vote of no-confidence, all the more reason to move forward with dispatch—and yet, unknown to him, the offer had been withdrawn.[15]

As he headed toward the bridges, Grabowski positioned himself with Bravo Company, his lead unit, commanded by Captain Tim Newland, a Kansas farm boy. To get to the Euphrates, the battalion had to cross a railroad overpass that was defended by nine Iraqi T-55 tanks, five of which were immobilized and being used as stationary pillboxes. The Marines could not tell which of the tanks were manned, so a team armed with antitank weapons blasted them all.

As the platoon of tanks from Peeples's company arrived to bolster Bravo Company, Grabowski radioed his regimental commander to say that, once the battalion captured both the northern and southern canal bridges, the rest of the regiment would be needed as reinforcement at the southern span. Bailey ordered 2/8, commanded by Lieutenant Colonel Royal Mortenson, to move up behind 1/2 so it could take on this mission. He also called for air support.

In the weeks leading up to the war, Grabowski had given considerable thought to how he would take the bridges if he was ordered to do so. He planned for Newland's Bravo Company and Dan Wittnam's Charlie Company to advance over the Euphrates bridge and then immediately turn right to avoid having to drive directly through the city. The route through the city, which the Marines had taken to calling Ambush Alley, was a two-and-a-half-mile, four-lane boulevard. It was exposed and dangerous, and no provision had been made to clear and secure it. By hooking right, Bravo and Charlie would move through an empty field on the outskirts of town. Having circumvented Ambush Alley, the companies would grab the northern bridge. While the platoon of Peeples's tanks would be attached to Bravo Company, the rest would take a position just south of the city to support the attack. Meanwhile, Captain Mike Brooks's Alpha Company would secure the southern bridge until it was relieved by Marines from Mortenson's battalion.

Having encountered not only a problem with refueling but also confusion over when his mission should start, Grabowski had been forced to attack without all the tanks his plan required. He would soon face another unwelcome surprise. After Bravo Company crossed the southern bridge and proceeded through the vacant field, it discovered it had driven into a marshy sewage area covered by a thin crust of earth that could not take the weight of the Marines' vehicles. All three tanks, two AAVs, two Combined Anti-Armor Team (CAAT) Humvees, and the company command AAV quickly sank in the vile muck.

As Bravo Company tried to extract itself, it called for a tank retriever, which in turn became stuck. As Grabowski sought to control the situation, his command vehicle was underneath high-tension wires that interfered with radio transmission. Finally, Newland met with Grabowski, who told him to dismount his troops, take what he had, and head north to the bridge over the Saddam Canal. The plan was barely under way and already Grabowski was calling audibles. Mike Brooks's Alpha Company quickly moved into defensive positions at the Euphrates bridge Bravo Company had just crossed.[16]

The Iraqis had expected the Marines to come directly through the city and had set up a defense in depth along the route. When they realized that the Marines were attacking on an unexpected axis, they began hastily relocating eastward to face them. "There was no fire initially," said Brooks. "I sat there for about five minutes watching a lot of activity. People in robes were running around, but they all seemed to have weapons. I was worried about it, but nobody was shooting at us. Then it was like making popcorn. It started slowly and then reached a crescendo within an hour. I thought, so much for Iraqi capitulation."[17]

With Bravo Company mired and Alpha Company holding the Euphrates bridge, Wittnam led Charlie Company over the span. A veteran of the Gulf War, Wittnam was surprised that he could not see Bravo Company and Grabowski's command group. "I'm expecting to see these last tracks, something moving that way, dust, something along those lines. I don't see anything," Wittnam recalled. Unable to locate Bravo, Wittnam guessed that they might have encountered so little resistance that they drove straight through Ambush Alley. Perhaps the CIA intelligence about the lack of resistance in Nasiriyah had been right after all. Wittnam's mission was to take the bridge over the Saddam Canal; he decided to "go straight up the gut." His was a spontaneous decision and a deviation from the original plan.

At about noon, Wittnam passed through Brooks's company and sped straight up Ambush Alley at forty-five miles per hour. Wittnam's company did not have its own forward air controller to call in air strikes. Lieutenant James Reid, the weapons platoon leader, planned to pick up Alpha's controller as they passed through its position. But Charlie Company was moving fast and did not stop. "I guess I was just too excited," Reid later said from his hospital bed at the Bethesda Naval Medical Center in Maryland. It was a fateful oversight. As Charlie Company approached the northern bridge, the last AAV in the column was hit on its door ramp by an RPG. The column had moved too fast and too far for the Iraqis to strike the lead vehicles, but the AAV carrying Lieutenant Michael Seely, the 3rd Platoon commander, had suffered a devastating blow. The vehicle limped to the northern side with four badly wounded troops, one with his leg all but blown off.

Once they were across the bridge, bad turned to worse. Wittnam's company was caught in a firestorm. It was hit by Iraqi army artillery and mortar fire from a T intersection to the north, by Fedayeen machine gun fire and RPG fire from southeast of the canal—an area known as the Martyrs District—and by assorted small arms fire from all directions. While the small arms, machine guns, and RPGs were inaccurate, the Iraqi artillery and mortar fire were deadly.[18] The company's radios came alive but with so many Marines trying to talk at once, the commander could not communicate with them or with battalion command to the south. Radio discipline had broken down. "Nobody realizes how much traffic is going to be on one net when you're getting shot at for the first time," said Wittnam.

Surprised by the fire, Wittnam's Marines jumped out of their vehicles and sought what little cover there was. Starnes's artillery battalion set up its counterbattery radar and commenced suppressing the Iraqi artillery and mortar fire, as Cobra gunships raked the area with rocket and machine gun fire. The Army's initial reservations about returning artillery fire into Nasiriyah when it bypassed the town were irrelevant in this rapidly escalating fight. Soon the radio jam eased. Wittnam got through to Grabowski's forward command post and learned that Bravo Company was still south of the Saddam Canal. There was some discussion about sending a Medevac helicopter to evacuate Wittnam's casualties. "There's no way," Wittnam responded. The area was too hot. The helicopter would be blown away.

Wittnam managed to disperse his vehicles in herringbone fashion, his troops dismounted in defensive positions on either side of the berm along the bridge approach. Seely's AAV sat burning in the middle of the road. The company's first sergeant set up a casualty collection point and Navy corpsmen treated the wounded.

After the battle the Marines discovered a sand table that laid out the Iraqis' defensive positions. From it and interrogations of captured officers, it emerged that the Iraqi 11th Division had expected an American heliborne assault north of the canal bridge and planned to catch their opponents in a fire sack. CENTCOM's deception plan had sought to throw the Iraqis off balance by aggravating their fears of an airborne assault. For one reason or another, this had become the main Iraqi concern in Nasiriyah. The Iraqi 11th Division's 23rd Brigade positioned three battalions around the presumed American landing zone.

Wittnam had driven right into it and was in serious trouble. He was taking casualties and, to make matters worse, did not have a forward air controller in his company to call for air support. As he coordinated defenses, Wittnam had to move back and forth from one side of the road to the other, where for all practical purposes two separate wars were being fought. Unaware of Bravo Company's plight, he planned to hold out until the unit came over the bridge to help. Wittnam alerted his mortar men to the dangerous possibility of an exchange of friendly fire.[19]

As Reid, the weapons platoon leader, stood up to call for fire over the battalion tactical net, First Lieutenant Frederick Pokorney Jr., a big man of linebacker proportions and the company's FO, or forward artillery observer, tackled him and said, "Get the fuck down, you're drawing fire." The Iraqi gunners were bracketing the Marine position. As the Iraqi mortars zeroed in, they exacted a terrible toll. Once the Iraqis had the range, a mortar round that nearly severed Reid's arm was shot. Within seconds, one of his two mortar positions took a direct hit, killing a staff sergeant and two other Marines. Three more were wounded. The Iraqis fired additional rounds in rapid succession. Reid sought help when yet another mortar round found him. "I was up in the air all of a sudden and when I landed I was staring at the dirt and saw a bunch of blood dripping on the ground from my face," he recalled. Within minutes another Marine in the vicinity was struck down. One casualty of the barrage was Pokorney, who was killed while rushing from position to position locating targets and calling in fire.

On the verge of shock, Reid managed to reach an AAV carrying ammunition, and told a corporal who was breaking out mortar rounds to get the track over to the mortar position and help out. Reid himself then headed back to where he had directed the corporal. There he told the corporal in charge that help was on the way and to load the casualties in the AAV. If he did not make it back, Reid said, the corporal should "get these guys back to the BAS [battalion aid station] south of the Euphrates." Reid was looking for Wittnam when he was rocked by a nearby explosion and wounded a third time. The company gunnery sergeant rushed to give him first aid. "I told the gunny to see if my eye was still in my head and he said he thought so," Reid recalled.

As the company first sergeant, who had established the casualty collection point, covered the dead with ponchos, an NCO approached Wittnam and urged that the bodies be sent back across the bridge. "Absolutely not," Wittnam replied. "We need to fucking hold right where we're at." Wittnam was afraid that a mechanized vehicle heading back over the bridge would be mistaken by Bravo Company for an Iraqi tank coming in the opposite direction and be blown away. No sooner did Wittnam decide against evacuating the casualties than he saw one of his company's AAVs heading south across the bridge. Wittnam tried without success to contact the vehicle. He was distressed to see several other vehicles follow it. Wittnam had lost control of his company: some Marines were trying to evacuate casualties, in accordance with Reid's instructions "if he did not make it back"; others saw the AAV leave and figured the company was pulling back; some thought they were getting in formation to attack Iraqi positions at the T intersection to the north; others assumed that Wittnam himself had been killed.

Wittnam was in the fight of his life, and with a dwindling force. "So I'm thinking, holy shit, there goes half my fighting power over the bridge," he recalled. "I was angry, I mean, incredibly angry, but there was nothing I could do. I tried to get those guys on the net—nobody's talking on the net, nobody's listening, and they're gone. The only thing you could do was focus on the guys you have at hand. You could try to keep everybody focused on what's going on."[20]

The first AAV to run the gauntlet south had taken advantage of the element of surprise and gotten through to the safety of Alpha Company's position at the Euphrates bridge. But the second, AAV 208, loaded with mortar ammunition, took a catastrophic hit. It exploded in a huge fireball, incinerating eight Marines and wounding two. The third AAV took a mobility hit, stopping dead in its tracks on the boulevard. The squad it was carrying, four of whom were wounded, scrambled out and took refuge on the second floor of a building off the boulevard, which the battalion called the Alamo. The fourth AAV nearly made it all the way before it was hit by an RPG. Its rear ramp blown open, it was exposed and vulnerable: easy pickings for the Iraqi fighters. From his position on the Euphrates River bridge, Brooks, the commander of Alpha Company, saw the next blow. "A second RPG comes through the open troop hatch and just destroys it, collapses the whole structure," Brooks recalled. "It's a burning mess and looks pretty shocking." Gunnery Sergeant Justin Lehew, who had helped to rescue wounded soldiers from the 507th Maintenance Company earlier in the day, rushed forward and spent an hour under fire recovering nine wounded Marines from the wreckage, including carrying a six-foot-four, 240-pound corporal who had been trapped. Lehew would later be awarded the Navy Cross for his bravery.

Alpha Company called for a Medevac helicopter. Because of the heavy fire, the pilot was told not to attempt a touchdown on the highway, but to instead land at a partially protected spot on the east side of the road. When the CH-46 arrived, the pilot, Captain Eric Garcia, landed right where the AAV had just been destroyed. Brooks felt sick to his stomach; it was just a matter of seconds, he thought, before the helicopter would be blown up before his eyes. To the astonishment of the entire company, the casualties were loaded on board the helicopter, which managed to take off and evade a hail of gunfire. "I just couldn't believe it," Brooks recalled. In a day of calamities, the Marines could occasionally catch some luck.[21]

The battalion's troubles, however, were far from over. In the early afternoon, the fierceness of the fighting in the vicinity of the canal prompted the regimental air officer at Bailey's forward command post to call for air support. Two Air Force A-10s, whose call sign was Gyrate 73, flew to the scene. Control of the aircraft was turned over to Bravo Company's forward air controller—Charlie Company having no forward air controller or direct communications with the aircraft.[22] The A-10 flight leader reported that north of the canal bridge he had seen a number of vehicles, including one on fire. The Bravo Company controller, whose call sign was Mouth, could see only a rising pillar of smoke.

Grabowski knew that Wittnam's company had seized the northern bridge, and assumed that Captain Newland, Bravo's commander, knew so as well. In his urgent efforts to contact Grabowski, Wittnam had talked on the battalion net. Since Grabowski and Newland were moving in vehicles that were just yards apart, the battalion commander thought they shared the same "situational awareness." Moreover, Grabowski had given instructions that, without his approval, no air strikes—known as Type 3 close air support[23]—were to be called in against targets not observable by a ground controller.

As close together as they were, Newland and his battalion commander had radically different notions about what was happening on the battlefield. As a result of the chaos of urban warfare and the jammed radio nets, Newland and his controller still had no idea that Wittnam had run the gauntlet and was north of the Saddam Canal bridge. He assumed that Wittnam, in accordance with the original battle plan, was somewhere behind Bravo Company, probably stuck in muck. Newland believed he was the lead element in the fight and the controller thought the vehicles the pilot reported north of the canal bridge must be Iraqi armor poised to strike south. When the A-10s sought to to engage enemy targets north of the bridge, the controller told the A-10 that there were no friendly forces at that location and cleared them to attack.

Customarily, Marine vehicles displayed bright, six-foot-long fluorescent panels on their tops for easy identification from the air. But at the outset of the war, McKiernan's command had replaced the fluorescent panels with state-of-the-art tan thermal panels that were supposedly more easily identifiable by friendly aircraft, particularly at night. Unfortunately, the A-10s were not equipped with the system to do so; they assumed the vehicles they saw were Iraqi. On the ground, Wittnam heard the A-10s and was relieved that they were on station. Finally, he would have real support. Then there was a loud explosion. The A-10s rolled in "hot" and made multiple passes through the target area, firing 30mm cannons, dropping eight bombs, and launching three Maverick missiles. They were targeting Wittnam's vehicles. "I could hear the A-10s," said one Marine, "and then remember seeing the big green tracers skipping off some of the parked tracks. The first time I heard it, nothing hit around me. The second time, the world went black. Staff Sergeant Torres sitting next to me was hit. It tore him from the pelvis all the way to the back of his calf."[24]

The beleaguered Marines desperately fired half a dozen red pop-up flares to signal they were friendlies. It was to no avail: the A-10s attacked again. Finally Charlie Company was able to raise the battalion on its radio and pleaded for the air attack to be called off. On the ground, the company had been hit from all sides by the Iraqis; from the air, it had been pounded by the U.S. Air Force. An exhaustive investigation of the ill-fated air attack, which was later conducted by the Air Force itself, concluded that there were numerous contributing factors, but that the "primary cause of the incident was a lack of coordination regarding the location of friendly forces." In short, the Marines had called the air strike on themselves.

During the course of the fighting on either side of the canal bridge during the afternoon of March 23, eighteen Marines were killed, and seventeen wounded. The Air Force investigation was unable to precisely determine how many casualties were attributable to friendly fire by the A-10s. Evidence, the report stated, indicated that eight of the killed were victims of enemy fire, but that it was impossible to determine the sources of the fire that had killed the other ten. As for the seventeen wounded, the best the investigators could do was conclude that thirteen casualties were the result of enemy fire. Despite the hundreds of pages of the investigation, it is still a matter of conjecture as to how many Marines were killed and wounded by the A-10s. Marines with non-life-threatening wounds were moved to the Marine hospital at Camp Commando in Kuwait. Some Marine helicopters also dropped off casualties at a 3rd Infantry Division field hospital in Tallil.[25]

Wittnam was shaken by the turn of events, but exhorted his troops to hang on. Help finally came in the form of Peeples, the reservist who had switched tanks and rushed to join the fight. As the fighting unfolded, Peeples had driven to Brooks's position at the Euphrates River bridge with three of his company's tanks and provided Alpha Company with some badly needed support. While engaged, Peeples heard over the tactical radio net that Charlie Company also needed tanks north of the canal bridge. "I don't know who said it," Peeples recalled, "but took it as an order to move north to assist Charlie Company."

Leaving two tanks to support Brooks, Peeples decided to charge forward through Ambush Alley and over the canal bridge. He called Captain Scott Dyer, his executive officer, and ordered him to join him in the rush north. "Hey, XO, punch it," Peeples instructed. "We're going to run down this damn alley as fast as we can and hope we don't get hit." Firing their machine guns right and left, the two tanks ran through a hail of machine gun and RPG fire, past the burning and disabled AAVs and the Marines holed up in the Alamo, and crossed into Charlie Company's position. Peeples's forward air controller, Major Scott Hawkins, was riding in Dyer's tank. Hawkins took on the role of both air controller and artillery forward observer, assuming the duties of the dead Pokorney and severely wounded Reid.

When Peeples's M1 arrived, Wittnam climbed on the back of the tank and pointed out targets for the main gun. The suppressive fire had its effect. As enemy activity subsided, Peeples was told of wounded Marines on the south side of the bridge—the Marines in the Alamo. Convinced that nobody in dire need of help in Ambush Alley could survive the night, Peeples told Wittnam he was going for them. He backtracked over the bridge. Peeples drew up to the building from which the Marines from the disabled AAV were firing. Positioning his tank between the building and the enemy fire, Peeples dismounted and ran into the building. He told the small Marine contingent to hold tight while he loaded their four wounded on the back of his tank and brought them safely south of the Euphrates bridge. Later in the day, a CAAT team recovered the isolated squad. Peeples's role was a graphic demonstration of what tanks could do against the Fedayeen. But it also showed the cost of rushing the attack on the bridges of Nasiriyah.[26]

Mortenson, the commander of 2/8, had been told by Bailey to follow 1/2 and clear enemy positions that Grabowski bypassed as he went north. He was also to relieve Brooks's Alpha Company at the southern bridge, so that Brooks could join Wittnam on the north side of the canal. Beyond that, Mortenson had a "be prepared" mission to move up to a canal bridge. His was a tall order, especially since Mortenson's battalion, unlike Grabowski's unit, was not mechanized and had to move in trucks or on foot. Led by Captain Tim Dremann, F Company proceeded in their trucks up the highway toward the Euphrates, as the other two companies cleared either side of the road. Brooks knew that Wittnam's situation was dire and was anxious to move forward. As the minutes dragged on, Brooks gave up waiting for Mortenson and ordered his company to move in its AAVs "at best possible speed" up Ambush Alley, accompanied by two newly arrived tanks from Peeples's company and supported by Cobra gunships.

Backed up by the extra firepower, Brooks ran the gauntlet without taking a shot. He reached Wittnam at 4:00 p.m. and took up defensive positions. Although Brooks's initiative violated his orders to wait for Mortenson's Marines, he knew they were on their way and that it was vital to come to Wittnam's assistance in his hour of need. Besides, moving up to the canal bridge would ensure the success of the battalion's larger mission. Newland's Bravo Company and Grabowski's command group crossed the bridge an hour and a half later. By late afternoon of March 23, Grabowski had secured the northern bridge, had his battalion intact, and had organized a perimeter defense.

When Dremann got to the bridge only to find that Brooks had already taken off, he pulled back about 500 yards south, began clearing buildings on either side of the road, and radioed Mortenson's battalion to say it would take about six hours to finish the job. With no Marines securing the Euphrates River bridge, Dremann was ordered to get back on it. As he moved across the span, he came under machine gun fire. Once more, Eddie Ray was on the scene to assist at a critical moment. During the confusion over the Euphrates River bridge, Ray had again approached Bailey to offer him a platoon from his 2nd LAR Battalion. Bailey again had gratefully accepted and, this time, Ray was not countermanded. The LAR platoon was sent to the Euphrates to support Mortenson's battalion.[27]

As night fell on the twenty-third, Bailey's battalions were in place. Grabowski's held the bridgehead over the canal, and Mortenson's the bridge over the Euphrates. But neither commanded territory beyond the bridges or the narrow strip of highway on either side. While firing from Ambush Alley had diminished, the area was still not secure. Donahoe's 3/2 was still at the Highway 1 bridge to the west. Nobody was sure of the number of American casualties suffered during the daylong battle. Brooks and Newland were able to account for all their men, but the flight south of the AAVs from Wittnam's company, multiple reports of casualties from various sources, and the rapid evacuation of the dead and wounded made it difficult for an accurate reckoning of Charlie's casualties. Some dead Marines were still in the smoldering wrecks of the AAVs in Ambush Alley and not all of their remains were easily recognizable. "When you say dead Marines, we're really talking about a spine with some tissue on it," said one officer. "Most of the guys were burned so severely that you wouldn't even know they were human beings."

Eddie Ray—less the platoon he volunteered at the Euphrates bridge—and his LAVs were able to race through Ambush Alley that night and head ten miles up Highway 7, the first unit of Dowdy's RCT to go north. But the battle for Nasiriyah was not over. Grabowski still had to expand his bridgehead to secure the T intersection and eliminate the Iraqi 23rd Brigade positions, both on the north side of the canal. Mortenson needed to deal with the Fedayeen in his sector south of the Euphrates.

That night, Task Force Tarawa got a clue about what was emboldening the Iraqis. An Iraqi ambulance ran a Marine roadblock under fire, but was stopped at the northern end of the bridge as it tried to get back into Nasiriyah. One of the Iraqi paramedics seemed highly suspicious and the Marines captured him. He turned out to be the commanding officer of the Iraqi 23rd Brigade, who was trying to get back into the city, presumably to reorganize the Iraqi resistance. The officer said that his men had been apprehensive about facing U.S. forces but, when they ambushed the wayward 507th Company, they thought they had won the first round in the American attempt to take their city and were encouraged to keep up the resistance. When the Marine reinforcements arrived, however, their spirit was broken.[28]

The Iraqi soldiers might have lost heart, but the Fedayeen were still full of fight. The Americans were facing a determined foe. The Iraqis were sending civilians to observe the Marines' positions and then were carefully charting them on a large sand table, a primitive but effective way to locate their enemy. After securing the northern bridge, the Marines at Grabowski's position could see armed men in civilian clothing sneaking in and out of buildings, and engaged them with sporadic tank, artillery, and machine gun fire throughout the night and following day. But as far as Grabowski was concerned, he had fulfilled his mission. The bridges had not been blown up; his battalion had taken them intact. As the fighting appeared to be trailing off, he assumed that the route between the two bridges was relatively safe.

Now that Natonski's forces had secured the bridges in Nasiriyah, Dowdy's regiment could drive over them north through the town toward Kut. But while Bailey believed he had finished his job by securing the two bridges, Dowdy noticed an all too obvious problem. To be sure, Task Force Tarawa had fought hard for the bridges, but it did not control anything in between. Task Force Tarawa had still been operating with limited intelligence; even on March 24 it had no access to UAVs to provide surveillance. At Natonski's command center, Apodaca, the intelligence officer, urged his commander to press Conway for more support. Nasiriyah was the Marines' main battle now and the terrain was hazy and dangerous.

Dowdy had first planned to fight his way through Nasiriyah with his mechanized and armored units, sending his soft-skinned support vehicles the long way around, over the Highway 1 bridge to the west. But, aware that Bailey had not secured Ambush Alley, Dowdy was reluctant to add to the mayhem by intervening in the ongoing battle. Conway began to wonder why Dowdy was not moving up the alley. Mattis, for his part, was also getting impatient. He had moved two regiments over the Highway 1 bridge and was heading north. He was worried that his right flank would be exposed unless Dowdy made a parallel move up Highway 7 toward Kut to cover him. Mattis was famous for his aggressiveness, and his frustration over the situation in Nasiriyah bubbled over. Mattis ordered Brigadier General John Kelly, his assistant division commander, to go to Dowdy's regiment and "get them moving." Late in the afternoon of the twenty-fourth, Kelly arrived in Nasiriyah, where he huddled at the southern bridge with Conway, Natonski, Bailey, and Dowdy. Kelly pulled Dowdy aside and urged him to push hard.

"This is a simple tactical problem and has a tactical solution," Kelly told the regimental commander, giving him a tutorial on combat in an urban area. Dowdy was caught off balance. To pass through another regiment in the middle of a battle was no small matter, especially since the two units were operating with different radio cryptological protocols and could not talk to each other. Nor did it appear to Dowdy that Task Force Tarawa had the situation in hand. But Mattis was desperate to get him on the road to Kut, and Eddie Ray had managed to scamper through the city and was in a defensive coil ten miles north of the canal.

Kelly told Dowdy he had two hours to get going. As darkness fell, Dowdy met with Lieutenant Colonel Lew Craparotta, the commander of the regiment's 3rd Battalion, 1st Marines, and told him he had an hour to saddle up and clear the two-and-one-half-mile stretch of Ambush Alley. Craparotta's battalion had been together as a unit for eighteen months and had recently completed a six-month deployment at sea. Although it had yet to see combat, it was a cohesive and seasoned outfit. Craparotta asked for a company of tanks.

Within two hours he started to wage a night attack with the tanks and two of his companies mounted in AAVs. The battalion rolled down the left lane of the boulevard between the bridges, firing as it went into the darkness. Craparotta ordered the opposite lane kept open for the upcoming passage of the regiment. Wherever a street or alley opened onto the boulevard, he dropped off a tank or an AAV team to cover it, creating a series of strongpoints along the road. Craparotta situated his command group at a major intersection halfway to the northern bridge. "Every once in a while a guy would pop out of an alley for an RPG shot and he'd be zapped," he recalled.

Shortly after midnight Craparotta waved the rest of Dowdy's regiment through, cautioning them that because his men had the left flank covered, they should not fire in that direction. At daylight, Craparotta brought in his 3rd Company and Cobras to help suppress the Iraqis. Ambush Alley was cleared by noon on the twenty-fifth. Craparotta's job was done and his unit fell in behind Dowdy's thousand-vehicle column, which had successfully crossed over the northern bridge. The lone glitch was another instance of friendly fire when Dowdy's regiment wounded a corporal from Grabowski's air defense team as it drove north. Mattis's confidence in Dowdy, however, had eroded. Mattis told Kelly to stay with Dowdy and act as his "link" to the regiment.[29]

As Dowdy's regiment rolled that night, an Iraqi approached Captain Dremann and in fluent English identified himself as a doctor from a nearby hospital. He said that civilians were in the building and he could not leave it for long for fear of looting. He simply wished for the Americans not to attack it. U.S. intelligence concluded from the incident and from other reports that survivors from the 507th might be there. When Mortenson's battalion expanded its perimeter that night, it came under fire from the hospital, among other directions. Mortenson was careful not to use artillery near the facility and held off trying to seize it, but authorized mortar fire to silence Iraqi machine gun fire. During the firefight, a colonel from the Special Operations Forces arrived at Bailey's headquarters and said he wanted to scout the hospital for possible American POWs. Told that the Marines were still fighting in the area, he departed.

Once again the Iraqi "doctor" appeared out of the darkness and asked permission to move his patients to another hospital in the city. This time he was declared an enemy prisoner and was sent back to regimental headquarters to be questioned. He was subsequently released and given the permission he had requested. The following morning, the Marines decided to take action against the hospital. After aiming mortars at the building perimeter, Dremann's company took fire as it attacked the two-story complex. Once the hospital had been seized, it was clear that it was a military and not a civilian hospital, and that it was also an Iraqi strongpoint, well stocked with weapons, ammunition, and suits to protect against chemical weapons. The hospital's grounds also featured a T-55 tank that was missing its engine but had both a main and a machine gun in working order.

Dremann concluded he had been hoodwinked by the mysterious doctor, who more than likely was a senior Iraqi officer who had escaped with wounded Iraqi soldiers and Fedayeen. But U.S. intelligence later established that Private Jessica Lynch of the 507th had been treated at the hospital before being moved to another in the center of the city. They also recovered several uniforms of the 507th soldiers. They had been doused with oil to be burned.[30]

Recovering from the shock of the Marine attack in the city proper, the Iraqis began infiltrating Nasiriyah, seeking to resume the fight. It was just three days into the ground war, but the CIA's anticipated victory parade through town and the Army commanders' reluctance to fire artillery into urban areas had long been forgotten. To stop enemy movement, Cobra pilots were now being told that all colored taxis, seen as Iraqi reconaissance vehicles, were fair game—an order that bothered some of the pilots who were trying to limit civilian casualties. As the fighting continued, the electrical grid near Nasiriyah was bombed, an exception to Moseley's decree to limit damage to Iraq's infrastructure. Gradually, the Marines gained control of the city, but not without snafus. When some of Grabowski's Marines moved east through the town, they were surprised to discover that the other bridge in the center of the city, being used by the enemy as an infiltration route, was not guarded. There was so much confusion among the rank and file about what roles the Army and Marines were to play in the city that some of Grabowski's company commanders erroneously assumed that the Army was securing the other main bridge in the town.

On March 24, the Marines endured yet another costly round of friendly fire. In light of reports that Iraqi fighters were massing near the railroad, the Marines pounded the area with artillery. No bodies were found there the following morning, but the possibility of an Iraqi night attack put the Marines on edge. When an engineer unit came under fire at a highway intersection late in the day, chaos reigned, resulting in Marines firing at one another, with thirty wounded.

By the twenty-seventh of March order seemed to have been largely restored in Nasiriyah as Tarawa expanded its control. But Apodaca, Natonski's intelligence officer, was concerned. City residents were reporting that many of the enemy had not been destroyed, but had vanished into sanctuaries in nearby villages and towns, including the enemy stronghold in Suq Ash Shuyukh, southeast of Nasiriyah. Apodaca sent an Iraqi agent to the town and he later reported that much of the Fedayeen leadership had set up operations there. The Fedayeen were monitoring the Marines' movements, sending teams of fighters to attack their checkpoints.

With CENTCOM's strategy to push to Baghdad as quickly as possible to destroy the regime's center of gravity and Mattis doing his best to fulfill the Marines' contribution to the plan, there were no Marine forces left over to track down the bands of Fedayeen that had moved to the surrounding countryside. Apodaca feared that they would return to Nasiriyah to engage the Marines, which could haunt the coalition effort to stabilize Iraq after the war. He joked to his comrades that the Marines would be fighting the same Iraqi fighters after Saddam was toppled and the MEF headed back to Kuwait. The Fedayeen ran away and came back when you weren't looking, he jested.

Apodaca drafted a classified assessment for Natonski that was subsequently forwarded to Conway, officers at McKiernan's command, and the National Ground Intelligence Center in the United States. The intelligence officer compared the Fedayeen attacks to insurgencies in Nicaragua, El Salvador, and Colombia, pointing out similarities and differences. Unless the allies went after the Fedayeen in smaller villages and towns and cleared out adjoining areas, hit-and-run attacks on personnel and infrastructure would persist. This would hamper the war effort and, more important, the stabilization of Iraq after the war.[31]

Nasiriyah was a shock to the Marines. Although marked by acts of impressive heroism, the engagement was not an auspicious beginning for the overall campaign. Intelligence was faulty. The Marine plan, which called for coordination among multiple commands, was overly complicated and badly coordinated. Notwithstanding the surprising intensity of enemy resistance, the engagement was marked by confusion, indecisiveness, and costly mistakes. The casualty count was high and it remains uncertain exactly how many killed and wounded were the result of enemy or friendly fire. As for the Iraqis' tactics, they were a portent of things to come. The Iraqis were not going to fight on the Americans' terms. The enemy faced by U.S. forces would be largely amorphous, not in uniform, and rarely part of an organized military force. This enemy would level the battlefield by ignoring the rules of conventional warfare; it would fight using guile, deception, and ambush. Samawah and Nasiriyah had made that clear. The Marines and soldiers would adapt on the battlefield, but Apodaca's e-mail raised an important question: if the Fedayeen had disappeared into small villages and towns to regroup to fight another day and were to be hunted down, did the United States have the right strategy for that, as well as sufficient forces?

CHAPTER 14

Vampire 12

On the afternoon of March 23, Dave McKiernan flew north from Kuwait to meet with Scott Wallace in Iraq and assess the progress of the campaign. The fighting at Samawah had been surprisingly sharp and had forced the V Corps to defer its plan to conduct a feint up Highway 8. The reports about bloody fighting in Nasiriyah were disconcerting. But the land war plan still seemed to be on track. McKiernan's helicopter flew over long columns of Army vehicles and muddy villages before landing in an empty patch of desert south of Najaf with nary a soldier in sight. McKiernan lit up a cigarette as his aides tried to establish radio contact with Wallace's command vehicle to locate the V Corps commander, but Wallace had already moved on. McKiernan and his team saddled up and flew to a new rendezvous point. Spider Marks, McKiernan's intelligence officer, would later refer to the trip as the Lost in the Desert episode.[1]

When the two generals finally linked up, Wallace was sick and speaking so hoarsely that he could barely be heard. He told McKiernan that the Fedayeen had been venturing out of towns and cities to attack Army supply columns. Wallace was still sticking to his plan, which was to take the fight to the Iraqi Republican Guard. Colonel William Wolf's 11th Attack Helicopter Regiment would fly deep into Iraq to attack the Medina Division that night.

At CENTCOM, despite the appearance of the Fedayeen on the battlefield, the focus was still on the threat the command had scripted before the war: Iraq's Republican Guard, its army units, and the prospect that they would employ chemical or biological weapons. Franks pressed his officers to be aggressive and press ahead. U.S. forces, Franks said, needed to maintain pressure on Iraq's 10th and 6th divisions in the east, while moving on the Republican Guard in the west. Wherever and whenever possible, caches or WMD should be seized. "We are where we want to be," Franks assured his officers. "Move to accelerate."[2]

Army aviation had had its share of setbacks in recent years. Wolf's regiment had prepared extensively for NATO's war in Kosovo, but never managed to get in the fight. Transported to Albania at enormous effort— hundreds of C-17 flights were required—the regiment was blocked from attacking by Pentagon leaders who feared it would be too vulnerable to the Serbs' wide-ranging air defenses. The episode had been a source of some embarrassment to Army aviation and had raised questions about the feasibility of launching Apache helicopter attacks deep into enemy territory. The opening night of the Iraq land war had added insult to injury when the strike against the Iraqi 11th Infantry Division in and around Nasiriyah had been canceled.

But the upcoming attack against the Republican Guard divisions was to be one of the most celebrated missions of the war. The Apaches would fly far in front of the ground troops, hover at a safe distance from the enemy, and fire their tank-killing missiles at the Iraqis' T-72s and artillery. These were tactics the Army had planned to use against Warsaw Pact tanks if a shooting war had erupted during the Cold War, and they seemed optimal for the sort of desert war the United States had waged when it evicted Iraqi troops from Kuwait.

The regiment had practiced deep attacks in Poland during the fall of 2002, and this time had a weapon that would make its strikes even more effective: the Longbow RF missile and targeting system, which gave the Apache a "fire and forget" capability. It was the perfect system to attack enemy armor at long range and its use in the Iraqi war would mark another first.[3] The V Corps planned to conduct repeated deep helicopter attacks against the Republican Guard, strikes that Wallace's planners believed would be all-important because the land invasion had not been preceded by a prolonged air campaign.

With Buff Blount's 3rd Infantry Division determined to race to Baghdad and destroy the Medina Division along the way, many in the regiment felt the upcoming mission might be their last chance for major combat. Their mission would be challenging under the best of circumstances. The regiment's Apaches were based at Udairi, an airstrip carved out of the Kuwaiti desert that had a deserved reputation as an inhospitable dust bowl. To attack the Medina, the Apaches would have to fly to Objective

Rams, the assembly area south of Najaf that the 3rd Infantry Division would have recently secured, link up with the regiment's refueling convoys that had left days before and were still en route, and fly another 60 miles north to strike the Medina Division tanks.

On the morning of March 23, however, the Medina mission had become even more problematic. The deep attack was slated for the evening of the twenty-fourth and the military's weather forecasters were predicting violent winds and sandstorms that were bound to ground the Apaches. Colonel Wolf was not about to stand still for this; he decided to try to beat the bad weather by advancing his regiment's attack. "Planning has turned extremely serious since there is a sense we failed to even start the first mission," Major Michael Gabel wrote in his diary. "Lots of discussion on getting into the fight. The regiment and corps do not want the war to pass us by."[4]

The lead role in the Medina attack was assigned to 1-227, a Longbow Apache squadron from Fort Hood, appropriately nicknamed First Attack and under the command of Dan Ball, a lieutenant colonel from East Texas. Ball's squadron had been attached to Wolf's regiment to augment its fleet of Longbow-equipped aircraft. The 1-227 Squadron's target would be the 2nd Brigade of the Medina Division, which was supposedly loading tanks onto railcars to fortify Baghdad or to stiffen the southern defenses.

Ball had given considerable thought to how to conduct the attack, but his plans had run afoul of the V Corps and his own regiment. Ball's original plan was to strike the division on its flank and sidestep Iraq's air defenses by swinging west of Najaf over Milh Lake and attacking the Medina's 14th Brigade. But that target and area was later allocated to Dave Petraeus's 101st Airborne, which was still grappling with logistics but pressing to get in the fight. Next, Ball drew up plans to attack the Medina on its left flank, flying east to west. This time his commander, Wolf, rejected the idea. The colonel wanted to squeeze all three of his squadrons, including the regiment's two Germany-based units, into what he thought might be the regiment's one and only real fight.

Ball was left with the most undesirable option: his attack would be a plunge straight up the middle, and into the teeth of whatever defense the enemy had managed to put together. Ball's Apaches would fly routes in the western part of the zone, while Mike Barbee's 6-6 squadron and Scott

Thompson's 2-6 squadron maneuvered in the east. That meant that Ball's pilots would be flying northward over urban areas near Karbala and Hillah.[5] "The approved routes were north–south approaches that we didn't want to do," Captain Karen Hobart, the regiment's intelligence officer, said after the war. "We tried to make the best of approach routes to avoid flying over urban areas. The Mesopotamian valley was populated. We put in nine routes and only three were approved."[6]

Ball was also worried about V Corps's plan to suppress Iraqi air defenses before the Apaches arrived on the scene. At Fort Hood, the thinking was that ATACMS missiles carrying cluster bombs should rain down on the enemy just minutes before the Apaches reached the target area. Brigadier General Daniel A. Hahn, the V Corps chief of staff, had decreed that the ATACMS should be fired thirty minutes before the attack. It was a measure that reflected not only Hahn's faith in the killing power of the ATACMS—Hahn was an artilleryman by training—but also the corps's effort to reduce the risk of friendly fire to an absolute minimum. Air strikes by Mosely's warplanes in support of the Apache mission were to be carried out an hour before the helicopters took off. The timing might have been appropriate for a military exercise in Europe, but to Ball, it seemed poorly suited for war. He figured it would simply alert the Iraqis to the impending Apache attack, giving them time to prepare for it. He wanted the air and artillery and Apache strike to be carried out near simultaneously to overwhelm the foe.[7]

The regiment did not have detailed intelligence on the enemy, except for one disturbing fact: the Iraqi military's air defense school was near Karbala and close to the targets the Apaches were to attack. Chief Warrant Officer 5 Lance V. McElhiney, who had thirty-four years in Army aviation and was one of its most experienced pilots, had read through the intelligence and been struck by this fact. McElhiney had fought in Vietnam, been shot down three times in three days during the incursion into Laos, and did a tour training Iranian pilots during the reign of the shah. Having fought with the 101st Airborne during the Gulf War, McElhiney recalled how the Iraqi forces began to move into towns and set up positions next to houses and schools at the end of the conflict, which made the fight entirely different from open desert warfare. The new Longbow radar and missile systems, he thought, were twelve years too late. McElhiney told his company's aircrews that they should forget about the regiment's plans to lob missiles at vulnerable T-72 tanks from afar. The Iraqis had had a dozen years to improve their tactics. The Apaches should not hover, which would make them sitting ducks. The aircrews needed to fix bayonets and prepare for close fighting. "This is going to be a knife fight," McElhiney said.[8]

Logistics were also of immediate concern. Having learned days earlier that he would be doing battle against the Medina Division, Ball had already pulled out all the stops. Captain Andy Caine was dispatched with a load of fuel on a bone-jarring, dusty trek to Objective Rams behind Dave Perkins's 2nd Brigade Combat Team. The rest of the regiment's fuel trucks would take the more conventional, longer route and might not make it to Rams in time. A West Point graduate who had been trained as an Apache Longbow pilot, Caine had been thrust into an unglamorous and unfamiliar mission—and a seemingly impossible one. As the leader of the 3-5 Support Platoon, he was to lead a convoy of twenty-eight fuel and ammunition trucks and eighty-two soldiers across 330 miles of southern Iraq, including through the town of Salman and past the city of Samawah. Major Charles Adkins, the battalion operations officer, would go along, but running the convoy was Caine's responsibility.

None of Caine's vehicles was armored, and only three were mounted with .50 caliber guns. Most of the route would not be paved. He would be out of range for radio contact with the regiment for much of the time. The convoy was to cross into Iraq on March 21 and be at Rams two days later. To motivate his soldiers, he brought them together and told them they had been given the sexiest mission in the regiment. It was very simple: "No fuel, no fly." The attack could not proceed without them. The motto of the platoon was "Stick 'em deep"; many indeed thought they were being stuck deep in Iraq without much backup. Displaying a sense of irony, some in the platoon scrawled "Sexy Mission" on their trucks.

Even before he crossed the border, Caine ran into a complication. He had been summoned to refill the auxiliary's fuel tanks for Ball's squadron after other fueling arrangements had fallen through. This left him short of what he would need at Rams, but Ball reassured him that he would be able to pick up more fuel from Perkins's brigade when he stopped for a planned rest near Samawah. The regiment planned to take off from its base at the Udairi Range in Kuwait in mid-afternoon on March 23 and link up with Caine's supply convoy at Rams by sunset.[9]

Rams was one of those places that had no intrinsic value to the Iraqis but was vital for the Army's push north. It was a sparsely populated stretch southwest of Najaf where the V Corps planned to catch its breath and refuel before making its big push through the Karbala Gap toward Baghdad. Reflecting its strategic significance, a long-range surveillance team—specially trained commandos who hid by day and scouted the enemy at night—had been inserted into Rams several days earlier to ensure that there were no enemy forces in the area. Rams seemed as advertised: a vacant space that the Army could use as a springboard north.

That was good news for Perkins's 2nd BCT, which was to be the first conventional unit to drive to Rams. Its scouts and Eric Schwartz's 1-64 battalion led the brigade. Terry Ferrell's 3-7 Cavalry had tangled with the Iraqis in Samawah, but the 2nd BCT had driven 300 miles and had yet to fight anybody. It was driving west on what it thought would be an unopposed road march. Anticipating little resistance, Schwartz's battalion was moving on the road in a line and even had several broken-down tanks in tow. With a big battle ahead near Baghdad, the battalion was determined not to leave any potentially useful piece of hardware behind. Rams seemed to be the perfect place to try to fix maintenance problems. "Rams was really not supposed to be more than a confirmation sweep. We were going to clear this area very quickly and continue our move northward. It was supposed to be sort of a distraction, if you will," said Captain Andy Hilmes, commander, A Company, 1-64 Armor.[10]

As the commander of E Troop, 9th Cavalry, Scott Woodward was with the scouts at the head of the column. As he approached Rams, Woodward noticed that a makeshift blockade, consisting of several two-and-a-half-ton trucks and men in civilian clothes, had been erected across Highway 28. Woodward was reluctant to attack until he determined who was manning the roadblock: were they the Iraqi freedom fighters the soldiers had heard about, or enemy combatants?

When Woodward's soldiers were 700 yards or so from the blockade, the Iraqis at the roadblock opened fire. "It was our first two-way engagement, where the enemy was firing back. They were in civilian clothes, not in uniform. It was like, What do I do? Can I shoot at these guys? There were an awful lot of them returning fire," said Staff Sergeant Dwayne Thacker, senior scout, E Troop, 9th Cavalry. The Iraqi intentions became clearer when a white pickup truck approached the blockade from the east and dropped off reinforcements. Woodward's scouts responded with everything they had: .50 caliber machine guns, Mark 19 grenade launchers, and M240B machine guns. The roadblock and its fighters were no longer an obstacle.

Woodward was uncertain of what to expect beyond the roadblock, but figured it was probably more of the same. So he stopped and waited for Schwartz's 1-64. Schwartz had picked three objectives in order to secure Rams: a radio tower, a pump house, and some trenches farther north. The first two were easily taken, though after being told for weeks that the intelligence showed they would be facing an ill-motivated enemy, some of his soldiers had trouble adjusting to their first taste of combat. "This task force had not really had a fight to this point, so we hadn't killed any enemy," Schwartz recalled. "The first time we came into a direct fire, we had someone on the radio who said, 'I've got somebody out here that's shooting an RPG at me.' They were basically looking for guidance. 'Do I close a little farther? Do I maintain standoff? Do I bring in CAS [close air support]? What do you want to do?' I remember telling him, in a very basic call, 'Well, then, kill him.' "[11]

The third objective—the trenches south of Najaf—was stoutly defended by fighters armed with mortars and RPGs. Fedayeen reinforcements streamed in on pickup trucks shortly before dawn on March 23, during a lull in the fighting. Few seemed to have any idea that Schwartz's soldiers could detect them in the dark with night vision goggles. Perkins, who had positioned his command vehicle near Schwartz to monitor the battle, summoned his two remaining battalions to finish the fight and secure the area. "Welcome to the war," Perkins said.[12]

Intelligence gathered from twenty-seven captured fighters indicated that Iraqi commanders had expected the Americans to conduct an airborne assault—a paratroop drop or heliborne attack—at an airstrip south of Najaf. An Iraqi general had come to the area two days before to tell the fighters precisely where to defend. Another senior officer later came and drew circles in the sand to site RPG positions. In the wake of the battle in Nasiriyah, here was more evidence of how much regard the Iraqis had for the 82nd and 101st Airborne. CENTCOM had made elaborate efforts to persuade the Iraqis that it planned to drop the 82nd Airborne north of Baghdad and use the 101st Airborne to attack north of Basra, but the Iraqis were concerned that a paratrooper division might also be deployed south of Najaf, and had prepared accordingly. Like Nasiriyah, the fight near Najaf showed how each side was surprised by the enemy it encountered: the Americans were not expecting to be harassed by guerrilla fighters; the Iraqis were not expecting a U.S. armored brigade to drive into Rams.

Even though Perkins's brigade had made quick work of the Iraqis at Rams, the V Corps now had to wrestle with the fact that there were more enemy in the area than it had anticipated—no small consideration, as Rams was to be the site of the temporary V Corps command post, the 3rd Infantry Division's rear logistics, and a base for the 11th Attack Helicopter Regiment, which, lacking the ability to mount a ground defense of its own position, planned to use Rams that night as a launching pad for its upcoming attack against the Medina Division.

Perkins assigned Philip "Flip" DeCamp's 4-64 battalion to protect Rams with the understanding that it would soon be relieved by another unit. The plan had been for the regiment's helicopters to rendezvous with their logistics at Rams, but Caine was still struggling to reach the site. Caine's convoy had experienced every bit of the unwelcome adventure he had feared. As it headed north, an Iraqi in civilian clothes shot at the convoy and then disappeared. Caine was puzzled. Again, American intelligence had said that the Iraqis in the south would be welcoming. "Why would the Iraqis shoot at us? We are the good guys," he thought. As he struggled to stay on schedule, Caine pondered going around Salman. But that would have meant having to drive on rough sand and forfeiting the possibility of finding a road. As the convoy approached the town, crowds began to line the road. Caine grabbed the tear gas and smoke grenades at his side. He ordered his soldiers to prepare to go "weapons hot." But for once, the invasion went according to script. The Iraqis were mostly curious; some even started cheering.

Things, however, began to fall apart as Caine approached Samawah and learned that Perkins's 2nd BCT was already on the move toward Rams and was in no position to give Caine extra fuel as Ball had planned. Caine's platoon would not be able to fuel more than one squadron's aircraft. When Ball heard this, he was not amused: he didn't care if Caine had to steal a 5,000-gallon tanker; Caine had to get the fuel.

As he rushed to Rams, Caine grew increasingly frustrated with the stop-and-start military traffic ahead of him. Every time the forces at the front ran into strong resistance, the columns would come to a halt. Desperate to be on time, Caine decided to take his chances in the desert and drive on a stretch adjacent to the road. The convoy began to move past M1 tanks and was soon ahead of the scouts at the front of the column. "The scout soldiers seemed a little surprised and maybe a little hurt to be passed by an element of refuel trucks," Caine recalled. "The officer in the lead just shook his head and wished us luck."

For two hours, the convoy drove without spotting another American vehicle. Caine finally reached the rendezvous point, which was grassy terrain. Two of the regiment's squadrons were coming from Germany and had less desert experience than did Ball's squadron; they had chosen to land on as much grass as possible to avoid the brownouts that can occur when a chopper's rotor whips up sand. Caine soon discovered why the area was green: it was crisscrossed by one-foot-wide irrigation ditches. After Major Adkins reported this to Ball by satellite phone, the refueling site was changed to a nearby stretch of sand. As Caine prepared for the incoming aircraft, he finally received some good news. One of his soldiers had made contact with a battalion commander from Will Grimsley's 1st BCT. The commander had agreed to give the convoy 5,000 gallons of his fuel, but warned Caine's soldiers to act fast, before he changed his mind. As evening approached it was clear that Ball had been wise to give Caine his mission. The rest of the regiment's refueling trucks were nowhere in sight. It looked like there would be enough fuel for the regiment to attack.

At precisely 5:00 p.m. the first aircraft from 2-6 Cav could be heard in the distance. Caine instructed it to land at the new refueling site but the squadron commander responded that his unit would be landing on the grassy area as originally planned. The two other squadrons followed its lead. Sergeant First Class Ernest Dudley looked at Caine in shock. Since the fuel trucks would have to navigate around the irrigation ditches, the supply company would not be able to distribute fuel to all of the battalion's aircraft in time. Further complications abounded. There was at least one Black Hawk more than had been planned and, even though four CH-47s arrived with bladders of fuel and other equipment needed by the regiment, they in turn had to be refueled in order to be able to return to their base. At the insistence of Major John Lindsay, the regiment's operations officer, some of Caine's supply had to be diverted to the CH-47s— each of which required as much fuel as two Apaches.

Adding to the fuel crunch, some pilots had conducted long pre-flight checks prior to leaving Kuwait and had had only enough left to make it to Rams. Soon there was an ugly free-for-all for gas among the squadrons, with each insisting that it had priority. After days of little or no sleep, and unable to contact Wolf to straighten things out, Caine finally lost his cool and got on the radio to make some announcements to the three squadrons.

"Guidons, Guidons, Guidons, this is Attack 3-5," he said, identifying his supply unit. "Since you can't agree to who should have priority for refuel and Colonel Wolf is off the net, I am going to determine it off the operations order that I am currently holding. First Attack, as the main effort, will get gas first. 6-6, as supporting effort one, will be next. Medevac helicopters will be next, and then Command and Control and Personnel Recovery Black Hawks. 2-6, you're not getting gas. If you don't like it, tough! Go talk to the regimental commander. If you all hadn't figured it out, we are short fuel and I am the only show in town. If you want fucking fuel, you are going to have to get it from me! If you order my 3-5 personnel to do anything different than what I just said, I will report you to Colonel Wolf and you can explain to him how your selfish acts caused the mission to fail! Unless you are updating me on your fuel status, get off my net!" Caine waited for a higher-ranking officer to threaten him with insubordination, but there was no response. Ball's 1-227 would have first call on fuel.[13]

Faced with a fuel shortage at Rams and communication glitches with the V Corps headquarters, Wolf called his commanders together to discuss options. Option one was to take off on schedule and somehow muddle through the attack. Option two was to request a two-hour delay. Ball proposed a third option: to use the whole evening to complete the refueling process and go at first light. In taking the fight to the Medina, the Apaches would have to ensure that they were targeting enemy tanks and not civilian vehicles. On McElhiney's advice, Ball had felt from the start that it would be easier to identify targets in daylight, and safer, too, as increased visibility would enable the helicopters to fire from a greater distance. It would also give the regiment more time to update its intelligence and resynchronize the attack with artillery and air strikes. But, again, Ball's option was vetoed.

Wolf decided to launch the nighttime attack after a two-hour delay. With fuel tight and time running out, one of the squadrons, the 2-6, had to be cut from the mission. Without the communications suite that was still on the road, Captain Hobart was compelled to receive the intelligence update from the V Corps headquarters on her TacSat instead of downloading it. V Corps was able to provide only four-digit grids for the targets, which were far less specific than the eight-digit coordinates the regiment was accustomed to using. No UAVs were available to survey the helicopter routes or the target site. The UAV teams were either on the move or providing surveillance for the coming air strikes near Baghdad. As was the case with Task Force Tarawa, the 11th Attack Helicopter Regiment would be proceeding without the benefit of a reconnaissance drone, a surprising development, since the Apache attack was to be the corps's main effort that day.

As the pilots prepared to take off, the aircrews were startled to see missiles streaking overhead. It was the ATACMS launch that was supposed to occur thirty minutes prior to the attack. Because of communications problems, the artillery had never gotten the word that the deep attack had been delayed by two hours. When it was time to take off, all of Ball's helicopters had taken gas, but 6-6 discovered that only fourteen of its twenty-one helicopters had been refueled; the regiment's command and control helicopter had also not received fuel. Wolf, who was to orchestrate the attack from his Black Hawk, would not be able to take off and supervise the operation. The colonel spent the first thirty minutes of the attack on the ground and out of touch with his forces. His Black Hawk was ready only for the final minutes of the battle.

With the Americans aloft and headed north, the Iraqis put their own plan into place. As U.S. intelligence would learn after the fall of Baghdad, the Iraqis had begun thinking about new ways to counter U.S. helicopter strikes soon after the Gulf War. The issue was worked on by the Republican Guard staff, the Iraqi military's School of Advanced Armor and Infantry, the Air Defense School, and Al Bakr University. To counter the choppers, the Iraqis reorganized air defense battalions into twelve to eighteen antihelicopter ambush teams. Each team had five vehicles—military as well as civilian trucks—and its weapons included machine guns, ZPU-23-2 cannons, S-60 guns, and SA-7 and SA-14 surface-to-air missiles. Each team had a spotter section of Iraqi Special Forces equipped with communication systems and deployed along likely attack routes. The teams were trained to fire in the general direction of hovering helicopters, move on, and fire again. Their goal was not to strike the helicopter, but to throw up a wall of fire through which the helicopter would have to fly. Some of the ambush teams also had night vision equipment and could fire antiaircraft guns with tracers. Iraqi soldiers without night vision gear would aim at the tracer fire, hoping to get lucky and strike an aircraft. To provide early warning of the Apache attack, the Iraqi defense plan called for 485 observation points in southern Iraq, manned by spotters with cell phones.

Having studied U.S. tactics, the Iraqis knew that the Americans always worried about the possibility of flying into telephone or electrical wires and would always be at pains to fly over them. So the Iraqis concentrated their firepower at locations where the American helicopters would be flying over suspended wires. Their S-60s—high-altitude air defense weapons—would be adjusted to set off bursts at 500 feet, forcing the Americans to fly at a lower altitude, making them more vulnerable to ground fire. The 11th Attack Helicopter Regiment knew none of this. American intelligence had suggested that the Iraqis had not trained seriously for more than a decade, were reluctant to activate their radars for fear of being detected and attacked, and were no match for Longbow Apaches.

Commander of 6-6 Mike Barbee's helicopter had been among those not refueled, so he scrambled to find a fueled one to lead his Apaches into the fight. Barbee was surprised by how urbanized the terrain appeared to be. No sooner was he under way than he heard that one of his Apaches had crashed: loaded to the gills with ammunition, the helicopter had had trouble taking off in the talcum-like sand churned by the refueling vehicles. As he flew north, Iraqi fire became increasingly concentrated. It seemed as if the lead helicopters in his formation had put the Iraqi defenders on alert and triggered the fire at the aircraft that followed. Barbee lost another helicopter when the aircraft was shot up twenty minutes into the attack, had its primary flight controls disabled, and was forced to turn back. One of Barbee's commanders went so far as to ask if the mission should be aborted. Barbee rejected the idea. His Apaches were distributed all along the route and it would not be easy to reverse course safely. Barbee instructed his squadron to fly east of the assigned route, away from the urbanized areas.[14]

Chief Warrant Officer John Tomblin and First Lieutenant Jason King were maneuvering in Palerider 16 when they noticed an odd sight. The lights in Haswah and Iskandariyah were ablaze at 1:00 a.m. As their helicopter climbed to 200 feet to clear some telephone wires, the lights in one town suddenly went out. When they were turned back on a few seconds later, there was a fusillade of small arms fire and antiaircraft artillery. Palerider 16, the second helicopter in Barbee's squadron to take off, had flown straight into an ambush. The light had been a signal for the Iraqis. Although the Apaches were blacked out, they were silhouetted against the clouds by the lights of the Iraqi towns. The Iraqis were engulfing the Apaches in fire, determined to strike them as they moved to their targets.

Like the 3rd Infantry Division soldiers at Rams and Samawah, Barbee's aircrews were initially uncertain about how to respond under the rules of engagement. They had been instructed to identify their targets before attacking. Numerous "no-strike" areas, including gas stations and mosques, had been designated. Wolf had even cautioned his pilots at Udairi that their combat recordings might be inspected for infractions of the rules of engagement. But with the enemy firing at night from buildings, roadways, and palm groves, it was difficult to identify the foe. The pilots who relied on the FLIR system, which generated images from sources of heat, could not even see the red, yellow, and white tracers. Only those in front seats with night vision goggles could see the streams of fire. Nonetheless, Barbee exhorted his aircrews to return fire; it was now a matter of survival. They were simply to shoot at Iraqi attack positions. Suppress the small arms fire and return fire for your wingman, he yelled into the radio.

But for Palerider 16, it was already too late. As Tomblin took evasive maneuvers, the crew detected a burning smell. Some of the helicopter's electrical equipment was on fire. With his night vision goggles, King was pointing out to Tomblin where the fire was coming from when radio transmission stopped.

"Are you okay, sir?" Tomblin asked.

There was no response. A bullet had ripped into the cockpit and struck King in the neck. Tomblin reported that his front-seater had been hit, that his condition was not known, and that he was turning back. As Tomblin pulled behind his wingman he saw that the other Apache's engine was on fire. One of the hydraulic lines had been severed, making it impossible for the wingman to return fire. Tomblin would have to shoot for both of them. As Tomblin fired at the enemy, King managed to get hold of a pressure bandage and apply it to his neck wound. The bullet had just missed King's windpipe. He was bloody but once again able to speak. Palerider 16 headed back to Rams. Soon after, Barbee ordered his squadron to abort their attack. 6-6 had lost one helicopter on takeoff, all the others had been shot up, and a crewmember had been seriously wounded—all before the squadron reached the Medina Division tanks it was supposed to strike. Now Barbee would have to run the gauntlet back. If the 11th Regiment was going to achieve its mission, it would be up to Ball's 1-227.[15]

Ball had devised a three-prong attack. Charlie Troop would guard the regiment's western flank in case the Iraqis began to shift forces from Karbala and along Highway 9 across the Euphrates. The main attack would be conducted by Bravo Troop. Alpha would maneuver in the east and join Bravo if the latter needed extra firepower. Ball would be flying between Bravo and Alpha so he could coordinate the fight. As Colonel Wolf had yet to take off in his command and control Black Hawk, Ball had no way of communicating with his superior.

McElhiney was flying one of the four helicopters on Charlie Troop's mission in the west. With his experience running fire in Vietnam, in what he called "high-energy tactics," he was convinced he would have to maneuver now. Anticipating that he would be doing a lot of shooting, McElhiney had removed some of his antitank missiles from his aircraft at Rams and added 30mm ammunition. Now he yelled to the lead craft in formation that he needed to keep moving and not hover. Within seconds the Iraqis began to attack. It was the most fire he had seen in his life, more even than during the invasion of Laos. Two of the four helicopters were too damaged to continue the fight.

McElhiney could tell that he was taking on a clever foe: by firing S-60s the Iraqis were pressing the Americans to fly at lower altitudes, where they were more vulnerable to ground fire, much of it coming from a mosque. McElhiney realized he would have to fight in close quarters and destroy the Iraqi air defenses one at a time. Using 30mm guns and rockets, he took out the mosque. His wingman launched a Longbow Hellfire into an S-60 battery. As the firefight continued, McElhiney saw a train moving through town and attacked it. McElhiney recalled that he had seen a ZSU-24 gun on the back of a train during the 1991 Gulf War and did not plan on taking any chances. As in Nasiriyah, the ROE were getting considerably looser as the fighting went on. All of Charlie's aircraft were hit. McElhiney's lost its primary hydraulics system. He was able to make it back to base, landing near the 6-6 Apache that had crashed upon takeoff.[16]

Eastward, Alpha also ran into heavy resistance. Its mission was to protect Bravo Troop's eastern flank and to carry out a supporting attack. In the rush to carry out the mission, none of the Alpha pilots had been told that 2-6 squadron had been scratched, a conspicuous omission, as Alpha Troop pilots assumed they were operating to their east. Chief Warrant Officer 3 Olin Ashworth piloted the lead Apache. He was flying over urban sprawls and palm groves not depicted on the Joint Operations Graphic maps that back-seaters generally used. As the Apaches approached their targets, Ashworth saw lights in the city below go out. Ashworth thought that CENTCOM had somehow destroyed the Iraqi electrical grid to facilitate the Apaches' mission. Then, as before, the lights came on and the firing started.

One Alpha helicopter, Avenger 26, turned back early, after its engine caught fire and it lost its hydraulics. The company had been told to look for an Iraqi armored battalion in defensive positions along Highway 1, which went from Baghdad to Hillah and Iskandariyah. There were many unoccupied fighting holes, but no tanks or enemy forces. Alpha fought on until it ran low on fuel. On the way back, one pilot heard an F-15 pilot talking on Guard, the emergency frequency. "Got 7 down." He was shocked. Had the battalion lost seven Apaches?

To carry out the main attack, Bravo Troop had been augmented with two Apaches from Charlie, bringing its formation up to eight. Bravo's target was thirty T-72 tanks, part of the Medina Division, which the battalion had been told had moved south to bolster the defenses around the Iraqi capital. First, the scouts in the formation would find the tanks. Then the rest of the Apaches would fly in and strike. Joe Goode and Cynthia Rosel had been scheduled to be part of the attack formation, but five minutes before taking off from Rams they had been reassigned to the scout formation because one of its helicopters was still being refueled.

Goode and Rosel reached their target area without incident, but Rosel saw no tanks, only a few trucks. Lieutenant Joe Bruhl, in a nearby helicopter, was convinced he saw a truck with some kind of weapon system and launched a Hellfire. Suddenly, Iraqi fire broke out in all directions, forcing the Apaches to scatter. The Apaches had stumbled on the Iraqi Air Defense School. With the Apaches dispersing in all directions, Rosel was initially reluctant to fire back. She was not sure where her fellow pilots were positioned. Goode and Rosel flew to Waypoint 19, a designated location along the route, and circled back.[17]

As for the rest of Bravo's Scout section, it was also being hit hard. Chief Warrant Officer Sean Wojansinski was flying with Justin Taylor in Reaper 11, and its number one engine and cockpit displays were disabled by ZPU antiaircraft rounds. Flying on a single engine, the crew had to jettison their wing stores to stay aloft. Even so, they were flying dangerously low, sometimes just fifteen feet off the ground, between houses and along the riverbank. Taylor, a strapping former Marine, hit the floor microphone to talk on Guard and broadcast that Reaper 11 was going to try to make it back to Rams. Unbeknownst to Taylor, his microphone became stuck in the open position. Taylor was hot-miking. He guided Wojansin-ski on how to dodge the RPGs, and also spoke to Karma 1, a British offi-cer on a JSTARS Air Force plane monitoring the fight, who dispatched a pair of F-15s to provide support for Reaper 11 on its way back to Rams. Taylor's hot-miking was disconcerting to the rest of the troop: his under-standable anxiety had been transmitted throughout the regiment to everyone who was listening—the Iraqis included. It had also drowned out other emergency communications.[18]

Dave Williams and Ronald Young flew in Vampire 12, a Charlie Apache that had been allocated to Bravo for the main attack. Williams had wanted to get into the fight in the worst way. He had been in the Army for almost fourteen years and had worked in Special Operations. He served with Mike Durant, the helicopter pilot who was shot down in Somalia. Williams and Young flew to their target area in silence, going over tactical procedures in their heads. Williams found the situation sur-real. Cities and towns were lit up. People were walking around with rifles. He was astonished to see so many people in the streets. Williams had heard other pilots report that they were taking fire, and had even heard one say he was going down. Now all of a sudden a wall of antiaircraft ar-tillery appeared in front of their chopper. "Don't fly through that," Young yelled. Before Williams could react, there was more fire; tracers went past the canopy, past the windscreen, past the fuselage and the rotor disc.

Williams rolled the aircraft to the left. Young yelled out that they were taking more fire at one o'clock. Williams contacted his wingman for fire support. "3-0, I need you," Williams said. "I am trying to hang with you," the wingman shot back.

Williams spent the next forty minutes dodging Triple A—or at least trying to. His Apache was so damaged that Young could not fire back. Young tried to guide Williams to less vulnerable locations, but it seemed that every way Williams turned they ran into antiaircraft fire. During one banking maneuver, a round broke into the cockpit, ripped across the top of Williams's boot, split the shoe open, and grazed his left foot on the flight control pedal. As it was not a debilitating wound, he was able to keep going.

As he approached his attack-by-fire position, where he was to shoot at his prescribed target, he, too, lost his number one engine. The Apache Longbow is a sophisticated aircraft. It does not have conventional dials. It has two computer screens called Multipurpose Displays (MPD) con-stituting a "glass cockpit." If an engine goes out, the onboard computer autopages to a set of instructions to the engine and rotor. Williams was able to keep his other engine going and to continue jinking and jiving. On one of his passes Young slowed to 100 knots and flew at an altitude of fifty feet. Young watched through his FLIR as a group of Iraqis tried to adjust an antiaircraft gun in front of a house. Williams fired his 30-millimeter gun at the enemy. But the Iraqis were firing, too. The Apache's flight management computer went out. Its hydraulics were disabled. The evasive maneuvers were too much for the stricken aircraft. An automated voice announced: "Rotor RPM low. Rotor RPM low."

The chopper came down in a rice paddy, gliding to the ground. It was one of a pilot's worst nightmares: to be trapped behind enemy lines. Williams and Young had to scramble to evade capture, and hope that Special Operations search-and-rescue teams would find them before the enemy did. "Get out, get out, get out," Williams yelled to Young, who was six feet four. No sooner did Williams open the canopy than Young was already out, telling his fellow pilot that they had to run fast—the Iraqis would be on their tail. Williams's foot wound, however, slowed them down. His boot was blown apart, the top of his foot cut open; he was in pain. Williams and Young got on their survival radios and made several distress calls as the Triple A fire continued over their heads: "Vampire 1-2, heading on foot . . . Request Hasty Pickup." Later, they made another call, using the theater call sign. "This is Pantry 70. I am on foot. I need help."

They did not get 100 yards from the aircraft before the Iraqis were all over it. Williams and Young slogged southward through the rice paddy, desperately looking for vegetation that would provide cover. With a three-quarter moon in the sky, it was distressingly bright—so bright that Williams and Young were casting shadows. As the drama unfolded, the Iraqis broke into the emergency frequency to denounce the "infidel Americans." Rosel had caught a snippet of Vampire 12's emergency broadcast: "we're on foot." She had assumed it came from Taylor, who had been hot-miking Reaper 11's efforts to stay aloft. Rosel radioed Captain J. B. Worley III, the Bravo commander, and his pilot, Chief Warrant Officer Paul Dean, and mistakenly told them that Taylor and Wojansinski were down.

Flying in Reaper 6, Worley and Dean went to look for the downed helicopter. There was a means for an Apache to rescue a pilot by strapping him on the wing. It was a hell of a ride, but it was better than being left behind for the Iraqis. The rescue effort soon turned into a near disaster. Reaper 6 had already taken a hit to its TADS targeting system earlier in the fight, but Captain Worley had stayed on station to command his troop. Now his Apache was hit again: fire struck three of the main rotor blades and the hydraulic system. The helicopter shook violently, its instruments all but impossible to read. Dean worried that they would have to land before getting to Rams. As it struggled to save itself, Reaper 6 was in no position to go to the assistance of Williams and Young.[19]

Dan Ball now moved in to help the downed pilots. His command and control helicopter had loitered to direct the attack and thus had some fuel at its disposal. It would be the last chance for immediate rescue. Ball was crewed with Chief Warrant Officer 4 John Davies, one of the most experienced pilots in the squadron. They hoped to surprise the Iraqis by approaching the area from a different direction, but as they climbed over a utility pole their Apache was hit by either a shoulder-fired missile or an RPG and caught on fire. Ball jettisoned his stores. Word trickled back to Rams. The 1-227 squadron commander might be another casualty. Before he headed back, Ball punched in the coordinates of his location in an encrypted system, hoping that search-and-rescue teams could somehow make it there to rescue Williams and Young.

At Rams, John A. Carey, the rescue coordination director for V Corps, was monitoring the situation. He knew that Reaper 11 and Palerider 16 were in trouble, though it took a while for him to determine if theirs had been a call sign for a jet or helicopter. When he heard about Vampire 12 he tried to pin down its location. In the heat of battle, Ball had entered the code incorrectly, but after some effort, Special Operations Forces were able to identify the location. As the emergency beacon of the Apache helicopters was weak and its pilots were not equipped with advanced survival radios that also transmit GPS coordinates, the SOF had to know not only the location but whether the distress call was authentic and not an enemy ploy to lure them into a trap. Initially, they knew neither. But even with that information, it would have been difficult, if not impossible, for them to carry out the rescue. The Iraqis were right on the heels of the downed Americans.

Running for their lives, Williams and Young came upon an irrigation canal. Williams was reluctant to jump in, fearing they might perish from hypothermia if they were forced to hide in the water. But there was nowhere else to go. Williams and Young managed to move almost a mile through the water before becoming so cold they had to climb out. Moving south, they came upon a lake. Wet, cold, and miserable, they walked south on the shore. If it looked as if the Iraqis were on their trail, they would get back in the water and hide there if need be.

The Iraqis were hot on their tracks—so close the downed pilots could hear enemy soldiers talking. Williams and Young got facedown in the mud to evade detection. Williams glanced over his left shoulder. He saw three soldiers just fifty yards away, armed with rifles. As they got closer, they looked in the direction of the Americans and started pointing. Willams prayed that they would walk on by. Young had taken his pistol out of its holster, but that would be no match against Iraqi soldiers with AK-47s. Soon the Iraqis fired a round near the Americans. They moved closer and started yelling. Williams and Young had been discovered.

Williams slowly raised his left hand in surrender, to little avail. One soldier took a rifle and struck Young in the back of the head. Another wielded a rifle like a baseball bat, coming down hard on Williams's lower back. Then an Iraqi put a knife to Williams's neck. Williams thought of his family and hoped the Iraqis would be quick about it. Another soldier fired a round right past Young's head. But the Iraqis intended not to kill Williams and Young but to terrify them. After their hands were tied, the two pilots were hauled into the town of Karbala in the back of a blue pickup truck and taken to a government building, where there was only one Iraqi who spoke a smattering of English.

"What country are you from?" he asked. "Where are the American forces? What are you doing in my country?"

Williams tried to be tactful. He had been taught that if a pilot is captured, the start of his ordeal is the most dangerous. If a prisoner was to be killed, he would die early on—before being passed up the chain of command. Williams said he was just flying around and following orders. The Iraqi did not like his answers.

"Do you expect me to believe you were just flying around and not shooting anybody?" the interrogator shot back. "You are not being honest with us." Williams and Young were later blindfolded, thrown in an ambulance, and driven to Baghdad. They had survived the most dangerous phase of their captivity, but their long and punishing ordeal had just begun.[20]

At Rams, the rest of the regiment's supply column had finally begun to trickle in. When the soldiers arrived, Captain John Cochran was stunned.

As the assistant operations officer for the regiment, Cochran had been driving for four days. He had snaked his way north past blown-up Iraqi trucks, overturned and wrecked Army trucks, and the earth-shattering explosion of an oil storage tanker in Samawah, which had sent up a 400-foot wall of flame. But nothing had prepared him for what he encountered when he reached the assembly area at Rams. Helicopters were strewn everywhere. After a few near collisions, the returning pilots had put down wherever they could, the exhausted crews curled up underneath their aircraft with no security. Cochran ran up to Captain Gary Morea, the chief planner for the Medina attack. Morea was near his TacSat radio and appeared to be shaken. "It was a bad mission, a really bad mission," Morea said.

John Lindsay, the operations officer for the regiment, wrote in his diary that U.S. intelligence had left the regiment utterly unprepared for the mission. "G2 really screwed the pooch on this one," he wrote. "No assessment ever accounted for the threat we faced." Said Hobart, the intelligence officer or S-2 for the regiment, "This ambush was rehearsed. It was trained for. This was asymmetrical warfare at its best. They had decided they can't turn on their radars because they knew we would kill them, but they knew we were going to send Apaches in to clear the way."[21]

Still, the damage had been extensive. One Apache had crashed on take-off; another had been shot down and its crew captured. Virtually all of the thirty aircraft had returned with bullet holes. With the helicopters all over the assembly area, it took hours even to determine how many aircraft had managed to return. As the count proceeded, Lindsay was relieved to find a Black Hawk with seven unaccounted-for personnel parked in the distance. In Ball's squadron alone, aircraft had cumulatively been hit more than 300 times by enemy air defense and small arms fire. The list of problems that the regiment had encountered was long: sixty-two rotor blades were hit; seven fuel cells were banged up; eight engines were stuck; and six canopies were damaged beyond repair. The night flight systems of some helicopters were knocked out. The Iraqis had also targeted the weapons mounted on the Apaches: eight damaged Hellfire missiles caused three in-flight fires. As if this were not enough, the Iraqis were able to move the captured Apache—with its sophisticated suite of electronic aviation and fire control systems—before CENTCOM could destroy it. Special forces eventually went in to try to locate Williams and Young but had to be pulled out when they heard that V Corps was planning to fire ATACMS missiles at the position to destroy the helicopter and deny the Iraqis an intelligence bonanza. But U.S. fire came too late.

The mission had failed: the Medina Division had been hard to locate and had barely been attacked. "Any damage we did to them was fairly minimal," Wolf concluded. There was one comforting development: the Air Force report about seven downed Apaches turned out to be inaccurate; the Air Force pilot had mistaken seven Apaches sitting at Rams for downed aircraft.[22]

On the night after the deep attack, Wallace visited the 11th Attack Helicopter Regiment. He told them that the mission had been compromised by a cell phone call. According to 6-6 squadron's after-action report, the Iraqis turned the electrical power off and on as a signal. Then they would unleash fire, aimed at creating an impenetrable "wall" for the approaching Apaches. The Iraqis had two- to three-man teams in vehicles along canals, in open fields, and in urban areas, following the anticipated flight path. Fire from the vehicles had been so accurate as to prompt the suspicion that the Iraqis were using night vision equipment. "These vehicles provide a moving platform for ground forces which are not targeted or tracked by intel assets," the report noted. And because the Apaches came and went along the same routes, they were even more vulnerable. Subsequent intelligence analysis based on interrogations of Iraqi officers and captured documents was more detailed.[23]

Ball and the other commanders had a long session to pass on the painful lessons they had learned to the 101st Airborne, slated to carry out its own deep attack in a few days. While the attack highlighted the valor and flying skills of the aircrews, as well as the durability of the Apache aircraft in the face of enemy fire, the pilots considered it a minor miracle that only one Apache was shot down. When the Army looked back at the episode, it identified a confluence of errors: an underestimation of the enemy; logistical problems; overly restrictive rules of engagement; unimaginative attack routes; the long delay between the firing of the ATACMS missiles to suppress enemy defenders and the attack itself; the absence of any close air support aircraft ready and on call; and, most of all, an intemperate rush to get into the fight without adequate preparation. As one member of the regiment later put it, the regiment was looking for 100 percent success with a 50 percent plan.

But the failure of the mission suggested something fundamental. The V Corps's plans for mounting deep helicopter attacks were ill suited for the fluid battlefield on which the U.S. military now found itself and the mélange of the Iraqi troops and paramilitary fighters it faced. Its tactics may have worked well against Soviet armor, Iraqi tanks in the desert, and in the exercises in Poland. But they needed to be overhauled in taking on the Iraqis armed with shoulder-fired missiles, RPGs, and AK-47s.

There had been much training, but for the wrong type of war. The exercises in Poland simulated long attack routes, but those routes were, needless to say, not heavily defended. According to one after-action report, "this gave the staff the illusion that if there are no ADA [air defense artillery] systems along the route then it is a safe route when in reality the most deadly system for the AH64 is not an ADA system but an AK47." The report also noted that "massed small arms fire is so distracting that it causes mass confusion when unprepared." The Air Force, V Corps, and regiment "did not rehearse their mission in the manner required for real world execution."[24]

Having started out well, the first week of the war had taken a turn for the worse. The first part of the war was supposed to have been little more than a race to the Red Zone. But Terry Ferrell's 3-7 Cavalry had engaged in an unexpected firefight in Samawah; Rams had been infiltrated by small groups of Fedayeen; and the battle in Nasiriyah had become a bloody brawl. Now, the V Corps's vaunted 11th Attack Helicopter Regiment had come up short.

CHAPTER 15

A Sanctuary for the Fedayeen

As the V Corps rumbled north, Scott Wallace still considered the Republican Guard to be the main enemy, the threat of chemical weapons in the Karbala Gap to be the greatest danger, and the capture of Baghdad to be the principal objective. But the Fedayeen attacks were becoming increasingly difficult to ignore. None of the fighting so far had dampened the Fedayeen's ardor to do battle with the Americans. If anything, the Fedayeen seemed more emboldened than ever.

With fighters in Najaf, the Fedayeen were within striking distance of Objective Rams, where the V Corps was marshaling its logistics and in position to strike the Army's supply lines. The decision to defer Terry Ferrell's feint up Highway 8 toward the Medina Division was understandable given the enemy resistance in Samawah, but it also meant that the area between the Euphrates River and Highway 8 had become a veritable Fedayeen sanctuary. Towns like Hillah and Diwaniyah seemed to be teeming with fresh fighters eager to head west to strike the V Corps, or east to harass Jim Conway's Marines.

The job of securing the V Corps's right flank was left to Buff Blount's 3rd Infantry Division. With its focus on getting to Baghdad and its forces spread out from cliffs north of Najaf to Tallil, the division was not eager to devote too many forces to its new mission. But for the V Corps to advance, the division needed to isolate Najaf, strangle the resistance there, and prevent the flow of Fedayeen reinforcements from the east.

To carry out the screening operation, Lloyd Austin, Blount's assistant division commander for maneuver, turned to Will Grimsley's 1st Brigade Combat Team. Leading the division's charge, the brigade had made its way along a narrow sabkhah-lined causeway and up a 250-foot-high escarpment north of Najaf. The landscape was strangely familiar to some officers. The Army had built a close replica of the terrain leading to the escarpment at its National Training Center in California, and Grimsley's brigade had trained on it in the fall of 2002. No sooner had Grimsley fought his way up than Austin called to tell him that some of his forces would have to reverse course and move southeast to block the Fedayeen from crossing east at Kifl.

Grimsley did not know much about Kifl, nor could he have been expected to. The town on the east bank of the Euphrates River had never been an important objective for the Americans. Its most noteworthy feature—from the American point of view—was its Class 70 bridge, a span strong enough to bear the weight of U.S. armor. But since the V Corps had not planned to use it as an invasion route, neither SOF nor conventional Army reconnaissance teams had been in or around Kifl. To the Iraqis, however, Kifl was vital terrain. It was a smaller version of Samawah or Nasiriyah, a Euphrates River crossing point that they planned to defend at all costs to prevent the Americans from advancing on the main highways that led to Baghdad. Holding it also protected the network they relied on to funnel Fedayeen reinforcements into the fray.

Focused on consolidating his position on the escarpment for the upcoming push north through the Karbala Gap, Grimsley assigned Captain Charles Branson, the commander of a "linebacker" air defense artillery battery, to advance toward the Kifl bridge. For reinforcement, Grimsley gave him a small group of scouts from the Brigade Reconnaissance Troop, including observers to call in artillery. To Grimsley it seemed sufficient force for what he regarded as a relatively minor mission. The air defense battery had no other pressing duties, as the Iraqis were not flying combat aircraft, and the battery was equipped with Bradleys and Avengers, which had night vision capability.

There had been a hint that Kifl might be connected to the broader Fedayeen network: the religious leaders of the town had asked for and received a temporary cease-fire to recover the remains of some of the Iraqi fighters killed on the escarpment. As a precaution, Grimsley ordered Lieutenant Colonel Rock Marcone's 3-69 Armored Battalion to provide backup if needed. Marcone, in turn, told Captain Dave Benton, the commander of Bravo Company, 3-7 Infantry Battalion, to be prepared to serve as a quick reaction force in the event things heated up at Kifl, but assured him there was no reason to lose sleep over the assignment. It did not look as if there would be much of a fight there.[1]

Branson's battery moved out around midnight, passing muddy fields and small towns, but soon ran into ferocious resistance from, among others, paramilitary fighters firing from buildings and sandbagged positions. Having no infantry, Branson pulled back and called for artillery fire. By dawn, it was clear that Branson would need help to make it to Kifl, and Benton's infantry company was ordered into the fight. With two mechanized platoons and a tank platoon, Benton had wisely decided to lead with his tanks. On the move for less than a mile, his company, too, ran into fighters armed with RPGs and mortars. To escape the ambush, Benton ordered his tanks to get going. As the company approached a small town along the road, he got his first look at the enemy: men in civilian dress, armed with AK-47s and RPGs, scurrying around farmhouses and other structures.

With the fighting intensifying, Marcone ordered Major Mike Oliver, his operations officer, to head east. The air defense battery and the mechanized infantry company were not accustomed to working together; so, as the battle intensified, a more senior officer would need to take command. Setting out alone in his tank, Oliver soon came upon Branson, whose vehicle had thrown a track in the rough terrain. According to Oliver's map there were two bridges in Kifl. Oliver told Branson to take his air defense company south of the spans and block any Iraqi fighters heading north, a task that seemed commensurate with their limited capabilities. Benton's company would deal with the bridges.[2]

On his way south, Second Lieutenant John Rowold, the tank platoon commander in Benton's company, tried to take the measure of his foe. Enemy bullets were whizzing over the top of his tank. At first Rowold thought the shooters might simply be bad shots. But it occurred to him that, as overmatched as they were—equipped with only RPGs and small arms—they might be trying to take out the tank commander as he stood in his turret or shoot up the "Doghouse"—the sights and laser range finder atop the tank—one of the few ways at their disposal to stop an M1.

When Rowold got to the bridge, his first encounters with the Iraqis suggested that they were hopelessly outclassed by the Americans. Rowold watched as a truck stopped on the span and a group of men with weapons jumped out. The tanks opened up on the truck. Next a car started to cross. The tanks raked it with coax machine gun rounds; the occupants got out and ran. Rowold could not see if they were armed and ordered his platoon to cease fire. It was not always easy to tell fighters from noncombatants on the battlefield. Rowold's next sighting was the strangest of all. Eight Iraqis—the first uniformed soldiers he had come across all day—

started walking across the bridge almost as if in formation. Rowold was not sure how to respond to these enemy fighters who seemed so oblivious to the danger they faced. But after a Bradley from Benton's company began to fire, the tanks followed suit, killing the soldiers. In a matter of minutes, the span at Kifl was covered with corpses and mangled vehicles. It had been a one-sided fight to this point.[3]

Oliver arrived on the scene and was surprised to discover that there was just one bridge, not the two indicated on his battle map. He ordered a scout to check for demolitions. None were reported; they found only burlap sacks, which appeared to be filled with rice or grain. At 9:30 a.m., Oliver radioed Marcone and asked if he should establish a foothold on the other side. Marcone gave Oliver the go-ahead to send a tank platoon across and then called Grimsley's headquarters to ask for guidance. Major Morris Goins, Grimsley's operations officer, told Marcone that the battalion should not have ventured to the other side. Marcone asked sarcastically if he should give the bridge back to the Iraqis. Then Grimsley got on the radio and instructed Marcone to take the bridge but not to get decisively engaged. The main focus was still on heading north through the Karbala Gap.

At 10:00 a.m., Rowold's tank platoon began to rumble across the bridge. Two tanks with mine plows pushed the truck and car wreckage from the span, as the rest of the platoon followed in single file. Standing in his turret, Rowold was annoyed that he had not thought about having his camera at the ready. As he was thinking about reaching down to retrieve it, there was an explosion directly underneath his M1. Rowold felt his tank tilt backward until his driver hit the gas; the tank tread hugged the concrete and the seventy-ton vehicle pulled itself forward and onto the far bank. Rowold reported that the bridge had been partially blown up, and ordered the column of vehicles behind him to halt.

The three tanks came to a T on the far bank and split up to guard the access roads to the left and right. Rowold positioned himself in the middle. Rowold's platoon proceeded to leave a calling card: a depleted uranium sabot antitank round smashed into a government building displaying an Iraqi flag. With the thunderous arrival of the tanks, two Iraqis hopped in a jeep parked in front of the building and drove away. The tanks blasted the jeep, turning it into a mass of crumpled metal. Detonating equipment was later retrieved from the ruins of the vehicle and

Rowold figured these were the Iraqis who had probably tried to blow up the bridge. The tanks also machine-gunned a car that was moving toward their position. Confused and in a state of shock, its driver got out and opened his hood to check his engine before he dropped to the pavement as a result of his wounds. In this town that had abruptly been transformed into a battlefield, was this Iraqi an innocent civilian or the enemy?

On the near bank, Oliver was relieved to see that none of the tanks had sunk into the Euphrates, but was distressed to discover that three of his tanks were trapped on the far side of the river; he had no clear way to get them back or to send reinforcements. Oliver radioed Marcone with the news and the report sped up the chain of command. At V Corps, Wallace was worried that he had a Mesopotamian Black Hawk Down situation on his hands: U.S. forces cut off in enemy territory. It was the sort of battlefield drama that could overshadow the sad saga of the wayward 507th Maintenance Company in Nasiriyah.

As he surveyed the battlefield, Oliver grew concerned that the Iraqis would finish off what was left of the bridge and told Rowold to check the far end to see if it was also wired for demolition. Rowold reported that he saw some wires but balked at Oliver's order to cut them. Rowold was not an ordnance expert and was afraid that he would set off the explosives. Scanning his map, Oliver told him there was a bridge five miles to the north and one four miles to the south, but U.S. forces controlled neither. Disconnecting the wires, Oliver said, was the best way to get back home, assuming the bridge didn't explode in the meantime. Rowold grudgingly agreed and climbed underneath the bridge to cut the wires. As the tank crews tried to cope with their predicament with some black humor, Sergeant Frank Munley wondered whether they would be getting their mail on the far side of the bridge.[4]

As soon as he heard that he had tanks stuck on the wrong side of the Euphrates Marcone hopped in his own and raced to Kifl. Grimsley did the same, bringing his combat engineer battalion commander with him, hoping the man might be able to improvise a new span. That was easier said than done. The brigade had three bridge companies, but none had made it to the escarpment yet, and were hours away from Kifl. Since the division had not been planning to cross at the town, nobody had anticipated that a bridge company would be needed so soon.[5]

Arriving at the bridge at 10:30, Marcone inspected the span. The Iraqi demolition plan was not the work of amateurs. It was more elaborate than the U.S. troops had anticipated. The supporting columns for the span were pre-chambered—they had hollow spaces in which the Iraqis had inserted plastic explosives and covered them with rice bags both as camouflage and to direct the blast directly at the column instead of outward. Heavy guard wires ran under the bridge, which U.S. combat engineers later determined was a German-made detonation system activated by a high-voltage source of power. The far side was outfitted with explosives as well. The Iraqis appeared to have waited until the tanks were on the bridge for maximum effect. But the well-conceived plan had failed somewhat in its execution. The near end of the bridge had slumped on its now shortened supports, but it had not collapsed. Marcone asked where the bridge had been blown and a scout pointed to the truncated column. "This is it?" Marcone exclaimed. "A tank can drive over this." Grabbing his M4 carbine, he decided he would be the first to try. Marcone told his tank gunner that he would lead the tank over the damaged portion of the bridge so the battalion could set up a defensive position at the end of the span and get Rowold's platoon back.[6]

Rowold was up in his turret scanning the town while the two tanks ahead of him were buttoned up. "Guys, you are not going to believe this," Rowold told them. Power 6 (Marcone's call sign) was coming across, ground-guiding his tank. The tank crews thought he was joking until Sergeant Schwartz opened his turret to look for himself. "Well, this will play well in the movie," he said.

As Marcone walked ahead of his M1, the tank suddenly raced past him, rushing to strengthen the defenses on the far side. Marcone completed the crossing solo on foot under the gaze of the enemy. Having made it to the far bank, Marcone commanded Rowold's platoon to return to the near bank and ordered a portion of Benton's infantry company and their Bradleys forward. Walking to his tank, Marcone was surprised by several enemy fighters hiding behind a wall and shot and killed one of them. Securing the foothold would be a task for the infantry.

When Grimsley arrived on the scene at 1:00 p.m., he joined Marcone on the far bank: Kifl had been considered a sideshow before; it was a major cause of worry for the V Corps now.

As dangerous an adventure as Kifl had become, Benton comforted himself with the thought that reinforcements were on the way, that allied warplanes were at his disposal, and that the mission would soon be over. The brigade's plan was to replace Marcone's battalion as soon as possible so it could focus on the Karbala Gap. "My understanding at that point was I was going to be relieved early that evening," said Benton. He put one infantry platoon on the road north and one on the road to the south. He had scouts guarding the underside of the bridge itself to make sure that the Iraqis did not sneak up to ignite any explosives hidden inside the columns on the far side.[7]

First Lieutenant Brad Castro, platoon leader, Bravo Company, had the dubious distinction of guarding the northern position facing the road to Hillah, the town from which enemy reinforcements were most likely to come. Within minutes, he spotted a white car headed straight for his Bradley at sixty miles an hour—a civilian vehicle. His platoon, which had already mistakenly shot up two civilian vehicles, was unsure about what to do. "An alarm went off in my head. This is a threat," Castro recalled. He feared the car might be trying to pin his Bradley so RPG teams could attack it. The platoon opened fire and the car swerved, colliding with a telephone pole. The soldiers ran over to see who was in the car and reassure themselves that the platoon had not just inadvertently slaughtered a family. The driver had a military pistol and holster and was still alive; his passenger was dead.

U.S. soldiers finished the driver off, putting several bullets in his back. It was the first time they had faced such fanatical opposition, and they were afraid he might be a suicide bomber with a detonator in his hand and a trunk full of explosives. The car burned for hours; some soldiers took this as a telltale sign that explosives were in the trunk after all. But as the fighting picked up, nobody was able to investigate, as the once restrictive rules of engagement quickly gave way to rules for survival. There was a distinction between desperate fanaticism and the nihilistic impulse for self-destruction of a suicide bomber. At Kifl, it was hard for the soldiers to tell them apart; no one was ready to try. Fanatics, even wounded ones, would not be given the benefit of the doubt.[8]

With their visibility obscured by smoke and fog, the platoon was increasingly relying on its heat-sensing devices. The next threat was 400 yards in front of them and seemed to have the heat signature of an armored vehicle. The platoon blasted it with armor-piercing rounds, setting it aflame. Castro's gunner identified it as a Montero Sport. By this time the platoon was operating on the assumption that any vehicle that was zooming toward the U.S. positions was hostile.

By early evening, when Benton had expected to be relieved by a fresh unit, a sandstorm set in. It was the start of a furious three-day-long storm that would turn the sky an eerie orange. Oliver warned that there would be a delay of several hours. The platoon would have to hang on for a little longer. But the company's position was far from enviable. Even the seemingly indomitable Marcone was now out of action: a mortar blast had knocked him unconscious and forced his temporary evacuation. Within hours, Marcone would be back in the fight, but with the pounding he had taken and his hearing impaired he would later turn the battle over to Oliver.

As the fight dragged on, the brigade began to form a picture of its enemy: it was a mix of Fedayeen fighters who had headed south from Baghdad and Republican Guard soldiers, including a lieutenant colonel who was captured as he tried to orchestrate the fight from a building in the town. Several of the prisoners were convinced that Marcone, a dark-haired West Point graduate of Sicilian descent, was actually an Arab.

Farther south, Lieutenant Colonel J. R. Sanderson had refueled his armored battalion at Rams and then joined in the hellish road march north, jostling with other units to get on the narrow file leading to the escarpment. Under the 3rd Infantry Division plan, Sanderson's battalion was to be attached to Grimsley's 1st BCT for the next stage of the fight. Sanderson's most pressing problems were bringing up his logistics so his battalion could be at full strength and clearing the Fedayeen fighters—who, he feared, might be communicating the battalion's location to Iraqi artillery units—wandering around the escarpment. .

When Sanderson reported to the brigade commander, Grimsley informed him of his new mission: securing Kifl. After a long and trying day, Sanderson was to send a company that night to relieve Benton's. Sanderson's Assassins Company had led the way for the battalion, but only seven of its tanks were in good enough condition to keep rolling. Sanderson told Captain Stu James, the company commander, that he was to relieve Benton's infantry company in Kifl and that the battalion operations officer would be joining him.

As James drove east, the sandstorm intensified into a Shamal. Sanderson noted that tactical radio was buzzing with reports of Fedayeen attacks and rapidly deteriorating, eerily apocalyptic weather. As it rumbled along, Assassins Company received a Frago, or change in orders. It would attack into Kifl, then immediately swing southward to support Terry Ferrell's 3-7 Cavalry. As part of the plan to isolate Najaf, Austin had ordered 3-7 Cav, which had attacked northwest from Samawah along Route Appaloosa, to cross the Euphrates south of Najaf and block the key intersections at the bridges that connected Najaf to Diwaniyah. The move was also supposed to put Ferrell in position to help the U.S. forces at Kifl. But now the tables were turned: the 1st BCT had been told it was the cavalry squadron that needed help.

At Kifl, Mike Oliver passed the bad news to Benton. After trying to hang on for the required few extra hours, the promised relief would not be coming that night. Benton would just have to hold the town, stop infiltrators from trying to blow up the bridge, and wait. Benton used the waning hours of daylight to close the formation, refuel, and rearm. As night fell and the sandstorm grew worse, he had trouble seeing as little as 50 yards ahead. Benton tried listening for sounds of enemy activity. He would turn off the Bradleys' engines and keep the infantry out, securing the flanks with their ears to the ground for a sneak attack. Castro saw movement down a road and was able to spot enemy infantry getting out of trucks. As Iraqi RPG fire heated up, two of the platoon's Bradleys pushed into an alley in an evasive maneuver. Castro pulled up to support them, only to get a call from Benton: RPGs or no, he had to get his Bradleys moving to block the road north.

In the darkness, the Iraqis tried to sneak up on the U.S. troops. Some crawled on the ground with packs of dogs. One Iraqi fighter poked his head out of an alley and waved his hands, trying to determine if the platoon could sense him with their thermal imaging system. It could. The platoon held its fire as the Iraqi beckoned his comrades to slip down the street, then unleashed its fusillade. The platoon was holding its own but it was going to be a long night.[9]

For Terry Ferrell's 3-7 Cavalry Squadron, the first few days of the war had turned out to be a nonstop fight. After their harrowing night of miscues and dead-ends on Route Appaloosa, the division's plans to give the squadron a brief rest at Rams had been upended by the unexpected battle at Kifl and the initial reports that M1 tanks were stranded on the eastern side of the Euphrates. Instead of a respite, Ferrell's new destination was a position east of the Euphrates that was code-named Objective Floyd. In addition to blocking the routes there to Najaf, the move offered the possibility of a linkup with the forces at Kifl and kept alive the possibility of a feint on the east side of the Euphrates, which had been an important element of Wallace's plan to deceive the Iraqis about the main direction of his attack.

Ferrell cobbled together a plan. His Bonecrusher Troop was closest to Objective Floyd, so it would be charged with seizing the span. Apache Troop would cross the bridge and head north twenty-five miles on the highway. It would be just six miles from Grimsley's forces at Kifl and in position to move farther.

Subsequently, Crazy Troop would replace Bonecrusher on the bridge, enabling Bonecrusher to head west to block the two major roads leaving the city. According to intelligence, the bridge was likely to be the most secure spot. Crazy Troop had borne the brunt of the fighting in Samawah and Ferrell was still trying to give it a break. Ferrell moved out at 9:30 a.m. His units were to be in place by 4:00 p.m.

The Shamal was now so fierce—with gusts of up to forty-five knots—that the soldiers could barely see twenty-five yards. When Bonecrusher Troop reached the span, engineers quickly discovered that 2,500 pounds of explosives were sitting in crates under the north end. The explosives were not wired and it appeared that the Iraqis had planned to rig the bridge for demolition but somehow had never gotten around to it. Iraqi reluctance to destroy their bridges had played into the hands of the Americans. Saddam's regime intended to keep as many bridges whole as possible to be able to transport forces to quash a possible Shiite rebellion. The kind of extensive bridge demolition the Americans feared had yet to occur. So far, the Kifl bridge was the lone exception.

In keeping with the plan, Bonecrusher moved forward, swung left at a fork in the road, and almost immediately stumbled into an ambush. Gary O'Sullivan, the company commander, got on the radio: he had two tanks that were catastrophic kills. Ferrell tried to calm him down. O'Sullivan was still agitated. The tanks were destroyed and on fire. They were trying to get the crews out. The situation was bad, but not as disastrous as O'Sullivan feared. The M1 tank was designed with special blowout panels that shed when the tank was struck so that the explosive force of ammunition would be directed outside the vehicle and not at the crew. The panels had blown off, but the tanks themselves had not been blown up. All but one crewmember in the two tanks had taken cover on the far side of their vehicles. The driver of one of the M1s was trapped when the main tank gun fell on his compartment.

Sergeant First Class Javier Camacho in a tank and Sergeant First Class Steven Newby in a Bradley climbed out of their vehicles and wrested open the driver's hatch with a pry bar to rescue him. The driver was alive but groggy from smoke inhalation. Scouts quickly led the shaken soldier and his fellow crewmembers into their Bradley, raising and lowering the rear hatch as bullets pinged off the metal. Private First Class Raymond Smith, driver of another Bradley, pulled in front of the second tank to block enemy fire and retrieve the remaining tank crew. But as Smith drove away, he discovered that his night vision equipment was jammed, obscuring his view. Staff Sergeant Brian Borden crawled atop the Bradley and, with his own night vision goggles, guided Smith out of the firefight as bullets whizzed around him.

Bravo retreated, leaving behind the two stricken M1s and a damaged Bradley. Ferrell told O'Sullivan to let him know when all his soldiers were out of the battle zone and then called division. The squadron's artillery battery was out of range, so Ferrell asked for division artillery to pound the abandoned position since the enemy still occupied strongpoints along the route. The division's Multiple Launch Rocket Systems fired shells with thousands of tiny cluster bombs. It was the ultimate antipersonnel weapon, and lethal. Military procedures called for a minimum 2,100-yard separation between the artillery barrage and friendly forces. This time the separation would be no more than 1,300 yards—too close for comfort, but a risk Ferrell had to take to keep the enemy at bay. Colonel Tom Torrance, the division artillery commander, had the coordinates of the abandoned Bradley and used it as the target. The artillery fire was on target, so much so that when soldiers later went to look for the vehicle, as well as the enemy nearby, they found that the Bradley was completely destroyed.

After the battle, the Army would determine that Bonecrusher Troop's engagement was not the squadron's finest hour. The stricken M1 tanks had been hit by fire from the troop's own Bradleys as well as by enemy fire. O'Sullivan, Ferrell concluded, had lost control of the fight. When the tank crews evacuated the M1s they had grabbed personal items. Though the troop reported that it had taken all the sensitive material, some was left behind. Two weeks later, when Sanderson made it to Baghdad, an Iraqi showed him a piece of American equipment that he had picked up in a local bazaar. It was the hard drive for the FBCB-2, a computer in one of the abandoned M1s. Sanderson powered it up only to discover that it contained the 3-7 cavalry squadron graphics showing the invasion route and operations for the entire war.[10]

· · ·

As Bonecrusher Troop engaged the Iraqis in combat, Apache Troop fought its way north, trying to close the gap with Grimsley's soldiers at Kifl. For more than twenty miles, the troops encountered small arms fire, including fire from fighters in pickup trucks and in one case on a motorcycle with a sidecar on which was mounted a 30-millimeter gun. The Americans had trained to fight "open protected"—their hatches were open only a hand's width. But the severity of the sandstorm and the worsening visibility compelled the troops to emerge from their hatches. They were hanging over the sides of their Bradleys and tanks and firing away with M4s, M16s, and 9mm pistols at muzzle flashes. Enemy RPGs were bouncing off the U.S. vehicles. The Iraqi fighters were shooting from such close range that they did not have time to arm their RPGs. One of Apache Troop's biggest spoils would be an Iraqi warrant officer and a private captured with a truckload of rockets on its way from Hillah to Najaf.[11]

According to Ferrell's plan, Captain Jeff McCoy's Crazy Troop had the easiest task: protecting the bridge secured by Bonecrusher. Dillard Johnson, the troop's senior scout, who had led the way to Samawah, was again up front, along with another Bradley and an M1. As soon as he moved onto the bridge and started to cross, RPGs came flying. He called in a contact report to Crazy 6, McCoy's call sign. As in Samawah, the bridge was teeming with enemy. "Unfortunately I was on the eastern side of the bridge and my other two elements were still on the western side of the bridge. There was a large volume of fire on the bridge itself," Johnson said. "I called up to Crazy 6 and told him I was being engaged by RPGs and small arms fire." McCoy ordered the scouts back. Given the ferocity of the fighting, McCoy decided they should hold on to what they had: an intersection just east of the span. The soldiers established blocking positions in all directions.

Soon a bus drove over the bridge toward the troops. The soldiers fired tracers in front of the vehicle, signaling it to turn back, but to no avail. Rumbling down the road, the bus rammed into a taxi and began pushing it toward the soldiers. Johnson's gunner raked the bus, which smashed into a Bradley, stunning the crew inside and almost knocking them unconscious. The Bradleys ran into the bus, pushing it sideways to block the route. The unconventional Iraqi battering ram had become an American fortification. Things did not stay quiet for long. A tan Toyota pickup truck appeared. Johnson and his fellow soldiers waved at the driver to turn around. But like the bus, the truck seemed headed on a one-way trip. It stopped abruptly and a group of Fedayeen with AK-47s and RPGs jumped out. The Americans made quick work of them. Now a heavy truck barreled down, smashing into the bus the Americans had turned into a barrier, backed up, and rammed it again. The soldiers unloaded on the truck with coax machine gun fire and disabled it only to discover that a fuel tanker was headed their way—too great a threat to allow to get close. The troops turned it into a flaming wreck, so hot it was impossible to use their thermal systems.

McCoy commanded a cavalry troop, but his soldiers needed to become infantrymen to hold the intersection. They could not afford to sit in their vehicles and allow the Iraqis to sneak up on them. McCoy needed dismounts of his own, boots on the ground. Climbing out of the tracks, First Sergeant Roy Griggs and others in the troop's logistics trains began digging foxholes. Worried about their supply of ammo, some soldiers picked up the AK-47s of the dead Iraqi fighters. Griggs had to remind the troops how to throw a fragmentation grenade. The last time some had done that was in basic training.[12]

"All the other fights we had were rolling fights," recalled Griggs. "We would roll into an area, we would return fire. There was never a point defense per se. We were always on the move, closing the area. This is the first chance that we had gotten to literally sit somewhere for thirty-six to forty-eight hours, whatever the hours came out to now, and us be in contact that whole time. So this is the first time that we were able to really secure ourselves."[13]

In the heat of the fight, McCoy called Ferrell on the air controller's radio net, the only communications link that could operate at such long distances. McCoy had been hardened by the fighting in Samawah but was looking for assurance that the squadron had this fight under control. The troop was encircled. It had been in contact for two days, facing wave after wave of Fedayeen from all directions. He described the Iraqi vehicular battering rams. Ferrell told him he would come through all right. "I said, sweetheart, you're okay," Ferrell recalled. "He said, 'Sir, I got it, I just want to hear from you that I'm okay.' " As the Iraqis began to retrieve their dead, visibility improved to more than 400 yards. Several new vehicles had approached the bridge, but had turned around. Johnson secured the far side and it seemed as if the troop might have the situation in hand after all. But as night fell, neither Ferrell nor McCoy was sure.

A JSTARS radar plane picked out a convoy of twenty vehicles headed east toward McCoy's position. McCoy reconfigured his defense and oriented his tanks to the west. His soldiers thought they saw the infrared searchlights of Iraqi T-72 tanks. The Iraqi column was later identified as four T-72s and several BMPs and trucks, all of which were moving out of Najaf. Whether they were looking to escape from the 3rd Infantry Division or to attack Crazy Troop's position was not clear. What was clear was their collision course with McCoy's unit.

Ferrell called Torrance, the division's artillery commander. He needed fire, and quickly. The fire would be "danger close," well under the minimum separation distance. There was no time to waste. Broadhead, a platoon sergeant with McCoy's unit, was reporting that he could see the Iraqis' tanks. Within minutes, an artillery barrage landed 1,200 yards or so from McCoy's forward positions. There were no friendly casualties, but the advancing Iraqi column took plenty. But the barrage failed to stop the westward incursion. Iraqi vehicles and soldiers were still on the move toward McCoy. The Shamal had precluded air support earlier, but Ferrell's air controller was able to call in a strike with B-1s armed with satellite-guided munitions. They unloaded three JDAM satellite-guided bombs to blast the road. The Iraqi vehicles stopped moving. It was 3:30 a.m. For the first time, it seemed, Crazy Troop would receive a bit of a respite. "I don't like to say we were surrounded, but we were being fired at from all directions," McCoy said, looking back on the episode.[14]

That morning, the tank company from J. R. Sanderson's battalion arrived after a long night of fighting its way south through the sandstorm and linked up with Apache Troop and Ferrell's command post. Filling a gap on the eastern side of the squadron's formation, the tank company finally enabled Ferrell to establish defenses on all avenues of approach. After a day and night of hard fighting, the U.S. troops had defended their positions in Kifl and at Objective Floyd. It had been a much harder battle than anticipated, and the fighting was not yet over.

On the escarpment, Sanderson prepared to join the fray. After his Alpha Company had been dispatched south to help Ferrell, Sanderson grew concerned. He did not want his battalion to be broken apart and used piecemeal as reinforcements. It would be better if it were kept together and assigned a zone of its own. Grimsley heard Sanderson out and gave him a six-square-mile zone, which included the strongpoint Benton was defending in Kifl. But the zone also included unsecured territory farther east, where there was a north–south highway from Hillah being used by the Fedayeen to funnel troops into the fight. Sanderson had received the battle space he sought; now he would have to make good use of it. Grimsley told Sanderson that the battalion would represent the main effort of the division and probably V Corps. The fighting in Kifl had become more of a battle than the division or corps had expected. Both sides had raised the stakes.

Sanderson drew up a plan and had it photocopied and distributed to his officers. Despite the efforts to clear the center of Kifl, the Iraqis were still firing from government buildings. Those would have to be cleared— again. Worse, the engineers were not sure the Kifl bridge would continue to hold up. The passage of vehicles over the past few days had strained the span even more. Sanderson's battalion would have to cross it one tank at a time before massing. Cobra Company, with two M1s abreast, would conduct a high-speed run through the town. Cobra was what Sanderson called a "tank pure" unit, one that was made up entirely of seventy-ton M1s. Supplemented by engineers, Cobra's job was to secure the key highway link by 8:00 p.m. that night. Based on Marcone's experience Sanderson anticipated tough going.

"Normally as a task force commander I will give one of three weapons control status," Sanderson recalled. "The first is 'weapons hold,' which is you will not fire unless fired upon; the second is 'weapons tight,' which means that you fire only at a clearly identified enemy; and the third is 'weapons free,' which means that you will fire at anything that looks suspicious and/or dangerous or about to kill you. So we went into Al Kifl weapons free."

Sanderson's battalion began moving toward Kifl at 3:00 p.m. on March 26. The Shamal was still raging; visibility was under 150 feet. The sunlight shining on particles whipped up by the Shamal had turned the sky an eerie red. Even the Iraqis were struck by the phenomenon, describing it as an omen. The loader on Sanderson's tank, Specialist Jeremiah Bateson, asked what was going on. Like the rest of the forces, Sanderson had seen a steady diet of reports about possible Iraqi WMD. "Maybe somebody is popping a nuke," Sanderson replied. The crew went deathly quiet.

Cobra Company attacked straight across the bridge. The tanks started attracting fire from rooftops and both sides of the road. If a tank could see the enemy five blocks down, it could fire its main gun. Otherwise, tank crews used their machine guns to suppress enemy fire. Carter fired two tank rounds randomly, hoping it would frighten the enemy from firing back. The psychological operations unit attached to Sanderson's battalion broadcast appeals in Arabic: "Surrender, surrender, surrender. Further resistance is futile." The message seemed to have the opposite effect. The Fedayeen poured it on. The Iraqi fire was so intense that Cobra had to go to "open protected," preventing the tankers from firing back with their tank-mounted machine guns.

When Sanderson reached the intersection, he laid out his tanks in a pattern he called the "Death Star." The tanks formed a circle to defend against threats from any point on the compass. Engineers manned defensive positions with .50 caliber machine guns. With their thermal systems the tanks could detect objects only up to about fifty feet. Night vision systems that relied on magnified ambient light did even less well. Sanderson prayed for the sandstorm to end so he could see the enemy. While Cobra settled in, Sanderson's infantry company relieved Benton's at the bridge. After a long night and a day, Benton was finally able to pull out.

Sanderson got a phone call. A JSTARS radar plane had detected 1,000 enemy vehicles heading south from Hillah. JSTARS had been wrong before, but if a force that large was moving south the battalion alone would not be able to stop it. Sanderson's engineers exploded shaped charges into the road, cratering it. Sanderson also asked for aircraft to bomb the roads to stop the Iraqi advance. The weather was starting to get better and the soldiers soon saw their adversary—more Iraqis mounted on trucks riding to the fight, planning not only to retake the intersection to open up the route from Hillah, but also to infiltrate Kifl and move on the bridge. Sanderson left a tank platoon on the bridge and ordered the infantry to start clearing nearby buildings. He needed to keep the RPG fire away and create more battle space for his unit. He also brought his TOC—tactical operations center—to the east side of the river and set up in an abandoned school, leaving his fuel and ammunition on the west side. He was hoping the Iraqi fighters would somehow back off if they saw that the battalion had consolidated its position and had plenty of air and fire support.

In the effort to control the bridge, two of Sanderson's soldiers were shot by an anxious tank gunner who did not realize that U.S. troops had dismounted their vehicle. It was a rare breakdown of discipline in the midst of a nerve-racking firefight. The infantry company had violated the battalion's rule that it would send out an alert when it put troops on the ground. Sanderson was thankful that neither of the soldiers had been

killed. As Sanderson solidified his hold, Grimsley and Blount came forward to visit the troops. The officers walked through the abandoned
town. Grimsley noticed a barbershop that had a tourist picture of the
World Trade Center in New York. Was it a decorative picture of an exotic,
far-off attraction, or some sort of celebration of the Al Qaeda attack?
There was nobody at the shop to ask. It was four days after the first river
crossing on the twenty-fifth that U.S. troops saw civilians in any large
numbers. They reported that the Fedayeen and Baath Party militia had
moved in before the fight, given weapons to the men in the town, and ordered them to defend the city.

Sanderson was relieved by newly arriving soldiers from Dave Petraeus's
101st Division. Ferrell's squadron in the south, meanwhile, was replaced
by a battalion from Dave Perkins's 2nd BCT. As Sanderson was meeting
with Joe Anderson, the commander of the 101st's 2nd Brigade, to talk
about the handoff, the Iraqis unleashed a brutal barrage on Sanderson's
tactical operations center, burying shells with delayed fuses into the
ground. Immediate and massive counterfire was aimed at the Iraqi battery. Sanderson was struck by the boldness and aggressiveness of his foe at
Kifl. As he prepared to pull his battalion out and resume the march north,
he told Grimsley that he needed to get his battalion ready for the upcoming battle with the Republican Guard. Grimsley thought that the unanticipated battle they had just fought against a mix of Iraqi soldiers and
Fedayeen might, in retrospect, turn out to be one of the major battles of
the war. "This may be decisive," Grimsley said. After the war, Grimsley
felt more strongly than ever that Kifl had been a turning point. "This became decisive for the division even though it was never intended to be," he
told Army historians.[15]

At the MEF headquarters, Conway, too, was alarmed by the Fedayeen.
The Marines had received intelligence that buses and trucks were bringing reinforcements from Baghdad to Diwaniyah. Like Najaf in the Army
sector, Diwaniyah was becoming a hotbed of enemy activity, no small
concern since it flanked the Marines' path north. Jim Mattis planned to
lead two Marine regiments on Highway 1 past Diwaniyah, going as far as
Hantush, a small town with an airfield and a contingency airstrip—a reinforced stretch of highway with a removable median allowing aircraft to
take off and land. With sparse logistics, he planned to grab the Hantush
airfields so C-130s could fly in supplies, enabling Blue Diamond to

restock, before suddenly changing direction northeast to cross the Tigris and then hooking left toward Baghdad. Lieutenant Colonel Stacy Clardy's 3rd Light Armored Reconnaissance Battalion would be at the lead of the Marine attack. Before the Marines had crossed the Highway 1 bridge outside Nasiriyah, Mattis had asked Clardy if he would get all the way to Diwaniyah that night. "His intel was that there was nobody along Highway 1," Clardy recalled. "I told him logistically that I had enough fuel and everything I needed."[16]

While Task Force Tarawa was fighting in Nasiriyah, and Blount's division headed north on the western side of the Euphrates, Mattis's regiments had begun their northward trek. In addition to the bridge seized by J. R. Sanderson's battalion, there was an older span nearby of questionable load-bearing capability. In view of the monumental traffic jam south of the bridge, Mattis needed both. The backed-up traffic was vulnerable to enemy artillery—and, more important, to a chemical or biological attack—though there was no Iraqi barrage.

Crossing the Euphrates was not the only immediate concern. Highway 1 was in a deplorable state of repair. A JSTARS plane claimed to have tracked an Iraqi vehicle going sixty miles per hour down the road before the war, but the intelligence had been misleading. In fact, the highway was under construction and much of the pavement was broken up. The area transited was largely unpopulated, with marshes and berms on either side of the road.[17]

On the morning of March 23 and under orders to get to Hantush as quickly as possible, Clardy moved fast with his LAR battalion and was soon beyond the range of the division's supporting artillery. At nightfall, the LAR battalion was out of the division's radio range. Marine Cobra helicopters, which had prowled the highway earlier in the day, had reported indications of enemy activity. Soon, the LAR battalion came upon a suspicious vehicle, which took note of the Marines before quickly driving away. Like Ferrell's soldiers outside Samawah, the Marines were reluctant to fire, even though some were convinced the passengers had acted suspiciously.

Moments later, tracers began to stream across the road and the Marines came under fire from mortars, machine guns, and RPGs. The air officer attached to the battalion, overreacting to the unexpected attack, grabbed his radio and called out "Slingshot!" This was the emergency code for units on the verge of being overrun by the enemy; it electrified the division.[18]

The terrain was too muddy to allow the battalion to drive off the road and outflank the enemy. Fending off the Iraqis, it responded with its own barrage from 25mm chain guns. The fighting spread. "We hammered them along the three-mile length of the column," said Clardy. Within thirty minutes a dozen attack aircraft arrived and contributed to the carnage by bombing, rocketing, and strafing Iraqi positions on both sides of the road. The violent fight was short and one-sided; only one Marine was wounded. Not having accompanying infantry, Clardy could not pursue the Iraqis into the marshes.

Clardy hunkered down for the rest of the night. Given the array of fighting positions farther north, RCT-5's infantry was better suited than an LAR battalion to clear the path. The road to Hantush would be a running gun battle. Midmorning the following day, Lieutenant Colonel Sam Mundy's 3rd Battalion, 5th Marines, arrived to take over the division's lead. "Stacy Clardy told me if we were looking for a fight, we'd soon find one," recalled Mundy.[19]

The Marines had been sobered by the night's events. Unlike the reluctant Iraqi soldiers they had met along the Kuwaiti border, the Fedayeen they encountered on Highway 1 were full of fight. While not particularly skilled, they were courageous and did not hesitate to charge the LAVs in the face of withering fire. The Marines, like their Army counterparts, sensed that unlike the Gulf War, this would not be a head-to-head engagement with the Republican Guard. It would be a close-fought war of ambush and deception against paramilitaries not adequately profiled by the intelligence. The Marines concluded that it was vital to keep up their pace of attack and strike the enemy before it had time to stiffen its defenses.

Both the Army and Marines had superior battlefield technology. The Marines had classified e-mail. Global positioning systems helped them pinpoint their position in the barren Iraqi countryside. Drones like the Dragon Eye, which were used by small units, and the Predator, which the Air Force operated, proved invaluable. Blue Force Tracker was another battlefield innovation that rated high marks from commanders who had them. Like a GPS, the Tracker's satellites triangulated the location and movement of friendly forces and displayed near-real-time data to all units. Still, "situational awareness," in the argot of the military, was proving to be more theoretical than actual, especially when it came to ferreting out the Fedayeen. "When do we get Red Force Trackers?" quipped one Marine.

As the Marines drove north, the Fedayeen headed south to Diwaniyah, determined to bloody the invaders. Mattis had lost whatever element of surprise he was planning on. Cargo trucks and buses were heading for Diwaniyah to drop off fighters, then shuttling back to pick up more. Gun-mounted "technical vehicles," reminiscent of those in Somalia, were prowling the road along with Iraqi armored vehicles. The Iraqi tactics were basic. They would ambush the road-bound Marines from successive positions, many of them hastily prepared, and then fall back to the next set of emplacements. Supported by Cobra attack helicopters and artillery, Mundy's battalion soon found itself locked in one engagement after another. "It was the Fedayeen guys that were the masterminds," recalled Duffy White, commanding the 1st LAR battalion. "They would grab whatever Al Qud, militia, or army forces that hadn't deserted and put them into position saying, 'Okay, Give 'em hell!' Then they would leave and go organize the next series."[20]

On March 25, just short of Diwaniyah, the battalion ran into a group of particularly well-entrenched Iraqis near a cloverleaf intersection of Highways 1 and 17. The tank platoon at the head of the column was swarmed by Iraqi fighters just as the furious sandstorm descended on the area. Soon the battalion was engaged along their entire axis. Dismounting from their AAVs, the Marines began to fire at point-blank range across the berms. Led by First Lieutenant Brian Chontosh, a veteran of the Gulf War, the Combined Anti-Armor Team, which was attached to 3/5, was thrust into the battle. Accustomed to scouting for enemy tanks, the team—mounted in several Humvees and armed with TOW antitank missiles, .50 caliber machine guns, and MK19 grenade launchers—came under fire from berms to the right and left. One of Chontosh's vehicles was hit by an RPG, killing a Navy corpsman and wounding a Marine.

The lieutenant ordered his driver to head through a break in the berm. Jumping out of his Humvee, Chontosh leapt into a trench and, followed by his driver and a gunner, ran down the length of the channel, killing Iraqis with his M16 and pistol. When he ran out of ammunition, he picked up an enemy AK-47 and even an Iraqi RPG, firing them at his foes, killing twenty before resuming the drive north. Chontosh was later awarded the Navy Cross.[21]

Caked with mud and enveloped by an eerie haze called an "orange crush"—resulting from the driving sandstorm and rain—Dunford's

RCT-5 took the Hantush airstrip twenty-two miles to the north on the morning of March 27 after a spirited defense by Iraqi company-sized units supported by armor. The action was not without cost: a Marine gunnery sergeant, who was directing fire from his AAV, was killed by small arms. Soon, though, C-130s would be landing with supplies and ammunition. By the end of the day, Mundy's battalion had also taken the cloverleaf intersection at Highway 17 near Diwaniyah.

It was clear to Mundy from the intensity of enemy resistance near the city that Diwaniyah was an assembly area for Iraqis rushing to contest the Marine drive up Highway 1. Terry Ferrell had fought to block the Fedayeen from sending fighters west from Diwaniyah to Najaf. Now the Marines had to contend with the Fedayeen heading east from the town. For the Marines, taking the fight to the Fedayeen in the town of Diwaniyah was not a simple matter.[22]

Highway 8, running by the town, was the north–south route the Fedayeen were using to reinforce and reposition their fighters, and was in the V Corps zone. With the vast majority of Blount's 3rd ID far west of the Euphrates and Wallace's decision to forgo Terry Ferrell's squadron's feint up Highway 8, there was a gap between the Army and the Marines, which at one point was fifty miles wide. The area unoccupied by the Army was beyond the Marines'assigned zone of action. The efforts to apportion the battlefield had inadvertently created a Fedayeen sanctuary. Mattis's division could not fire or cross the boundary without permission. "We were briefed that the only unit the Army had on our left flank was one battalion from the 7th Cav. That was all. Basically we played it as if our flanks were open and not secure," said White, 1st LAR battalion commander.[23]

The problem came to a head when Mundy's battalion captured an Iraqi special forces brigadier general who revealed that the stadium in town was being used as a staging ground for the Fedayeen and Al Quds militia. To deal with the Iraqis in the stadium, the Marines flew one of their Pioneer drones over the city to confirm the target and passed the information to the V Corps. Next, the V Corps sent one of its Hunter drones to again confirm the target before calling in an air strike. The A-10 air strike that finally followed killed dozens of Fedayeen and several antiaircraft guns and, as Mundy recalled, "was quite a show." But the episode proved that there was still a way to go before the military was able to practice joint warfare. The Army and Marines were fighting their own wars. Eventually, the boundary between V Corps and I MEF (Marine Expeditionary Force) was modified to include Diwaniyah in the Marines' zone of action, authorizing the Marines to fire into the city and run combat patrols into the outskirts of the city.[24]

To protect his open flank on Highway 1 against Fedayeen attacks, Mattis ordered SEAL, Force Reconnaissance Marines, and infantry patrols to conduct "hunter-killer" missions. Colonel Steve Hummer's RCT-7 was ordered to protect the highway up to Diwaniyah. Chris Conlin's 1st Battalion, 7th Marines, which had seized the Crown Jewel in the Rumaylah oilfields during the "opening gambit," was one of the units securing the supply route. On the morning of March 26, one of the patrols saw four men in civilian clothes walking south. As the Marines neared them, the Iraqis tried to flee but were captured. A Marine intelligence team later determined that the four men were Iraqi intelligence officers. During interrogation, they disclosed that an American from the ill-fated Army 507th Maintenance Company had been moved to the Saddam Hospital in Nasiriyah. The information was passed up the chain of command. U.S. military intelligence now had a fix on Jessica Lynch.

CHAPTER 16

Back to the Drawing Board

At Camp Doha, McKiernan was intently following the push north. The Shiite uprising and widespread surrender of Iraqi forces that the CIA had anticipated had not occurred. The Fedayeen had prevented V Corps from crossing the Euphrates and conducting its feint up Highway 8. The Army and Marines had used everything from M1 tanks, artillery, and B-1B bombers to hold off the Iraqi fighters, and the better part of an Army brigade had been positioned outside Samawah simply to contain the enemy forces and prevent them from severing the Army's vulnerable supply lines. In a March 26 telephone call, Scott Wallace had even suggested delaying his attack on the Republican Guard until the Army's 4th Infantry Division arrived in Kuwait, a process that would take weeks. The V Corps commander did not want to continue the march to Baghdad until he had additional forces to cope with the difficult fight he expected ahead, safeguard his logistics, and help deal with the threat in the rear. While McKiernan rejected Wallace's suggestion, he knew that the battlefield conditions had changed and concluded that the plan needed to be adjusted.

Huddling with his staff, McKiernan declared he was going to direct "a little focus change." While McKiernan believed the main battle lay ahead with the Republican Guard, he was also convinced it would be reckless to plunge ahead until Wallace's V Corps and Conway's Marines stepped up their fight against the Fedayeen and blunted the paramilitary attacks along the lengthening supply lines. J. D. Thurman, McKiernan's hard-charging operations officer, heartily supported the change in strategy. "I talked to the CG quite a bit about it," Thurman recalled. "We have to clear this enemy in zone, which means we're going to have to get in these towns and clear the enemy out of there. The enemy was fighting in our rear."[1]

McKiernan sketched out a concept of operations that he planned to present to Franks titled "The Way Ahead: The Destruction of the Republican Guard." The title was carefully chosen. On the computer screens at CENTCOM's headquarters in Qatar, Iraq's Republican Guard and Regular Army divisions were represented with bold red icons. Franks had repeatedly touted the value of audacious attacks and taking risk, and he considered the Fedayeen to be little more than a speed bump on the way to Baghdad. McKiernan and his principal field commanders, however, viewed the fighters as a threat to be ignored at the coalition's peril, and their best hope of winning Franks over was to assure him that taking on the Fedayeen was not a diversion from the main event but a requirement for the push north.

To keep the pressure on the Republican Guard, McKiernan's briefing noted, Dave Petraeus's 101st Airborne would conduct a deep attack that night against the 14th Brigade of the Medina Division. It would be the first deep Apache attack since the one by the 11th Attack Helicopter Regiment on the Medina regiment and would incorporate all the lessons of that ill-fated operation. Meanwhile, allied warplanes would continue to pound the Republican Guard. When the battle damage assessments indicated that the Republican Guard division had been reduced to about 50 percent of their original fighting strength, Army and Marine ground forces would head north to destroy what remained, not slowing until Baghdad itself had been cordoned off and its major roadways interdicted.

While airpower and the Army's choppers were pounding the Medina, a parallel effort would be launched to take on the Fedayeen. A brigade of the 82nd Airborne would be flown to Tallil and driven to Samawah, where it could clear out the Fedayeen once and for all. The 82nd would also relieve Dan Allyn's brigade of the responsibility of dealing with Samawah, enabling it to join the rest of Blount's 3rd Infantry Division for the final push to Baghdad. The 82nd Airborne brigade was the only reserve that McKiernan had and his most effective means of rapidly securing the Baghdad airport in the event that Saddam's regime unexpectedly collapsed. But the notion that Saddam's regime would implode—the "early regime collapse" scenario that had been promoted so persistently by White House and Defense Department officials in Washington—seemed more unlikely with each passing day. Committing McKiernan's only reserve was a critical decision, but if ever there was a time to call in the 82nd this seemed to be it. McKiernan also arranged for a squadron of the 2nd Armored Cavalry Regiment to be rushed from the United States along with its Humvees on C-17s. It would be sent north to help guard the supply lines.

To McKiernan's frustration, there was one division that would not be arriving anytime soon: the 4th Infantry Division. McKiernan had argued for months that it was vital that there be a continuous flow of combat power into the fight, and he wanted the 4th ID in time for the assault on Baghdad. The division's tanks and equipment had been floating on more than thirty ships in the Mediterranean for weeks, while the Bush administration sought to persuade Ankara to open a northern front. That, McKiernan argued, did nobody any good. He wanted the ships to head south through the Suez Canal and around to Kuwait so the division could attack north. In Washington, Colin Powell also repeatedly urged that the ships be sent to Kuwait. As secretary of state, Powell believed that getting the Turks on board was difficult to the point of being impossible and, as former chairman of the Joint Chiefs of Staff and a strong proponent of dominating the enemy with overwhelming force, he had repeatedly argued that the military needed more troops in Iraq. His military experience informed his opinion that moving a division across Turkey and then south to Iraq would be a daunting logistical task.

Unlike Powell and his land war commander, Franks was persuaded that there was no immediate need for the division and that the ships' holding pattern in the Mediterranean was useful in deceiving Saddam into thinking a major attack might still take place in the north, thus encouraging the Iraqis to keep many of their divisions there. Months later, Franks would insist he had been right all along. "My experience from Afghanistan made me more comfortable with the hard decisions I had to make in OIF [Operation Iraqi Freedom]," Franks noted. "For example, I learned to live with small formations in OEF. Had I not had that experience I would have been forced to make a premature decision to get the 4th ID's combat power in too early. I would have caved to its early commitment because I would have been afraid of the risks involved with small formations. I would have missed the whole strategy piece by holding Iraqi forces in the north by delaying the decision. I knew that getting 4th ID in early mattered less due to my Afghan experience."[2]

But McKiernan and Thurman remained just as convinced that withholding the most technologically advanced division in the Army when it might have done the most good was one of the biggest mistakes of the war. "We wanted more combat power on the ground," Thurman said. "The decision was made way late to move the 4th ID south."[3]

The debate over the 4th ID was another example of the differences between Franks and his subordinates about the nature of the enemy and what it would take to defeat him. McKiernan had to accept Franks's decision as a fact of life, like bad weather or sandstorms. The 4th Infantry Division would eventually be shifted to Kuwait, but not in time to help Wallace deal with the upsurge of fighting in the south.

McKiernan presented "The Way Ahead" at an evening video conference, which Franks and his senior deputies attended. John Abizaid, Franks's deputy, raised a point. Since the BDA (bomb damage assessment) was so problematic, how would CENTCOM and McKiernan know when the Republican Guard had been reduced by 50 percent, the trigger point for the attack to Baghdad? It was a good question and McKiernan did not have an easy answer. Neither McKiernan nor Moseley had accurate and timely BDA. While CENTCOM was formally in charge of BDA, the component commanders would need to act on their best estimates and instincts.[4]

Franks appeared to accept McKiernan's general plan, but peppered him with skeptical questions. Franks liked the idea of mounting the deep Apache strikes on the Medina, and heartily endorsed bombing the Republican Guard. But Franks was not keen on holding the V Corps back while Buzz Moseley's warplanes decimated the Republican Guard. "We are parked," Franks complained. The 3rd Infantry Division, Franks continued, was a "shit magnet"—it was largely stationary and a potential target for Iraqi WMD and artillery. Of the 3rd Division forces, Franks exclaimed, only Terry Ferrell's 3-7 Cavalry Squadron had been in the fight. But Franks was overlooking Grimsley's battle in Kifl, the role of Perkins's brigade near Najaf, and the Marines' fight up Highways 1 and 7. Nor was Franks happy with the planning for using the 101st, which he still thought was a prime candidate to take the Baghdad airport. Franks was clinging to the hope for a dramatic air insertion, which would bring the war to the enemy's doorstep, and wanted Petraeus ready for the mission. Neither McKiernan nor Wallace thought that such a mission was likely, certainly not after the problems the 11th Attack Helicopter Regiment had experienced in trying to fly deep into enemy territory. The Baghdad airfield was surrounded by all kinds of air defenses.

Franks also wondered whether the 82nd Airborne and 2nd Cavalry were too "thin-skinned" to control the supply lines and clean out Iraq's southern cities. Those were, however, the only forces of choice for McKiernan and Wallace. Instead, Franks pushed for more SOF backed up by AC-130s, as well as CIA operatives, which the CENTCOM command thought should be patrolling the routes and taking the fight to the Fedayeen in the southern cities. Franks's view was that SOF and CIA paramilitary units should be able to tie up the Fedayeen, freeing conventional Army and Marine forces for the push north. Franks's take on how the war should be conducted was not shared by McKiernan and his field commanders. Unlike the Afghan conflict—where SOF collaborated with the anti-Taliban Northern Alliance and a variety of warlords and mujahidin—there were no comparable indigenous opposition forces to rely on in Iraq. The Fedayeen were numerous and tough and the few Special Operations Forces and intelligence agents in the south had had little success against them to date.

After criticizing McKiernan's plan, Franks assigned some new tasks. He was concerned that the southern oilfields might not be sufficiently protected, and he was worried about the Iraqi formations north of Basra, especially the 10th and 6th divisions, which were deployed near the Iranian border in southern Iraq, though neither the Marines nor McKiernan regarded them as much of a threat. Franks wanted Task Force 20 to attack along Highway 6 running north from Basra, and he wanted Tomahawk cruise missiles fired at the Nebuchadnezzar Republican Guard Division, which, unbeknownst to CENTCOM, had moved troops south of Baghdad but which U.S. intelligence believed was still stationed in northern Iraq.

Franks's barbs aside, McKiernan still believed that he had sufficient support from the CENTCOM commander to put his plan into action. Even as Franks did not like the idea of pausing the attack north, McKiernan thought there really was no alternative. McKiernan was insistent that the right conditions needed to be set before U.S. ground forces locked horns with Republican Guard defenses around Baghdad. Midday on March 27, the V Corps and the MEF received the order from McKiernan's command: they were to halt their advance north and focus on clearing the pockets of resistance in their rear to secure the supply lines.

Wallace, for his part, was heartened to be getting more firepower. When he heard that he would be reinforced by a brigade of the 82nd he scribbled a message for Chuck Swannack, the two-star general who commanded the division, and had been itching to get into the fight: "Get your ass up here."[5]

. . .

On March 28, McKiernan flew to Conway's field headquarters at the Jalibah air base in Iraq to meet with the Marine commander and with Wallace. McKiernan brought Thurman and Terry Moran, his special adviser. Now that the attack north had been halted, the commanders needed to plan their next steps. McKiernan opened the session, which was chronicled in notes taken by several aides. The forces, he said, now faced two enemy "centers of gravity": Saddam's Republican Guard forces, which were arrayed near Baghdad, and the "paramilitary" Fedayeen. The American forces would need to deal with both; they could not race to Baghdad while neglecting the dangerous threat in their rear. Still, McKiernan noted, the commanders themselves would have to resolve the issue of acceptable degree of risk in the rear areas. The forces needed to blunt the Fedayeen threat, but could move north without eradicating it altogether.

With regard to the ultimate objective, the Republican Guard, McKiernan outlined the disposition of the units near Baghdad. Karbala, Hillah, and Kut, McKiernan said, constitued a "red line." By moving north beyond the line, the United States might prompt the Iraqis to fire their chemical weapons, the general said, reflecting the prevailing intelligence. When the V Corps and Marines did head north to destroy the Republican Guard, they would establish a cordon around Baghdad. The major routes in and out of the city would be cut off. That would set the stage for the raids into the capital that Wallace was contemplating to bring down the regime. This was all in keeping with the plan the V Corps had developed months earlier and that Franks had presented to the White House.

McKiernan said there were two conditions for resuming the attack north. The Republican Guard would have to be reduced to half strength, and the 82nd and 101st would need to shore up the V Corps's rear. The general anticipated two more days of reconnaissance and air strikes before resuming the main attack, but he wanted to hear the assessment of his field commanders. "I need to hear your views on timing. I will be very resistant until the RGFC [Republican Guard Forces Command] is at 50 percent," McKiernan said.

Wallace, who was overseeing the main attack, spoke next. The Iraqi paramilitary forces were contained but the U.S. hold on them was tenuous, the V Corps commander said. There were paramilitary forces in Samawah and Najaf and they were moving between the two towns. Wallace was not certain how many fighters he was up against. "I am not sure how many of the knuckleheads there are," he said. As for the Shiites, Wallace thought some were willing to help the Americans, but had been intimidated by the Fedayeen. There were plans to provide arms to the Shiites, but some of the Special Operations Forces were reluctant to bail out their new allies if they got in over their heads. Wallace thought he had made progress in protecting his supply lines and that V Corps would have the logistics in place to continue the push north by March 30 or March 31. But he warned that dealing with Karbala could be more difficult than Najaf and that it would take a few days to insert reconnaissance teams.

The V Corps commander added that he thought the Fedayeen might be providing intelligence to Iraqi missile batteries and noted that the enemy was even ferrying supplies across the Euphrates by boat. Wallace talked about his plan to attack the Baghdad airport. If the 82nd and other units arrived soon to shore up the rear, Wallace thought he might be able to attack north as soon as April 1. But he also noted that if the pause went on he would be better able to counter the Fedayeen threat in the south. "If I have more time I can be more aggressive with the cities," Wallace said.

As for Conway, he somewhat echoed Wallace. The Marine commander said that the enemy "hardheads" were harder and their command and control tougher than he had anticipated. Bypassed enemy units were still fighting. The enemy was in a "deliberate defense." The "rolling start force" with which the U.S. had begun the war, Conway said, was "inadequate." As for the Marine supply lines, they were brittle and truly secure only where the Marines had forces—what Conway called "armored bubbles." With their organic air support, the Marines were in good shape when the weather was clear, but sandstorms, hail, and rain changed the equation. Conway said he still had several days of fighting ahead of him before the Marines could renew their push to Baghdad. That would give Moseley time to pound the air defenses and Republican Guard units around Baghdad. Conway indicated that he still wanted the Air Force to blow up a few bridges to protect the Marine advance. McKiernan agreed.

Conway also expressed specific concerns about Diwaniyah, which the Fedayeen were using to challenge RCT-5 on Highway 1 and to send fighters to contest V Corps near Najaf. The Marines were worried about the seam that had opened between V Corps and the Marine formations. The Marines were emphatic on this point: one Marine general, who was part of Conway's team, said that "seam" was too gentle a term: it was really a "chasm." McKiernan turned to Wallace and asked what he could do about the problem. There was a discussion about possibly inserting reconnaissance teams and setting up blocking positions on Highway 8, but neither McKiernan nor Wallace saw the seam as a major impediment to the push north, and no decisions were made.

The bottom line was that the Army's and the Marines' push toward Baghdad would be paused so V Corps and MEF could go after the Fedayeen and, when resumed, synchronized so that both forces would converge on the Iraqi capital at the same time. The "red zone" fight was expected to be fierce and, according to McKiernan, the Army and the Marines could not afford to be out of step. McKiernan, who never accepted Franks's view that commandos and CIA operatives could cope with the Fedayeen threat, said that it would take time to make effective use of the intelligence operatives and Special Operations Forces in the south. Wallace and Conway would step up attacks in the cities and against communication networks, while V Corps helicopters conducted reconnaissance in the vicinity of Milh Lake. At the end of the meeting, the generals discussed how to proceed if the Fedayeen did not crack in the next few days. "I don't know where we go from there," Wallace said.

"That's when we wait for the 4th ID and the 3rd ACR," McKiernan responded.[6]

When he returned to Camp Doha, McKiernan received an angry phone call from Franks at 5:25 p.m. Wallace had given a joint interview to the *New York Times* and the *Washington Post* the day before in which he had shared some of his concerns about the Fedayeen. On the face of it, Wallace's comments were not controversial. "The enemy we're fighting," Wallace told the reporters, "is a bit different than the one we war-gamed against, because of these paramilitary forces. We knew they were here, but we did not know how they would fight." Enemy fighters in light trucks with .50 caliber weapons were charging American tanks and Bradleys, a tactic Wallace termed "bizarre." That resistance, plus the need to build up logistics and a blinding sandstorm, was forcing a pause.[7]

"We've got to take this pause," Wallace added. "We're still fighting the enemy every night. We're doing things to keep him operating at a higher tempo than the one we're operating at." The V Corps commander made no mention of his recommendation to McKiernan that the V Corps await the arrival of the 4th Infantry Division before resuming its march to Baghdad, but he indicated in response to a question that it was beginning to look like the war would last longer than anticipated. On the battlefield, Wallace's remarks seemed to be a recognition of the blindingly obvious. In Washington, at the NSC, staff aides found them helpful. They did not feel like they were getting the straight story about the war from Rumsfeld. For once, they had the unvarnished truth from the field. Wallace had not been despairing and, at the very least, his comments explained the recent engagements on the battlefield.

At the Pentagon, however, Rumsfeld and his aides took Wallace's remarks as a vote of no confidence in their strategy. The defense secretary raised the issue with Franks, who had assured his subordinates and Rumsfeld before the war that he expected U.S. forces to be in Baghdad within two weeks. "Rumsfeld talked to Franks, and wanted to know who is this guy and why is he saying that. He thought the plan was good and was frustrated that a commander in the field could say that," recalled one senior aide to General Franks.

McKiernan did not know what Franks and Rumsfeld had discussed, but he knew the CENTCOM commander was agitated. Franks interpreted Wallace's remarks to the press as nearly disloyal, a repudiation of Franks's insistence that the war be "fast and final." Franks indicated to McKiernan that Rumsfeld, too, was upset, and the CENTCOM commander said he was considering relieving Wallace of his command immediately.

"Wow," McKiernan said loudly. His aides knew something bad was up, for their commander was usually taciturn, almost always unflappable. Franks's threat to relieve Wallace shook McKiernan, who thought it was not only unjust but impractical in the middle of a war. McKiernan and Wallace had known each other for years, and McKiernan had strong confidence in the V Corps commander. McKiernan had endured Franks's bluster before, but he was worried that the CENTCOM commander's threat was more than a scare tactic, given his allusion to Rumsfeld.

McKiernan told Franks that the matter should not be resolved in a phone conversation and that he would fly to Qatar the next day to talk face-to-face at Franks's command post. McKiernan then got on the phone to Abizaid, a fellow three-star officer and friend, to express his incredulity about what Franks had said. "That the 3-7 Cavalry was doing all the fighting was B.S. Talk about unhinging ourselves," McKiernan told his inner circle. What was needed was patience, control of the southern cities and highway approaches to Baghdad, and concerted efforts to shape the fight around the Iraqi capital.[8]

Before he set off for Qatar, McKiernan fired off a quick message to Franks, defending Wallace and making the case once again for slowing the push to Baghdad in order to defeat the paramilitary foe in the south. McKiernan said that he had told Wallace not to talk to the press until further notice, but insisted that Wallace was an aggressive leader, regardless of how his press interview may have been perceived. McKiernan argued that the enemy was fighting an urban-centric battle, starting from the Euphrates. There had not been a Shiite uprising, and Saddam's ability to command his forces was still intact. Iraq's Regular Army divisions had neither surrendered nor capitulated.

McKiernan assured Franks that although the fight would not be fast, it would be victorious. U.S. forces were now fighting in multiple directions for valid reasons and Washington needed to understand that. McKiernan stressed that the additional forces that were to be deployed were essential. He wanted the 3rd Armored Cavalry Regiment and particularly the 4th Infantry Division for the "red zone" fight in the approach to Baghdad.

McKiernan's message was confident even as it argued for additional forces and a little patience. Franks was not persuaded and fired back a terse e-mail. The CENTCOM commander did not believe the situation in the south was serious. The problem was not the Saddam Fedayeen but the V Corps's lack of aggressiveness, which Franks compared unfavorably to that of the Special Operations Forces, and further complained that McKiernan was paying excessive attention to the rear.[9]

During his video conference that night, Franks kept the pressure on, insisting that McKiernan answer a series of questions. Franks wanted to know the pluses and minuses of having Petraeus's 101st Airborne Division take Baghdad, and of focusing V Corps energy not on the Fedayeen, but on the lake region near the Karbala Gap and Baghdad. Franks wanted to know when Blount's 3rd Infantry Division was going to engage the enemy again. And he wanted to know what McKiernan thought about having the Marines attack the Iraqis' 10th and 6th divisions from the rear and pushing the British forces north of Basra.

The next morning, Colonel Dave Halverson, one of Franks's chief planners, called Terry Moran. Even though the 101st had conducted a deep attack, Franks was still unhappy. The BDA was minimal. The 101st had little to show for its operation. That suggested, Franks said, that the V Corps had lost contact with the enemy and did not know where enemy forces were positioned.[10]

McKiernan flew secretly that day to Franks's headquarters in Qatar and suffered the commander's wrath against the V Corps commander Wallace. McKiernan would later tell Thurman that he "ate a shit sandwich." McKiernan reassured Franks everything would work out if Wallace were just allowed to fight his fight. Gary Luck, the retired four-star general who was serving as General Franks's mentor, also spoke up for Wallace and helped calm Franks down. Wallace, Luck said, was not one to shrink from battle. Once he was back at Camp Doha, McKiernan called Wallace and repeated that he was not to talk to the media. McKiernan did not mention that Franks had been thinking about firing him, as Wallace was already under enough pressure.

But McKiernan made a telling comment to his staff: "Blue Force Tracker drives the CINC." The instantaneous ability to transmit information on the location of U.S. units had drawbacks. It was one of the pitfalls of Rumsfeld's exaggerated claims for transformation. On the CENTCOM computer screens, the blue icons that represented the Army had not been moving north, and it was easy to conclude that fighting had ceased when in fact the Army had been contending with the Fedayeen. If the scale of the map was reduced to a specific area, however, the screen showed considerable activity. The blobs of blue icons on the screens—representing all of southern Iraq—at CENTCOM headquarters in Qatar or at the Pentagon had been interpreted incorrectly, McKiernan thought.

The ground war had started fast and accelerated. Mattis had grabbed the oilfields and Dan Allyn had taken the Highway 1 bridge in a matter of hours. But the speedy attack had stalled when the Fedayeen had surprisingly struck back. The top military commanders at CENTCOM and the land war command were at odds as to what to do next. Franks and McKiernan had divergent views of the battlefield. Spider Marks was struck by this. "Seeing disconnect," he wrote in his diary. "McKiernan wants to control battlespace. CINC says keep moving."[11]

Even as Franks pressed McKiernan to drive on, CENTCOM was looking for other ways to speed up the war. John Abizaid, deputy CENTCOM commander, thought he had one. Abizaid had studied at the University of Jordan in Amman and was attuned to the sensitivities in the region. Abizaid had advised Joe Collins, the Pentagon's chief civilian peacekeeping expert, that U.S. forces would be an "antibody" in Iraqi society and it would be important to put an Iraqi face on the occupation. Now, he thought it might be critical to put an Iraqi face on the invasion as well.

Zalmay Khalilzad was in Ankara when he received a call from Abizaid. As the senior National Security Council staff member for Iraq, Khalilzad had been meeting with Iraqi exiles and opponents of Saddam for months. The White House had also kept Khalilzad in Ankara with instructions to use his skills to persuade the Turks not to send troops into northern Iraq in an attempt to preempt any Kurdish move to declare independence. Abizaid asked Khalilzad if he could arrange a meeting of Iraqi exiles in the liberated port of Umm Qasr, the Iraqi port city. He thought that it would be easier for the Iraqi army to surrender if they could do so to fellow Iraqis. Khalilzad was stunned by the call, as well as by the difficulties in rounding up the exile leaders on short notice and finding a way to get them to an American-controlled part of Iraq. But he knew CENTCOM was serious when Franks called as well.

Khalilzad was not the only official who got a call from CENTCOM. As there had been no signs of mass capitulation, Abizaid had contacted Feith's office, looking for Iraqis who would fight alongside the Americans. William Luti, one of Feith's deputies, put Abizaid in touch with Colonel Ted Seel, a former defense attaché at the U.S. Embassy in Egypt and the CENTCOM liaison to Ahmed Chalabi, the head of the Iraqi National Congress.

Seel had entered northern Iraq from Turkey, along with Lieutenant General Henry "Pete" Osman, the Marine officer who was supposed to help coordinate U.S. policies in the north. After hooking up with Chalabi, Seel moved to their headquarters—a former recreation site for Baath Party leaders. Seel submitted daily reports to CENTCOM's planning office on the status of the Chalabi forces, their equipment and morale. On March 27, Seel was told to contact Abizaid's office. When Abizaid got on the line, the general told Seel that if he was following the news he probably knew that the U.S. forces had run into much opposition. He said that he was aware of Seel's reports that Chalabi had a large number of fighters in northern Iraq. Abizaid wanted to know if Chalabi would raise an Iraqi military force that could be employed in the south to help turn the situation around. Would Chalabi be willing to deploy them? the general asked. Seel said that Chalabi was standing right next to him and he would ask him.

"Yes, he has got them," Seel replied. Abizaid said he needed a realistic appraisal of the number of fighters Chalabi could send south within the next twenty-four to forty-eight hours. Chalabi said he could field as many as 1,000 fighters, but Seel thought a more accurate count would be 700.

The U.S. Air Force could transport them in three flights of C-17s to the Tallil air base just south of Nasiriyah.[12]

Franks was first to break the news to a nervous White House. Anxious to reassure the president and his staff that he had the means to overcome Fedayeen resistance, Franks told Bush in a video conference that 1,000 Iraqi freedom fighters would be joining U.S. troops. Frank Miller, the senior National Security Council deputy for defense issues, was taken aback by the development. It was the first he had heard of the plan.

At the insistence of Wolfowitz and Feith, the Pentagon had intended to train Iraqi freedom fighters in Tazar, Hungary, a scheme that Abizaid had welcomed, but which Franks had treated with disdain. But in the wake of logistical problems, the need to vet applications to ensure that no foreign agents were included, and differences with the administration about the value of the plan, there had been only a trickle of recruits—seventy-three personnel—who had since been distributed among American units as interpreters. But what CENTCOM was now proposing was different. It was a plan conceived in haste to deal with unexpected difficulties. Unlike the Iraqis processed in Hungary, these fighters had been neither screened nor trained. Nobody in Washington seemed to know anything about them. This was extraordinary improvisation at a critical moment.

After the video conference with Franks, Miller approached George Tenet, the CIA director. Who are these freedom fighters? Miller wanted to know, assuming that the CIA had had a covert role in the business. "I have no fucking idea," Tenet responded. So Miller called Luti's office to find out, but even Luti was not sure what was going on. Also in the dark was Secretary of State Powell. Even after he left office, Powell wondered how Chalabi's fighters got into the war.[13]

Before Chalabi's men were flown south, the deal was almost queered when a CIA operative sent a cable to Washington warning that the force included Iranians and that Chalabi had paid them $5,000 each. The message was that they were unreliable mercenaries, a time bomb that could blow up in CENTCOM's face. But Seel kept the plan on track by challenging the CIA assessment and vouching for the men—a collection of pro-Chalabi fighters, including some who had returned from their exile in Iran, and a few Kurds. When the airlift finally started in early April, the total number of fighters transported was somewhat more than 570.

Once the airlift was under way, Chalabi insisted that he go as well. Abizaid had not bargained for that and objected. Sending Iraqi freedom fighters into the fray was one thing, but transporting a would-be president of Iraq on an Air Force plane was another. Abizaid argued in a tense phone conversion with Wolfowitz that CENTCOM should not be taking sides in future Iraqi politics. Wolfowitz did not yield. It was Abizaid who had solicited Chalabi's fighters in a moment of anxiety about the war, and the fighters did not want to go without their leader. When Abizaid awoke the next day, Chalabi was at Tallil.[14]

When flying the fighters on C-17s, the Air Force and CIA insisted that the Iraqis leave their weapons behind. They did not want an armed, untested force on their planes. Chalabi's men agreed; they would have to come up with their own weapons at their destination. The fighters arrived with virtually no provisions, and no welcome. They were ushered into a busted-up hangar where a sympathetic Army supply officer gave them humanitarian rations, prepackaged meals that contained no culturally insensitive foods like ham—rations intended for the hordes of refugees that had failed to materialize. McKiernan, for his part, was blindsided by the development and saw Chalabi's fighters as an unwanted burden, apparently unaware that it was Franks and Abizaid who had sought them. For weeks, Thurman scrambled to find a way to arm and equip them. Chalabi's men were neither effectively trained nor supervised by the U.S. Special Forces responsible for their crash course. They never played a significant military role during the war. Chalabi, however, was undeterred; he took full advantage of the situation. Driving to Nasiriyah, he delivered a rousing political speech to potential supporters.[15]

In Washington, McKiernan's decision to pause on the way north to Baghdad shook the Pentagon. Barry McCaffrey, the former commander of the Army's 24th Mechanized Division and one of the most aggressive generals of the Persian Gulf War, lambasted Rumsfeld for sending too few troops. Striking back, Myers, the JCS chairman, asserted that any criticism of the planning would undermine morale, an assertion that made second-guessing of the Pentagon decision about how many troops to send tantamount to disloyalty. Fending off his critics, Rumsfeld insisted to the Pentagon press and several television interviewers that he was not the author of the war strategy. Everyone had agreed that Zinni's plan was flawed, Rumsfeld argued. The new plan that followed had been produced by Franks. "I keep getting credit for it in the press, but the truth is I would be happy to take credit for it, but I can't," Rumsfeld said. "It was not my plan. It was General Franks's plan, and it was a plan that evolved over a sustained period of time, which I am convinced is an excellent plan."[16]

Rumsfeld also defended his management of the deployment. "The logistics train was designed to be either everything went or nothing went," he said, alluding to the TPFDL. "And in fact, the president wanted to support the diplomacy in the United Nations. So he wanted things to flow in over a period of time. But everything that they've asked for is in process. It's all arriving." These were extraordinary statements from a man who had thrown out Tony Zinni's 1003-98 war plan, insisted that Franks start afresh, dispatched Doug Macgregor to CENTCOM to tout the advantage of attacking Baghdad with less than a division, faxed Franks to proclaim the virtues of "shock and awe," spurned the TPFDL, and hesitated to alert the reserves. For eighteen months, CENTCOM had been bombarded with questions from Rumsfeld on why the command could not deploy more quickly and fight with fewer troops. It was Franks's plan, but Rumsfeld had been a powerful and insistent influence.[17]

Behind closed doors, Rumsfeld let his anger show. With the secretary of defense under fire, Newt Gingrich approached Macgregor, the iconoclastic Army officer, and asked for a supportive memo he could slip to Rumsfeld. Macgregor was more than happy to oblige. Macgregor had heard that some generals wanted to wait for more forces before advancing to Baghdad and was convinced that this was yet another example of the Army's risk-averse mentality. Macgregor drafted a blistering memo on why halting the march north was a bad idea.

The coalition force, he wrote, was massive and had taken almost no casualties. The logistical strains could be dealt with by flying parts and supplies on C-130s and better protecting the supply convoys. Holding one's nerve is fundamental, he wrote. Tikrit should be flattened. The Republican Guard should be destroyed. Urban resistance should be eradicated with armor and precision bombing. Saddam was winning the media battle and should the U.S. stop its advance, he would win a psychological victory. Stopping would damage the morale of the troops. It would send the wrong signal to the Kurds and Shiites. It would tempt the French and the Germans to interfere diplomatically and undermine support for the war at home. "The soldiers," Macgregor wrote, "are out to win and will win if allowed to but they need momentum on their side."[18]

Rumsfeld was impressed and sent a reply to Gingrich a day later: "Thanks for the Macgregor piece. Nobody up here is thinking like this."

As the pause in the war continued, the generals in the field began to debate when it would be time to resume the march. Blount was unhappy with the pause and becoming impatient. He had two brigades on the escarpment south of the Karbala Gap, and was concerned that they might be an easy target for Iraqi artillery and possibly chemical or biological weapons. He feared that the Iraqis would use the time more vigorously to defend the Karbala Gap. So far, U.S. intelligence indicated that the gap was wide open. Instead of waiting for Dan Allyn's brigade to arrive, Blount pressed the V Corps to allow him to take two brigades and the 3rd ID logistics through the gap. The V Corps nixed the idea, arguing that it would be too risky until the Medina Division was reduced by 80 percent through air strikes—a virtual impossibility and 30 percent more than McKiernan's goal.

Eager to maintain some momentum, Blount proposed a feint at the Euphrates River town of Hindiyah, by having Dave Perkins's 2nd Brigade Combat Team attack to the bridge in the center of the town, thereby creating the impression that the division was planning to cross the Euphrates for its push toward Baghdad. The maneuver, Blount calculated, would prompt the Iraqis to fire their artillery. Blount's division would use its counterbattery radar to pinpoint the Iraqi guns so they could be bombarded by U.S. artillery and air strikes. Destroying the Iraqi artillery would substantially neutralize the enemy's ability to defend the Karbala Gap. Mindful of what had happened at Kifl, Blount instructed Perkins not to cross the bridge to the far bank. He did not want to risk having U.S. forces cut off on the other side.[19]

Wallace liked the idea and amplified it. He drew up plans for four additional attacks, including a feint by the 101st from Kifl toward Hillah. Wallace also wanted the 101st to isolate Najaf and clear the Fedayeen out of the city, and he wanted the 101st to conduct an armored reconnaissance to the west. The brigade from the 82nd would start to clear Samawah. The plan, known as the "five attacks," was to be carried out on March 30.[20]

On March 29, Wallace, his division commanders, and McKiernan met to review the situation and discuss their next moves. Blount pressed for resuming the attack north as soon as possible. By now, Dan Allyn's brigade had moved from Samawah to Karbala, where it would protect the right flank of the division as it moved through the Karbala Gap. If the 101st were to take on the Karbala mission, Blount's entire division could move forward. Blount knew Terry Moran, McKiernan's adviser, from the general's days in Saudi Arabia. Doing an end run around the V Corps commander, Blount told Moran that it was time to start moving north again.

To carry out the feint, Perkins arranged for two infantry battalions to secure the roads to Hindiyah, while Phil DeCamp's 4-64 battalion attacked into the town. Eric Schwartz's 1-64 was held in reserve. As the brigade pushed into Hindiyah, Captain Phil Wolford's tank company came under RPG and small arms fire. Captain Chris Carter's infantry company pressed on and seized the bridge. At the span, combat engineers quickly checked to see if it was rigged for demolition. The engineers found some wires under the bridge and readily severed them; the Iraqis had not yet placed their explosives.[21]

With the troops in town, Iraqi fighters on the other side were using civilians as shields. A frightened woman began to run across the span and was shot in the buttocks. Braving the Iraqi fire, Carter rushed onto the bridge to rescue her. The event was captured by an AP reporter who was accompanying the unit and chronicled for the world.[22]

When the Iraqi fighters tried to cross the river by boat, Perkins called an end to the feint. The plan was not to hold the town; he did not want civilians caught in a bloody fight. As it withdrew, the battalion destroyed large caches of arms—and then blew up the Baath Party headquarters. The attack prompted the Iraqis to use their artillery, though not to the extent that Blount would have liked. The 3rd ID fired twenty counterbattery artillery missions and called in thirty air strikes. It also acquired a useful piece of intelligence. One captured Iraqi was a platoon leader from the Nebuchadnezzar Republican Guard Division, which was supposedly deployed north of Baghdad. Republican Guard troops had moved south, undetected, to join the Fedayeen.[23]

The other V Corps operations were carried out against substantial resistance. One soldier was killed and another wounded when the 101st began its feint from Kifl toward Hillah. The commander of one of the division's Apache helicopter companies supporting the attack was also wounded. Like Perkins's brigade, the soldiers determined that troops from Iraq's Nebuchadnezzar unit were among the defenders. The fighting in Samawah and Najaf was also stiff.

In the east, Mattis was as unhappy as Blount with the pause and equally eager to see it lifted. Like Blount, he feared that waiting too long would forfeit the momentum of his attack and leave his Marines vulnerable to an Iraqi strike with chemical or biological weapons. Intelligence reports showed that the Iraqis were rushing fighters to stiffen their defenses on Highways 1 and 8, and Mattis had 20,000 Marines downwind of any WMD the Iraqis might use. Having fought to seize Hantush, Mattis decided to recall Joe Dunford's 3/5 battalion south after the pause was ordered. Mattis figured that the division needed more defendable positions, and he was worried that leaving part of his division so far north might give away the plan for advancing on Baghdad. Dunford and his officers were stunned by the order to fall back and consolidate at the Diwaniyah jumping-off point. Giving up hard-fought ground for which one Marine had died was distasteful to the troops. Beyond that, Dunford believed the airfield was needed for aerial resupply. He also thought that seizing Hantush would not give away the division's strategy but would deceive the Iraqis about Mattis's plan to move west and cross the Tigris.[24]

While McKiernan, Wallace, and Conway discussed how best to proceed, Mattis used the pause to clear up pockets of resistance. Lieutenant Colonel Bryan "Baseplate" McCoy's 3-4, part of RCT-7, conducted an armed reconnaissance up Highway 17 to Afak, where he ran into some enemy forces. Attacking from the east, Colonel Joe Dowdy's RCT-1 raided Fajr on the same route to root out Baathists, an operation that led to the death of one Marine and serious injury to another.

While the land war generals debated the pause, Buzz Moseley's air war command was trying to keep the pressure on the enemy. The Bush administration had taken twenty-two leadership and communications targets that carried the potential of high collateral damage off the target list for the A-day strike, an exercise in restraint that reflected Washington's hope that Saddam had only a fragile hold on power.

With the frustrations on the battlefield and no mass surrenders on the part of the enemy, though, the gloves were coming off. Bit by bit, the targets had been put on the hit list. Washington had been readily approving all of them, and Franks was urging Moseley to strike them as soon as possible. Moseley ordered the F-15E pilots in particular to "fly them hard until they whine." The F-15Es had the longest combat radius of all the fighters and were the least reliant on tankers for support. The CENTCOM commander was also unhappy about Saddam's television broadcasts exhorting Iraqis to resist the invaders and celebrating the shoot-down of Dave Williams's Apache helicopter. The CIA was reporting that the broadcasts were making it harder to win over the Shiites, who seemed uncertain who was winning the war. Franks wanted Moseley to knock Saddam's television off the air. Attuned to the public relations of the war, Franks cautioned his commanders that they needed to be careful how they publicly portrayed the attacks on Saddam's television and radio capability. "Everybody needs to recognize that we don't want to talk about 'media' or 'propaganda' at all," Franks noted in a video conference with his commanders. "Use 'command and control' instead. Treat 'em rough."

By March 27 Franks was beginning to get frustrated. He wanted to pummel the Republican Guard divisions that were defending the approaches to Baghdad. His priorities were to strike the Medina, Hammurabi, and Baghdad divisions—in that order. But Franks was not happy with the lack of timely BDA. The bad weather was interfering with the satellite reconnaissance, and the chronic difficulties in processing the bomb damage assessments had left CENTCOM in the dark. A lot of bombs were being dropped, but it was not clear what the effect was. "The BDA process is not serving us well," Franks told Moseley in a March 27 video conference. "Let's play like there are no satellites and use other means to find the missing elements of the RG. It is appalling that we don't know where six units of the Republican Guard are."[25]

Moseley, for his part, was eager to help the ground troops get to the Iraqi capital. Unlike some of the air commanders in the Gulf War, he did not expect to win the war single-handedly with a knockout punch in downtown Baghdad. He was determined to pave the way for the V Corps and Marines. In his country twang, Moseley had promised that the air attacks would be so effective that McKiernan's forces would not need to stop on their way to Baghdad unless they wanted to drop by the nearby drive-in for a cherry limeade. The criticism that Rumsfeld had sent too few troops, Moseley had opined, was no more significant than a cow peeing on a flat rock. The defense secretary loved the put-down, commented on it in a video conference, and even faxed a congratulatory note to Moseley, which the Air Force general later framed and hung in his Pentagon office.[26]

The word at Moseley's command was to find ways to put more "warheads on foreheads." For all the bravado, however, the land forces had their hands full with the Fedayeen and were paused on the way north. The Fedayeen were not a threat to Moseley's warplanes, and the Iraqi air force was not flying. But Moseley worried about the Russian-made GPS jammers that the Iraqis had mounted on towers, according to U.S. intelligence, to try to impede the Americans from using their JDAM satellite-guided bombs. Moseley was also concerned that the Iraqis would mount terrorist or even WMD strikes in the rear to knock his bases out of commission. On March 28, the biological sensors the United States had installed at the Al-Dhafra base in the United Arab Emirates sounded an alarm: terrorists had unleashed the plague. Like the many other reports of WMD, the alert turned out to be false. Still, the report forced airmen to scramble into their protective suits and don gas masks. Tensions were running high.[27]

Moseley also faced some difficult constraints. A big one was the limited number of refueling tankers and the farflung network of bases where they were deployed, including Egypt, which quietly allowed the use of an airfield. The tanker problem had thrown a monkey wrench into the F-117 strike on A-day and also reduced the number of air strikes that could be conducted against Iraqi ground forces.

Nor had the synchronization with the land forces come as smoothly as Moseley had hoped. To coordinate air strikes and avoid friendly fire the V Corps used a long-established system in which a dividing line was drawn; this was dubbed the fire support coordination line, or FSCL for short. Enemy units north of the line could be bombed with abandon but air strikes south of the line could not be conducted without coordination with the V Corps. The system was a holdover from the days of the Cold War and U.S. plans for the defense of Europe, which anticipated clear defense lines and massive tank armies on both sides.

Air crews, however, found the V Corps procedures enormously frustrating. Initially, the V Corps placed the FSCL so far north that warplanes had only several minutes of loiter time to drop their bombs before they had to turn south to refuel. As for attacks south of the line, the V Corps was only able to coordinate six flights an hour during the early days of the war. Moseley's command and Conway's Marines favored a different system, in which all of Iraq was divided into a series of thirty-mile by thirty-mile grids, or "kill boxes." The boxes were further divided into ten-mile by ten-mile squares, or "keypads." The sectors were to the front as well as the rear of Marine positions and afforded the air war commanders more flexibility in carrying out bombing attacks. Not surprisingly, the Marines received a disproportionate share of the air strikes as they moved north.[28]

With Franks's injunction to flatten the Republican Guard and with the advance of the V Corps and Marines to Baghdad on hold there was no time to argue about targeting procedures. Moseley had to find a way to increase the pressure. One step was to move the fuel closer to the bomb-droppers by ordering refueling tankers north into Iraq. The KC-10 and KC-135 tankers carried no missiles or guns. They did not have warning systems to sound an alert if the plane was being painted by a SAM radar, nor were their aircraft outfitted with chaff or flares to spoof enemy radar-guided or heat-seeking missiles. They were little more than flying gas stations. Moseley began moving the tankers north on March 26 and was so enthusiastic about the idea that he later jumped on one of the planes and called Franks as he orbited over western Iraq. Moseley made plans to follow that up by basing A-10s at Tallil in early April. The planes were well suited for close air support but had a relatively short range. By moving them to southern Iraq, they would be closer to the fight.[29]

As for the GPS jammers, they were obliterated by Colonel McKeon's F-117s. Captain Ian Phillips and Lieutenant Jeff Strange used a pair of EGBU-27 bombs to blast the towers they were mounted on. Since the bombs only occasionally used GPS data to update their position and could also be guided by a laser, they were not thwarted by the jamming. In one of the war's ironies, the GPS jammers were put out of action by GPS bombs.[30]

There was another innovation. Before the sandstorm settled in, a military weather forecaster at Moseley's headquarters had alerted the air war command, which responded by ordering his reconnaissance planes to take photographs of the enemy positions. The theory was that once the bad weather came in, U.S. spy satellites and drones would use their radars to map the ground. Objects that appeared to match with the enemy locations in the photos would be pounded with satellite-guided bombs. The officers at Moseley's command had a fitting name for the procedure: "smack-down" targeting.

The weather took its toll on the pace of the air campaign—one quarter of the scheduled strikes were canceled on March 27 alone—but the bombing never stopped. By March 31, 1,861 satellite-guided JDAMs had been dropped, including 260 on the night of March 30. In its enthusiasm to add to the ordnance that was being dumped on enemy forces, a B-2 Stealth bomber was even dispatched to drop a load of MK-82 "dumb" bombs. That mission drew a complaint from the air staff at the Pentagon, who questioned the wisdom of sending a $2 billion plane to drop unguided bombs.[31]

To the great frustration of Franks and the air war command, Saddam was never knocked off the air for long. The Iraqis had their workarounds, too, and had an array of antennas to beam their message throughout the country. Franks's expectations for the next phase of the war were plain. "I think the intent is pretty clear," he told his commanders. "Offensive spirit, shock action, drive on."[32]

On March 31, Franks flew to McKiernan's headquarters in Kuwait. The CENTCOM commander was all smiles as he greeted the battle staff in the command center. Things took a different turn, however, when he met with McKiernan and his key deputies in McKiernan's office. Franks was direct in his criticism of his land commanders. Only the British and the Special Operations Forces had been fighting, he said. The 3rd Infantry Division was acting like a bunch of "eaters and shitters" and needed to be turned into war-fighters. Franks said he doubted that the forces had even had a serious tank engagement and warned them to pay attention to the embarrassment that would follow if they failed. The resistance around Karbala was minor, and destroying it would be "crust work." The commanders needed to figure out how to use Ray Odierno's 4th Infantry Division, which would be arriving soon in Kuwait. It would not be needed to clean up the mess along the supply lines. Franks said that the Baghdad International Airport could be taken sooner than McKiernan and his commanders believed. It could be done now, Franks insisted, and Task Force 20 and Petraeus's 101st were still the right units to take on the job.[33]

Franks was frustrated that neither McKiernan nor the Marines had heeded his suggestion to destroy the Iraqi 10th and 6th divisions; something needed to be done about those red icons on his screen. He was surprised that the generals did not perceive a threat from the 10th. Highway 6, which ran north from Basra, had to be controlled. "Basra did not feel isolated," he said.

The most striking moment of the meeting came when Franks said he did not want to hear about casualties, even though no one had mentioned any. At that point, he put his hand to his mouth and made a yawning motion, as if to suggest that some casualties were not of major consequence to the attack. Nobody argued openly with Franks. The CENTCOM commander was unloading on them and they would ride out his behavior. McKiernan's deputies who attended the meeting, however, were shocked. Albert Whitley, McKiernan's top British deputy, was furious at Franks's cavalier attitude about casualties—Royal Marines had been killed on the opening night of the war and an American Patriot unit had mistakenly shot down a British Tornado, killing its two-man crew. Spider Marks was also put off by the tone of Franks's presentation. He felt as if Franks had simply taken all of Rumsfeld's frustrations with the war and dumped them on his subordinates.

In addition, Whitley and other members of McKiernan's team felt that Franks was taking a scattershot approach to the prosecution of the war. He was asking for action on all fronts. He wanted to move on Baghdad and simultaneously take on the 10th and 6th divisions, which both the Marines and McKiernan considered to be fixed, of no threat, and all but out of the war. The U.S. forces were not to concentrate their efforts on a main goal, but to take on an array of tasks. The guidance to do everything at once was no better than issuing no guidance at all.

After Franks left, McKiernan, who felt he enjoyed a solid relationship with his commanders and had endured Franks's tirades before, sought to calm his team and stem any rumors of differences within the command. The land command was still on track, he said, and it was important to maintain a sense of unity. McKiernan approached Whitley, his deputy and friend, with whom he had served in Sarajevo. "That conversation never happened," McKiernan said.[34]

In the months after the invasion, the assaults by the Fedayeen, the furious sandstorms, the stretched logistics, the wrong intelligence projections, and the absence of a Shiite uprising would all be dismissed as the inevitable friction of war. The plan, Franks, Cheney, and Rumsfeld would argue, had been sound from the start. Only a bunch of armchair generals had thought otherwise.

Inside CENTCOM, the situation had been more complex. Franks had threatened to fire the V Corps commander. Franks and Abizaid had been sufficiently concerned about setbacks on the battlefield to bring in Chalabi's fighters on U.S. Air Force C-17s. The effects of the bombing of the Republican Guard had yet to be properly assessed. And Franks had chastised his top generals for being overly cautious and worrying too much about the Fedayeen. For his part, McKiernan remained convinced that he had to deal with the threats in the rear and the Iraqi defenses on the road to Baghdad. He agreed that speed was imperative, but there was a huge difference between viewing icons on a computer screen and moving large formations on the battlefield as they were fighting a paramilitary foe over extended distances. Despite the tension with Franks, he believed his instinct had been right, that he had done the right thing by ordering a pause and taking the time to shape the next phase of the fight. As McKiernan reminded his staff at the daily battle update, "Make no mistake about it, we're in a goddamn war!"

CHAPTER 17

Team Tank

While the Army and Marines were working to blunt the Fedayeen attacks in the south, Colonel Pete Blaber was running his own small war in the west. Under CENTCOM's division of labor, western Iraq had been designated an arena for the Special Operations Forces, and Blaber commanded a sensitive unit: a squadron from the 1st Special Forces Operational Detachment commonly called the Delta Force.

Franks had been greatly impressed by the role the Special Operations Forces had played in toppling the Taliban in Afghanistan, and the commandos had been given a big piece of the war against Saddam Hussein. The 5th Special Forces Group had been stationed in Jordan. Led by John Mulholland, its job was to scour the western Iraqi desert for Scuds and ensure that the Iraqis did not manage to lob any missiles at Israel, as they had in 1991. It was to carry out the task along with warplanes from Buzz Moseley's command, which had overall authority for the counter-Scud mission. In northern Iraq Charlie Cleveland's 10th Special Forces Group was working with the Kurds. But there was also another conglomeration of Special Operations Forces stationed at Ar'ar, a secret base in western Saudi Arabia. Virtually everybody who was anybody in the shadowy world of "black SOF," the most covert Special Operations Forces, was there. In addition to the Delta Force, Ar'ar hosted the 75th Ranger Regiment, Combat Talon MC-130s and Little Bird helicopters from the 160th Special Operations Aviation Regiment, as well as a battalion from the 82nd Airborne Division, a conventional unit, which was placed under the operational control of the special operators to beef up their ability to seize sites deep in Iraq.[1]

The presence of the U.S. Special Operations Forces on Saudi territory was such a carefully guarded secret that it would not be officially acknowledged even after the war. As far as the unclassified annals were concerned, Ar'ar simply did not exist. The Ar'ar forces were under the command of Major General Dell Dailey, who oversaw the Joint Special Operations Command at Fort Bragg. During the Iraq War, Dailey's forces would be known simply as Task Force 20. When Tommy Franks posed for a photo opportunity with his top commanders at the Abu Ghraib North Palace after the seizure of Baghdad, he made sure that Dailey was not in the frame.

Much of Dailey's focus was on taking down Baghdad International Airport, which was not surprising given his background as a helicopter pilot, his experience with large-scale military operations, the fact that the Rangers had specialized in this kind of mission during the invasions of Panama and Afghanistan, and the Bush administration's obsession with early regime collapse. Two major rehearsals were conducted at Fort Benning in Georgia and, later, at Fort Bragg in North Carolina to practice taking the airport and clearing it of obstacles and debris, so that the commandos and McKiernan's reserve force, the 2nd Brigade from the 82nd Airborne, could parachute or fly in. If Saddam's regime collapsed like a house of cards, Dailey's Task Force 20 would have a starring role in the drama.

The airfield seizure mission was controversial. Buff Blount's 3rd Infantry Division figured that its armored vehicles would make it to the airfield first and would be in a much better position to secure the massive airport and deal with the enemy's defensive positions. The division's vehicles gave it more mobility and it did not need to worry about Iraq's extensive air defenses. The division let CENTCOM and the special operators know it could do the mission more effectively and with less risk. But Dailey was known as a pit bull: once he latched on to a concept he would rarely let it go—or as Dailey's own staff quipped, he was determined to shove a marshmallow into a piggy bank.

A veteran of Afghanistan, Somalia, and the Balkans, Blaber had a much less visible mission. Blaber had spent thirteen years in Delta Force, fought in operations around the world, and spoke two languages. He also relied heavily on the experience of Delta's noncommissioned officers, who were allowed to stay in the unit their entire careers if their bodies could withstand the punishing regimen. Blaber's partner was Sergeant Major Iggy Balderas, one of the most experienced soldiers in the Army. The Delta squadron was not going to parachute into Iraq or advance on the Iraqi capital. The squadron, some seventy-five commandos in all, would blow a gap through the sand berm that marked the Iraq-Saudi border and drive into western Iraq one day before the official start of the war in fifteen Pinzgauers, rugged six-wheel, Swiss-made vehicles, and two civilian SUVs that could blend into Iraqi traffic. The team was also equipped with Javelin antitank missiles and a reconnaissance drone, which could be launched to peer at the terrain ahead. Gaining permission from his superiors to drive into Iraq had not been easy. Dailey, for one, had been opposed. He maintained that Delta and the other commandos should be based at Ar'ar and chopper in and out to check WMD sites and conduct raids. Blaber countered that the best way to gather intelligence would be to get in on the ground and develop the situation. Only after Franks himself intervened was Blaber's mission approved. The CENTCOM commander knew Blaber from Afghanistan, had a high opinion of the Delta Force's ability to swiftly execute operations, and expected much of the commandos this time as well.

Delta's initial task was to investigate several suspected WMD sites in the west and then push east toward the Haditha Dam, a massive structure that was constructed by the Soviets in the 1970s to provide electrical power and facilitate irrigation, and stood at the head of the Qadisiyah Reservoir near the town of Haditha. It was not entirely clear what Blaber was supposed to do when he got to the dam, but the Kuwaitis had told Franks that Saddam might have hidden his WMD there, and somehow the dam had become a part of the general search for Saddam's hidden caches. To exploit whatever information about WMD and Saddam's regime the Delta squadron could obtain from local Iraqis, the commandos were accompanied by a battlefield intelligence team, including a psychologist, two military intelligence officers, and several dogs. The dogs would serve as sentries and assist in catching "squirters," enemy soldiers who tried to run away.

The Delta squadron's most important intelligence asset, however, were two Iraqi-Americans: a veterinarian from Philadelphia; and Saif Ataya, a real estate agent from San Francisco who had once been a private in the Iraqi army and had escaped from Saddam's Iraq by trekking through the desert after the Gulf War, eventually making his way to the United States where he had become a successful businessman. The Iraqis would be more than interpreters; they were to serve as the Delta Force's cultural advisers and guides. Not everyone at Ar'ar was enamored of the idea. When one ranking intelligence officer learned about the men, he demanded to know how the most secret organization in the U.S. military could take two civilians without security clearances into a combat zone. Blaber told the intelligence officer that the Iraqi-Americans were committed to the overthrow of Saddam, loyal to the United States, and essential to the mission. "They're Americans. I trust them, and I need them to ensure my men are successful and stay alive," Blaber said, as the intelligence officer marched off in frustration.[2]

For all his lobbying to get Delta Force in on the ground, Blaber was skeptical about finding much in the way of WMD, regardless of how convinced the U.S. intelligence agencies were that the Iraqis had chemical weapons and mobile biological factories. Blaber's Delta experience had taught him to put himself in the shoes of his adversary, and it seemed illogical that Saddam would stash such a critical capability in a remote and poorly defended stretch of desert that was only loosely controlled by the regime in Baghdad. But Blaber recognized that WMD was a convenient rationale for Delta's role in western Iraq.

Blaber and his men were brainstorming about alternative operations in March when American intelligence intercepted the phone calls of a senior Iraqi general as he drove toward Syria on Route 12 and back. That had prompted speculation that the Iraqi leadership was scouting potential escape routes to the west. Will H., a fire support officer on Blaber's staff, developed a plan that relied on the SOF's experience in Afghanistan. With support from Moseley's warplanes and help from other commando units, Delta Force could cut off the road to Syria and generally create the impression in Baghdad that a sizable invasion force was moving on the capital from the west. With more than forty allied teams moving around western Iraq, there would be a lot of activity.

Five days before the war, Delta officers flew to FOB (Forward Operating Base) 51, the secret 5th Special Forces base in Jordan, to exchange radio frequencies and discuss with them the potential for joint attacks. While Delta was pushing north from Ar'ar, the commandos in Jordan would be mounting a three-prong attack from the west, with the 5th Special Forces in the south, the Australians in the center, and two British teams in the north. The Special Forces and Delta units had fought side by side in Afghanistan, and, although they were compartmented and had not been instructed to plan joint missions, they believed they could take advantage of their numbers and routes if opportunities presented themselves to swarm their foe from all directions.

Blaber was hoping to take the plan a step further. To him, the Iraqi units that had been arrayed around Baghdad in accordance with Saddam's ring defense plan looked like a series of four fence posts, each anchored at a key geographical location. After kicking up a ruckus in the western desert, Blaber wanted to use Delta Force and Moseley's warplanes to batter the northwest fence post. He believed that this would create an impression in Baghdad that allied forces were everywhere, confusing and panicking the enemy. Marauding would become a strategic principle.

On March 19, with temperatures in the low twenties, the Delta squadron drove from Ar'ar under the cover of darkness and blew a corridor through the forty-foot-high sand berm that ran along Iraq's border with Saudi Arabia. They were the first force to enter Iraq; Blaber and his small staff remained behind at the Ar'ar command site. To carry out their plan, they would need to lobby for additional Delta Forces still in the United States and fight for a bigger share of the war—linking up with the squadron. At the assigned suspected WMD sites, the Delta Force as expected turned up nothing but a group of Iraqi troops who were equipped with German gas masks, but who claimed to know nothing about chemical or biological weapons. Within minutes of talking to the corpulent and disheveled Iraqi major who was in charge of the site, Ataya told Bill C., the lieutenant colonel who led the Delta squadron across the border, that there was no way these men would ever have come into contact with WMD, much less been charged with guarding them. As a small force on the move, the Delta squadron was not interested in taking prisoners: the Iraqis were told the Americans were just the reconnaissance for a multidivisional attack from the west and were let go.

After firefights at Rutbah and the H-3 airfield in western Iraq, and several days of ambushing Iraqi convoys while trying to dodge Bedouin tribes loyal to Saddam, the Delta team moved toward the Haditha Dam—in Blaber's view the northwestern fence post. It was protected by Roland air defense missiles and a nearby Iraqi mechanized company of tanks and BMPs. With B-1 bombers and F-15Es with satellite-guided bombs orbiting western Iraq, the Delta team had plenty of airpower to call on in overtaking a substantial target.

After night fell, Delta commandos advanced in nine all-terrain vehicles equipped with special noise-suppressing mufflers and Blue Force Tracker, which enabled Blaber and his officers to track their movement. Using their advanced night vision systems, they drove through the Iraqi defensive perimeter and used handheld laser devices to identify Iraqi vehicles, artillery, and tanks for destruction from the air—precision fire combined with precision maneuver, in accordance with Will H.'s plan. With both laser-guided bombs and satellite-guided JDAMs, the aircraft destroyed twenty-three enemy armored vehicles and seventeen ZSU air defense guns, along with numerous trucks and barracks. The Delta team repeated the exercise the next night. The episode made a big impression on Franks, who repeatedly used it to pressure McKiernan to speed up the march to Baghdad.

Blaber and his men recognized that the area around the dam was an important piece of terrain. But the Delta Force was in fact too small to seize and hold the dam, and Blaber was anxious to hand off the mission so his team could swing east and begin to harass Highway 1 north of Baghdad. He needed additional forces. Blaber called up Colonel Frank Kearney, the chief operations officer for the Joint Special Operations Command, and asked for another squadron of Pinzgauer-equipped Delta commandos, a battalion of Army Rangers, and a company of M1 tanks. Kearney backed the request and Franks quickly approved it.

Within hours, a Delta squadron was loaded onto two C-17s, which took off from North Carolina and flew nonstop to a dirt airstrip in Iraq established by the Delta commandos. It was the first time a U.S. mechanized force had flown directly from its home base into a combat zone and driven from their planes to fight, a feat that would be acknowledged only in the classified annals of the war. Commanded by Lieutenant Colonel Mark O., the squadron added to Delta's marauding potential.

The Rangers were happy to join the expanding mission in the west. By March 27, it seemed clear that the Bush administration's hope for early regime collapse had faded and that Dailey's Task Force 20 would not be capturing the Baghdad airport. The one mission the Rangers had conducted had been a dubious affair: two Rangers had been seriously wounded and two Chinooks and three Black Hawks damaged by armor-piercing rounds in a raid on a suspected chemical and biological weapons testing facility near the Qadisiyah Reservoir that turned out like other sites to be bereft of any signs of WMD. The war plan's assumption that Iraq had WMD had resulted in American casualties.

With no airport mission or obvious caches of WMD to seize, Dailey was busy designing a series of alternative raids, calling for sweeping into Saddam's now empty palaces, filming the operations, and distributing video as part of a psychological operations campaign. As it was all but official that the seizing of the Baghdad airport was off the table, capturing the Haditha Dam seemed the next best thing to the Rangers. When Blaber asked the Ranger regimental commander if he could spare any troops, the officer responded with a slight hint of sarcasm, "Sure, how about an entire regiment?" CENTCOM would later portray the seizure of the Haditha Dam as a strategically vital step that prevented Saddam from flooding the western approaches to Baghdad, including the all-important Karbala Gap. But the dam capture mission was an improvisation.[3]

On March 27, three C-17s jammed with Rangers flew toward the H-1 airfield in western Iraq, a sprawling facility that was to serve as a staging area for the push toward Qadisiyah. Dodging antiaircraft fire, the C-17s descended to 500 feet and the Rangers, each of whom carried hundreds of pounds of gear, and combat engineers jumped out into the desert night. There was no enemy to be found, but the hard sand and sharp rocks led to a fair number of broken legs and sprained ankles. Within hours the engineers had cleared the runway of debris and H-1 was operational. The first plane in was an MC-130, which arrived to evacuate the casualties.

Like the Tallil and Jalibah airfields in southern Iraq, the United States now had another Iraqi base under control—and a means to fly in additional forces. Two days later, a company from the 3rd Ranger Battalion flew into H-1, linked up with its fellow Rangers, and began to head east toward the dam. Little Bird helicopters were flown in as well to give the Rangers more air support for the mission.

Still more force was on the way. Captain Shane Celeen, the commander of C Company, 1-41, was at Objective Rams on April 1 when he was tapped to join the covert war in the west. As the commander of a company of M1 tanks, Celeen had helped to contain the Fedayeen around Samawah. But none of the planning had prepared him for the mission that was about to unfold. Celeen was instructed to leave a platoon at Rams and take the rest of his company sixty miles southeast to Tallil for a special mission. Intending to ease wear and tear on his M1s, Celeen waited for tank transporters to haul them south, but they never arrived. So he road-marched his company to Tallil.

Many of Celeen's soldiers had never flown in a C-17 before. Now they would be flown to H-1 to fight with the SOF. Putting an armored unit under the command of a Special Operations Force was an unorthodox move not made since World War II. The tanks packed a lot of punch but they consumed a lot of fuel and had no real supply lines to fall back on. But Blaber figured that if anything would create the impression that an American division was slicing through western Iraq it would be M1 tanks. The seventy-ton tanks were flown in one by one on a C-17 after most of their fuel was drained. All told, ten M1 tanks, three APCs (armored personnel carriers), one fire support tracked vehicle, three trucks, two fuelers, and a Humvee were flown west to H-1 over three days.[4]

On April 1, the Rangers swooped in to take control of the dam, the nearby power station building, and the transformer yard. Before departing the area, the Delta commandos escorted the first Ranger platoon up to the edge of the dam. Smashing into the main administration building, the Rangers began to clear the building room by room, eventually finding and detaining the dam manager and twenty-five other civilians. Within four hours, the Rangers were able to report that the building was clear of explosives. Outside, however, fighting raged, spilling into the day. Iraqi soldiers were firing RPGs from the west side of the dam and lobbing mortars and artillery. To silence the enemy, the Rangers called on A-10s to blast the Iraqis, blowing out all the windows of the administration building in the process.

The Iraqis continued to shell the Americans for days, scoring a lucky hit on a Ranger mortar position and severely wounding a soldier. The Little Bird helicopters helped suppress the enemy fire, but struck a nearby gas main. The fire, which burned for a week, was visible for seventy miles. But now that the Rangers had seized the dam, they found themselves with a big problem on their hands: none of the Americans knew how to operate the dam, which was old, poorly maintained, had been damaged in the fighting, and needed to be run properly to avoid its collapse from uncontrolled water flow.

A company of the 96th Army Civil Affairs Battalion had been attached to the Rangers and was back at H-1, but it had no expertise in operating and running dams. The closest thing the civil affairs unit had to an expert was Sergeant First Class Kevin Camp, who had been an engineer in the Special Forces for twelve years, but whose only experience consisted of three months working on a dam in Virginia after high school. His limitation acknowledged, Camp was instructed to fly to the site, take photos of the huge, Soviet-made dam, and return to H-1 so his superiors could figure out what to do.

Camp's flight was delayed for two days by enemy mortar and artillery fire, and when he arrived on an MH-47 Chinook the situation at the Haditha Dam was not looking good. A critical transformer had been hit by Iraqi fire and power to the dam was shut down. When power was restored, only one of the five turbines was working and its shaft was so warped that it shook the entire structure. The seals in the dam leaked and unless the pumps worked the water level inside the dam would rise. As Camp was surveying the dam with another soldier it seemed to shudder. The soldier began to make a break for it, fearing the massive structure would give way. Camp calmly informed him that if the dam was on the verge of collapse it was already too late to get away; Camp kept working. The Americans would have to rely on those who knew the dam best: the Iraqis.

The Iraqi workers, who had been detained inside the dam, were also afraid that the dam might give way and were desperate to leave. After persuading the Iraqi manager that the U.S. troops did not intend to destroy the dam and denying the Iraqi request to evacuate, Camp and the Iraqis worked hard to keep the dam working. The Army Corps of Engineers later sent in a team, which arranged a video conference with experts in the United States to get their ideas on how to fix it. Brigadier General Vincent Brooks, the CENTCOM spokesman, praised the seizing, saying that destruction of the dam by the Iraqis would have led to a devastating flood. But the Iraqis had had no intention of so doing and the U.S. military had initially been ill equipped to maintain it. Saving the dam had been a closer call than many realized; the battle over it had put American lives in danger. U.S. forces had essentially saved the dam from themselves.[5]

During the first weeks of the Iraq campaign, much of the war in the west was carried out beyond public view. For all their efforts, however, the 5th Special Forces Group, and the Australian and British commandos who attacked from Jordan, found no Scuds. The National Intelligence Estimate that was provided to Congress in October 2002 reported that Saddam had up to several dozen Scud missiles with ranges of 400 to 550 miles. The threat that Saddam might fire Scuds with WMD warheads at Israel had been one of the Pentagon's biggest worries and extensive training had been carried out at Nellis Air Force Base on operations to hunt the weapons. But in the years since the Gulf War, U.S. reconnaissance had not snapped a single picture of a Scud. The estimate was based on the CIA's insistence that there was a gap in accounting between the number of Scuds the Iraqis were thought to have acquired before the Gulf War and the number that they expended and destroyed. The mission of the 5th Special Forces Group was a sensible precaution but also another case in which the prewar intelligence was way off base.

Yet some operations received more publicity than the allies would have liked. The British inserted two teams in the west: a Special Air Squadron unit and Task Force 7, which was made up of commandos from the Special Boat Service, the British equivalent of U.S. Navy SEALs. Task Force 7 had not conducted desert operations prior to the mission, a fact that irritated some in the British Special Air Service who had pioneered many desert tactics and developed them with their American counterparts in Delta years earlier. The day after Task Force 7 ventured into the northern part of the Sunni Triangle, it ran across a small group of Bedouins and decided to talk to them over tea. A much larger group of Bedouins, meanwhile, sneaked up on the British forces and opened fire. In the confusion, the British commandos fled, abandoning their combat vehicles and their sensitive equipment, including radios programmed with the Delta Force frequencies. The British commandos were eventually able to reorganize themselves and call in helicopters to whisk them to safety, but the episode proved to be an embarrassment, especially when Al-Jazeera showed Iraqi tribesmen driving some of their vehicles.[6]

Later Delta would have its own encounter with the Bedouins. While the Delta squadron was planning its next night's mission, a sentry noticed a large group of the tribesmen approaching. Ataya went out to talk to them. The Bedouins wanted to know who the mysterious visitors were and why they were there. Concocting a cover story was not easy. Two of the squadron's Pinzgauers were clearly visible. Following instructions from Bill C., Ataya told the Bedouins that the force was in Iraq to help their people get out of the embassy. "So you are Russian," the Bedouins said, aware that the Russians had one of the few still functioning embassies in Baghdad. Before leaving, the Bedouins gave Ataya advice on the safest route to the capital and wished him luck.

Blaber had accomplished one of his principal missions. He had created a commotion in the west and put his Delta squadron in a position to continue their raids along Highway 1, north of Tikrit, in the days ahead. The recently arrived armored unit dubbed Team Tank would have its day. While the Rangers fought for the dam, the Delta team drove across the Rawa River bridge toward Tikrit. McKiernan had instructed the Army and Marines not to display American flags to avoid creating the perception that the U.S. forces were occupiers, but Delta Force had a compelling reason to be an exception, flying large American flags on their vehicles. There were times when it was safer for the squadron to hide its identity and times when it was safer to advertise it: flags were to be unfurled when the Delta commanders knew that allied warplanes were within fifty miles of their location. The commandos had learned from painful experience in the mountains of Afghanistan that it was important to take every possible measure to reduce the risk that they would be mistaken by allied pilots for an enemy column as they navigated far behind enemy lines.

While the Delta Force was operating in western Iraq, six MC-130 Combat Talon aircraft had headed south across the Mediterranean. U.S. forces had encountered no problems in entering western Iraq from Jordan and Saudi Arabia, but Turkey was altogether another matter. After months of negotiation and promises of billions of dollars in aid, the failure of the Turkish government to authorize an American attack from its territory was a disappointment. The setback had not only prevented Ray Odierno's 4th Infantry Division from opening a northern front but, less visibly, had thrown a monkey wrench into CENTCOM's fallback plan to secure northern Iraq with Special Forces.[7]

Under the terms of the Turkish decision, the U.S. could not carry out air attacks from bases in Turkey or search-and-rescue missions on Turkish soil; initially, it could not even fly over Turkish territory. U.S. diplomats worked feverishly to secure overflight rights, the bare minimum needed to operate effectively in the north, and a day after the setback in parliament the Turks finally granted the rights, greatly easing the deployment of some of Cleveland's Special Forces and making it possible for U.S. aircraft carriers in the Mediterranean and B-52s in Britain to carry out bombing strikes in northern Iraq.

Still, as the war approached, the bulk of Cleveland's 10th Special Forces Group was still at Constanza, Romania, with no direct air route to Iraq. In an extraordinary move, the 352nd Special Operations Wing resorted to a circuitous and high-risk air route. On March 22, the MC-130s began transporting the 2nd and 3rd battalions of Cleveland's troops, sometimes at an altitude below 500 feet, over the Sinai Peninsula, Saudi Arabia, and Jordan, skirting the Syrian border just inside Iraqi airspace to reach Bashur and Sulaymaniyah in the Kurdish zone of northern Iraq. The route was fittingly dubbed Ugly Baby. The first flight of MC-130s came under Iraqi antiaircraft fire and took a few hits. One plane was so badly damaged it was forced to make an emergency landing at a U.S. Air Force base in Incirlik, Turkey. The Turkish politicians may have kept their distance from the American-led operation, but Turkey was not about to close their airspace to a U.S. military aircraft in distress.[8]

Nonetheless, the Bush administration's inability to win over the Turks meant that the U.S. force in the north was necessarily small and not well protected by U.S. airpower. The only way to support the U.S. soldiers and their Kurdish allies was with air strikes by warplanes dispatched north from bases in the Arabian Peninsula. The commandos in the west were fighting under a virtual umbrella of allied warplanes; the Special Forces in Kurdistan could call in air strikes, but the response time was as long as ninety minutes, an interminable wait for lightly armed commandos dependent on airpower. But Cleveland was operating with one important advantage. Unlike the U.S. forces in the west, he had allies who had defended a quasi-independent enclave in northeastern Iraq under the protection of allied airpower since shortly after the 1991 Gulf War. His big disadvantage was that these same allies could pose a major problem.

The Special Forces mission in the north was as much political as military, far more complex than the shoot-'em-up unfolding in western Iraq. Kurdistan was controlled by two Kurdish factions: Masoud Barzani's Kurdistan Democratic Party and Jalal Talabani's Patriotic Union of Kurdistan. Barzani's sector, with its base in Irbil, was along the mountainous border with Turkey. Talabani's was to the southeast and was anchored in Sulaymaniyah. Although longtime rivals, Barzani and Talabani cooperated in a shaky alliance against their common enemy, the Baathist regime in Baghdad. Each controlled Peshmerga fighters. Lightly armed but respected warriors, there were some 60,000 in all.[9]

Saddam took the Kurds seriously and stationed twelve divisions, some 150,000 troops, in the north, backed up by Iraq's ever-present irregulars, the Fedayeen. The Iraqi divisions were lined up along the 100-mile demarcation line known as the Green Line, between the area controlled by Saddam Hussein and that controlled by the Kurds. The Iraqi area south of the Green Line included Mosul, Iraq's third largest city, and Kirkuk, with its 300 oilfields, second in size only to the Rumaylah fields along the Kuwait border. Much of the region was populated by Kurds and minority Turkomans, but Saddam in an ethnic cleansing program had expelled many Kurdish and Turkoman communities and replaced them with loyal Baathist Sunni Arabs. The western half of Mosul, divided by the Tigris River, was turned into a Baathist stronghold.

For most of the previous decade, the Turks, Iraqis, and Kurds understood the unspoken ground rules. The status quo was largely maintained along the Green Line, and each side stayed in its own backyard. Cleveland's job would be not only to pin down the Iraqi divisions along the Green Line, but prevent the delicate Iraqi-Turkish-Kurdish balance from being upset while Saddam's regime was being removed. The American presence in the north, small as it was, was intended to boost the Kurds' morale and help convince them of the president's commitment to defeat Saddam's regime.

But the Bush administration also sought to keep the Kurds in line. Washington did not want the Peshmerga to become too aggressive for fear of provoking the Turks, who were determined to prevent the Kurds from declaring an independent state, a move Ankara feared would inspire the Kurds in Turkey to secede. A Kurdish drive to seize the Kirkuk oilfields was a casus belli for the Turks. The last thing CENTCOM needed was a war within a war. Cleveland's job was to take on the Iraqis and to sit on the Kurds. He embedded his SOF troops with the Peshmerga to reinforce this message and provide essential support—command and control, intelligence, and the ability to call in air strikes—for the Kurdish fighters.

When Lieutenant Colonel Robert Waltemeyer, a Special Forces officer who commanded a base in Barzani's territory, encountered the Kurds he discovered they had plans to head south. So when he met Barzani he used the opportunity to lay down the law. Barzani asked him what message President Bush had for him. Waltemeyer told the Kurdish leader that the White House wanted the Kurds to protect key urban areas but to avoid any action that would give the Turks a pretext to intervene. The Peshmerga should not move south of the Green Line without American approval. There would be no unilateral entry into Mosul or Kirkuk and no human rights violations. "I made that message up on the fly," Waltemeyer later confessed.[10]

While Cleveland focused on the war-fighting, the delicate task of implementing American policy was overseen by two-star Marine General

Pete Osman, who infiltrated northern Iraq from Turkey and served as the head of something called the Military Coordination and Liaison Command. The command was a fiction, as Osman commanded nothing more than the five members of his immediate staff. Osman's role was to roam among the various Kurdish factions, keeping peace among them, restraining them from upsetting the territorial status quo, and reporting on their activities to U.S. officials in Turkey.[11]

When it was clear that Turkey was not going to allow the 4th Infantry Division on its territory, General James Jones, the NATO commander and head of the United States European Command, had proposed sending the Italy-based 173rd Airborne and the newly arrived 26th Marine Expeditionary Unit afloat in the Mediterranean as a stopgap measure. McKiernan also wanted the 173rd Brigade and decided that it would be placed under the control of Cleveland, who would be the senior military commander in the north. That meant that an airborne brigade colonel would be under the command of a Special Forces colonel. Some of McKiernan's fellow Army generals in Washington were aghast at the notion and warned McKiernan against it. But McKiernan stuck to his decision, figuring the two colonels would work everything out on the ground. The 173rd, like Team Tank, would be commanded by the SOF.[12]

On March 26, 1,000 soldiers of the 173rd took off in C-17s from Aviano, Italy, and parachuted onto an airstrip at Bashur in the Kurdish zone. This was not Normandy. The landing zone was protected by Kurdish militiamen, CIA operatives, and Special Forces soldiers. Still, it went down in the books as a combat jump. Some of the 173rd soldiers missed the drop zone by eight miles. But four days later, 2,160 soldiers and 381 pieces of equipment were on the ground at Bashur. The paradrop was later followed by air-landed reinforcements, including a modest number of tanks, armored personnel carriers, and artillery.[13]

The unit had little mobility, but its presence signaled to the Iraqis that the United States had indeed opened its northern front and the Kurds were its ally. Osman, for his part, made an elaborate public show of the arrival of the 173rd. Three days before the jump, he had held a press conference to announce that American paratroopers were about to enter the war, conveniently ignoring the small size of the contingent. Like Blaber, Osman wanted the Iraqis to think the force was more formidable than it was. "It led one to believe that something really big was going to generate from the north," Osman recalled.[14]

Before Cleveland could move against the Iraqi forces along the Green Line he had to secure his rear area and deal with Ansar al-Islam. An independent affiliate of Al Qaeda, it and a smaller Iranian-backed group, the Islamic Group of Kurdistan, which was positioned along the Iranian-Iraqi border, posed a threat to the back of Talabani's Peshmerga. Destroying both groups would not only eliminate them as a threat, but also test the ability of the Americans and Kurds to fight together. In U.S. military circles Ansar al-Islam was known simply as AI. Cleveland gave the mission, code-named Viking Hammer, to Lieutenant Colonel Kenneth Tovo's Special Forces 3rd Battalion. Tovo attached one of his companies to a 6,500-strong Kurdish contingent, commanded by Nasrudin Mustafa. Talabani's Peshmerga were eager to wreak revenge on AI, which had assassinated Shawkat Haji Mushir, one of the founding fathers of the Patriotic Union of Kurdistan.

The operation was preceded by cruise missile attacks on both renegade groups. On the morning of March 26, Mustafa attacked a mountain redoubt along six different routes. U.S. air strikes and deadly AC-130 gunships supported the Kurdish assault. Four days later the battle in the mountains was over. AI was defeated, though some of its fighters managed to flee across the border into Iran where they regrouped and plotted to return to Iraq. The intensified air campaign, the simultaneous American paratroop operation, and the Peshmerga attack had a profound effect on the Iraqis, who began abandoning their positions east of Kirkuk, falling back into defensive lines on its outskirts and, in many cases, deserting their positions. The battle cemented mutual confidence between the Kurds and their American allies, who were now free to turn their attention to the Green Line.[15]

Osman, meanwhile, sought to orchestrate the Iraqis' capitulation. Virtually all of the Iraqi forces on the Green Line were conscripted Regular Army troops, and Osman did not relish visiting war on a group of ill-motivated troops. Using Kurdish contacts as intermediaries, he told the Iraqi commanders to surrender or face destruction. But the Iraqi forces were so infested with Saddam loyalists that their commanders were afraid to act. Small skirmishes occurred along the Green Line while SOF and Peshmerga patrols, working out of forward operating bases, found gaps between Iraqi units and infiltrated their front lines. A clash at Sifini early in April illustrated the Peshmerga's ability to move behind the Iraqi lines. The Iraqi positions were softened up by F-14s and F/A-18s and then successfully attacked by Kurds accompanied by a Special Forces team. In clearing the town, the Americans noticed that some houses were locked and some were not. The Peshmerga passed by the unlocked ones but broke into those that were locked. Asked by Special Forces soldiers the distinction, the Peshmerga explained that Kurdish residents had been alerted to the attack in advance and told to leave their doors open. Locked doors meant the houses were occupied by Iraqi Arabs.[16]

Pummeled by air strikes and pressed by the Peshmerga, the Iraqi army in the north frayed quickly, as the Army and Marines in the south advanced toward Baghdad. Demoralized Iraqis continued to desert in droves despite the presence of Saddam's security services and the Fedayeen's best efforts to round them up and return them to the front. But some Iraqi units still had some fight left. The Iraqi 1st Mechanized Division decided to make a stand at the Tebecka Crossroads, located on the main road connecting Mosul, Irbil, and Kirkuk. The key to the crossroads was Zurkah Ziraw Dagh, a long ridge three miles to the northeast, which the Americans simply called Dog Ridge. The local Kurdish commander told his Special Forces counterpart, Major Eric Howard, that he was going to attack the ridge with four simultaneous assaults and would rely on the Americans to provide the necessary air strikes.

The attack got under way on the morning of April 6, but quickly ran into resistance. For once, the air strikes were ineffective. Howard called in B-52s and F/A-18s while the Kurds fell back, regrouped, and prepared for another assault. When the Kurds attacked again, accompanied by a Special Forces team, they managed to take the crossroads. But the Iraqis counterattacked with tanks and BMPs and forced the Kurds and the Special Forces back to some nearby ridges. Outnumbered and outgunned, they tried to fight off the Iraqis with a fusillade of Javelin antitank missiles and machine gun fire. Trying to speed up the air strikes, the Special Forces air controller with the Peshmerga radioed two Navy F-14s. The enemy, he said, was at a crossroads in front of his position. There was no time to follow the standard target identification procedures. Cleared to attack, an F-14 unleashed a 2,000-pound bomb, aiming it at a cluster of fighters. Howard was hurt and more than a dozen Peshmerga killed or wounded in the blast, including a close relative of Masoud Barzani. The Navy pilot had misidentified a group of Special Forces and Peshmerga, who had retreated to Dog Ridge, as the Iraqis.

The Iraqis continued to attack and the Kurds and Special Forces team were again forced to fall back to another ridge. Repeated air attacks on the Iraqis began to take a toll and their counterattack stalled. After re-grouping, the Iraqis made a third attempt to dislodge the Kurds, but the combined air and ground fire proved too much for them. The Iraqis called off the attack as darkness fell. The following day the Peshmerga moved closer to the crossroads, but the battle ended in a stalemate until it was settled by the general disintegration of the Iraqi northern army.[17]

For all the complications, the northern front—an "economy of force" operation, in military parlance—was surprisingly successful. After concluding that the 4th Infantry Division would not be part of a northern attack and influenced by CENTCOM's deception campaign, the Iraqis shifted their two Republican Guard divisions, their premier units, from north to south. The Adnan Division moved near Tikrit, the site of an 82nd Airborne assault, according to CENTCOM's deception campaign. In interrogations conducted after the war, U.S. officers learned that the Nebuchadnezzar Division had moved south of Baghdad between March 19 and March 24 in civilian vehicles, abandoning much of their logistics and artillery to avoid detection by U.S. reconnaissance—a fact that CENTCOM missed and the V Corps did not discover until March 27, when it began to capture Nebuchadnezzar officers near Hindiyah and Kifl. Nevertheless, a modest contingent of Special Forces and airborne infantry, together with Kurdish allies, had succeeded in pinning down the bulk of the Iraqi forces. The political mission had also been fulfilled: the Peshmerga had been kept in check.

As Osman and other officers concluded after the war, the Turkish refusal to admit Odierno's division also had a silver lining. In their efforts to win over the Turks, the Bush administration had offered the Turks billions. An October meeting chaired by Condoleezza Rice had settled on a package of $3 billion in aid, $3 billion in financing, and a promise to make a concentrated effort to persuade Persian Gulf states to provide $1 billion in free oil and to help Turkish companies secure reconstruction contracts in Iraq and Afghanistan. It was a far cry from the $25 billion in outright grants the Turks had once demanded from Colin Powell in an 11 p.m. meeting at the home of the secretary of state, but it was still a considerable offer. As a result of Turkey's rejection of the northern front, the United States would save money. It would also avoid introducing another wild card into the politics of northern Iraq. During the secret negotiations, the United States had discussed a deal that would have allowed the Turks to send a 20,000-strong combat force in on the Iraq side of the Iraq-Turkey border, ostensibly to stem a potential tide of refugees. After the negotiations between Turkey and Washington collapsed, the Turks continued to press for money and to send troops, but the Bush administration held firm. The Turks were forced to keep their army on their side of the border.[18]

Tension between the Americans and the Turks persisted. Two cruise missiles the Navy had lobbed from the Mediterranean fell short, landing in Turkey. The weapons caused no damage, but the episode led the Navy to stop firing the missiles over Turkish territory and to move all its cruise missile vessels in the Mediterranean to the Red Sea. After several more missiles inadvertently landed in Saudi territory, the Navy limited its firing of cruise missiles to ships in the Persian Gulf and Arabian Sea.[19] For their part, the Turks stirred things up by sending agents to infiltrate northern Iraq. Franks was hardly amused. The CENTCOM commander was vocal in his criticism of Ankara and believed the Turks were doing everything they could to be uncooperative. Franks's enmity, if not his words, became known to the Turks, further exacerbating Turkish-American relations. General James Jones, NATO commander and head of the United States European Command—who was responsible for military relations with Turkey—was upset by the turn of events. He went to Ankara several times to salvage something from the strained relationship, setting up a small liaison headquarters in Ankara under Lieutenant General Colby Broadwater, who served as his conduit to the Turkish General Staff. "I was willing to be the good cop in this thing, since he'd obviously selected his role as the bad cop," Jones said of Franks.[20]

CHAPTER 18

The Red Zone

After monitoring American moves in the south, Lieutenant General Raad Majid al-Hamdani thought he had sized up the enemy. As the commander of the II Republican Guard Corps and the Iraqi officer responsible for the southern zone defenses, Hamdani had prepared a situation report on March 23, concluding that Buff Blount's 3rd Infantry Division was aiming for the Karbala Gap. At an April 2 war council in Baghdad, Hamdani pressed the point, according to the classified analysis of interrogation prepared for the U.S. Joint Forces Command. Standing before a map, Hamdani identified the Karbala Gap as the bottleneck that the U.S. Army had to pass through to get to the capital. There was a secondary attack along the Tigris that would be coming at Baghdad from the east.

To block the Americans' main advance, Hamdani asked for command of the Hammurabi and Al Nida Republican Guard divisions, and for permission to blow up the al-Kaed bridge at the 3rd Infantry Division's projected crossing point over the Euphrates. The fate of the Iraqi capital, he said, stood in the balance. Lieutenant General Hashim Ahmad, the Iraqi defense minister, was not persuaded. Hamdani, he confidently declared, was overreacting to the American units in the south. "The last two weeks were a strategic trick by the Americans," he declared. The main American attack would come from the west.

Saddam had given his son Qusay authority over the Republican Guard, and it was Qusay who settled the argument. The plan for the defense of the capital, he explained, had already been decided and Hamdani's role was not to challenge it but to carry it out. The Hammurabi Division would defend along the Fallujah–Ramadi highway west of the capital, and the Al Nida Division would move from the eastern side of the capital to Abu Ghraib, just southwest of the city. Saddam was convinced the main U.S. attack would come from the west, and Qusay, the defense minister, and the Republican Guard chief of staff had backed him up.

Hamdani was given little more than a sop. Instead of two Republican Guard divisions he received a company of Iraqi Special Operations Forces. Hamdani was also given permission to destroy the al-Kaed bridge. Bridges were among the most strategically important assets in Iraq. Saddam's regime needed them to rush forces south to quash any Shiite efforts to organize a rebellion and to reinforce his defenses in the south. The regime was loath to blow up the spans unless absolutely necessary. Bridges were not to be sabotaged without an explicit order from Saddam and any officer who ignored that directive was subject to execution, according to interrogations of Iraqi officers after the fall of Baghdad.

As he left the meeting, Hamdani tried to make the best of the situation. He ordered his demolition commander to take out the al-Kaed bridge when it was clear the Americans were moving to seize it. He sent a Special Forces regiment with artillery and antitank weapons to Aziziyah to obstruct the Marine attack from that direction. But these were small steps, and the hour was late.[1]

A combination of inadvertent moves, the CENTCOM deception plan, and deliberate ploys had left Saddam and his most senior aides confused about the U.S. strategy. Saddam and his inner circle were conditioned by their experience in fighting the United States during the Gulf War and believed that Washington was practiced in the art of deception.

Military plans marked secret and slipped to the Iraqis as part of Franks's deception scheme had further confused the Iraqis. They indicated that the 1st Cavalry and 1st Armored divisions were to be part of the fight and those divisions had not arrived. To the Iraqis the apparently mysterious movements of the 4th Infantry Division seemed to be another surprise in the making. The Iraqis were well aware that it had the most modern equipment in the U.S. Army, and assumed that the main attack could not begin without it. At the same time, the Delta Force and Ranger attacks in the west had fortified the impression in Baghdad that the main U.S. attack would be coming from Jordan.

Beyond that, the fighting at the Euphrates River towns had strengthened the impression in Baghdad that U.S. forces had been determined to cross the river and had been repelled. Terry Ferrell's 3-7 Cavalry Squadron had tangled with the Fedayeen at Samawah only to withdraw. After fierce battles at Kifl and Objective Floyd, no V Corps troops had crossed the

Euphrates and advanced too far north. That was all part of the plan to isolate Najaf, but the Iraqis read it as a retreat. The Apaches from the 11th Attack Helicopter Regiment had faced a wall of lead and one of its helicopters had been shot down. Then, Blount's troops, mounting a feint at Hindiyah, had attacked the bridge but stopped short of securing the eastern bank of the river. One of the principal Iraqi worries continued to be an airborne assault, but so far no such attack had taken place. Muhammad Said al-Sahaf, Iraq's information minister, "Baghdad Bob," was roundly ridiculed in the West for his assurances that the American attack had faltered short of Baghdad, but the Iraqis treated the Euphrates as a major defensive perimeter and had ample reason to believe they had defended much of it successfully. To many Iraqi commanders, the operational pause on the approach to Baghdad that McKiernan had ordered seemed to be the end of the ground war in the south.

The one part of the plan that the Iraqis got right had to do with the north. The Iraqis understood that there would be no major offensive from Kurdistan, given Turkey's decision to bar Odierno's 4th ID. The commander of the 1st Republican Guard Corps, which had responsibility for the northern part of the country, correctly concluded that the U.S. SOF operations were not part of a push south. Two Republican Guard divisions that were normally near the Green Line, the Adnan and the Nebuchadnezzar, had been moved south. Working on these assumptions, Saddam and his inner circle had ignored the assessment of Hamdani, the Iraqi military's most talented commander. Republican Guard units were being moved around as though they were chess pieces—and all going in the wrong direction.

There was one fact Hamdani and Blount agreed on: the al-Kaed bridge was critical and crossing it would put the Americans within striking distance of Baghdad. Blount viewed the attack north as one continuous operation. The 3rd Infantry Division would drive through the Karbala Gap, an agricultural area squeezed between Milh Lake and the city of Karbala, which at one point was as narrow as 2,000 yards. To move through it, the forces needed to use several small roads that crossed an irrigation canal. Keeping up the attack, it would then maneuver through an old Iraqi military training area, seize the al-Kaed bridge, continue northeast to take the Baghdad airport, and grab the key crossroads at the intersection of Highways 1 and 8. With one big push, Blount would have outflanked the Medina Division, which was guarding the southern approaches to Baghdad, seized the airport, and be poised to take the fight to the capital itself.

While Blount's plan reflected his offensive style of warfare it went beyond what had been decided by V Corps. Wallace had not yet determined whether Blount's division or Petraeus's 101st Airborne would take the airport. But the first step was to secure the bridge. The Army's previous fights along the Euphrates had either been feints to fool the Iraqis about the main direction of the attack or temporary crossings to stanch the flow of Saddam Fedayeen fighters headed south. This was different: to take the fight to Baghdad the entire division had to cross the river and keep rolling north.

With the lifting of the pause on the evening of April 1, Blount's forces would begin to move forward. The 3rd Infantry Division commander had been anxious to head north. Sitting in place had created some vulnerabilities. On March 29, soldiers from Scott Rutter's 2-7 Infantry Battalion had stopped a taxi at a checkpoint. When the driver opened the trunk so it could be inspected, the vehicle exploded, killing four of Rutter's soldiers as well as the driver and charring a passenger bus on the other side of the highway. It was one of the first unambiguous cases in which the U.S. forces had been attacked by a suicide car bomb—and a harbinger of some of the guerrilla tactics to come.

Grimsley's 1st BCT would lead the division through the Karbala Gap and had the job of seizing the bridge. To keep the Iraqis off balance, Grimsley ordered Rutter's battalion to conduct a feint at the Euphrates River town of Musayif, southeast of the bridge. Rock Marcone's 3-69 Armored Battalion would secure the span. Grimsley planned to oversee the bridge fight from his assault command post on the near shore. If the Iraqis were ever going to use their stocks of poison gas this would be their last opportunity before the Americans got into heavily populated areas. The crossing point itself was given an anodyne code name. As the 3rd Infantry Division was based in Georgia, the river crossing was called Objective Peach.

Marcone commanded more than 1,100 soldiers, including two tank companies, two infantry companies, engineers, and smoke and chemical reconnaissance platoons, all of whom were backed up by artillery and Apache attack helicopters. For all of the confusion, the fight at Kifl had been an important learning experience. Combat engineers had discovered that their enemy used a modern German-made demolition system and appeared to have designed their bridges so they could be quickly destroyed.

Meeting with his battalion staff, Marcone hashed out a plan. Based on the discovery of the German firing mechanism at Kifl, the battalion estimated where the Iraqi demolition teams would set up. Those areas would be pounded by artillery and by JDAM satellite-guided bombs. Then combat engineers would make their way across the Euphrates and cut any demolition cables they could find on the far side. To cross the river, Marcone arranged to borrow several inflatable RB-15 boats and motorboat engines from the 299th Multi-Role Bridge Company. Rock Marcone's 3-69 Armor Battalion would secure the near bank. When the bridge was pronounced safe by the engineers, the battalion would roll across.

The terrain on the other side included a sprawling compound that U.S. intelligence had listed as a suspected WMD site. After the toppling of Saddam, the Iraqi Ministry of Science and Technology reported that 350 tons of high explosives—powerful enough to initiate a nuclear weapon and material the U.S. government was eager to keep out of the hands of terrorists—was later looted from the site. But on the push to Baghdad neither the 3rd Infantry Division nor any other V Corps unit knew what was located there or had orders to secure it. The division was worried about being targeted by WMD, not about securing them. The only explosives the soldiers worried about were the ones they assumed the Iraqis had affixed to the Objective Peach bridge.

As the battalion advanced, it left behind the familiar desert terrain for the palm trees, rice paddies, and canals of the Euphrates region. To Marcone, it looked like Vietnam. None of the maps he had studied had prepared him for what he found. Soon the battalion's scouts came under fire and had to call on help from M1 tanks, Bradleys, and Apaches to break contact. The skirmish prompted Marcone to move a tank company to the head of the formation. Though Marcone had a lot of firepower at his disposal, there was one deficiency. The Army was adept at using its Q36 counterbattery radars to locate the source of enemy fire so that it could respond in kind, but the battalion's counterbattery radar was broken and the division's Q37 radar, which was supposed to be in position, had yet to arrive. The forward elements of the battalion arrived at the near end of the bridge at 3:00 p.m.[2]

. . .

Dan Hibner, the commander of A Company, 11th Engineer Battalion, got to the near bank shortly after it was secured. Marcone's battalion had moved fast, but as Hibner peered through his binoculars he was worried it might not have moved quickly enough. The bridge, in fact, consisted of two spans, and the northern one appeared to have been recently blown up. Having received last-minute authority to destroy the al-Kaed bridge, Hamdani had issued written and verbal orders to the demolition commander, Major Rawkan al-Ajeeley, to blow it as U.S. forces approached, but the job had been only partially accomplished.

The southern span, a three-lane-wide structure, was still intact, but for how long? As Hibner wondered whether the southern span was about to vanish in a cloud of smoke, the engineers jumped out of their trucks and lugged the first of the inflatable boats 300 yards to the riverbank. The boat's motor had yet to be carried forward but Hibner was worried that there was no more time to wait. He ordered a team of sappers and infantrymen to climb into the boat and paddle over to the far side, while Marcone's troops provided covering fire and a smoke platoon tried to generate enough of a haze to obscure the vulnerable craft. The U.S. military had the world's most advanced military technology but this operation depended entirely on the ability of soldiers to paddle their way across the Euphrates in an inflatable boat. Forty-five minutes after Marcone's troops had secured the near side, the first boat was in the water.

As the sappers tried to make their way across the Euphrates the boat began to drift. The current was swift and the boat was weighed down by troops with body armor, equipment, and ammunition. No matter how hard the soldiers paddled, the boat continued to flow downstream, moving away from the span and toward a two-story building 200 yards south of the bridge from which the Iraqis were unleashing bursts of machine gun fire. First Lieutenant Kevin Caesar, an infantry platoon leader in the boat, felt it was beginning to sink. In all the confusion, his platoon sergeant had fallen out and was hanging on to the back of the boat. Adding to the danger, the cloud of smoke seemed to dissipate. Caesar had expected about fifty minutes of cover, but it seemed to him like there was only about ten minutes' worth. The engineers were moving away from their objective, into clear view and headed for disaster.

Surveying the fight from the near bank, Hibner ordered his troops to cease fire so as to pinpoint where the enemy fire was coming from. For nearly a minute there was an eerie stillness until a burst of machine gun fire erupted from the northern part of the building. Marcone's battalion on the near bank and the engineers poured fire fiercely, hoping to silence the enemy as the boat drifted closer and closer to the building.

Meanwhile, Hibner rushed to get more of his engineers to the far shore. A second boat set off, this time with a motor. But no sooner did the boat push out into the river than the motor sputtered and stopped running. In the rush north, sand had crept into the engine. The second boat also began to drift south. Even the sappers seemed struck by the absurdity of the situation. "We're all saying, 'Oh, we're going to float down here; we're dead.' Things like that," recalled Sergeant Jay Bliss. "It was to kind of ease the situation and take your mind off it."

Hibner jumped into a third boat that was not sinking and was equipped with a motor that worked. By the time he arrived on the far side, the sappers from the first two boats had landed, trudged several hundred yards north to their objective, and begun to cut the detonation wires. Sergeant Robert Stevens, a sapper with Alpha Company, had the toughest task. Venturing into ten feet of water to cut a final wire, he disappeared beneath the surface and nearly drowned only to be pulled out by an embedded reporter.

After securing the span, the infantry began clearing out the nearby bunkers and launched a Javelin antitank missile into the two-story building, demolishing the structure. Afterward, Caesar saw two Iraqis gingerly approach the Americans with a wheelbarrow. One Iraqi was lying in the wheelbarrow with his guts hanging out; the other was missing part of his ear. The soldiers turned them over to the medics and continued to clear the far bank.[3]

Hibner reported that the southern span was trafficable, but there was a large hole in the northern span. At 4:35 p.m. Hibner could hear Marcone's armor coming across. It was not clear if the battalion had thwarted the Iraqis from blowing up the bridge or whether the Iraqi demolition teams, who had a tendency to literally get their detonation wires crossed, had simply done a bad job of rigging the explosives. Either way, the soldiers had secured the bridge.

The Iraqis, however, had not given up the fight. As Marcone's battalion began to move forward, Iraqi artillery fired several massive volleys, sending as many as 200 shells flying at the M1 tanks and Bradleys as they waited to cross on the near side, scarring many of the vehicles. Grimsely's assault command post was among the vehicles that came under fire. Fortunately, as they moved forward the Iraqi gunners failed to adjust their fire. After reaching the far side, Marcone's battalion began to expand its bridgehead, destroying the Iraqi II Corps Reconnaissance Battalion and Iraqi infantry that were assigned to defend the span.

The 3rd ID attack had unfolded at the al-Kaed bridge, as Hamdani had anticipated. But he had far fewer forces than he wished at his command, and just about any forces that were on the move seemed to be hit by U.S. warplanes. Still, he struggled to put together a counterattack. At 9:00 p.m. Marcone received a report based on signals intelligence that a Special Republican Guard commando brigade would attack from the Baghdad airport to retake the bridge. Marcone's battalion did not receive any intelligence about an Iraqi armored attack, but after 3:00 a.m. it heard the rumble of the Iraqi T-72s and M113s. Hamdani had also ordered the 10th Brigade of the Medina Division and the 22nd Brigade of the Nebuchadnezzar Division into the fray.

The much vaunted theory of military transformation held that near-perfect intelligence about the disposition of enemy forces on the battlefield, as well as the ability to communicate that data nearly instantaneously, had changed the nature of warfare, stripping away the fog of war and enabling a relatively small number of U.S. troops to score decisive victories. But on the battlefield in Iraq the theory was not up to the challenge. Data about the location and strength of the Fedayeen was often lacking and even the movement of troops from the Nebuchadnezzar Division south of Baghdad had gone undetected. When U.S. commanders did have up-to-date information about the movement of conventional Iraqi units, they often were not able to transmit it to their lead forces in time. The result was that many U.S. troops got their first clue about enemy resistance when they bumped into their foe.

Now Marcone's armor battalion was involved in a "movement to contact," but it was the Iraqis who were on the move. The Iraqis tried to use artillery, armor, and infantry to break the line in two places. Marcone used tank and infantry companies to block the attack from the north. The Iraqi armor was coming from the east. To stop the Iraqis' T-72s and M113s, Marcone used a two-prong defense. M1s, Bradleys, and mortars and hovering Apaches represented the first. The second involved alternating artillery barrages and air strikes. It took thirty-three seconds for the U.S. artillery rounds to land, as they were fired from guns 7 miles away. Each time the artillery fired, Marcone's air liaison officer would call "shot" and the warplanes would be told to stay clear of the battlefield. As soon as the rounds landed, the planes would resume their attack. By 5:30 a.m. the battle was over.

During the fight, a map was recovered from a Republican Guard commander who had been killed. The map had a large red circle at Kifl and also highlighted the bridge crossing at Musayif, where the 14th Brigade had been defending against Rutter's feint. Despite Hamdani's analysis, the local Iraqi commanders had been confused by the 101st's feint toward Hillah and 2-7's ploy at Musayif. The map showed that the al-Kaed bridge had only been lightly defended.[4]

While Marcone's forces were fighting off the counterattack at the al-Kaed bridge, the division was taking a hit toward the rear. Battery D of the 1-39 Field Artillery Battalion had been shelling the enemy to help Blount's brigade get past Karbala and up toward Baghdad. Worried about attacks by the Fedayeen, the battery had tightened the distance between its twenty-five vehicles and MLRS launchers. The battery was worried that paramilitary fighters might sneak into their position. Intelligence reports indicated that enemy snipers might have night vision gear so the battery turned off its "fireflies," strobe lights the battery used to identify itself to other allied forces. The vehicles were still equipped with thermal panels and special reflective tape as signals and were well behind the front lines.

At 2:47 a.m. on April 3, the battery fired six MLRS rockets at the Iraqi artillery location. Ten minutes later an incoming round struck the hood of a Humvee, blowing up the ammunition stowed inside. Three soldiers were killed and four wounded, including Lieutenant John Fernandez, a platoon leader who lost both feet as a result of the blast. A demolition expert from the division surmised that the Humvee might have been attacked by an RPG. It was a tough blow and came on the heels of a Black Hawk helicopter crash that killed six more of Blount's troops.

The attack turned out to be one link in a series of events. At the start of the war, Patriot antimissile batteries had been rushed forward to defend the troops. The Iraqi air force was not flying but the Iraqi missile batteries, and their presumed chemical or biological warheads, were still a worry. CENTCOM had made elaborate plans to use SOF as well as air strikes to silence the Iraqi missile crews in the west. But the Iraqis were actually firing from a swath of territory in and around the southeastern city of Basra and along a stretch north to Amara. There were no U.S. SOF in the area to hunt the Iraqi missile launchers and it was difficult for aircraft alone to strike them. After the initial Iraqi missile attacks following the F-117 raid at Dora Farms at the beginning of the war, the Iraqis had lobbed Ababil-100s and Al-Samoud missiles at Camp Doha, Udairi, and other military targets in Kuwait. On March 27, an Ababil-100 had been intercepted only two miles from McKiernan's headquarters, where its top officials and hundreds of staff had gathered for a morning command meeting. Analysis after the firing indicated that the missile was dead on target when it was intercepted.

Now the chief concern was that the Iraqis would launch Ababils and Al-Samouds at the Army and Marine forces on the move. On April 1, an Ababil missile had been lobbed toward a logistics area near Najaf and was shot down by a Patriot PAC-3 battery. On April 2, Patriot batteries defending the Karbala Gap identified what they thought was an incoming Iraqi missile. Blasted out of the sky, it turned out to be a U.S. Navy F/A-18. It was the second deadly episode of friendly fire for the Patriots. The downing of a Tornado nine days earlier by a Patriot battery that mistook the plane for an antiradiation missile fired from an Iraqi jet had killed the two-man British crew. That mistake was the more surprising as the Iraqi air force had not conducted a single flight and it was far from clear that the Iraqis had any antiradiation missiles in their inventory. In that case, there had been a series of snafus. The Tornado's electronic identifying system that marked it as a friendly aircraft was not working, and the Patriot battery was not able to communicate electronically or by radio with other Patriot units to check its reading. But the F/A-18 had been misidentified by two Patriot batteries, and the mystery of the shoot-down was never solved.

The Patriot had been effective against the Iraqi missiles. All nine Iraqi missiles that were close enough to be engaged by the Patriot batteries were successfully shot down. (The Patriots could do nothing against the Seersucker cruise missiles like the one that landed near Camp Commando and another that later hit a mall in Kuwait City.) But friendly fire remained a worry. Allied planes were the only ones in the air, but as U.S. forces closed in on Baghdad, two allied aircraft had been shot down and three pilots lost, all by the Patriots. (The Patriot had been at risk from friendly fire as well. On March 26, an F-16 blasted a Patriot radar after its pilot feared his plane was being tracked by an Iraqi surface-to-air missile. Miraculously, no one was hurt in that episode.)

With the downing of the F/A-18, the air war commanders ordered a pair of F-15Es from the Al Udeid Air Base to search for the wreckage of the plane and any evidence that the pilot might have survived. No word was passed that the shoot-down had already been identified as the probable result of friendly fire. Seeing flashes on the ground, an F-15E crew concluded that it was being targeted by the same Iraqi SAM battery that had downed the F/A-18. The F-15 sought and failed to establish contact with V Corps, which coordinated strikes behind the front Army positions. So it contacted an AWACS, which cleared the attack on the suspected SAM position after checking with an officer at Moseley's command in Riyadh. Within five minutes, the F-15 had targeted Battery D with a GBU-12 bomb.

One instance of friendly fire had begotten another. Investigators never solved the riddle of why the Patriot misidentified the F/A-18 as an incoming missile, a disconcerting fact for future operations. But they identified a number of factors that led to the mistaken attack on the artillery unit, including the decision not to let the aircrews know immediately that the downing of the F/A-18 was suspected as a case of "blue on blue"—an act of friendly fire. At the time, however, Blount knew none of these details. He was focused on what was ahead.[5]

Blount's next objectives were the Baghdad International Airport and the critical intersection of Highways 1 and 8 south of the city. Blount's plan was for Dave Perkins's 2nd BCT to cross the al-Kaed bridge on the heels of Grimsley's 1st BCT. But Perkins was lagging way behind schedule, the result of one of Blount's brainstorms. To make sure that the traffic in the Karbala Gap did not slow the rush north, Blount directed Perkins to take a parallel route to the east. The idea looked good on paper. But the route ran into a swamp, and several of the brigade's tanks were quickly mired. Lieutenant Colonel Charlton's 1-15 Infantry Battalion was forced to fight its way through the marshy ground, leaving its less mobile command post behind. Confronted by boggy terrain, Eric Schwartz's 1-64 Armored Battalion turned around and headed west through Karbala only to become engaged in a firefight with the enemy. With his column headed in two different directions, Perkins, on a satellite phone, called Flip DeCamp, who led the 4-64 Armored Battalion, and told him to stick to the original route behind Grimsley's 1st BCT. DeCamp needed to pass the word to Stef Twitty, who commanded the 3-15 Infantry Battalion, to do the same.

Perkins called Lloyd Austin and broke the bad news: the brigade had executed a starburst maneuver and was going along separate routes. All night long Perkins's brigade fought the enemy as well as the terrain. At 8:40 a.m., April 3, Perkins's lead elements reached the bridge only to discover that, with one of the spans damaged by the Iraqi demolition teams, it would take seven hours to pass the 2nd BCT over the bridge, assuming the entire brigade was even ready to cross. The lightning attack to Baghdad was beginning to look like a ponderous rush-hour commute. Seeking to maintain momentum, Perkins decided to attack from the march. Instead of consolidating his forces on the near bank, he sent the units across company by company as they arrived, piecemealing his force, and regrouping on the far side. Charlton's soldiers were the first to cross and found themselves battling the remnants of the Iraqi defenders within an hour.

With the staggered arrival of Perkins's brigade, Blount was in position to resume the attack north—at least in the opinion of the 3rd ID commander. That morning Blount and Pete Bayer, the division G-3, or operations officer, went to Grimsley's TOC, which was located about 100 yards from the bridge on the east side of the Euphrates. Blount wanted to resume the attack north in the afternoon and hit the Baghdad airport that night. He was anxious to keep the pressure on the enemy and not give him time to reposition his forces. "You're going to Lions," Blount said, using the code name for the Baghdad airport. "We're not waiting. Can you do it?"

It was an acceleration of the original plan, but not a complete surprise given the huddle Blount had conducted with his commanders before moving through the Karbala Gap. Soon after, Blount talked to Wallace, who was concerned that the 3rd Infantry Division not move forward unless its supply lines and flanks were secure. Blount explained that one of Perkins's battalions—Stef Twitty's 3-15 Infantry Battalion—would protect the al-Kaed bridge and screen the right flank in case what was left of the 14th Brigade of the Medina Division tried to attack. "Sir, we trained for this," Blount said. "We're ready for this. We need to go now." There was a pause on the other end until Wallace announced his decision: "Have a good fight. Victory 6. Out."[6]

Exhausted by his ordeal at the bridge, Marcone was woken up out of a dead sleep on the roof of his Humvee by an FM radio call. Grimsley told him that Terry Ferrell's 3-7 squadron would pass his position shortly to screen the division's left flank and that he was to begin his march to the airport right after that. Marcone was not happy to get the call. After thirty hours of continuous fighting his soldiers were trying to get a few hours' rest and Marcone was low on supplies. Attacking so soon meant that other units that were to join the attack on the airfield would not be there. Marcone had argued for attacking the airfield at dawn. Attacking earlier meant that he would need to resupply on the move and conduct a night attack with little intelligence.

Marcone's battalion led the way toward the airport with the rest of the brigade following behind, all driving along narrow roads bounded by canals and irrigated fields. As the battalion moved forward, an armored scout Humvee was hit by two RPG rounds and one soldier was seriously wounded. The battalion killed the RPG team and blasted enemy positions with a main tank gun and .50 caliber machine gun. The M1 tanks missed one of their targets: a vehicle that was headed toward the battalion at high speed. It was the only time that Marcone was thankful that his tankers had missed: the vehicle turned out to be a bus full of women and children who, like the commanders in Baghdad, were oblivious that an invasion force was closing in on the capital.

The electrical grid in the capital had collapsed, shrouding the outskirts of the city in an inky darkness. The battalion moved through some palace grounds and paused so the airfield could be prepped by MLRS rockets and other artillery. Navy F/A-18s provided cover. When the battalion reached the airport it could not find the gate. One of Marcone's companies fired two tank rounds to blow a gap in a wall. The blast started a fire that provided enough illumination to find a nearby gate. It was not the subtlest way to find the entrance, but it worked.[7]

In Baghdad, the Iraqi commanders thought the only immediate threat to the airport could come from an airborne assault. The airport, in fact, was defended by antiaircraft artillery and soldiers who had dug trenches in the middle of the runways. Iraqi tanks were positioned on the airfield with their engines off so they would be harder for the Air Force's heat-sensing signals to detect. The Iraqi plan was to throw up a wall of anti-aircraft artillery and shoot down U.S. planes and helicopters transporting troops and then use Special Republican Guard soldiers and armor to kill any American soldiers that had managed to parachute in. They were not expecting a tank-on-tank engagement. The Iraqis had an inflated view of the utility of U.S. airborne operations and underestimated the reach of armored forces, all of which led Saddam and his aides to believe that they had the situation at the airport in hand.

The Iraqi airport staff had taken their own precautions. They had removed the engines from the civilian aircraft to demonstrate to U.S. warplanes that the planes were neither a threat nor a means of escape. Their effort had its intended effect. CENTCOM had decided that the aircraft were not to be destroyed but preserved for the post-Saddam Iraqi government. There was no way for the aircraft to take off anyway. American warplanes had cratered the runways.

After weeks of fighting, the battalion had reached its most important objective, and some of the soldiers had a moment of elation. As the companies ventured on the tarmac the soldiers began clearing the airfield. Many of the Iraqi soldiers, however, seemed to be asleep. Their commander, a colonel, was killed as he tried to race to his car, keys in hand. A tank blasted one of the Iraqi jetliners before Marcone angrily ordered it to stop. The tank crew had not gotten the word that the engine-less planes were not fair game. A Republican Guard T-72 tank platoon was on the west runway; three tanks were destroyed and a fourth captured.

For its part, the 3-7 Infantry Battalion, which was rushing to join the fight, attacked the VIP and main airport terminals. When Rutter's 2-7 Infantry Battalion arrived at the airport early in the morning of April 4, it set up a blocking position on the way leading to the city, a prime route if the Iraqis were to mount a counterattack. A number of Saddam's palaces were located near the airport, which made the area off limits to many Iraqi units. This measure to protect the regime in peacetime was now an impediment. Still, it was not off limits to the Special Republican Guard, as Rutter's soldiers would soon discover.[8]

On April 4, Captain Matthew Paul, the commander of a mortar platoon, was patrolling with another soldier about 300 yards from the airport. An M1 hauling a disabled U.S. tank drove by. Soon after, they heard the rumble of another armored vehicle and figured it was also an M1. Paul waved. The tank crew waved back. Then he realized what he had done. Paul cried out, "T-72!" There were two T-72s headed their way. Paul scrambled into the grass and dove behind a berm. He called on his radio to the platoon and warned them. He told them there were T-72s and they needed to contact higher headquarters. The T-72s went looking for Paul, firing their 7.62 guns. The platoon sent a Humvee out to draw the tanks' fire, darting in and out to distract the crews and take the heat off Paul.

As the mismatch continued, Paul heard an M1, the tank he had seen earlier. He also heard the Iraqi tank crews yelling, then the firing of a main tank gun and a sound of glass shattering—the sabot round hitting a T-72. In a matter of seconds both T-72s were destroyed. The Iraqis had not expected to see American armor. They seemed to think the soldiers had arrived at the airport as part of an air assault. The episode was a revelation for the battalion as well: its forces were jumbled with the enemy.[9]

The point was driven home when one of the battalion's Fox reconnaissance vehicles, trying to detect traces of poison gas or germs, was nearly struck by an Iraqi tank round. First Lieutenant Paul Milosovich ordered his Bradley onto a highway overpass to respond and was immediately hit by another Iraqi tank round. The impact tossed Milosovich out of his turret and onto the front deck of his vehicle. The crew's rucksacks, which were draped on the sides of the vehicle, exploded in flames and were hurled into the air. Private First Class Wendell Gee, the Bradley driver, drove the vehicle off the overpass before the Iraqis could get off another shot.

A four-man Javelin antitank team rushed to the scene and, although they did not find the tank that had shot the Bradley, they soon uncovered three T-72s behind a wall less than a mile from the battalion's command post. The team fired a Javelin missile, which soared over Rutter's command center, and smashed into one T-72, sending its turret fifty feet in the air. Another tank was also hit while the third was damaged but managed to drive away.[10]

Not all the U.S. soldiers were so lucky. At the airport, the 11th Engineers Battalion arrived to fix up the runways and get power and water running. Ordered to construct an enclosure to hold prisoners, the engineers from Bravo Company began to string barbed wire along a military compound nearby. As one of the engineers' armored personnel carriers smashed through the gate so the soldiers could get inside, a contingent of Republican Guard troops hiding inside opened fire. The Iraqi soldiers raced up a tower in the compound and began shooting at the engineers with RPGs and small arms. Three U.S. soldiers in the APC were immediately wounded.

Sergeant First Class Paul Smith lobbed a grenade at the Iraqis, dragged away some of the American wounded, and then jumped in the APC and drove it backward into the center of the compound. Positioning himself behind the .50 caliber machine gun, Smith held off the Iraqi soldiers until he was mortally wounded. The engineers withdrew from the compound and U.S. warplanes and artillery pummeled the Republican Guard troops. Smith received the Medal of Honor posthumously, the only one awarded in the war.[11]

Grimsley had accomplished his mission. Apaches soon began to arrive, and a large number of SOF and CIA operatives began to filter in. The American-controlled airport became a natural rallying point for the clan-

destine forces that had been moving around the capital. Grimsley assigned the 3-7 Infantry Battalion to the SOF to beef up its firepower. Following the model of Team Tank in the west and the 173rd Brigade in the
north, it was another example of partnership between the conventional
forces and the special operators.

While Grimsley was moving on the airport, Perkins gathered his 2nd
BCT and headed toward the intersection of Highways 1 and 8 south of
Baghdad, a junction the V Corps had dubbed Objective Saints. The division had received intelligence that the Medina Division's tanks and BMPs
were headed north on Route 8. The long-awaited tank battle with the
Medina Division—or the little that was left of it—was about to begin.
Perkins sent Schwartz's 1-64 Armored Battalion south on Route 8 and
DeCamp's 4-64 Armored Battalion down Route 1. This time he had good
news to report to Blount. The brigade had moved south about eighteen
miles, halfway or so to the Medina Division's headquarters, destroying
the enemy along the way. Much of the Republican Guard's equipment
was parked under the palm groves along the highway and abandoned.
The main battle had occurred at the bridge the day before.

Declining morale and an abiding fear of U.S. airpower had clearly taken
their toll on what was supposed to be one of the premier Republican Guard divisions, a big surprise to the Americans. The 3rd Infantry
Division had battled a paramilitary foe that had been largely ill-defined
before the war but two of the principal threats it had expected to encounter had evaporated: WMD and the much touted Republican Guard.
Perkins planned to spend the night at the intersection outside Baghdad,
bring up his fuel trucks, and press farther south to destroy the remains of
the Medina the next day.[12]

Hamdani considered the battle all but lost. The crossing of the
Euphrates at Peach had been the general's worst nightmare. "On this
night the enemy broke through fiercely," Hamdani later recalled. "We
learned that the Americans had crossed the bridge with about 150 tanks
and armored vehicles and had a big leap to the eastern side of the Euphrates. Our forces were shaken. This bridge is as important as the al-Kifl
Bridge . . . its width was enough for armored troops to cross fast and in
large numbers." Hamdani himself had had a close call. Returning to the
front, his jeep was riddled with bullets and an aide killed. Hamdani knew
his situation was hopeless when he arrived at his field headquarters only

to see an M1 tank parked there. Determined not to be captured he had run across the fields and canals. Ten days later he surrendered.[13]

Like Buff Blount's 3rd Infantry Division, the Marines faced a tricky river crossing on their way to Baghdad. Mattis hoped to throw the Iraqis off with a few head fakes. On April Fools' Day, he sent the 3rd LAR north on Highway 1 back toward Hantush to give the Iraqis the impression that Marines were taking that road directly to Baghdad. Then Joe Dunford's RCT-5 and Steve Hummer's RCT-7 made an abrupt turn east on Highway 27 and headed for the Tigris, which they planned to cross at Numaniyah. Crossing at Numaniyah would enable the regiments to get astride Highway 6 for the final spring to Baghdad from the east. It would enable the Marines to stay outside the range of the artillery of the Baghdad Infantry Division at Kut, no small concern since American intelligence had reported that the unit was equipped with chemical artillery. The Marines would also be temporarily out of range of the Al Nida Division's artillery, which was closer to Baghdad. The Marines would split the seam between the Iraqi units.

To discourage the Baghdad division from moving west to interfere with the crossing, Joe Dowdy's 1st RCT attacked up Highway 7 from Nasiriyah toward Kut to hold the Iraqi division in place. Despite all the feints and emphasis on deception, some of the Marines were convinced that the Iraqis had an idea where the division was headed. "All of this was supposed to fool and confuse the Iraqis, but I'm not sure it did. They seemed to always have a pretty good fix on where we were and what we were doing," said Lieutenant Colonel Duffy White, the 1st LAR commander. Two RCTs equipped with tanks and AAVs were a difficult force to disguise.[14]

As critical as the Tigris crossing was, Mattis would take no chances. The operation required the Marines to cross the Saddam Canal and drive over an island just to get to the river. When the Marines arrived in Kuwait and unloaded the supply ships coming from Diego Garcia, they were pleasantly surprised to discover caches of Mark 77 bombs, or napalm. Major General Jim "Tamer" Amos, the Marine air wing commander, thought it was as good as gold and shared the find with his fellow officers. As Mattis focused on the Numaniyah bridges, he asked Amos if his warplanes could use the napalm and incinerate the enemy defenses on the way to the Tigris. "Sounds good to me," Amos replied.

For Amos, the bloody slugfest at Nasiriyah had been a signal event, which made him more determined than ever to use Marine air aggressively. "I still had this belief, until we came out the other side of An Nasiriyah, that we were going to be able to fight this war, and preserve a large chunk of the Iraqi army," Amos said. "When the Saddam Fedayeen came down and they were picking up our Marines, they became in my mind cannibals. My whole perspective of how we were going to fight this war changed. I decided that I was going to try to destroy every single piece of Iraqi military equipment, and I was going to personally kill every single Iraqi soldier that fought back. . . . It certainly changed in my mind when I started looking at the targeting and how we were going to do business in the future. We went after the Iraqi army for vengeance after that."[15]

Marine aircraft ran two missions to pave the way for RCT-5's Tigris crossing. During the first mission, the aircraft, still wary of the Iraqi air defenses, dropped the napalm from 4,000 feet with no effect. So aircraft flying at 500 feet napalmed the southern side of the bridge and the island. Mattis's strategy emphasized finesse, but was buttressed by a reliance on brute force.

Even the napalm did not eliminate all the resistance. As his battalion advanced toward Numaniyah on April 2, Lieutenant Colonel Fred Padilla's 1/5 ran into a company-sized Iraqi defense at a bridge over the Saddam Canal. Padilla quickly defeated the resistance and Marine combat engineers rushed to install a second bridge so the regiment would have two routes east. Then Dunford organized an impromptu task force to race to the Tigris, which was led by 2nd Tank Battalion. The force quickly covered the twenty-five miles from the canal to Numaniyah and the bridge over the river. A battalion's worth of paramilitaries was waiting for them.

"They had no idea of the power of a massed tank battalion and were knocked back on their heels," according to Lieutenant Colonel Mike Oehl, the battalion commander. With the loss of one tank, the Marine armor penetrated the Iraqi defenses. Supported by Cobra attack helicopters, the Marine tank battalion cleared the town of Numaniyah and secured the Tigris crossing site. Again, the Marines found indications that the Iraqis had anticipated the attack. "Despite the claim that the Iraqis did not know the Marines were coming, one of our company commanders brought a captured Iraqi map to the CP that showed what appeared to be a detailed and fairly accurate map and overlay with the position of the U.S. forces."[16]

With Dunford's regiment in the lead, Colonel Steve Hummer's RCT-7 was next to cross the Tigris. His regiment joined some of Dunford's forces in clearing Numaniyah and the adjoining airfield. Then Hummer turned to attack into the rear of the Baghdad Infantry Division, which intelligence reported was still at Kut. The V Corps's strategy to squeeze through the Karbala Gap had not fooled the II Republican Guard Corps commander and the series of Marine fakes had not deceived the Iraqi defenders near Numaniyah. The speed of the U.S. ground attack and air superiority, however, had enabled the U.S. forces to penetrate deeply before the Iraqis could react. The Marines were now at Highway 6 severing the primary road that ran from Baghdad to Kut, Amara, and Basra. The Iraqi forces to the south and east were cut off from the capital. Another bridge was laid over the Tigris to facilitate the march north.

At Conway's headquarters, the Marine success caused trepidation. Having received a steady stream of U.S. intelligence reports, Conway was convinced that Iraq possessed chemical weapons and germ weapons and intended to use them as his Marines closed in on the capital—the Red Zone. The risk of a chemical attack was considered to increase exponentially after the Marines crossed the Tigris and threatened Baghdad from the southeast.

On April 2, U.S. signals intelligence intercepted the Iraqis calling for "blood," which according to U.S. intelligence was the Iraqi code name for the long-dreaded chemical weapons attack. Conway told his officers that the Marines were about to be attacked with poison gas. U.S. forces had not uncovered any caches of WMD, but Conway was convinced his Marines were about to find the evidence—the hard way. After the war, however, it became clear that Saddam's assertions to his commanders that he had no WMD had been truthful. General Amar Husayn al-Samarrai, head of Iraq's chemical corps, told his American interrogators that it was his job to ensure that the army was equipped to handle a coalition chemical attack, but was not aware of any plans for chemical warfare against Iraq's enemy.[17]

In the east, Dowdy fought his way up Highway 7 against a surprisingly resilient enemy. The terrain between Nasiriyah and Kut was unlike the desert Dowdy's regiment had seen when it crossed into Iraq. The roughly triangular region—about the size of Massachusetts and bordered by Basra, Nasiriyah, and Kut—was known as the Mesopotamian Marshes. It had been home to about 250,000 Ma'dan Shiites, who had never accepted the authority of the Baathist regime. In the 1990s Saddam Hussein had tried to destroy the "Marsh Arabs," by bombing them and draining the marshes. Ninety-five percent of the marshes were destroyed, leaving largely inhospitable terrain.

Seventy-five miles to the east of Highway 7 was the Iraqi 10th Armored Division at Amara, which could potentially attack the Marine flank. As doubtful as this was, given the terrain and the Marines' absolute air control, Dowdy wanted flank protection. So Lieutenant Colonel Steve Ferrando and his 1st Reconnaissance Battalion left the highway and headed west into the unknown. On either side of the highway, the ground was hard on top and soft underneath. It was dotted with cultivated family and tribal farmlands, laced with wagon trails, small canals, and irrigation ditches. It was exotic, but hardly conducive to mechanized warfare. There was no possibility that the Iraqis could use it to mount a tank attack.

Ferrando decided to grind his way forward until he could reconnect with the highway. As the reconnaissance battalion emerged from the swamp, he heard firing ahead. Lieutenant Colonel John Mayer's 1/4 Battalion had led RCT-1 up Highway 7 and run into an ambush just short of the village of Gharraf. Mayer had fought his way through the village and kept moving. But the Fedayeen and Iraqi soldiers were biding their time and using an orange and white taxi as a lookout. When Dowdy's forward command group arrived with an accompanying infantry company and an artillery battery, the enemy sprang into action. Their opening salvo severed the hand of the captain commanding the artillery's advance party. The battle was so hotly engaged that the Marines lowered several 155mm howitzers for direct fire.

Ferrando ordered his Alpha Company to attack through the town despite the risk of friendly fire. As the Recon Marines drove through the narrow streets of the town, they were met by AK-47 rounds. The Iraqis stretched a cable across the road to behead gunners standing up in their Humvees. It caught a Bravo Company Marine in the chest, but did not kill him. The attack from an unexpected direction unnerved the Iraqis and they fled. That evening RCT-1 closed the gaps between its spread-out units and consolidated its position just south of Ash Shatrah.

The Marines were learning something about the Iraqi tactics. When the local farmers were friendly, it was a good sign. When they were subdued or women and children were seen heading down the road, it meant Fedayeen were in the area. Open country was good, towns bad. The Fedayeen had good command and control over their fighters, disposed them cleverly, and sought to attack the least defended elements of the convoy. The Marines assumed that the ubiquitous white and orange taxis were part of an Iraqi early warning network. Dowdy expected more Gharrafs on his march to Kut. To counter the Iraqi tactics and on their own initiative, battalion commanders took a page out of Craparotta's book from Ambush Alley in Nasiriyah. They would leapfrog the route. A lead unit would fall out and provide security as the column passed. It would then fall in at the end of the column while the next lead unit assumed picket duty.

Dowdy released Ferrando from his picket duties at the village of Rifa and sent the Recon Marines back into the off-highway morass for yet another scouting mission, this time at night to the Qalat Sukhar airfield. The British 16 Air Assault Brigade was to land at the field to cover Highway 7 in case the Iraqi 10th Armored Division made a move out of Amara. By dawn Ferrando reached the airfield, and saw no sign of any Iraqis. But as Ferrando said in his raspy voice, "That didn't mean they weren't there waiting for us. They seemed to know our every move."

Soon he received orders to assault and seize the airfield. "I knew my lightly armed Marines would be blown away if there were tanks hiding out here and held my breath." Two companies abreast, the Marine vehicles charged like the Light Brigade. They secured the airfield without a shot. It was deserted and littered with old and useless equipment. One unfortunate incident marred the charge. Told that anyone in the area was to be considered hostile, Bravo Company Marines spotted movement in a palm grove on the way in and opened fire. Later they found that they had hit some hapless shepherds. The Marines sat on the airfield for two days before they found out that their British comrades were not coming after all. The airfield was restored and turned into a receiving point for airlifted supplies. Ray's and Craparotta's battalions pushed on toward Kut.[18]

A short distance beyond Qalat Sukhar was the hamlet of Fajr, a key road junction on Highway 7. It was the intersection with Highway 17, which ran west to link up with Highway 1, the main route of the Marine Division seventy miles away.[19] RCT-1 set up its main command post at the road junction only to get a rude surprise during the night of the 30th: a Russian-made BM-21, hidden in a field, launched a full salvo of forty

122mm rockets at the encampment. "All I could see was a wall of red, orange, and purple flame lighting up the night," said one Marine. Fortunately, the BM-21's aim was bad and the rockets exploded harmlessly more than 200 yards from the CP. Artillery counterbattery fire responded immediately and destroyed the launcher.

The town of Hayy was next on the road to Kut and, as expected, the Iraqis had fallen back on prepared positions to defend it. At a sharp turn in the river, the Iraqis had set up a kill zone with 82mm mortars firing from one side and an antiaircraft gun lowered for direct fire from another. A Marine Recon platoon leader was awed by the AA fire. "I didn't know what it was. It just looked like flaming pumpkins coming at us." Cobras were called in and cleared the area. Surprisingly, the Iraqi paramilitaries were still in place holding their ground. All through the night firefights flared as hundreds of Iraqis abandoned their heavy weapons and managed to use a bypass road to head north in trucks while being pounded by artillery fire.

When the fighting was over, the locals told the Marines that the Fedayeen were mostly foreigners, and they had retreated to a suspected camp at Muwaffaqiyah, a few miles northwest of Hayy. The regiment's 2nd LAR and Recon moved on the town border, which was skillfully and tenaciously defended. Covered by Cobras, the Marines headed north to the town from the western side of the Gharraf River, paralleling Highway 7. Craparotta's 3/1 moved up and passed through Ferrando and cleared the town. As was becoming common throughout Iraq, very large ammunition and weapons depots were uncovered. Some of the defenders killed at Hayy and Muwaffaqiyah were Syrians in well-tailored civilian clothes. According to their passports they had arrived in Iraq as a group during the first week of the invasion. All had visas stamped with their entry location, al-Qa'im where the Euphrates crossed the Syrian border. In the section for "Purpose of Visit," the Iraqi control officer had penned in, "Jihad."

Craparotta soon received unexpected orders. He was told to go back down the highway to Ash Shatrah to support a force of émigré Ahmed Chalabi's Iraqi freedom fighters. They were the Iraqi fighters that had been flown to Tallil on the U.S. C-17s after Abizaid sought a way to put an Iraqi face on the invasion. The fighters had contributed little since they arrived at Tallil; now they were to attack regime holdouts still in the town—or so Craparotta was told. When he got to Ash Shatrah, Chalabi's freedom fighters never materialized, but, indeed, Baathists were still holed up there. After an air strike on their suspected hideout, Craparotta's Marines entered the town without difficulty. Craparotta then hurried back north, but not before he saw an orgy of looting and pillaging of the town by the local populace. It would become a familiar sight to Marines and soldiers when they arrived in Baghdad.[20]

There was a much bigger issue, however, concerning Kut. Despite many months of planning, there was unusual confusion within the division on how to handle the city. As far as Dowdy understood, the plan was for his regiment to push to the outskirts, skirmish with the Iraqis, and then pull back for a long detour around the city to the Tigris River crossing established by his brother regiments. Dowdy believed his mission was to pin down the Baghdad Division while avoiding getting tangled up in the fighting inside the city. Mattis himself agreed with that and had earlier made the decision that Kut was not to be fought over. Wary of a costly fight with the Fedayeen, he did not want to divert forces to occupy Kut and be saddled with the responsibilities of occupation.

Brigadier General John Kelly, Mattis's assistant division commander, however, had a different view. Kelly had become concerned that Dowdy's regiment was too slow to make its way through Nasiriyah after Task Force Tarawa's bloody fight there and had stayed with the regiment to keep his eye on Dowdy ever since. Dowdy's push up Highway 7 had done nothing to reassure Kelly. Initiative and aggressiveness, Kelly thought, were being exercised at the battalion, not regimental, level. Kelly's assessment was that the enemy in Kut had run away or been destroyed from the air. As Dowdy approached Kut, Kelly wanted him to take a bridge on the southern part of the city to test the enemy defenses. If the enemy had faded away, as Kelly suspected, he wanted to exploit an opportunity and recommend that the regiment skirt the city. That would avoid a lengthy detour, quickly reunite the division, and ease the logistics burden. Mattis, concentrating on the attack on Baghdad, knew nothing of this.

Dowdy did not buy the idea and was mystified by Kelly's pressure to push into the southern part of the city. He had already organized his logistics for the detour to the east and was worried that he might confront the type of heavy fighting that had engulfed Task Force Tarawa in Nasiriyah. Moreover, no Frago, or written order, to attack through Kut had been issued. "There was uncharacteristically a lot of back and forth between the division and us about whether or not to go," Dowdy recalled.

"It could have been a confused, jackass circus. I still don't think that it would have worked."[21]

To encourage the Baghdad Division to surrender, Mattis had composed a message reminiscent of the one the Germans sent to Major General Anthony McAuliffe, the commander of the 82nd Airborne Division at Bastogne during the Battle of the Bulge in World War II. "To the commander of the Iraqi forces in Al Kut," the message read. "You are surrounded. There is no hope for your forces to be reinforced or re-supplied. We will continue to attack unless you choose to stop the unnecessary killing. If you choose not to surrender, all of the killing will be your responsibility and yours only." The message was sent over multiple frequencies; there was no response.[22]

Dowdy's regiment fought to the southern outskirts of Kut, cleared a minefield, lost an armored bulldozer, and tangled with the enemy until it received an order from Division two hours later to pull back and make the long-planned detour. Dowdy had prevailed on the plan for Kut, but after a difficult couple of days the tension between Dowdy and Kelly reached the boiling point. As Dowdy headed south from Kut, he discovered that Kelly had arranged for a helicopter to take him to Mattis's headquarters. As Dowdy got out of the helicopter, he was attacked by a stray dog. It was a bad omen.

When he met with Mattis, the general seemed sympathetic, as if dealing with a combat fatigue casualty. Mattis gently asked Dowdy what was wrong. Dowdy said he had not slept in two days and was tired. Mattis asked why Dowdy was not pressing more into the cities. Dowdy thought Mattis was talking about Kut and said that he loved his Marines. Dowdy never saw the sense of attacking into Kut, since Mattis's own plan called for making a wide detour around it. Only later did it dawn on Dowdy that Mattis was probably referring to Nasiriyah. Mattis asked why Dowdy had been telling his staff that he might be relieved of command. Dowdy based that on Kelly's insinuations. Mattis asked if Dowdy had previous combat experience. Dowdy said he had been in Lebanon and Somalia, but Mattis dismissed that. It was not Desert Storm.

Trying to demonstrate that he had the right fighting spirit, Dowdy said he had been euphoric when his regiment arrived up north. Mattis responded that Rommel had had a commander who was euphoric and had made decisions that got many of his men killed. Then Mattis came to the point. "He said that, by being too cautious, I was going to cause the death of my Marines," Dowdy recalled.

Mattis left his tent and walked around to think. When he returned he told Dowdy that he was going to be relieved as commander of RCT-1. Dowdy began to plead for his job, asking Mattis to spare his family and career. Mattis was about to upend his life. But Mattis's decision was final. Dowdy offered to stay with the division and work in the command center, but Mattis told him it would be best if he had another assignment. Mattis asked Dowdy if he should confiscate his ammunition. Dowdy thought the gesture was melodramatic: "I said that I wasn't a coward, I wasn't going to kill myself."

Dowdy was then taken by Kelly via helicopter to Hantush, and from there to Camp Commando in Kuwait. After showering, Dowdy called his wife, who was already being bombarded with calls from Paula Zahn at CNN and producers from *Larry King Live*. The media were after the story. Dowdy spent the rest of the war in a P-3 helping to identify enemy positions. He was replaced by Colonel John Toolan, Mattis's chief operations officer.

The episode marked the only time that a senior officer was relieved of command during the war and was the kind of career-ending decision called for by only the most serious infractions. Mattis said he needed three aggressive regimental commanders for the upcoming battle for Baghdad. Dowdy believed that his initial reluctance to run the gauntlet in Nasiriyah after Task Force Tarawa stumbled into the unanticipated battle there had set a tone and that he was unfairly depicted as too hesitant by Kelly regarding an operation in Kut that Mattis himself had never planned.[23]

With all of his regiments separated and going in different directions, and despite the confusion within his command over Kut, Mattis's audacious and convoluted plan was nonetheless working. Having driven the Iraqi defenders into the center of Kut, he concentrated artillery and hundreds of air strikes, including B-52s, on them. When he was satisfied that its remnants would not pose a threat to his move on Baghdad, Mattis recalled his disparate units so they could move on the Iraqi capital.

Under its new commander, RCT-1 carried out its old plan, accomplishing its disengagement from Kut and the 150-mile road march to rejoin the division at the Tigris River crossing in twenty-four hours. All three RCTs were reuniting for the drive on Baghdad. The fancy maneuvering was over. It was time for the full division and air wing to move on the capital.

After the war, interrogation of Iraqi officers revealed that the enemy the Marines had planned so hard to thwart, and which U.S. intelligence had mistakenly endowed with chemical artillery, was not even there. The feared Baghdad Infantry Division was ordered by its superiors in Baghdad to leave Kut on March 30 and move along the Tigris toward Baghdad. It was replaced by the 34th Division, a Regular Army unit that was at 40 percent strength and which had been deployed near the Iranian border. The Iraqi army defense of Kut was much weaker than the Marines knew, though the Fedayeen almost certainly were there in force. The Marines had designed an entire strategy around an Iraqi unit that had already left.[24]

It was not the only time that strategy had been devised around a non-existent threat. Under persistent pressure from Franks to attack Iraq's 10th Armored Division at Amara, McKiernan instructed Conway to finish off the unit. Conway considered the mission to be a distraction and a diversion of combat forces he could put to better use in the drive toward Baghdad. After arguing futilely against the mission, Conway assigned the operation to Task Force Tarawa. Tarawa arrived to find that there was no resistance. Later, the commander of the 10th Division told the Marines that he had no orders to mount an attack against the Marine flank, as Franks feared, and had been instructed to defend against Iran.[25]

As Mattis pressed toward Baghdad, he was anticipating a head-on collision with the Al Nida Division, deployed south and east of the city. Up to this point in the campaign, the Marines had faced Fedayeen almost exclusively. They were brave but not very skilled. Now that the Marine division was in the Red Zone, they would confront not only the paramilitaries, but the Regular Army and, most important, the Republican Guard. How hard would they fight and would they use WMD in a last-ditch effort to keep the Americans out of Baghdad? In command of the Al Nida Division was one of Saddam's cousins, and he had far more authority than his counterpart in the Baghdad Division. Despite air attacks, the division was assessed by the U.S. as being at 80 percent strength.

Dunford's RCT-5 attacked along Highway 6 north of the Tigris with its tank battalion in the lead. After forty miles, the Marines on Highway 6 approached the small town of Aziziyah. When the tanks arrived on the scene, they were met by heavy fire from mortars, artillery, and entrenched Iraqi troops. Marine tanks and infantry, supported by Cobra attack helicopters and warplanes, took on the enemy, sweeping through the town and moving six miles beyond it.

Even so, getting to Baghdad looked easier on the map than it was in practice. Mattis had only the vaguest intelligence on the disposition of the Al Nida Division and the terrain was difficult. The Marine forces south of the Tigris ran into enormous problems. While Dunford was moving on Highway 6, the remainder of the regiment attacked on a parallel route on the south side, figuring it would rejoin its parent units later for the final push to the capital. But as Duffy White's 1st LAR looked for a way to cross the river, it found that the bridges were either destroyed or too light to bear heavy equipment. So Mattis ordered the unit to return fifty miles to the Numaniyah site and cross the river to join the two battalions already on Highway 6. Anyone monitoring a Blue Force Tracker at that point would see major Marine elements retracing their steps.[26]

At Camp Doha, McKiernan tried to orchestrate the final assault on Baghdad. In the weeks leading up to the war, a variety of plans had been considered to divide the battle space. At one point, Wallace had proposed that the Marine regiments be put under his control for the climactic battle in the Iraqi capital. The Army and Marines would set up five bases on the outskirts of the capital, all under Wallace's command. It was all part of Wallace's plan to establish cordons around Baghdad and run raids in and out of the city, and it would establish unity of command. But Conway had pushed back. The communications used by the Marine regiments were not compatible with those used at V Corps. Moreover, putting regiments under Wallace's command, the Marines argued, would split the Marine ground units from the Marine air units that supported them and undermine the Marines' way of going to war.

On April 4, McKiernan flew to Numaniyah to meet with Conway and, among other things, settle the issue of how to attack the capital. The Tigris was defined as the boundary between the Army and the Marines: the Army would take Baghdad west of the river; the Marines would control the city east of the Tigris. It was a crude but effective way of reducing the risk of friendly fire, and reflected the limits of joint warfare. For all the talk of joint operations, the V Corps and Conway's Marines had fought two separate campaigns on their march to Baghdad and they would fight two separate campaigns when they got there.

In the planning for Baghdad, Conway was initially told that his Marines should attack the city from the northeast through the Saddam City sector of the capital, which was dominated by Shiites and presumably anxious to be liberated by the Americans. But following the Numaniyah meeting, the CIA reported that the Iraqi military appeared to have anticipated that possibility and had prepared defensive positions in that part of the capital. The strength of the Iraqi defenses there was not clear, but it was enough to prompt McKiernan to rethink and alter his plan.

McKiernan directed Conway that Mattis would be entering Baghdad from the southeast. To get into position, Mattis needed to rush to the Diyala crossroads and eventually drive to the Rasheed airfield, which was on the southeast corner side of the Diyala River, code-named Objective Ravens. It was part of the plan to cordon off the capital and establish forward operating bases around it so the Marines could join the Army in conducting raids into the city.

Mattis sent scouts forward to look for the Al Nida while he held up short of the airfield and consolidated his supply lines. On the morning of April 4, McKiernan talked by phone with Conway to complain that Mattis had not made it to Ravens the previous night. "The expectation is to press this up to Ravens," McKiernan said tersely. "Get back to me as soon as you can." Conway did not know why Mattis had not reached the objective the previous evening, but figured the aggressive commander had a good reason and never passed on McKiernan's displeasure. It was one of the few times that McKiernan had been unhappy with the pace of attack.

That day the Marines moved up to clear the southeastern approaches to Baghdad. With Oehl's tank unit leading the way, it was not long before the Marines ran into fiery resistance from irregulars near the town of Jubayr. A roadside truck bomb, which was remotely detonated, disabled two tanks, damaged other vehicles, killed four Marines, and seriously wounded eight more. It was another indication of the guerrilla war that was in the offing and a preview of the tactics that insurgents would later use to great effect, but was just one event in a whirlwind of ambushes and counterblows.

Sam Mundy knew about the engagement by listening in on 2nd Tank's radio traffic. He then rushed forward with two of his companies. The Marines dismounted their AAVs and attacked both sides of the highway in an eight-hour battle, with Cobra gunships providing very close support and the 11th Marines massing four battalions of artillery fire on the Iraqis. The highway was finally cleared and when prisoners were rounded up, the Marines were surprised to find that they were not Iraqis. The column had run into fighters from Syria, Jordan, Egypt, and other Middle Eastern nations. In the fighting in and around the approaches to the Diyala it was apparent that the jihadists were better marksmen than the

Iraqis. Most of the killed and wounded Marines were shot in the head or neck.

As Oehl's 2nd Tank Battalion drove on to a critical crossroads just short of the Diyala River, the jihadists ignited fire trenches on each side of the road to reduce visibility. The Marines encountered ambushes and yet another truck bomb. A scout platoon leader and a tank crew member were killed. At one point, Dunford's regimental command post came under attack and was hit by two 122mm rockets from a Soviet-made BM-21, the kind of weapon fired at Dowdy's command post on his march to Kut. The enemy was adept at identifying field headquarters and was trying to take Dunford's out.

With 2nd Tanks advancing, 3/5 became involved in a brawl. In the midst of the turmoil, a Republican Guard general in a car tried to run a Marine blocking position and was cut down. He was later identified as the chief of staff of the Special Republican Guard entrusted with the defense of Baghdad. The site was quickly nicknamed "The Dead General's Corner."

Intelligence gathered after the war indicated that while the fighting in Aziziyah was stiff, the Al Nida was nowhere near full strength when Mattis's division smashed into it. The commander of the unit later told his interrogators that the leaflets dropped on his troops telling them to depart or be bombed by U.S. warplanes had had a tremendous effect. The soldiers became demoralized when they realized that allied aircraft could fly over their position with virtual impunity and that the leaflets could just as easily have been bombs. Originally a division of 13,000 soldiers and 500 vehicles, it had been reduced to 2,000 troops and 50 vehicles of all sorts by the time the Marines closed in on the Iraqi capital, according to the classified JFCOM report.

Like the Medina Division, the Al Nida was just a shell of itself when it was attacked by U.S. troops. But the Republican Guard was not the main foe. The truck bombs, guerrilla tactics, and alliance between foreign fighters and Baathists were a portent of the resistance to come. The number of casualties and disabled Marine tanks and other vehicles left no doubt that RCT-5 was breaking through the crust of Baghdad's outer defenses. But Iraqi resistance was intensifying and U.S. forces had yet to venture into the city.[27]

CHAPTER 19

The Thunder Run

As the Army and Marines advanced deep into the Red Zone, Scott Wallace prepared to attack the Iraqi capital. From the start, top military planners and the president himself had been worried about Fortress Baghdad: the prospect that Saddam would reinforce his capital and engage the Americans in deadly house-to-house fighting. The United States military's experience in urban warfare, in fact, gave reason for concern. The loss of eighteen Army soldiers in Mogadishu and the Marines' bruising fight for Hue during the Vietnam Tet Offensive of 1968 weighed heavily on the mind of the military, as did the Russian experience in Chechnya and the Israeli military's in the Jenin refugee camp. There was no easy way to conquer and control a city, even with the best of troops, equipment, and high-technology support.

Wallace and his V Corps staff had studied the problem intensively and developed a methodical plan. The five forward operating bases set up by the Army and Marines on the outskirts of the city were code-named after NFL football teams. To prevent Iraqi reinforcements from getting in and to stop Iraqi leaders and suspected caches of WMD from getting out, the forces would also establish an outer cordon thirty-five miles from the capital and an inner cordon twenty miles from the city. Then, the Americans would run raids in and out of the city, using mechanized infantry, armor, helicopters, SOF, psychological operations units, and support from the Air Force to attack command centers and other carefully selected targets. Over time, it was assumed that the cohesion and combat capability of the Iraqi defenders would fracture to the point that Baghdad could be occupied at acceptable cost. Wallace, in essence, would pick and poke at the regime until it collapsed. The raids could take weeks but Wallace consid-

ered it preferable to plunging headlong into the capital and becoming en-
snared in house-to-house fighting. To facilitate the raids, V Corps planners had diagrammed the entire city, dividing it into fifty-five zones, and
numbered each block and building so the attacks could be precisely
planned. Wallace had also instructed Colonel J. D. Johnson, one of his
former staff officers, to war-game the raids and present the results to
Army and Marine commanders in a briefing in the auditorium at Camp
Doha before the war.[1]

Wallace was so confident of the strategy that he openly discussed it before the war. More important, the entire scheme had been briefed up the
chain of command. Following several sessions with Wallace, McKiernan
approved the tactical plan and ensured that the zones were adopted by
Moseley's command center and the SOF. In December, McKiernan had
briefed the plan at CENTCOM, and Franks had presented it at the White
House after President Bush had expressed concerns about the possibility
of a bloody fight to take the capital. Along with Franks's Inside-Out Plan
to pin the Republican Guard with airpower and stop them from taking up
positions inside the capital, Wallace's plan represented the coalition command's most comprehensive strategy for taking Baghdad.[2]

But while the strategy was embraced by senior commanders, it made
no sense to Blount or Mattis. By waiting to wear the enemy down, they
thought, they would be forfeiting the initiative to the Iraqis and giving them time to thicken their defenses. By occupying static positions on
the outskirts of the city coalition units would be easy targets for Iraqi
artillery and missile fire. By running raids in and out of the city their
troops would be faced with the demoralizing prospect of giving up
ground taken and being forced to fight for the same piece of terrain over
and over again. It would also encourage the Iraqis to think they were
beating the Americans.

After Johnson briefed the plan for the takedown of Baghdad in the
auditorium at Camp Doha ten days before the war, Blount confided his
misgivings to his planners and command group, which included Dave
Perkins, the 2nd BCT commander. Perkins wholeheartedly agreed with
Blount. Perkins thought the V Corps approach risked losing momentum.
During training exercises in his career, Perkins had seen many a battle get
to a point where it could go either way. In every case he could remember,
the side that won was led by a commander who saw opportunity and
quickly took advantage of it. Those who paused usually lost. The time
that the U.S. forces took to set up their bases and conduct their in-and-out
raids would be time that the Iraqis could use to their advantage as well. In

the words of one 3rd ID officer, Wallace's methodical approach stemmed from the "tyranny of synchronization."

Although they were from different services, Blount and Mattis were very much alike. Both were tactically skilled and very aggressive. In the months leading up to the war, the V Corps and 3rd ID had had their differences. Blount had worked hard to shape the V Corps plan to maneuver to Baghdad. When Scott Wallace proposed at a January meeting in Germany that the 3rd ID take the direct route up Highways 1 and 8 to Baghdad, Blount argued that the Army's war-gaming showed that fighting through the towns and cities along the way would slow the attack. After pressing his case, Blount's proposal to swing west of the Euphrates, race through the Karbala Gap, and strike the Republican Guard in the rear became the centerpiece of the V Corps attack. But to the consternation of Blount and Mattis the plan to take the city was all V Corps.

Having advanced to the outskirts of Baghdad, Blount's troops were already occupying two of the five operating bases near Baghdad under Wallace's plan: the Baghdad airport, code-named Objective Lions, which Grimsley's 1st BCT controlled, and the critical intersection of Highways 1 and 8, Objective Saints, which Perkins's 2nd BCT controlled. With the Marines yet to make their way over the Diyala River, and the 101st trying to keep order in Najaf and Karbala, the rest of the cordon had not been set. Blount, however, believed that the division had arrived at the outskirts of Baghdad before the Iraqis had had time to prepare and did not want to wait to cordon off the city and carry out Wallace's methodical plan. The differences over how to take the city were now coming to the fore.

Blount's first move was to take advantage of the broad four-lane road that sliced through western Baghdad and send an armored task force on armed reconnaissance through the edge of the city. His purpose was threefold: to take the measure of his foe, destroy as many of the enemy as the U.S. soldiers could find, and send a message to the Iraqis that the Americans were at their doorstep. Since arriving at the airport, Blount's command had set up a satellite dish and TV, which it had used to monitor the claims by Iraq's information minister that the division was being destroyed by Iraqi forces. Blount calculated that the armed reconnaissance would show the people that their government was lying to them about the status of the war and would demoralize the Iraqi military.

Worried that it might not be easy to sell the V Corps on his Thunder

Run, Blount downplayed the potential risks. He made the mission sound more like an effort to secure the route between his two brigades and help build the cordon around Baghdad than the start of the battle for the capital—an alteration of V Corps's carefully crafted plan. "Well, this was my plan, basically letting him [Wallace] know we were going to open our MSRs [main supply routes] between the objectives of Saints and Lions, that's about all I told him. Not sure how much he understood on it, but he didn't come back and tell me not to do it, so we went ahead and executed," Blount later told Army historians.[3]

On the afternoon of April 4, Blount called Perkins at his TOC, or tactical operations center, a series of vehicles and makeshift shelters set up at Objective Saints. The 2nd BCT had begun to strike the Medina Division in the rear, delivering the final blow to the main Republican Guard unit that stood between the U.S. Army and Baghdad, which was all according to plan. Blount was still determined to finish off what was left of the Medina. But the 3rd ID commander also had another task for the 2nd BCT. Perkins was to conduct an armed reconnaissance to the Baghdad airport, where Blount and Grimsley's 1st BCT were located. Perkins had already conducted a series of these heavily armored, fast-moving attacks into built-up areas, starting in Najaf, which was when he had started calling them Thunder Runs.

Perkins decided to send a tank battalion to the airport. The battalion was ordered to attack only with their M1A1 tanks and Bradleys; they were to leave their wheeled vehicles and fuel trucks behind. Blount cautioned Perkins to avoid any gaps and watch his flanks as they passed through the four major intersections on the way to the airport. Perkins would have first call on the Air Force A-10s that were allocated to support the division and would also be supported by the division's artillery. By conducting the Thunder Run, the division would learn how the Iraqis planned to defend the city, how they used their tanks and BMPs, what kind of obstacles they had emplaced, and how they used the highway overpasses. Perkins would then exploit that information in his next attack. There was limited to no intelligence on any of this from the UAVs, satellites, or human sources. If Perkins ran into trouble, Blount assured him, Grimsley's 1st BCT would attack from the airport and pull his task force out.

Perkins, an armor officer like Blount, embraced the mission. The New Hampshire native was a devout Christian who read *The Daily Bread* each morning and rarely lost his temper. But like Blount, Perkins was convinced that a display of audacity would shorten the war. Not all of the brigade's officers were convinced of the wisdom of the strategy. Perkins summoned Lieutenant Colonel Eric Schwartz, the commander of 1-64 Armored Battalion, to his brigade TOC to give him his new mission. Taking off his Kevlar, Schwartz noted that the atmosphere in the TOC seemed to be unusually quiet and even somber. After a day of shooting up Medina Division armor and artillery along Highway 8 south of Baghdad, Schwartz had anticipated that his battalion would refuel and then head back south on a route for more of the same. "What's it look like?" Schwartz asked. "What are we doing?"[4]

Perkins told Schwartz, "I need you to attack along Highway 8 tomorrow." This is what Schwartz was expecting, but then Perkins took his finger and traced the stretch of highway that ran north through Baghdad. "I need you to attack north into Baghdad tomorrow morning at first light, not south."

"You must be fucking crazy . . . sir," Schwartz said. No U.S. forces had ventured into the city yet and there was no solid intelligence on the enemy defenses in the city.

The entire TOC was now silent waiting for Perkins's response. "I don't think so, and I am coming with you," he said.

Perkins's 2nd BCT had several missions to accomplish in one day. It had to complete the destruction of the Medina Division, secure the east side of the Euphrates, and attack through Baghdad to the airport, all simultaneously. Instead of massing the brigade's combat power, all of the battalions would be going in separate directions. Flip DeCamp's 4-64 Armored Battalion would drive in a big loop south of the capital to finish off the 2nd and 10th brigades of the Medina Division. Stef Twitty would take 3-15 Infantry Battalion from the bridge at Peach and attack the 14th Brigade of the Medina Division, securing the east side of the Euphrates.

Schwartz's 1-64 would have the hardest and most dangerous mission: the attack through Baghdad. As he headed back to his battalion, Schwartz was wondering how he would explain the mission to his troops. Once the attack began, the column would stay on the move. The battalion would attack with twenty-nine tanks, fourteen Bradleys, and a handful of other armored vehicles, including M113s. The vehicles would move at 9 miles an hour and there would be a 55-yard space between them. To maintain momentum, the tank and Bradley crews would shoot what they could and then pass off the targets to the soldiers behind them.

What really concerned Schwartz was not just that the mission was high-risk but the virtual certainty that he would lose soldiers. In battles so far, there had always been the danger that some of his troops would be killed, but in the Thunder Run it seemed to be a grisly inevitability. Schwartz did his best, however, to hide his worry and projected confidence when he briefed the mission to his officers. Schwartz did not have all the answers, but he assured his soldiers that surely somebody must. "Somebody at headquarters has done the analysis," he said. "They are not going to send us in to fail." Many of the soldiers were apprehensive about what was in store, but not all. The plan to swing through Baghdad appealed to Staff Sergeant Stevon Booker, a tank commander and section leader in Alpha Company, 1-64 Armor. "About time," he said.[5]

The morning of April 5 was just another day for many of Baghdad's residents. Despite three weeks of war, the broad four-lane highway that swung through western Baghdad was full of morning commuters and civilian traffic. The Iraqi information ministry had assured the Iraqi public and the international media that the Americans had been kept at bay. But even though Baghdad was not at battle stations, the city was swarming with thousands of troops: Special Republican Guard soldiers as well as Saddam Fedayeen, Syrians, and other foreign fighters who had come to wage a jihad against the Americans. The Thunder Run was intended to be a wake-up call to the Iraqi people, and Schwartz's battalion would be stirring up a veritable hornets' nest.

Red Platoon was in the lead as Schwartz's formation drove north into Baghdad at 6:00 a.m. Second in the order of march was an engineer platoon, which had been turned into a rolling fort. Four or five engineers were crammed into each of three open M113s: one engineer would man a .50 caliber machine gun mounted on the vehicle while the rest would fire away with machine guns or M4 carbines. The engineers had developed this way of fighting in Najaf. Tanks could focus in only one or two directions. The engineers could fire in five or six and at all elevations. The engineers debated whether to take the MICLIC, a rocket on wheels that when fired unleashed a line of explosives, to blow a lane through a minefield or any obstacles the Iraqis might erect in their path. But they were afraid that enemy fire might ignite it. So they left it behind. If they had to breach any fortifications, they would have to use artillery or air strikes or blast their way through with their own weapons.

Schwartz was at the head of the formation with Alpha Company, nicknamed the Wild Bunch. Perkins was in the middle in his command track. A-10s were overhead, ready to strike any Iraqi units making a beeline for the Americans' flanks. Tank and Bradley crews arrayed their carbines, 9mm pistols, and hand grenades atop their turrets, knowing full well that the fighting might be so close that they would not be able to depress their coax machine or main guns to engage enemy soldiers attacking the vehicles' flanks.

Schwartz's soldiers struck the first blow: machine-gunning a group of surprised Iraqi soldiers who seemed oblivious to the approaching American task force as they sat on the side of the road drinking tea to warm up in the early morning chill. Within minutes, the front of the column was met with a blizzard of fire from AK-47s, RPGs, and mortars. As in the south, the enemy was not operating in any discernible formation. There were RPG teams, fighters in civilian vehicles, trucks, and buses, and defenders operating from nearby buildings, overpasses, and fighting positions only yards away from the road. Some were wearing uniforms, others not.

C-12, Staff Sergeant Jason Diaz's tank, had been shot at for weeks as it drove from Kuwait and seemed to be all but invulnerable. Buttoned up in his M1, Diaz felt a thud but assumed that his wingman, First Lieutenant Roger Gruneisen, had fired a main gun round and that he had been buffeted by the aftershock. After 500 yards, however, Diaz's tank rolled to a stop and smoke began curling from the back. It was one of a tanker's worst nightmares: Diaz's tank was immobilized and on fire. A round had hit the auxiliary power unit on the back of the turret. Fuel had spilled into the engine compartment, which set the engine ablaze, which in turn ignited more fuel lines. Diaz's tank was at a complete standstill, with what seemed like the entire Iraqi army firing at him. Even worse, Diaz knew that the rest of the column had to keep moving or possibly suffer further casualties.

Diaz jumped out along with his driver, loader, and gunner. He yanked the emergency fire handle on the exterior of the tank to activate the Halon fire-extinguishing system, but it did not put out the fire. The task force had traveled just 4 miles and had reached the first of the four intersections and already Schwartz faced a key decision: whether to abandon the tank or stop and try to save it. Schwartz ordered the formation to halt. M1s created a perimeter around the stricken tank while soldiers rushed forward with extra fire extinguishers and water cans to tamp down the flames. The fire died down but as soon as Diaz's tank was hooked up for towing to the airport, it was aflame again. Frantically, Diaz and Major Rick Nussio, the battalion executive officer, began pulling the air cleaners from the tank and heaving them to the ground, hoping to starve the fire of vital kindling. Still, the fire refused to die.

While the soldiers struggled to save the tank, Perkins was becoming increasingly uneasy. The enemy was massing their fire on the marooned tank and the soldiers who were trying to rescue it. RPGs were skipping off the pavement. Enemy vehicles were crashing into the American armor, which was staggered in a column along the road. The Americans had lost the element of surprise and would soon lose the initiative. The column had been stalled for more than twenty minutes.[6]

Blount, with Austin in the assault command post at the airport, could hear the battle raging only a few miles away from the airport. Monitoring the attack by TACSAT, Blue Force Tracker, and a V Corps UAV, he saw a gap developing in the column and was worried that Perkins would get bogged down trying to recover Diaz's tank in the middle of the intense firefight. Blount called Perkins and asked him for a status report. Perkins assured him that if he could not quickly remedy the problem with the tank he would leave it behind. Blount was restless sitting in the CP while this critical battle was going on, so he moved up to the front of the airport to link up with Grimsley's tank brigade, which was ready to move out to help Perkins if needed.

Perkins directed his M113 driver to head toward Diaz's tank. He hollered at the soldiers to abandon the stricken M1, and ordered Schwartz's task force to start rolling again. Diaz and his crew removed their maps, codebooks, and other documents from the tank, and grabbed the loader's M240 machine gun from its mount. Diaz and his gunner, Sergeant Jose Couvertier, climbed into Gruneisen's tank while Diaz's driver, Private First Class Chris Shipley, and his loader, Private First Class Donald Schafer, raced to the first sergeant's M113 armored personnel carrier.

Sergeant Carlos Hernandez, Gruneisen's gunner, raced to the burning tank and tossed two thermite grenades inside. A following tank blasted C-12 with a HEAT round. The soldiers were following their training and trying to prevent the M1 from falling into the hands of the enemy, but the actions irked Perkins. He had not ordered the tank destroyed and fully intended to recover it on a future Thunder Run. Like Blount, Perkins was confident that the division would soon be attacking again into the city.[7]

Before the battalion got moving again, a car driven by a hapless Iraqi brigadier general slammed into a Bradley. The officer was captured by the Americans and thrust into the back of a Bradley so he could be brought to the brigade's human intelligence teams. The general was later identified as one of the principal logistics officers for Baghdad. He had no idea the Americans were in Baghdad and had been on his way to work. Other drivers were not so lucky. The firefight was being conducted on one of Baghdad's main thoroughfares. Civilians were caught in the crossfire. The explosion and fire from one enemy vehicle that was targeted engulfed a nearby car.

"As I drove by the destroyed enemy truck I saw the most horrible thing I have ever seen in my life," Eric Olson, a tank platoon sergeant with Alpha Company, confided in his diary. "Behind the enemy truck was a blown up civilian car that had a family in it. The father was twitching on the ground with no skin on his body, I'm pretty sure he was dead. The mother was sitting on the ground rocking back and forth, her body was smoking, and in her arms she cradled an infant. The other casualty I believe was a boy about ten years old. He had no hair and very little skin left. His eyes were fused shut as he walked around aimlessly, with layers of skin hanging off of his body. I wanted to help them, even if I could do something I wasn't allowed to. We had to keep pushing forward."[8]

Now that Schwartz's column was on the move again, it needed to navigate a major intersection, which the soldiers had dubbed Spaghetti Junction after one of the most intricate overpasses in Atlanta. First Lieutenant Robert Ball, who commanded the lead tank in the formation, was looking for a sign to the airport. Ball had fired a main gun round, which had kicked up a lot of dust. He blew past the turnoff, leading the column away from the road to the airport and was now headed north in the direction of downtown Baghdad. After several hundred yards, Ball figured out that he was headed the wrong way. Ball plowed over the guardrail, pulled a U-turn, and got the task force back on track—or, at least, most of the task force.

Perkins was toward the end of the column, and his M113 had followed the preceding vehicles through the U-turn. After making the turn, a truck full of Iraqi soldiers came flying toward him. The Iraqis were trying to pick off a vehicle toward the end of the column. Nussio, the executive officer with 1-64, fired at the truck, which crashed. But one fighter, with an AK-47, decided to make a run at Perkins's command vehicle. Startled by the one-man attack against an armored vehicle and out of ammunition, Captain John Ives, Perkins's intelligence officer, who was doubling as the .50 caliber gunner, threw an empty ammo can at the Iraqi. Perkins pulled out his 9mm pistol and shot the fighter, the only time he needed to use the weapon during the war.

Most of the high drama, however, was yet to come. When Diaz abandoned his tank and jumped into Lieutenant Gruneisen's tank the soldiers had lost time. The tank was extremely cramped—too cramped to operate efficiently. There were five solders in a tank built for four, so the sensitive items and baggage were lodged on the front deck. With the extra passenger and baggage on top of the tanks, the driver's observation was impeded. Worse, Gruneisen was the commander of the lead platoon in the column—it would be hard to command and control his platoon from the rear of the formation. Gruneisen's tank had gone from the tip of the spear to last in the queue. It was well behind the column and would have to scramble to catch up.

As the column advanced along Highway 8, each tank alternated its turret, ensuring that its main gun was pointed in a direction opposite to that of the main gun of the vehicle in front. Gruneisen's main gun was traversed to the left, with the gunner scanning for the enemy, driving in the far right lane. Gruneisen's gunner, Sergeant Carlos Hernandez, caught a glimpse of an upcoming bridge pillar and yelled for the crew to move the gun, but it was too late. The barrel clipped the edge of the pillar and sent the turret spinning wildly. The crew later reported the turret had spun around about twenty times in less than a minute. The sensitive items and machine gun they had rescued from Diaz's tank and stored on the hull were now strewn all over the highway. The jolt had also ripped up the metal teeth that held the turret, making it impossible to traverse the gun. Gruneisen halted the tank and the crew ran along the road gathering what documents they could. Then they locked the turret so the gun stayed in place. The crew seemed hopelessly behind now and struggled to make time.

Captain Jason Conroy, the commander of Charlie Company, told Gruneisen to look for a statue, which was the only marker indicating the way to the airport that Conroy could think of. But it was too late: Gruneisen's tank had already passed it. Conroy told Gruneisen he needed to turn around right away. Conroy then called Schwartz and told him the convoy needed to slow down. "I've got a tank heading into downtown Baghdad," the captain explained. From the start, Blount's main concern was that gaps might develop in the column. This was worse. A tank had split off and was headed straight toward the heavily defended palace area. The Thunder Run was supposed to be audacious, but not that audacious.

Gruneisen saw a traffic circle ahead, which was occupied by an array of

Iraqi vehicles. There were trucks and cars full of soldiers. Gruneisen quickly sized up the situation. His main gun had been knocked out of commission by the collision with the pillar; his main weapon was the loader's M240 machine gun. There was no time to stop and turn around. He ordered his driver to speed to the traffic circle and drive around it. The Iraqis seemed to be as surprised at the turn of events as the Americans and were too startled to open fire. A car full of soldiers slammed into the side of the tank. "Just keep on going, just keep on going," Gruneisen yelled. The tank drove over the front of the car, killing the driver, and kept rolling. A bleeding passenger got out with an AK-47 to fire at the tank, but was quickly shot. A near disaster had been averted.[9]

As Gruneisen rushed to join the column, the Iraqis were pouring on the fire. They had even taken RPG warheads, wrapped them in clothes, and thrown them in the middle of the road, hoping that they would blow off a Bradley or M1A1 track. The use of these improvised roadside bombs was a glimmer of a tactic that the Iraqis would later perfect and use with much greater effect after the fall of Baghdad. Gruneisen was not the only one who had a problem. Blue 4, a Bradley from Charlie Company, 3-15, which was attached to the formation, was hit by a rocket-propelled grenade. The RPG round penetrated the Bradley armor, hit the fuel cells, went through the outer wall, ricocheted to the left and hit the bottle of Halon fire-suppressant, which exploded. In the process, Private First Class Sean Sunday was wounded: his leg was broken, his ligaments torn. Thinking the Bradley was on fire, Sunday jumped out of the hatch and fell onto the highway, unable to walk and caught in the middle of a firefight. Sergeant First Class David Wayne Crotus radioed Black 6, his commander, Captain Larry Burris, and told him that his Bradley had no power and that his driver might be dead. Crotus could not get the driver to respond on the internal vehicle net that is piped into the combat crewman's helmet and had no idea he was lying on the road.

Crotus popped his commander's hatch to assess the situation. When he looked out he saw Sunday on the ground. A Bradley and tanks had pulled up to provide protective cover. Riding in his Bradley, Staff Sergeant Jeffery Empson also saw Sunday. He did not want to open the ramp and let his infantry squad rush out. He was afraid that the enemy would fire into the track as soon as the ramp opened only to be engulfed in a firefight that would produce U.S. casualties and slow the column down even more. So Empson jumped out, raced 30 yards to Sunday as enemy fighters tried to shoot him. With Sunday hopping on one foot, he brought Sunday to his vehicle. Empson then towed the stricken Bradley.[10]

. . .

Toward the front of the column the fighting was just as intense. Schwartz's formation was in a rolling firefight, and Sergeant Booker from Alpha Company was in the thick of it. The platoon sergeant was a larger-than-life character and one of the most popular men in the battalion. Early in the Thunder Run Booker had discovered that his .50 caliber machine gun was jammed, so he took advantage of the delay caused by the fire in Diaz's tank to exchange ammunition with Sergeant First Class Ronald Gaines. Gaines took all of Booker's .50 caliber ammunition and handed Booker all of his M4 carbine rifle ammo. He was making full use of the additional ammo. Booker was up in the turret firing away with his M4 at enemy fighters that were as close as 10 to 16 yards from the vehicle, all the while bragging over the radio to Gaines when he got a kill. "I don't want to die in this fucking country," he exclaimed to his tank crew. It was his jocular way of justifying his determination to fight. Some soldiers later wondered why Booker was taking such a risk, but the sergeant wanted to stay in the fray.

Sergeant David Gibbons, the gunner, was scanning, when he felt Booker fall on his back. Gibbons looked at the loader, who seemed to be in a state of shock and was staring at Gibbons. When Gibbons saw Booker he was shocked, too. It looked like he had been hit right in the face. With injuries that extensive, Gibbons concluded that he had to be dead. Gibbons radioed the news. The platoon sergeant told Gibbons that it was too dangerous to bring the medics up to extract the body. Gibbons would have to take command and keep going. Gibbons was trying to figure out how best to position Booker's body when he saw Booker's tongue moving. It looked like he was gasping for air. Gibbons immediately radioed the news: Booker was alive and gasping for air.

The medics were sent. Firefight or not, Booker would have to be evacuated. Gibbons turned to his loader. He would get on top of the tank and they would pass Booker's body through the hatch. The loader was so upset that Gibbons had to call him back and remind him to put on his CVC helmet. They put some straps under Booker's arms and hauled him out of the tank, a drill they had often practiced in training never realizing they would have to do it for real while under fire one day. Command Sergeant Major William Barnello ran over to help with the stretcher. "Hold on, Book, we're gonna get you. We got you. Hold on, Book," he said.

The line medics, Specialist Shawn Holland and Private First Class Joe

Hill, tended to Booker. They placed him in the medical track, opened his airway, and administered CPR. Then Captain Mike Dyches, the physician's assistant and the most experienced medical professional in the brigade, arrived. He had been a Navy corpsman and had worked in a hospital emergency room before joining the Army. If anyone could save Booker it would be he.

Dyches climbed into their vehicle, but concluded that there was nothing that could be done for Booker. There no longer was a pulse. It looked as if an RPG had hit the tank and then careened up and struck Booker smack in the face. As they drove toward the airport, Dyches tried to hold Booker's hand but discovered his thumb was missing. It had been blown away by the RPG. The medics wrapped bandages around Booker, but it was primarily for the benefit of the soldiers who were still alive and who would have been shocked by the gruesome death of the popular sergeant.[11]

The task force was in the home stretch now and driving for the airport. At the final intersection, the Iraqis had pushed three-foot-high cement barricades across the road. At the airport, Blount was getting reports from a V Corps UAV that the Iraqis were also barricading the route behind the task force. Enemy fighters seemed to be streaming toward the area from the flanks. For the second time in the Thunder Run, Blount had serious concerns. The Iraqis were trying to block the force, break it into pieces, and then mow it down, as they had done with the wayward 507th Army logistics column in Nasiriyah. Blount had alerted Grimsley to get an armored battalion ready to attack toward the city if Perkins's situation became desperate. Now it looked like Grimsley might need to carry out the rescue.

Blount called Perkins on the radio and asked him if he wanted to turn around. Perkins knew he had to press on. If he started to turn around, he would lose momentum, and expose his flanks and rear to the enemy. He also knew it would be a major psychological advantage for the Iraqis. "Negative," Perkins replied. "We will continue the attack to the airport as planned and link up with Raider [Grimsley's 1st BCT]".[12]

At the head of the column, Schwartz was trying to figure out how to get past the cement barricade, no small task since the MICLIC line charge had been left behind. Schwartz wondered if it would be possible to move the barriers or drive around them. He decided to crash through and pray that the tank he would use as an armored battering ram would not be knocked out of action. Ball's tank, which was still at the head of the task force and was equipped with a plow to push aside mines, was quickly nominated for the assignment.

Ball gathered up a head of steam and drove headlong into the barrier. The seventy-ton tank literally flew through the air before plopping back down intact on the highway. Several tanks followed. Gibbons's tank rocked so much when it went over the barrier, he thought the driver had become distraught from seeing Booker killed and had driven the tank off the road and collided with another vehicle. "Stop, stop, stop," Gibbons yelled. But the intercom system was not working. Only later did he learn they had cleared the barrier. "It felt like we hit another tank almost, it was pretty rough, and then I could feel the tank, the front end dip down. That's why I thought we'd run off road. I thought we'd hit something and went off the side of the road. It was a pretty good hit."

The Iraqis seemed to sense that this was their last crack at the intruders and were pulling out all the stops to hit the Americans before they escaped to the sanctuary of the airport. They were firing from the rooftops, from the bushes, from the overpasses. Sergeant Olson with Alpha Company told his soldiers to go "open protected." "When you can hear the bullets whizzing by, does that mean they're close?" asked Specialist Brian Lawlor, the loader on the tank. It did. Moments later, one of Olson's tanks took a direct hit from an Iraqi RPG team that had positioned themselves in an apartment building. The M1 put a main gun round into the building and kept going.

As the column moved forward, Ball's gunner in Red 1 saw another potential problem ahead. "I have tanks," he called out over the radio. A ripple of apprehension went through the task force. The battalion had dealt with RPG teams, fanatical fighters, and obstacles. So far, there had been no large formations of Republican Guard troops or Iraqi armor. Were the Iraqis now bringing their T-72s into play? The column slowed down while Schwartz tried to identify the armor. Red 1 checked the distance to the tanks with his laser range finder. It was 2 miles away. The distance fit the data from the Blue Force Tracker in Schwartz's tank. The tanks were M1s from Grimsley's brigade, which were guarding the approaches to the airport and had been ready to come to Schwartz's aid.[13]

The fighting was not over yet. The uncertainty over the tanks had forced the column to slow down. It was particularly intense near First Sergeant

Jose Mercada's M113. The crew had left the hatch open for better observation and so an embedded reporter from the *Atlanta Constitution* could
see out. It had also taken on Shipley, the driver from Diaz's tank, and
Schafer, Diaz's loader. Shipley was on the left and Schafer on the right,
protecting the reporter on each side. Specialist Shawn Sullivan, a medic,
was shooting over them. A bullet penetrated Shipley's Kevlar, went
through his head, and came out through his right eye. Schafer was struck
in the back and the round went through his lung before exiting through
his side and striking his right arm. When the column reached the airport,
the M113 raced ahead, looking for the Medevac helicopter to evacuate
the two wounded soldiers. It seemed like it took forever to find it at the
large airport. The rest of Schwartz's column pulled on line motor-pool-
style by company team.[14]

The task force had suffered one dead and two seriously wounded.
They had lost one tank. All of their vehicles had scars from the fight.
Most of the externally secured equipment and baggage had been burned
or blown off the vehicles. As the crews surveyed the damage, many came
to the realization that the externally mounted storage cages, rucksacks,
and duffel bags deflected a lot of the RPGs fired at the vehicles. Had it not
been for that, the Bradleys and M113s may have suffered far greater damage. At the airport, the ground was covered with shell casings as the soldiers emptied out their ammo cases. Schwartz's task force figured that it
had killed as many as 2,000 of the enemy and destroyed one Iraqi tank, a
BMP, thirty enemy trucks, and several air defense systems. The lopsided
results were reported up the chain of command.

Blount's M113 was on the airport's east-side road to meet Perkins's column. Standing by his vehicle, Blount surveyed the formation, trying to
gain a sense of the severity of the morning's attack. It was one thing to
track it on a computer screen or hear the ebb and flow of the battle on the
radio from a few miles away, and another to see it firsthand. Blount re-
mounted and followed the tail end of Perkins's column and then went to
talk to the soldiers. Some were crying, some laughing, some hugging, and
some still shaking. The division's command sergeant major, Julian Kell-
man, gave the soldiers what little water he had stockpiled, since most of
theirs had been blown off the vehicles. Captain Erik Berdy, Blount's aide,
went to find two of his closest friends—Larry Burris and Andy Hilmes—
to make sure they were all right.[15]

Schwartz had been shaken by the episode. When he was at the airport, he had gone from soldier to soldier and apologized for leading them into the maelstrom. When he embraced Olson, Schwartz's voice was quavering as if he had been crying. "I should have never sent you guys in there," he said. Afterward Olson confided the episode to his diary along with this note: "There is a horrible rumor that they [the brigade commander and the division commander] want us to do another raid into Baghdad. I hope and pray that it is just a rumor. For I don't ever want to go through that 'HELL' again."[16]

That afternoon, as the battalion was getting ready to return to Objective Saints, Blount approached Perkins to talk about follow-up missions. Perkins told him that the key to the city was the regime district downtown, and that he had driven by the exit to that area on the way to the airport. Blount told him he would discuss this with the division staff and get back to him with guidance. When Perkins got back to the tactical command post, Blount called to tell him that he wanted to follow up soon with another attack into the city, one that would involve not just one tank battalion but the entire brigade.

CHAPTER 20

The Accidental Victory

On April 6, Saddam gathered his top aides and high command. The Iraqi leader had been moving among a network of safe houses in Baghdad, including one that had a satellite dish, which allowed him to receive international cable news. For this session, the most stringent security precautions were in effect. Tariq Aziz, Saddam's deputy prime minister and longtime aide, arrived in a van with windows covered to prevent the passengers from identifying the secret meeting place, but when he got out of the vehicle Aziz was able to determine that the site was a small home in the Al-Mansur district, the most affluent and pro-regime area in Baghdad. Aziz later told U.S. interrogators that at Saddam's behest he had read aloud an eight-page letter that the Iraqi leader had composed and prepared for the session. Saddam showed no emotion, which he considered a sign of weakness, but Aziz thought the letter had a desperate tone. Aziz considered the session as Saddam's way of saying goodbye to his top aides and the letter that of a defeated man who had lost the will to resist. As Aziz read it, he sensed that the regime was coming to an end.

The same day, "Baghdad Bob," Iraq's information minister, Muhammad al-Sahaf, led a group of Western reporters to view Diaz's abandoned tank. By this time, the heavily damaged M1 had also been hit by a Maverick antitank missile. Ignoring Perkins, who was convinced he could recover the tank when he next attacked into the city, an air strike had been ordered to destroy the M1. Using the tank as exhibit A, Sahaf cast the Thunder Run as a defeat. Blount and Perkins thought the Thunder Run demonstrated that they could enter Baghdad at will, but Sahaf was telling the media that the Americans had been repulsed. The Iraqi senior leadership did not believe the line, but Sahaf was putting the best face on a deteriorating situation.

Late that night, Saddam held a war planning session with his sons and military commanders at yet another safe house. The topic was urban operations, and the Iraqi leader ordered the Republican Guard and Fedayeen to prepare to fight the Americans in the streets of Baghdad. For years, the Republican Guard units had been positioned away from the capital to diminish the risk of a coup. An Iraqi decision to bring Republican Guard troops into the capital was one of McKiernan's worst nightmares. But it was a step that Saddam was only prepared to take in extremis and in fact had come too late. The meeting went on into the early morning hours.[1]

Fortified by the success of the Thunder Run, Perkins was making plans for another raid into Baghdad. The 2nd BCT commander saw it as a chance to deliver a body blow to Saddam by grabbing control of the Baath Party headquarters and some of the regime's buildings. Perkins was enthusiastic about the task. He was irritated by Sahaf's claims that the Americans had been routed and wanted to put an end to the Iraqi spin control once and for all. When Perkins took his soldiers downtown he would make sure that the international media saw them. Perkins even thought about crashing the site where the Iraqis held their press conferences. The Thunder Run had proved that there was still a lot of fight left in the enemy, and Perkins did not relish the idea of fighting his way into the city only to relinquish the territory. If the brigade went to downtown Baghdad Perkins wanted to go to stay.

Collaborating with Lieutenant Colonel Eric Wesley, his executive officer, Perkins began sketching out the plan. Perkins figured that the Iraqis were expecting the Americans to fight their way in street by street, but had no plan for an adversary who set up camp in the heart of Baghdad. So his strategy was to race to the core of the city, establish a base, and fight from the center out. Grabbing the city center would ensure that the Americans could not be outflanked and would establish interior lines. The parade grounds and parks near the Republican Palace also offered Perkins clear fields of fire against Iraqi counterattacks. After consolidating their position, Perkins's soldiers would begin to push out. The joke within the brigade was that Perkins would have the enemy right where he wanted: he would be surrounded by them.[2]

In fleshing out the plan, the brigade put to use some valuable lessons it had learned from the April 5 Thunder Run. It was, for example, vital to maintain momentum. If a vehicle stopped, the enemy would quickly converge with RPGs and trucks full of soldiers. This time, Perkins's soldiers would have to keep moving. It was also clear that the overpasses on the way downtown were key pieces of terrain. The Iraqis had a penchant for taking positions on the top of the bridges to fire down at the American vehicles. They also liked to hide under the overpasses for protection. South of Baghdad, the Iraqis had used the palm groves to hide their armor from allied warplanes. In the city, they used the overpasses to protect their tanks, BMPs, and infantry fighting positions. Beyond that, each cloverleaf raised the risk of an open flank. The Iraqis could use the on- and off-ramps to attack, which was what had happened when the soldiers struggled to recover Diaz's tank.[3]

Meeting with his planners later that night, Perkins laid out the key decisions he would have to make to carry out his ambitious plan. If the brigade went in to stay, how would it refuel? Should it bring fuel and ammo into the city, or should it replenish its fuel and supplies at a site outside the city? Perkins was inclined to bring fuel and ammo along. Otherwise, he would be weakening his defenses by sending tanks and Bradleys out of downtown Baghdad.

Perkins also needed to figure out how to distribute forces, what to do with his artillery, how to use the close air support, and where he would deploy his reserve, such as it was. His planners' initial recommendation was to lead with Twitty's 3-15 Infantry Battalion, which would secure the overpasses so that the armored battalions could move through unmolested. But Perkins was worried that it might take too long to gain control of the overpasses. While Twitty's soldiers were fighting for the intersections the tank battalions would be waiting to attack and out of the fight.

So Perkins turned the plan on its head. The brigade's artillery would fire airbursts over the key intersections to kill as many Iraqi defenders on the overpasses as possible. Then the tank battalions would blow through the intersections. Schwartz's 1-64 Armor would have the dubious honor of leading the attack once again. Its soldiers knew the way. Schwartz would head to the monument area, a relatively open piece of terrain, which featured the enormous crossed sabers and the Iran-Iraq War Memorial near the Tomb of the Unknowns, Iraq's tribute to its unknown soldiers, which looked like an enormous concrete flying saucer. Schwartz's terrain would also include a park, the zoo, and the Al-Rasheed Hotel, which Perkins believed was filled with the international media. It would be like seizing the Mall near the Washington Monument. There were no alleyways or apartment buildings in which the Iraqis could hide. It would be defensible terrain and would also provide the psychological effect of owning the symbols of Iraqi power.[4]

DeCamp's 4-64 Armor Battalion would follow on Schwartz's heels and race to the Republican Palace and the complex of government buildings and luxury villas that abutted the Tigris River, thus seizing the administrative heart of the capital. The tank battalions would have to control nearby intersections and bridges. Perkins told his commander that they would need at least a platoon to control an intersection. That would enable them to station four tanks in four different directions, their rears abutting each other so that the enemy could not get behind them to strike the sort of blow that had disabled Diaz's tank.

Twitty's 3-15 Infantry would come last and would hold the intersections so that there would be an open supply line to the tank battalions downtown. With a secure route to the center of the city, the brigade would be able to stay the night. There were three intersections 3-15 would need to control and the battalion code-named them Moe, Larry, and Curley. Wesley would run the brigade tactical operations center, which would call in air strikes and coordinate the artillery. The brigade moved the TOC to a walled Iraqi military compound on the outskirts of the city. Perkins did not know if he could pull it off. The moment of decision would be at the four-hour mark. A tank consumed fifty-six gallons of fuel an hour when it was fighting, which translated into eight to ten hours of operations. At the four-hour mark the brigade's M1s would be halfway through their supply of fuel. If Twitty's battalion did not control the Highway 8 intersections by then, Perkins would have to pull the tank battalions out. The brigade would have conducted a dramatic raid, but not the decisive war-ending maneuver Perkins intended.[5]

While Perkins was consumed with planning, Blount briefed the operation to Wallace. The V Corps commander was pleased with the Thunder Run, but considered an attack downtown and the occupation of the regime area too much of a reach. The division, Wallace told Blount, was not ready to go downtown and stay. Wallace authorized the division to seize several of the main intersections that Perkins had passed through on his Thunder Run to the airport, stay several hours, and then come back out. It would be, in effect, another Thunder Run, one in keeping with

Wallace's original plan to set up five forward operating bases around the city and run raids in and out of the capital. There was reason to be cautious. If Perkins became ensnarled in an urban fight it would not be easy to reinforce the 2nd BCT. Grimsley was at the airport and Dan Allyn was fighting on the northwest outskirts of the city.[6]

"We had a UAV flying overhead during the first Thunder Run," Wallace later recalled, "and my G-2 [intelligence officer] reported back to me we had observed the enemy folding in behind 1-64 as they went along Highway 8 and placing obstacles in the road behind them, under the assumption that they would be coming back the same way. And that in turn led me to believe that maybe the notion of having to hold terrain and hold a cordon all the way in so you could come back out was something we might ought to take a look at before we went in to stay. My thought was that Perkins was going to attack in along Highway 8 about to that second main intersection and then extract himself coming out the same direction. A kind of a limited-objective attack, still an armed reconnaissance, but using a different technique than you're just driving down the road and taking a left. That was my expectation."

Blount had his operations center pass the word to Perkins's 2nd BCT: attack to the intersections and then pull out. Perkins would conduct another armed reconnaissance, but would not stay in the city. It would be an in-and-out raid, nothing more, nothing less. "Wallace said, 'Don't go to stay. We are not ready to go to the palace yet,' " Blount recalled. "I am sure the division told the brigade to just go to the intersections and seize them. I always thought Perkins understood to stop at the intersections."[7]

Perkins, who was not in his tactical operations center when Blount's staff called, never got the message. He assumed everybody was in agreement that he was to attack downtown. The contentious issue, he thought, would be winning permission from V Corps to stay the night. When he discussed his plan that night with Lieutenant Colonel Pete Bayer, Blount's chief operations officer or G-3, Perkins talked about the route he intended to take to reduce the risk of friendly fire, but did not go into the details of his criteria for determining whether the brigade would remain overnight.

Perkins later explained his approach: "It definitely wasn't the focus of my conversation. Quite honestly, I did not want them to get fixated on me staying downtown because I wasn't really sure what was going to occur and I was afraid they would start overanalyzing that portion of it. If that opportunity developed I would then report to them as it was unfolding and lay out all the options available." In effect, Perkins had treated his superiors at the division much the way Blount had dealt with Wallace at V Corps in seeking permission for the April 5 Thunder Run. Perkins had given a barebones description of how he planned to conduct the mission inside his battle space. To minimize the chances that the division would limit his options, Perkins had downplayed just how ambitious an operation he had in mind.[8]

As with the first Thunder Run, Schwartz's 1-64 Armored Battalion would lead the way with Red Platoon and their mine-plow-equipped tanks. To synchronize the artillery fire, Lieutenant Colonel Kenneth Gantt, the brigade's fire support coordinator and commander of the supporting field artillery battalion, planned to bombard four major overpasses on the route downtown so that the shells would fall thirty seconds before Schwartz's and DeCamp's battalions reached them. His batteries would fire HE—high-explosive, variable-time rounds, airbursts that would explode two to three yards off the ground and send shrapnel radiating downward. Gantt figured that the airbursts would take care of the Iraqis and other Arab fighters without damaging the overpasses. The tank battalions could button up in their M1 tanks and Bradleys.[9]

The brigade was not sure what to expect. Captain Felix Almaguer, the 3-15 intelligence officer, learned through contacts with the special forces that there were numerous foreign fighters in the city and put out the word that the soldiers would encounter Syrians, Jordanians, Sudanese, and Yemenis. The brigade had picked up two new embedded reporters, foreign press who had seen Schwartz's battalion come into the airport and wanted to be closer to the action. As Perkins prepared to attack on the morning of April 7, they decided to stay with Wesley at the TOC. They could monitor the action and avoid the outsized risks.[10]

The Iraqis anticipated that the Americans would soon be back and used the time to lay a long field of antitank mines, less than one mile from Perkins's northernmost positions on Objective Saints. The minefield was deep—there were some 400 mines—but no efforts appeared to have been made to bury them. They were lying on the highway. Fearing that the antitank mines might be booby-trapped, the engineers started by lassoing the mines and pulling them gently to the side of the road. Time, however, was running out, and they soon began carrying them to the side of the road after swiping them quickly with their fingers.

As the attack began on the seventh, it looked like a repeat of the first

Thunder Run. Red Platoon went through the breach lane in the minefield, leading with its number two tank, the only one with a mine plow that had not been dented or destroyed in the April 5 raid. It pushed aside a concrete barrier and came under fire from small arms and RPGs. Staff Sergeant Joe Jerril fired back. During the first Thunder Run, the bullet casing had backed up and jammed his coax machine gun. So this time he attached a laundry bag at the base of the gun to catch the shells.

Again, a tank was hit in the rear, this time by two RPG-7s. The projectiles penetrated the fuel cell and fuel began leaking. "The platoon sergeant called up and said, 'You've been hit real bad,' Gibbons recalled. "I was like, no shit, and then not too long after that we got hit again on the right side, he called and said, 'You got hit again, you're on fire.' " The crew managed to put out the fire, but the tank was stuck in the middle of the road with no power or hydraulics. This time the attack would not wait. Gibbons and his crew watched the battalion pass by. They would have to defend themselves until a tank came later to tow them back for repair. The Iraqis and their foreign fighters who were battling with them were prepared for another Thunder Run. The enemy was better hidden in the palm groves, on the side of the road, and on rooftops. There were fewer cars and civilians on the road. Still, Schwartz did not think the enemy fire was as intense as on his April 5 push to the airport.[11]

From his assault command post at the airport, Blount was monitoring the column on Blue Force Tracker and looked at Pete Bayer as the line of blue icons swung right at Objective Moe and headed toward the palace area. Blount told Bayer he did not think Perkins was going that far. Blount told Austin to call Perkins and find out where he was going. Going downtown was not part of the plan. Perkins was following Schwartz and as he made the turn at Moe, he got a call from Division. Perkins was surprised by the question. He had never gotten the word that the attack downtown was off. "Sir, I am heading downtown," he told Austin.[12]

There was a pause at the other end. An attack to the heart of Baghdad was under way, but Blount could not authorize such an audacious operation on his own. He had to consult Wallace. Already, there was confusion at the V Corps headquarters as to what was going on. The battle captain on duty complained to the civilian technical support contractor that Blue Force Tracker was generating a screwy report. There were crazy icons indicating two battalions were in the center of Baghdad. Blount called Wallace and told him that Perkins had gone downtown. He did not explain why. The 2nd BCT commander had inadvertently created a new situation and V Corps needed to decide how to play it. "I'm watching FBCB-2 and I see this column taking a right at Moe and heading downtown," Wallace said, referring to the Blue Force Tracker that monitored allied positions. "I got a call from Buff, and I don't remember his exact words, but he notified me that Perkins was en route downtown. . . . And at that point, from my perspective, we were committed to doing what Perkins was doing. So there was no choice other than to reinforce the success he was having."[13]

Schwartz's column passed the Crossed Sabers and came under recoilless rifle fire as it approached the Tomb of the Unknowns. The Americans fanned out to the Al-Rasheed Hotel, the Tomb of the Unknowns, and the Azura Zoo, where the Iraqis had cached some of their arms just inside the zoo fence. Schwartz had been worried that the international media was concentrated at the Al-Rasheed Hotel, as they had been during the 1991 Persian Gulf War. But it soon became clear that the media was not there, instead enemy soldiers were gathering. Meanwhile, DeCamp's 4-64 battalion fought its way toward the Republican Palace, which was decorated with four massive helmeted heads bearing the likeness of Saddam.

Wallace called McKiernan's headquarters at Camp Doha and reached J. D. Thurman, McKiernan's operations officer. "Okay, Bubba," Wallace said. "We're here. Now what?" As Perkins's battalions raced into the city the issue was how long the brigade should stay. Thinking that Perkins would soon withdraw, McKiernan told Wallace to have Perkins find a statue at Saddam's palace gate to blow up and have the operation filmed so that the United States could counter the Iraqi information minister's claims that U.S. troops were not in Baghdad. Blount passed this on to Perkins. The 3rd ID needed to leave its calling card. A Fox television crew accompanied the brigade and was standing ready for live TV.[14]

While Perkins was talking with his officers, Chris Tomlinson, an AP reporter with the brigade, called a colleague at CENTCOM on his Thuraya. He told them he was on the parade grounds. The colleague checked with CENTCOM and said that nobody was going downtown that day. Tomlinson repeated that he was already downtown. The colleague checked again. CENTCOM told him that the brigade would be coming right out. Tomlinson said: "I think he is staying."

Perkins was happy to find and blast a statue of Saddam. Schwartz's 1-64 battalion found the perfect photo op: a Saddam monument on the

parade grounds with the Crossed Sabers in the background. A tank took
it out with a 120mm round. DeCamp was also trying to help with the information war. He told Perkins that he had a group of Iraqis who wanted
to tear down a poster of Saddam. But the embedded television correspon-
dents were with Perkins. The brigade told DeCamp that the TV crew
would be right over. But the photo op disappeared when the Iraqis spied
several refrigerators in a nearby building and rushed off to loot them. It
was a small indication of the disorder to come. When the 3rd Infantry Division went by a week later the poster was still there.

Still, Perkins did not want to pull out. Sahaf would again be boasting
to the world that the Americans had been repulsed and the 3rd Infantry
Division would end up fighting its way downtown again. Perkins's plan
had been to stay and build up a base of operations inside the city. But that
would depend on Stef Twitty's success in controlling the three principal
intersections on the route downtown and keeping the supply lines open.

While much of the world's attention was riveted on the M1s prowling
downtown Baghdad, Twitty was fighting for the intersections. He had divided his battalion into three parts, one for each intersection. Team
Gator, commanded by Captain Josh Wright, consisted of two mechanized infantry platoons and a tank platoon, and was assigned to Objective Moe, the final intersection before the right turn to Baghdad. It was
the main effort. Team Rage, commanded by Captain Dan Hubbard, consisted of two tank platoons and a mechanized rifle platoon, and was assigned to Objective Larry, the second of the two intersections. The task of
securing Objective Curley, the first intersection on the route, was given to
a hodgepodge of units, called Team Zan for Captain Harry "Zan" Hornbuckle, the senior operations officer in the battalion. Hornbuckle, who
had been a Ranger instructor, pulled together his team in six hours. It
consisted of a rifle platoon riding in four Bradleys, the mortar platoon,
an engineer platoon, and 3-15's forward aid station, its TOC, and an
extra Bradley that the battalion had acquired in Kuwait. A veteran of
the Mogadishu battle, the battalion's senior NCO, Command Sergeant
Major Robert Gallagher, also joined the team. Gallagher traveled in an
M88 recovery vehicle and tried to position himself at the key fights. As the
battalion prepared to attack, a detachment of Special Forces asked to
come along. They wanted to make contact with the locals, explaining
that if they could just talk to the "men in beards," Team Zan might not

have to fight after all. To facilitate the interaction with the Iraqis, the Special Forces soldiers were deliberately not wearing all their body armor.[15]

The hope of avoiding a fight evaporated almost immediately. The enemy recognized the significance of the supply route and was determined to close it down. As Team Zan rolled into Curley it came under intense fire. The soldiers had to fight just to get to the area under the overpass where they intended to station their command post. Hornbuckle had about 80 soldiers on his team and estimated that he was up against 150 to 200 very determined fighters. It was what the military called a 360-degree fight. The enemy was attacking from all directions.[16]

Doing the best with his limited manpower, Hornbuckle ordered the rifle platoon from the Bradleys to defend east and west, instructed the engineers to defend to the north, and had the mortar platoon and scouts defend south. To clear the enemy from a series of nearby trenches, he ordered the drivers and radio operators from his M577 command vehicle into action. The Special Forces threw on their body armor and went to clear some of the nearby buildings as well. After the Special Forces troops charged into a building, the troops at Curley heard a flurry of shots. Then they saw the Special Forces soldiers dragging out two of their wounded comrades.[17]

Over the next three hours, Hornbuckle's team blasted one pickup truck after another charging their position, including one that zoomed down an on-ramp on the cloverleaf and almost attacked the M577 command vehicle. Hornbuckle ordered the engineers to use their armored bulldozer to knock down nearby light poles and push them across the road so the enemy technicals could not drive in. There was so much machine gun fire from some of the nearby buildings that they appeared to be twinkling. Enemy fighters also began to sneak back into the trenches near the cloverleaf and started edging in toward the intersection. They were "hugging" the American position, situating themselves so close that it was all but impossible for Hornbuckle to call in air strikes or artillery. In the midst of the fighting, Gallagher spied the broken-down M1 from Schwartz's position, which was being towed south. He wanted to use it to transport the wounded. In all the confusion, the tank left before the wounded could be loaded on board.

Twitty had positioned himself at Larry, the middle of the two intersections, so he would be within radio range of his entire task force. After three hours of fighting, Twitty called Hornbuckle. "Zan, just tell me. Do you need extra help?" Hornbuckle did not say yes, but Twitty could hear the shooting, so he called Gallagher, the most experienced and combat-hardened member of Team Zan. Gallagher had already been wounded in the leg and was standing near his M88 vehicle and firing his M4 when Twitty called. "We need help, and we need it now," Gallagher said. Twitty called Perkins and asked him to send the mechanized infantry platoon that was protecting the Highways 1 and 8 intersection. Captain Ronny Johnson went one better. He suggested sending the entire rifle company. Perkins called Wesley and told him to send everything he had left over to Objective Curley. The 2nd BCT had now launched its only reserve and was fully committed. Twitty reinforced the message. "Get to Curley! ASAP!" Twitty said.[18]

While Twitty was trying to manage the fight on Highway 8, Perkins drove down to the parade grounds to consult with Schwartz and De-Camp. The news was troubling. Fuel gauges were down to half empty. Perkins had arranged for additional fuel and ammunition to be driven in, but he did not want to order them sent until Twitty had the intersections under control.

Perkins radioed Twitty. It was not what he wanted to hear. Twitty was one of the brigade's most unflappable officers, but he could not guarantee that he could hold Highway 8. Curley was in danger of being overrun. The soldiers at the other intersections were having plenty of trouble as well. At Larry, Twitty himself was firing so much his fighting vehicle had to be reloaded with 25mm ammunition. At Moe, like Curley, the combat engineers had knocked down light poles to block the enemy's attack routes. After hours of fighting, however, Josh Wright reported that he was "black" on main gun ammunition in the tank platoon, "black" on coax machine gun ammunition for the Bradleys and tanks, and "black" on small arms ammunition for the infantrymen. In other words, they had about an hour of ammo left.

Perkins got on the phone to Wesley, who was at the brigade TOC, which was installed in the former Iraqi military compound near the intersection of Highways 1 and 8 to shield it from Iraqi RPGs and small arms fire. Wesley congratulated Perkins on making it to the heart of the regime in Baghdad. Perkins said he had some challenges and talked about the fuel problem. He was asking about the status of the R2 (rearm and refit) resupply package and how quickly he could launch it. All of sudden there was static on the radio. "Sir, we have been hit," Wesley said. Perkins knew that the TOC had been taking mortar and artillery fire and figured the new attack was not that serious. "Roger, get an assessment and give me a call back," Perkins said.

A surface-to-surface missile had come screaming in from the northwest and scored a direct hit on the brigade command center. The missile left an enormous crater seven feet wide and ten feet deep. Before the brigade moved into the compound, it had been used by the Iraqis to store plastic bags full of rice. After the explosion, sheets of burning plastic were strewn about. It was what the military called a MASCAL, or mass casualty, situation. Many of the soldiers inside the walled compound had taken off their body armor and Kevlar helmets, making them more vulnerable to the blast.[19]

Alexander Gongora, the brigade's operations sergeant major, was covered in blood and shaking. He went to see if the driver of a mangled vehicle was all right. But all he found was a headless torso under a burning truck. The chaplain began putting white tape on the pieces of flesh so the remains could be recovered. Captain William Glaser, the commander of the headquarters company at the site, had been knocked unconscious and was caught underneath the collapsed operation center's main tent. As he extricated himself he was shocked to see wounded soldiers and vehicles and equipment melted beyond recognition. Across his path, Private First Class Conrad Camp was walking with no weapon and a single boot, bleeding from shrapnel in his back. "Where the hell are you going?" Glaser asked. "I have to pull security, sir," he responded. Glaser persuaded the stunned soldier to go with a medic. Corporal Henry Brown, the brigade commander's driver, had been evacuated across the street to an aid station and was positioned near two of the Special Forces soldiers who had been wounded at Curley. The medics were having trouble putting an IV into Brown, who was burned and dehydrated. So one of the SF soldiers ordered the medics to bring Brown over. Full of morphine and with a round in his leg, the Special Forces soldier pulled out his Leatherman knife, cut Brown's leg open, stuck a catheter in a vein, and got the IV started.[20]

Twenty minutes later Wesley called Perkins from an Iridium satellite phone to give him a report. "Sir, we really got hammered," he said. All told, there were five dead, seventeen wounded, and twenty-two vehicles destroyed or damaged. The dead included the two foreign journalists, who had joined the brigade at the airport but elected to stay behind in what they thought was the relative safety of the command post. Also im-

portant, the brigade's primary command and control system for calling
in air strikes and artillery was out of action.

Perkins told Wesley to salvage what he could, put the TOC back together, and concentrate on evacuating the casualties. Perkins had an Air
Force captain and artillery officer with him and would directly coordinate
any air strikes. Wesley thought the Iraqis had scored a one-in-a-million
shot and decided to reestablish the TOC in the same vicinity instead of
taking time to search for a new site. The move did not sit well with some
soldiers, including one military intelligence officer who thought it had
been a mistake to use the facility in the first place. The Iraqis, he reasoned, might not be able to track the U.S. forces as they closed in on Baghdad, but they knew the geographic coordinates of their own facilities and
could easily target them.

With all the problems he was having—the tanks downtown running out
of fuel, Twitty afraid of being overrun, and the brigade TOC in ruins—
Perkins was still determined to stay. If anything, the strike on the TOC
persuaded him that it was more dangerous to sit on the outskirts of the
city than to fight inside of it. He considered his options for reinforcing his
supply link; there were not many good ones. His reserve had already been
sent to Curley. Perkins could take a company from Schwartz or DeCamp
and send it to Moe to shore up the defenses there, but he had only six
companies downtown and sending one to Moe might create a gap in the
defense.

The brigade had its R2 package, the convoy of fuel and ammo
HEMTT trucks that would enable it to rearm and refit. The twenty-truck
convoy, which was under the command of First Lieutenant Aaron Polsgrove, could carry forward 20,000 gallons of fuel and 110 tons of ammunition. But it was highly vulnerable and accustomed to operating beyond
the front lines, not in front of them. Perkins decided to order the ammunition trucks through the gauntlet. Meanwhile, he would have his forces
downtown shut down their tanks to conserve fuel.

As with the first Thunder Run, Blount had told Grimsley to be ready to
come to Perkins's aid if he needed help. Grimsley was ready to attack
from the airport and establish control of Highway 8 and the overpasses.
Perkins preferred that Scott Rutter's 2-7 Infantry Battalion be sent instead
and placed under the 2nd BCT's control. After a short discussion, Blount
agreed to Perkins's request. Rutter was told to go to Curley and take control of the intersection so Twitty's soldiers could move up to Larry and

Moe to strengthen the defenses there. Rutter's troops would provide some badly needed firepower, but they would not arrive until after the R2 package was on its way. Blount himself would be going with 2-7 Infantry in an attempt to link up with 2nd BCT in Baghdad, feeling he could get a better assessment of the situation if he was with Perkins in the center of the city.

While Wallace had never anticipated that his soldiers would be battling to hold on to downtown Baghdad that day, he approved the division's decision to stay the night. "I've got a brigade commander who has seized the initiative, went downtown, seized the new presidential palace, he's now on national TV," Wallace recalled. "I'm listening to the 3rd Infantry Division command net all of this time. Frankly Buff Blount and the 3rd ID was asking Perkins exactly the questions I would have been asking. Can you stay? Do you have enough fuel? Do you have enough ammunition? Can you get your casualties out? Can you get supplies in and out and do you have sufficient combat power to stay where you are? And that running commentary went on for probably a good two or three hours in late afternoon of the seventh. Dave Perkins convinced Buff Blount that he could stay. . . . The second thing was that once he got downtown all of us realized that his fields of fire, his ability to employ his weapons systems in this part of Baghdad because of the parks and the long roads and wide avenues, was actually better than what he had back at Objective Saints. And so he made the recommendation to Blount to stay and Blount made the recommendation to me and I approved it."[21]

Still, getting to the fuel downtown was a risky endeavor. Captain J. O. Bailey, the battalion logistical officer for 3-15 who was to lead the R2 convoy, did not want to set off until he had an escort to protect the convoy and some notion of where he could park the vulnerable fuel and ammo vehicles at Curley. What was the point of bringing fuel and ammo forward if it got blown up along the way? He requested an armored escort from the task force. Major Denton Knapp, the battalion's executive officer, denied the request. As he saw it, the defenders at Curley were in the fight of their lives and there was no armor or mechanized force to spare. The R2 package would have to head north and take its chances. The only help would come from the scouts. The main defense would be from the three scout vehicles, an M577 command track and the .50 caliber machine gun on the maintenance M113.

Sergeant First Class John Marshall, the scout platoon sergeant, picked up the escort mission and was directing the defense of the convoy by radio from the exposed gunner's position in his armored Humvee. Steve

Hommel, the battalion chaplain, was determined to go north to the medical stations that had been set up at Curley and Larry to tend to the wounded. He left his soft-skinned Humvee behind and hitched a ride on the maintenance M113.

For all the valor, Captain Bailey was convinced that he would be involved in a bloody and all but impossible mission—a view he retained well after the fall of Saddam. When an Army historian asked Bailey what he might have done differently, Bailey said that the column should not have been rushed forward until additional forces were brought to escort them and better secure the route. "If I went back in time, I would not have left," he said. "I would have disobeyed an order."[22]

As they prepared to go north the column came under mortar fire. The Iraqis seemed to be waiting for the resupply package to run the gauntlet. Enemy spotters with radios or cell phones were calling in mortar strikes. The American soldiers fired a few bursts to try to suppress the spotters. Before the convoy was even a third of the way to Curley, however, it started taking machine gun and RPG fire as well. There were enemy fighters on the upper stories and roofs of buildings. There were fighters in trenches along the road, who would pop up and shoot. There were fighters mingling with civilians on the street.

Marshall was standing in the turret, firing his MK19 grenade launcher, when an RPG struck him in the upper torso and blew him out of the vehicle. Even though he was wearing body armor his body was nearly severed in half. The driver was dazed and seemed to stop. Polsgrove's vehicle pulled up and the lieutenant told him to keep going. Now was not the time to go back for Marshall's body. They had to get out of the kill zone.

Staff Sergeant Robert Stever was next. He was firing his .50 caliber on the maintenance M113 when an RPG crashed into the butt of the gun and detonated, blowing off his right arm. Stever's torso fell into the M113, which veered left and crashed into the median in the center of the road. But the driver, who was wounded by shrapnel, regained his composure and pressed ahead. The battalion's maintenance tech, Chief Warrant Officer 3 Angel Acevedo, took over the .50 caliber and began to return fire as the M113 continued to move.

As the R2 convoy drove into Curley, it seemed like all hell was breaking loose. The troops were taking fire from all directions. Bailey tried to cram the fuelers and ammo trucks into a spot just off the right side of the road near the overpass. There was little protection, but Bailey would try to get whatever shelter he could. The soldiers parked the vehicles in a coil inside the on- and off-ramps, jumped out, and began to help defend the perimeter.

It was a dire scene with the bodies of dozens of enemy fighters strewn across the intersection. The fighters had made it inside the perimeter before they were cut down. About thirty prisoners, stripped naked to ensure that they were not suicide bombers, had been corraled. Some of the U.S. troops were in nearby trenches, having pushed the enemy dead out of the holes to make room for themselves. RPGs were being fired from such close range that their warheads did not have time to arm. Bravo Company soldiers were throwing hand grenades over mounds at Syrian and Iraqi fighters not more than ten feet away. In their haste some of the U.S. soldiers forgot to "cook off" the grenades—allow two or three seconds of the five-second fuse to elapse before tossing them—giving the enemy a chance to throw some of them back or run away before the grenades exploded. The soldiers from the mortar platoon were especially glad to see the R2 convoy and raced up to the ammo truck to grab several rounds. The platoon had already fired seven "danger close" missions to defend the position at Curley and was running out of ammo.[23]

Hommel, the chaplain, rushed to the medical aid station, where the wounded were gathered. Chief Acevedo, who was in the M113 when Stever was killed, was among the ranks of wounded. He had taken shrapnel in his side and seemed to be in a state of shock. Stever's torso had been placed in a human remains bag. Also among the wounded was an enemy fighter, burned and moving in pain, who made eye contact with Hommel and indicated with his hands that he wanted the Americans to help him or shoot him. The chaplain went and got some stretcher-bearers to take him to the aid station, which was under direct and indirect fire. The battalion surgeon station tried to insert a breathing tube into the wounded fighter, but the tissues in his throat were beginning to swell. There were two dead and about forty wounded, including enemy fighters.

Hommel was a combat veteran. Before he became a chaplain he had served as an infantry sergeant. As he surveyed the melee around him, he was afraid the U.S. troops would be overrun. Army chaplains were under instructions not to bear arms. In the most extreme circumstances, where their lives were at stake, chaplains could declare an exception. It was called the "moment of decision" and was a judgment each chaplain had to make for himself, but one the Army Chaplain Corps discouraged. Hommel decided it was time to fight. He picked up a weapon and started firing at the enemy. "At one point, I thought, you know, we just CAN'T be overrun. It just isn't supposed to happen. And surrendering to those guys—it was just out of the question," Hommel recalled after the war. "I picked up a weapon and I was firing, and I have no problem with that in my conscience. I think I was the first chaplain to do that since Vietnam," Hommel continued. "The policy didn't change until the early '80s, when it came out that chaplains could not carry weapons. Prior to that, you could if your conscience allowed it. And I really believe that we should go back to that. Because in a war like this, and in the foreseeable future we're going to have wars like this, where you don't know where the front lines are, suddenly they're all around you."[24]

In the midst of the fighting, Major Rod Coffey, the battalion operations officer from 2-7, arrived in a Bradley to coordinate the relief with Denton Knapp and 3-15. He was upset by what he saw. Some of the soldiers at Curley seemed to have been worn down by the fighting and were hiding behind any cover they could find. Coffey began exhorting the soldiers to keep firing. Help was on the way and the only way the troops at Curley would survive was by becoming more aggressive. As Coffey was climbing through a Humvee, the vehicle was hit. The explosion broke his foot and speckled him with shrapnel. Coffey's gunner shouted over the 2-7 Infantry command net to report that the officer was down, all the while firing the Bradley's 25mm cannon to hold off the enemy. Coffey managed to return to the Bradley and quickly took control of the net to update Rutter: a by-the-book relief was just not possible.

As if to underscore that point, an RPG hit one of the ammo trucks, stunning Private Joseph Gilliam, who had been firing a .50 caliber machine gun from the vehicle. The truck was chock-full of munitions: 120mm tank rounds, 25mm ammunition, hand grenades, claymore mines, and more. The ammo on the stricken truck began to cook off. The seventeen ammo and fuel vehicles were bunched together. As the ammo exploded it ignited two adjacent fuel trucks. Now 4,600 gallons of fuel had ignited and exploded. None of the forces had yet been refueled and the R2 package was in danger of burning up. Soldiers raced to the remaining trucks to drive them away before they exploded. But it was too late for two of the vehicles. They, too, burst into flames. Now altogether five trucks were flaming wrecks.

Special Forces vehicles on the scene met with a similar fate. Their Toyota trucks, which had arrived at Curley hours ago with Team Zan, also started to take fire. One loaded with ammunition was ablaze. A nearby Bradley was also struck. This time the fire was coming from a new direction: south. "We started receiving fire from the south," recalled Staff Sergeant Leo Aime Levesque III. "So our mortars and our scouts started to engage to the south. I looked and noticed that we had friendlies down there. So we started screaming 'Cease fire.'"

The 2-7 soldiers coming to relieve the troops at Curley had mistaken the Special Forces pickup trucks for enemy technical vehicles through their thermal sights. Here was yet another instance of "blue-on-blue": friendly fire. Curley was getting too hot. There was as much danger from exploding ordnance as from enemy fire. It was time to pull out and let Rutter's 2-7 take over. Knapp and Gallagher ordered the 3-15 soldiers to depart. The seven American casualties and the medical team got into the M577 command vehicle and the M113 tracks. Stever's remains were placed in an ammo truck. They would be dropped off at the next aid station and brought back to mortuary affairs the next day. The 2-7 liaison team also piled into the evacuating column. The enemy wounded were abandoned. Then 2-7 moved in.[25]

Tucked in with 2-7 Infantry was Erik Berdy, Blount's aide, who had Ted Koppel, ABC's *Nightline* anchorman, and the rest of Koppel's crew with him. Though Blount had wanted to move forward with Rutter's unit and eventually link up with Perkins, the 3rd ID commander had revised his plans. The strike on Perkins's TOC and his concern that he might have spotty communications with Wallace if he ventured downtown convinced Blount that he should stay at his command post at the airport. But Blount was still eager to counter Iraqi reports that U.S. forces were being repulsed back across the Euphrates. Blount gave Berdy the mission of getting Koppel downtown to see for himself and Berdy packed the ABC newsman and his crew into a Bradley and linked up with Rutter's battalion.

When 2-7 Infantry occupied Curley, the battalion came under heavy fire. Rutter's Bradley destroyed an enemy vehicle as it was trying to attack Berdy's vehicle. Scanning the area, Berdy recognized an old acquaintance. In front of Berdy's Bradley was a U.S. Special Forces technical vehicle packed tight with Special Forces soldiers and CIA operatives. In the driver's seat was "Bob," the CIA operative who had promised to facilitate a link-up with anti-Saddam Iraqis after the division crossed into Iraq and whom Berdy attempted to call repeatedly for Blount without success.

The vehicle was so full that it looked to Berdy like the sort of car that clowns pile into in a circus. Berdy thought the Special Forces soldiers and agency operative seemed anxious. Not only had the Special Forces lost their other vehicle at Curley, but they were in a vulnerable, unarmored one in the middle of a firefight. Berdy wanted to find out what had happened to the CIA in Nasiriyah. What had happened to the CIA plans to facilitate the Iraqi surrender and line up allies among the Iraqi tribes weeks earlier? Why had his phone calls to "Bob" gone unanswered? But there was too much mayhem to pose the question. Berdy made eye contact with "Bob" but never had a chance to exchange words. Fortunately for "Bob" and his passengers, the route beyond Curley was too dangerous for Berdy's Bradley to travel by itself: Koppel would not be making it to downtown Baghdad. Berdy would be able to escort "Bob" and his comrades south toward 2nd BCT's original attack positions near Objective Saints.[26]

Before the push downtown, the U.S. military had expected that the main battle would be with the Special Republican Guard. At Curley, however, most of the fighting had been against foreign Arabs and jihadists. Interrogation reports indicated that the Arab fighters were organized into platoons of thirty to forty and that there were an estimated 200 to 300 at Curley. Many had been brought over from Syria in buses and trucks and had only been in Iraq a few days. Some had military training but none were professional soldiers. Of the thirty enemy prisoners of war captured at Curley, twenty-eight held Syrian passports and neither of the two Iraqis taken prisoner was a soldier.[27]

"Most of what we found was Syrian, Syrian mercenaries, that had been recently conscripted to come over here and fight us," recalled Felix Almaguer, the intelligence officer. "This was based on the interrogations we had during the actual battle. The leaders were generally individuals who had some experience in some kind of Hezbollah or Hamas militia. It was very easy to spot them. We had been told by Special Operations Forces the night prior, look for older gentlemen with beards that look distinguished, look like they could be a religious leader, or a spiritual leader. And in fact when we found the EPWs [enemy prisoners of war] it was very easy to find the leader, because he pretty much matched the description word for word and we selected the individual that we believed to be the leader, and sure enough, he was the leader."

According to the enemy's defensive scheme, there were fewer Arab fighters proportionately at the intersections closer to the center of town and more of the Special Republican Guard. At Larry, Arab fighters made up about half of the resistance. At Moe, the majority of enemy combatants were from the Special Republican Guard. "As you moved along it became more and more of an Iraqi fight," Almaguer recalled.[28]

While Perkins was battling downtown, the CIA received a tip that Saddam and his two sons were meeting at a house around the corner from the Al-Saa restaurant in the Al-Mansur district of Baghdad. The CIA report was received at 12:45 p.m. The restaurant, the CIA also noted, had traditionally been used by the Iraqi Intelligence Service for meetings. Within an hour a B-1 bomber dropped four 2,000-pound satellite-guided bombs on two separate buildings, turning them into a mountain of debris. It was an impressive feat of airmanship and one of the most notable decapitation strikes of the war. The Air Force had worked hard to reduce the "sensor to shooter" time to the bare minimum when striking what it called TSTs, time-sensitive targets. The B-1 crew were awarded Distinguished Flying Crosses for their efforts.

In Washington, U.S. officials hoped the fate of the Iraqi leader and his sons had finally been sealed. After the fall of Baghdad the U.S. Army would truck away the ruins to the Baghdad airport so intelligence experts armed with the latest DNA technology could sift for signs of Saddam and his aides. The staff of the restaurant, however, said that eighteen innocent Iraqis had been killed in the blasts.

Interrogations conducted by U.S. intelligence after the war pinpointed the numerous safe houses Saddam had been shuttling among during the war. According to the classified study by the Joint Forces Command, Saddam was not in the area at the time of the attack. Like the strike at Dora Farms, the bombing had been based on faulty CIA intelligence. On April 7, Saddam had in fact met early in the day at a safe house Qusay used as an alternative Republican Guard command post, which was far from the site of the air strike. Saddam convened a meeting after that at the former residence of the Spanish ambassador, who had evacuated the capital. The Iraqi leader stayed that night at the home of Abd Hameed, his personal secretary. The CIA's informant who provided the original tip may have been the victim of a ruse by Saddam's intelligence operatives to expose disloyal Iraqis and may have been executed, the JFCOM study noted.

In all, Moseley's command carried out 156 TST attacks during the war. Of these, fifty were against targets where the Iraqi leadership was thought to be, four were against "terrorist" targets, and 102 were against suspected infrastructure for WMD or the artillery and rockets to deliver them. As it turned it, "most of the leadership strikes were offset from where Saddam stayed during the war, denying him use of government buildings, but not threatening his life," the JFCOM report noted.

Despite repeated attempts to decapitate the regime, none of the top fifty-five officials in the Iraqi government were killed by an air strike. The TST attacks could only be as good as the intelligence they were based on. The postwar interrogations also showed that, by chance, Perkins's two Thunder Runs had come within one and a half miles of two locations where Saddam stayed during the war, including the house where Aziz had read Saddam's eight-page letter. None of this was known to the U.S. ground commanders at the time. All they knew was that the Iraqi resistance had not ceased. Twitty's battalion had done its job. Most of the R2 package made it through. Perkins was able to stay the night. The 2nd BCT had claimed a portion of western Baghdad. But the eastern part of the city was still up for grabs.[29]

At the land war command headquarters in Kuwait, McKiernan sensed that Baghdad was falling and the regime was dissolving. The conditions had radically changed from the prewar planning, but it now looked like the V Corps and Marine forces would be able to gain control of Baghdad far more rapidly than anticipated. McKiernan was thinking about his next steps. When could he get into Baghdad himself with his forward command post to start working with those Iraqis who would be part of the post-Saddam solution? Where was Saddam? How could the 4th ID be quickly projected into northern Iraq? When would the rest of the forces flow into Kuwait and on to Iraq? As a result of Perkins's unexpected fight to the heart of Baghdad, McKiernan and Franks faced some new opportunities and decisions.

CHAPTER 21

The Second Battle for Baghdad

Jim Mattis liked to command from the front and as his division closed on Baghdad he positioned his command post on Highway 2, just east of the Diyala River, the last obstacle between the Marines and the capital. Marine artillery fire reverberated through his field headquarters as he gathered his commanders to go over his plan to attack into the eastern sector of the city. For all the detailed preparation the Marines had done to get to Baghdad, surprisingly little planning had been done for how to take the city when they got there. The general idea was for the 1st Division to attack from the northeast to cordon off the northern part of the city and then conduct raids in and out of Baghdad on critical targets.

Meeting with his commanders on April 6, Mattis sketched out his plan. Joe Dunford's RCT-5 would carry out the main attack, crossing the Diyala River to thrust into the capital from the northeast. Steve Hummer's RCT-7, meanwhile, would cross the Diyala in the south and attack into the Al-Rasheed military complex—a secondary attack to distract the enemy and pin down the Iraqi defenders. The trouble was that after racing toward Baghdad, Mattis's attack was in danger of becoming stalled at a critical moment. As it fought north on Highway 6 the day before, Lieutenant Colonel Bryan McCoy's 3/4 had flown a Dragon Eye drone near two bridges that crossed the southern stretch of the Diyala and was surprised to see that they were still intact. McCoy thought about seizing the spans before the Iraqis destroyed them but the bridges were beyond his limit of advance. Mattis, who was wary about seizing the bridges while the bulk of his combat power was still battling its way up the highway, decided he needed more time to get ready for the push across the river.[1]

By April 6, however, gaping holes had been blown in the spans. Compounding the Marines' problems, there were no bridges at all on the northern stretch where Mattis wanted to launch his main attack. A fifty-yard-wide channel stood between the Marines and the Iraqi capital. Waving his hand over a map, Mattis gave an urgent set of instructions: "Find me crossing points." The job of spanning the Diyala fell to Lieutenant Colonel Niel Nelson, the commander of the Marines' bridge battalion. Laying bridges had not been one of the Marines' priorities before the war, but Nelson had worked hard to prepare his unit. He had canvassed the military establishment for spare parts and practiced river crossings with Blount's 3rd ID in North Carolina. In the months leading up to the war, Nelson had drawn up plans to lay bridges across the Euphrates, Tigris, and the Gharraf canal, which ran toward Kut. It seemed that he had plans to cross every body of water but the Diyala. Crossing the Diyala was an unexpected assignment.

When Mattis asked him how long it would take to find a crossing point for Dunford's RCT-5, Nelson estimated that the job could be done in six hours. In reality, neither he nor anybody else in Mattis's division knew much about the terrain to the north, but he felt he had to tell the general something. Nelson was improvising now. Reconnaissance units from RCT-5 and RCT-1, as well as engineers from Nelson's battalion, would move north along a twelve-mile stretch of river and somehow find a way across.[2]

The intelligence at the Marines' command post indicated that the northern stretch of the Diyala was defended by Iraq's 42nd Armored Brigade, but as the Marines' 1st Light Armored Reconnaissance Battalion headed north on Highway 2 it was clear that the Iraqi resistance was breaking down. The Iraqi brigade had dispersed to make itself less of a target for U.S. air strikes and, after being hammered by B-52s, Iraqi soldiers had quickly abandoned their armor. The Iraqi tanks were still warm when the Marines got to them. As with the Medina and Baghdad divisions, the Iraqis' fear of U.S. airpower was as crippling as the air strikes themselves. The 1st LAR got a small taste of that airpower when a Navy F-14 Tomcat suddenly appeared, mistook the Marine reconnaissance unit for the enemy, and without clearance from forward air control unleashed a 500-pound bomb. Fortunately, the F-14's aim was bad and the bomb landed on the far side of a sand berm, shielding the Marines' LAVs from the effect of the blast. One mistake had canceled another; a potential friendly fire disaster became a minor footnote.[3]

While Iraqi resistance was crumbling, so was the terrain. Two obstacles stood in the way of suitable crossing sites. One was the fragile, steep riverbanks, which required a major engineering effort to emplace a bridge across the Diyala. The second was the lack of suitable roads to the river. Some routes were little more than donkey trails and others were crisscrossed with irrigation canals and culverts—some made of wood and tin—capable of withstanding at best five to ten tons, far too little to support a seventy-ton tank. To even get to the crossing site the engineers would have to construct an approach from scratch.

After several hours of searching, an impatient Mattis pressed Nelson for a fresh estimate when the elusive crossing point would be found. Trying to buy some more time, Nelson said he needed another six hours. Still, it was beginning to dawn on Nelson why there were no Iraqi bridges in the vicinity: the river in that area was virtually unbridgeable. "The Babylonians hadn't found crossing points there in 2,000 years," Nelson recalled. "The banks were made of brittle hard-packed clay that had been used and reused over centuries."

While Nelson's search went on, Marine units were stacking up on Highway 6. Instead of thrusting into Baghdad they were caught in the mother of all traffic jams. "The place looked like a parking lot," recalled one Marine officer, who noted that the division had inadvertently created "a potentially lucrative target for the Iraqis." Mattis had touted the value of speed to unhinge the enemy and reduce the vulnerability of his forces, but now his division was stuck at the doorstep of the capital.

After twenty hours of futile searching, Nelson drove south to Mattis's command post and recommended that the division abandon its effort to bridge the Diyala in the north. Attacking from the east, lower on the river, would still enable Dunford's regiment to enter the capital through Saddam City, the Shiite-dominated area that would hopefully be sympathetic to the Americans. It would also put the regiment in position to move north to Kirkuk should McKiernan call on the Marines to secure the oilfields there, a mission that the Marines had already learned might be handed to them after the battle for Baghdad was won.

There was a way to traverse the lower Diyala. With air and artillery support and the help of mine-clearing gear, Marine combat engineers had been able to reach the damaged bridges on the southern stretch of the river. A quick inspection of tunnels on the near side of the river found no evidence of additional explosives. The southernmost span could be made usable by installing a ribbon bridge over the gaps. A nearby footbridge could be made passable by gathering debris from the near riverbank and stuffing it in the holes. To the north, the Marines planned to bring up an AVLB, a collapsible bridge that is carried folded up in an armored vehicle, and lay it over the large breaks in the span.

As Perkins was preparing to attack downtown on the evening of April 6, Mattis finally discarded the northern attack route. He decreed that the Diyala would be bridged in the south at first light the next day and that Hummer's RCT-7 would lead the attack. After almost a day of delay, the Marines would turn the southern Diyala into a major thoroughfare.[4]

As the Marines planned their next move, McCoy moved stealthily and alone to the Diyala to size up the damaged bridges for himself. While prone on the ground he was startled to see a French news photographer in bright civilian clothes taking his picture. McCoy was worried that the photo shoot would give away his position, but quickly calculated the photographer was between him and any fire from Iraqi defenders on the far bank. The media had its uses on the battlefield. If the photographer was prepared to serve as an unwitting decoy, McCoy was not about to complain. The battered bridges were just part of the problem. The Iraqis had also laid a minefield on the far side, which the Marines would have to make their way through as well. Hummer would have plenty of firepower to draw on when RCT-7 fought across the bridges. Cobra attack helicopters, with Hellfire missiles, would hover, M1 tanks would scan the far bank, and artillery would engage in counterbattery missions.[5]

Colonel John Toolan, who had replaced Joe Dowdy as commander of RCT-1, would also do his best to help. To take some of the pressure off Hummer's regiment, Toolan offered to conduct a supporting attack: his amphibious AAVs would swim across the river and attack into the city on the northern flank. The Marines had traveled hundreds of miles in the aluminum AAVs, but this would be the only amphibious operation of the war. The maneuver would not be without risk. Some of the AAVs had been received so soon before the war that the Marines had not had a chance to check their seals and bilge pumps. Toolan figured he would hedge against that by ordering the crews to ford the river with the top hatches open so they could jump out if the armored vehicles began to sink. Fording the river meant that Toolan's assault force would be separated from fuel, ammo, and other logistical supplies that would have to link up later once the far bank was secured. It was the sort of bold move

Lieutenant Colonel J. R. Sanderson (LEFT). His 2-69 Armor Battalion secured the Highway 1 bridge and fought a tough battle at Kifl before heading to Baghdad. (U.S. ARMY PHOTOGRAPH)

Lieutenant Colonel Rock Marcone (CENTER, WITH CIGAR), commander of the 3rd Infantry Divison's 3-69 Armor Battalion. His soldiers took the Kifl bridge and later seized the Euphrates River crossing that enabled U.S. troops to head to Baghdad. (U.S. ARMY PHOTOGRAPH)

U.S. soldiers with a wounded Iraqi during the battle for Baghdad (DENNIS STEELE)

Iraqi prisoners taken by the 3rd Infantry Division's 2nd Brigade Combat Team during the fight for Objective Curley in Baghdad (DENNIS STEELE)

Major General James "Tamer" Amos (RIGHT), commander of the 3rd Marine Air Wing, discusses air support with Colonel Joe Dunford, commander of the 5th Marines. Dunford's regiment was in the lead during the Marines' charge to Baghdad. (SERGEANT KEVIN R. REED/U.S. MARINE CORPS PHOTOGRAPH)

Though wounded, Command Sergeant Major Robert Gallagher (STAND-ING) kept on fighting to hold Objective Curley during the April 7, 2003, Thunder Run to downtown Baghdad. (PHOTOGRAPH BY DENNIS STEELE, FROM *Army Magazine*, COPYRIGHT © 2003 BY THE U.S. ARMY AND REPRODUCED WITH PERMISSION)

Colonel Dave Perkins, the commander of the 2nd Brigade Combat Team, surprised the Iraqis and some of his superior officers by leading the April 7 Thunder Run to the heart of Baghdad. (U.S. ARMY CENTER FOR ARMY LESSONS LEARNED)

During the April 7 Thunder Run, an Iraqi missile scored a direct hit on Perkins's tactical operations center on the outskirts of Baghdad. (U.S. ARMY CENTER FOR ARMY LESSONS LEARNED)

Fedayeen fighter, RPG in hand, battles near the Sinak bridge in Baghdad on April 8, 2003. (PATRICK ROBERT/CORBIS)

Colonel Curtis Potts (LEFT), the aviation brigade commander for the 3rd Infantry Division, accepts the surrender of an Iraqi general, Muhammed Thumayla, outside Ramadi on April 15, 2003. It was the only time that Iraqi forces formally capitulated. (SPECIALIST DAN WILTSHIRE/U.S. ARMY PHOTO-GRAPH)

Franks meets with his senior commanders on April 16, at the Abu Ghraib North Palace. LEFT TO RIGHT: Brigadier General Gary Harrell, Lieutenant General David McKiernan, Franks, Marine Lieutenant General Earl Hailston, Vice Admiral Tim Keating, and Major General Dell Dailey. (SERGEANT 1ST CLASS DAVID DISMUKES/CFLCC PUBLIC AFFAIRS)

Tommy Franks tours the Abu Ghraib North Palace on April 16, 2003. (SERGEANT 1ST CLASS DAVID DISMUKES/CFLCC PUBLIC AFFAIRS)

With their previous deployments in Northern Ireland and the Balkans, British forces had ample experience in postwar operations. (USMC PHOTOGRAPH BY CORPORAL ANTHONY BLANCO)

U.S. forces were not prepared for the looting of the capital and initially did little to stop it. (U.S. ARMY PHOTOGRAPH)

Major General David Petraeus (FOREGROUND, SECOND FROM LEFT), the commander of the 101st Airborne Division, with L. Paul Bremer. Petraeus warned an aide to Bremer that the decision to dissolve the Iraqi army and leave Iraqi soldiers without a livelihood was jeopardizing the safety of American soldiers. (U.S. ARMY CENTER FOR ARMY LESSONS LEARNED)

Jay Garner (LEFT) pressed to take his postwar team to Baghdad, only to find that he lacked the resources and security to do the job. (U.S. ARMY CENTER FOR ARMY LESSONS LEARNED)

Colonel Dave Perkins (LEFT) and Lieutenant Colonel Mike Presnell explore one of Saddam's Baghdad palaces, April 7, 2003. (PHOTOGRAPH BY 3RD INFANTRY DIVISION)

Saddam's dismal spider hole was his last refuge before his capture on December 13, 2003. (CAPTAIN TROY LEACH/U.S. ARMY PHOTOGRAPH)

that Toolan's predecessor would have been unlikely to propose; Mattis quickly approved the plan.

The Iraqis, however, sensed the attack coming. Intelligence reports indicated that the Iraqis were rushing to stiffen their defenses at the anticipated crossing points. That evening, the Marines and the Iraqis engaged in a two-hour firefight as Iraqi forces moved to the far riverbank to prepare for the Marine crossing. Iraqi observers hidden in buildings on the far side were directing artillery and mortar fire at the Americans. One round scored a direct hit on an Amtrack, killing two Marines.

Corporal Jeremiah Day had helped to clear Iraqi mines on the way to the Diyala the day before and knew that his platoon would be needed again. The platoon prepared for the day by wolfing down an MRE. Most of the platoon had only had one meal the day before and they did not know when they would have a chance to eat again. Day's platoon received a welcome order to shed their cumbersome chemical protective gear and fight in their camouflage uniforms. If the Iraqis had not used chemical or germ weapons against the Marines while they were parked on Highway 6, it was doubtful that they would do so now. That was one fewer danger to worry about.

Two M1 tanks were the first to arrive at the damaged bridge. They immediately began scanning for the enemy on the far bank and provided covering fire while the AVLB bridge was installed. Rolling across the span, a platoon of tanks established a 180-degree defense to guard the flanks. The external fuel bladders had been removed from the tanks. An M1 had been hit and burned up on Highway 6 and with the bladders in place enemy fire could turn a tank into a blazing inferno.

The protection provided by the tanks was all to the good, but Day's platoon needed to advance in front of the armor to clear the minefield. The most lightly protected Marines would be at the tip of the spear. Riding in their thinly armored AAVs, the platoon approached the mines and fired a MICLIC line charge. The charges were effective when they worked. This one did not. Though the line shot forward, the charge failed to detonate. The platoon had two additional MICLIC charges, but wanted to save them in case it ran into more mines on the way to downtown Baghdad. There was another way to set off the charges: what Marines called a "Medal of Honor run," a reference to the battlefield medal, which was almost always awarded posthumously.

Lance Corporal Biamchimano grabbed a stick of C4 plastic explosive and a timing device, raced to the butt of the line charge, placed the charges, and then scampered back unscathed to the AAV. There was a huge sympathetic explosion as the MICLIC blew a channel through the mines. As the dust cleared, the platoon could see that some mines remained. The minefield had been dense and even the blast from the line charge had not destroyed all of them. The platoon would need to make a few more Medal of Honor runs. Corporal Cobian and Lance Corporal Eubanks prepped two Bangalore torpedoes in the back of the AAV. The Bangalore, which was first devised by the British army to blow gaps through barbed wire and used by the U.S. Army for the D-Day invasion in World War II, was essentially an explosive at the end of a long, expandable tube. It was also a simple but effective means of breaching obstacles, but required that the Marines run up to the minefield to employ it. The Bangalore blasts widened and deepened the lane.

With a path blown through the minefield, the Marines left the AAVs again to mark the lanes, sticking flags in empty, upended cans of ammo to designate the entrance, left side, and exit of the route the vehicles were to take. As Day and his comrades were checking the lanes, they were surprised to see that some of the mines had survived the MICLIC and the Bangalores and were sitting on the fringe of the lanes, close enough that they could blow the track off a wide vehicle like an M1 or damage any vehicle that strayed ever so slightly from the path. Sergeant Adam Lauritzen bent down to move a mine and cast a fatalistic glance at Day. It was a look that said "if it happens it happens." Lauritzen would either get the job done or he would be "a pink mist and a memory," Day recalled. Lauritzen moved the mine without any harm to himself, and then moved two more. Day and Lance Corporal Diaz joined in. By noon the lane was clear and the follow-up units were able to cross.

When the Marines reached the far side they began to explore some of the tunnels on the far bank only to discover five charges that had not detonated but were wired to explode. Gunnery Sergeant Smith followed the wires tied to one explosive until it led to an enemy fighter who had been killed by fire from the M1s before he could blow up the final section of the bridge. By the end of the day Hummer's RCT-7 had crossed the Diyala and all but captured the Rasheed airfield complex, which was the regiment's limit of advance in accordance with McKiernan's intent to establish the Baghdad cordon, but not to occupy the city itself. Scouring the Rasheed medical facility, the Marines found five pairs of camouflage trousers, some with traces of blood, which came from U.S. troops. The Marines had stumbled on the trail of the U.S. soldiers from the 507th and aircrew from the ill-fated Apache deep attack, who had been captured early in the war. The American prisoners were nowhere to be found, but the Marines found three truckloads of decomposing Iraqi bodies near a mortuary.[6]

Toolan's supporting attack was also successful. Marines cheered as each AAV made its way across the river without sinking. The Iraqis were astonished by the "floating tanks." Once across the Diyala and under intermittent sniper and mortar fire, RCT-1 moved quickly north and crossed a canal[7] to cut off Highway 5, a main highway into Baghdad from the north.

By the time Perkins had fought his way downtown, Mattis's division had crossed the river and begun to cordon off the city from the north. The engineers of the 8th Engineer Battalion made bridge repairs and installed additional expeditionary bridges to accommodate the traffic of supporting and logistics units. Mattis's Marines ringed Baghdad from the east and were ready to attack into the city. U.S. signals intelligence was reporting that the Iraqi communications were in a state of panic. In a video conference among the commanders, John Abizaid cautioned that the fighting would become more difficult as the U.S. forces proceeded downtown. The regime was still intact, and the shrinking battlespace increased the possibility of "blue on blue."[8]

As Mattis edged in from the east, Perkins was struggling to hold on to his foothold in the regime area. Perkins had played to the international media. By April 8, the entire world knew that the Americans were in downtown Baghdad. But while Perkins's brigade controlled an important swath of the capital, his unexpected arrival meant he was the only force in a city the land area of Boston but with a population of some six million.

With the Tigris as a boundary for U.S. Army forces and the Marines largely on the eastern fringe of the capital—the eastern bank of the Tigris—the Al-Mansur district and most of the eastern sector of the capital had become a temporary sanctuary for the Fedayeen and Special Republican Guard troops. By coordinating with Division, Perkins could call in air strikes and even artillery on targets on the eastern side of the Tigris and his tanks and soldiers could shoot across. But the U.S. Army had to stay on their side of the river. The battle for Baghdad was messy enough without allowing Army thrusts across the river into the Marine sector, possibly resulting in fratricide.

The Iraqis and their foreign jihadist allies, however, were under no such restrictions. At the Republican Palace, Flip DeCamp was worried about the Iraqi counterattacks. His 4-64 Armor Battalion had easily taken the palace grounds, but there were five bridges just north of the palace complex that facilitated west-to-east traffic across the Tigris, and Perkins's brigade did not control any of them. The Al-Jumhuriya bridge, which fed into a major intersection just north of the Republican Palace, gave cause for worry. The brigade was getting reports that dozens of vehicles were driving across this and other bridges, dropping off fighters who would pick up RPGs and AK-47s from the numerous caches hidden on the west side of the city and then head back to get more reinforcements. DeCamp was also concerned about a park on the other side of the major intersection just north of the palace area, which was dotted with Iraqi bunkers and fighting positions.

As Iraqi fighters streamed across, Perkins tried to shore up his position by requesting an air strike to take out one of the bridges. This time, Blount endorsed the request only to have McKiernan turn it down. Destroying bridges in downtown Baghdad was not a step McKiernan was prepared to take at this point. He did not want to destroy the capital to save it. Perkins had gotten his brigade downtown; now his soldiers would have to stanch the flow of Iraqi fighters across the Al-Jumhuriya. The only way to block the fighters was to get the brigade's tanks and fighting vehicles on the bridges—or at least at the intersections near them. Eric Schwartz's 1-64 Armor Battalion had its hands full clearing the parade field and Crossed Sabers monument area, and was not in a position to help. DeCamp's battalion would have to take on the job itself.

DeCamp delegated the seizing of the intersection adjacent to the Al-Jumhuriya bridge to Captain Phil Wolford, one of his most aggressive company commanders. The intersection was on the other side of a triumphal arch known as Assassins' Gate, where Haifa and Yafa streets crossed. Wolford called on his mortar platoon to fire on the intersection and did not halt the mortar attack until he was 200 yards away. First Lieutenant Maurice Middleton, the commander of an infantry platoon attached to Wolford's company to provide more foot soldiers, had the lead for the company. As Middleton approached the arch, jeeps were dropping off enemy fighters who were toting RPGs and taking up positions in the archway. The platoon shot several TOW antitank missiles at their foes near the arch and Wolford's tanks fired its main guns as the company moved into the intersection.

The thrust into the intersection put Wolford's company in the center of a giant kill sack. The Iraqis were firing from bunkers directly ahead in the park. The company was taking fire from recoilless rifles to the left. Enemy fighters were also shooting from the roof and upper floors of the Ministry of Planning and other buildings in the intersection. "We were pretty much receiving fire from all directions," Middleton recalled. The company did not have fire superiority. The Iraqis were giving as much as they were getting.

Within minutes, a tank platoon sergeant was wounded by a sniper. Wolford's tank was hit by enemy fire, which blew out the driver's vision blocks and knocked out the sight for the .50 caliber machine gun. One enemy shot caused a spent shell casing to ricochet off Wolford's neck, which sent him reeling. The company commander slammed his head against the hatch as he fell down and blacked out. The soldiers feared their company commander had been mortally wounded. As Wolford regained consciousness he started to reload his .50 caliber, but saw that his tank loader had been shot. The company now had two wounded soldiers and no way of stopping the enemy fire or controlling the intersection. Wolford needed some serious help from the Air Force. For the first time in the war, Perkins's soldiers pulled back, returning to the palace area to clear it so that close air support could be brought in.

Soon, four A-10s arrived and began to shoot up the park with their Gatling guns. The Ministry of Planning was pulverized by JDAM satellite-guided bombs dropped by an F/A-18. Wolford called on his mortar team again to hit the Iraqis. By the time the company returned, enemy resistance had been sharply reduced. The company shot its way through the park and then turned its attention to the RPG teams prowling the riverbank and small boats of Iraqi fighters trying to get across.[9]

After fighting through the intersection, the next step was to take control of the bridge. As Wolford moved his tank into position he was concerned about fire from a tall building at the far eastern end of the bridge and wanted the brigade to call in an air strike on the structure. Meanwhile, soldiers in Schwartz's battalion found a Motorola radio the Iraqis had been using and turned it over to the battalion's intelligence officer. Major Rick Nussio, the executive officer for the battalion, was told that the radio chatter indicated that the Iraqis had a spotter who appeared to be monitoring the brigade and directing fire. The spotter was reported to be in a building with a Turkish restaurant. The information was passed to DeCamp's battalion.

When Lieutenant Middleton received the word about the Iraqi spotter, he forwarded it to the rest of his platoon on the bridge, including Sergeant Shawn Gibson. Gibson's M1, Red 2 had moved onto the bridge. The air was hazy but Gibson's tank systems gave him a good look. He saw a figure in a building in the distance looking at him with binoculars. He hit the zoom button to bring his scan to 10-power magnification. The figure was standing on a balcony and pointing. Gibson called Middleton, the platoon leader, and reported what he had seen. "Roger, I see it," Middleton replied, who asked how far away the observer was. "1,760 meters," Gibson replied. Middleton told Gibson to stand by. Less than ten seconds later, he told him to take out the target. Red 2 lased and fired his main tank gun. Wolford thought they had taken out the forward observer.[10]

In his command track, Perkins had fielded Wolford's request for an air strike on the tall building at the far end of the Al-Jumhuriya bridge and was trying to coordinate the attack. As he was discussing the strike, Greg Kelly, a correspondent for Fox News and a former Marine, approached Perkins. Perkins needed to be careful so as not to hit the Palestine Hotel. Western journalists were gathered there. That was the first time Perkins had heard of the Palestine Hotel. The hotel was a strange place. The international media had moved there from the Al-Rasheed, after being quietly alerted by the Pentagon it might be a target. The Pentagon knew that the Americans were concentrated at the Palestine. It was on the no-hit list for Moseley's command center. Iraqis had also calculated that the Americans would be unlikely to strike the hotel and had been using it for their press operations. Other unsavory visitors had also moved into the hotel for the same reason.

As Perkins sorted out the situation, Chris Tomlinson, the Associated Press reporter who was embedded with the brigade and a former Army captain, tried to contact the AP reporter at the Palestine by e-mail. The message bounced back, so Tomlinson called an AP colleague in Qatar, who in turn tracked down an AP employee in Amman, Jordan, who had stayed at the Palestine. While Perkins listened on a Thuraya satellite phone, the employee described the Palestine, depicting the tan hotel as pink. Perkins was still struggling to identify the buildings on the far side when Tomlinson called his AP contact in Qatar and suggested that it pass on a message to the reporters at the Palestine. They should mark their position by hanging white bed sheets out the windows. He was told it was too late. The hotel had been struck. Smoke was pouring out of the hotel and journalists were running out the front.

Hearing that the hotel had been hit, Perkins turned to his ALO, the air liaison officer who traveled with the brigade and coordinated the air strikes. Did the Air Force bomb the Palestine? No such air strike had been conducted, the officer insisted. Perkins called DeCamp. Did 4-64 fire on the Palestine? DeCamp had no idea. He too had never heard of the Palestine. With the brigade commander demanding an answer, DeCamp pressed Wolford: "Did you fucking hit the Palestinian hotel?" Like De-Camp, Wolford drew a blank. Apart from the general injunction against destroying mosques and cultural sites, the only building his company was specifically ordered not to damage was the Republican Palace along the river. As Wolford sought to figure things out, scouts reported sheets hanging from a building across the river. Wolford told DeCamp that was the building the tank had struck. "Okay, cease fire on that building. I'm coming over to talk to you," DeCamp said.[11]

A CENTCOM spokesman initially justified the attack on the Palestine, asserting that the soldiers had been fired at by enemy fighters in the hotel. Further investigation later determined that there had been no fire from the hotel. A military inquiry absolved the tank crew, concluding that in attacking a suspected spotter it had been acting within the rules of engagement. Still, the inquiry sidestepped the main reason for the episode: the failure to alert the ground forces attacking into Baghdad about the unique status of the hotel. The brigade had been careful not to attack the Al-Rasheed Hotel until it determined the media was not present and would have been cautious in its approach to the Palestine as well had it known about it. CENTCOM and the Pentagon knew that American and other journalists were based in the Palestine, but neither Blount nor his brigade commanders were made aware of this.

For Perkins, the episode was replete with irony. He had sought to turn the tables on the Iraqi information ministry by showing the media his soldiers had made it to the heart of Baghdad. He wanted the international media to cover the brigade's exploits and the professionalism of his soldiers. That was also Blount's reason for ordering Erik Berdy to try to get Ted Koppel to downtown Baghdad. Now one of the brigade's tanks had inadvertently attacked the media that he was hoping would chronicle his success. Taras Protsyuk, a Reuters cameraman, and José Couso, a cameraman for Spain's Telecinco, were fatally wounded.

· · ·

As the Marines were battling their way across the Diyala, Dan Allyn was maneuvering to isolate the city from the west. Under Wallace's original plan to ring Baghdad with U.S. military units, Dave Petraeus's 101st Airborne was to seize the Iraqi military base at Taji on the northwest outskirts of the capital. That would have provided Wallace with an additional airfield and enabled U.S. forces to cut off the routes leading to the capital from the west and north. But the problems the Army had encountered with Iraqi air defenses had led Wallace to turn again to the tanks and Bradley Fighting Vehicles in Buff Blount's 3rd ID. With Grimsley at the airport and Perkins attacking into the city, the task had been handed to Allyn.

Allyn had played a supporting role since taking the Highway 1 bridge and the Tallil air base, first fighting to contain the Iraqis at Samawah and then penning in the Fedayeen at Karbala. Throughout the push to Baghdad, his brigade had been used as something of a 3rd ID reserve with battalions loaned to Perkins and Grimsley to reinforce their attacks. Now, for the first time since the Highway 1 bridge, his brigade would be at full strength again. Allyn's command M113 had broken down on his final day of operations in the Karbala Gap, so he headed north in an unarmored Humvee. With the collapse of Baghdad seeming close at hand, Allyn was not to occupy Taji, but to block two bridges and an intersection that led west and north from the city. The hope was that this would not only stop Saddam and his cohorts from fleeing west but would also put Allyn in position to drive into the capital himself. It was a small but important change that would draw Allyn's brigade into the battle for Baghdad.[12]

The first leg of the journey took Allyn to Terry Ferrell's 3-7 Cavalry Squadron, which had been sent west of the capital on April 3 to cut the routes there and protect the division's western flank from the Hammurabi Division, which had been positioned west of the capital as part of Saddam's misguided effort to guard against an attack out of Jordan. In his push west of Baghdad, Ferrell had gotten himself into more of a fight than he had anticipated. U.S. F-16s, A-10s, and British Tornados had targeted Iraqi T-72s on the western outskirts of the city and Ferrell headed to the area soon afterward to confirm the battle damage. As the squadron drove to the supposed site of the destruction it discovered that a battalion of the Iraqi tanks was not only intact but positioned behind a sand berm to the right. The Americans had blundered into a confrontation with Iraqi armor.

With his tanks and artillery, Ferrell made short work of the T-72s, destroying some twenty tanks. It was a small taste of what the Americans had once thought would make up most of the fight: a head-on clash with Iraqi armor and another object lesson in both the U.S. proficiency in mechanized warfare and the gaps in battlefield intelligence. After the episode, Ferrell had continued to screen the division's left flank, going as far as the intersection of Highways 1 and 10 east of Fallujah. But despite the skirmishing in the west and north by Blaber and other Special Operations Forces, the territory beyond was a veritable no-man's-land. Allyn's route to the northwestern bridges passed right through it.[13]

As Allyn arrived at Ferrell's forward checkpoint, the brigade's scouts pulled their Humvees over to the side of the road so that J. R. Sanderson's armored battalion could take the lead. As Sanderson's battalion moved forward, Captain Clay Lyle, the Apache Troop commander in Ferrell's squadron, came on the radio and cautioned that Allyn's 3rd BCT would be in contact with the enemy within 400 yards. The warning turned out to be uncannily accurate. Sanderson's soldiers came under RPG and machine gun attack from both sides of the road, and later took fire from Iraqi BMPs and tanks. As Sanderson's battalion moved through an S-turn, Private Brian Huxley was hit squarely by an RPG as he was returning fire from an M113. Huxley was part of the engineer unit that dismantled obstacles the Iraqis had erected to slow the American advance. Sanderson had sought to use a series of code words for casualties so as not to unnerve his troops, but the word soon spread on the net: just twenty minutes into its drive north Allyn's brigade had its first KIA of the war.

With artillery and A-10s softening the resistance ahead, the brigade pressed on, bypassing resistance whenever possible to maintain momentum. With little intelligence on the enemy, Sanderson relied on reports from the pilots to gauge his foe. "It was all movement to contact," he recalled. "There was very little intelligence and what we did get was often wrong. The best intel came from talking to the pilots." Six hours after Sanderson forged ahead, Allyn's brigade received an intelligence report identifying the enemy it had already faced. Here was yet another example of how the speed of the attack exceeded the ability of the intelligence systems to support it.

Sanderson's battalion fought its way through a company of Iraqi BMPs and an air defense battery, and then hooked right to block a major highway bridge over the Tigris, as well as a secondary bridge 3 miles to the north, another potential escape route from Baghdad. Baghdad was now isolated from the northwest—if the U.S. troops could solidify their control.[14]

Like Perkins, Allyn sought a secure place to lodge his command post and decided to move it inside an Iraqi building: the Arab Petroleum Institute, a modern one-story structure off a highway. "We had been through direct fire engagements throughout the day," recalled Allyn. "I think everybody had finally taken a breath and said, 'Okay, we own this ground.' " After determining the area was reasonably secure, Sanderson ordered his ammunition and fuel trucks to drive up to the site. The brigade was running low on fuel and ammo and the institute appeared to be away from the main fight.

About forty-five minutes later, an Iraqi advanced toward the Americans motioning as if he wanted to surrender. The Americans ordered the Iraqi to lie prone on the ground, a precaution against suicide bombers, and kept their guns trained on their would-be prisoner. Almost immediately, they came under fire. The Iraqis were trying to blow up the fuel and ammunition used to support the American advance. There were no front lines and rear areas in the battle for Baghdad. Allyn's brigade command post and the supply trucks were in the middle of a firefight.[15]

Private Kelly Prewitt was in the front seat of the ammo truck at the head of a five-vehicle supply column. Just nineteen, Prewitt had joined the Army to find himself and had been trained as a tanker. With the division's tank crews at full strength the new recruit was given the seemingly safer job of driving supply trucks. As the supply trucks came under fire, Prewitt and the other drivers jumped out to take cover in the institute's compound. Prewitt did not get far before a tracer round tore a hole in his right thigh. Wounded, Prewitt began to drag himself along the road using his arms and hands. He was in the middle of a shooting gallery, severely injured and alone. As bullets whizzed across the highway, Sergeant Jimmy Harrison heard somebody yelling for a medic and was alarmed to see a soldier crawling in the street and nobody rushing to help him. Harrison left his M16 behind with a comrade providing covering fire and climbed over the fence outside the institute. Doffing his helmet, Harrison started to crawl forward before sprinting the last 30 yards to the injured private.

Prewitt reported that he felt numb and could not see. His pupils were dilated and he was in shock. With bullets flying around them, Harrison gave Prewitt his 9mm pistol while he tried to administer first aid. Harrison had his hands full dealing with Prewitt. If the Iraqis approached, Harrison would tell him where to aim. "You'll be okay," Harrison said.

"If I tell you, just squeeze the trigger." As the drama unfolded in the middle of the highway, other soldiers from the brigade staff ran out to help Harrison carry Prewitt back to the institute and drive away the vulnerable supply trucks. But they could only salvage three of the vehicles. As ammunition in Prewitt's truck began to cook off, it ignited the fuel truck directly behind it. For hours, the area was racked with fiery, secondary explosions.

Two of the brigade's Bradleys and J. R. Sanderson's M1 helped to repulse the attack. Now the race was on to save Prewitt, who needed to be urgently evacuated to the division rear. A request was made for a helicopter. The soldiers marked out a landing zone and waited. Eventually, the soldiers got the word. The Medevac helicopters were not flying. The news went down hard with Harrison and the rest of the soldiers. Prewitt's situation was desperate and they would have to drive him sixty miles to the rear. The private died en route. This brief episode in the war spoke volumes about the nature of the conflict. The brigade had suffered two dead in the battle for Baghdad—a truck driver and an engineer. The Iraqis had tried to stifle Perkins's attack by lobbing a missile at his command post and cutting his supply line to the city. Now, Allyn was encountering similar tactics.[16]

"After several weeks of fighting our tanks and Bradleys, the enemy knew he could not do anything significant to our tank and Bradley formations," recalled Allyn. "So he had begun targeting our soft-skin vehicles and our logistics vehicles. I am absolutely convinced that once they infiltrated this location here to the northwest, they surveyed it and figured out where they could do some damage to us. Their intent was not just to kill one or two Americans. It was to attempt to cause a situation that would kill a large number of Americans and also hurt our supply status."

With Perkins downtown and the Marines pushing in from the east, the Tigris River bridge was one of the few spans under Iraqi control. Captain Stu James's Assassins Company had rapidly seized the near side of the bridge, but it would have quite a fight on its hands to stop the Iraqis from coming across. Iraqi armor and vehicles were prowling the far bank along with hundreds of fighters in and out of uniform. The Iraqis had not seemed to appreciate the importance of the bridge until the Americans showed up on the western bank and were now preparing a major counterattack to recapture it.

Sanderson was worried an enemy attack would overburden his overstretched force. Sanderson had just four companies to secure about 2 square miles of battle space. He had encountered fanatical fighters in Kifl and knew it would take a lot to prevent the Iraqis from overrunning his position. At Kifl he had fought to save a bridge; now he wanted to drop it. Dropping the bridge would leave Sanderson with one less problem as he struggled to control his interior lines. Sanderson called Allyn and urged an air strike to take out the Tigris bridge. During the Gulf War, the Air Force had bombed bridges with abandon; in this war the destruction of a bridge was not a decision to be taken lightly. Allyn, however, agreed with Sanderson's assessment. The bridge had to go. Allyn took his request to Blount. The word came down that higher-level commanders had given permission to drop a small bridge to the north. The Iraqis were not massing to counterattack across that span, but bombing it would give the brigade one less objective to defend and allow it to shift forces. In Blount's view, the bridge Sanderson was on was key to the link-up with the Marines and the encirclement of Baghdad.

Even so, holding the Tigris bridge required all the firepower Allyn could muster. Desperate to hold off the Iraqis, Sanderson called for "final protective fires," a last-ditch artillery and mortar barrage to prevent friendly forces from being overrun. It was the only time that the Army used the procedure during the war. The brigade's artillery began an intensive thirty-minute bombardment, supported by some of the division's artillery. A-10s swooped in to bomb the far bank. All told, more than seventy enemy vehicles were destroyed.[17]

The Iraqis, however, were not through. A T-72 started to cross the bridge and was knocked out by an M1. First Lieutenant McKinley Wood, a platoon leader with Alpha Company, was ordered to cross the bridge and see if the Iraqis were forming yet another counterattack. As Wood led two tanks onto the bridge, there was a large explosion followed by another. Having failed to mount a counterattack and open a route to the west, the Iraqis were trying to destroy and deny the bridge to the Americans. As at Kifl, the demolitions failed in their objective. Wood pulled back and began firing at the Iraqis across the river. Iraqi soldiers began taking off their uniforms so they could blend into the population. Baghdad was isolated from the west and east now.[18]

In the final days, it was impossible to tell from the air which Iraqi tanks were operational and which had been abandoned, so Moseley instructed his aircrews to "keep killing it all." Moseley's warplanes also kept pounding Iraqi airfields. The Iraqi air force had not sent a single plane aloft, but

Moseley would not take any chances. He would hit the airfields until Franks told him to stop. Still, the upsurge of fighting on the northwest outskirts of Baghdad led to the loss of an allied plane: an A-10 that had been shot down by a Roland antiaircraft missile while supporting Allyn's brigade. Another barely managed to make it back to base. The aircraft were flying low and had been silhouetted against clouds. It was the first U.S. warplane to be knocked out of the sky by the enemy. The pilot ejected and was in hiding and trying to elude capture until he heard the unmistakable shout of a 3rd ID team that had been sent to rescue him: "Hey, pilot dude."

At CENTCOM, Franks and his top aides were struggling to keep up with the rapidly changing developments on the battlefield. Franks had made his first visit to the U.S. forces in Iraq on April 7. Overcome by emotion, Franks had drawn his generals together at Conway's field headquarters at Numaniyah, instructing them to hold hands and say a prayer thanking God for the looming victory. With Perkins's rush downtown, Iraqi fighters launching counterattacks from the eastern section of the city, and Mattis and Allyn itching to get downtown, the idea of conducting raids in and out of the city had been overtaken by events. In a morning teleconference on April 9, McKiernan, Wallace, and Conway settled on a new plan to assault Baghdad. Mattis would be given a green light to attack from the east and would seize the Directorate for General Security, the air force headquarters, the Ministry of Intelligence, the Ministry of Oil, and the Fedayeen command center. The Army would push from the west and the forces would meet in the middle. By this plan, they would capture the key city locations. All three leaders recognized that they had very little solid intelligence to shape their attacks but also knew the time was at hand to push hard to exploit the crumbling regime's defensive efforts.

RCT-7 headed downtown. Lieutenant Colonel Chris Conlin's 1/7 seized Baghdad University on a peninsula-like spit of land opposite the Republican Palace. In doing so, Conlin also overran the home of Iraq's deputy prime minister, Tariq Aziz. McCoy's 3/4 and tanks from 1st Tank Battalion drove into the city's riverfront complex of embassies and hotels. Continuing the attack, 3/7 captured government buildings, including the high-rise Ministry of Information, which was cleared of snipers floor by floor.

To the north, Toolan's RCT-1 advance in its zone was opposed only by snipers until Lieutenant Colonel Jeffrey Cooper's 2/23 came upon the Directorate for General Security, the walled headquarters of Saddam Hussein's internal security police off the Al-Dawrah Expressway. Cooper's Marines were met by heavy fire from approximately 100 loyalists within the compound as well as attacked outside by gun-mounted technicals. Nine Marines were wounded before the compound was taken. Iraqis not killed in the engagement blended into the neighborhood. The Marines received a friendly reception in Saddam City, but were astonished by the wholesale looting. In the absence of any guidance about looting, Mattis ordered his Marines to do what they could to protect hospitals and critical installations as long as it did not interfere with their combat mission. As for looters in general, Mattis said, "We didn't come to Iraq to shoot some fellow making off with a rug." Focused on digging out the last of the defenders, the Marines did little to restore order.

To the west of the city, Allyn dispatched a battalion toward the airport on April 8. Blount wanted to clear the battle space that existed between 3rd BCT in the northwest, 1st BCT at the airport, and 2nd BCT in the center of Baghdad. The next day, Sanderson's 2-69 Armored Battalion charged downtown from the northwest. The forces were converging on the city from all sides.

It was Corporal Edward Chin, a tanker with 3rd Battalion 7th Marines, who stole the spotlight by hooking a cable from a tank retriever to a statue of Saddam—draping the head of the monument with an American flag—so that it could be hauled to the ground. As soon as Franks saw the flag on CNN he called McKiernan. McKiernan had already called Conway. Displays of the U.S. flag were officially forbidden. CENTCOM did not want to be perceived as an occupying army. There was a sense that Baghdad had been captured, but the battle for the capital was not over yet.[19]

In the early hours of April 10, Lieutenant Colonel Fred Padilla moved west around Baghdad's outskirts to seize one of Saddam Hussein's opulent palaces on the northern bank of the Tigris River. Earlier, the battalion had been welcomed after they crossed the Diyala. In one instance, Padilla and his sergeant major, Kenneth Jones, were brought to an ominous-looking walled compound by a group of agitated Iraqis who crossed their hands at the wrists as though handcuffed and lowered their hands knee-high. The two Marines interpreted the crossed hands to signify prisoners, but the other signal was unclear. As the Iraqis grew more agitated, Padilla called for some Marines to break through the heavy gate of the compound. About 150 dirty, bruised, and malnourished children, some as young as seven, rushed out and ran screaming to the open arms of the waiting crowd. What the Marines had uncovered was a children's prison, whose inmates were presumably locked up as punishment for their families' disloyalty to the regime. Their warders had fled, but left the children imprisoned. Upon reunion with their families, grateful parents descended on the colonel and his sergeant major with kisses of gratitude. "I don't go for that shit," Jones said to one. "Go kiss the colonel."

The mission to take the palace was different. Padilla was faced with uncertainties. His maps were not detailed and there was very little intelligence about the enemy. He had no idea about the loyalties of the population in that part of Baghdad. He had decided to attack at night when few civilians would be on the streets and to take advantage of the battalion's night vision capability. Anticipating a tough fight, Padilla left most of his soft-skinned vehicles behind. One Humvee per company was loaded with emergency ammunition and other supplies to help sustain the attack.

With Captain Blair Sokol's Alpha Company in the lead, the battalion plunged south into the darkness on Highway 2 beginning what Padilla called "the longest night"—a nine-hour running gun battle. Concealed in the buildings on either side of the four-lane highway, the enemy opened up on the column with small arms, machine guns, and RPGs. Firing right and left the column drove deeper into the city until the entire battalion was engaged and casualties were mounting. According to Padilla's map, there was a three-way intersection four miles down the road. The battalion was to turn right at a mosque and follow Antar Street to the palace. As Sokol approached the mosque, he ran into a blizzard of fire and hooked right. In the confusion of battle, however, Sokol had turned too far. He had led the battalion onto a road heading northwest, away from the palace. Realizing his error, Sokol ordered his company to jump the median to head back to the intersection. With the battalion now moving in both directions on a divided highway, Padilla screamed an order over the radio: "Fire only outboard!" Already taking enemy fire from both sides, there was danger of the Marines firing into each other as they reversed course past one another. Compounding the problem, Alpha Company's command AAV was hit by an RPG, lost a track, and ground to a halt.

Trying to salvage the situation, Captain Jason Smith, the Bravo Company commander who was positioned at the rear of the column and knew where the palace was, offered to take the lead. "I've got the route up to the palace," he radioed his battalion commander. Unlike Sokol, Smith had no tanks but at least he knew where to go—or thought he did. After reaching Al-Maghrib Square, Smith himself took a wrong street under fire at a traffic circle. He, too, quickly realized his error and also reversed direction. More than ever, the attacking column was in disarray. Padilla was worried that things might get out of control and he might not make it to the palace.

Making matters worse, Padilla received a new order from Joe Dunford, his regimental commander, directing him not only to capture the palace but also seize the Iman Abu Hanifa Mosque, a mile and a half beyond the palace around a bend in the Tigris, where Padilla was told Saddam might be taking refuge. Padilla was also told to grab some Baath Party buildings a half-mile northwest of Al-Maghrib Square, where American POWs were thought to be imprisoned.

Padilla ordered Bravo Company to continue to the palace and followed behind. He sent Alpha to attack the mosque. Shawn Blodgett's Charlie Company was ordered to seize the suspected POW site. The battalion commander now had three companies under heavy fire going in three different directions, none in a position to provide support for the others and no reserve. In retrospect, Padilla thought the confusion might have had a silver lining: any Iraqi defenders trying to divine the Marine plan would have been thoroughly mixed up. "I think it may have unhinged their defensive game plan," Padilla said. "There were Marines everywhere. They [the Iraqis] must have thought the entire 1st Marine Division had hit them."[20]

At early dawn the Marines could see the Tigris River and the palace, an elegant complex surrounded by a high wall. Smith's Marines dismounted and attacked the defenders, who were dug in outside the wall. An armored bulldozer was ordered up to smash down the gate, but the Marines found the gate open. Bravo Company rushed into the palace complex and began clearing it building by building, room by room. To the Marines' surprise the palace was empty. All the defenders were fighting from outside the complex and continued to do so. Even with the capital full of invading soldiers and Marines the Iraqis were wary of entering one of Saddam Hussein's residences. Padilla established his command post in the palace and, protected by its walls, called for a helicopter medical evacuation for twelve of his increasing casualties.

Meanwhile, Sokol's company followed the road abutting the river to the mosque, where he ran into intense fire from the mosque and the adjoining buildings. His gunnery sergeant, Jeffrey Bohr, was killed while evacuating a wounded Alpha Company Marine. A tank and two or three AAVs were also knocked out. (Thirty-three RPG hits were later counted on the tracked vehicles.) Padilla was afraid Sokol would be pinned down and exhorted him to keep moving.

The battle seemed to hang in the balance when Dunford radioed that he was sending a company of M1s from the 2nd Tanks. Padilla immediately dispatched it to reinforce Alpha Company. By this time it was daylight. Alpha Company's forward air controller called for air strikes from F-14s, F/A-18s, and A-10s stacked overhead. The A-10s marked the enemy locations and the fixed wing aircraft made multiple runs at "danger close" range. With the arrival of the tanks and air support, the tension disappeared from the company commander's radio reports. Although mosques were protected sites, this one had been turned into a fortress, abrogating its sacrosanct status. Supported by air and M1 tanks, Sokol launched his assault on the mosque, hoping to kill or capture Saddam. After a four-hour fight and under covering fire from the tanks and AAVs, the dismounted Marines blew a hole in the wall of the mosque, rushed in, and overran it.[21]

Facing furious firefights and cut off from the bulk of their supplies, Padilla's Marines were short of ammo. There was a way to rush ammunition to the Marines but it was risky: a section of vulnerable CH-46 Sea Knight helicopters under the command of Captain Larry Brown had landed at the Iraqi Airborne Training Facility in Baghdad. They were better suited to flying supplies in the rear than dashing without an armed escort into a hot landing zone. Brown's crews began breaking out the pallets of ammo and packing machine gun rounds and smoke grenades on the choppers—some 3,000 pounds of ammunition in all. Then, flying fifty feet over buildings and dodging electrical wires, Brown took the first CH-46 in, landing at a designated spot near a swimming pool.

As the Marines unloaded the helicopter, a second CH-46 anxiously waited to land. As the firing picked up, the pilot decided that he was better off landing in a marshy area away from the main landing zone and taking his chances on the ground than providing the enemy with an easy target in the sky. In all, the helicopters made five runs, only one of which was escorted by Cobra attack helicopters. The Marines captured twenty-two prisoners at the mosque, all armed, many dressed in black and identified through documents as Syrians. But once again there was no sign of

Saddam Hussein. A CH-46, on the final run of the day, picked up most of them, as well as a trove of secret papers and files. All the litters on the chopper had been stripped to make more room for cargo. So the crew chief had the prisoners lie down sideways, stacked them like Lincoln Logs, and strapped them down with cargo straps.[22]

Charlie Company had no luck in locating the American POWs at the Baath headquarters. Under fire, but supported by air strikes, Blodgett's Marines stormed the Baath Party buildings. They found evidence that the captured Americans had been there, but had been moved. The "Battle of the Mosque," as it became known, was over. It had cost seventy-seven casualties and was the last major battle for Baghdad. By April 10, it was clear that Baghdad had fallen to the Army and Marines.

At his air war command post near Riyadh, Buzz Moseley had been keeping up the pressure. He was still concerned that the Iraqis might have some Scud missiles squirreled away in western Iraq and he was determined to keep the Iraqi airfields out of action and deprive the Iraqi air force of any opportunity to take to the skies. He also had an unusual problem. Rumsfeld's aides had pressed CENTCOM to drop a new bomb: the "Massive Ordnance Air Blast Bomb," a 21,700-pound behemoth of a weapon that had been promoted by J. D. Crouch, a senior civilian official. The huge bomb was a successor to the "Daisy Cutter" that had been used to create landing zones in Vietnam by eviscerating swatches of jungle. The weapon was designed to produce a large mushroom cloud and the theory was the massive blast would frighten the enemy into submission and have the psychological effect of a nuclear blast.

John Jumper, the Air Force Chief, thought the weapon was hardly needed in Iraq. "I was not excited about it," he recalled. But Franks had been inclined to placate the civilians at the Pentagon by giving the weapon a try. The CENTCOM commander had told Moseley that the Air Force should bring two of the MOABs to the region "so we can help the designers do their work." Two of the bombs had been transported to Al-Udeid while several Daisy Cutter bombs were shipped to Romania on their way to the Gulf.

Finding targets for the weapon was no easy matter. The MOAB was designed to be dropped from a vulnerable and slow-moving C-130, and it seemed singularly inappropriate for an air command that was committed to precision warfare and limiting collateral damage in Iraq. Moseley dutifully discussed a plan to drop the MOAB and Daisy Cutters for three days and to monitor the effects, but he remained unenthusiastic. "Unless we have a different mind-set, dropping them in a city with a CEP of about 3,000 feet does not make much sense," Moseley said. CEP was a technical term that signified the radius of a circle in which the weapon could be expected to fall 50 percent of the time. In other words, the MOAB would produce a mammoth bang, but it was hardly an accurate weapon. To the relief of the Air Force, the war ended before the bomb was used. The Iraq War would record a number of air war firsts, including the first time that B-1, B-2, and B-52 bombers were all in a single bombing raid, but the MOAB would not be one of them.[23]

As he watched Iraqis celebrating Saddam's fall on television, Moseley decided to catch one of the first C-17s to the Baghdad airport to get a firsthand look at the victory his aircrews had worked so hard to achieve. Before he left, he mused about the war. The air war commander was conflicted. "I've got mixed emotions about this," he confided to an aide. "We've conquered a country today and for the first time we started it."

The aide quickly corrected the general: Iraq had been "liberated."

"You're right," Moseley added. "That's a better way to describe it." One day, Moseley ventured, Iraq would become the jewel of the region.

On April 12, McKiernan's early entry command post was loaded into C-17s, which made a blacked-out, eerily quiet flight to the Baghdad airport. The vans of communication gear were moved into an airport hangar that months before had been picked from reconnaissance photos as the site of his initial headquarters. Now that the capital was in U.S. hands McKiernan would direct the final stages of the war in the north and the beginning efforts to rebuild the country from his new headquarters on the outskirts of the Iraqi capital. He would be the senior general on the ground.

Wandering around the pitch-black airfield with Command Sergeant Major John Sparks, a close friend and adviser, McKiernan surveyed the destroyed planes and debris around him. McKiernan had no idea how many Iraqis might come forward to help or who they might be. There was no provisional government in waiting. Jay Garner was still organizing his team in Kuwait and there was very little direction from on high. McKiernan was entering a new and very uncertain phase.

CHAPTER 22

Saddam's Great Escape

On April 9, Saddam made his last appearance before the faithful. Riding in a Mercedes he stopped in the Al-Adhamiya district of northwestern Baghdad, jumped out of the vehicle, and vowed to carry on the struggle. Then he vanished as quickly as he had appeared, returning to one of his numerous safe houses in the sprawling Iraqi capital. It was clear to the Iraqi leader that the noose around his neck was tightening. One member of Saddam's party later told U.S. interrogators that the group decided it was time to get off the street after spying U.S. tanks maneuvering across the river in the Al-Azimiyah district, where the Marines were battling for the mosque. The day that Saddam had thought would never come was at hand: Baghdad was overrun with U.S. troops. It was time to abandon the capital.[1]

The next day, Saddam, his two sons, his personal secretary, Abd Hameed, and his bodyguards set off in a convoy of a dozen or so vehicles. The convoy came under fire and the entourage forced their way into a residence and hid there until the following morning. Saddam's massive palaces and government buildings had long since been abandoned. The Iraqi leader was on the run now and heading west.

Saddam's next destination was Anbar Province, a vast Sunni region west of Baghdad that contained the restive cities of Ramadi and Fallujah and offered the best refuge in Saddam's hour of crisis. The region was friendly to Saddam and had a long, porous border with Syria, Jordan, and Saudi Arabia. It was also largely void of allied forces. The only coalition troops in the region were the teams of U.S., British, and Australian commandos that were roaming in search of WMD and regime leaders on the run—what the military called "high value targets" or HVTs. They were a danger for Saddam but were too few to seal off all his possible routes for escape.

Saddam proceeded to a safe house in Ramadi, which turned out to be not nearly as secure as the Iraqi leader would have had it. After he got to the sanctuary on April 11, the building next door was bombed at 2:00 a.m. An hour later, Saddam and his sons hit the road again, spending the night in their vehicles, parked in an orchard. Allied warplanes were prowling the skies and hunting for Iraqi convoys. This was one time when there was no safety in numbers: Saddam and his sons decided to split up.

Qusay and Uday hopscotched their way across western Iraqi, moving from Bija, Mayadin, and Maah until they made their way to what they thought would be a safe haven in Damascus, Syria. For all of their difficulties with Washington, however, the Syrian authorities decided that Saddam's sons were too hot to handle. They forced Qusay and Uday to return to Iraq, where they made their way to the northern city of Mosul. Saddam, for his part, sought refuge initially in the western Iraqi town of Hit.[2]

Now that Baghdad had fallen, McKiernan needed to seize the northern oilfields near Kirkuk and take Tikrit, Saddam's regional base of support and a potential rallying point for his loyalists. He also needed to deploy American troops in the north to augment the modest Special Forces there so that the region would not dissolve into bitter ethnic fighting among the Kurds, Arabs, and Turkomans. Before the invasion, McKiernan's staff had identified the ethnic fault lines in the north and fretted about the potential competition for control of Kirkuk and Mosul and the threat of Turkish intervention. McKiernan was convinced that he needed a U.S. ground presence north of Baghdad, all the way to the Turkish border.

McKiernan did not have the 380,000 troops that Zinni had determined in his 1003 plan would be needed to control all of Iraq. The allied troops would be distributed in a wide belt that extended from Mosul and Kirkuk in the north to Basra and the Shiite area in the south. As for western Iraq, the U.S. military would have to cut some corners and Anbar would be one of them. The U.S. military presence there would be an "economy of force." As for sealing the borders, Dell Dailey's Task Force 20 and later the 3rd Armored Cavalry Regiment could try to patrol them, but there were nowhere near enough troops. That was a task that McKiernan hoped would be taken up, in time, by a new Iraqi military and whatever troop contributions could be rustled up from allied nations.

Franks endorsed McKiernan's strategy and passed on his guidance in a video conference. As U.S. forces ventured north, Franks wanted them to cut off the pipeline that was transporting Iraqi crude to Syria. The Syrians had allowed foreign fighters to cross into Iraq and were no friends of the Pentagon. "Find out where the knobs are to shut off the oil to Syria—they've been assholes, they continue to be assholes, so I want to turn off their oil," Franks said.

Franks also had another matter on his mind. With Saddam out of power, the Turkish government was beginning to complain that Turkomans in northern Iraq were being harassed by the new law in the area: the Kurds who were allied with the U.S. Franks had little sympathy for Ankara's position. "Tell the Turks they can kiss my ass," Franks said. The CENTCOM commander was still smarting from Turkey's refusal to let the coalition open a northern front. As for the enemy, Franks made it clear that the remaining pockets of Iraqi forces were to surrender promptly or be destroyed. "I'm interested in exploitation, in killing those who need to be killed and targeting what needs to be targeted. Let the youngsters know that they should be as lethal as they need to be. We need to still be very much offensively inclined. The only negotiating we'll do is either you capitulate or we'll kill you. Don't get jerked around, be tough in negotiations, either you surrender or we kill you period."

On April 10, McKiernan told Jim Conway that the Marines would have the Kirkuk mission. Buff Blount's 3rd ID had its hands full trying to maintain order in western Baghdad. Dave Petraeus's 101st was busy dealing with Karbala and Najaf and had temporarily contributed a brigade to Blount's efforts in the Iraqi capital. Shortly after Conway was given the Kirkuk assignment, however, it was switched. The Peshmerga and the SOF forces that were working with them had already raced ahead to Kirkuk. The Marines would take Tikrit instead. The next day, John Kelly, the Marine assistant division commander, was told he had twelve hours to organize a task force and set off.

Because of the need for speed and the uncertainty of bridges ahead, Kelly decided not to bring any tanks, AAVs, or other tracked vehicles. They were too heavy, required regular maintenance, and guzzled lots of fuel. Instead, the task force would be a form of light cavalry built around the division's three Light Armored Reconnaissance battalions supported by a company of truck-mounted infantry, an artillery battalion, a service support unit, a detachment of SEALs, and an air control and support team. All told, the force numbered 4,000 troops and 600 vehicles. Kelly named it Task Force Tripoli, alluding to First Lieutenant Presley O'Bannon's Barbary war exploit. Tikrit was on the western side of the Tigris, while the Marines were on its eastern bank. The fastest and most secure route was to use the northern Baghdad bridge to cross the river and zoom up Highway 1. This, however, meant passing through the U.S. Army zone. When Kelly proposed the route he was told it would take twelve hours to coordinate the passage. Clearly, joint operations still had a way to go. "I was in disbelief that it would take that long, so I said screw it. If we have to, we can build a bridge in twelve hours." The task force would find a crossing point farther north.[3]

How much fighting Kelly would have to do along the way was uncertain. Saddam was born in the village of Awja, just south of Tikrit, and the city was a bastion of support for the Iraqi leaders and home to many of the leading figures in the regime. The Marines had already made a few shallow probes north and had encountered enemy resistance. While the Marines had been taking control of Baghdad, Lieutenant Colonel Steve Ferrando, the reconnaissance battalion commander who had protected Joe Dowdy's flank on the way to Kut, had been ordered to go twenty-five miles north to Baqubah, where a Republican Guard brigade headquarters was reported. Just ten miles into the journey, Ferrando ran into Iraqi forces in one of the stiffest defenses he had encountered in the war. The Iraqis were in fortified positions, supporting one another. Withdrawing for the night, Ferrando assaulted the positions at daylight with substantial support from Cobra helicopter gunships. To Ferrando's surprise an Iraqi approached him afterward and warned of an ambush site at a crossroads just south of Baqubah, the first time he had received a tip from a local. The tension heightened when the lead squad leader rounded a turn in the road in his Humvee and started screaming into his radio, "Tank! Tank!" Circling the area a Cobra pilot asked dryly if the supposed T-72 was to the "right or left of the irrigation pipe propped up in the road."

The Iraqi had been truthful regarding the ambush at the crossroads. An Air Force F-16 and other air support were used to take out the Iraqi defenders. After Ferrando seized the Republican Guard headquarters he discovered two trailers in a palm grove—trailers that resembled the mobile germ warfare labs Colin Powell had warned of in his February address at the United Nations. Ferrando thought he had hit the jackpot until the Marines broke into the trailers and discovered they were nothing more than Russian-made field kitchens.

Another probe took place on the morning of April 12 when Lieutenant Colonel Dan O'Donohue's 2nd Battalion, 5th Marines, supported by a battery of artillery, drove north to check out a report on American POWs and to investigate an old pontoon bridge that crossed the Tigris at Swash. The POW report turned out to be groundless. The bridge was a different story. Captain Myle Hammond's Golf Company was in the lead and the first to arrive at Swash. Two AAVs from 1st Platoon were sent to secure the far side of the bridge, which was part of another town named Tarmiya.

Hammond did not have an Iraqi interpreter with him, but an artillery forward observer who was mingling with the people in the town found an Iraqi who spoke some English. As the Marines were monitoring the bridge, a car crossed the far bank and the Iraqi driver made a hand motion as if firing a gun. Pressed into service, the English-speaking Iraqi talked to the driver, who explained that there were large caches of weapons on the far side of the river. Assuming the weapons had been abandoned, Hammond asked the driver when he had last seen Iraqi soldiers. The driver said the Iraqi troops were there now. After the driver left, the residents of the town also began to move east. It seemed clear that something was about to happen. Hammond went back to his vehicle, but before he could radio the platoon on the far side, two RPGs struck one of the AAVs. The Marines on the far side were pinned down by small arms and RPG fire.

The Marines on the near side provided supporting fire and Hammond called for artillery and air strikes. As the Marines pounded the enemy, the Marines left Tarmiya and returned to the east bank of the Tigris. The Marines had four wounded, some seriously, but estimated that they had killed some sixty enemy fighters. Clearly, the fall of Baghdad had not signaled the end of enemy resistance.[4]

That afternoon Task Force Tripoli headed north with Lieutenant Colonel Duffy White's 1st LAR in the lead. With no electricity and therefore no operating traffic lights, the traffic on the outskirts of the city was a nightmare. Units snarled in the crush of automobiles were simply told to catch up with the main column as soon as possible. As the task force drove north through narrow village streets, Marines used poles to raise the sloping utility wires so the vehicles, and their radio antennas, could pass. Kelly made no effort to secure a supply line to Baghdad. He cut his lifeline, counting on Marine aircraft for needed support. By the time the task force reached Swash, there was no more resistance. The main danger was the bridge itself. It was so rickety that each of Tripoli's 600 vehicles had to cross one at a time. The drivers were under orders to keep their doors open so they could jump out if the bridge began to collapse, but it never did.

After crossing the river at a snail's pace, Tripoli sped through the night without opposition to Samarra, the only town of consequence before Tikrit. The route was littered with abandoned Iraqi armor and artillery. By dawn on April 13, Kelly had bypassed Samarra to the west and was racing the remaining twenty miles to the southern outskirts of the city. As Kelly moved north, Lieutenant Colonel Stacy Clardy's 3rd LAR was left behind at Samarra to establish a blocking position outside the town and prevent attacks against the task force. That day, a group of sheiks from Samarra approached Clardy's unit to ask the Marines to stay clear of their town. The sheiks insisted there were no Baathists there and Clardy assured them he would not attack the town if the Iraqis did not cause any trouble. Staff Sergeant Randy Meyer, a member of a human intelligence team, made contact with an Iraqi policeman who insisted that there was something of interest to the Americans in the town after all: U.S. prisoners of war.

Ever since the ambush of the 507th Maintenance Company in Nasiriyah and the shoot-down of Dave Williams's Apache helicopter, the rescue of U.S. POWs had been a top-priority mission. But as the Marines put it, POW sightings seemed as frequent as Elvis sightings. For the most part, these leads had been tantalizing but unfruitful. After an hour of questioning, Meyer gave the Iraqi informant his GPS receiver and instructions to go to where the Americans were being held and enter the coordinates into the device. The Iraqi did as instructed and upon returning sketched the location. The Iraqi captors, the informant said, wanted to get rid of the prisoners but were scared that the U.S. would kill them. They also were equally concerned that if they surrendered the prisoners, the Baathists would kill them. Clardy remained skeptical. The task force had passed Samarra and his blocking mission was over. Earlier reports that prisoners were being held in Baqubah had been untrue. But if there was the remotest chance to free American prisoners, Clardy did not want to leave any stone unturned. "I had orders to go to Tikrit and be there in four hours," Clardy recalled. "We sent a platoon from Delta Company with the coordinates, the Iraqi sketch map with a description of the house."[5]

Since his Apache had been shot down and he was taken captive near Karbala, Dave Williams had been through a punishing ordeal. Williams and his fellow crewmate, Ron Young, had been hauled to Baghdad, where they learned a few days into their captivity that there were other American prisoners nearby. Yelling out to them, Williams learned they were soldiers who had been ambushed on Saturday morning, but communication was difficult as Williams was generally kept several cells away from the other prisoners. Subsisting on a bowl of rice a day, Williams lost twenty-five pounds. He was subjected to death threats. His captors had taken his Seiko watch in Karbala and given him nothing more than a thin blanket. He slept on the floor. The walls of one of his cells were splattered with bloodstains, pieces of skin, and hair. Like all pilots, Williams had heard the story of Michael Scott Speicher, the Navy lieutenant commander whose F/A-18 was shot down on the first night of the Gulf War and who had been declared missing in action. There had been no definite proof that he was alive or dead and some in the Pentagon had wondered if he might have been held prisoner for thirteen years. Williams did not see how he could endure a lengthy captivity in such conditions. "I don't know how those guys did it in Vietnam," Williams said. "I really don't. Because I didn't feel like I was going to make it a year, or certainly any longer than that. You're totally helpless . . . dependent on your captors for even the basic necessities. I hardly ever slept, and we were getting bombed all the time. I wouldn't wish my treatment on my worst enemy."

On the twelfth day of his captivity, he suffered a distressingly close call when the Iraqis set up an antiaircraft gun on the roof of his Baghdad prison and began to fire away at the U.S. planes. Williams could hear the empty cartridges clattering on the tin roof overhead. With air raid sirens blaring Williams was back in the war again, but now he would be on the receiving end of U.S. fire. Confident that the U.S. planes would be striking back, Williams ran to each corner of his cell, trying to figure out which might be safest. The first bomb threw him to the floor. The second bomb landed nearby. "Afterward, I lay there for a minute or two," Williams recalled. "Then I stood and brushed off some of the bricks and debris. I started yelling out to the other kids, and Ron answered. The bombs had ripped the welded tin roof off my cell room, and I could see clouds."

Some of the walls of the building had tumbled down from the blast. When the Iraqi captors returned they seemed surprised to find their American prisoners alive. Gathering the prisoners, they moved them to an array of Baghdad facilities until Williams was handcuffed, blindfolded, and driven out of town in an ambulance. Williams was afraid that the American prisoners might be on their way to Syria or perhaps being hauled off to a remote spot of the country for execution. He knew he was moving north because the setting sun was always to his left.

When the POWs arrived at their destination they were put in a single room. Williams was the senior officer present and began to take responsibility for the five young soldiers from the 507th, several of whom had been wounded in their ordeal. Edgar Hernandez had been hit by a bullet in his right arm, Shoshana Johnson, an Army cook, in both legs. Joe Hudson had taken three rounds to the lower back. It had been four days since their bandages had been changed. Williams insisted that the Iraqis provide fresh bandages. After claiming that all the pharmacies were closed, one of the Iraqis secured those and other medical supplies that night. "The Iraqis had a hard time understanding something," Williams recalled. "Shoshana is Panamanian. Edgar is Hispanic. Joe is Philippine, and Patrick [Miller] is from Kansas. The Iraqis could not conceive how we could all have been in the same army and not fight one another. One Iraqi said to me, 'You no fighting each other? Why?' "

The POWs had just received their morning bowl of rice when they heard the roar of diesel engines outside the door. After getting lost a few times in a warren of streets and alleys, a Delta Company platoon, led by Second Lieutenant Brett Eubanks, had found a house matching the informant's description. The Marines pounded on the door. After receiving no answer, they burst in. "The door crashed open and Marines stormed in, yelling, 'Get down! Get down! Get down!' They looked just like the steely-eyed killers you'd imagine them to be," Williams recalled. "The Iraqis got down quicker than we did, and rightfully so." Then the Marines began shouting, "If you're American, get up."

Williams stood up and declared, "I'm Chief Warrant Officer Dave Williams, United States Army." A Marine responded, "You're going home, bud." As the Marines brought the POWs to the waiting LAVs, the soldiers could see where they had been kept: in a house in a walled compound on a Samarra street. The ambulance that had brought Williams there was next to the house, its siren and rooftop light covered by a green blanket. Johnson began crying from sheer relief.[6]

Kelly had led Task Force Tripoli to the outskirts of Tikrit when he got a call from Clardy. "The battalion commander was saying, 'We've got POWs,' " Kelly recalled. "And I was saying to him, 'How the hell could you have POWs? You never reported any contact. How the hell did these guys get captured?' I thought he was telling me that Marines had been captured." Clardy explained that he had freed seven American POWs and asked what he should do with them. Kelly said, "I think we ought to send them home." The POWs were given a quick medical checkup and flown to safety in Marine CH-46 helicopters. After Clardy's Marines rounded up the Iraqi captors, some of the POWs entreated the Marines to let them go. "I guess they treated the prisoners decently and they didn't want anything to happen to them," Clardy said. Clardy acquiesced and freed the Iraqis. His focus was catching up with the rest of the task force and getting to Tikrit.[7]

Like Tarmiya, Tikrit had already been the scene of a violent skirmish. After leaving the Haditha Dam, Blaber's Delta Force had continued to swing north. In early April the Delta Force had been involved in a serious firefight. When half a dozen Iraqi SUVs maneuvered toward C Squadron, the commandos blasted the two lead vehicles with Javelin missiles, triggering a violent brawl. The squadron took casualties: one soldier suffered a broken jaw when he was grazed by a bullet and another was shot just below his body armor. The squadron broke contact while other Delta troops killed and captured some of the enemy. While interrogating the prisoners, Saif Ataya discovered that they were members of a 100-strong force from the town of Seniya, 25 miles to the east.

Back at Ar'ar, Sergeant Major Iggy Balderas coordinated the air attack. Armored MH-60 helicopters attacked the enemy along with F-16s and other aircraft. Franks himself was at the Delta command center at Ar'ar when the clash was taking place and checked on its progress. It was a lopsided battle. More than sixty enemy fighters were killed. Despite the victory, the episode had a sour outcome for Delta.

To Medevac the critically wounded soldier, Balderas called on Black Hawks, which were at Ar'ar and ready to go. But they were on call for another mission: a Dell Dailey operation to film one of Saddam's empty palaces as part of an information operations campaign. It took four and a half hours to Medevac the injured Delta operator, who later bled to death. Later that night the Black Hawks flew Dailey's commandos to the empty palace and a combat camera crew filmed every bit of the staged attack. The tape was flown to a psychological operations team based in Kuwait, but never used.

A week later, Delta set up a desert encampment, which they called Grizzly, 13 miles to the west of Tikrit. Delta was joined by Rangers, Army Special Operations helicopters, Team Tank, and human intelligence teams. Leaving the Ar'ar command post, Blaber flew there to run the operation. He was in control of a small but lethal force he called Wolverines, after the teenagers who took on an invading Soviet army in the B movie *Red Dawn*. The mission was to raid Highways 1 and 12 north of Baghdad, capture senior Iraqi officials who were trying to escape, and generally sow panic and confusion in enemy rear areas.

The move was not without its drama. On April 9, Captain Shane Celeen, along with his fellow tankers, was heading to seize a nearby airfield when his M1 vanished into a forty-foot-deep hole and flipped over. The plunge nearly severed the hand of the tank loader and trapped the crew. Upside down, out of radio contact, and operating by flashlight, the crew administered first aid and tried to figure a way out of its predicament. Finally, Private First Class Christopher Bake wiggled through the driver's hatch and dug a tunnel through the sand beneath until he was clear of the upended tank. The injured loader was passed through the tunnel. Celeen had to doff his bulky chemical protective suit to squeeze through and emerged in nothing more than combat boots and underwear, soaked in blood and spilled diesel fuel. Team Tank later blasted the M1 with two main gun rounds to prevent any sensitive materials from falling into the hands of the Iraqis and then pressed on.

On April 11, after a week of marauding on the outskirts of Bayji and Tikrit, Blaber and Delta officer Bill C. decided it was time to begin encroaching on Tikrit. Before departing, Blaber explained his strategy. His intent was to instill fear and panic in the enemy forces occupying Tikrit. At no time would the Delta Force allow itself to be decisively engaged by larger enemy forces, or get caught in an urban area that would allow the Iraqis to cut them to pieces. Blaber's final words to the assembled force were, keep your backs to the desert at all times.

Led by Bill C., the force departed Grizzly under the cover of darkness and drove to their objective: a highway cloverleaf on the edge of Tikrit. Bill C. positioned one tank on each ramp of the cloverleaf covering all four cardinal directions. The enemy quickly began swarming to the area. Bill C. noted that all the roads leading into town had been either blocked or barricaded so that only a single vehicle could pass. Trenches dug along the road were stocked with weapons and ammunition.

A complex situation suddenly became worse when one of the M1's tracks became snarled in a strip of utility wire, and two Delta soldiers had to brave enemy fire to cut the cable to free the tank. As Delta fought off the Iraqis, Blaber received a call from Major General Dell Dailey, who was monitoring the melee from his command post at Ar'ar. Dailey had his own idea of how the operation was to proceed: Delta was to fight its way north and do a Thunder Run through Tikrit. Like Dave Perkins's Thunder Run through Baghdad, it would shock the enemy and test their defenses.

Delta was not the 3rd ID and Blaber had no intention of engaging in a slugfest in urban terrain. Blaber told Dailey that he was willing to talk about a future operation in the heart of Tikrit but this would not be it. The Delta team planned to pull back into the desert. "Negative! Negative!" Dailey shot back. He wanted Delta to attack through downtown Tikrit now. Blaber stood his ground and said that Bill C. had already been ordered to return to Grizzly. Dailey was furious. As a member of Dailey's staff described the scene, just as Dailey was about to respond, the radio in his Ar'ar command center blew a fuse. Dailey slammed his radio headset down in disgust.

Over the next several days, Delta continued to conduct raids on the outskirts of the city, with mixed results. It searched in vain for Speicher, the missing Navy pilot from the Gulf War, and hunted for an underground facility that the CIA believed might contain WMD. The suspected prison where Speicher was supposedly being held turned out to be a hospital that had never treated an American. When he got to the suspected underground structure, Bill C. called Blaber with the results of the raid. Bill C. said sarcastically that his soldiers were looking at dead coals. The site was actually a barbecue pit—the most mundane structures had been cast as part of an ominous WMD infrastructure by American intelligence.

Several days later, Delta and Team Tank raided Highway 1 near Bayji, a town north of Tikrit, the first of numerous forays into Bayji. With the help of Saif Ataya and Nazzar, another Iraqi-American attached to Delta, the commandos were able to learn about the Baathists in the area and where to find them. The result was the capture of five of Saddam's bodyguards, the chief of staff of the Iraqi air force, and numerous ministers in Saddam's inner circle.

By and large, Delta's collaboration with Team Tank had been a plus. It gave the commandos more firepower and surprised the Iraqis by deploying M1 tanks in their rear. The combination of SOF and conventional forces was precisely the sort of imaginative thinking that the Pentagon had promoted as part of its program of transformation and reflected the trust that McKiernan had developed with Dailey.

But there was a setback. Team Tank and the SOF were also not always familiar with each other's tactics, all of which led to disaster one night. A Ranger commander made the mistake of sending a Humvee in front of the tanks without informing Team Tank. When the enemy began shooting at the tanks, one of the M1s mistook the Ranger vehicle for the enemy and blasted it with a main tank round, killing one of the Rangers' controllers who was responsible for calling in air and artillery strikes. When the Special Operations Command put out its official history of Team Tank, the deadly episode of friendly fire went unmentioned.[8]

Two days after Delta's raid on Highway 1, Task Force Tripoli arrived on the outskirts of Tikrit with Duffy White's 1st LAR in the lead. White ran into some resistance, killing some and taking prisoners, including foreign fighters. "We got passports from them; they were Syrians, Jordanians, and some others," he recalled. The 2nd LAR under Lieutenant Colonel Eddie Ray, whose battalion had distinguished itself earlier on the march to Kut, swung north and blocked Highway 1. That cut the road north. A city bridge across the Tigris was bombed, restricting access to the east—one of the few occasions when U.S. forces struck a bridge.[9]

Kelly spent part of April 13 investigating a new intelligence tip: Saddam was dead and buried in a village south of Tikrit. Kelly was given the grid coordinates of the suspected burial site. When the Marines arrived at the site the neighborhood was abandoned. There were no residents and no freshly dug grave. After finishing with the detour, Kelly was ready to move north again. The sudden appearance of the Marines caught the local Iraqis by surprise. Many were on their way to work when the LAVs appeared. One gas station owner drove up to find a command group parked at his pumps. "He was astounded and didn't know what to do," Kelly recalled. "So after hesitating, he simply unlocked the door to his office and opened up for business."

By dawn on April 14, the main body of Kelly's task force began to enter the city. Monuments and tributes to Saddam Hussein were seen on every street, leaving no doubt about Tikrit's allegiance. West of the city, tanks and artillery were spotted in revetments. They appeared unmanned, but were hit by Tripoli's covering aircraft as insurance. The Marines had little need for air support in Baghdad and had dozens of warplanes and helicopters scouring Tikrit for targets. But as 1st LAR passed through the city's gates it came under machine gun and RPG fire, which damaged one LAV. What ensued was a running gun battle, but opposition was spotty and was quickly ended by overwhelming Marine air and the accompanying infantry. The Marines were amazed at the number of weapons and ammunition depots abandoned in and around the city. White stated, "We even found thirty-one helicopters parked in the trees, half of which were probably still flyable. They were American-made, some German, some Russian ones, and a Hind or two."

The anticipated battle for Tikrit had not amounted to much. After the initial firefights, the Baathist forces had either fled or gone underground. Getting Tikrit back on its feet was a priority. Kelly installed his command post in the opulent palace above the Tigris but did not allow Marines to bed down in them for fear of appearing too much like conquerors. Kelly met with the local sheiks and urged them to form an interim council. He wanted them to take responsibility for the restoration of services to the city and manage its day-to-day affairs. Meanwhile his Marines set up checkpoints throughout Tikrit and began to track down regime holdouts. Much of the population had fled the city upon the approach of the Americans, but came back in droves days later. Their fear of the Marines was overridden by fear that Kurdish renegades would swoop down from the north and catch them undefended outside the city. With the Marines there, their anxiety over the Kurds was allayed and some semblance of order was restored. But on the outskirts of Tikrit, there were robberies, looting, and shootings.

Nonetheless, Kelly decided he had entered the postwar phase of operations. He ordered his Marines to take off their flak jackets and helmets and circulate among the locals. An ad hoc Tikriti police force was organized. Vigilante checkpoints were disbanded. The Marines, who had been involved in pacification programs in Central America during the 1920s and 1930s and later in Vietnam, had drawn upon this experience when planning in Iraq. Yet it was clear that loosely organized resistance groups—known as "the Shadow Regime"—still intimidated the population. They were hunted down, but were not eliminated.[10]

· · ·

Within a few days, Task Force Tripoli received orders to turn over their area of operations to Ray Odierno's 4th ID. Now that he had an additional Army division at his disposal, McKiernan had divided the battle space in accordance with his original campaign plan: the Army would secure northern Iraq and Baghdad while the Marines and British controlled the south. Cooperation between the Army and the Marines had been good from the outset of the campaign to the seizure of Baghdad, though at Tikrit there was disharmony: Kelly believed he had already transitioned to postwar operations; Odierno thought that his late-arriving division was still in the combat phase of the campaign. Odierno had been told his mission was to attack north, seize the Iraqi military complex at Taji airfield at Balad, and then advance to Tikrit as quickly as possible.

Apache helicopters from the 4th ID flew into the Marines' battle space without coordination with Kelly's task force and began to strafe abandoned enemy armor, vehicles that were close to the Marine LAR units. Major Ben Connable of the Marines said that Odierno's staff "felt they were coming to Tikrit not to relieve us, but to rescue us." A draft history prepared by the 1st Marine division was equally critical. "US 4th ID had missed the combat phase of OIF [Operation Iraqi Freedom] and was determined to have a share in the 'fighting.' . . . Stores that had reopened quickly closed back up as the people once again evacuated the streets, adjusting to the new security tactics. A budding cooperative environment between citizens and American forces was quickly snuffed out." According to the Marines, a senior officer with the 4th ID made it clear that the Army had a different prescription for Tikrit when he remarked, "The only thing these sand niggers understand is force and I'm about to introduce them to it."

Lieutenant Colonel Gian Gentile, the executive officer of the 1st BCT of Odierno's division, confirmed that the 4th ID went into Tikrit "hard" but insisted it was for valid reasons. He said that the Marines, in their zeal to demonstrate that the war was over, had limited the number of checkpoints and did not patrol at night. "The velvet glove applied by the Marines in Tikrit covered up some dangerous problems and conditions," Gentile noted. "The perception among Iraqis was that the American occupation forces would do from little to nothing to stop them from looting ammunition and weapons." On his first night in Tikrit, Gentile said, a combat patrol from his brigade came upon thirty Iraqis looting weapons from an abandoned Iraqi base. A sharp firefight ensued and about fifteen Iraqis were killed.

The differences between the units were evident on April 19 when a traditional tribal feast was arranged between the Marines and Sheik Fahran al-Sudaid and important Kurdish and Arab tribal leaders in northern Tikrit. The goal was to facilitate the transfer of command. Kelly and his staff attended the dinner. Odierno's division was represented only by his sergeant major.[11]

On April 21, the relief in place was completed and Task Force Tripoli made its way south to the 1st Marine Division staging area at Diwaniyah. It left convinced that the good work it had done would soon be undone by 4th ID heavy-handedness. For its part, the 4th ID was convinced that the Marines were naive in thinking they had left matters under control. The question of how best to deal with Iraq after the regime's fall remained a matter of dispute as resistance persisted and grew in subsequent months.

North of Tikrit and Baqubah, U.S. forces had an entirely different issue to deal with. When Baghdad fell, the Iraqi resistance there crumbled, dissolving the Green Line. In Kirkuk, Iraqi soldiers had shed their uniforms and blended into the populace. The police had disappeared from the streets. Along with a delirious celebration, rioting and looting were rampant. The problem the Americans faced was not pushing the Iraqis out, but controlling the Kurds who were rushing in to fill the power vacuum in the north.

In the Kurdish city of Sulaymaniyah, Lieutenant General Pete Osman, heading the largely symbolic Military Coordination and Liaison Command, had worked hard to keep the Kurds in line. But when Jalal Talabani, head of the PUK, called he knew he had trouble. "They're looting! They're rioting in Kirkuk!" Talabani exclaimed. "We need to do something! I've got to send Peshmerga." Kirkuk had been home to thousands of Kurds until Saddam began to push many out and bring in Arabs in a calculated effort to alter the ethnic balance and solidify his hold on the oil-rich region. The Americans were afraid that the Peshmerga would try to expand the Kurdish sphere of control southward, possibly provoking a Turkish military intervention. Osman urged Talabani to stay calm and let the U.S. military deal with the unrest in Kirkuk—to no avail. Talabani's Peshmerga rushed forward.

Unable to restrain the Peshmerga, Osman contacted Colonel Bill Mayville, the commander of the 173rd Airborne Brigade, which was headquartered at Bashur, and warned him that the Kurds had rushed south. Mayville, in turn, contacted Lieutenant Colonel Ken Tovo, the commander of the Special Forces 3rd Battalion, which had been working with the Kurdish forces in that area. The 173rd was under the SOF's command in the north. Mayville wanted to know what he was to do about the Kurds. He did not have enough forces to "capture" the city. Mayville had been preparing to fight Saddam's forces, not restore law in an area that was now officially in friendly hands. Tovo replied that, as Mayville did not have a combat mission, his job was to "just stabilize the situation." "The 173rd was having a very difficult time accepting what they were facing. They were all about fighting Iraqis and force ratios and how they were going to handle the threat. They just couldn't come around to the realization that wasn't their problem."[12]

Mayville got the 173rd on the road and, by the end of the day on April 10, advance elements entered Kirkuk. The following morning, to the surprise of the Americans, Kirkuk was returning to normal with only pockets of disorder, mostly the doing of Peshmerga. "There had been a good deal of rioting and looting, but there was a sense of calm," said Osman. "The people seemed happy. They had gotten the rioting out of their system and seemed ready to settle down." Some Kurdish police from Sulaymaniyah arrived to help restore order.

But the crisis was not over. A 173rd roadblock on the approaches to the city reported that Talabani and "a huge escort" were heading for the city center. By the time Osman arrived on the scene, Talabani was already giving a speech and taking questions from the media at city hall. Osman was alarmed at how this would play in Ankara. The Kurdish leader was not only in Kirkuk but acting very much as if he was now in charge. An SOF officer managed to whisk Talabani away from the microphones and cameras and into the mayor's office, where Osman confronted him. Osman told him his presence as head of the PUK, the Patriotic Union of Kurdistan, was going to give the Turks the excuse they were looking for to cross the border. "But this is my home," retorted Talabani. "I don't give a damn if this is your home," shouted Osman. "Get your guys and get out of town before you cause a war we don't need." A chastened Talabani left the city. Forty-eight hours later calm had fully returned to Kirkuk. The police slowly reemerged while paratroopers of the 173rd patrolled the streets and chased renegade Peshmerga out of town.

In Washington, Colin Powell made an urgent phone call to Abdullah Gull, Turkey's foreign minister, promising that the Peshmerga would be persuaded to leave. Powell also agreed that a small number of Turkish officers could accompany U.S. forces into the city. By April 9, U.S. forces had taken control of Kirkuk's 300 unscathed oilfields. On April 11, Gull expressed satisfaction with the situation, saying, "There is no need at this time for intervention on our part," while clearly implying that the option remained.[13]

Mosul proved to be a bigger challenge than Kirkuk. Even as the battle for the Tebecka crossroads was taking place, the Peshmerga attacked and captured the town of Ayn Sifni, thirty miles north of Mosul. The Kurds closed in on the beltway around Mosul, which was designated the limit of advance. At a joint meeting with Waltemeyer the two Kurdish groups got into an angry shouting match. Masoud Barzani's KDP people had heard that Talabani's PUK was in Kirkuk in violation of all agreements. Officials from the two groups were at each other's throats and neither side was particularly interested in talking with Waltemeyer. Frustrated, Waltemeyer went to Dohuk, where he met with two dozen representatives of various regional factions. He told them that the Americans were going into Mosul and solicited their assistance. By day's end, however, he had no commitments. That night Waltemeyer received reports that Mosul was on fire and being looted.

The next morning Waltemeyer learned that the commander of the Iraqi V Corps, which had defended Iraqi territory south of the Green Line, wanted to formally capitulate at a designated meeting point south of Dohuk. When Waltemeyer arrived, he recalled, "it looked like Woodstock with guns." Waltemeyer was not the only one who had been informed of the event. The surrounding hills were covered with trucks and thousands of Peshmerga. It was soon apparent that the Iraqi general had nothing to surrender but himself. The Iraqi V Corps had evaporated and was a corps in name only. Sensing this, the Kurds began mounting their trucks for a drive into Mosul. It was clear the door to the south was wide open.

Waltemeyer grabbed a rifle and ran to the front of the column and aimed at the lead Kurdish vehicle—a dramatic confrontation between two allies. To his relief the column came to a halt and three hours of parlaying ensued. It was clear to Waltemeyer that somebody would have to go to Mosul and that he should be the one. Trying to stop the Kurds from claiming the city, Waltemeyer rounded up about thirty SOF troops and headed toward the city with American flags flying from the vehicle antennas. The goal, he said, "was to drive to city hall and plant an American flag." Waltemeyer had made himself clear but was in no position to control the city. Mosul was the third largest city in Iraq and multiethnic. To secure Mosul the SOF desperately needed to be reinforced.[14]

Jim Jones provided the initial help. With few forces in the north the NATO commander and four-star Marine general had come up with a stopgap: the 26th Marine Expeditionary Unit, which was afloat in the Mediterranean. Franks and the CENTCOM headquarters reluctantly accepted the offer. Commanded by Colonel A. P. Frick, the unit consisted of an infantry battalion, attack and transport helicopters, fixed wing AV-8 Harrier jets, tanks, LAVs, and artillery—some 2,200 Marines in all. An early plan had called for the MEU to block senior Iraqi officials from fleeing across the Iraqi-Syrian border. With the chaos in the north, Frick was ordered to deploy his Marines to Irbil "by the most expeditious means available." Given the considerable distance the MEU had to travel, that was easier said than done.

As a decision had been made to get as many boots on the ground as quickly as possible, the infantry debarked from their amphibious ships at Souda Bay, Crete, where they were to fly by C-130 and helicopter on a circuitous route to Irbil. Lieutenant Colonel David Hough, his command group, and 128 members of a rifle company were on the first flight. The next day twelve of their transport helicopters took off to begin a hopscotch journey to the landing strip at Bashur, the first step in a troop airlift that would take days. CENTCOM refused the Marines' request to bring along their Harrier jump jets and Cobra attack helicopters, saying they would not be needed. "We had no idea what our new mission was at that point. We were completely in the dark," said Major Paul Brickley, the battalion operations officer.

When Colonel Charlie Cleveland, the commander of the 10th Special Forces Group, told Frick he was going to Mosul, the Marine commander had one paramount question: "Where is that?" The Marines had no way to get there, so Cleveland said he would provide transport, which turned out to be Special Forces Pave Low helicopters and local buses. "What are we supposed to do?" Frick asked. "Link up with 5102 and work it out with them. There's civil unrest in the city," Cleveland said. "Who's 5102?" was the next question. "Special Forces," was the answer.[15]

At the Mosul airfield, Waltemeyer told Hough he wanted the Marines to establish a footprint at the airfield and set up a presence in the city to let the residents know the Americans were there. Early the following morning, SOF and Marines established checkpoints over the Tigris and, on April 14, a company of Marines and SOF drove to Mosul's city hall through an angry crowd protesting the lack of water and electricity. The situation turned deadly when Mishan al-Jabouri, a notorious local businessman, was seen entering city hall, which enraged the crowd. The Jabouri tribe had a Mafia-like reputation with ties to Saddam Hussein, and Mosul residents believed Jabouri's presence indicated that he was about to be installed as head of a regional government. Ignorant of local politics, the Marines made the mistake of letting Jabouri address the throng in the belief that this would somehow calm it down. Cars were overturned and set afire and the Marines reported taking small arms fire. They responded by firing over the crowd, but when a mob rushed city hall they lowered their sights and killed seven of the attackers. SOF put out a call for air support. In sequence, F-14s, F/A-18s, and F-16s arrived and made threatening low passes over the crowd, temporarily dispersing it. But soon the aircraft were gone.

By noon things had quieted down. When a relief convoy arrived, Waltemeyer and Hough decided to hold their position for the night. But things became worse the next day when firing at the beleaguered company and command group resumed with increased intensity. Frick, Hough, and Waltemeyer realized that a couple hundred Marines in the third largest city in Iraq were in an untenable position. Under cover of an SOF AC-130 gunship, the Americans withdrew to the Mosul airport when it became dark. Meanwhile in Ankara, U.S. officials were busy assuring the Turks that all was under control and that the Americans and not the Peshmerga were in charge of Mosul.

The Marine Expeditionary Unit commander sorely wished he had been allowed to bring his Cobra helicopter gunships, Harriers, and LAVs. He was further dismayed when on April 17 the Sixth Fleet commander ordered the Marines to halt further deployments to Iraq. The flow of his battalion was stopped in midstream. The 26th MEU had received little guidance about its mission and only a fraction of what it needed to do the job. Thereafter, the 750-man force had to content itself with providing security for the airfield. The deployment of the 26th MEU had been Jones's brainstorm, not CENTCOM's. Without strong backing from Franks or any real coordination with McKiernan's staff, the plan did not get very far.[16]

Osman, too, was convinced that the U.S. still needed more troops, and firepower, in the north. Already Turkish Special Forces operatives had been picked up in Kirkuk, disguised as humanitarian aid workers. Osman believed the Turks were meddling and that the threat of a Turkish intervention, if the Peshmerga took control of Mosul, was real. Osman called Abizaid and told him, "You've got to get a larger force in here and give them some tanks. They've got to see we're serious about this." The deputy at CENTCOM responded that he would send Petraeus's 101st Airborne Division. McKiernan was thinking the same thing. With its heliborne forces and long reach, the 101st was ordered to conduct the longest airmobile operation in history, moving from well south of Baghdad to Mosul, with multiple refuelings en route.[17]

Overseeing Mosul was just about the last thing the 101st had had in mind when American forces invaded Iraq. Petraeus had been convinced his soldiers would be among the first to get to Baghdad. But after the American military was attacked by paramilitary forces in the rear, the 101st was ordered to clear the southern Iraqi cities of Najaf and Karbala before moving north. The 101st's new orders were to take charge of Mosul, the territory to the west that stretched to the Syrian border, as well as Kurdish areas to Mosul's north and east. Petraeus had a large area to cover—the entire Ninawa Province—but he had a full division of soldiers and firepower with which to do it.

Colonel Joe Anderson, the commander of the 2nd Brigade of the 101st, led his soldiers to the Mosul airfield on April 22. The situation did not appear encouraging. The Marines were hunkered down at the airport. The city was still in an uproar. Many of the Peshmerga had left, but not before looting the Iraqi V Corps's supply depot and retiring to the mountains with purloined artillery and every other piece of useful weaponry and equipment they could get their hands on. As a farewell salute they had also blown up the Iraqi ammunition dump, which exploded and burned for days.

Colonel Anderson quickly moved more than 1,600 soldiers into the city center. Within a few days, General Petraeus began negotiations with the various ethnic groups and tribes to form a local governing council and convene a caucus so the Iraqis could pick a new mayor. Petraeus had his troops assume a no-nonsense but nonaggressive posture. He himself took off his helmet and flak jacket while he walked through the streets and talked with neighborhood leaders. "He did it right and won over Mosul," said Osman. It was a far different approach from the one taken by Odierno in Tikrit.[18]

The campaign in northern Iraq relied more on finesse than speed or firepower. More so than the campaigns in the south or west, it validated the strategy employed in the earlier war against the Taliban. As in Afghanistan, SOF forces relied on indigenous forces supported by American airpower to hold in place and ultimately defeat a 150,000-man Iraqi army along the Green Line. The political challenges had been more daunting than the military ones. Still, a handful of officers from different commands managed to tamp down ethnic tensions. The liberation of Iraqi Kurdistan owed much to their ingenuity and adaptability.

While Osman and his fellow officers were struggling to keep the lid on northern Iraq, the British were securing the southeast. Robin Brims, the British major general who commanded the 1 U.K. Armoured Division, had faced a different strategic situation than had most of his American counterparts. Unlike Buff Blount or Jim Mattis, Brims's goal was not to seize the enemy capital, defeat the Republican Guard, and throw Saddam out of power. The British mission was to stabilize and ultimately liberate the Shiite-dominated corner of Iraq.

In the opening days of the war, the British had quickly taken the Faw Peninsula and assumed control of the Rumaylah oilfields from Mattis's division. Taking advantage of the newly seized port of Umm Qasr, Albert Whitley, McKiernan's British deputy, scored an early public relations coup by organizing a very visible delivery of food and humanitarian assistance. Whitley had initially approached the Americans, who had tons of aid stockpiled but were slow to respond. The British government had little to offer. So Whitley convinced the Kuwaiti Red Crescent to donate aid and arranged for it to be loaded on the *Sir Galahad*, a British vessel. The arrival of the ship on March 28 was, as Whitley hoped, an international media event, though more show than substance.

After its initial operations, the British offensive had been methodical, even patient. Franks had pressed McKiernan during his visit to Camp Doha to seize Basra faster. But when McKiernan went to see Brims, he left the timing up to the British. As far as McKiernan was concerned, the British had already accomplished their main strategic purpose by fixing the Iraqi forces in Basra and in eastern Iraq. On Franks's computer screens in Qatar, the red icons looked like menacing formations but McKiernan saw them as hollow symbols of divisions that had little will to fight.

For Brims, the pace of the attack was less important than risking the destruction of Basra, Zubayr, and other southern cities. The population in the region was deemed to be largely anti-Saddam, presumed to be receptive, if not friendly, to the coalition but also under the thumb of hard-nosed Baathists who reported to Baghdad. Ali Hassan al-Majeed, Chemical Ali, who was in control of the network of Baath militia and Fedayeen in the south, was operating out of Basra.

Brims did not want to lay siege to Basra and cut off the city from food and other supplies. Nor was his goal to trap all the Baathists in the city. For Brims, it was enough to take the city more or less intact. The British commander was careful to leave an escape route for many of the regime forces—the road north of Highway 6 leading to Amara—unlike the Americans, who had hoped to set a cordon around Baghdad and trap as many senior officers as they could. Unlike Mattis, who gave orders to his commanders to destroy the enemy units they faced and not let them retreat to fight another day, Brims said, "I knew that they didn't want to fight, and I wanted to give those who didn't want to fight the opportunity to escape. So I exercised restraint there. I could mention any number of occasions when I restrained. But it was not because I was given 'limited freedom of action,' nor for 'legal reasons,' but because that is how we wanted to fight the war."

The strategy minimized the chances of a slugfest in Basra but allowed the Fedayeen to live to fight another day. In another contrast with the Americans, Brims also applied stricter rules of engagement. The V Corps and Marines routinely relied on counterbattery radar in their artillery duels with the Iraqis. Brims was reluctant to rely on unobserved fire, a procedure that was effective in quickly responding to enemy barrages but which increased the possibility of civilian casualties. The British general was also determined to draw on the lessons of Zubayr, which had been a hotbed of Fedayeen resistance. Instead of racing into the city, the British 7 Armored Brigade had set up checkpoints on the outskirts, gathered intelligence about the resistance in the city, and ambushed the Iraqi fighters who came out to contest their positions. Brims did much the same at Basra. The British conducted raids in and out of the city and gradually moved into the outskirts.

During the Army's and Marines' approach to Baghdad, the British had received intelligence pinpointing the location of Chemical Ali. Within minutes, an air strike had been authorized. An American F-16 dropped two JDAM satellite-guided bombs. The first was a dud, but the second hit and blasted the suspected hideout. On the morning of April 6, the Black Watch was conducting a raid in northern Basra, penetrating the city. After meeting no resistance in their Challenger tanks and Warrior armored vehicles, the British drove farther until they encountered Iraqi soldiers and

Fedayeen at concrete pillboxes and in fortified houses. After attacking the enemy positions it was clear that the Iraqi defense was coming apart. Constant pressure from the British and the attack on Chemical Ali had undermined enemy morale. Brims could see that the Iraqi defense at Basra was hollow and it was time to strike. Officially, the decision to attack into Basra was McKiernan's, so Brims called McKiernan's command and was given the green light.

At 11:00 a.m., Brims finally gave the order for British forces to move deep into the city. The 7 Armoured Brigade, commanded by Brigadier Graham Binns, drove over the western bridges while Brigadier Jim Dutton's 3 Commando Brigade attacked from the south. The 16 Air Assault Brigade under Brigadier "Jacko" Page simultaneously moved into Diya, a town about ten miles north of Basra that British intelligence indicated was the headquarters for the Iraqi military's III Corps. Brims could have attacked the headquarters but held back. By now it had been abandoned. The mayor of the town came out waving a white flag. The Iraqi command had left several hours earlier.

The attack into Basra made for a long day of fighting, but only three British soldiers were killed. The division commander was duly proud of its accomplishment. "If you had said to me on March 19 that you could attack into a defended city of one and a quarter million people and only have three of your own soldiers killed I'd have taken it. I deeply regret the three but I think it was a pretty remarkable achievement by 7 Armoured Brigade."

At the Pentagon, officials released video of the strike on Chemical Ali's house. "We believe that the reign of terror of Chemical Ali has come to an end," Rumsfeld said. U.S. intelligence, however, later discovered that the Iraqi official had survived the attack and escaped the city. Like the failed F-117 strike at Dora Farms and the April 7 B-1 attack in Baghdad, the air strike had been precisely delivered but the target had eluded them.

Brims, who had also believed the early intelligence reports, was philosophical about the episode. The British general thought that the final collapse of the Iraqi defenses in Basra had been precipitated by reports among the residents of Basra that Chemical Ali had been killed. Here was an inadvertent case of psychological warfare. The Pentagon, CENTCOM, and the British Ministry of Defence were convinced that Ali was buried under the debris of his Basra headquarters, and for a while the Iraqis were as well. His body, however, was not found. Chemical Ali was still alive and well. Saddam and his top officials had scattered to the four winds, but they were not finished yet.[19]

CHAPTER 23

Hello, I Must Be Going

On April 15, President Bush convened a meeting of his top aides to consider the plan for withdrawing U.S. forces from Iraq. In his Citadel speech before assuming the presidency, Bush had vowed to avoid open-ended peacekeeping operations and massive nation-building operations. Rumsfeld had echoed the same themes in his address "Beyond Nation-Building" just a month before the war. With the Iraqi capital in American hands the administration was moving to put its precepts into action.[1]

Prepared by the Joint Staff, the plan was confidently titled "Iraq Phase IV: Gaining Coalition Commitment." There were to be three foreign divisions: a British-led division that would include other allied forces, a Polish-led division, and a Muslim force that would be led by the Saudis and Arabs from other Persian Gulf States. In addition, the administration would solicit foreign constabularies to help keep order and train the Iraqi police. The Italian carabinieri were high on the wish list, as were constabularies from Denmark, Italy, Portugal, South Korea, and Singapore. Few of the potential contributors had been wholehearted supporters of the war, but the administration assumed they would be willing to help keep the peace in a relatively benign Iraq, which controlled some of the world's largest oil reserves and which would be ruled by a new enlightened government.

The president applauded the plan to seek foreign troops, and the meeting yielded three additional decisions on post-Saddam Iraq. The United States would collect and publish information on Saddam's brutality. It would upgrade the Iraqis' health care system and accept an offer from Saudi Crown Prince Abdullah to establish a hospital in Baghdad.[2] In the early days after the fall of the capital, Baghdad had been racked by a spasm of looting, but the Bush administration was convinced its strategy was still on track. There would be no Balkans-like peacekeeping operation. The Iraq War would be like a thunderstorm: a short, violent episode that swept away the enemy but would not entail a burdensome, long-term troop commitment.

The next day, Tommy Franks flew to the Iraqi capital to discuss the path ahead. It was the CENTCOM commander's first flight to the sprawling Baghdad airport, which American forces had turned into a transportation hub for liberated Iraq. As Franks emerged from his C-130 he pumped a clenched fist into the air. Though the airport was in U.S. hands, Franks's security detail was not taking any chances. Apache attack helicopters prowled the skies as Franks made the ten-minute drive to Cobra Base, the new forward headquarters for McKiernan's land war command.

Cobra Base was situated at the Abu Ghraib North Palace, a massive white edifice set in the middle of an azure man-made lake. The war had robbed the palace of much of its splendor. Anticipating that the palace would be a target, the Iraqis had removed nearly all of its furnishings—paintings had even been taken from their frames—turning the once grand residence into a dusty hulk. One wing of the structure had been turned into a heap of rubble three weeks earlier thanks to a GBU-10 that Major Steven Ankerstar, the F-117 pilot, had dropped as "a show of force." When the palace was seized by Buff Blount's 3rd ID, its only residents were a small group of Syrian jihadists, one of whom was found hiding in a refrigerator, and some stray goats. The palace did not have electricity or even working plumbing. The U.S. soldiers who now occupied it had transformed its cavernous chambers and grand balconies into crowded dormitories and had taken to washing their clothes in the increasingly foul moat.

Franks took a quick tour of the grounds and then gathered his commanders in an enormous drawing room. Buzz Moseley had flown up from his command post in Saudi Arabia. Vice Admiral Tim Keating, who oversaw the naval campaign from his headquarters in Bahrain, made the trip. So did Major General Dell Dailey, who commanded the most secret Special Operations Forces. McKiernan was the host. It was the first time the commanders had gathered in person since before the war. After embracing the officers, Franks issued his classified set of instructions.

The combat forces that had battled their way to Baghdad, Tikrit, Karbala, and Najaf should prepare to pull out within sixty days. New units would arrive to help stabilize the country but most would stay no longer than 120 days. Cutting back so quickly would leave much of Iraq uncovered, but Franks laid down the rule that was to guide the next phase of the operation: the generals should be prepared to take as much risk departing as they had in their push to Baghdad. The U.S. forces in Iraq should expect some form of functioning Iraqi government in thirty to sixty days.[3]

After their discussion Franks and the commanders sat down in front of a screen for a satellite video conference with President Bush. Turning his attention to Franks, the president asked about the effort to recruit a multinational force. Franks said he would give it a 6 on a scale of 1 to 10, noting that Colin Powell and Don Rumsfeld would be approaching allied nations while Franks himself would be lobbying the United Arab Emirates, which had expressed interest in sending a force of Arab peacekeeping soldiers to Iraq. As the Baghdad meeting drew to a close, the president congratulated the commanders. Afterward, Franks and his team posed for photos and puffed on victory cigars.

Rusty Blackman, the two-star Marine general who served as McKiernan's chief of staff, was dumbfounded by Franks's emphasis on a speedy U.S. troop withdrawal. The Army and Marines had taken the Iraqi capital just a week earlier. The U.S. had yet to send troops to cities like Fallujah and there were regions of the country—and even neighborhoods in Baghdad—that were still not secure. McKiernan had planned to oversee forces in Iraq for as long as six months before transitioning to a new command and nothing he or his staff had seen so far had suggested that it was time to think about leaving. If Franks's guidance was carried out, the more than 140,000 troops in Iraq could be down to little more than a "division-plus," about 30,000 troops, by September.

After the session, Blackman told Terry Moran about Franks's surprising guidance. Moran, in turn, called Mike Fitzgerald, the chief CENTCOM planner. "What the hell is going on?" asked Moran. McKiernan had just been told that U.S. forces would soon begin to leave Iraq. "Who said that?" Fitzgerald asked. "CENTCOM said that," Moran replied.[4]

After he retired, Franks explained that the guidance was part of the broader Bush administration effort to convince allied countries that Iraq was stable and encourage them in thinking that it was safe to send troops. "I wanted our troopers to work up their transportation plans, work up a process whereby they could begin redeployment in as little as sixty days," Franks said. To reinforce the point, Franks recommended that the White

House proclaim that the major hostilities had come to an end. The idea, Franks said, was "to have the old man declare the end of major combat operations on the first of May because it opened the bank, so to speak, for us to go after additional international forces."[5]

Though Franks did not mention it, the CENTCOM commander had outlined his strategy in a private e-mail to Rumsfeld on the day of his Baghdad visit. Franks recommended that the United States declare a military victory in Iraq and announce that it was transitioning to post-war operations. To drive the point home, Franks's e-mail further recommended that Jay Garner move his team to Baghdad and that McKiernan be designated as the head of CJTF-Iraq—or Combined Joint Task Force Iraq.[6]

Several days later, McKiernan received another surprise. When McKiernan pitched Cobra II in December 2002 he had insisted that the initial invasion force be followed by the 1st Armored Division and the 1st Cavalry. Iraq was a big country with long, unsecured borders. The Fedayeen attacks in the south had only reinforced his assessment that the occupation could be more challenging than anticipated and that the follow-up troops were needed. Even with the reinforcements, McKiernan would have only half the 380,000 troops that Zinni had once determined would be necessary to secure the entire country. McKiernan hoped to strengthen his hold with the help of reconstituted Iraqi troops and foreign forces, but they were not available yet. For the foreseeable future, the only significant forces he had to control the country would be the Americans and British. Even if allied forces were to be drawn down soon, McKiernan still wanted all of the forces that were earmarked for the Cobra II plan.

Rumsfeld, however, had made it equally clear that he might off-ramp some Army units if Saddam's forces were quickly defeated. From the time he was briefed on Zinni's 1003 plan, Rumsfeld saw force requirements more in terms of what was needed to win the war than to secure the peace. Even before the war began Rumsfeld had discussed the possibility of off-ramping units if they were not needed to defeat Saddam. On February 20, the Joint Staff had developed a list of units whose deployment could be canceled or reversed: the 173rd Airborne, the 3rd Armored Cavalry Regiment, the 101st Airborne, the 1st Armored Division, and the 1st Cavalry Division. On March 8, Rumsfeld sent a note to Myers expressing his view that the flow of forces should be carefully metered so that an excessive number were not deployed. "I think I need a good deal more understanding of the units we may decide not to send over," Rumsfeld wrote, "so we make intelligent decisions and don't get stampeded into just sending them over." In response, the Joint Staff prepared weekly briefings on the subject. With victory seemingly at hand and the Republican Guard vanquished, the defense secretary had begun to press the issue again in video conferences with Franks, asking why the Pentagon needed to send both the 1st Armored and 1st Cavalry divisions. Rumsfeld had never accepted Shinseki's suggestion that more troops might be needed to stabilize postwar Iraq than to prosecute the war, and he was no more convinced now.[7]

Initially, Franks took the position that he needed both divisions: they would extend the military's reach into northern and western Iraq and enable CENTCOM to devote more resources to retraining the Iraqi army. But after discussing the matter for several days with Rumsfeld, Franks relented. The 1st Armored Division was sent, but the deployment of the sixteen-thousand-strong 1st Cavalry Division was officially canceled on April 21. Franks justified his change of heart on the grounds that allied forces would soon be on the way and that McKiernan and other commanders could manage with the divisions they had. While Franks insisted that he had not been browbeaten into going along, he acknowledged that Rumsfeld was the impetus behind the decision. "We had First Armored and First Cav in the flow," Franks said. "Don Rumsfeld did in fact make the decision to off-ramp the First Cavalry Division."[8]

Tom White, the civilian Army secretary, had a less charitable view. "Rumsfeld just ground Franks down," White said. "If you grind away at the military guys long enough, they will finally say, 'Screw it, I'll do the best I can with what I have.' The nature of Rumsfeld is that you just get tired of arguing with him." Since Rumsfeld and his aides were determined to keep the American troop presence in Iraq to a minimum, the decision was all but pre-ordained. White explained, "Our working budgetary assumption was that ninety days after completion of the operation, we would withdraw the first fifty thousand and then every thirty days we'd take out another fifty thousand until everybody was back. The view was that whatever was left in Iraq would be de minimis."[9]

For his part, McKiernan was unhappy with the decision, which was made without his consultation, but he did not fight it. Making the best of the forces he had on hand, he decided how to distribute his troops. McKiernan told his Army and Marine commanders that the troops' main focus would be on keeping order in Iraq's cities. The rest of the country would be "economy of force" and there would be no more than an armored cavalry squadron in western Iraq. While military commanders would be making preparations to leave the country, McKiernan cautioned that the redeployment could be delayed or even halted if security in Iraq deteriorated or if the Bush administration failed to recruit the allied forces. The success of Jay Garner's postwar team, McKiernan noted, would facilitate the redeployment.[10]

One region with the smallest U.S. troop presence was the Anbar Province, which included Fallujah and Ramadi, where unbeknownst to the Americans Saddam and his sons had initially taken refuge. In mid-April, the United States had gotten by with a modicum of troops when an Iraqi general in the west indicated he was prepared to formally surrender his division. Colonel Curtis Potts, the commander of the 3rd Infantry Division's Aviation Brigade, flew on April 15 to an outpost in the Anbar region where he was joined by some of Terry Ferrell's troops. General Mohammed Jarawi officially submitted his surrender over a small folding table. The Iraqi troops in the division had already gone AWOL, but U.S. forces drove around the region afterward and destroyed the seventy-odd armored vehicles that were officially under Jarawi's command before dropping off the general at his home in Ramadi. It was the only time that an Iraqi unit had formally surrendered during the war. Though hailed as a confirmation of the U.S. victory, the Iraqi troops in the unit had blended into the population, and the U.S. did not have nearly enough troops to establish a presence in the province, let alone impose order. It was a grand photo op, but not much of a bellwether of what was to come.[11]

On April 24, troops from the 82nd Airborne took up positions in a schoolhouse in Fallujah, the first time that U.S. forces had installed themselves in the Sunni city. During an angry demonstration against the U.S. troops six days later, shots rang out. The 82nd fired back, killing seventeen Iraqis and wounding more than sixty. The 82nd insisted it had been fired at. The Iraqis claimed that the soldiers had overreacted. The next day, as angry protests continued in the city, seven soldiers from the 3rd Armored Cavalry Regiment were wounded by a grenade attack. "It's just a reaction to the shootings," said Emad Hassan, a well-dressed civil engineer. "If you kill my brother, then I will kill yours." On a wall outside the mayor's building next to the Army's makeshift compound protesters hung a sign in English that proclaimed, "U.S. killers, we'll kick you out." The region that the United States had hoped to control with just a smattering of forces was soon a tense battleground.[12]

Two days later, Bush flew to the deck of the *Abraham Lincoln* aircraft carrier. Standing before a banner announcing "Mission Accomplished," the president said that the major combat phase of the war had been completed and noted that U.S. forces were bringing order to the country and pursuing Saddam's henchmen. The White House was making an effort to suggest that Iraq was stable enough for allied nations to volunteer troops, but events on the ground were sending the opposite message.

At his hotel headquarters in Kuwait, Jay Garner was anxious to get to Baghdad. The day after Franks returned from the meeting with his commanders, Garner had contacted Franks and urged him to fly the postwar team to the fallen capital. Under CENTCOM's original plan, Garner and his team of postwar advisers and administrators were not to arrive until sixty days after the war. Franks and his staff figured that military civil affairs teams and combat engineers would do the heavy lifting in the early days. Garner and his civilian aides would come later.

With the rapid demise of Saddam's regime, however, Garner lobbied to get his Office for Reconstruction and Humanitarian Assistance to Iraq sooner rather than later, and Franks agreed. Garner's plan was to attach advisers to the Iraqi ministries and manage the country until an Iraqi government was put in place, a government that would be expected to include Ahmed Chalabi, Iyad Alawi, and the other exiles who had been meeting with Bush administration officials in Washington, London, Kurdistan, and Tallil.[13]

It was assumed that the dramatic ouster of Saddam would create a "*Wizard of Oz* moment" in Iraq, recalled Carl Strock, the two-star general from the Army Corps of Engineers and a Garner deputy. After the wicked dictator was deposed, throngs of cheering Iraqis would hail their liberators and go back to work under the tutelage of Garner's postwar organization and its teams of advisers attached to the Iraqi ministries—in some cases, no more than a single individual. It was, Strock acknowledged, a "simplistic approach." But simplistic or not, the strategy had been embraced by the White House. "The concept was that we would defeat the army, but the institutions would hold, everything from ministries to police forces," Condoleezza Rice had noted. "You would be able to bring new leadership but we were going to keep the body in place." Garner, for his part, was not anticipating that he would be taking on the political and physical reconstruction of Iraq, and he was hoping to find a partner among the Iraqis.[14]

Still, Garner thought Franks's admonition about risk-taking on the way out was plain crazy. Garner did not relish the prospect of watching U.S. forces leave just as he was setting up shop. Franks's embrace of audacity was fine for the invasion, since a U.S. victory had been all but preordained, but Garner thought it was reckless to take risks in postwar Iraq. Holding the country together and installing a democratic government in the heart of the Arab world would be hard enough without removing forces from the field. "There was no doubt we would win the war," Garner recalled telling McKiernan, "but there can be doubt we will win the peace."[15]

As unsettling as Franks's comments were, it was not the first time that Garner's team had heard that the U.S. might diminish the number of its troops in Iraq. In mid-April, Lawrence Di Rita, one of Rumsfeld's closest aides, had arrived in Kuwait to join Garner's team. Speaking to a group of Garner's aides, Di Rita had outlined Rumsfeld's vision. The Pentagon was determined to avoid open-ended military commitments like those in Bosnia and Kosovo, and to withdraw the vast majority of the American forces in three to four months. The State Department had mismanaged the postwar efforts in the Balkans, and Afghanistan was headed the same way. With the Defense Department now in charge of Iraq after the fall of Saddam things would run more smoothly. "The main theme was that DOD would be in charge, and this would be totally different than in the past," said Tom Gross, who was also at the session. "We would be out very quickly. We were very confused. We did not see it as a short-term process." In another meeting with Garner's team, Di Rita had also rejected the notion that the United States would supervise a lengthy and costly reconstruction of the country. Paul Wolfowitz had initially suggested that much of the long-neglected repair and upgrading of Iraq's infrastructure would be paid for by its oil proceeds; Di Rita stressed this with more passion. Garner's team had projected no more than $3 billion in reconstruction costs over three years at the February Rock Drill, but as the reconstruction plan was being laid out Di Rita slammed his hand on the table and erupted: "We don't owe these people a thing. We gave them their freedom." Rumsfeld's loyal lieutenant was passionately championing his boss's "Beyond Nation-Building" doctrine. Di Rita's views were much remarked on by Garner's aides, though he later insisted he had not made the statement, or he had been misinterpreted.[16]

· · ·

There was a vicious circularity to the military and civilian planning. CENTCOM was hoping that the success of Garner's team would speed the withdrawal of U.S. troops; Garner was hoping that CENTCOM would provide the security he needed to begin to fashion a new Iraqi government, deliver humanitarian aid, and begin to rebuild the country.

When Garner's team flew to Baghdad on April 18, they stayed at the Abu Ghraib North Palace before moving into the Republican Palace, which Flip DeCamp's battalion had seized on the April 7 Thunder Run. Garner immediately took off on a nationwide tour, heading to Kurdistan, where he was greeted as a hero by throngs of pro-American Kurds who had been living in a virtual American protectorate for more than a decade and were grateful for Garner's role in managing the relief program after the Persian Gulf War. It was a veritable *Wizard of Oz* moment.

Baghdad, however, was nothing like Kurdistan. The Iraqi ministries Garner had hoped to use to run the country had been ransacked and looted. Communication systems were in shambles. When the Iraqi resistance had stiffened and Saddam had taken to the airwaves, Moseley had stepped up his efforts to cut Saddam off from his troops. The twelve telephone switching centers in Baghdad were hit hard and disabled. In its zeal to knock Saddam and his propaganda broadcasts off the air—and to sunder the regime's ability to command its forces—the U.S. had in effect disabled what Garner now needed. Moreover, the Iraqi electrical grid had become unstable, and the Iraqis had shut it down only to discover it could not be switched back on. It was all but impossible for Garner to communicate with officials across town, let alone get his message to the capital's residents. Two of the three sewage treatment plants in Baghdad had to be extensively rebuilt as a result of the looting. Security was tenuous.

Robert Gifford had been one of the first members of Garner's team to arrive in Baghdad. He was a longtime deputy in the State Department's Bureau for International Narcotics and Law Enforcement Affairs, and his job was to advise Iraq's Interior Ministry and get its police force up and running. Garner had given Gifford explicit instructions to arrange a "police event" as soon as he got to Baghdad: a public demonstration that the police were returning to work, a potential photo op for Garner shown meeting with Iraqi cops in charge of keeping the peace.

It did not take long for Gifford to discover that the Iraqi police force had abandoned their posts and that their police stations had been picked clean by looters—electrical wires, phones, light fixtures, even some of the door jambs had been stolen. If the police were not able to protect their own stations it did not look like they would be helping the Americans keep order in Iraq anytime soon. Without reliable information on Iraqi personnel, Gifford was also worried that Iraqi law enforcement officials might rustle up tainted loyalists of the old order for the new police force—hardly the kind of people Garner should publicly embrace.[17]

The dearth of qualified Iraqi police in the opening weeks and months of the occupation was precisely the kind of problem that Dick Mayer, the Justice Department expert, had anticipated in February when he pushed at the Rock Drill for a 5,000-person international civilian police force. Bob Perito had warned of it as well in his presentation at the Pentagon. The reluctance of the White House to plan for this scenario, in fact, had led David Kay to resign his position on Garner's team months before. Mayer's recommendation to deploy an international constabulary had been rebuffed by the White House, which was determined to rely on the Iraqis to get the job done and which took comfort from a CIA assessment that Iraq's police were true professionals.

Soon officers from U.S. military units across the country were trekking to Gifford's office asking him for help in organizing the Iraqi police in their areas, but he had nothing to offer. Gifford was still operating with a mere $25 milion in seed money. Only the thirty-four-member assessment team that was to address Iraq's law enforcement needs and 150 private contractors still on standby in the United States had been authorized and funded.

When the assessment team showed up in May, Gifford immediately sent many of them into the field to try to encourage returning police station commanders, establish traffic control, help police leadership, and start training at the police academy. Appealing for more resources, Gifford and other experts prepared an internal report painting a bleak picture of the Iraqi police. The Iraqi police, the assessors noted, were corrupt, unprofessional, and untrustworthy. In fact, they were little more than traffic cops, were despised by the population, and were without any investigative competence. Molding them into a modern police force would be difficult work. The assessment recommended that 6,663 police advisers be sent. In effect, the report was making recommendations that had been rejected months before.[18]

Critics have complained that the Bush administration did not have a plan for postwar Iraq. But insofar as rebuilding the Iraqi police was concerned, the White House had not neglected the issue. It had considered and rejected the proposal by midlevel Justice and State Department officials for five thousand U.S. law enforcement personnel. It chose instead to rely on Iraqi forces, whatever gendarmes could be solicited from foreign countries, and several hundred U.S. contractors who would be sent only if the need arose. Looking back on the summer of 2003, Perito said, the Bush administration "did not have a training mission set to go." "Instead, they decided to do an assessment, offer recommendations, have them adopted, and then go for the money," he said. "What that does, it loses you the first six months of the operation. The doctrine on peace operations is that the initial month or so is critical."[19]

When Major General Carl Strock first joined Garner's team, he had been given an intelligence briefing on Iraq's electrical grid, but the intelligence focused on potential war damage to the system, not on the dilapidation of the power plants and generators—comprised of a hodgepodge of parts from Europe and Asia—that had suffered as a result of more than a decade of economic sanctions and inadequate investment.

The infrastructure was not only antiquated but had collapsed. U.S. troops approaching Baghdad might have thought that Saddam had blacked out the city, but in fact the Iraqi shutdown of the electrical grid had been purely technical. The U.S. policy had been not to target Iraq's power plants or electrical system. But U.S. air strikes had undermined the system in two ways: fuel lines to power plants, as well as electrical transmission lines, had inadvertently been damaged in bombing raids. Under the strain, the already fragile system had begun to experience power surges. When the chief engineer of the south Baghdad plant shut it down as a precaution, the entire grid had collapsed. Adding to the difficulties, much of the system had been undergoing its annual spring maintenance when the war approached. Some of its machinery had been disassembled and was undergoing repair when the foreign contractors who were hired for the job evacuated the country. Compounding the problem, the main expertise of the Army Corps of Engineers in charge of rectifying matters was in hydropower.

The looting in Baghdad made the task of restarting the system all the more difficult. The computerized control center in the capital was stripped bare. "You have to have some kind of control to stop generators or raise it or throw a switch—it was gone," recalled Thomas Wheelock, a senior official with the U.S. Agency for International Development. Even the transmission lines, which contained copper and aluminum, were stolen. "They just started at one end of the transmission line and worked their way up, taking down the towers, taking away the valuable metals, smelting it down, selling it into Iran and Kuwait," Wheelock added. "The price of metal in the Middle East dropped dramatically during this period of time."[20]

In January 2003, the National Intelligence Council, a CIA-led panel of intelligence specialists, had cautioned that building democracy in Iraq would be difficult because of its authoritarian history and warned of the risk that the American forces would be seen as occupiers. "Attitudes toward a foreign military force would depend largely on the progress made in transferring power, as well as on the degree to which that force were perceived as providing necessary security and fostering reconstruction and a return to prosperity," it said. The report also noted that quick restoration of services would be important to maintain the support of the Iraqi public. It was a useful point, but had not spurred any extraordinary efforts on the part of the Pentagon and other agencies. Strock and his engineers had been prepared for a patch job, not an overhaul.[21]

The absence of electricity further undermined an already burgeoning security problem, encouraged crime, made it hard for Garner and McKiernan to communicate with the Iraqi public over television and radio, and rendered the oppressive summer heat more trying for the Iraqi citizenry. Saddam had been brutal, but at least he had kept the capital supplied with electricity, even if it meant diverting power from the Shiite-dominated south. Now the capital's residents were mystified that a nation that had sent a man to the moon could not supply electricity. Sensing the urgency of the situation, McKiernan ordered Steven Hawkins, the brigadier general who was picked by Casey to head JTF-4, to form a task force and get Iraq's electrical system working again. Hawkins plunged into the job, beginning with no funds or even radios for his team. Working with Iraqi engineers to the point of exhaustion, Hawkins gradually restored electricity on a part-time basis, but the system remained vulnerable to sabotage and blackouts.[22]

In allocating his forces, McKiernan continued to view Baghdad as the political center, symbolically and in practical terms. Even so, the U.S. military was hard put to keep order in the capital. Buff Blount's 3rd Infantry Division had plenty of tanks and Bradleys but relatively few infantry. While the division had about eighteen thousand troops, only ten thousand or so were in a position to patrol Baghdad after the collapse of the regime. Of these, just twelve hundred would be dismounted infantry. With little guidance, the division took on the mission of guarding several hundred critical sites in the city, including hospitals, clinics, banks, government offices, palaces, refineries, shopping centers, and museums. There were also other sites that needed to be secured until the WMD investigation teams cleared them. Using tank crews to add to the foot patrols was easier said than done. There were only several hundred sets of body armor for the entire division. The Marines had lots of infantry, but they were needed to secure the Shiite-dominated area and moved south. The dearth of troops on the ground was only partially remedied by the arrival of the 2nd Armored Cavalry Regiment and other units in the capital.

The troops' considerable burden was aggravated by the need to protect Garner's teams. Each time one wanted to drive to an Iraqi ministry, two Humvees with soldiers had to be provided as escorts. "The moment I got there I put a demand on them for somewhere between fifty and sixty armed Humvees a day," Garner said. "That's a big demand. Plus, I put a demand on them for pretty much an infantry battalion to protect the palace that we had our people living in, had our office in. So there was instantly a huge security requirement."[23]

"We simply did not have enough forces for a city of six or seven million," Strock said. "The forces were stretched too thin and the troops on the ground often did not understand the significance of the stuff they were guarding." Wheelock noted that U.S. forces guarded the Oil Ministry and key power plants. "For the power lines we did not have enough assets," he said. "We didn't have enough troops in the country to provide security. They could not protect the power lines and they were not about to devote resources to them."[24]

As U.S. forces gradually extended their presence throughout Baghdad, the extent of weapons and munitions caches they discovered was enormous, and well beyond the intelligence estimates. Truckload after truckload of munitions were moved out of the city just to get them away from heavily populated areas. There was no way coalition forces could secure all the weapons and munitions storage sites across Iraq, a problem that grew over time. One of McKiernan's first major challenges was how to get weapons off the streets in a society where everyone seemingly had access to guns, there were barely contained ethnic tensions, and looting was still prevalent. He tried proclamations and meetings with political leaders, who were more concerned about arming their personal security teams than disarming the society. It was a seemingly impossible task.

While the Americans struggled with Iraq's infrastructure, their efforts to organize an interim government faltered. When U.S. forces had encountered the Fedayeen, Franks and Abizaid had implored Khalilzad to organize a series of meetings among the Kurds and exiles, and sessions were conducted at Tallil and later in Baghdad. The appeal to the resistance leaders was also a linchpin of the Pentagon's strategy for a quick turnover of the country to the Iraqis and for the rapid exit of most U.S. forces from Iraq. During his swing through Kurdistan, Garner had also urged Talabani and Barzani to come to Baghdad and work with members of the Iraqi resistance like Ahmed Chalabi and Iyad Alawi. Given their long-awaited opportunity to run the country, however, the eclectic collection of Iraqi leaders and opposition figures was hobbled by rivalries and ethnic politics. The hope to rapidly put an Iraqi face on the occupation was hampered by the Iraqi exile leaders themselves.

Qubad Talabani, the son of the Kurdish leader and a Kurdish representative to Washington, said that the American shortfalls were magnified by the failure of the Iraqi resistance to work together. "The first failure was an Iraqi failure," he said. "We were collectively unable to form this government because of what has plagued Iraq since then, quotas and who gets what share and what responsibility. This sent a message to Washington that the Iraqis were unable to administer themselves."[25]

While Garner and his team officially expressed confidence despite the challenges they faced, some began to fear that their reconstruction and political mission verged on the impossible. "It was supposed to be a Chalabi-centered effort with the five other parties," recalled Robin Raphel, a former U.S. ambassador to Tunisia and a senior member of Garner's team. "It was very obvious to me that we could not run a country we did not understand. We were not prepared. We went too soon. We should have waited until we built an international coalition." The White House had spurned the United Nations, but Raphel jested darkly to her colleagues that the United States would be on its knees in a week begging for help from the world body.[26]

The Bush administration's doctrine of preemption held that while the United States might act unilaterally, the success of its military operation would attract allies to share the postwar burden. Wolfowitz had even speculated before the war that France might be among those willing to

send forces to post-Saddam Iraq. In foreign capitals, word soon spread
that the United States was fumbling in Iraq. The country was disorderly,
the interim Iraqi government had not congealed, and the invasion did
not have the United Nations's imprimatur. There did not, as yet, seem to
be an organized insurgency, but the proclamation that major combat
operations had ended seemed hollow.

Talk of a Muslim peacekeeping division soon faded. The Saudis imposed all sorts of conditions on their participation, including the requirement that they not be under U.S. command. Even the hospital the Saudis
volunteered was a worry after Washington became concerned that Wah-
habis, Muslim zealots, had infiltrated it. Quiet discussions to deploy
troops from the United Arab Emirates to protect the southern Iraqi oilfields also came to naught.

E. J. Sinclair, a brigadier general with the 101st Airborne, was ordered
to New Delhi to try to secure India's agreement to deploy an entire division in northern Iraq. Dressed in his desert camouflage, the general flew
from Mosul to Kuwait on a C-12 plane only to struggle with Kuwaiti officials who were reluctant to allow him to board a commercial flight to
India without a passport. The U.S. embassy had to intervene to get Sinclair on the flight. The absence of a U.N. endorsement for the invasion
was a major political obstacle for the Indians and nothing came of the
trip. Turkey later offered peacekeeping troops, but the Iraqis saw their
offer as an attempt by Ankara to meddle in Iraqi affairs and would not
accept them. The Poles agreed to lead a division, but it was of uneven
quality. At Washington's insistence, a contingent of Spanish troops was
put under Polish command but they were limited by restrictive rules of
engagement. A Ukrainian brigade was stationed in Kut, but they were
barely able to defend themselves and retreated during their first serious
challenge. Only the British-led division, fortified by Italian and other
troops, became a reality.[27]

In early May, Tony Blair's government made John Sawers, the British ambassador to Egypt, its point man in Iraq. Four days after arriving, Sawers
sent a confidential cable to top officials at 10 Downing Street, the British
Foreign Office, the British Ministry of Defence, and the British International Aid Agency. His message was entitled "Iraq: What's Going
Wrong?" It painted a bleak picture and noted that the U.S.-led coalition
was gradually losing public support.

"A Baghdad First strategy is needed," Sawers wrote. "The problems are worst in the capital, and it is the one place we can't afford to get it wrong. But the troops here are tired, and are not providing the security framework needed. We need a clear policy on which Baathists can return, a more concerted effort on reconstruction, and an imaginative approach on the media. For all this, money needs to be released by Washington. The clock is ticking."

Sawers contended that Garner's team was ill suited for the challenge ahead. "Garner's outfit, ORHA, is an unbelievable mess," he wrote. "No leadership, no strategy, no coordination, no structure, and inaccessible to ordinary Iraqis. . . . Garner and his team of 60-year-old retired generals are well-meaning, but out of their depth."

The effort to reconstruct the country needed to be stepped up to gain public support. Forty percent of Baghdad's sewage was pouring into the Tigris untreated. Garbage was piling up in the streets. A mobile phone system was desperately needed. Bechtel, the contractor the United States had turned to for its major reconstruction projects, was moving far too slowly. Water was running but not potable. Electrical power was intermittent. "We need visibly successful projects, however small: schools and hospitals re-opening, new bakeries, food distribution points."

There was no television in the capital and no way for the coalition to get its message to the Iraqis. "Baghdad has no TV, and no newspapers apart from party political rags. I was given two fliers yesterday by an Iraqi, one calling for the assassination of all Baathists, the other for the killing of all U.S. forces. That, and rumour, are the only information flowing. An ORHA TV project is due to get going next week, but its content will be tightly controlled by ORHA, and it risks not being credible. I have pressed them, as a start, to broadcast a Premier League [British soccer] game each day, but the Americans don't yet get it."

Funding was scant. Unlike the British in Basra, the Bush administration was reluctant to use confiscated Iraqi funds to pay police and government workers. Security in the capital was a huge worry, as it did not seem that the United States had control of the city. The 3rd ID was exhausted by the fight to Baghdad and tied to their armored vehicles. "No progress is possible until security improves," Sawers warned. "Crime is widespread (not surprising as Saddam released all the criminals last autumn). Carjackings are endemic, with the cars driven to Iran for sale. Last week, the Ministry of Planning was re-kitted out ready to resume work; that night it was looted again. The evening air is full of gunfire. There is still a climate of fear on the streets, because of the level of crime, and that is casting a shadow over all else.

"Frankly, the 3rd Inf Div need to go home now, and be garlanded as victors," Sawers wrote, adding that the British should consider sending some troops of its own to Baghdad. "We, the Brits, do not have all the answers, but an operational UK presence in Baghdad is worth considering, despite the obvious political problem. Transferring one of our two brigades is presumably out of the question, but one battalion with a mandate to deploy into the streets could still make an impact."[28]

It was an uncharitable view of the army division that had been the first to get to Baghdad and which had struggled to keep order without sufficient assets and no guidance from on high.

There were also limits to how much the British government would help. That month Albert Whitley and a visiting British general advocated extending the tour of duty of the 16 British Air Assault Brigade and moving it to Baghdad so it could assist in training the Iraqi police and help the Americans safeguard the capital. The request was enthusiastically supported by McKiernan. But the war in Iraq was controversial in the United Kingdom and Baghdad was dicier than Basra. British officials in London overruled their British commanders in Iraq and decided against extending the brigade's tour of duty. For all of Sawers's warnings, the United States would continue to shoulder the burden in the Iraqi capital.

Four days after Sawers sent his cable, Franks met at his Tampa headquarters with Edmund Giambastiani, the head of the Joint Forces Command. Days before, Franks had briefed the Joint Chiefs. Relations between Franks and the JCS had been strained throughout the planning and execution of the military plan, and Jim Jones, the NATO commander, had sought to lighten the mood by buying purple T-shirts with "TTMF" emblazoned on the front and arranging for the chiefs to wear them when Franks arrived. "TTMF" alluded to Franks's denunciation of the chiefs as "Title Ten Motherfuckers." Franks recounted the episode to Giambastiani as the generals discussed lessons learned in the Iraq War. The private meeting also included Gene Renuart and Gary Luck, Franks's mentor, and an aide took notes.

Franks touted the virtues of joint military operations among the Army, Navy, Air Force, and Marines and dismissed his critics as behind the times. "The SECDEF has made his mark on the future, more joint, not less joint," Franks said, referring to Rumsfeld. "Where is the center of gravity of the U.S. military? It is jointness."

As the meeting proceeded, Franks discussed how operations in Afghanistan had influenced his strategy in Iraq. Afghanistan had taught him that relatively small groups of forces, coupled with precision weapons, could be effective against the enemy.

In the middle of the discussion, Franks was interrupted by a phone call. Franks's guidance to prepare for rapid deployment and his fascination with small formations—views supported at the highest levels of the Bush administration—no longer seemed so prescient. "That was the SECDEF," Franks confided to the group. "He said he's getting the hell beat out of him about the Baghdad security situation. He wanted to know if we needed more divisions in country. Tell John Abizaid to pick a brigade-size unit and get it to Baghdad now. I am not gratified by enough forces on the ground. Lawlessness is a problem and we need more people to accomplish the task."[29]

CHAPTER 24

Starting from Scratch

With Baghdad in disarray, the White House opted for a major course correction: Jerry Bremer would be brought in to oversee Iraq. L. Paul Bremer had worked as Henry Kissinger's chief of staff, served as ambassador to the Netherlands, and headed the State Department's office on counterterrorism. In Bremer, the administration saw a hands-on and assertive administrator: a veritable proconsul who would grab hold of the turmoil that was Iraq and get the Bush administration's program there back on track.

Bremer auditioned for the job by meeting with Rumsfeld, whom he knew from the Ford administration three decades earlier. Bremer was not an expert on the Middle East and in his years as a diplomat had never been posted in the region, but in Rumsfeld's Pentagon that was considered a plus. Rumsfeld had sought to block some of Jay Garner's picks because they were State Department Arabists who might be less than ardent supporters of Bush's bold plan to remake Iraq. With Bremer, he would not have that problem.

The day after Bremer's meeting with Rumsfeld, Bush offered him the post, stressing that it was important to take the time to build a broad-based government. Bremer fully intended to assert his authority. The initial version of the administration's plan called for Bremer to share responsibilities with Zalmay Khalilzad, who had been meeting with Iraqi leaders on the political arrangements for a new government. Bremer vetoed the collaboration. There would be a single chief in Iraq and he would be it. Khalilzad learned he had been excluded just minutes before Bremer's appointment was announced on May 6. At the State Department, Colin Powell was stunned by the decision to remove Khalilzad from the administration's team in Iraq. The matter had never been discussed in interagency meetings. Powell called Rice and asked for an explanation. Khalilzad, Powell said, was the only guy who knew the Iraqi players well and who was regarded by them as a trusted representative of the White House. Rice replied that she had nothing to do with the move. Here was yet another example of how the national security apparatus was sidestepped.[1]

Before he headed to Iraq, Bremer consulted with Rumsfeld's aides about the next moves in Iraq. Doug Feith's policy shop had been drafting an order that would bar senior Baathists from power. The concept of de-Baathification was not a new one and had in fact been approved by Bush when he was briefed on it in March. It had been understood all along that Saddam's power structure had to be eliminated. But how deeply did the U.S. need to dig? There was a balance between purging the old order and depriving the new Iraqis of the human capital they needed to run the country.[2]

Saddam's opponents themselves had been divided on the question. At the December meeting of the Iraqi opposition that Khalilzad had convened, Iyad Alawi had pushed for limited de-Baathification and an appeal for Iraqis affiliated with the old order to switch sides. There was a measure of self-interest in Alawi's position. Alawi had contacts among the Baathists and the Iraqi military and had calculated that they could be part of his power base. Ahmed Chalabi, for his part, had pushed for a strong de-Baathification policy and for disbanding the Iraqi military, figuring this would not only remove the vestiges of Saddam's regime but also undermine his rival. In London, Khalilzad had been more influenced by Alawi's position than Chalabi's.

During his first weeks in Iraq, Jay Garner had taken a pragmatic approach toward de-Baathification. Seeking to work through the ministries, Garner had planned to lop off the top organizational layer or two but keep most officials in place. Evicting the Baath Party loyalists would be more a matter of compiling a blacklist than a full-fledged purge. But Khalilzad and Garner were now out. Bremer was in. Not only was Bremer entirely comfortable with a strict de-Baathification policy but he wanted to be the one to issue the edict. As Bremer put it in a memo to his Pentagon colleagues, he wanted to ensure that "my arrival in Iraq be marked by clear, public and decisive steps to reassure Iraqis that we are determined to eradicate Saddamism." Bremer was not anticipating any *Wizard of Oz* moments. The edict on de-Baathification would be a way for Bremer to demonstrate his authority and take control. If Saddam's supporters thought they could take advantage of the confusion in Iraq to claw their way back to power, Bremer would demonstrate that the Baathists were through, once and for all.[3]

There was one important decision that gave Bremer pause: the number of U.S. military forces in Iraq. Bremer was friendly with James Dobbins, who had served as the Bush administration's special envoy for Afghanistan and had also done stints as a State Department troubleshooter for Kosovo, Bosnia, Somalia, and Haiti. Dobbins declined Bremer's invitation to join him in Baghdad as a senior deputy, but he provided Bremer with a forthcoming study he had overseen for the RAND Corporation on nation-building exercises from World War II through Afghanistan. Nation-building was an area Bremer had not been involved in during his earlier career as a diplomat.

The message of the RAND study was that large peacekeeping forces were better than smaller ones. Not only did small forces encourage adversaries to think they could challenge the peacekeepers but they also led the occupation force to rely more on firepower to make up for their limited numbers. That raised the risk of civilian casualties and increased disaffection among the population. "The highest levels of casualties have occurred in the operations with the lowest level of U.S. troops, suggesting an inverse ratio between force levels and the level of risk," the RAND study noted.

Beyond that, Dobbins thought the Bush administration was neglecting the lessons of the Balkans at its peril. Rumsfeld had portrayed the Balkans in his February speech "Beyond Nation-Building" as a textbook example of postwar policies gone wrong. But Dobbins thought there was much to learn from the NATO operations there. Like the former Yugoslavia, Iraq was a multiethnic state that had been held together by a dictator. Like Bosnia and Kosovo, it had a Muslim population. Unlike postwar Germany, which some in the Bush administration cited as an important historical baseline, Iraq did not have an ethnically homogeneous population or a First World economy. Nor had it been totally devastated by war. To safeguard the peace in the Balkans, NATO had deployed about twenty peacekeepers for every thousand civilians. In Iraq this rule of thumb would have yielded a peacekeeping force of more than 450,000, about three times the force commanded by McKiernan. The numbers were sim-

ilar to those in the study that had been prepared in February for Rice and
Hadley by the young Marine major on the NSC staff.

In its argumentation and analysis, the RAND study ran directly
counter to the Bush administration's policy for securing postwar Iraq.
If the study had been applied, Rumsfeld would not have off-ramped the
1st Cavalry Division but would have sent even more forces. Bremer sent
an executive summary of the RAND study to Rumsfeld, but never received a response. When Bremer arrived in Baghdad on May 12 and was
driven to his headquarters at the Republican Palace, he was struck by the
paucity of U.S. forces in the streets: soldiers seemed glued to their tanks
and were not patrolling. To Bremer, the situation appeared to confirm the
cautionary lessons of the RAND report.

The next day, Bremer convened his staff and signaled that it was time
for a no-nonsense policy on crime and looting in the capital. In Haiti, as
the RAND report noted, the Marines had fired on a group of Haitian soldiers who made threatening gestures five days into the occupation. Seven
of the Haitians were killed and the episode sent a signal that the United
States was not to be trifled with. Bremer thought it might be time to send
a similar message in Iraq by shooting some of the looters. His closed-
door comments were leaked almost immediately and made headlines:
Bremer had promulgated a new policy under which Iraqi looters were
now to be shot. Bremer's position came as a surprise to Buff Blount, who
soon made clear that his soldiers had no intention of using deadly force to
stop stealing by the impoverished Iraqis his soldiers had liberated. The
military's general policy was not to talk about its rules of engagement,
but Blount did not want any of his soldiers to confuse Bremer's tough talk
with their actual instructions. "Unless the soldier's life is threatened, we
are not going out and shooting looters," Blount said. Mattis expressed
similar sentiments. It was not an auspicious start to the Bush administration's corrective policy and served only to indicate dissonance between
Bremer and the generals. As impressed as Bremer was with Dobbins's
work, the episode suggested that Bremer had not examined the RAND
report carefully enough. Using firepower to compensate for an inadequate number of troops was not the best way to win over an occupied
population.[4]

Wearing his trademark Brooks Brothers suits and hiking boots, Bremer
established a new organization: the Coalition Provisional Authority. Garner stayed on for a while to smooth the transition, but he had been surprised that his role as the civilian administrator in Iraq had ended so soon

and was unhappy when Bremer began to turn many of his policies on their head. On May 15, Bremer nullified a commitment by Garner and Khalilzad to convene a meeting in Baghdad by the end of May to set up an interim Iraqi government, opting instead for a methodical step-by-step approach in which a constitution would first be drafted and, ultimately, elections held. The delay in transferring control to the Iraqis was a change but not a new option for the Bush team. Just eleven days into the war, Rumsfeld sent a classified paper to Cheney, Powell, and George Tenet, the CIA director, stating that it could also be risky to hand over power too quickly to the Iraqis. Washington needed to first assure itself that the new government would be friendly to the United States.[5]

The next day, Bremer issued Order No. 1: "De-Baathification of Iraqi Society," promulgating the policy drawn up by Feith's staff. As Bremer interpreted the order, the top four levels of the Baath Party were to be barred from government jobs. Garner was with the CIA station chief when the de-Baathification order was issued. Bremer, the station chief opined, had just disenfranchised more than 30,000 people.[6]

The change in approach was fundamental and much more than a matter of differing personalities and administrative styles. When the Bush administration became anxious about the staunch resistance it encountered from the Fedayeen during the early days of the war, it was eager to put an Iraqi face on the problem. The United States decided to convene a meeting of Iraqi resistance leaders at the Tallil air base and pushed for the early establishment of an Iraqi interim government. But when Baghdad was quickly captured and Iraqi opposition leaders began to bicker, the administration became more confident that it could and should shape events in Iraq. The United States tugged on the reins of power and put off the day when the Iraqis would be entrusted to run their own affairs. With Bremer's appointment, the pendulum had swung back toward Washington. Despite the disorder and confusion, the Bush administration was convinced that it could dictate the terms of the peace.

Nowhere was the policy difference starker than on the plans to rebuild the Iraqi army. CENTCOM had hoped that there would be wholesale capitulations of Iraqi units. The forces would serve as the building blocks of a new Iraqi military, which would supplement the U.S. troops and help them to secure Iraq. Even though there had only been one such instance of capitulation—in Anbar Province when an Iraqi general had formally surrendered without his troops to Colonel Potts—Abizaid, McKiernan, and Garner calculated that they would still be able to recall AWOL soldiers and begin to put the Iraqi military back together again. They had a powerful incentive to do so.

Abizaid and McKiernan were looking for troops, as well as a means of avoiding the taint of occupation. From the start, they had counted on Iraqi troops and allied units to supplement the overstretched American forces. The use of Iraqi troops was vital for security and an eventual exit strategy. On April 17, little more than a week after American troops first entered Baghdad, Abizaid told a satellite video conference that a three-division interim Iraqi military should be formed using units that had "self-demobilized" as well as members of opposition groups, who would be invited to appear at processing centers. Abizaid was under no illusion that the new military would instantly be transformed into a crack fighting force and the idea was to initially arrange for the Iraqi soldiers to undertake minor tasks like guarding government buildings and monitoring border crossing points. But he believed that Arab armies were not just military organizations—they provided jobs, helping to hold Arab societies together. His goal was to field three divisions in three months.

McKiernan had sought to recruit a new Iraqi general staff after his arrival in Baghdad. On May 9, he and a select few senior U.S. officers met at the Abu Ghraib palace with Faris Naima, a former Iraqi officer, in a meeting coordinated by the CIA. Naima had the professional bearing of a soldier and spoke fluent English. He had been the commander of al-Bakr Military College, a training ground for Iraq's top officers. Suspect politically, but a Sunni who was still valued by Saddam's government, he was appointed as the Iraqi ambassador to the Philippines and then Austria. Naima later told Americans that working for Saddam's Stalinesque regime was a nerve-racking ordeal. When he was invited to one of Saddam's palaces for a meeting he was never sure whether he was going to be promoted or bundled off for execution. When Qusay ordered him and his wife to return to Baghdad after their tour in Vienna, Naima decided it would be safer to break with the regime and stay abroad.

Wearing a frayed business suit at the meeting with the American generals, Naima pulled out a folded piece of paper from his jacket that outlined his plan for how to proceed. Because looting had broken out in Baghdad and crime was rampant, a show of power was needed. The most important thing was security. Naima urged the Americans to establish three Iraqi military divisions to be deployed in northern, central, and southern Iraq. An army company would be stationed in each major town to back up the police. Naima said there were plenty of potential military leaders who were not committed Baathists. The idea, he said, would be to start at the top, create a new Iraqi Ministry of Defense, and then work down. All officers would be required to denounce the Baath Party.

When the Americans wondered where they would find the officers, Naima had an answer: "I can bring them to you." He also offered some political advice. The United States, he stressed, needed to pay the military, the police, and the bureaucrats. Iraq was a nation of civil servants, he said, and they needed their salaries to survive. Beyond that, the Americans should announce a departure plan so Iraqis did not view them as occupiers. McKiernan was impressed. It looked like he could work from the top down as well as from the bottom up to summon Iraqi soldiers to duty, screen them, and quickly install a new force.[7]

While McKiernan and the CIA were working on reviving the army, Jay Garner's team had been making a parallel effort. Garner still wanted to use the former Iraqi army as a source of labor. To that end, he had arranged for contractors to retrain the Iraqi troops. RONCO, a Washington consulting company, had developed a proposal to screen Iraqi soldiers so they could join a new fighting force or be retrained for other duties. The company drew up a detailed plan for three screening centers in northern, central, and southern Iraq. MPRI, a consulting company that was run by Carl Vuono, the former Army chief of staff, had been awarded an initial contract for $625,000 to help prepare Saddam's former troops for reconstruction duties. As a preliminary step, it had sent a nine-member team to Kuwait.

Soon after arriving in Baghdad, one of Garner's top planners, Colonel Paul Hughes, heard that some former Iraqi officers had approached U.S. troops in Baghdad to ask how they might receive their salaries. After securing approval from senior officers, Hughes met with the group at one of the Republican Guard's officers clubs. Calling themselves the Independent Military Gathering, the Iraqi officers indicated that they wanted to cooperate with the Americans. Though many wanted to work outside the military, they were willing to supply names of potential recruits, including lower-ranking noncommissioned officers. Anticipating that the Defense Ministry would be bombed, they had wisely removed the computers containing military personnel records. Eventually, they gave the Americans a list of some 50,000 to 70,000 names, including the military police. The United States may not have had a ready-made military force but it seemed to have some of the pieces—if, that is, it wanted to use them.[8]

As with Bremer's edict on de-Baathification, the groundwork for the

Coalition Provisional Authority's position on building a new Iraqi military had been laid in Washington. Before leaving for Iraq, Bremer had consulted with Walter Slocombe, who had held Feith's defense policy position in the Clinton administration. Though a Democrat, Slocombe had supported the Bush administration's decision to attack Iraq and had maintained cordial relations with the Rumsfeld team. One day as he was coming out of the Pentagon gym, Slocombe had run into Steve Cambone, one of Rumsfeld's closest aides, who asked him if he would be willing to join Bremer's team. Within a few days, Feith invited Slocombe to come in and talk about the possibility of running Iraq's new Ministry of Defense. Before leaving for Iraq, Slocombe and Bremer discussed the idea of formally disestablishing the Iraqi army and starting from scratch. In a sense, the proposal was part of Bremer's crusade against "Saddamism." With one blow he would purge the Baathists from their government posts and eliminate Saddam's army. Keeping a Sunni-dominated military, Bremer and Slocombe reasoned, would outrage the Kurds. The Shiites would refuse to join, creating more of an ethnic imbalance. Moreover, by dismantling the army, the United States would be relieved of the obligation to pay AWOL Iraqi officers and soldiers. There would be provisions for making termination payments, but no arrangements would be made to pay salaries to those ushered out of the force. What was the point of paying an army that had fled its post and did not exist? they thought. Nor was there a system on hand to retain former troops for other jobs, an important omission in a nation with a soaring unemployment rate.[9]

Bremer and Slocombe's position completely reversed the plan that Feith himself had briefed to Bush in March. The president, in fact, had been told that it would be reckless to throw 300,000 Iraqi soldiers out of work amid the confusion of postwar Iraq and far preferable to screen the force to identify Saddam loyalists. Feith, however, became a supporter of the new tack. Now that the Iraqi army had gone AWOL, Feith figured that the advantages of trying to recall it were not worth the potential liabilities of recruiting a military that might include officers loyal to Saddam. The Pentagon's closest Iraqi ally, Chalabi, had been pushing for months to do away with the old Iraqi army, as had the Kurds.

Once Slocombe arrived in Iraq, McKiernan made an effort to win him over by inviting him to a session with Naima and other former Iraqi officers. Slocombe heard the officers out, thanked them for their time, and made it clear that he did not view them as the nucleus of a new Iraqi command. Using ranking Iraqi officers to rebuild the Iraqi military, Slocombe reassured, would simply produce another Sunni-dominated force.

Sticking to his position, Slocombe drafted an edict—Order No. 2, "The Dissolution of Entities"—formally abolishing the army, the Defense Ministry, and Iraq's intelligence agencies. There would be a new force—the New Iraqi Corps, which would be "professional, non-political, militarily effective and representative of all Iraqis." Slocombe sent the text of the order to the Defense Department, where it was scrutinized by Rumsfeld's staff. Bremer secured Rumsfeld's consent. Plans for the new corps that were to follow were discussed with the Pentagon, too.

On May 19, Rumsfeld himself sent a classified set of planning instructions to Bremer on how to establish the New Iraqi Corps. "The NIC will contribute to setting the conditions necessary for a stable, self-sustaining Iraq, with a viable governing body," Rumsfeld's message noted. "Endstate is a viable force that is a source of Iraqi national pride, contributes to national unity and provides a model for ethnic cooperation." Rumsfeld added that the corps should initially consist of three motorized battalions that would be eight hundred strong. One battalion would be in the north, one in the central part of the country, and one in the southern region. Rumsfeld's message envisioned that it would take six months to field the initial force, which would be put under the control of a new Ministry of Defense. The corps would eventually grow to three divisions and forty thousand personnel. For all the talk of building Iraqi pride, the name of the new force betrayed a certain cultural insensitivity: NIC, when pronounced, sounded very much like "fuck" in Arabic. It was a graphic demonstration of just how little the liberators understood the nation they occupied.[10]

On May 23, Bremer formally issued Order No. 2. While Rumsfeld had been consulted in advance, other key players were blindsided by the edict. Peter Pace, the vice chairman of the Joint Chiefs of Staff, said later that the Joint Chiefs were not consulted about the decision. Powell did not know about it in advance. Condoleezza Rice was caught off guard but comforted herself with the thought that the White House needed to respect the judgment of their man in Baghdad. "I don't think that anybody thought it was wildly out of context with what we were trying to achieve, and the whole structure had been set up so that some of those decisions could be made in the field or through the Pentagon chain," she said later.[11]

In fact, Abizaid and McKiernan did consider the decision an abrupt and unwelcome departure from their previous planning. Just how great a departure became clearer when Slocombe outlined his plans for forming the New Iraqi Corps. To avoid the taint of Baathism, it was decided that no one from the rank of colonel and above could join without extensive vetting. Building the corps battalion by battalion meant that it would take a full year to field the first division of infantry—about 12,000 Iraqi troops—and two years to train and equip a three-division force. The generals wanted to use Iraqi forces as a means to generate the troop levels that would be needed to guard the borders and establish a military presence throughout the country. The decision to abolish the Iraqi army not only risked alienating some 300,000 Iraqi troops but upended CENTCOM's postwar plan. "We wanted to rapidly call the soldiers back, get them on our side, and then sort out who could and could not be trusted," said John Agoglia, the CENTCOM planner who became the command's liaison to Bremer's authority. "It would have been a lot faster than building one battalion at a time. And we wanted to send a psychological message that they were going to be part of the new Iraq, to prevent them from turning against us."[12]

Franks and his commanders were in an awkward position, trying to influence a decision that had already been made. In late May, Rear Admiral James Robb told Slocombe that Abizaid believed that former senior Iraqi officers should not be disqualified and that the training should be accelerated. Franks followed up in a video conference on June 2 with Bremer. "I think the velocity of doing it can be characterized as a miscalculation," Franks said after the war.[13]

The reaction to Order No. 2 in Iraq was incendiary. The decree prompted angry demonstrations in Baghdad. In Mosul, Petraeus's 101st had been working tirelessly to win the support of Iraqis. But the announcement led to violent protests that wounded sixteen of its soldiers. On June 14, Petraeus spied Slocombe at a change-of-command ceremony for Scott Wallace at the Abu Ghraib palace. He told him that the decision to leave the Iraqi soldiers without a livelihood had put American lives at risk. Trying to calm the roiling waters, Bremer later decided to pay the Iraqi troops, which gave the United States the worst of both options: it was paying money to a bitter, demobilized army but was getting nothing in return, and had created a situation in which the soldiers were unsupervised, had no stake in the new order, and were free to create mischief, or worse.[14]

Soon after Bremer issued his order abolishing the army, the occupation authority made a discovery. Bremer's de-Baathification program had disqualified Iraqis who held the top party ranks from holding posts in the new Iraq—a policy that had mechanically been applied to the military, barring the recruitment of all senior Iraqi officers. After the Americans acquired and examined the military's personnel records, they learned there were fewer Baathists among the top ranks than they had thought. Only half of the major generals were committed Baathists, and only a small percentage of the brigadier generals. Only some 8,000 of the 140,000 officers and NCOs were committed enough Baathists to be disqualified. That was one of the points Naima had made with McKiernan, and in a sense it was not surprising. Saddam had been so distrustful of the Regular Army that he made sure the divisions were stationed far from Baghdad. Even the supposedly loyal Republican Guard had not been allowed to take up positions inside the capital. Bremer had denied top-level officers a role in the new Iraqi army based on a misunderstanding of the Iraqis' civil-military relations.[15]

In his memoirs of his tour of Iraq, Bremer made much of the fact that Rumsfeld and his aides had signed off on the decision to abolish the Iraqi army, but he did not note the deep unhappiness of the U.S. military about the move.[16] Under pressure from Abizaid and Rumsfeld, Bremer sought to speed up the training of the new Iraqi forces. The Americans also created a new militia—the Iraqi Civil Defense Corps—but this militia was of widely inconsistent abilities, it was not a national force, and it was unable to fill the gap.

In fact, in their own way, Rumsfeld and Bremer each contributed to the security problem. Rumsfeld limited the number of American troops in Iraq, and Bremer limited the number of Iraqi forces that were immediately available. The two decisions combined to produce a much larger security vacuum.

Bremer's CPA, the Coalition Provisional Authority, was not the only organization that was starting from scratch. Before the war, the Joint Staff suggested that a new military organization be established and staffed in advance to control postwar Iraq. Abizaid had suggested that the task might be allocated to the III Corps. There were attempts to get a running head start. The idea, however, had gone nowhere. When Baghdad fell it was still unclear how long McKiernan's land war command would be in charge or what would follow.

In late April, Franks had gathered his officers to discuss the sort of organization that needed to be established and it was agreed that the military would establish a new Combined Joint Task Force, an organization that would be headed by a three-star general, would have a staff from throughout the services, and would oversee all the military units in Iraq.

When the time came to pick a name one aide suggested CJTF-13, a bit of black humor that pointed to difficulties ahead. Franks chimed in, "Let's make it CJTF-1369, unlucky cocksuckers." Gene Renuart, ever the dignified Air Force officer, quickly restored some civility to the conversation: the organization would be called CJTF-7. Renuart picked the number 7 because that was the number his son had worn on his soccer uniform. Still, the episode was indicative of Franks's attitude about the postwar administration. For Franks, anything other than war-fighting was an unglamorous and thankless burden. Franks was already considering retiring and negotiating a multimillion-dollar deal to write his memoirs, much as Schwarzkopf had done after the Gulf War. "I am going to get my mains," he told one of his senior officers. For Franks, postwar Iraq would soon be somebody else's problem.[17]

In Washington, Jack Keane thought that this was a time for continuity in command in the Iraqi region. A gruff but articulate New Yorker, Keane took over as the acting head of the Army after a period of considerable turmoil in the top ranks. Two weeks after Baghdad was taken, Tom White had been told to report to Rumsfeld's office for a five p.m. meeting. When the civilian Army secretary walked in, Rumsfeld came right to the point. "I want to make a change," he said. "Fine, that is your choice," White shot back. White's alliance with Shinseki had become an unpardonable offense for the defense secretary, who continued to believe that the service was too enamored of large forces and slow to change. White told Rumsfeld he would write a short resignation letter that day. The army secretary had planned to stay through the end of Shinseki's terms, but a week later Wolfowitz called to say that was no longer acceptable, and White left on May 9. When Shinseki retired the next month he lauded White for his principles. Rumsfeld, who was traveling, did not attend the event.[18]

Keane's big worry was not about the changes in Washington, but the ones that were being planned in the Persian Gulf region. Keane had contacted Myers and suggested extending Franks's tour at CENTCOM, which would enable Abizaid to focus more on Iraq. But Myers told Keane that that was not an option. Franks seemed exhausted by two wars and Myers was frustrated with trying to convince him to stay on and focus on the postwar situation.

Keane was also concerned about who was going to run CJTF-7. Keane's own choice—and that he presumed of the administration—was McKiernan. In mid-June, however, Keane was dumbfounded to learn that McKiernan was on his way out of Iraq and that the post was going to Ricardo "Ric" Sanchez. The two-star commander of the 1st Armored Division had replaced Scott Wallace as the head of the V Corps, a move that Wallace had only learned about two weeks earlier. Sanchez was now going to be elevated yet again to the head of CJTF-7. Almost overnight the commander of the last arriving division in Iraq would become the senior military commander for the most sensitive part of the operation. Compounding the problem, Sanchez would have to build a new team, drawing on the V Corps and senior officers from elsewhere in the army. McKiernan already had a team of general officers, one that had been focusing on Iraq. Keane called Abizaid and asked what the hell was going on. Keane respected McKiernan. Had Keane accepted Rumsfeld's offer to stay on as the Army Chief, he planned to make McKiernan the Vice Chief. Abizaid replied that the arrangements had been agreed upon between Franks and McKiernan.

In fact, it was something of a garble. McKiernan was prepared to stay on, but had asked that much of his staff, which had been deployed for almost two years, be rotated home. A larger factor seemed to be the attitude of civilians in Washington. McKiernan had decidedly less support from Rumsfeld and his staff than from his Army superiors. Larry Di Rita, a top Rumsfeld aide, had been overheard at Bremer's headquarters telling officials in Washington that McKiernan was not the right general to run the operations in postwar Iraq. It also did not help when Rumsfeld returned from an April 30 meeting with McKiernan and Wallace in Iraq and complained about the Army generals he had encountered there. Washington was prepared to rely on an untested general who was not the choice of the head of his own service.[19]

On the morning of June 15, McKiernan and Terry Moran said their goodbyes to Bremer. McKiernan gave Bremer an overview of the operation that the 4th ID was about to undertake near Taji and Baqubah to search for members of Saddam's regime. Bremer was comfortable with the plan. McKiernan then offered two pieces of advice. Bremer needed to increase the money provided to brigade and division commanders for projects in their area. They knew the country, had the security and the contacts. Bremer's office, in contrast, was Baghdad-centric. It had no representative in most of Iraq's eighteen governorates.

McKiernan also raised again his concern over the Army. Bremer needed to go "bigger and faster." He could establish an Iraqi general staff, recall the Iraqi soldiers and officers to their garrisons, and arrange for the Iraqi forces to conduct "low-risk" missions like guarding gas stations, power plants, government buildings, and bridges. It would not be pretty. The vetting would have to be carried out quickly. The United States would need to sort out those with "blood on their hands" over time. But Iraqi brigades could quickly be deployed near Mosul, Baghdad, and Basra. Bremer listened, but made no promises.[20]

Personalities aside, the summer of 2003 had been a time of enormous turbulence in the American command. Franks was preparing to leave his post to be replaced at CENTCOM by Abizaid. Garner had been replaced by Bremer. McKiernan and Wallace had left. The newest general on the block was in charge, and his relations with Bremer were soon strained. The changes and sheer transport of staff to and from Iraq was time-consuming and distracting. At Bremer's headquarters, John Agoglia was concerned that Americans were so preoccupied with rearranging their headquarters that they were losing touch with the deteriorating situation in Iraq.

Ten days after McKiernan left, John Sawers sent another confidential cable to London. The message was entitled "Iraq: Progress Report," but there was not much progress to speak of. Sawers noted that Bremer had become concerned that the U.S. troop withdrawals had gone too far, prompting him to call the president. Unemployment was running at 60 percent. "It has been a difficult week in Iraq. Fire fights between Coalition forces and Iraqi groups have been more frequent, with the Majar al-Kabir incident the worst. That seems to have been due to local causes and is in a known volatile area, but it shows how thin is the veneer of security in many parts of Iraq," he wrote.

"The new threat is well-targeted sabotage of the infrastructure. An attack on the power grid last weekend had a series of knock-on effects, which halved the power generation in Baghdad and many other parts of the country. That, in turn, cut off the water supply. Much of Baghdad has been without electricity and running water for the last three days. The oil and gas network is another target, with five successful attacks this week on pipelines. We do not yet have an answer to this threat. We are also seeing the first signs of intimidation of Iraqis working for the Coalition.

"Bremer's main concern is that we must keep in-country sufficient military capability to ensure a security blanket across the country. He has twice said to President Bush that he is concerned that the draw down of

US/UK troops has gone too far, and we cannot afford further reductions. US forces are down to 60 percent of end-conflict levels, UK forces have reduced further to 40 percent. While other national contingencies are welcome, he questions whether they will be sufficiently robust when push comes to shove.

"In the medium term, my main concern is the Shia. The continued problem with security and essential services means that moderate Shia leaders are coming under pressure as their communities question whether supporting the Coalition is the right approach. Meanwhile, the Iranians are adding to their options in Iraq by cultivating the young Najaf radical, Muqtadr Al-Sadr, and that is worrying the moderate clerics. SCIRI, the pro-Iran party we are working with, are facing some tricky decisions. Iraqis remain resistant to Iranian attempts to exert influence. But the biggest threat in the next year is that, for a mix of reasons, we lose the Shia heartlands. The Iranians seem to be positioning themselves so they can make that threat more real."[21]

On July 16, John Abizaid used his debut press conference after taking over as CENTCOM commander to deliver a message of his own. U.S. forces in Iraq were now under attack from "a classical guerrilla-type campaign." The account was the first time that a senior officer had openly stated that the U.S. confronted an insurgency and made headlines. Rumsfeld, who had been stating for weeks that the U.S. was merely conducting mopping-up operations against "dead-enders," privately expressed his unhappiness to Abizaid about his blunt comments, military officials said.

Six days later, the Americans thought they might have struck a decisive blow. After escaping to Syria, Uday and Qusay Hussein had been turned away and found their way to Mosul. Tipped off by their anxious host, soldiers from Colonel Joe Anderson's brigade surrounded the house. In Baghdad, Dell Dailey's Task Force 20 began to head north. After a series of miscues the timing of the raid was delayed until daylight the next morning. Having surrounded the house, the Americans asked the Iraqis to come out peacefully. Then TF-20 went in after them. Four U.S. troops were wounded and the insertion force withdrew.

After a second failed attempt to attack the house, the TF-20 commandos told Anderson they wanted the building leveled by air strike and M1 tanks. "They come to me and say, 'We want tanks, we want CAS [close air support]. We want to level the building.' The reason is that they say they are in some fortified, interior bunker, bulletproof." Anderson was not about to launch an air strike in the middle of a crowded site. So he ordered his soldiers to launch ten TOW antitank missiles at the structure. When the soldiers finally took the building, they determined that there was no interior bunker, but Uday, Qusay, and Uday's fourteen-year-old son were dead. The damaged building was razed several days later. After months of growing insurgent activity, the Americans thought they might finally have reached a turning point. But the resistance continued to build.[22]

As the long, hot summer dragged on, Bremer sought to maintain tight control over the political life of Iraq. Since his Coalition Provisional Authority had little presence outside Baghdad he worked through the U.S. military.

To the south, Lieutenant Colonel Chris Conlin, whose battalion had taken the Crown Jewel on the opening day of the invasion, was given authority for Najaf. Conlin arrived to discover that the CIA had installed a Sufi as mayor who not only was unpopular with the city's residents, but was receiving bad notices in the Western media. Soon word came down from Bremer's office that Conlin was to fire the mayor.

Conlin suggested that an election be held and Mattis's and Bremer's staffs endorsed the idea. The Marines and an Army reserve unit from Green Bay, Wisconsin, devised a plan to register the Iraqis and build wooden ballot boxes. The upcoming balloting stimulated enormous interest and intensive campaigning. The Shiites had been repressed for years by Saddam and now, having been liberated by the Americans, they would finally have an opportunity to govern themselves. Just a day before the registration process was formally to begin, however, Conlin received a call from Mattis. The election had to be canceled. Bremer was concerned that an unfriendly Islamic candidate would prevail.

With election fervor running high, Conlin urged Mattis to allow him to announce that the election had been postponed, not annulled. Appearing on local television, Conlin took the blame, saying that he had pushed the Iraqis to vote before they were ready. There would be an election, but not yet. Then Conlin went with Jim Conway, the top Marine commander, to Baghdad to plead the case for an election with Bremer. Bremer was not available, and the Marine officers had to settle for a deputy, who matter-of-factly explained that Bremer would not allow the wrong guy to win the election. The Marines were advised to select a group of Iraqis they thought were safe and have them pick a mayor. That way the United States would control the process. The Marines did not like the idea. That was not what the Marines had in mind after hearing the White House talk about bringing democracy to the Middle East. "A window of opportunity existed when the regime fell," Mattis recalled. "When the Marines went south I reminded my commanders that the kinetic phase was over, that we had come to Iraq to liberate and they should take off their helmets and help the people with what they need. It worked. Two things then created major problems: disbanding the Iraqi army and putting proud soldiers on the street unemployed. The other was shortstopping local elections."[23]

North in Tikrit, Ray Odierno was having his own problems. Unlike the Marines, Odierno was not operating in the Shiite heartland, but in the Sunni north. After a month of relative peace, insurgent activity had begun to heat up, and Bremer's de-Baathification edict was making things worse. In Saddam's old stomping grounds everybody who was anybody was Baathist. As the schools prepared to reopen, Odierno was instructed to fire a thousand schoolteachers in the province on the grounds that they were committed Baathists. Meanwhile, Bremer's authority cut off their pay. Odierno retained the teachers while he sought to argue the case with Bremer. The decision on the teachers had rippled through the community and fortified support for a growing resistance. It was jeopardizing the security of American soldiers. An exception was eventually made, but the episode had hardly improved the division's standing with the Iraqis.

Odierno fought a similar battle over the Iraqi police. Again, Bremer's authority said they were riddled with Baathists. Odierno went to Baghdad to plead his case with Bernie Kerik, the former New York City police chief who had taken over from Robert Gifford. Again, Odierno prevailed, but the wrangle had its cost. Relations with the Iraqis were soured and for weeks the police stopped coming to work. Odierno later concluded that it would have been better to let the U.S. military call the shots on such important policy issues. It was dispersed around the country and was working hard with the local communities. Bremer's CPA had been entrusted with important governance issues before it was ready to exercise the responsibility. "Decisions were taken out of our hands," Odierno recalled. "We lost the window of opportunity when it would have done the most good."[24]

In the west, Buff Blount had sent Perkins's 2nd BCT to Fallujah to restore order after the 82nd and 3rd Armored Cavalry Regiment had come under attack. Perkins had an entire brigade of troops. The brigade also reached out to the Iraqis. Blount authorized the payment of "blood money" for the Iraqis who had been shot by the 82nd, hoping to head off further revenge killings. The division's soldiers sought to cooperate with

the local imams and to train the police. By July, however, it was time for
the 3rd ID to return to the United States.

But Blount was worried that the inroads his soldiers had made with the
Iraqi population would be erased if his soldiers were replaced by troops
from the 82nd, whom the residents of Fallujah still hated with a passion.
Blount went to see Sanchez and explained the sensitivity of the situation.
As much as Blount wanted to take his soldiers home, he offered to extend
the 3rd ID deployment in Fallujah. If the 82nd returned, there would be
fewer forces in the area and fewer soldiers with a history of troubled relations with the Iraqis.

Sanchez was not sympathetic. It was time for the 3rd ID to leave and
the 82nd was the only unit that was available to take over. Within weeks
of the 3rd ID's departure, the 82nd shot and killed some of the policemen
the 3rd ID had worked so hard to train after mistaking them for Iraqi insurgents. Hostility against the Americans continued to grow in Fallujah.[25]

After his marauding in the north, Pete Blaber made his way to Baghdad, where he and his Delta team were conducting operations. Stopping
by the Green Zone with Saif Ataya, Blaber approached a CPA official and
identified himself as the Delta commander to a State Department official
on Bremer's staff. Blaber explained that Ataya had been useful to Delta
and could guide the civilians in dealing with the welter of clashing cul-
tures that is Iraq. Blaber was told that Ataya's services were not needed.
The only job that the CPA could offer was working as an interpreter for
$60 a day.

Ataya eventually found a role for himself funneling intelligence about
terrorist cells and the situation to the U.S. military. No Iraqi had been
more supportive of the invasion than Ataya, but what he found in Baghdad worried him greatly. There was no security on the streets, just the law
of the gun. The people felt cut off from the Americans and their own interim government. There were few jobs. For $50 or $100, groups could
hire local Iraqis to take a shot at the Americans. Corruption was rampant. Before he fled Iraq, Ataya recalled that Saddam had staged events,
appeared on television, and masqueraded as a man of the people. It was
all a charade but at least he had made the effort. But Ataya felt that the
new Iraqi leaders who were setting up the interim government seemed as
isolated as the Americans in the Green Zone and were not getting their
message out.

When Ataya returned from Iraq in 2004 he was invited to the Pentagon
to offer his impressions to Wolfowitz and Blaber. Ataya still held out hope

that democracy would take root in Iraq and spread through the Middle East. But he warned that things were deteriorating. "I told them the situation would be worse because of the evidence of corruption." Returning to California, he got a job teaching Arabic to U.S. military personnel and rebuffed several lucrative offers to return to Iraq.[26]

In December 2005, McKiernan was awarded his fourth star and took command of U.S. troops in Europe. Looking back at the summer of 2003, McKiernan later saw the period as a lost chance to build support and to prevent the insurgency from gaining momentum. "With few exceptions we were not being shot at. I could walk the streets anywhere in Baghdad. Most Iraqis there still viewed us as liberators, even if they did not particularly like us culturally," said McKiernan. "From the beginning in planning for a post-Saddam Iraq, we failed to seize a window of opportunity to get military, political, economic, and informational effects harmonized to bring order to a chaotic situation. While the Baathist hard-liners would have opposed the coalition under any circumstances I believe the insurgency's mosaic of affiliations was not a preordained event."[27]

Some of McKiernan's aides were blunter still. With limited American troops, few allies, and no Iraqi army to draw on, the United States had lost the initiative at a critical moment. "My position is that we lost momentum and that the insurgency was not inevitable," said Spider Marks, who retired from the military after a stint running the Army's intelligence school. "We had momentum going in and had Saddam's forces on the run. But we did not have enough troops. First, we did not have enough troops to conduct combat patrols in sufficient numbers to gain solid intelligence and paint a good picture of the enemy on the ground. Secondly, we needed more troops to act on the intelligence we generated. They took advantage of our limited numbers."[28]

Jim Conway, who was later made the senior operations officer for the Joint Chiefs, agreed with McKiernan that while some level of resistance was inevitable, political, economic, and military steps could have been taken to mitigate the virulence of the insurgency. Preventing the Iraqis from holding local elections, he said, was a major blunder. "I think we underestimated the importance of Iraqi pride in our dealings with them," Conway said. "When we denied Iraqis the opportunities to elect local officials—vice appoint them by the area commander—we were increasingly seen as occupiers."

Like other senior military officers, Conway believed that the disestablishment of the army reinforced the impression that the U.S. was intent on acting like an occupying power while depriving the U.S. of security forces at a critical time. "We should have capitalized on—not dissolved—the Iraqi army," he said. "The most respected institution in the country was the army. It has been said that they 'melted away' during the initial fighting. That is only partially true. Nevertheless, I am certain that had we seriously attempted to reassemble them—and dismiss those with blood on their hands from the Saddam era—that could have been accomplished. We had no problem rounding them up to pay for no work done when that became the CPA policy."

Beyond that, the problems in winning the support of the Iraqi public, he said, were aggravated by the inability of Bremer's Coalition Provisional Authority to meet the Iraqis' expectations for rebuilding their country. Even the Marines were taken aback by the CPA's poor state of preparation and its inability to operate outside Baghdad. Conway's officers kept waiting for civilian "local governance teams" that never arrived, forcing Marine battalion commanders to become city managers, chiefs of policy, and agricultural experts.[29]

Brigadier General John Kelly, Mattis's assistant division commander, was made the Marines' chief liaison to Congress after his two tours in Iraq. Like Marks, he believed that the limited number of troops made it hard to contain the insurgency. "Numbers count. One of the truisms I found in my studies and experience is if you are forced to shift forces around in an insurgency to plug holes, you lose," Kelly observed. "No cooperation from the locals who need the presence and security." The multinational forces the United States recruited were often not very effective. Most of the newly arriving foreign troops were not authorized to conduct offensive operations by the governments that sent them and had to check with their respective capitals before they could carry out many of their orders. With little involvement with civil affairs and local Iraqis, they did not provide much of a stabilizing influence. The civilian effort in Baghdad never seemed to get organized. Frustrated with the insurgent attacks and unprepared to deal with the complexities of Iraq, there was a "default to meet violence with violence on the part of some U.S. forces," Kelly observed, which led to civilian casualties and hardened the attitudes of many Iraqis against the Americans.[30]

Buff Blount also thought the United States had missed an opportunity. "There was a time when the insurgency could have been headed off or greatly reduced and contained," he said. Blount cited several factors that allowed the insurgency to develop. One was the change in personnel. "There were several leadership changes that are questionable," Blount said. "The first is letting McKiernan and his headquarters go back to Kuwait and giving the responsibility for CJTF-7 to V Corps. McKiernan and his staff were the Army's experts on the Middle East. V Corps is European-based and had no experience in the region. You also had a brand new corps commander who had not participated in the first phases of the war and had all the responsibility Bremer was soon to thrust on him. In the same time frame, Bremer replaced Garner and within a week or two all the people that the U.S. military and the Iraqis had been dealing with were replaced and everything started over."

Like the other generals, Blount said the decision to dismantle the Iraqi army and his de-Baathification decree made the military's job harder. "For a period of time we were perceived as and acted like liberators, but as more and more combat troops came, there was a shift to an occupation or fortress mentality."[31]

Jack Keane retired from the military after running the U.S. Army through the troubled summer of 2003. The United States mission in Iraq, he recalled later, was made all the more difficult by the administration's aversion to nation-building and its determination not to study the lessons of its predecessors. That attitude set the stage for many of the problems that were to come. "It was an ideology they came in with and an overreaction to the Clinton administration," Keane said. "The Bush administration looked at the Bosnia/Kosovo model and decided that it was fundamentally flawed. They concluded that it encouraged an artificial dependency on the part of the host country by committing a larger footprint of U.S. troops. They preferred a small presence to force the host country to do its own nation-building. I believe this is desirable but only if there is security. Without security, the model breaks down quickly, which was the case in Iraq."

Keane said military leaders, including the Joint Chiefs of Staff, the Vice Chiefs, and Franks, share responsibility for the problems in Iraq by not considering that guerrilla war was a serious possibility. "The fact is that the Baathist insurgency surprised us and we had not developed a comprehensive option for dealing with this possibility, one that would have included more military police, civil affairs units, interrogators, interpreters, and Special Operations Forces. If we had planned for an insurgency we probably would have deployed the First Cavalry Division and it would have assisted greatly with the initial occupation. This was not just an intelligence community failure, but also our failure as senior military leaders, including myself."[32]

Colin Powell left the administration soon after Bush's reelection. At the State Department, Rich Armitage, Powell's top deputy, stayed on for a month and made several fact-finding trips to Iraq before he also left government. Armitage had no love for Saddam and was happy to see him overthrown. He had questioned the timing of the invasion but not its purpose. Still, he was troubled by the way the transition was going. Reconstruction projects had slowed as a result of the violence. The insurgents seemed to know where the U.S. forces were and where they were headed. Time was not necessarily on the U.S. side. Meeting with Bush and his National Security Council in November 2004, Armitage provided his unvarnished assessment.

"We are not winning," Armitage stated. The president seemed taken aback.

"Are we losing?" Bush asked.

Armitage's reply was not reassuring: "Not yet."[33]

Epilogue

On December 5, 2005, Donald Rumsfeld visited the Johns Hopkins School of Advanced International Studies to give his appraisal of events in Iraq. Asked about the lessons of the still unfinished war, the defense secretary was quick to tout the virtues of military transformation. "I think if I had to pull out one lesson that we've learned over the past four or five years, it would be that in the twenty-first century we're going to have to stop thinking about things, numbers of things, and mass, and think also and maybe even first about speed and agility and precision."

It was the same message that George W. Bush had delivered in a Citadel speech in 1998 and the one lesson that Rumsfeld had sought to drum into the Pentagon. The secretary of defense, however, was only partially right. As a consequence, the United States has yet to achieve its victory and U.S. troops and the Iraqis themselves have paid an unnecessarily high price. The violent chaos that followed Saddam's defeat was not a matter of not having a plan but of adhering too rigidly to the wrong one.

From the start, American political objectives were bold and extraordinarily ambitious. The military operation was intended to strike a blow at terrorism by ousting a long-standing adversary, eliminating Iraq's weapons of mass destruction, and implanting a moderate and pro-American state in the heart of the Arab world. It was also to be a powerful demonstration of American power and an object lesson—for Iran, Syria, and other would-be foes—of the potential consequences of supporting terrorist groups and pursuing nuclear, biological, and chemical arms. The United States would not just defeat a dictator. It would transform a region and send the message that the American intervention in Afghanistan was not the end but just the beginning of Washington's "global war on terror."

But President Bush and his team committed five grievous errors. They underestimated their opponent and failed to understand the welter of ethnic groups and tribes that is Iraq. They did not bring the right tools to the fight and put too much confidence in technology. They failed to adapt to developments on the ground and remained wedded to their prewar analysis even after Iraqis showed their penchant for guerrilla tactics in the first days of the war. They presided over a system in which differing military and political perspectives were discouraged. Finally, they turned their back on the nation-building lessons from the Balkans and other crisis zones and fashioned a plan that unrealistically sought to shift much of the burden onto a defeated and ethnically diverse population and allied nations that were enormously ambivalent about the invasion. Instead of making plans to fight a counterinsurgency, the president and his team drew up plans to bring the troops home and all but declared the war won.

There is a direct link between the way the Iraq War was planned and the bitter insurgency the American-led coalition subsequently confronted. The ambitious plans that the president announced to transform American defense proved to be at odds with his bold plan to transform a region.

THE MISREADING OF THE FOE

Rumsfeld and his generals misread their foe by viewing the invasion of Iraq largely as a continuation of the Persian Gulf War. During the Desert Storm campaign Saddam Hussein's Republican Guard was the best equipped and most loyal force. Tommy Franks and his generals continued to regard the Republican Guard as their principal adversary. The allied ground forces, as few as they were, expected to run roughshod over the Guard units with a combination of maneuver and firepower and drive directly to Baghdad. Bypassed Iraqi units would be left to die on the vine. As it turned out, the generals were well prepared to fight the enemy that they had war-gamed against. But it would be the paramilitary Fedayeen that represented the principal challenge in Nasiriyah, Samawah, Najaf, Kifl, and Diwaniyah, and that fought tenaciously in Baghdad as well. The failure to understand the foe in part reflected a failure of intelligence. The CIA in particular was not only wrong on WMD, but failed to identify the importance of the Fedayeen or to uncover the tons of arms that had been cached in the cities and towns of southern Iraq. The CIA's assurances that the Iraqi military would capitulate and that the Army and Marines would be welcome in the southern cities were misleading and dangerous. Field commanders lost confidence in the agency and came to depend upon front-line reporting to gain knowledge of their enemy in the unexpected war they were fighting.

Just as Rumsfeld and Franks failed to understand the enemy, they also did not understand the actual structure of political power in Iraq. Rumsfeld and Franks believed that their victory would be sealed with the seizing of Baghdad, which was identified as Iraq's "center of gravity." But from the first day of the invasion the United States was not fighting a purely conventional war, one that would be suddenly brought to an end when the regime's ministries were seized and its leader toppled. The attacks by the Fedayeen on the road to Baghdad demonstrated that the American-led coalition was contending with a decentralized enemy that was fanatical, not dependent on rigid command and control, and whose base of operations was dispersed throughout the towns and cities of Iraq. The "center of gravity" was not a single geographic location—the Iraqi capital—but the entire Sunni Triangle and more broadly the Iraqi people themselves. The Fedayeen would not be defeated and the war not won until the Sunni region was under control, and the Iraqi population supportive or at least not actively antagonistic.

THE OVERRELIANCE ON TECHNOLOGICAL ADVANCEMENT

The administration put far too much confidence in American military technology, Special Operations Forces, and clandestine operations. Rumsfeld's principles of transformation were in large measure a codification of the long-promised "revolution in military affairs." With the aid of high-tech reconnaissance systems, precision weapons, and advanced communications, relatively small units could be even more lethal. For Rumsfeld his vision had been realized in Afghanistan and would be adapted for Iraq.

During the march to Baghdad, the approach was effective. Saddam's regime was caught off guard when the United States invaded with a force that was far smaller than the one it amassed for the 1991 Persian Gulf War and without waiting to carry out a long, preparatory air campaign. Speed was a vital element of the campaign. The rapid pace of the Army and Marine attack enabled the United States to secure the critical bridges and assure the Iraqis could not destroy them. It also made it possible for U.S. troops to move into the Iraqi capital before the enemy could stiffen its defenses. Improved reconnaissance and surveillance and precision munitions gave well-trained U.S. forces a decisive edge. The expanded cooperation among the military services added to the efficiency of the effort. The military campaign was more "joint" than ever before. The establishment of McKiernan's allied land war headquarters, an innovation compared with CENTCOM's arrangements for waging the Persian Gulf War, helped to harmonize the Army and Marine attacks.

But after the fall of Baghdad in April 2003, the requirements were re-versed: mass, not speed, was requisite for sealing the victory. Military technology was less decisive against an opponent that faded away into Iraqi cities only to fight another day. Nor were SOF efforts and CIA operations generally effective against an elusive adversary. To gain control of the Sunni Triangle and pursue the Fedayeen, Baath Party militia, and enemy formations before they had a chance to catch their breath, rearm, and regroup, the United States needed more boots on the ground. As a re-sult of a deficit of forces, Anbar Province in western Iraq, the heartland of Sunnism and Baathist support, was treated as an "economy of force" op-eration and only sparsely covered by American troops. There were not sufficient troops to seal the borders, guard the copious arms caches, and dominate the terrain, all of which allowed the province to become a sanc-tuary for insurgents. The Bush administration's assumptions that it could solicit substantial coalition troops for the postwar and quickly reorganize and use defeated Iraqi military manpower were either proved wrong or derailed by ill-informed decision-making like Bremer's edict to abolish the Iraqi army. Without sufficient forces, there was a constant turnover of U.S. troops in Fallujah, a key city just a short drive from Baghdad, which impaired the U.S. military's ability to develop a good working relation-ship with locals. The problem was not just one of numbers. The United States also lacked the right sort of troops for the postwar phase: it needed to have more civil affairs units, military police, and interpreters. The re-sult was that Anbar Province became the seat of much of the resistance to the U.S. occupation and Fallujah became a metaphor for post-combat failure in Iraq.

THE FAILURE TO ADAPT TO DEVELOPMENTS ON THE BATTLEFIELD

There were numerous indications in the first days of the war that the United States was involved in a different war than it had anticipated. Instead of being welcomed at Nasiriyah, the Marines engaged in a bloody and casualty-inducing fight. After running into stiff resistance at Samawah, the V Corps dropped its plans for a feint up Highways 1 and 8. The clashes at Kifl and Objective Floyd were fierce. The first Marine to be killed in action died at the hands of an Iraqi dressed in civilian clothes who fired from a pickup truck, not a tank. Moreover, the Americans en-countered primitive roadside bombs, suicide car bombs, foreign jihadists, and guerrilla-style ambushes, hallmarks of the insurgency to come.

American troops themselves were quick to identify the nature of their enemy. Shocked by the early battles at Nasiriyah and near Najaf, they adapted and successfully developed tactics to deal with the real as opposed to expected enemy—tactics used effectively in the assault on Baghdad. The troops' training and the leadership in the field and at the allied land command paid off.

But the American war plan was never adjusted on high. Tommy Franks never acknowledged the enemy he faced nor did he comprehend the nature of the war he was directing. He denigrated the Fedayeen as little more than a speed bump on the way to Baghdad and never appreciated their resilience and determination. Franks threatened to fire Scott Wallace, the V Corps commander, when he noted publicly that his soldiers were battling a different enemy than the one that had been featured in the military's war games. Once Baghdad was taken, Franks turned his attention elsewhere in the belief that victory was his, never realizing the irregulars he maligned constituted the real military center of gravity, one that had not surrendered. In his book, *American Soldier*, Franks claims credit for a winning strategy. At best he had won the first round of the war thanks largely to his subordinate commanders, but neither he nor they had won the war.

More important, Rumsfeld failed to heed his own counsel on defense planning. From the day he returned to the Pentagon as George W. Bush's defense secretary, Rumsfeld underscored the need to be prepared for the unexpected. There were, Rumsfeld cautioned, unknown dangers so unanticipated that experts could not even imagine them. Success depended on agility: the ability to adjust the battle plan in the face of threats that could be neither predicted nor foreseen. Yet Rumsfeld was so confident of the validity of the prewar plan that he questioned the need to deploy the 1st Cavalry before Baghdad fell. Just a week after Baghdad was seized, the White House, Defense Department, and CENTCOM were focused on withdrawing troops and replacing them with less capable foreign troops instead of deploying the assets that would be needed to hedge against new threats.

The failure to read the early signs of the insurgency and to adapt accordingly was all the more surprising given the Bush administration's repeated assertions that Saddam's regime was allied with Osama bin Laden and terrorist organizations like Abu Musab al-Zarqawi's and given confirmed intelligence reports that jihadists had infiltrated from Syria. Had the administration taken its own counsel to heart, it would have been planning to wage a counterinsurgency and conduct antiterrorist operations as soon as Baghdad fell.

THE DYSFUNCTION OF AMERICAN MILITARY
STRUCTURES

During the Persian Gulf War, Defense Secretary Dick Cheney had a strong and independent-minded counterpart in Colin Powell, the chairman of the Joint Chiefs. The two differed over strategy and even the imperative of going to war. The dynamic provided for a more informed debate over strategy and force requirements. In the Iraq War, Rumsfeld and Franks dominated the planning; the Joint Chiefs of Staff were pushed to the margins and largely accepted their role. Richard Myers was picked to be the JCS chairman because of his track record as a team player and largely fulfilled Rumsfeld's expectations. Even Shinseki, who stirred up a debate over the number of troops needed for the postwar period in his remarks to Congress, did not press the issue inside the JCS, according to former chiefs.

With his experience as defense secretary, his ties to the Iraqi opposition, and his role as advocate of the war, Cheney had the authority to serve as a counterweight to the Pentagon's optimism on postwar planning. But the vice president never once challenged the realism of Rumsfeld's expectations. Rather, he ratified the hopeful and unrealistic plan. Colin Powell raised both the issue of insufficient troops and the difficulties the U.S. would encounter in postwar Iraq, but he was the odd man out in an administration that was dominated by Bush, Cheney, and Rumsfeld and later told the president that he considered the policymaking machinery to be broken. Given the many indications that Rumsfeld and his aides viewed the building of a new Iraq as a relatively undemanding pursuit, the nation would have been better served if Powell had objected when the secretary of defense moved to seize control of postwar planning.

The problem was compounded at lower levels by the improvised military and political structures that were established in Iraq by the Americans. No military headquarters or staff was selected in advance to secure postwar Iraq. The summer of 2003 was one of turmoil in which McKiernan's command, which was focused on the Middle East region, was supplanted by a command led by Ricardo Sanchez, a junior three-star general whose last assignment was in Europe. The changeover occurred as Franks was nearing retirement and preparing to hand CENTCOM over to John Abizaid, and as Jay Garner and his team were replaced by L. Paul Bremer and his Coalition Provisional Authority. Determined to solidify his authority, Bremer squeezed out Zalmay Khalilzad, the one official who knew the Iraqi politicians well. Exacerbating the situation, relations between Sanchez and Bremer were not strong. The personnel changes and infighting were distracting and diverted attention and energy from Iraq at the precise moment when the insurgency was beginning to gain traction.

THE BUSH ADMINISTRATION'S DISDAIN FOR NATION-BUILDING

When he first visited Kosovo, President Bush confided to the U.S. commander that his imperative was to extract American forces from the region while Rumsfeld publicly cast the Balkans as an object lesson of a policy gone wrong. Many critics have assailed the administration for lapses in its planning. But it is striking how much of the United States postwar strategy was the product of careful deliberation. The failure to organize a civilian constabulary for immediate duty in Iraq was not an oversight. Rejecting recommendations from officials of the Justice and State departments, senior administration officials decided they would not be needed and decided to rely on the Iraqi law enforcement apparatus. The cost of reconstructing postwar Iraq was assessed at no more than $3 billion, which assumed that Iraq would soon be on its feet and able to pay its own way. Bush received a comprehensive briefing on the postwar plans for Iraq on March 10 and 12, 2003, barely a week before the war.

Without a focused and realistically derived commitment to Iraq's future, the administration's political plan veered wildly from quickly transferring power and employing the Iraqi military to putting off Iraqi rule and formally disbanding the Iraqi armed forces. The disregard for the nation-building efforts of Bush's predecessor was largely an exercise in wishful thinking. The administration convinced itself it could dislodge the regime without doing the hard work of rebuilding a new Iraq or without committing itself to the troop levels that were needed in most other postwar conflicts, as documented in a study prepared for Condoleezza Rice and Steve Hadley by a young Marine on their staff, and by a RAND Corporation report provided to L. Paul Bremer.

The war planning took about eighteen months. The postwar planning began in earnest only a couple of months before the invasion. Bush, Cheney, Rumsfeld, and Tommy Franks spent most of their time and energy on the least demanding task—defeating Saddam's weakened conventional forces—and the least amount on the most demanding—rehabilitation of and security for the new Iraq. The result was a surprising contradiction. The United States did not have nearly enough troops to secure the hundreds of suspected WMD sites that had supposedly been identified in Iraq or to secure the nation's long, porous borders. Had the Iraqis possessed WMD and terrorist groups been prevalent in Iraq as the Bush administration so loudly asserted, U.S. forces might well have failed to prevent the WMD from being spirited out of the country and falling into the hands of the dark forces the administration had declared war against.

In making the case for its preemptive war, the Bush administration made it clear that it was prepared, if need be, to act unilaterally. But the consolidation of the United States's gains assumed that Washington would eventually elicit the cooperation of others: the Iraqis and allied nations that in the main were all too happy to keep their distance from postwar Iraq. There was a disparity of ends and means: the unilateral foreign policy required that others move in later to fill the security and nation-building void. Apart from the British, the "coalition of the willing" much touted by the United States was few in number, hobbled by restrictive rules of engagement that precluded them from launching effective offensive actions, or ill-prepared for the civil affairs requirements needed to stabilize Iraq after the war.

As for the Iraqis, Saddam Hussein's strategy was no more prescient than that of the Americans. Classified interrogations conducted after the war reveal that Saddam and his aides repeatedly dismissed the threat that the American-led forces in Kuwait posed to Baghdad. Saddam viewed Iran as his principal external enemy. The Iraqi leader had initially calculated that he could maintain the ambiguity over his WMD program to deter Iran, his opponents at home, and other adversaries even as he complied with the letter of the U.N. inspection demands. It was a fine line to walk and a misreading of his American adversary. The "deterrence by doubt" strategy encouraged suspicions within the Bush administration that the Iraqi leader really did have something to hide. Having publicly promulgated a doctrine of preemption, the Bush team was not about to be restrained by lack of support at the United Nations.

Saddam's military calculations were similarly deficient. Saddam's formative military crisis was not his lopsided defeat in the 1991 Persian Gulf War, but the sudden Shiite uprising in the south that followed. With preservation of his regime his top priority, Saddam oversaw the development of the Baath Emergency Plan, which called for squelching the sort of uprisings that the Shiites had mounted after the Gulf War. The idea was for the Fedayeen and other militia to contain any uprising long enough for Republican Guard units to arrive and crush the opposition. Saddam assumed that local Baathists would be cut off for a period of time and would have to survive on their own until the army or Republican Guard arrived to rescue them. Each village, town, and city would become a small semi-independent citadel. Fedayeen units would put down local revolts, drawing on caches of light weapons like AK-47s, machine guns, mortars, and RPGs, which would be kept under close guard by the Baathists. Ultimately, the very force designed to counter an insurgency became the regime's stoutest defender and ultimately the core of the insurgency against the Americans.

Saddam's preoccupation with internal security precluded him from taking measures that would have slowed the American advance. The Ring Plan he approved was a stolid positional defense that ceded much of Iraq, and was held in poor regard by his more capable generals; it stood a poor chance of thwarting the Americans. The Iraqi leader refrained from ordering the destruction of bridges early in the war, calculating that he would need them to rush his own forces south to quell a possible uprising. Fearful of the potential for a coup, he prohibited Republican Guard troops from taking up positions inside the capital. Distrustful of his own officer corps, he did not allow contacts among neighboring units. The scenarios that most worried the Bush administration—the willful destruction of the Iraqi oilfields and the blowing up of dams—were in fact never planned. Saddam's miscalculations were so great that he never expected to lose the war.

While there are indications that Iraq's intelligence service and other diehards prepared to battle after the regime was toppled, there is no convincing evidence that Saddam anticipated and planned a guerrilla campaign. As the CIA debriefings of captured regime officials made clear, Uday and Qusay were on the run with a meager support network after Baghdad fell while Saddam was apprehended in a spider hole. Saddam was no more farsighted than the Americans in preparing for the aftermath. But while the Fedayeen were not part of a deliberate plan to carry on a guerrilla war in the event the regime was toppled, it provided much of the wherewithal for an insurgency: thousands of committed fighters, decentralized command and control systems, and massive caches of arms.

. . .

The combination of miscalculations on both sides led to an outcome that neither expected. Saddam failed to prevent the fall of the capital, his own capture, and the ascendancy of Shiite and Kurdish groups that he had long suppressed. His supporters were forced to wage a bloody guerrilla war that threatened to tear the country apart and offered no promise of restoring the Iraqi leader to power. The United States's hopes for a lightning victory were quickly dashed and it suffered mounting casualties.

None of this was inevitable. The U.S military commanders who battled their way to Baghdad and endured the long, hot summer of 2003 believe that there was a window of opportunity in the early weeks and months of the invasion, which was allowed to close. Though some degree of opposition was unavoidable, the virulent insurgency that emerged was not inevitable but was aided by military and political blunders in Washington. Having failed to prepare for post-combat burdens, undertaken the war with the minimal acceptable forces, and canceled the deployment of badly needed reinforcements, the Bush administration compounded the problem by disbanding the Iraqi army, putting more than 300,000 armed men on the streets, and denying local elections that would have allowed the Iraqis a measure of control over their own affairs. When it looked like a candidate not to Washington's liking might win in Najaf, Bremer canceled the vote. The difficulties were compounded when Washington installed a new military headquarters and civilian authority that did not work well together and were ill prepared for their tasks.

As poorly positioned to keep order as the Americans were, many Iraqis at first were thankful for the removal of Saddam's regime or simply too numbed by the rapid turn of events and display of American power to complain. But when order and essential services were not immediately restored, American prestige eroded quickly. There was a chink in the victor's armor. As local Iraqis were quick to note, the Americans could put a man on the moon but could not provide electricity.

The cost to the administration's foreign policy was considerable: instead of sending a cautioning message of American strength to Iran and North Korea, the United States was bogged down in a conflict that absorbed its military efforts. Instead of demonstrating the liberating power of democratic rule, the United States had inadvertently sent a message that the transition to a representative government was fraught with peril. Instead of demonstrating the sort of success that would have attracted allies to send forces to share the burden of occupation, American and British forces found themselves virtually alone.

For all this, the future of Iraq still hangs in the balance. The determination of American forces to fill the void left by the civilian policymakers and to engage the Iraqis, as well as fight the insurgents, has kept alive the hope of an outcome that would justify their sacrifice. The valor and resilience of the Iraqis who have flocked to the polls have also preserved the possibility that a representative government may emerge from the ruins of Saddam's totalitarian Iraq. The price for the American and allied troops, and for the Iraqis themselves, though, was higher than it need have been: chaos, suffering, and a future that is still vexed.

Acknowledgments

This book is heavily indebted to the soldiers, Marines, airmen, and sailors, of all ranks and stripes, who fought in the conflict and met with us over the past three years. They spent hours telling their story, gave us access to their personal diaries and after-action reports. They were generous with their time and never asked anything in return other than our best effort to get the story right.

We owe a special thanks to David McKiernan's Coalition Forces Land Component Command, where Michael Gordon was embedded as a reporter for the *New York Times* during the war. McKiernan's staff there gave him extraordinary access and spent many months afterward answering questions about the complex events. Terry Moran, William Webster, James "Spider" Marks, J. D. Thurman, Robert "Rusty" Blackman, Kevin Benson, Albert Whitley, and Daniel Leaf were among the many who provided valuable insights during the war. Rick Thomas, Gregory Julian, and Dave Connolly provided public affairs support.

We are also grateful to Scott Wallace's V Corps, which granted interviews with key participants before, during, and after the invasion. Buford Blount's 3rd Infantry Division was particularly helpful. When the division sought to document its fights, it allowed Gordon to participate in the effort and visit the battlefields with the very soldiers who fought in the engagements. It was a unique opportunity to meet the participants and understand the clashes when memories were fresh right after the war.

All of the division's brigades and their commanders were extremely helpful, but a special appreciation must be extended to David Perkins's 2nd BCT, which allowed Gordon to live with its battalions in Baghdad and Fallujah. Rock Marcone's 3-69 Armored Battalion also allowed Gordon to visit briefly in Baghdad, and Terry Ferrell's 3-7 Cavalry Squadron facilitated interviews there. David Petraeus's 101st Airborne Division hosted Gordon after it moved to Mosul and other points north, and James Mattis's 1st Marine Division hosted him in Hillah. Timothy Keating was most helpful during visits to his naval headquarters in Bahrain and later at the Pentagon. Robin Brims and his able deputy Chris Vernon met with Gordon at the British headquarters in Kuwait before the war and Gordon was also able to speak with senior British officers during and after the capture of Basra.

In the United States, we traveled extensively to meet with a large variety of military units to fill in the story. The trips took us to Camp Lejeune to interview Richard Natonski's Task Force Tarawa Marines and Camp Pendleton and Twenty-nine Palms to interview Marines of Mattis's division. We visited Miramar Air Station to meet with Marine aviators from James "Tamer" Amos's 3rd Air Wing and Fort Hood to talk to some of the officers of the 4th Infantry Division, which Raymond Odierno had handed off to J. D. Thurman. At Fort Hood, we also interviewed the aircrews with Dan Ball's 1-227 Apache squadron. Special Operations Forces explained their war to us.

Our research also took us to CENTCOM's headquarters in Tampa, the Joint Forces Command near Norfolk, and Nellis Air Force Base, where T. Michael "Buzz" Moseley allowed Gordon to sit in on an internal briefing on the air war. We are also grateful to the assistance provided by officers from Moseley's Combined Forces Air Operations Center, which oversaw the air war, and to some of the F-117 pilots and aircrews who helped with our account.

The military's war colleges also allowed us to interview students and staff who fought in the war and, on occasion, consult their archives. Thanks to the Army War College at Carlisle Barracks, Pennsylvania; the Army Command and General Staff College at Fort Leavenworth, Kansas; the Naval War College in Newport, Rhode Island, and the Air War College at Maxwell Air Force Base in Alabama; and the Marine Corps Command and Staff College at Quantico, Virginia.

The services' historical centers were most helpful and allowed us to consult the work done by their industrious field attachments. Thanks to Frank R. Shirer of the U.S. Army Center of Military History and Vicki Hester, Fort Stewart Museum Historian. We would also like to extend our appreciation to Chuck Melson of the U.S. Marine Corps Historical Center. Gregory Fontenot and E. J. Degen, co-authors of the Army's official history of the conflict, *On Point,* were most helpful.

At the Pentagon, we were granted interviews with virtually all of the Joint Chiefs of Staff, as well as key members of the Joint Staff. Current and former Army, Navy, Marine, and Air Force officers patiently explained important decisions. Senior Defense Department officials made themselves available, including Paul Wolfowitz and Douglas Feith and his staff.

Thanks must also be extended to Condoleezza Rice and other White House officials who agreed to interviews on the war planning as part of a *New York Times* series that served as a foundation for some of our chapters, and to Richard Armitage and other senior State Department officials. Paul Pillar, formerly of the CIA, and other intelligence officials also provided their perspective.

Jay Garner, Paul Hughes, and other key members of the Office for Reconstruction and Humanitarian Assistance team were readily accessible. L. Paul Bremer and members of the Coalition Provisional Authority were helpful during their tour of duty in Baghdad. Rick Sanchez gave a *New York Times* interview to Gordon during his Baghdad tour, which was useful for this book.

Many of our important contacts cannot be openly thanked because of the documents and sensitive information they provided, information they believed should be made public to fill in the record of the war and enlighten the public on how the campaign in Iraq was actually planned and fought.

Some government and military officials chose not to cooperate. Secretary of Defense Donald Rumsfeld turned down a long-standing interview request. General Tommy Franks gave an hourlong interview in the fall of 2004 for a *New York Times* article on the postwar planning, much of which is drawn on in the book. But he did not agree to a follow-up session to go over issues in depth despite repeated requests. Vice President Dick Cheney also declined to be interviewed, a decision we were told was made after consultation with his then chief of staff, Scooter Libby.

This book would not have been possible without the support of the Center for Strategic and International Studies, where Gordon was a writer-in-residence from the fall of 2003 to the spring of 2005. John Hamre, the president of CSIS, and Kurt Campbell, a CSIS senior vice president and director of its international security program, were most supportive. Bruce Blair, the president of the World Security Institute, was also instrumental to the completion of the book. The institute named Gordon as its distinguished media fellow through the balance of 2005.

Jeremiah Cushman and Christopher Mann, our dedicated and talented research assistants, were indispensable. They scoured military archives, reviewed many hours of transcribed interviews, sifted through hundreds of documents, carried out vital research, and reviewed the book text. We were also aided by a variety of interns, including Mike Alpern, Tom Hommel, Sam King, Milady Ortiz, and Michael Petillo. Eric Schmitt, John Burns, and other members of the *New York Times* staff offered their insights. David Rampe, assistant foreign editor at the *Times,* read through the early drafts and provided helpful recommendations. Elisabeth Bumiller was an able guide to the White House.

Andrew Wylie, our erudite agent, guided us through the publishing world. Erroll McDonald, our patient publishing executive, had numerous perceptive and important suggestions as to how to improve the telling of a very complicated tale. Fred Chase, our keen-eyed copy editor, worked assiduously on the text. Joyce Pendola, our talented cartographer, prepared the maps. Thanks also to Pantheon's diligent production team: Peter Andersen, Lydia Buechler, Archie Ferguson, Avery Flück, Wesley Gott, Andy Hughes, Altie Karper, Maria Massey, and Robin Reardon.

Our heartfelt appreciation to many others, too numerous to name, who also helped us tell the inside story of the Iraq War.

Notes

CHAPTER 1: *Snowflakes from the Secretary*

1. Central Command, or CENTCOM, is the U.S. combat command assigned responsibility and authority for U.S. military operations in the Middle East.
2. Interview, Lieutenant General Gregory S. Newbold (Ret).
3. George W. Bush, "A Period of Consequences," 23 September 1999, the Citadel, available from http://citadel.edu/r3/pao/addresses/pres_bush.html, accessed 1 November 2005. Richard Armitage, who later served as deputy secretary of state under Colin Powell, drafted much of the text.
4. Interview, former Pentagon official. Also see James Mann, *Rise of the Vulcans* (New York: Viking, 2004), pp. x–xiii, and Midge Decter, *Rumsfeld: A Personal Portrait* (New York: Regan Books/HarperCollins, 2003), for accounts of Rumsfeld's career.
5. Interview, former senior military officer.
6. Interview, former senior official.
7. Quadrennial Defense Review Report, 30 September 2001.

   For the United States, the revolution in military affairs holds the potential to confer enormous advantages and to extend the current period of U.S. military superiority. . . . Moving to a capabilities-based force also requires the United States to focus on emerging opportunities that certain capabilities, including advanced remote sensing, long-range precision strike, transformed maneuver and expeditionary forces and systems, to overcome anti-access and area denial threats, can confer on the U.S. military over time.

8. Interview, Douglas Macgregor.
9. Dick Cheney, "Defense Strategy for the 1990s: The Regional Defense Strategy," DOD publication, January 1993.
10. Quadrennial Defense Review Report, 30 September 2001.
11. Interview, Tom White.
12. Donald Rumsfeld, "Bureaucracy to Battlefield," speech, 10 September 2001, available from http://www.defenselink.mil/speeches/2001/s20010910-secdef.html, accessed 1 November 2005.
13. Interview, Douglas Feith.
14. Thomas Kean et al., *The 9/11 Commission Report* (New York: Norton, 2004), pp. 559–60; Interview, Douglas Feith.

15. Letter to the authors from former President George H. W. Bush, as published in Michael R. Gordon and Lieutenant General (Ret.) Bernard E. Trainor, *The Generals' War* (New York: Little, Brown, 1995), p. 517.

16. The cease-fire arrangements agreed on at the March 1991 talks at Safwan also inadvertently gave the regime a badly needed boost. When the Iraqi generals complained that their bridges had been bombed and asked H. Norman Schwarzkopf, the chief allied commander, for the right to fly helicopters throughout southern Iraq, Schwarzkopf agreed. The Iraqi commanders quickly exploited the concession to mount ferocious helicopter attacks on the Shiites— including, American intelligence learned more than a decade later, with chemical weapons—prompting Schwarzkopf to complain that he had been duped. At the forward headquarters of the Third Army, Brigadier General Steve Arnold, the command's chief operations officer, drew up a top secret contingency plan to march on the Iraqi capital and dislodge Saddam, which he dubbed fittingly enough "The Road to Baghdad." Concerned that Saddam had survived the Desert Storm campaign and anxious to create problems for him at home, the Saudis proposed a covert program to arm the Shiite rebels during a visit to Riyadh by Secretary of State James Baker and a team of Bush officials. "The Road to Baghdad" plan, in possession of the authors.

17. Gordon and Trainor, *The Generals' War,* pp. 455–56.

18. Interview, Brent Scowcroft.

19. Wayne Downing, "An Alternative Strategy for Iraq" plan, in possession of the authors. It called for assembling a core of 300 to 500 Iraqi expatriates with military experience, which would be trained in the U.S. In addition, a 2,000- to 10,000-man force would be recruited and transported to a base in the Middle East. Two special units would be formed, including a 200-man Commando Company trained for raids and ambushes and strike operations, and a 150-man vehicle Anti-Tank Company armed with medium- and long-range antitank missiles.

20. William J. Clinton, "The Iraq Liberation Act," statement by the president, 31 October 1998, available from http://www.library.cornell.edu/colldev/mid east/libera.htm, accessed 28 October 2005.

21. Alfred B. Prados, "Iraqi Challenges and U.S. Military Responses: March 1991 Through October 31, 1998," *CRS Report for Congress,* 20 November 2002.

22. Interview, former Pentagon official.

23. Interview, former Clinton aide.

24. Interview, former Pentagon official; George W. Bush, "Remarks by the President to the American Troops in Kosovo," 24 July 2001, available from http://www.whitehouse.gov/news/releases/2001/07/20010724-1.html; David E. Sanger, "Bush, in Kosovo, Tells U.S. Troops Role Is Essential," *New York Times,* 25 July 2001, Section A, p. 1.

25. Interview, former member of the Joint Staff.

     Wolfowitz was influenced by the views of Laurie Mylroie, who argued that the 1993 attack was an Iraqi plot. As dean of the Johns Hopkins School of Advanced International Studies, a post he held after leaving the administration of George H. W. Bush, Wolfowitz informally looked into the matter. See Laurie

Mylroie, *The War Against America: Saddam Hussein and the World Trade Center Attacks: A Study of Revenge* (New York: Regan Books/HarperCollins, 2001).

26. Interviews, former Joint Staff officials.
27. Interview, Lieutenant General Gregory S. Newbold.
28. Saddam Hussein, "Open letter from Saddam Hussein to the American peoples and the western peoples and their governments," 15 September 2001, available from http://www.everything2.com/index.pl?node_id=1172306, accessed 20 October 2005. The second letter is available from http://web.archive.org/web/20010922151907/www.uruklink.net/iraqnews/enews12.htm.

> We say to the American peoples, what happened on September 11, 2001, should be compared to what their government and their armies are doing in the world, for example, the international agencies have stated that more than one million and a half Iraqis have died because of the blockade imposed by America and some Western countries, in addition to the tens of thousands who died or are injured in the military action perpetrated by America along with those who allied with it against Iraq. Hundreds of bridges, churches, mosques, colleges, schools, factories, palaces, hotels, and thousands of private houses were destroyed or damaged by the American and Western bombardment, which is ongoing even today against Iraq. . . . There is, however, one difference, namely that those who direct their missiles and bombs to the targets, whether Americans or from another Western country, are mostly targeting by remote controls, that is why they do so as if they were playing an amusing game. As for those who acted on September 11, 2001, they did it from a close range, and with, I imagine, giving their lives willingly, with an irrevocable determination. . . . Americans should feel the pain they have inflicted on other peoples of the world, so as when they suffer, they will find the right solution and the right path. . . . America needs wisdom, not power. It has used power, along with the West, to its extreme extent, only to find out later that it doesn't achieve what they wanted. Will the rulers of America try wisdom just for once so that their people can live in security and stability?

29. Interview, senior official.
30. Interview, former senior official.
31. Kean et al., *The 9/11 Commission Report*, 2004, p. 335.
32. Interview, Francis Brooke.
33. Interview, Lieutenant Colonel Charles Danna.
34. Interview, Lieutenant Colonel Chuck Eassa.
35. Review of Rumsfeld's talking points by the authors.

CHAPTER 2: *The Generated Start*

1. Tommy Franks, *American Soldier* (New York: Regan Books/HarperCollins, 2004).
2. Interview, former aide.
3. Interview, Newt Gingrich.
4. Interview, General (Ret.) Anthony Zinni.
5. Even after Clinton signed legislation giving him the authority to train and equip the INC, Zinni declared that the idea was a prescription for disaster. Invoking memories of the failed, CIA-sponsored Bay of Pigs invasion of Cuba, Zinni predicted it would lead to a "Bay of Goats" incited by Ahmed Chalabi's "Gucci Guerrillas." The comments sparked angry complaints from the Republican supporters of the plan, most notably John McCain, who, in a sharp exchange with Zinni, complained that the CENTCOM commander was not following the law. Zinni did little to defuse the confrontation by telling the senator that the Iraq Liberation Act had not revoked his constitutional right of free speech and that his responsibility as a commander was to call the shots as he saw them. The exchange upset the White House, which thought it had managed to finesse a potent political issue. JCS Chairman General Hugh Shelton, who agreed wholeheartedly with Zinni, later called him to say he had been asked by the White House to reprimand the CENTCOM commander. Shelton dryly told Zinni that he should consider himself chewed out.
6. Ibid.
7. Interview, General Anthony Zinni.
8. Plan details provided by former CENTCOM officials.
9. Interview, Lieutenant Colonel John Agoglia.
10. Interview, former CENTCOM official.
11. Franks, *American Soldier,* p. 198.
12. Ibid., pp. 346–56; Interview, former CENTCOM official.
13. Interviews, former CENTCOM officials.
14. Interview, Douglas Macgregor. The briefing provided to Rumsfeld was entitled "Transforming the Way America Fights," and contained the following slide:

What the Enemy Does Not Expect
- The enemy does not expect a swift, sudden ground attack without warning that begins without air or missile strikes.
- The enemy does not expect the United States to attack with a ground combat force of fewer than 100,000 troops.
- The enemy does not expect a ground attack aimed directly at Baghdad and its oil fields.
- The enemy does not expect US forces to rapidly "lean into" potential WMD fires making their use very unlikely.
- The enemy does not expect the United States to act without prior international sanction.

Therefore, that is exactly what the United States must do to swiftly remove the Iraqi regime.

15. Interview, Douglas Macgregor.
16. Franks was sent a summary of James P. Wade's "Rapid Dominance Concept," a strategy "based on four core characteristics—'total' knowledge, rapidity, brilliance in execution, and control of the environment." Also included was an article by retired Air Force General Charles Horner, who oversaw the air campaign during the 1991 Persian Gulf War. It was entitled "How and Where to Apply Shock and Awe." This six-page paper cited historical examples as far back as Genghis Khan and concluded with the passage, "In the end, if we are going to lead then we must be considered the madmen of the world, capable of any action, willing to risk any thing to achieve our national interests. It is only our ends that must be admired, if we seek to be loved then our capacity to act will be weak, as our threat will not be credible. If we are to achieve noble purposes we must be prepared to act in the most ignoble manner."
17. President George W. Bush, "State of the Union" speech, 29 January 2002, available from http://www.whitehouse.gov/news/releases/2002/01/20020129-11.html, accessed 1 November 2005.
18. Interview, CENTCOM official.

CHAPTER 3: *Smaller Is Beautiful*

1. Franks, *American Soldier*, pp. 372–73; Interview, former CENTCOM official.
2. Interviews, former State Department officials.
3. Interview, Dick Cheney, 1991.
4. Interviews, officials on trip and U.S. diplomats. Also see Michael R. Gordon, "Cheney, in London, Receives Strong Support from Blair on Tough Stance Against Iraq," *New York Times,* 12 March 2002, Section A, p. 14; Michael R. Gordon, "Saudis Warn Against Attack on Iraq by the United States," *New York Times,* 17 March 2002, Section 1, p. 16; Michael R. Gordon, "Cheney, in Jordan, Meets Opposition to Military Move in Iraq," *New York Times,* 13 March 2002, Section A, p. 12; Michael R. Gordon, "U.S. Offers Aid to Turkey to Lead Kabul Force," *New York Times,* 20 March 2002, Section A, p. 14; Michael R. Gordon, "Cheney Asks Yemen to Join the Pursuit of Al Qaeda's Remnants," *New York Times,* 15 March 2002, Section A, p. 10; Michael R. Gordon, "Cheney Says Next Goal in U.S. War on Terror Is to Block Access to Arms," *New York Times,* 16 March 2002, Section A, p. 8.
5. Interview, former CENTCOM official.
6. Interview, meeting participant.
7. Notes of a participant. A war game presentation at the Component Commanders' Conference, 23 March 2002, Ramstein, Germany, recommended a "near simultaneous" air and ground campaign. That is, one in which the air and ground action would be separated by twenty-four to sixty hours. But it noted that Moseley did not concur. It also noted that the summer months would reduce the ability to wage war. It supported the idea of attacking from Turkey if the air- and sea-lift could be worked out. It reported "no major holes in current plan."

8. Notes of a participant of the CENTCOM meeting.

9. John McCain, Senate Armed Services Committee hearing, 23 September 2004. After listening to Rumsfeld, McCain said: "I don't need General Myers' response. I know it will be exactly the same as yours. I would like the personal opinions—I would—and I don't mean that as in any way a criticism, General Myers. I would like the personal opinions of the other CINCs, if I could, since my time has expired."

10. Franks, *American Soldier,* p. 277; Interviews, former members of the Joint Chiefs of Staff.

11. Interview, General John Jumper.

12. Interviews, former CENTCOM officials.

13. Notes of a participant.

14. Interview, former CENTCOM planner.

15. Interview, former CENTCOM official.

16. White House transcripts: "President Bush Meets with German Chancellor Schroeder," 23 May 2002, available from http://www.whitehouse.gov/news/releases/2002/05/20020523-1.html, and "President Bush Meets with French President Chirac," 26 May 2002, available from http://www.whitehouse.gov/news/releases/2002/05/20020526-2.html. Bush made a similar comment to a reporter from ITN, the British television channel, on April 4. See "Interview of the President by Sir Trevor McDonald of Britain's ITV Television Network," available from http://www.usembassy.it/file2002_04/alia/a2040709.htm.

17. DOD news briefing transcript, CENTCOM CINC General Tommy Franks, Tuesday, 21 May 2002, available from http://www.globalsecurity.org/military/library/news/2002/05/mil-020521-dod01b.htm.

18. Notes of a participant.

19. Interview, former member of the Joint Staff.

20. No reliable census had been carried out for years. The Iraqi population was estimated variously at 24 to 25 million.

21. "Iraq: Prime Minister's Meeting, 23 July," memorandum prepared by Matthew Rycroft, a Downing Street policy aide, 1 May 2005, available from http://www.timesonline.co.uk/article/0,,2087-1593607,00.html.

CHAPTER 4: *The Other Side of the Hill*

1. "Comprehensive Report of the Special Advisor to the Central Intelligence on Iraq's WMD, with Addendums (Duelfer Report)," vol. 1, Regime Strategic Intent, 30 September 2004, p. 25.

2. "U.S. Joint Forces Command Combat Study: Iraqi Perspectives on Operation Iraqi Freedom Major Combat Operations," classified "secret." Reviewed by the authors. Much of the research was done for JFCOM by the Institute for Defense Analyses, a Pentagon-funded research center. The study also had the support of the CIA, the Defense Intelligence Agency, and the Iraq Survey Group, a panel that studied Iraq's WMD programs and efforts, and CJTF-7, the U.S.-led military command in Iraq.

3. Visit to Babylon by Michael Gordon.

4. "Comprehensive Report," vol. 1, pp. 11–12, 19, 72; Interview, intelligence official.

Reports that Saddam made extensive use of doubles, so prevalent in the West, however, were a myth, U.S. officials determined from their interrogations with the Iraqi hierarchy after the war. Saddam did not use doubles, perhaps because it introduced the potential for mischief by would-be coup plotters.

5. JFCOM briefing.

6. "Iraqi Perspectives," pp. 10, 26, 34.

While Saddam seems to have understood that those around him actively distorted their views to please him, after 1998 he became increasingly reclusive and less inclined to personally verify claims made by subordinates. Grossly exaggerated assessments were left unchecked, and few among Saddam's closest confidants risked bringing the dictator bad news.

7. Ibid., p. 36.

8. Ibid., p. 26.

9. JFCOM briefing; "Iraqi Perspectives," p. 10.

10. JFCOM briefing.

11. JFCOM briefing.

12. George W. Bush, graduation speech at West Point, 1 June 2002, available from http://www.whitehouse.gov/news/releases/2002/06/20020601-3.html, accessed 1 November 2005.

13. "Excerpts from Pentagon's Plan: 'Prevent the Re-emergence of a New Rival,'" *New York Times,* 8 March 1992, Section 1, p. 14.

14. The National Security Strategy of the United States, September 2002, available from http://www.whitehouse.gov/nsc/nss.html, accessed 1 November 2005; Michael R. Gordon, "In Bush's 'Axis of Evil,' Why Iraq Stands Out," *New York Times,* 9 September 2002, Section A, p. 8; Interview, senior administration official.

15. George W. Bush, "President Salutes Troops of the 10th Mountain Division," 19 July 2002, available from http://www.whitehouse.gov/news/releases/2002/07/20020719.html, accessed 1 November 2005.

16. "Iraqi Perspectives," p. 29; Interview, intelligence official.

17. Comprehensive Report," vol. 1, p. 25.

With sixteen of Iraq's eighteen provinces in open revolt, the Iraqi regime felt the urgent need to rapidly overpower the growing resistance movement. Husayn Kamil, head of a key military ministry and personal confidant to Saddam Hussein, first ordered a strike on rebel positions at Najaf using VX liquid. When the oily nerve agent could not be found, Kamil instructed subordinates to use mustard gas instead. This option was also ruled out, however, after Iraqi commanders considered the high risk of detection by coalition forces. Another substitute would have to be found.

In early March 1991, roughly a dozen Iraqi Mi-8 helicopters loaded with Sarin nerve gas launched from Tamuz air base and began a series of chemical strikes against rebel Shiite positions in the Karbala region. The attacks were judged to be ineffective—probably due to improper delivery—but the regime did not abandon its efforts to dislodge insurgents with chemical weapons. Several hundred more aerial bombs filled with CS (tear gas) fell on Karbala and Najaf over the following weeks. Anecdotal reports gathered from Iraqis fleeing the country after the Gulf War also described a variety of chemical strikes executed against Basra and Nasiriyah.

18. "Comprehensive Report," vol. 1, p. 58. Evidence suggests these resolutions were never implemented, and it remains a mystery what Saddam's real motivation in passing them had been.

19. JFCOM briefing.

20. USCINCCENT Commanders' Conference, Operation Iraqi Freedom (CENTCOM slides with backups), 1–2 August 2002, slides 19–21. The CENTCOM slides put it this way: "eliminate Saddam's regime through the destruction of his security apparatus, exposing Saddam to threat of a population uprising, coup, assassination, or direct attack by U.S. forces, while eliminating Iraq's WMD threat to neighbors."

21. USCINCCENT Commanders' Conference, 1–2 August. Slide 103 describes thirty-two to forty-five months of total Phase IV work and an additional American security commitment of two years.

22. Interview, James Moschgat, 26 May 2004. Aircrews grew increasingly frustrated as they were ordered to leave hostile (SAM) antiaircraft sites untouched in favor of alternative targets. Other operational constraints included a marked Saudi reluctance to allow offensive strikes from their territory. Also see Michael R. Gordon, "U.S. Air Raids in '02 Prepared for War in Iraq," *New York Times,* 20 July 2003, Section 1, p. 1.

23. Elizabeth Bone and Christopher Bolkcom, "Unmanned Aerial Vehicles: Background and Issues for Congress," *CRS Report for Congress,* 25 April 2003, p. 16.

24. Component Commanders' Conference, 1–2 August 2002, component commanders' meetings; notes of a participant.

25. Interview, senior British officer.

26. Interview, Richard Armitage. Other State Department officials say there was a general perception that the White House had concluded that military action had to occur no later than the spring of 2003 so the war would be won before the 2004 election. Robin Raphel, a senior State Department official who later served as an aide to Paul Bremer, said, "There were two pressures [on the administration to move forward]. One was the clear political pressure, election-driven and calendar-driven. And the other was, the troops were deployed forward for Afghanistan and to let that kind of fall back and then reenergize everybody is very difficult. That's a real issue." U.S. Institute for Peace oral history interview by Charles Stuart Kennedy, 13 July 2004. The USIP is a government-funded research center.

27. Interview, Lieutenant General Gregory S. Newbold.

28. A draft of the classified statement was read to the authors by a senior administration official.

29. George W. Bush, "President Discusses Security and Defense Issues," 21 Au-

gust 2002, available from http://www.whitehouse.gov/news/releases/2002/08/
20020821-1.html, accessed 1 November 2005.

30. Bush meeting with NSC on September 6, account from notes of a participant.

CHAPTER 5: *Back to the Future*

1. Notes of a participant.
2. Interviews, CENTCOM and CFLCC officials.
3. "Fortress Baghdad" slide, viewed by the authors.
4. "Report of the Select Committee on Intelligence on the U.S. Intelligence Community's Pre-War Intelligence Assessments on Iraq, Together with Additional Views," 7 July 2004.
5. Interview, Brigadier General James "Spider" Marks.
6. Interview, Colonel Kevin Benson.
7. Interview, Lieutenant General David D. McKiernan, Army oral history interview by Major John Aarsen, 30 November 2002.
8. Notes of a participant.
9. Some of McKiernan's staff, notably Benson and Marks, favored moving G-day ahead of A-day to gain surprise, as did Lieutenant General James Conway, but McKiernan did not go that far.
10. The CENTCOM commander was intrigued by early regime collapse. Gary Harrell, the commander of CENTCOM's Special Operations Forces, noted that Task Force 20 would need two days' heads-up to carry out the seizing of the Baghdad airport. He noted that he had plans to stop the flight of top Iraqi officials to Syria and Iran. Franks wanted the Navy to provide sufficient security to ensure that cargo ships could transit unmolested through the Suez Canal and the Bab al-Mandab Strait near the Horn of Africa. "Keep the ditch open," he said.
11. Notes of participants.
12. "Rumsfeld, Franks Address Press," CNN International transcript, 12 December 2002.

FRANKS: You know, for more than two years now we have talked a lot about transformation, and we have thought a lot about what transformation means, and we have thought about the way we field our assets, the way we train our people, the sorts of technologies we use, and a great many other things. The power of this Exercise Internal Look, in my view, has been—or is that it is giving us an opportunity to get at all those points. You know, the doctrines that existed for our armed forces several years ago really don't apply to the first war of the 21st Century.

Franks also suggested that there was not a link between the Internal Look exercise and tensions with Iraq. "Well, actually I wasn't aware that any threat had been issued. The purpose of the Internal Look exercise is as I described it: move the command post a long ways and gain the effect of this training and increased readiness."

13. Notes of a participant.
14. Franks and other CENTCOM officials provided a similar account to Bob Woodward, who wrote in *Plan of Attack* that the U.S. forces had executed the

Hybrid 5-11-16-125 Plan. Gregory Hooker, CENTCOM chief intelligence analyst, noted in his monograph *Shaping the Plan for Operation Iraqi Freedom* that a close examination of the record "runs counter to the frequently repeated suggestions by senior participants in OIF [Operation Iraqi Freedom] that the Hybrid plan was the version ultimately executed. Hybrid, with its thirty-two-day buildup to G-day and its sixteen-day separation between A-day and G-day, does not accurately describe OIF's execution." Hooker cites Franks's book, *American Soldier,* and Woodward's *Plan of Attack.* Bob Woodward, *Plan of Attack* (New York: Simon & Schuster, 2004), pp. 287, 401. Gregory Hooker, *Shaping the Plan for Operation Iraqi Freedom* (Washington, D.C.: Washington Institute for Near East Policy, 2005), pp. 32–33.

CHAPTER 6: *'Round and 'Round We Go*

1. Among other units, the MODEP sought theater missile defense systems that were to be deployed in Kuwait and other Arab nations offering bases, and Odierno's 4th Infantry Division.
2. Interview, Colonel Kevin Benson.
3. CFLCC briefing slide.
4. Interview, Major General James D. "J.D." Thurman, Army oral history interview by Lieutenant Colonel Steven Holcomb, 27 May 2003.
5. Interview, Lieutenant Colonel Thomas Reilly, Army oral history interview by Major Gregory A. Weisler, 15 May 2003.
6. "Final Report of the Independent Panel to Review DOD Detention Operations," August 2004, p. 54. The report wrongly blames the Army's Forces Command for failing to use the TPFDL system.
7. Interviews, CFLCC staff; Interview, Newt Gingrich.
8. Interview, senior civilian official.
9. Interview, Brigadier General Steve Hawkins.
10. "U.S. Senate Armed Services Committee Hearing on FY 2004 Defense Authorization," transcript, 25 February 2003. The exchange between Senator Carl Levin and General Eric Shinseki follows:
    SENATOR LEVIN: General Shinseki, could you give us some idea as to the magnitude of the Army's force requirement for an occupation of Iraq following a successful completion of the war?
    GENERAL SHINSEKI: In specific numbers, I would have to rely on combatant commanders' exact requirements. But I think . . .
    LEVIN: How about a range?
    SHINSEKI: I would say that what's been mobilized to this point, something on the order of several hundred thousand soldiers, are probably, you know, a figure that would be required. We're talking about post-hostilities control over a piece of geography that's fairly significant with the kinds of ethnic tensions that could lead to other problems. And so, it takes significant ground force presence to maintain [a] safe and secure environment to ensure that the people are fed, that water is distributed, all the normal responsibilities that go along with administering a situation like this.

LEVIN: And what effect would that type of an occupation to that extent have on two things, one is our OPTEMPO [operations tempo], which you've talked about, already stressed, and also on the ability of the Army to fulfill the other missions that we have?

SHINSEKI: Well, if it were an extended requirement for presence of U.S.-only Army forces, it would have a significant long-term effect. And therefore, I think the kind of assistance from friends and allies would be helpful.

11. Interview, Tom White.

12. Briefing reviewed by authors; Interview, senior administration official.

13. Unlike a "surrender," which makes the defeated combatants prisoners under the Geneva Convention and prohibits them from switching sides, when an enemy unit "capitulates," it can be enlisted to serve the victor.

14. Interview, General Anthony Zinni.

15. SCIRI, the Iranian-backed Supreme Council for the Islamic Revolution in Iran, had a militia dubbed the Badr Corps, but did attend the London meeting.

16. Interviews, Department of Defense and White House officials.

17. Interview, Kanan Makiya. Also Kanan Makiya, "Our Hopes Betrayed," *The Observer,* 16 February 2003, available from http://observer.guardian.co.uk/iraq/story/0,12239,896611,00.html, accessed 8 November 2005.

18. Interview, Colonel Kevin Benson.

19. Interview, senior official.

20. "Iraqi Perspectives," p. 13; Interview, General Michael Hagee, commandant, United States Marine Corps.

21. Notes of a participant at the CENTCOM meeting.

22. Notes of a participant.

23. Michael R. Gordon, "NATO, the Inside Story," *New York Times,* 25 February 2003; interviews with senior U.S. and NATO officials.

24. Notes of a participant.

25. Dexter Filkins, "Turkish Deputies Refuse to Accept American Troops," *New York Times,* 2 March 2003, Section 1, p. 1.

26. In the end, cooler heads prevailed and the United States offered the Turks $1 billion in credits despite their refusal to open a northern front. The credits were never used.

27. Interview, General J. D. Thurman, 27 May 2003.

28. Joseph Collins's memo, "Rear Area Forces Gap."

CHAPTER 7: *The Red Line*

1. "Comprehensive Report," vol. 1, p. 65.

2. Ibid.

3. Ibid., p. 63.

4. Ibid., p. 34.

Saddam never discussed using deception as a policy, but he used to say privately that the "better part of war was deceiving," according to Ali Hassan al-Majeed. He stated that Saddam wanted to avoid appearing weak and did not reveal he was deceiving the world about the presence of WMD. The U.N.'s inconclusive assessment of Iraq's possession of WMD, in Saddam's view, gave pause to Iran. Saddam was concerned that the U.N. inspection process would expose Iraq's vulnerability, thereby magnifying the effect of Iran's own capability.

5. "Iraqi Perspectives," pp. 39–42.

According to senior Iraqi officers, the plan was not drawn up through the customary deliberate staff process. A later study to support the new plan was in fact formalized by an al-Bakr University team on 23 February 2003, only weeks before the war. The February enemy courses of action study postulated multiple attacks on multiple fronts, south, west, and north.

6. Ibid., pp. 32–33. "Saddam: there is no way the air force would win a battle or a war as long as there is an infantry soldier," said the director general of the Republican Guard general staff.

7. Visit to the facility by Michael Gordon.

8. Philip H. Gordon and Jeremy Shapiro, *Allies at War* (New York: McGraw-Hill, 2004), p. 100.

9. Michael R. Gordon, "German and Spanish Navies Take on Major Role Near Horn of Africa," *New York Times,* 15 December 2002, Section 1, p. 36.

10. "Iraqi Perspectives," p. 11.

11. "Comprehensive Report," vol. 3, pp. 107–10.

12. Interview, General Anthony Zinni.

13. "Report of the Select Committee on Intelligence on the U.S. Intelligence Community's Pre-War Intelligence Assessments on Iraq, Together with Additional Views," 7 July 2004.

14. "Prior to the Gulf War, America's top intelligence analysts would come to my office in the Defense Department and tell me that Saddam Hussein was at least five or perhaps even 10 years away from having a nuclear weapon. After the war we learned that he had been much closer than that, perhaps within a year of acquiring such a weapon," Vice President Dick Cheney, 26 August 2002 speech to the Veterans of Foreign Wars, available from http://www.whitehouse.gov/news/releases/2002/08/20020826.html, accessed 3 November 2005.

15. "Report of the Select Committee on Intelligence," p. 276. The Bush administration was not alone in pointing to the risk. The Carnegie Endowment for International Peace, which was critical of many administration policies, issued a report in June 2002 entitled *Deadly Arsenals,* which asserted that Saddam was determined to develop nuclear weapons, may have hidden up to 600 metric tons [600 short tons] of CW agents, had the capability to conduct clandestine BW research, and quite possibly possessed an arsenal of two dozen Scud missiles. Joseph Cirincione et al., *Deadly Arsenals,* 1st ed. (Washington, D.C.: Carnegie Endowment for International Peace, 2002), pp. 271–80.

16. "Report of the Select Committee on Intelligence," pp. 307–12.

17. Interview, Paul Pillar.

18. Declassified version of October 2002 National Intelligence Estimate, "Iraq's Continuing Programs for Weapons of Mass Destruction." The estimate read: "Baghdad, for now, appears to be drawing a line short of conducting terrorist attacks with conventional or CBW against the United States, fearing that expo-

sure of Iraqi involvement would provide Washington a stronger cause for making war. Iraq probably would attempt clandestine attacks against the U.S. homeland if Baghdad feared an attack that threatened the survival of the regime were imminent or unavoidable or possibly for revenge," the NIE noted. "Saddam, if sufficiently desperate, might decide that only an organization such as al-Qa'ida—with worldwide reach and extensive terrorist infrastructure—and already engaged in a life-or-death struggle against the United States—could perpetuate the kind of terrorist attack that he would hope to conduct. . . . in such circumstances, he might decide that the extreme step of assisting the Islamist terrorists in conducting a CBW attack against the United States would be his last chance to exact vengeance by taking a larger number of victims with him."

19. Declassified National Intelligence Estimate, October 2002, and Senate testimony; George Tenet interview with Alison Mitchell, *New York Times* congressional reporter; "C.I.A. Letter to Senate on Baghdad's Intentions," *New York Times,* 9 October 2002, Section A, p. 12; Alison Mitchell and Carl Hulse, "C.I.A. Sees Terror After Iraq Action," *New York Times,* 9 October 2002, Section A, p. 1; Michael R. Gordon, "U.S. Aides Split on Assessment of Iraq's Plans," *New York Times,* 10 October 2002, Section A, p. 1. Tenet declined an interview request by the authors.

20. Senator Bob Graham voted against and was among the first to drop out of the campaign for the presidential nomination.

21. As Washington has no embassy in Pyongyang, the U.S. team was taken to the British consulate in two British Land Rovers, went to a secure room, and reviewed the statement again with three linguists. After studying the translation, James Kelly and other members of his delegation concluded that there was only one way to interpret it: North Korea had defiantly declared that it was pursuing nuclear weapons. The conclusion was transmitted via encrypted British communications to Washington.

22. Interview, Charles "Jack" Pritchard, former U.S. ambassador to the talks with North Korea. Also see articles: Barbara Slavin, "N. Korea Admits Nuclear Program," *USA Today,* 17 October 2002, Section A, p. 1; Ryan Lizza, "Nuclear Test," *New Republic,* vol. 227, no. 19, 4 November 2002, pp. 10–11. After being contacted for comment by Slavin and by Chris Nelson, who writes a daily e-mail newsletter on Asian policy, the Bush administration organized a 7:00 p.m. conference call with the *New York Times* and other major publications and disclosed the story. Senator Richard Lugar and Representatives Jim Kolbe and Jim Leach, all Republicans, were briefed in closed session by Kelly on the meetings, and they did not publicly discuss the events. No Democratic lawmakers were briefed prior to the news disclosures.

23. Cheney made the argument in a 26 August 2002 address to the Veterans of Foreign Wars. "Some concede that Saddam is evil, power-hungry, and a menace—but that, until he crosses the threshold of actually possessing nuclear weapons, we should rule out preemptive action. That logic seems to me to be deeply flawed. The argument comes down to this: yes, Saddam is as dangerous as we say he is, we just need to let him get stronger before we do anything about it.

Yet if we did wait until that moment, Saddam would simply be emboldened, and it would become even harder for us to gather friends and allies to oppose him."

24. Interview, Larry Wilkerson.
25. On January 27, Hans Blix told the Security Council, "Iraq appears not to have come to a genuine acceptance even today of the disarmament which was demanded of it and which it needs to carry out to win the confidence of the world and to live in peace." Text of speech available from http://www.globalpolicy.org/security/issues/iraq/unmovic/2003/0127entblixrep.htm, accessed 11 November 2005.
26. Interview, Larry Wilkerson. Also, see transcript of Wilkerson's 19 October 2005 talk, "Weighing the Uniqueness of the Bush Administration's National Security Decision-Making Process: Boon or Danger to American Democracy?," hosted by the New America Foundation, available from http://www.newamerica.net/Download_Docs/pdfs/Doc_File_2644_1.pdf, accessed 3 November 2005.

> The consensus of the intelligence community was overwhelming. I can still hear George Tenet telling me, and telling my boss in the bowels of the CIA, that the information we were delivering—which we had called considerably—we had called it very much—we had thrown whole reams of paper out that the White House had created. But George was convinced, John McLaughlin was convinced that what we were presented was accurate. And contrary to what you were hearing in the papers and other places, one of the best relationships we had in fighting terrorists and in intelligence in general was with guess who? The French. In fact, it was probably the best. And they were right there with us.
>
> In fact, I'll just cite one more thing. The French came in in the middle of my deliberations at the CIA and said, we have just spun aluminum tubes, and by god, we did it to this RPM, et cetera, et cetera, and it was all, you know, proof positive that the aluminum tubes were not for mortar casings or artillery casings, they were for centrifuges. Otherwise, why would you have such exquisite instruments? We were wrong. We were wrong. . . . He was going to wait until the international tension was off of him, until the sanctions were down, and then he was going to go back—certainly go back to all of his programs. I mean, I was convinced of that.

27. "Report of the Select Committee on Intelligence," p. 249.
28. Douglas Jehl, "Report Warned Bush Team About Intelligence Doubts," *New York Times,* 5 November 2005, Section 1, p. 14.
29. Interview, Paul Pillar.
30. "Comprehensive Report," vol. 1, p. 67.
31. Ibid., p. 62.
32. V Corps classified operations order in possession of the authors.
33. I Marine Expeditionary Force classified operations order in possession of authors.

34. Interview, Major General Robert "Rusty" Blackman, Marine Corps oral history interview by Colonel Nicholas Reynolds, 31 May 2003.

CHAPTER 8: *A Little Postwar Planning*

1. Interview, General Anthony Zinni.
2. Interview, Major Ray Eiriz, Operation Iraqi Freedom Study Group interview by Major Craig Borchelt, 28 May 2003.
3. Interview, Colonel John F. Agoglia, Office for Reconstruction and Humanitarian Assistance (ORHA) history interview by Gordon Rudd, 28 June 2003.
4. Interview, Pentagon officials.
5. Interview, senior military official.
6. General Richard Myers's notes on the October 16 meeting were described by a Pentagon official.
7. Interview, Condoleezza Rice.
8. Doug Feith's office also produced a seven-page PowerPoint brief dealing with their view of Phase IV, but it was not coordinated with the Joint Staff, and key planners, including Jewett, were not allowed to keep a copy of it. Military officials recall that it listed a number of long-term-objective bullets, including building a new Iraq that had no WMD, installing a government that was friendly to the U.S. and Israel, and the use of oil to pay for the reconstruction.
9. Interview, Brigadier General Steve Hawkins.
10. Interviews, CFLCC officials.
11. Briefing to CINC (28 February), "CFLCC Stability Operations," slide prepared 16 February 2003.

The CFLCC briefing on stability operations contained a number of slides. "Commanders' Intent" said the goal was to "Control as we go," "Rolling transition to stability operations," "Balance effects of control and destruction." The idea was also to use existing Iraqi organizations and administration. Before regime collapse, V Corps, I MEF, and 4ID would work with Iraqi provincial administrations. Following regime collapse, an interim national military authority would work with "Iraqi ministries." A proclamation would be issued to establish the authority of the interim military administration. The briefing proposed the establishment of a seven-member Iraqi council. Three members would come from the exile community. Four would come from Iraqis who had lived under Saddam. All main ethnic groups would be represented.

The priorities for the first thirty to sixty days included the following: Defeat pockets of resistance; Secure key infrastructure; Provide emergency HA (humanitarian assistance); Control DCs (displaced civilians)/secure EPWs (enemy prisoners of war); Locate/Secure WMD/Conduct SSE (sensitive site exploitation); maintain public order and safety; Empower selected Iraqi officials at local/state/national level (Provisional Commissions); Repair mission essential LOCs (lines of communication); Restore critical utilities/basic services; Support sustainment HA (humanitarian assistance); Exercise military authority at local levels; Begin reintegration of Iraqi military.

12. Interview, Colonel (Ret.) Jim Rabon.

13. Lieutenant Colonel Steven W. Peterson, "Central but Inadequate: The Application of Theory in Operation Iraqi Freedom," National War College, available from http://www.ndu.edu/library/n4/n045602I.pdf.

14. Interviews, Colonel Tom Greenwood, NSC officials.

15. Interview, Jay Garner.

16. Interview, Major General Carl Strock.

17. Donald Rumsfeld, "Beyond Nation-Building," speech given at the 11th Annual Salute to Freedom, Intrepid Sea-Air-Space Museum, New York City, 14 February 2003, available from http://www.defenselink.mil/speeches/2003/sp20030214 -secdef0023.html.

18. Interview, former official.

19. Interview, Colonel Paul Hughes.

20. According to Brookings's 14 November 2005 update of the "Iraq Index," the U.S. has thus far appropriated $20.9 billion, obligated $17.3 billion, and actually disbursed $11.5 billion under the Iraq Relief and Reconstruction Funds (IRRF I and II). Available from www.brookings.edu/fp/saban/iraq/index.pdf.

    According to the Center for Strategic and International Studies' Post-Conflict Reconstruction Project's December 2004 publication on reconstruction spending, $24.1 billion has been appropriated for the reconstruction of Iraq. ("Progress or Peril? Measuring Iraq's Reconstruction," available from www.csis.org/media/pubs/iraq_funds.pdf).

21. Briefing slides from the meeting obtained by the authors, as well as the review of an informal transcript of the meeting.

22. ORHA briefing prepared by Colonel Tom Gross and Colonel Paul Hughes, in the possession of the authors.
    ORHA Rock Drill briefing:

Law Enforcement

BACKGROUND: The early establishment of public order through the rule of law is critical to ORHA's effective execution of its civil administration tasks.
DISCUSSION: Several issues require decisions:

    1. Need to determine the legal code that will be employed by the coalition.

    2. Law enforcement personnel requirements must be resourced by the U.S.

    3. Funding must be secured ($30M for 1st 3 months; $93M for next 9 months)

    4. Premature to determine U.S. law enforcement footprint.

RECOMMENDATION: Develop these issues and present to the PC for decision.

Use & Reorganization of the Iraqi Army

BACKGROUND: The Iraqi military, principally the Army, must be reorganized and retrained. Selected portions of the military will be demobilized and abolished.
DISCUSSION:

    1. Necessary to keep Iraqi Army intact for a specified period of time.

    2. Serves as a ready resource pool for labor intensive civil works projects.

3. Provides a command & control structure and available mobility assets that can be used in Phase IV (under U.S. supervision).

RECOMMENDATION: Contract out this functional mission area as soon as possible.

Vetting Process & Coordination

- BACKGROUND:
  - Every functional area will require the use of indigenous Iraqis.
  - Coalition must weed out "bad" Iraqis.
- DISCUSSION:
  - Vetting process is lengthy and bureaucratic.
  - Refugee/IDP camps will register all Iraqi personnel.
  - Use of NGO/IO-built rosters for vetting purposes is not a certainty.
- RECOMMENDATION:
  - ORHA be granted control of vetting process and be resourced to do so.
  - State coordinate with NGOs/IOs to use their rosters.

Achieving the Use of Service from Neighboring States

(TURKEY, IRAN, SYRIA, JORDAN, KUWAIT, SAUDI ARABIA)

- BACKGROUND: The reconstruction of Iraq is costly and time consuming. Estimates to be over 3 billion dollars and 3 years to complete.
- DISCUSSION: There is significant potential that gaps will exist in requirements (use) of services (water, power, medical, and economic) and our ability to provide. It is important there not be a gap as it will be interpreted by the international community as a failure by the USG. Iraq's neighbors are capable of providing a level of interim service to bridge this gap and mitigate costs and time by the USG.
- RECOMMENDATION: Engage Turkey, Jordan, Syria, Iran, Saudi Arabia, and Kuwait to develop policy and plans for use of available water, power, medical and other goods and services.

23. Interviews, participants of the meeting.
24. Interview, Qubad Talabani, Washington representative of the Patriotic Union of Kurdistan and Jalal Talabani's son.
25. Interview, David Kay.
26. Interview, Robert Perito. Perito's memo is excerpted below:

> The US-military administration will be responsible for security, public order, and law enforcement. In meeting this responsibility, the US will not be able to rely on the local authorities. Saddam's security services must be disbanded. Prior experience indicates the regular Iraqi police will be unavailable, intimidated or unprepared to act in the chaotic postwar environment. . . . Given the political and practical realities, it's doubtful the US will be able to turn to the EU, NATO and OSCE, which provided police and legal experts in Bosnia and Kosovo. . . . Relying on Coalition military forces is not the answer. Experience in the Balkans demonstrated that regular soldiers are neither trained nor equipped to deal with mob violence or engage in law enforcement. . . . To ensure a stable postconflict environment in Iraq, the US should create a civilian US "Stability

Force." Such force should include civilian constabulary, police and teams of judicial and corrections experts to establish the rule of law. This force could work with Coalition military forces that will remain to ensure a safe and secure environment. . . .

For Iraq, a US civilian Stability Force would have the following components:
- CONSTABULARY: A force of 20 companies with appropriate headquarters and administrative staff for a total of 2,500 personnel. Primary deployment would be in Baghdad, with contingents in four regional centers (Mosul and Kirkuk in the North and Basra and Kut in the South). These forces would have access to a helicopter airlift to ensure maximum mobility.
- CIVIL POLICE: A force of 4,000 US civil police with its headquarters in Baghdad and contingents co-located in the regional and provincial headquarters of the Iraqi National Police. These officers would require wheeled transport, light weapons and effective communications to ensure coordination with constabulary and military backups.
- JUDICIAL TEAMS: There should be ten teams of twenty lawyers, judges, court administrators and corrections officers supported by a headquarters staff, paralegals, translators and a training unit for a total of 300 personnel. They would be deployed to major population centers where they would work directly with local judicial authorities.

. . . The fact that we may be within weeks of a decision by the President to intervene in Iraq should not deter us. Experience in the Balkans, East Timor and Afghanistan shows that Coalition forces will have to deal with high levels of violence for the first two years of the mission.

27. Interview, David Kay; "Future of Iraq Study," in possession of the authors.
28. Interview, Colonel Paul Hughes.
29. Presentation to the NSC on March 10 and March 12, reviewed by the authors; Interviews, senior NSC and DOD officials.
30. Joseph Collins memo, 7 March 2003.

CHAPTER 9: *Dora Farms*

1. Interviews, senior allied officials who participated in the meeting.
2. "Comprehensive Report," vol. 1, p. 66.
3. Interview, Chief Warrant Officer Henry Crowder.
4. Interview, Pentagon official.
5. Interviews, CFLCC officials.
6. Interviews, CENTCOM and military officials.
7. Interview, U.S. Air Force officer.
8. Informal transcript of Richard Perle's briefing by a participant.
9. Interview, Colonel Mace Carpenter.
10. Interviews, Air Force officials.
11. Interviews, Colonel Matthew McKeon, Major Steven Ankerstar.

12. Eric Schmitt, "Back from Iraq, High-Tech Fighter Pilots Recount Exploits," *New York Times,* 25 April 2003, Section A, p. 12.
13. Interviews, Navy officials.
14. Interviews, Colonel Matthew McKeon, Major Steven Ankerstar.
15. President George W. Bush, "President Bush Addresses the Nation," 19 March 2003, available from http://www.whitehouse.gov/news/releases/2003/03/200303 19-17.html.
16. "Iraqi Perspectives," p. 55.
17. Interview, Pentagon official.
18. Interview, Brigadier General Howard Bromberg. Also 32nd AAMDC Operation Iraqi Freedom briefing, available from http://www.globalsecurity.org/military/library/report/2003/32aamdc_oif-patriot_sep03.ppt

CHAPTER 10: *The Opening Gambit*

1. Major General James Mattis, e-mail to the authors. Also see 1st Marine Division draft history for other details.
2. Internal report acquired by the authors.
3. Interview, Lieutenant General James Conway.
4. Interview, Major General James Mattis.
5. Interview, Captain David Banning. Also see Captain David Banning, Marine Corps interview by Major Carol Harris, 1 June 2003.
6. Interview, Lieutenant Colonel Jerome Driscoll, Marine Corps oral history interview, date unknown.
7. Interview, Lieutenant Colonel Fred Padilla.
8. Ibid.; Hampton Sides, "The First to Die," *Men's Journal,* vol. 12, no. 11, December 2003.
9. Interview, Lieutenant Colonel Chris Conlin.
10. Interviews, CFLCC officials.
11. Interview, Lieutenant Colonel Jerome Driscoll. Also see Lieutenant Colonel James R. Braden, Marine Corps oral history interview by Lieutenant Colonel Michael D. Visconage, 24 April 2003.
12. Tapes of meetings of Marine commanders made available to the authors. See video conference meeting of USMC commanders, 21 March 2003.
13. Major Craig Wonson, e-mail to the author.

CHAPTER 11: *Objective Liberty*

1. Interviews, aides to Major General Buford Blount.
2. Remarks by Captain Douglas Phillipone and 3rd Infantry Division staff ride attended by Michael Gordon.
3. During a normal year a tank battalion puts 800 miles on its M1s. During the first six months in Kuwait, 2-69 Armor, part of Allyn's brigade, put 1,660 miles on its tanks. It also used three times its normal expenditure of ammunition.
4. Interview, Colonel Daniel Allyn.

5. Interview, Lieutenant Colonel Jeffery R. "J. R." Sanderson.

6. Interview, Colonel Daniel Allyn. Also Special Forces after-action report in possession of the authors.

7. 6-6 Battalion after-action report.

8. Interview, Colonel Thomas Torrance.

9. Interview, Lieutenant Colonel John D. Harding conducted by Michael Gordon during 3rd ID staff ride to Tallil.

10. Interviews, Colonel Curtis Potts, Major James Desjardin, and Sergeant First Class Juan Rodriguez; 1st Lieutenant William Adams, Army oral history interview by Sergeant Daniel Goerke, 24 April 2003; Staff Sergeant John Thompson, Army oral history interview by Sergeant Daniel Goerke, 25 April 2003.

11. Interview, Major James Desjardin.

12. Interview, James Roche.

13. Interview, Captain Michael Downs.

14. Notes of a military aide.

15. Interviews, Colonel Matthew McKeon, Major Steven Ankerstar.

CHAPTER 12: *Everyone Loves a Parade*

1. Interview, Lieutenant Colonel Terry Ferrell.

2. Interviews, soldiers of the 3-7 Cavalry Squadron. See also Colonel (Ret.) Gregory Fontenot, Lieutenant Colonel E. J. Degen, and Lieutenant Colonel David Tohn, *On Point: The United States Army in Operation Iraqi Freedom* (Fort Leavenworth: Combat Studies Institute Press, 2004), pp. 126–27.

3. Interviews, Staff Sergeant Dillard J. Johnson and Sergeant First Class Anthony Broadhead.

4. Ibid.

5. Fontenot, Degen, and Tohn, *On Point*, pp. 130–31.

6. Interview, Lieutenant Colonel Terry Ferrell.

7. Interviews, Lieutenant Colonel Terry Ferrell, Staff Sergeant Dillard J. Johnson, Sergeant First Class Anthony Broadhead, and Captain Jeff McCoy.

8. First Lieutenant Stephen C. Gleason, Army oral history interview by Major Norman Childs, 28 May 2003; Lieutenant Colonel Scott Rutter, Army oral history interview by Major Norman Childs, 28 May 2003; Captain James Lee, Army oral history interview by Staff Sergeant Aaron McLeod, 28 May 2003.

9. Interview, Lieutenant Colonel Terry Ferrell.

10. Interview, Colonel Daniel Allyn.

11. Interviews, Captain Clay Lyle, Lieutenant Colonel Terry Ferrell, and Sergeant First Class Paul Wheatley.

12. Interview, Colonel Terry Ferrell.

13. Ibid.

14. Ibid.

CHAPTER 13: *Task Force Tarawa*

1. Task Force Tarawa intelligence summary, S//MCFI 24–72 Hour Assessment:

> The 11th ID will remain in survivability positions to garrison locations and is expected to fracture once U.S. forces draw closer to An Nasiriyah. The 45th and 47th will most likely remain in their current locations in the marshes east of An Nasiriyah, which will enhance their survivability. The 45th and 47th will most likely capitulate once U.S. forces prosecute ground operations into Iraq. Iraqi intelligence, security, and paramilitary units attempt to set up defenses in An Nasiriyah in order to delay U.S. movement and to discourage civil uprisings. However, this is expected to be short lived due to HUMINT reporting and FIF debriefs, which strongly suggest that paramilitary groups closely allied with the regime will ultimately break and run for fear of retribution from the local populace.

2. Interview, Lieutenant Colonel Joseph Apodaca.
3. Interview, Colonel Ronald Bailey; Colonel Ronald Bailey, Marine Corps oral history interview by Colonel Reed Bonnadonna, 8 May 2003.
4. Interview, Major Andrew Kennedy, Marine Corps oral history interview by Colonel Reed Bonnadonna, 7 May 2003.
5. Interview, Lieutenant Colonel James Reilly.
6. Interview, Colonel Ronald Bailey; also Colonel Ronald Bailey, Marine Corps oral history interview, 8 May 2003.
7. Copy of I MEF Frago 017-03 in possession of the authors.
8. Interview, Colonel Ronald Bailey; Major Andrew Kennedy, Marine Corps oral history interview, 7 May 2003.
9. Interview, Lieutenant Colonel Rick Grabowski.
10. Interviews, Major William Peeples; Major William Peeples, Marine Corps oral history interview by Colonel Reed Bonnadonna, 1 May 2003.
11. "Attack on the 507th Maintenance Company, 23 March 2003, An Nasiriyah, Iraq," after-action report of the 507th, U.S. Army.
12. Major William Peeples, Marine Corps oral history interview, 1 May 2003.
13. E-mail from Lieutenant Colonel Andrew Kennedy, in possession of the authors.
14. Major William Peeples, Marine Corps oral history interview, 1 May 2003.
15. Interviews, Colonel Ronald Bailey, Lieutenant Colonel Eddie Ray, and Lieutenant Colonel Rick Grabowski.
16. Lieutenant Colonel Rick Grabowski, Marine Corps oral history interview by Colonel Reed Bonnadonna, 6 April 2003. Of eight vehicles mired in the sludge three had to be stripped of sensitive materials, their radios zeroed, and abandoned. The following day the Marines returned to retrieve them and found that during the night the Iraqis had looted them. In the words of one Marine, "You couldn't have a cleaner strip job in New York. These people definitely knew how to take stuff apart. They took every wire, radio, every instrumentation out of the panels . . . the Humvees . . . we couldn't get them out of the mud. Somehow they were able to jack those vehicles up, get the tires off them, and put them back down in the mud. These people just stripped *everything*. Engines, everything."

17. Interview, Captain Michael Brooks.
18. Later, trail marks of the Iraqi artillery indicated that the guns were oriented westward in the direction of the bridge connecting Highway 7 to the center of Nasiriyah. They were apparently hastily redirected toward C Company, further indication that the Iraqis expected the American attack to come through the middle of the city.
19. Interview, Captain Daniel Wittnam, Marine Corps oral history interview by Colonel Reed Bonnadonna, 1 May 2003.
20. Ibid.
21. Interview, Captain Eric Garcia; Lieutenant Colonel Rick Grabowski, Marine Corps oral history interview, 6 April 2003; Captain Michael Brooks, Marine Corps oral history interview by Colonel Reed Bonnadonna.
22. Under the Marine Corps Table of Organization only two of the three rifle companies had forward air controllers (FACs). C Company did not have one.
23. FACs employ three different types of close air support (CAS) control. Type 1 requires the controller to visually acquire the attacking aircraft and the target under attack. Type 2 control occurs when either visual acquisition of the attacking aircraft or the target at weapons release is not possible or when attacking aircraft are not in a position to acquire the target prior to weapons release. FACs were authorized to employ the first two types of CAS with approval of the Fire Support Coordination Center (FSCC). Type 3 is used when the attack imposes a low risk of fratricide. Authorization rests only with a commander, who, if he sees fit, can grant a blanket weapons release clearance. Prior to crossing into Iraq, Lieutenant Colonel Grabowski specifically reminded his FACs that only he could authorize Type 3 CAS.
24. USCENTAF Friendly Fire Investigation Board, "A-10 Marine Friendly Fire Incident," 6 March 2004.
25. Ibid.
26. Interview, Major William Peeples.
27. Captain Timothy Dremann, Marine Corps oral history interview by Colonel Reed Bonnadonna, 22 April 2003.
28. Interview, Lieutenant Colonel Rick Grabowski.
29. Interviews, Major General James Mattis, Brigadier General John Kelly, and Lieutenant Colonel Lewis Craparotta.
30. Interview, Task Force Tarawa officer.
31. Interview, Task Force Tarawa official.

CHAPTER 14: *Vampire 12*

1. Interview, Brigadier General James "Spider" Marks.
2. Video conference transcript, notes of a participant.
3. The regiment had two different types of Apaches: 1-227 and 6-6 had AH-64Ds, which could fire the Longbow, while 2-6 had the older AH-64A, which was not capable of firing the Longbow.
4. Notes taken from Major Michael Gabel's diary.
5. Interview, Lieutenant Colonel Daniel Ball. Also see Sig Christenson, "Flight

into Ambush," a three-part series in the *San Antonio Express News,* 21–23 March 2004, for a detailed and informative account, available from http://www .mysanantonio.com/news/military/stories/MYSA21.01A.Longbow_1_0321.7d2 4b3c.html. Also Fontenot, Degen, and Tohn, *On Point,* pp. 179–92; and "Battle Summary, 6th Squadron, 6th Cavalry Operation Iraqi Freedom" and "Battle Summary of Attack Conducted Against the Iraqi Republican Guard, 2d Ar Bde, Medina Divisions," 1-227 Attack Helicopter Battalion.

6. Captain Karen Hobart, Operation Iraqi Freedom Study Group interview by Major David Tohn, 8 May 2003.
7. Wallace knew nothing of the timing of the ATACMS firing.
8. Interview, Chief Warrant Officer 5 Lance McElhiney.
9. The regiment was assigned to go to Tactical Assembly Area Vicksburg, which was inside Objective Rams.
10. Interview, Captain Andy Hilmes; 3rd ID staff ride attended by MRG, Najaf.
11. Interview, Lieutenant Colonel Eric Schwartz; 3rd ID staff ride attended by MRG, Objective Rams.
12. Interview, Colonel David Perkins; notes from 3rd ID staff ride attended by MRG, Objective Rams.
13. Captain Andrew Caine, "Task Force 3-5: The Odyssey to Fuel the Deep Fight."
14. Lieutenant Colonel Michael J. Barbee, Operation Iraqi Freedom Study Group interview by Major Jonathan Gass; Colonel William Wolf, Operation Iraqi Freedom Study Group interview by Colonel (Ret.) Gregory Fontenot, 13 November 2003.
15. Interview, 1st Lieutenant Jason King; Chief Warrant Officer 2 John Tomblin, Operation Iraqi Freedom Study Group interview by Major Jonathan Gass, 16 May 2003.
16. Interview, Chief Warrant Officer 5 Lance McElhiney.
17. Interviews, Chief Warrant Officer 2 Joe Goode and Chief Warrant Officer 2 Cynthia Rosel.
18. Interview, Lieutenant Colonel Daniel Ball.
19. Interview, Chief Warrant Officer 2 Dave Williams.
20. Ibid.
21. Diary entry of Major John Lindsay reviewed by the authors; Interview, Captain Karen Hobart.
22. Interview, Colonel William Wolf, Operation Iraqi Freedom Study Group interview, 13 November 2003.
23. "Power Grid and ADA Ground Fire," follow-up report to 6-6 Cavalry Medina Mission. Also "Iraqi Perspectives," p. 51.
24. "AAR Comments from TF 11 AVN FSO/FSE," document in possession of the authors.

CHAPTER 15: *A Sanctuary for the Fedayeen*

1. Interview, Colonel Will Grimsley.
2. Interview, Lieutenant Colonel Ernest "Rock" Marcone.
3. Interview, 2nd Lieutenant John Rowold.

4. Interviews, Major Mike Oliver and 2nd Lieutenant John Rowland.
5. The bridging assets were for crossing at Objective Peach and were arrayed accordingly in the division's linear formation.
6. Interviews, Captain Dan Hibner and Lieutenant Colonel Ernest "Rock" Marcone; Captain Dan Hibner, Operation Iraqi Freedom Study Group interview by Lieutenant Colonel James Knowlton, 15 May 2003.

   Captain Hibner noted that the Iraqis crossed their detonation wires, which meant when one cord exploded, it rendered the second harmless, thus defeating the mechanism that would have destroyed the other side of the bridge.
7. Interview, Captain Dave Benton; 3rd ID staff ride attended by MRG.
8. Interview, soldier who participated in the action.
9. Interview, 1st Lieutenant Brad Castro; 3rd ID staff ride attended by MRG.
10. Interviews, Colonel Terry Ferrell and Lieutenant Colonel J. R. Sanderson.
11. Interview, Lieutenant Colonel Terry Ferrell.
12. Interview, Captain Jeff McCoy; 3rd ID staff ride attended by MRG.
13. Interview, First Sergeant Roy Griggs; 3rd ID staff ride attended by MRG.
14. Interviews, Lieutenant Colonel Terry Ferrell and Captain Jeff McCoy.
15. Interviews, Lieutenant Colonel J. R. Sanderson and Colonel Will Grimsley.
16. Interview, Lieutenant Colonel Herman "Stacy" Clardy.
17. Interview, Major General James Mattis.
18. Interview, Lieutenant Colonel Herman "Stacy" Clardy. Two weeks passed before Clardy's men admitted a call for Slingshot had been issued and subsequently aborted.
19. 1st Marine Division draft history.
20. Interview, Lieutenant Colonel Duffy White.
21. First Lieutenant Brian Chontosh, Marine Corps oral history interview by Lieutenant Colonel Nicholas Reynolds, 4 May 2003.
22. Interview, Lieutenant Colonel Sam Mundy.
23. Interview, Lieutenant Colonel Duffy White.
24. Ibid.; Lieutenant Colonel Sam Mundy e-mail to the authors. Also 1st Marine Division draft history.

CHAPTER 16: *Back to the Drawing Board*

1. Notes of a participant. Major General James D. "J. D." Thurman, Army oral history interview by Lieutenant Colonel Steven Holcomb, 27 May 2003; Interview, Lieutenant General William Scott Wallace; Major General Buford Blount, Army oral history interview by Major Norman Childs, 24 May 2003; Interview, Major General James Mattis. The commanders, Major General Blount and Major General Mattis, were of like mind. Slowing down or pausing would mean loss of momentum and make their divisions vulnerable to chemical attack.
2. Informal transcript of conversation between General Tommy Franks and Admiral Edmund Giambastiani on lessons learned from OIF, 14 May 2003; Interview, senior administration official.

3. Major General J. D. Thurman, Army oral history interview, 27 May 2003.
4. The following morning, General Conway relayed to his commanders the results of the meeting and estimated it would take another thirty days of air strikes before Iraqi forces could be reduced to 50 percent. Video conference transcripts.
5. Interview, Major General Charles Swannack; Lieutenant General William S. Wallace, Operation Iraqi Freedom Study Group interview by Lieutenant Colonel (Ret.) Gregory Fontenot, Lieutenant Colonel E. J. Degen, and Major David Tohn, 7 August 2003. Also Fontenot, Degen, and Tohn, *On Point,* p. 211.
6. Notes of a participant; Fontenot, Degen, and Tohn, *On Point,* p. 245.
7. Notes of a participant. Also see Jim Dwyer, "A Gulf Commander Sees a Longer Road," *New York Times,* 28 March 2003, Section A, p. 1; Rick Atkinson, "General: A War Likely; Logistics, Enemy Force Reevaluation," *Washington Post,* 27 March 2003, Section A, p. 1.
8. Notes of a participant.
9. Interview, senior military officials.
10. Notes of a participant.

   "Phone call with Dave Halversen—CC still unhappy with our temp; feel like we have lost contact with the enemy. 101 Deep Attack last night with moderate BDA [bomb damage assessment] confirms CINC suspicion that we do not know where enemy is."
11. Notebooks, Brigadier General James A. "Spider" Marks.
12. Interview, Colonel Ted Seel.
13. Interviews, senior officials.
14. Ibid.
15. Interview, Major General James D. "J. D." Thurman.
16. Donald Rumsfeld, DOD news briefing, 1 April 2003; available from http://www.defenselink.mil/transcripts/2003/t04012003_t0401sd.html.
17. Donald Rumsfeld, remarks on ABC's *This Week with George Stephanopoulos,* 30 March 2003, available from http://www.defenselink.mil/transcripts/2003/t03302003_t0330sdabcsteph.html.
18. In his March 25 memo, Macgregor wrote:

   The advance must continue without pause. There is no reason to stop. The force in place is massive, and so far has taken almost no casualties. True, there may be some supply problems, but hardening the supply convoys and implementing a C-130 airlift will solve that problem. Holding one's nerve is fundamental. Tikrit should be flattened. The RG [Republican Guard] should be destroyed. Urban resistance should be eradicated with armor and precision bombing. . . . Saddam, who is already winning the media battle, would win a huge psychological victory even if he hangs from a lamppost in a few weeks time. He will be seen as the Arab leader who is able to fight the United States to a stand-still. . . . Stopping will damage the morale of the average American soldier out there more than just about anything else. The soldiers are out there to win, and they will win if allowed to but they need momentum on their side. Stopping will be a betrayal. Stopping will send entirely the wrong message to the Kurds and the Shiites and the many Iraqis who hate Saddam. Stopping will be a signal that the United States absolutely cannot be trusted. Stopping will encourage the Turks to play games. Stopping will give more time for the Russians and the Iranians to interfere. Stopping will allow the French, the Germans, and world public opinion to have a field day at this country's expense to the point where a combination of world opinion and the United Nations may be able to prevent us from re-taking the offensive. Stopping will open the door to destructive partisan politics. Public support could well evaporate.

19. Interview, Major General Buford Blount. Also see Lieutenant General William S. Wallace, Operation Iraqi Freedom Study Group interview by Lieutenant Colonel (Ret.) Gregory Fontenot, Lieutenant Colonel E. J. Degen, and Major David Tohn, 7 August 2003; Colonel David Perkins, Army oral history interview by Major Norman Childs, 25 May 2003. Also, interview, Lieutenant Colonel Philip "Flip" DeCamp: "Our job was initially to seize the bridge, attack across the bridge and put almost two tank companies on the other side of the bridge."

20. Fontenot, Degen, and Tohn, *On Point,* pp. 245, 258.

21. Interviews, Colonel David Perkins, Captain Christopher Carter, and Lieutenant Colonel Philip "Flip" DeCamp.

22. Chris Tomlinson, "Battling for a Bridge and a Town, U.S. Troops Risk Their Lives to Rescue an Elderly Woman," Associated Press newswires, 31 March 2003; Interviews, Captain Christopher Carter and Sergeant Luis Javier Sanchez.

23. As American forces withdrew, Iraqi civilians poured into the streets, onto the Hindiyah bridge, and toward an arms cache collection point that had been wired for demolition. If one inattentive U.S. soldier had not prematurely detonated the captured Iraqi weapons, the subsequent explosion may have severely injured hundreds of civilian spectators.

24. Major General James Mattis, Marine Corps oral history interview by Dr. Gary Solis, 24 January 2004. On the final day of the pause, Iraqi tanks and school buses filled with infantry soldiers rushed to prevent the Marine advance, having apparently deduced the American path to Baghdad.

25. Notes of March 26–27 VTCs.

26. Interview with Moseley aides.

27. Air war briefing attended by authors.

28. Colonel Mace Carpenter. "Deliberate, Disciplined, Proportional and Precise: The Operation Iraqi Freedom Air and Space Strategy; Initial Assessment," draft copy, pp. 19–20. Interview, Major General James Amos.

29. E-mail to the authors from Brigadier General Kurt Chicowski and interviews with Colonel Mace Carpenter and Major General T. Michael "Buzz" Moseley.

30. Interview, Colonel Matt McKeon.

31. Notes of a Moseley aide and interview with Colonel Mace Carpenter.

32. Notes of March 27 VTC.

33. Interview, Major General James D. "J. D." Thurman; notes of a participant, 27 March video conference.

34. Interview, military official.

CHAPTER 17: *Team Tank*

1. Interview, military officer.
2. Ibid.
3. Ibid.
4. Ibid., Robert W. Jones, "Team Tank: Armor in Support of Special Operations," *Veritas: Journal of Army Special Forces History,* Winter 2005, pp. 69–73.
5. James Schroder, "The Rangers Take Hadithah Dam," *Veritas: Journal of Army Special Forces History,* Winter 2005, pp. 55–60. Also Michael R. Mullins and Cherilyn A. Walley, "Holding Back the Flood at Hadithah Dam," *Veritas: Journal of Army Special Forces History,* Winter 2005, pp. 65–68.
6. Interview, military officer.
7. While the Turkish parliament debated U.S. entry, prominent Kurdish leaders told Khalilzad they planned on attacking Turkish troops who entered northern Iraq.
8. Interview, Major General Henry "Pete" Osman.
9. Ibid.
10. Lieutenant Colonel Robert Waltemeyer, Operation Iraqi Freedom Study Group interview by Lieutenant Colonel Rob Walsh, date unknown.
11. Interview, Major General Henry "Pete" Osman.
12. Interview, General James Jones.
13. Fontenot, Degen, and Tohn, *On Point,* pp. 222–29.
14. Interview, Major General Henry "Pete" Osman.

    General Abizaid had suggested to Osman that inflating the importance of the 173rd would help to mislead and fix Saddam's defenses in the north. Osman's terse presentation from Salahuddin did receive significant press coverage. However, it could not have allayed Kurdish fears of a Turkish intervention. The meeting opened with a statement by Colonel Keith Lawless indicating the MCLC (Military Coordination and Liaison Command) would coordinate among "all the various factions in the north, including the Turks, if in fact Turkish forces cross."
15. Interviews, Major General Henry "Pete" Osman, administration official; Fontenot, Degen, and Tohn, *On Point,* p. 230; Kenn Finlayson, "Operation Viking Hammer: 3/10 SFG Against the Ansar Al-Islam," *Veritas: Journal of Army Special Forces History,* Winter 2005, pp. 15–18.
16. Interview, Major General Henry "Pete" Osman. Also see Kenn Finlayson, "This Is What You Signed Up For: The Attack on Ayn Sifni," *Veritas: Journal of Army Special Forces History,* Winter 2005, pp. 75–78.
17. Nathan S. Lowrey, "The Battle for Debecka Crossroads," *Veritas: Journal of Army Special Forces History,* Winter 2005, pp. 79–85. Also Harvey Morris, "Eighteen Kurdish Soldiers Killed, Many Injured in US 'Friendly Fire,' " *Financial Times,* 7 April 2003, p. 3.
18. Interview, U.S. State Department official.
19. Interview, Rear Admiral John Stufflebeam.
20. Interview, General James Jones.

CHAPTER 18: *The Red Zone*

1. "Iraqi Perspectives," pp. 25, 52.
2. Lieutenant Colonel Ernest "Rock" Marcone, Army oral history interview by Major Norman Childs, 30 May 2003. Also Lieutenant Colonel Rock Marcone, Army oral history interview by Colonel (Ret.) Gregory Fontenot and Lieutenant Colonel E. J. Degen, 22 October 2003.
3. Interviews, Colonel William Grimsley, Lieutenant Colonel Ernest "Rock" Marcone, Captain Dan Hibner, Sergeant Jay Bliss, First Lieutenant Ramon Brigantti, First Lieutenant Kevin Caesar, and Sergeant Robert Stevens.
4. Ibid.; Lieutenant Colonel Ernest "Rock" Marcone, Army oral history interviews, 30 May 2003, and 22 October 2003.
5. CENTCOM Patriot investigation report.
6. Interviews, Colonel Dave Perkins, Major General Buford Blount. Also Colonel William Grimsley, Army oral history interview by Lieutenant David R. Manning, May 2003.
7. Interview, Lieutenant Colonel Ernest "Rock" Marcone, 30 May 2003.
8. "Iraqi Perspectives," p. 44.
9. Captain Matthew Paul, Army oral history interview by Lieutenant Colonel (Ret.) Arthur A. Durante, 15 May 2003; Captain Matthew Paul, Army oral history interview by Sergeant Troy Hester, 28 May 2003.
10. First Lieutenant Mark Schenck, "2-7 Infantry unit history."
11. Sergeant First Class Paul R. Smith citation.
12. Interview, Colonel Dave Perkins.
13. Lieutenant General Raad al-Hamdani, *Frontline* interview, available from http://www.pbs.org/wgbh/pages/frontline/shows/invasion/interviews/raad.html
14. Interview, Lieutenant Colonel Duffy White.
15. Major General James Amos, Marine Corps oral history interview by Colonel Charles J. Quilter and Lieutenant Colonel Michael Visconage, 16 May 2003.
16. Interviews, Major General James Amos and Major Craig R. Wonson. Also see Lieutenant Colonel Michael Oehl, "2nd Tank Battalion Unit Chronology."
17. "Comprehensive Report," vol. 3, p. 110. Many Iraqi generals and high-level defense officials also believed that Saddam had some sort of plan to use chemical weapons despite his statements that he had no WMD. In a compartmentalized military, many officers accepted that there were secret plans of which they would have no knowledge and of which some other unit would have the task.
18. Interviews, Lieutenant Colonel Steven Ferrando and Lieutenant Colonel Lew Craparotta.
19. An Air Force A-10 mistakenly attacked the Marines' command group at the intersection due to erroneous coordinates. The attack was called off before it inflicted casualties.
20. Interview, Lieutenant Colonel Lew Craparotta.
21. Interview, Colonel Joseph Dowdy.
22. Interview, Major General James Mattis.
23. Interviews, Colonel Joseph Dowdy, General James Mattis, and Brigadier General John Kelly.

24. "Iraqi Perspectives," p. 52.

25. Interviews, senior CFLCC and Marine officials.

26. Lieutenant Colonel Carl E. "Sam" Mundy, Marine Corps oral history interview by Lieutenant Colonel Michael Visconage, 4 May 2003; First Lieutenant Brian Chontosh, Marine Corps oral history interview, 4 May 2003; Interview, Lieutenant Colonel Duffy White.

27. Lieutenant Colonel Carl E. "Sam" Mundy, Marine Corps oral history interview, 4 May 2003; First Lieutenant Brian Chontosh, Marine Corps oral history interview, 4 May 2003; Colonel Joseph F. Dunford, Marine Corps oral history interview by Lieutenant Colonel Nicholas Reynolds, 2 May 2003. Also see Oehl, "2nd Tank Battalion Unit Chronology."

CHAPTER 19: *The Thunder Run*

1. Interviews, Colonel J. D. Johnson, Lieutenant General William S. Wallace, and Major General Buford Blount.

2. Michael R. Gordon, "Baghdad Targets Picked if Hussein Holes Up There," *New York Times,* 7 March 2003, Section A, p. 11.

3. Major General Buford Blount, Army oral history interview by Major Norman Childs, 24 May 2003.

4. Interview, Lieutenant Colonel Eric Schwartz.

5. Sergeant First Class Eric R. Olson, "Operation Iraqi Freedom Journal."

6. Interview, Sergeant Jason Diaz; 3rd ID staff ride attended by Michael Gordon.

7. Interview, Colonel Dave Perkins.

8. Olson, "Operation Iraqi Freedom Journal," p. 42. Also see Steven Lee Myers, "U.S. Tanks Make Quick Strike into Baghdad," *New York Times,* 6 April 2003, Section A, p. 1.

9. Interview, First Lieutenant Roger Gruneisen; 3rd ID staff ride attended by Michael Gordon.

10. Staff Sergeant Jeffery Empson, Operation Iraqi Freedom Study Group interview; Interview by Lieutenant Colonel David Manning, 19 May 2003.

11. Interviews, Captain Jason Conroy and Captain Michael Dyches; 3rd ID staff ride attended by Michael Gordon.

12. Interview, Colonel Dave Perkins.

13. 3rd ID staff ride attended by Michael Gordon.

14. 1-64 Armor officers, Operation Iraqi Freedom Study Group interviews by Lieutenant Colonel David Manning, 18 May 2003. Also see Ron Martz, "I Owe These Heroes My Life," *Atlanta Journal-Constitution,* 6 April 2003, p. A1.

15. Interview, Captain Erik Berdy.

16. Olson, "Operation Iraqi Freedom Journal," p. 47. Also 3rd ID staff ride attended by Michael Gordon.

   For additional information on the Thunder Run, see David Zucchino, *Thunder Run* (New York: Atlantic Monthly Press, 2004).

CHAPTER 20: *The Accidental Victory*

1. "Iraqi Perspectives," p. 83. This site (33 17′29″N, 44 21′16″E) also served as an alternate Republican Guard command post for Qusay Hussein. During Saddam's visit, he commanded those present to begin coordinating Fedayeen and Republican Guard forces in urban operations against Americans.
2. Interview, Colonel Dave Perkins.
3. 3rd ID staff ride attended by Michael Gordon.
4. Interview, Colonel Dave Perkins. Also Perkins, Army oral history interview by Major Norman Childs, 25 May 2003; 3rd ID staff ride attended by Michael Gordon.
5. Interview, Colonel Dave Perkins.
6. Interview, Lieutenant General William S. Wallace. Also see Lieutenant General William S. Wallace, Operation Iraqi Freedom Study Group interview by Colonel (Ret.) Gregory Fontenot, Lieutenant Colonel E. J. Degen, and Major David Tohn, 7 August 2003.
7. Interview, Major General Buford Blount.
8. Interview, Colonel Dave Perkins.
9. 3rd ID staff ride attended by Michael Gordon.
10. Captain Felix Almaguer, Operation Iraqi Freedom Study Group interview by Major Daniel Corey, 19 May 2003. Some captured foreign fighters had both Saddam Fedayeen and Hezbollah tattoos.
11. Fontenot, Degen, Tohn, *On Point,* p. 352.
12. Lieutenant Colonel Peter Bayer, Army oral history interview by Major Norman Childs, 25 May 2003.
13. Interview, Colonel Dave Perkins; Perkins, Army oral history interview, 25 May 2003; Interview, Lieutenant General William S. Wallace.
14. Interviews, General J. D. Thurman, Major General Buford Blount, and Lieutenant General William S. Wallace.
15. Interview, Lieutenant Colonel Stephan Twitty; Command Sergeant Major Robert Gallagher, Operation Iraqi Freedom Study Group interview by Arthur Durante, 19 May 2003.
    "The Objectives were originally called Golf 231, Golf 232, and Golf 233. We changed the names . . . to add some humor into it," remarked Twitty.
16. Intelligence provided by Special Forces and extrapolated from the April 5 Thunder Run led Captain Felix Almaguer, the task force intelligence officer, to predict that each of the three objectives would be defended by 150 to 200 dismounted infantry. Interviews, Colonel Stephan Twitty and Captain Zan Hornbuckle.
17. Interview, Sergeant Major Robert Gallagher; Gallagher, Army oral history interview, 19 May 2003; Interview, Captain Zan Hornbuckle.
18. "Regime Isolation," 2 BCT history, pp. 23–25; Interviews, Captain Zan Hornbuckle and Sergeant Major Robert Gallagher; Gallagher, Army oral history interview, 19 May 2003.
19. Captain William Glaser, Operation Iraqi Freedom Study Group interview by Major Peter Kilner, 18 May 2003.

20. Interviews, Colonel Dave Perkins and Captain William Glaser; Glaser, Operation Iraqi Freedom Study Group interview, 18 May 2003.
21. Interview, Lieutenant General William S. Wallace.
22. Captain J. O. Bailey, Army oral history interview by Sergeant Troy Hester, 20 May 2003; First Lieutenant Aaron Polsgrove, Infantry School manuscript, pp. 7–8.
23. Polsgrove, Infantry School manuscript, pp. 8–10; Interviews, Major Everett Denton Knapp and Captain Steve Hommel.
24. Interview, Captain Steve Hommel.
25. 3rd ID staff ride attended by Michael Gordon.
26. Interview, Captain Erik Berdy.
27. Some of the foreign fighters had been paid to fight Americans. "They had the money on them," said Task Force 3-15's executive officer Major Everett Denton Knapp. "Syrians captured at Objective Curley indicated they had been paid thirty days before U.S. troops arrived in Baghdad."
28. Captain Felix Almaguer, Army oral history interview, 19 May 2003.
29. "Iraqi Perspectives," p. 17.

CHAPTER 21: *The Second Battle for Baghdad*

1. Draft 1st Marine Division official history, Chapter 6, p. 30.
2. Interview, Lieutenant Colonel Niel E. "Rick" Nelson.
3. Interview, Lieutenant Colonel Duffy White.
4. Interview, Lieutenant Colonel Niel E. "Rick" Nelson.
5. Draft 1st Marine Division official history.
6. Corporal Jeremiah J. Day, Marine Corps oral history interview by Lieutenant Colonel Michael Visconage, 12 June 2003.
7. The Army Canal, which ran northeast from the Diyala to Highway 2, became the boundary between RCT-1 and RCT-7.
8. Draft 1st Marine Division official history, Chapter 6, p. 44.
9. Captain Phillip Wolford, Army oral history interview by Major Norman Childs, 19 May 2003.
10. Interviews, Captain Phillip Wolford and Sergeant Shawn Gibson.
11. Interview, Chris Tomlinson.
12. Colonel Daniel Allyn, Operation Iraqi Freedom Study Group interview by Colonel Timothy Cherry, 13 May 2003.
13. Interviews, Lieutenant Colonel Terry Ferrell, Captain Clay Lyle, Sergeant First Class Matthew Chase, and Sergeant First Class Paul Wheatley. Also commanders and staff of 3-7 Cavalry, Operation Iraqi Freedom Study Group interviews by Major Peter Kilner, 25 May 2003.
14. Interview, Lieutenant Colonel Jeffrey "J. R." Sanderson.
15. Interview, Colonel Daniel Allyn.
16. Interview, Staff Sergeant James E. Harrison. Also see Staff Sergeant James E. Harrison, Army oral history interview by Sergeant Daniel Goerke, 14 May 2003.

17. Interviews, Lieutenant Colonel J. R. Sanderson, Colonel Daniel Allyn, and Captain Stu James.
18. 3rd ID staff ride attended by Michael Gordon.
19. Draft 1st Marine Division official history.
20. Interview, Lieutenant Colonel Frederick Padilla.
21. Ibid.
22. Captain Larry Brown, Marine Corps oral history interview by Lieutenant Colonel Michael Visconage, 18 May 2003; Hospitalman 2 Michael O'Leary, Marine Corps oral history interview by Lieutenant Colonel Michael Visconage, 12 May 2003.
23. Interview, General John Jumper; accounts by Air War Command officials.

CHAPTER 22: *Saddam's Great Escape*

1. Interview, Rashid Abudullah Ibrahim al-Huraymis; "Iraqi Perspectives," p. 80.
2. "Iraqi Perspectives," p. 80.
3. Interview, Brigadier General John Kelly.
4. Draft 1st Marine Division official history, Chapter 7, p. 9.
5. Interview, Lieutenant Colonel Herman "Stacy" Clardy.
6. Interview, Chief Warrant Officer 2 David Williams.
7. Interviews, Brigadier General John Kelly and Lieutenant Colonel Herman "Stacy" Clardy.
8. Interview, military official; Jones, "Team Tank," *Veritas,* pp. 71–72.
9. Interview, Lieutenant Colonel Duffy White.
10. Ibid.; Interview, Brigadier General John Kelly; Draft 1st Marine Division official history, Chapter 7, p. 32.
11. Interviews, Brigadier General John Kelly and Major General Ray Odierno; draft 1st Marine Division official history, Chapter 7, pp. 35–36. Also see Gian P. Gentile, "The Risk of Velvet Gloves," *Washington Post,* 19 January 2004, Section A, p. 21.
12. Interviews, Lieutenant Colonel Kenneth Tovo and Lieutenant General Henry "Pete" Osman.
13. Interview, Lieutenant General Henry "Pete" Osman. Also see Philip P. Pan, "Kurds' Seizure of City Alarms Turkey; Officials Threaten Force but Say U.S. Will Be Given Time to Urge Withdrawal," *Washington Post,* 11 April 2003, Section A, pg. 35.
14. Interview, Lieutenant Colonel Robert Waltemeyer, Army interview.
15. Interview, Major Paul Brickley. "The original MEU mission required ACE helicopters to pick up BLT Marines and equipment at Irbil, fly them to positions along designated 'rat lines,' and establish checkpoints to intercept HVTs attempting to flee Iraq. Having planned for the intended mission of establishing security checkpoints to stop HVTs from escaping Iraq, the MEU was surprised by the sudden change in mission. The environment was unknown to MEU Marines as they climbed on board civilian buses for insertion into Mosul." Captain Arnaldo L. Colon, "Marines in North Iraq: A Certain Force," 26 MEU(SOC) official report, p. 15.

16. Colon, "Marines in North Iraq," pp. 21–29.

17. Interview, Lieutenant General Henry "Pete" Osman. To help pacify the Turks, liaison officers were allowed to join U.S. forces in Kirkuk. Turkey also wanted to send humanitarian aid with a large military escort. They were told that was unacceptable, but they could send the aid trucks without the troops. That Turkish SOF were part of the contingent became known when a fifteen-year-old Turkish youth turned in an AK-47 to the Americans, explaining that he didn't know how to use it.

18. Interviews, Colonel Joseph Anderson and Lieutenant General Henry "Pete" Osman.

19. Interview, Major General Robin Brims.

CHAPTER 23: *Hello, I Must Be Going*

1. Donald Rumsfeld, "Beyond Nation-Building," speech, 14 February 2003, available from http://www.defenselink.mil/speeches/2003/sp20030214-secdef0023.html; George Bush, "A Period of Consequences," 23 September 1999, available from http://citadel.edu/pao/addresses/pres_bush.html.

2. Interview, Pentagon official.

3. Interviews, senior military officials. Lieutenant General Earl Hailston, the senior Marine in the Persian Gulf region, who operated out of Bahrain, and Major General Gene Renuart also attended the meeting.

4. Interview, CFLCC official.

5. Interview, General Tommy Franks, 5 October 2004.

6. Interview, Pentagon official.

7. Ibid.

8. Interview, General Tommy Franks.

9. Interview, Tom White.

10. Interviews, CFLCC officials.

11. Interview, Colonel Curtis Potts.

12. Ian Fisher, "U.S. Force Said to Kill 15 Iraqis During an Anti-American Rally," *New York Times,* 30 April 2003, Section A, p. 1.

13. Interview, Jay Garner, PBS *Frontline,* "Truth, War and Consequences," available from http://www.pbs.org/wgbh/pages/frontline/shows/truth/interviews/garner.html, accessed 9 January 2006.

14. Interviews, Major General Carl Strock and Condoleezza Rice. Also see Michael R. Gordon, "Poor Intelligence Misled Troops About Risk of Drawn-Out War," *New York Times,* 20 October 2004, Section A, p. 1, available from http://www.nytimes.com/pages/world/worldspecial3/, accessed 9 January 2006.

15. Interview, Jay Garner.

16. Interview, Colonel Paul Hughes.

17. Interview, ORHA official. Also see Michael R. Gordon, "For Training Iraq's Police: The Main Problem Was Time," *New York Times,* 21 October 2004, Section A, p. 13, available from: http://www.nytimes.com/pages/world/worldspecial3/, accessed 9 January 2006.

18. Also see "Iraq Police: An Assessment of the Present and Recommendations for

the Future," draft report, 30 May 2003, for the Coalition Provisional Authority Interior Ministry. Also "Iraq Police: An Assessment of the Present and Recommendations for the Future," draft, 2 June 2003.

19. Interview, Robert Perito.

20. Interview, Tom Wheelock, United States Institute of Peace Association for Diplomatic Studies and Training, Iraq Experience Project, by W. Haven North, 8 September 2004.

21. For an excerpt from the report, see "A Long, Difficult and Probably Turbulent Process," *New York Times,* 20 October 2004, Section A, p. 12, available from http://www.nytimes.com/pages/world/worldspecial3/, accessed 11 January 2006. The thirty-eight-page report, entitled "Principal Challenges in Post-Saddam Iraq," chronicled a long list of potential problems. It noted, but did not emphasize, the issues. The discussion of this threat was left to the last paragraph of the report. The key judgments of the report are the following:

> The building of an Iraqi democracy would be a long, difficult and probably turbulent process with potential for backsliding into Iraq's tradition of authoritarianism. Iraqi political culture does not foster liberalism or democracy. . . . The principal positive elements in any effort at democratization would be the current relative weakness of political Islam in Iraq and the contributions that could be made by 4 million Iraqi exiles. Iraq would be unlikely to split apart, but a post-Saddam authority would face a deeply divided society with a significant chance that domestic groups would engage in violent conflict with each other unless an occupying force prevented them from doing so.
>
> Sunni Arabs would face possible loss of their longstanding privileged position, while Shia would seek power commensurate with their majority status. Kurds could try to take advantage of Saddam's departure by seizing some of the large northern oil fields, a move that would elicit forceful responses from Sunni Arabs and from Turkey. Score-settling would occur throughout Iraq.
>
> Iraq's large petroleum resources, its greatest asset, would make economic reconstruction less difficult than political transformation. Iraq's economic options would remain few and narrow without forgiveness of debt, a reduction in reparations from the previous Persian Gulf war or something akin to a Marshall plan. If they remained relatively unscathed and any administrative issues involving organization of Iraq's oil industry were resolved, it would be possible to increase oil production in three months from 2.4 million barrels per day to 3.1 million barrels.
>
> The foreign and security policies of a new Iraqi government necessarily would defer heavily in the near term to the interests of the United States, United Nations or an international coalition. But it would also reflect many continuing Iraqi perceptions. Unless guaranteed a security umbrella against its strategic rivals, Iraq's interest in acquiring weapons of mass destruction would eventually revive.
>
> A new Iraqi government would have little interest in supporting terrorism, although strong Iraqi support for the Palestinians would continue. If

Baghdad were unable to exert control over the Iraqi countryside, Al Qaeda or other terrorist groups could operate from remote areas.

22. Interview, Brigadier General Steven Hawkins.
23. Interview, Jay Garner, PBS *Frontline,* "Truth, War and Consequences."
24. Interview, Major General Carl Strock; Interview, Tom Wheelock, Iraq Experience Project, 8 September 2004.
25. Interview, Qubad Talabani.
26. Interview, Ambassador Robin Raphel, United States Institute of Peace Association for Diplomatic Studies and Training, Iraq Experience Project, by Charles Kennedy, 13 July 2004.
27. Interview, Brigadier General E. J. Sinclair.
28. "Iraq: What's Going Wrong," cable from John Sawers to British officials, in possession of the authors.
29. Informal transcript of conversation between General Tommy Franks, Admiral Edmund Giambastiani, Major General Gene Renuart, Major General Gary Luck, Lieutenant General Michael "Rifle" DeLong, 14 May 2003, obtained by the authors.

CHAPTER 24: *Starting from Scratch*

1. Interviews, Coalition Provisional Authority, White House, and State Department officials.
2. Jeremiah Cushman, "The Ba'ath Party and U.S. De-Ba'athification Policy," unpublished paper, August 2004.
3. Interview, former CPA official.
4. Interview, James Dobbins. Also see James Dobbins et al., *America's Role in Nation-building: From Germany to Iraq,* RAND Corporation, 2003.
5. Interview, Pentagon official.
6. Interview, Jay Garner. Also Coalition Provisional Authority Order No. 1, "De-Baathification of Iraqi Society," issued May 16, 2003.
7. Michael R. Gordon, "Debate Lingering on Decision to Dissolve the Iraqi Military," *New York Times,* 21 October 2004, Section A, p. 1, available from http://www.nytimes.com/pages/world/worldspecial3/, accessed 11 January 2006. See also Coalition Provisional Authority Order No. 2, "Dissolution of Entities," May 23, 2003.
8. Interview, Colonel Paul Hughes.
9. Interview, CPA official.
10. "19 May 2003 SecDef Planning Instruction—Establishment and Training of the NIC," reviewed by the authors.
11. Condoleezza Rice, quoted in Gordon, "Debate Lingering on Decision to Dissolve Iraqi Military," 21 October 2004. Also see "A Conversation with Peter Pace," 17 February 2004, Council on Foreign Relations, available from http://www.cfr.org/publication/6785/conversation_with_peter_pace.html.
12. Interview, Colonel John Agoglia.
13. Interview, General Tommy Franks.

14. Gordon, "Debate Lingering on Decision to Dissolve the Iraqi Military," 21 October 2004.
15. Interviews, CPA staff.
16. L. Paul Bremer, *My Year in Iraq* (New York: Simon & Schuster, 2006).
17. Interviews, military and Pentagon officials.
18. Interview, Tom White.
19. Interviews, military officials.
20. Interviews, CFLCC and CPA officials.
21. "Iraq: Progress Report," 25 June 2003, John Sawers, confidential British diplomatic report obtained by the authors.
22. Interviews, Colonel Joe Anderson and officers of the 101st Airborne Division.
23. Interviews, Lieutenant Colonel Christopher Conlin and Major General James Mattis.
24. Interview, Major General Ray Odierno.
25. Interview, military official.
26. Interview, Saif Atiyah.
27. Interview, Lieutenant General David McKiernan.
28. Interview, Major General James "Spider" Marks.
29. Interview, Lieutenant General James Conway.
30. Interview, Brigadier General John Kelly.
31. Interview, Major General Buford Blount.
32. Interview, John Keane.
33. Interview, meeting participant.

Appendix

What follows are internal documents concerning the planning and execution of the war and the situation in Iraq following the fall of Baghdad. They have not previously been released. Also included is L. Paul Bremer's public order dissolving the Iraqi military.

Chronology of the war prepared for President Bush, May 6, 2003

6MAY CINC to POTUS Briefing
Author: CCF6-D USCENTCOM

CHRONOLOGY

28 Nov: OSW aircraft dropped 360,000 leaflets IVO Al Kut,Al Basrah.
01 Dec: OSW Coalition Aircraft targeted air defense near Tallil, Iraq.
02 Dec :   OSW aircraft dropped 240,000 leaflets IVO Al Kut Iraq.
6-16 Dec: Exercise INTERNAL LOOK at Camp As Sayliyah, Qatar.
16 Dec: The Iraqi opposition conference concluded in London, reps   from
            over 50 opposition parties met.
19 Jan: 350 personnel depart MacDill AFB to Al Saliyah, Qatar, CENTCOM's
            Forward HQ.
5 Feb: Colin Powell delivers remarks to UN.
25 Feb: Red Cross workers built warehouses in three
            countries next to Iraq in the event of war.
27 Feb: Blix on Iraq "Still hasn't committed to disarming".
1 Mar: Turkish Parliament voted no to U.S. troops being based along Iraq border.
17 Mar: UN orders all UN personnel out of Iraq.
            Pres. Bush addresses nation setting an ultimatum for Saddam
       Hussein.
19 Mar: **(D-DAY)**   - OIF War Begins.
       - SOF / OGA recon Iraqi units along Green Line.
       - SOF / OGA infils and link ups continue in the South.
       - CFACC initiates counter-TBM operations.
       - 2100L: 1) Special forces destroy VISOBS and assault into   western Iraq
(S-DAY), 2) TF-20 destroys western VISOBS and   moves into Iraq, 3) Ground forces
recon into southern oil fields with SOF / OGA; I MEF conducts RIP with Kuwait forces.
20 Mar (D+1):   - Robust counter-TBM operations.
       - 0001L: TF-20 raid on Ar Rutbah
       - 0530L: TST 2 X F-117 and 24 TLAMs attack leadership target.
       - 2000L: Aerial and ground recon into southern oil fields.
       - 2100L: Air operations conducted to shape the battlespace; 537 air strike sorties;
34 TLAMs; 143 PGMs.
       - 2200L: SOF forces attack to; seize Tallil AB and Euphrates river crossings, and
secure MABOT/KABOT and Al Faw Manifold.
21 Mar (D+2): - Coalition forces seize Iraqi tugboat with 50 naval mines in Khor Abd
Allah waterway; 20 enemy detained; first evidence of mine warfare.
       - 0600L: I MEF seizes western Rumaylah oil fields. Accepts surrender of the
senior ledership of the 51st Iraqi Mech Inf DIV   **(G-DAY)**.
       - 2100L: Initiate strategic air operations **(A-DAY)**; 832 air strike sorties, 381
TLAM's, 124 CALCM's, 231 PGM's.
       - 2200L: Strike on Khurmal terrorist facility.
22 Mar (D+3): - 0700L: V CORPS seizes Tallil AB; controls Euphrates river
       crossings; establishes a FARP south of An Nasiriyah.

- TF TARAWA conducts RIP with 3rd ID to secure Euphrates crossing sites.
- CA Teams begin food and water deliveries and restoring local
- Continue air operations; 878 air sorties, 45 TLAMs, 3 CALCMs, 644 PGMs, 15 ATACMS.
- General Franks met with journalists for the first time since war began.

23 Mar (D+4): - Ground forces attack toward Baghdad
- Military Coordination and Liaison Command infiltrates into Northern Iraq.
-UK SOF and OGA with Iraqi assets expand the interdiction of HVTs.
- CA teams facilitate humanitarian support in southern and northern Iraq.
- Twelve soldiers assigned to the 507th Maint Comp, 3rd ID missing near An Nasiriyah. Iraqi's take PFC Lynch and five other soldiers prisoner.
- Conducted strategic air operations; 827 air strike sorties, 72 TLAMs, 690 PGMs.
- Weather and dust storms impact operations.

24 Mar (D+5) : - Damage Assessment Response Team made final preparations   to support the Iraqi people.
- US SOF and OGA insert assets into An Najaf; TF-7 (UK)
emergency exfil from western Iraq.
- TF-20 conducts raid on Thar Thar Palace; H2 AB surrenders.
- Conducted strategic air operations: 944 air strike sorties, 11
TLAMs, 2 CALCMs, 559 PGMs.
- CFLCC continues attack toward Baghdad; holds Euphrates
crossing sites and attacks north toward Al Kut with I MEF.
- 11th AHR attacks RG Medina DIV south of Baghdad; 1 AH-64 shot down; 2 POWs.
- CA teams restore local government and identify seaport workers in Umm Qasr; facilitate humanitarian assistance in southern Iraq.
- "Boots and Coots" begin oil field fire fighting.
- Engineers from International Red Cross repaired water facilities   in Basrah to 40% capacity.

25 Mar (D+6) :- TF-20 attacks H1 airfield.
- Mamals begin Mine Counter-measure operations at Umm Qasr.
- 1st UK Armored DIV secures Al Faw southern oil fields.
- Blacklist issued to components.
- V (US) CORPS seizes An Najaf, continues ops to secure city.

26 Mar (D+7) :   - 4th Inf DIV decision made to move to Kuwait.
- Began lethal aid to PUK in norther Iraq IVO Bashur airfield.
- 1st UK Armored DIV isolates Basrah.
- 173rd Airborne BDE executes airborne assault into Bashur   airfield via 15 X C-17.
- Dr. Khalilzad and LTG Broadwater infiltrate northern Iraq IVO   As Sulaymaniyah.
- Umm Qasr port open and ready for HA delivery.
- V (US) CORPS defeats enemy forces vic An Najaf and As
Samawah.

27 Mar (D+8) :   - 24th MEU commences offload.

28 Mar (D+9) :   - Mine clearing operations in KAA complete; channel open to   Umm Qasr.

- Khurma assault/sensitive site exploitation commences.

29 Mar (D+10) :   - A-10 refueling opds begin at Tallil AB.

- 101st Air Assault DIV conducts deep attack vicinity Karbala.

- 4th Infantry DIV ADVON commences RSOI in Kuwait.

- TLAM shooters move from Eastern Med and Red Sea to NAG.

- H1 airfield seized.

30 Mar (D+11) :   - Thar-Thar Palace direct action by TF-20.

- V (US) CORPS and I MEF occupy attack positions vicinity Karbala and Al Kut.

31 Mar (D+12) :

- First HA ship (UK) at Umm Qasr offloads.

1 Apr (D+13)   - TF-20 seizes Hadithah Dam.

- PFC Lynch rescued and remains of 11 soldiers recovered.

- 3 ID attacks north through Karbala Gap to secure Baghdad

- I MEF attacks north towards Al Kut to secure Baghdad.

2 Apr (D+14):   - 3 ID secures Euphrates crossing site 17 miles south of Baghdad.

3 Apr (D+15):   - 1st UK DIV begins Phase IV transition VIC Umm Qasr.

- I MEF cuts Hwy 6 to isolate Baghdad from southeast.

4 Apr (D+16):   - Operation MOUNTAIN THUNDER--air strikes against Iraqi V Corps in the north.

- Khurma samples and 11 human remains enroute to CONUS.

- 3 ID attacks to seize Al Hillah (Medina DIV) and BIAP.

- I MEF attacks to seize Al Kut (Baghdad DIV).

- 82 ABN attacks north of As Samawah.

- UK raid Said traffic circle in Basrah.

5 Apr (D+17):   - FIFF move from northern Iraq to southern Iraq.

- 1st "Thunder Run" into central Baghdad by 3 ID.

- I MEF isolates Baghdad from the southeast.

6 Apr (D+18): - 1st UK DIV executes attack into Basrah.

7 Apr (D+19):   - EUCOM heavy and medium immediate reaction company begins flow into Bashur airfield. **CHRONOLOGY (CONT)**

7 Apr (Cont):   **- CDR USCENTCOM visits Coalition troops in Iraq.**

8 Apr (D+20):   - I MEF raids Rasheed district.

- TF-20 armed recce along Syria/Iraq border.

- 3 ID completes outer cordon of Baghdad from Tigris north to   Tigris south.

- 2nd "Thunder Run" into central Baghdad by 3 ID.

- TF-20 commences Hwy 1 interdiction ops north of Baghdad.

9 Apr (D+21):- I MEF secures Al Rasheed complex southeast Baghdad.

- 2 MOABs arrive Al Udeid.

- Spanish ship delivers HA to Umm Qasar.

- Regime fractured; Saddam statue toppled by people of Baghdad. 10 Apr (D+22) - All roads leading into Baghdad interdicted.

- 3 ID holds BIAP, completes outer cordon from Tigris to Tigris.
- BIAP open for Intra-theater lift.
- Kirkuk and northern oil fields secured by JSOTF-N.

11 Apr (D+23): - 1 UK DIV secures the west Qurna and Majnoon oil infrastructure.
- JSOTF-N accepts surrender from Iraqi V CORPS Cdr.
- MV Manar (UAE) delivers HA to Umm Qasr.
- CFLCC early entry command post flows to Baghdad.
- CFSOCC jump command post flows to Baghdad.
- CENTCOM releases "playing cards" displaying the55 most wanted members of Iraqi regime.

12 Apr (D+24): - I MEF attacks north toward to Baqubah and Tikrit.
- 26 MEU commences air movement from Cyprus to Bashur.
- Civilian authorities turn Mosul over to Coalition.
- USS Abraham Lincoln CVBG outchops.

13 Apr (D+25): - Ar Ramadi surrenders to OGA and Tribals.
- Oil flow to Syria stopped.
- 18 of 27 population centers under Coalition influence.
- Naval mine clearing begins north of Umm Qasr.
- 4th ID starts movement into Iraq.
- 7 POWs recovered VIC Tikrit.

15 Apr (D+27): - MEK signs "Cease Fire" agreement.
- Interim Iraqi Authority conference held at Tallil.
- CFLCC begins repositioning of forces to Phase IV stance.
- CDR USCENTCOM announces counter-TBM mission in west is   complete.

16 Apr (D+28): - 3/7 CAV secures Ar Ramadi.
- **CDR USCENTCOM visits Baghdad.**

19 Apr (D+31): - USS Kitty Hawk CVBG outchops.

20 Apr (D+32): - USS Constellation CVBG outchops.
- 1.0 CVBG presence USS Nimitz CVBG in NAG.

21 Apr (D+33): - 101st RIP with TF-20 at H1 airfield and Hadithah Dam.
- ORHA begins insertion into Baghdad.
- 1st UK AR DIV secures Umm Qasr.

22 Apr (D+34): - JOR and KSA field hospitals arrive Baghdad.
- 1st Shia pilgrimage in 25 Yrs commences between karbala and An Najaf; 82nd ABN provided security.
- 101st air assaults into Mosul.

24 Apr (D+36): - 26 MEU commences reconstitution.

26 Apr (D+38): - 3 ID secures 125 sites in support of SSE and ORHA.

27 Apr (D+39): - TF-Tarawa hires 100 police officers; curfew in Al Kut to stabilize civil unrest.
- Central Iraq meeting in Baghdad (IIA).

1 May (D+43): - CJTF-7 established.
- POTUS announces end of major combat operations while aboard   USS Abraham Lincoln.
- **CDR USCENTCOM visits Basrah.**

3 May (D+45): - I MEF and V (US) CORPS conduct SASO throughout the battlespace.
4 May (D+46): - CJTF-7 assumes West Iraq battlespace.
    - 3 ID seizes Republican Presidential Palace in Baghdad.
    - 3 ID isolates Baghdad from the northwest
    - USS Nimitz CVBG inchop.

PERSONNEL (as of 5 MAY)

– Total military supporting OIF in AOR: 359,029
– US - 316,260
– Coalition - 42,769
– Military in Iraq: 173,218
– US - 150,816
– Coalition - 22,402
– Total Nations in Tampa: 52
– Total Nations in Iraq Theater: 23
– 12 in Iraq – US, AL, AU, CZE, IT, JO, LI, PO, SA, SP, UAE, GB

OIF CASUALITIES (as of 5 MAY)

- Total Deaths: 171
  - US - 138
  - UK - 33
- Total KIA: 138
  - US - 110
  - UK - 28

BOMBS DROPPED/SORTIES FLOWN
(as of 2 MAY)

Bombs Dropped:	30,501
PGMs:	20,142 (67%)
TLAMs: 802	

Sorties Flown:	47,694
- Strike:	16,969
- Refueling:	9,656
- Cargo:	9,974
- Reconnaissance:	1,795

TONNAGE MOVED (as of 2 MAY)
559,622 short tons (includes OEF; sea, air, rail and ground transport)

SENSITIVE SITE EXPLOITATION
(as of 2 MAY)

Major actions in CENTCOM's campaign. Prepared by
the Coalition Forces Land Component Command.

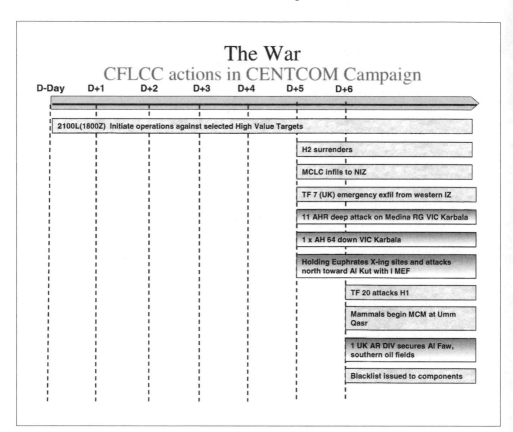

The War
CFLCC actions in CENTCOM Campaign

| D-Day | D+1 | D+2 | D+3 | D+4 | D+5 | D+6 |

2100L(1800Z) Initiate operations against selected High Value Targets

H2 surrenders

MCLC infils to NIZ

TF 7 (UK) emergency exfil from western IZ

11 AHR deep attack on Medina RG VIC Karbala

1 x AH 64 down VIC Karbala

Holding Euphrates X-ing sites and attacks north toward Al Kut with I MEF

TF 20 attacks H1

Mammals begin MCM at Umm Qasr

1 UK AR DIV secures Al Faw, southern oil fields

Blacklist issued to components

D+7	D+8	D+9	D+10	D+11

4 ID south decision made

Begin lethal aid to PUK in NIZ VIC Bashur

1 UK DIV isolates Basrah

173rd executes Paradrop in Bashur (15 x C-17)

Khalizad and Broad water infil to NIZ VIC Al Samamaniyah

Umm Qasr port declared open and ready for HA

24th MEU commences offload

Mine detonation in KAA. Channel free to Umm Qasr

Khalizad and Broadwater exfil from NIZ

Karma SSE/ASLT commences

A-10 refueling ops begin at Tallil

101st deep attack VIC Karbala

4 ID commences RSOI at KU

Decision to move TLAM shooters from Eastern Med and Red Sea to NAG

H1 seized

Thar-Thar DA by TF 20

Occupying attack positions for attack on Baghdad

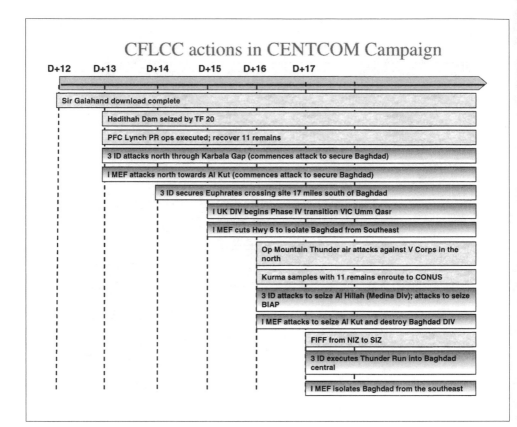

CFLCC actions in CENTCOM Campaign

D+12   D+13   D+14   D+15   D+16   D+17

Sir Galahand download complete

Hadithah Dam seized by TF 20

PFC Lynch PR ops executed; recover 11 remains

3 ID attacks north through Karbala Gap (commences attack to secure Baghdad)

I MEF attacks north towards Al Kut (commences attack to secure Baghdad)

3 ID secures Euphrates crossing site 17 miles south of Baghdad

I UK DIV begins Phase IV transition VIC Umm Qasr

I MEF cuts Hwy 6 to isolate Baghdad from Southeast

Op Mountain Thunder air attacks against V Corps in the north

Kurma samples with 11 remains enroute to CONUS

3 ID attacks to seize Al Hillah (Medina Div); attacks to seize BIAP

I MEF attacks to seize Al Kut and destroy Baghdad DIV

FIFF from NIZ to SIZ

3 ID executes Thunder Run into Baghdad central

I MEF isolates Baghdad from the southeast

CFLCC actions in CENTCOM Campaign

D+18   D+19   D+20   D+21   D+22

I UK DIV executes attack into Baghdad

HIRC/MIRC begins flow into Bashur

3 ID seizes Republican Presidential Palace in Baghdad

3 ID isolates Baghdad from the northwest

I MEF raids Rasheed district

TF 20 armed recce along Syria/Iraq border

3 ID completes outer cordon of Baghdad from Tigris North to Tigris South

3 ID commences thunder runs north into Baghdad Central

TF 20 commences HWY 1 interdiction ops north of Baghdad

I MEF secures Al Rasheed complex SE Baghdad

2 MOABs arrive Al Udeid

SPS Galicia delivers HA to Umm Qasr

All roads leading into Baghdad under coalition control

BIAP open for Intra-Theater lift

Kirkuk secured

CFLCC actions in CENTCOM Campaign

D+23   D+24   D+25   D+26

MV Manar (UAE) delivers HA to Umm Qasr

CFLCC early entry Command Post flows to Baghdad

CFSOCC Jump Command Post to BIAP

F-15 crew remains recovered VIC Tikrit

I MEF attacks north toward Baghdad

26 MEU commences air movement from Cyprus to Bashur

Mosul turned over to coalition by civilian authorities

Ar Ramadi surrenders to OGA/Tikrit

Oil flow to Syria stopped

18 of 26 population centers under coalition influence

MCM opens north of Umm Qasr commences

4 ID commences movement into IZ

7 POW's recovered VIC Tikrit

26 MEU deployment into NIZ complete

Northern oilfields assessed as operational

CFLCC actions in CENTCOM Campaign

D+27 D+28 D+29 D+30 D+31 D+32 D+33

MEK signs "cease fire" agreement

IIA conferences commences

CFLCC commences movement to Phase IV stance

CTBM mission in west IZ stance

3/7 CAV secures Ar Ramadi

1 CVBG presences

101st RIP with TF 20 at H1 snf Hadithah Dam

CFLCC actions in CENTCOM Campaign

D+34	D+35	D+36	D+37	D+38	D+40

Jordanian and KSA field hospitals arrive in Baghdad

Arbaeen pilgrimage commences

101st air assaults into Mosul

Arbaeen Pilgrimage complete without incident

First UAE ferry delivers Iraqi ex-patriots to Umm Qasr

26th MEU commences reconstitution

CIM in Baghdad

JTF-7 activated

Evolution of the land war plan. Prepared by the
Coalition Forces Land Component Command.

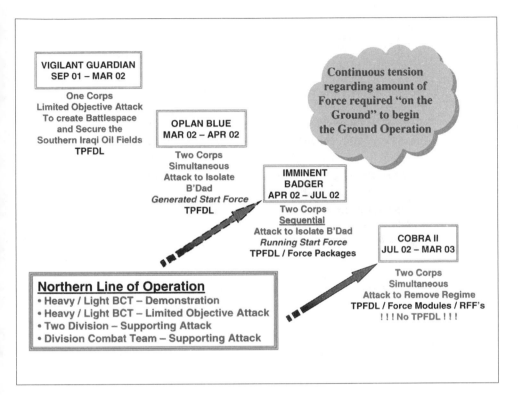

Plan to use the Iraqi army after the war. Prepared by Jay Garner's postwar team and presented at the February 2003 Rock Drill.

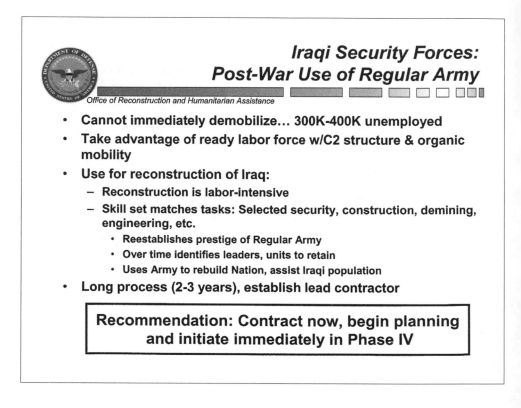

Iraqi Security Forces: Post-War Use of Regular Army

Office of Reconstruction and Humanitarian Assistance

- **Cannot immediately demobilize... 300K-400K unemployed**
- **Take advantage of ready labor force w/C2 structure & organic mobility**
- **Use for reconstruction of Iraq:**
  - **Reconstruction is labor-intensive**
  - **Skill set matches tasks: Selected security, construction, demining, engineering, etc.**
    - **Reestablishes prestige of Regular Army**
    - **Over time identifies leaders, units to retain**
    - **Uses Army to rebuild Nation, assist Iraqi population**
- **Long process (2-3 years), establish lead contractor**

Recommendation: Contract now, begin planning and initiate immediately in Phase IV

Briefing on the need for civilian constabulary to keep order in postwar Iraq

DEFENSE POLICY BOARD
BRIEFING
FEBRUARY 28, 2003

EASTABLISHING POST-CONFLICT SECURITY IN IRAQ

Robert M. Perito
United Institute of Peace

- If the President decides to take military action, the US will quickly face the challenge of creating post-conflict security in Iraq. This task will be difficult, confusing and dangerous for everyone involved.

- The US-military administration will be responsible for security, public order, and law enforcement.

- In meeting this responsibility, the US will not be able to rely on the local authorities. Saddam's security services must be disbanded. Prior experience indicates the regular Iraqi police will be unavailable, intimidated or unprepared to act in the chaotic postwar environment.

- Given the political and practical realities, its doubtful the US will be able to turn to the EU, NATO and OSCE, which provided police and legal experts in Bosnia and Kosovo.

- Relying on Coalition military forces is not the answer. Experience in the Balkans demonstrated that regular soldiers are neither trained nor equipped to deal with mob violence or engage in law enforcement.

- There is also a distinct difference between military and police forces. Military forces are trained to concentrate mass and firepower and to destroy the enemy.

- Police are trained to deal with civilians, to preserve and protect and to use only the amount of force required to control the situation.

- LA Rodney King Riot or Montgomery County sniper.

  - The US has the world's finest military, but the US military has no civilian security partner. There is no federal department or agency that has responsibility for post-conflict stability.

  - The US does not have civilian constabulary forces. It lacks a national police force.

  - The US is the only country that uses commercial contractors to staff its police contingents in UN peace operations.

- There is no Federal agency authorized to provide prosecutors, judges and corrections officers for stability operations. However, experience in Kosovo has shown that such personnel are needed to perform judicial functions and to reform local judicial and penal systems.

US STABILITY FORCE

- To ensure a stable post-conflict environment in Iraq, the US should create a civilian US "Stability Force." Such force should include civilian constabulary, police and teams of judicial and corrections experts to establish the rule of law. This force could work with Coalition military forces that will remain to ensure a safe and secure environment.

- A civilian Stability Force would provide the US military with an effective civilian partner. Establishing the rule of law from the outset will free the military to perform its duties and speed its withdrawal.

- Creating the rule of law will provide a foundation for political, economic and social reconstruction.

- The civilian Stability Force would consist of three elements:

Constabulary Units

- Constabularies are police forces with military characteristics.

- They are formed units that fill the place in the force continuum between the military and the civil police.

- In Kosovo, the UN and NATO deployed highly mobile, company-size constabulary units that operated independently or in combination with other forces.

- These constabulary forces were equipped with armored vehicles and heavy weapons and could fight as light infantry, if required.

- Their primary function was civil disorder management and they were highly trained and properly equipped with non-lethal weapons for crowd control.

- They were also trained and equipped to perform police functions and could engage in law enforcement.

- In Kosovo, these "UN Special Police Units" handled crowd control, but they were also able to perform a long list of other functions.

- They protected the airport, guarded prisons, escorted convoys, protected refugees, provided close protection for officials and patrolled the border. Of particular importance was their ability to conduct high-risk arrests of organized crime figures and terrorists.

Civil Police

- The US Stability Force should include civil police (street cops). Like the UN Police in Haiti, Kosovo and East'Timor, these police officers should be armed and have 'executive authority' to make arrests, conduct investigations and use deadly force.

- This would enable them to engage in police operations and to operate independently, if required. The civil police contingent would include a liaison and training unit to train and monitor the local police.

- The US has several thousand police officers that have served in UN police missions. These veterans could form the core of the police component of the US Stability Force.

Judicial Teams

- Constabulary and police are important, but they cannot function without the other parts of the judicial system, courts and prisons. The US Stability Force would include teams of prosecutors, defense attorneys, judges, court administrators and corrections officers.

- As in Kosovo, these teams could act independently and could decide to handle sensitive cases on their own authority. Their primary mission, however, would be to ensure that local courts function fairly and effectively.

- Judicial teams would deal with war criminals, ensure respect for human rights and assist with judicial reform. They would also train local attorneys, jurists and court administrators.

- Corrections officers would ensure the proper handling of war criminals, release of political prisoners and the rehabilitation of prison facilities.

- A cadre of American legal veterans with experience in Haiti, Bosnia, and Kosovo is available and could be recruited to perform these functions.

Iraq

- For Iraq, a US civilian Stability Force would have the following components:

- Constabulary: A force of 20 companies with appropriate headquarters and administrative staff for a total of 2,500 personnel. Primary deployment would be in Baghdad, with contingents in four regional centers (Mosul and Kirkuk in the North and Basra and Kut in the South.) These forces would have access to a helicopter airlift to ensure maximum mobility.

- Civil Police: A force of 4,000 US civil police with its headquarters in Baghdad and contingents co-located in the regional and provincial headquarters of the Iraqi National Police. These officers would require wheeled transport, light weapons and effective communications to ensure coordination with constabulary and military backups.

- Judicial Teams: There should be ten teams of twenty lawyers, judges, court administrators and corrections officers supported by a headquarters staff, para-legals, translators and a training unit for a total of 300 personnel. They would be deployed to major population centers where they would work directly with local judicial authorities.

BENEFITS

- Creating a US Stability Force will be challenging. Its contribution to creating post-conflict stability would more than justify the effort.

- Such a force would:

  (1) Join together all of the elements required to effectively achieve sustainable security under a single, unified authority;

  (2) Close the security gap that has plagued previous peace operations by providing for a smooth transition from war fighting to institution building;

  (3) Establish police and judicial authority from the outset, thus freeing the military to perform its functions and speeding its withdrawal;

  (4) Establish the rule of law as a platform from which the other aspects of political, economic and social reconstruction could go forward in an environment conducive to achieving success; and,

  (5) Provide the US with a force that could partner with similar forces from other countries or international organizations.

CONCLUSIONS

- Given the operational realities, the US must take responsibility for establishing the rule of law in Iraq. Other countries may play a role and contribute as conditions stabilize.

- If previous experience is a guide, countries will be more willing to contribute personnel, if the US participates and Americans provide leadership.

- This would mean assuming additional burdens, but it would prevent mistakes and shorten the period before the US can hand off to international or local authorities.

- The challenge is getting started. The people, skill sets and equipment exist in civilian law enforcement, but they need to be brought together by a federal government agency. This will require new funding and, possibly, new legislation. The key ingredients will be leadership and political will.

- The fact that we may be within weeks of a decision by the President to intervene in Iraq should not deter us. Experience in the Balkans, East Timor and Afghanistan shows that Coalition forces will have to deal with high levels of violence for the first two years of the mission.

- The faster we begin, the faster the US will be able to deploy effective civilian security forces and rule of law teams. The faster these units begin their work, the faster Coalition military forces will be able to withdraw and responsibility can be passed to a new Iraqi government.

PRINCIPAL CHALLENGES IN POST–SADDAM IRAQ

In January 2003, the National Intelligence Council issued a thirty-eight-page classified report entitled "Principal Challenges in Post-Saddam Iraq." The report noted that the failure to provide security, restore basic services, and make progress in transferring power to the Iraqi people would lead to the perception that the United States was an occupying power. But the report did not emphasize the possibility of an insurgency. Key sections of the report follow.

—"The building of an Iraqi democracy would be a long, difficult, and probably turbulent process, with potential for backsliding into Iraq's tradition of authoritarianism. Iraqi political culture does not foster liberalism or democracy. Iraq lacks the experience of a loyal opposition and effective institutions for mass political participation. Saddam's brutal methods have made a generation of Iraqis distrustful of surrendering or sharing power. The principal positive elements in any effort at democratization would be the current relative weakness of political Islam in Iraq and the contributions that could be made by four million Iraqi exiles, many of whom are Westernized and well educated, and by the now impoverished and underemployed Iraqi middle class. Iraq would be unlikely to split apart, but a post-Saddam authority would face a deeply divided society with a significant chance that domestic groups would engage in violent conflict with each other unless an occupying force prevented them from doing so.

—"Sunni Arabs would face possible loss of their long-standing privileged position while Shia would seek power commensurate with their majority status. Kurds could try to take advantage of Saddam's departure by seizing some of the large northern oil fields, a move that would elicit forceful responses from Sunni Arabs and from Turkey. Score settling would occur throughout Iraq between those associated with Saddam's regime and those who had suffered most under it.

—"Iraq's large petroleum resources, its greatest asset, would make economic reconstruction less difficult than political transformation. Iraq's economic options would remain few and narrow without forgiveness of debt, a reduction in reparations from the previous Persian Gulf War or something akin to a Marshall plan. Iraq's economic and financial prospects would vary significantly depending on how much damage its oil facilities sustained in war. If they remained relatively unscathed and any administrative issues involving organization of Iraq's oil industry were resolved it would be possible to increase oil production in three months from 2.4 million barrels per day to 3.1 million barrels per day. A less oil-dependent economy with a strong private sector would be required to generate the more than 240,000 new jobs needed each year to accommodate the rapidly growing labor force.

—"Major outside assistance would be required to meet humanitarian needs. Increasing numbers of refugees and internally displaced persons combined with civil strife would strain Iraq's already inadequate health care services, food distribution networks and supplies of potable water. Most Iraqis depend on government food rations and are not equipped to deal with hoarding, looting or price gauging. Rapid reconstitution of the distribution system would be critical to avoiding widespread health problems. Iraqis have restored their physical infrastructure quickly after previous wars. The difficulty of restoring such services as water and electricity after a new war would depend chiefly on how much destruction was caused by urban combat.

—"The foreign and security policies of a new Iraqi government necessary would defer heavily in the near term to the interests of the United States, United Nations or an international coalition. But it would also reflect many continuing Iraqi perceptions and interests. Those perceptions, particularly of threats from regional states, such as Iran, Turkey and Israel, would increasingly shape the Iraqis' policies as they reasserted their independence. These threat perceptions along with a prideful sense of Iraqi's place as a regional power probably would sustain Iraq's interest in rebuilding its military. Unless guaranteed a security umbrella against its strategic rivals Iraq's interest in acquiring weapons of mass destruction would eventually revive. A new Iraqi government would have little interest in supporting terrorism, although strong Iraqi support for the Palestinians would continue. If Baghdad were unable to exert control over the Iraqi countryside Al Qaeda or other terrorist groups could operate from remote areas.

—"Once the most pressing needs became less of a worry for most Iraqis, however, politics and the nature of the ruling authority would become increasingly important to them. Iraqis would expect progress in transferring power from foreign occupiers, however much they had been welcomed as liberators, to indigenous leaders. Attitudes toward a foreign military force would depend largely on the progress made in transferring power as well as on the degree to which that force were perceived as providing necessary security and fostering reconstruction and a return to prosperity."

Personal message from David McKiernan, Commanding General, Coalition Forces Land Component Command, to all personnel assigned, attached, or supporting Operation Iraqi Freedom. It was issued on March 19, 2003, on the eve of the war.

RMKS/1. YOU ARE ABOUT TO REMOVE THE REGIME OF SADDAM HUSSEIN AND ELIMINATE THE THREAT OF HIS WEAPONS OF MASS DESTRUCTION.

2. HE IS A BRUTAL DICTATOR WHOSE REGIME HAS A HISTORY OF RECKLESS AGGRESSION, TIES TO TERRORISM, ATTEMPTS TO DOMINATE A VITAL REGION OF THE WORLD AND A HISTORY OF DEVELOPING AND USING WEAPONS OF MASS DESTRUCTION. THERE ARE NO FURTHER OPTIONS OTHER THAN MILITARY OPERATIONS. TO DATE, NOTHING HAS RESTRAINED SADDAM HUSSEIN FROM PURSUING HIS GOALS OF INTIMIDATING NEIGHBORING STATES AND ATTACKING AND TYRANNIZING HIS OWN PEOPLE. HIS CONTINUING REFUSAL TO DESTROY WEAPONS OF MASS DESTRUCTION, TO FULLY COOPERATE IN INSPECTIONS TO VERIFY COMPLIANCE WITH UNITED NATIONS' MANDATES OR DESIST FROM ACQUIRING NEW WEAPONS PROVIDES NO REAL ALTERNATIVE TO THE ATTACK THAT WE WILL EXECUTE.

3. YOUR TASK WILL NOT BE AN EASY ONE, BUT IT IS JUST AND YOU WILL TRIUMPH. YOUR ARE A MEMBER OF THE BEST TRAINED AND EQUIPPED MILITARY FORCE IN HISTORY. THIS CAMPAIGN WILL PLACE EXTRAORDINARY DEMANDS ON INDIVIDUAL SOLDIERS, SAILORS, MARINES, AIRMEN AND SMALL UNIT LEADERS WHO MUST BE PREPARED TO FIGHT AS THEY HAVE BEEN TRAINED, WHILE, AT THE SAME TIME, PROVIDING A HELPING HAND TO THOSE IRAQIS THAT WELCOME THE COALITION AS LIBERATORS. YOUR COURAGE, TRAINING AND DETERMINATION, BACKED BY THE WILL OF ALL FREEDOM LOVING PEOPLES, ENSURES YOUR VICTORY.

4. WITHIN THIS FORCE, EACH OF US HAS A JOB TO DO, AND EACH OF US SERVES THE WHOLE. EVERY SINGLE CFLCC UNIT IS IMPORTANT IN THE CAMPAIGN TO REMOVE THIS DICTATOR AND RESTORE IRAQ TO THE PEOPLE OF IRAQ. LIKEWISE WE ARE PART OF A LARGER JOINT AND COALITION TEAM UNDER COMCENT. EACH OF US HAS A DUTY TO OUR UNIT, OUR SERVICE, AND OUR COUNTRY, BUT WE HAVE AN EQUALLY IMPORTANT DUTY TO EACH OTHER. YOUR COURAGE WILL BE TESTED BUT YOU WILL DRAW STRENGTH FROM THOSE ON YOUR LEFT AND RIGHT. YOU WILL NOT FALTER. I KNOW THAT ALL OF YOU WILL REPRESENT YOURSELVES, YOUR UNITS AND YOUR RESPECTIVE COUNTRIES WITH HONOR AND VALOR IN THE DAYS AHEAD. WE WILL FIGHT AS A TEAM AND WILL BE VICTORIOUS AS A TEAM THAT IS FIGHTING FOR A COMMON AND JUST GOAL.

5. I HAVE TOTAL CONFIDENCE IN YOU. THERE IS NO FINER TEAM GATHERED ANYWHERE IN THE WORLD; NO TEAM MORE CAPABLE OF ADDRESSING THE TASK AT HAND. WE ARE COMRADES IN ARMS AND I HAVE UNBOUNDED PRIDE IN LEADING YOU. TRUST YOUR INSTINCTS, TRAINING AND LEADERSHIP IN THE DAYS AHEAD. YOU ARE WARRIORS IN A HISTORIC CAMPAIGN THAT WILL BENEFIT OUR FAMILIES, LOVED ONES AND OUR COUNTRIES, AS WELL AS THE PEOPLE OF IRAQ.

6. STRIKE FAST AND HARD! MCKIERNAN

Marine e-mail from Lieutenant Colonel Andy Kennedy, the operations officer for RCT-2, on confusion during the battle at Nasiriyah

```
                              RE concern.txt
From: RCT-2 S3
Sent: Wednesday, June 04, 2003 02:50
To: Starnes LtCol Glenn T; 2 MEB 1/2 BN CMDR
Subject: RE: concern

Gentlemen,
Why did we not pass the timeline for siezing the bridges?
I'm not sure.  I thought I passed we would attack them after we gathered
ourselves at the 20 northing.  I may not have done so.  I wanted to see what
the situation was in the area before we went to attack the bridges (all
concerned about level of violence and urban suck etc.).  The MEB had told me
verbally to plan to attack them "sometime around 04-0700 if possible".  I
did not produce any written orders and did not recieve any from the MEB so I
have nothing to fall back on but my memory of the events.  It is possible
that I never mentioned attacking the eastern bridges, I can't remember.  My
intentions were to not go in half cocked but to assess the situation.  The
orders we'd recieved (verbally) were sufficiently annoying that I did not
want to execute them as briefed and so I asked Col J about why and when.  He
got me to shut up by telling me we need not attack until we were ready.  In
the rush of events that night I have no idea why I did not mention the fact
that MEB wanted us to attack the bridges.  I thought I passed this.  I have
no excuse except the press of events.  I am not trying to "soft pedal" this
in any way.  I obviously did not convey everything properly to our
subordinate units. I know it does no good to say so, but I am sorry.
Semper Fi
the newest LtCol on the block
```

British assessment by John Sawers on waning Iraqi suppport for the coalition and the need to improve Baghdad security, May 11, 2003

```
CONFIDENTIAL
PERSONAL
FM IRAQREP
TO IMMEDIATE FCO
TELNO 2
OF 111430Z MAY 03
INFO IMMEDIATE BAGHDAD, UKMIS NEW YORK, WASHINGTON
INFO IMMEDIATE ACTOR, DFID, MODUK, WHIRL, NO 10


PERSONAL FROM SPECIAL REP FOR IRAQ FOR:

NO 10: POWELL, MANNING, CAMPBELL, RYCROFT
FCO: PS/SOS, PS/O'BRIEN, PUS, RICKETTS, EHRMAN, CHAPLIN, CHILCOTT
MOD: PS/SOS, CDS, CGS, PUS, WEBB, PIGOTT
DFID: PS/SOS, PUS, BREWER, MILLER, AUSTIN

SUBJECT: PERSONAL: IRAQ: WHAT'S GOING WRONG?

SUMMARY

1. A Baghdad First strategy is needed.  The problems are worst
in the capital, and it is the one place we can't afford to get
it wrong.  But the troops here are tired, and are not providing
the security framework needed.  We need a clear policy on which
Ba'athists can return, a more concerted effort on reconstruction,
and an imaginative approach on the media.  For all this, money
needs to be released by Washington.  The clock is ticking.

DETAIL

2. Four days in Iraq has been enough to identify the main reasons
why the reconstruction of Iraq is so slow.  The Coalition are
widely welcomed, but are gradually losing public support.

3. Garner's outfit, ORHA, is an unbelievable mess.  No
leadership, no strategy, no co-ordination, no structure, and
inaccessible to ordinary Iraqis.  Bremer's arrival is not a day
too soon, and he needs to be radical.  Garner and his top team
of 60-year old retired generals are well-meaning but out of their
depth.  Tim Cross is widely seen as the only senior figure
offering direction to the many able individuals here from the US,
Britain and Australia.  Garner points to a glass half-full, but
much of this is despite, not because of ORHA.  The political
point is that progress is lagging behind the reasonable
expectations of ordinary Iraqis.

4. I have not yet been out of the capital, but it is clear that
Baghdad is the biggest problem.  Other parts of Iraq are getting
organised: there are minimal Shia/Sunni tensions; town councils
have been agreed in the sensitive cities of Mosul and Kirkuk;
and so on. But Baghdad has the worst security, a poor level
of essential services, and no information flow.  I will
recommend to Bremer a Baghdad First strategy.  We can afford
some of the regions to languish.  But failure in Baghdad would
be fatally undermine our success in the conflict.  What
would such an approach require?

SECURITY
```

5. No progress is possible until security improves. Crime is widespread (not surprising as Saddam released all the criminals last autumn). Car-jackings are endemic, with the cars driven to Iran for sale. Last week the Ministry of Planning was re-kitted out ready to resume work; that night it was looted again. The evening air is full of gunfire. There is still a climate of fear on the streets, because of the level of crime, and that is casting a shadow over all else.

6. A big part of the problem is the US Third Infantry Division. They fought a magnificent war, exhausted themselves and now just want to go home. Unlike more mobile US units like the marines (now gone) and the 101st Airborne Division (in Mosul), 3rd Inf Div are sticking to their heavy vehicles and combat gear, and are not inclined to learn new techniques. Our Paras company at the Embassy witnessed a US tank respond to (harmless) Kalashnikov fire into the air from a block of residential flats by firing three tank rounds into the building. Stories are numerous of US troops sitting on their tanks parked in front of public buildings while looters go about their business behind them. Every civilian who approaches a US checkpoint is treated as a potential suicide bomber. Those trying to set up Baghdad's police find the military here a hindrance, not a help. Frankly, the 3rd Inf Div need to go home now, and be garlanded as victors, but sadly that isn't due for several weeks. Can it be brought forward?

7. The military culture in the capital needs to change before their replacements (another heavy armour division) arrives. We, the Brits, do not have all the answers, but an operational UK presence in Baghdad is worth considering, despite the obvious political problem. Transferring one of our two brigades is presumably out of the question, but one battalion with a mandate to deploy into the streets could still make an impact. CGS saw the problem last Friday and can offer more professional advice. There are US units who could also contribute if there is any gap in coverage to be filled.

8. Re-forming the Baghdad police has begun, but needs to be accelerated. I visited them today and the work is being pushed forward by an excellent team of US military police and two civilian advisers (one a Brit). It is beginning to happen but is not getting the priority it needs. The police need to start patrolling with sympathetic soldiers, rather than with one police car sandwiched between four Humvees. Weapons, uniforms, funds, vehicles, access to fuel and a functioning judicial process are all problems. Bringing Kurdish Peshmerga down to the capital, as Barzani and Talebani are suggesting as a stopgap, would be at best only one small part of the solution. There is already a risk of Iraqi Arabs reacting against the prominent Kurdish role in the apres-guerre.

DE-BA'ATHIFICATION

9. The other fear among ordinary people in Baghdad is that the Ba'athists could still come back. ORHA have made mistakes here, appointing quite senior party figures as their main partners in the trade and health ministries, at Baghdad University and so on. Several political leaders I have seen say a line should be drawn at the "firqa" level of the Ba'ath Party and all those at that level and the three above should be excluded, about 30,000 in all.

This would represent between five and ten per cent of total party membership. But it is still a lot of people and may be one level too many, at least for now. Whatever, we need to set out a clear policy, plus a process for dealing with contested cases, even though it means starting again in some institutions.

RECONSTRUCTION

10. With security and credible de-Ba'athification will come the chance for durable reconstruction. Power is back, though the network is not robust. Water is running but is not potable. 40% of Baghdad's sewage is said to be pouring into the Tigris untreated, contributing to disease downstream. Garbage is piling up on the streets, and will be a health hazard here. A GSM mobile phone system is desperately needed in the capital as communications are dire. And so on. Bechtel, who have the main contract for re-connecting essential services, are moving far too slowly. They need to swamp Baghdad with engineers and skilled labour. They will have no difficulty in finding local workers.

11. Quick results projects are also needed to show there is progress on the way. We need visibly successful projects, however small: schools and hospitals re-opening, new bakeries, food distribution points. That is not a substitute for long term development, but it would meet genuine needs and also the political requirement. DfID and USAID could play a role here, as well as NGOs and the UN.

INFORMATION

12. Baghdad has no TV, and no newspapers apart from party political rags. I was given two fliers yesterday by an Iraqi, one calling for the assassination of all Ba'athists, the other for the killing of all US forces. That, and rumour, are the only information flowing. An ORHA TV project is due to get going next week but its content will be tightly controlled by ORHA, and it risks not being credible. I have pressed them, as a start, to broadcast a Premier League game each day, but the Americans don't yet get it.

13. More progress is being made with radio: the BBC (English and Arabic) should be up on FM this week. But, as all political leaders have stressed, Baghdad needs independent newspapers, radio stations and terrestial TV stations. One idea is to give satellite dishes and screens to cafes so that people can have access to pan-Arab channels - but it needs funding.

14. ORHA also needs a public face. Bremer's people already have this in mind, as ORHA's bunker image is painfully apparent. Security and the threat of swamping are real problems. But they are better than isolation and ignorance.

FUNDS AND PUBLIC SECTOR SALARIES

15. Finally, money needs to be available, not least to pay police and public service workers. This is held up in Washington (as ORHA gleefully point out). First, the US Administration are refusing to release Iraqi money to pay salaries - even the $740m in cash found here is being blocked (unlike the cash our troops found in Basra). That on its own should be enough to pay salaries into 2004. Second, early decisions are needed on salary levels and which

currency (dollars, Saddam dinars, or new Swiss dinars) should be used. The actual decisions are less important than getting them taken, so that a big information campaign can begin to distribute back pay in mid-June.

15.   There are hundreds of small problems needing attention - petrol and cooking fuel distribution, paying farmers for this season's harvest and so on.   But the big five are as set out above, and security is both the most important and the most sensitive.   There will be an instinct in Washington to allow Bremer time to find his feet and reach his own conclusions. But that will take another week or more - and the clock is ticking. I will talk to him once he gets here, but will have to feel my way at first.   No harm if the ground in Washington can be prepared.

16.   I am reporting separately about politics.

Contact: iraqrep@gtnet.gov.uk.; +88 216 521 00272

SAWERS

YYYY

SVLNAN 7523

NNNN

British assessment by John Sawers on declining security
and Bremer's argument for more troops, June 25, 2003

SIC
FROM SPECIAL REPRESENTATIVE FOR IRAQ

SUBJECT: IRAQ: PROGRESS REPORT

SUMMARY

1. Security has worsened in Baghdad, especially at night. Continued attacks against the Coalition in the Sunni triangle. Majar al-Kabir was the first major incident in the Shia south. Sabotage of the infrastructure is a new threat. Law and order capability is slowly improving, but Bremer is concerned that the troop draw down may have gone too far.

2. Unemployment remains very high. Salaries and pensions help keep people going but aren't substitute for economic activity. CPA economic policy is becoming more coherent. We have to resolve whether our net obligations are to help reform the economy or preside over the Saddam era structures with minimum change. De Mello is inclined to the former.

3. The political process is edging forward. The UN are on board and would like to move more quickly. A big effort will be needed to line up all the party leaders in an agreed Political Council by mid-July. Moderate Shia leaders are coming under pressure as problems persist with essential services. With Muqtadr al-Sadr's return from Iran, the Shia radicals are becoming more active. Retaining Shia support is a sine qua non.

DETAIL

4. It has been a difficult week in Iraq. Fire fights between Coalition forces and Iraqi groups have been more frequent, with the Majar al-Kabir incident the worst. That seems to have been due to local causes and is in a known volatile area, but it shows how thin is the veneer of security in many parts of Iraq. Our law and order capability in Iraq is slowly improving, with police numbers rising and retraining beginning. The Courts and prison systems are also edging

back up bit by bit. The need to transform Saddams brutal structures makes it a slow process.

5. US operations against hostile targets in the Sunni areas seem to have had some effect. Only two US soldiers were killed in action in the last week, but the number of incidents remains high—over 20 a day. Fortunately, ethnically-mixed cities like Kirkuk and Mosul remain calm and there are no significant Arab/Kurd or Shia/Sunni flashpoints.

6. The new threat is well-targeted sabotage of the infrastructure. An attack on the power grid last weekend had a series of knock-on effects which halved the power generation in Baghdad and many other parts of the country. That in turn cut off the water supply. Much of Baghdad has been without electricity and running water for the last three days. The oil and gas network is another target, with five successful attacks this week on pipelines. We do not yet have an answer to this threat. We are also seeing the first signs for intimidation of Iraqis working for the Coalition.

7. Bremer's main concern is that we must keep in-country sufficient military capability to ensure a security blanket across the country. He has twice said to President Bush that he is concerned that the draw down of US/UK troops has gone too far, and we cannot afford further reductions. US forces are down to 80 percent of end-conflict levels, UK forces have reduced further to 40 percent. While other national contingents are welcome, he questions whether they will be sufficiently robust when push turns to shove. General Reith assured Bremer today that we have the necessary forces in the south, and can reinforce if necessary.

The Economy

8. The attacks on the infrastructure are making it more difficult to build up electricity supply and to restart Iraq's economy. Food distribution is running smoothly, and the CPA are catching up with the backlog of salary payments to the public sector. The decision on military pensions has gone down well and protests on that front have gone quiet. But unemployment remains at an estimated 60 percent, and handouts arent a substitute for economic activity.

9. Economic policy making in the CPA is beginning to come together. As usual with the Americans, they start with the most radical ideas but usually end up with a more modest decision. An emergency budget for the rest of the year should be finalised in two weeks. A limited IMF-backed currency reform is in hand. Bremer is working up plans for a social safety net.

10. But there are big issues ahead: how do we get Iraq's state-owned industries running again? Can we attract foreign investment? How can the controls on the Iraqi economy and society be lifted to encourage enterprise? The World Bank and the IMF are pressing for reform of Iraqs state-controlled economy. Some say this would be contrary to our legal obligations. Others point to the requirements of SCR 1483 where the Coalition must promote the welfare of the Iraqi people, must effectively administer the country, and must restore conditions of security and stability (which covers the economy as much as civil society). De Mello told me today he favours more change, not less, and he regrets not doing more in East Timor when he had the power. We need to engage in this debate and do so in the knowledge that failing to get the economy moving will make it more difficult to achieve a successful transition. Political Process

11. Standing up a roughly 25 member Political Council by mid-July remains the goal. The main party leaders are playing hard to get. The Americans will need to twist Chalabi's arm to get him to take part personally. If he distances himself, then it will be harder to get other party leaders to join up. The UN Representative, de Mello, is supportive of our approach and asked me today why we couldn't move more quickly. I explained that we had to allow internal figures to come forward, and work for broad consensus among the parties, but we were stepping up the pace.

12. In the medium term, my main concern is the Shia. The continued problem with security and essential services means that moderate Shia leaders are coming under pressure as their communities question whether supporting the Coalition is the right approach. Meanwhile, the Iranians are adding to their options in Iraq by cultivating the young Najaf radical, Muqtadr Al-Sadr, and that is worrying the moderate clerics. SCIRI, the pro-Iran party we are working with, are facing some tricky decisions. Iraqis remain resistant to Iranian attempts to exert influence. But the biggest threat in the next year is that, for a

mix of reasons, we lose the Shia heartlands. The Iranians seem to be position-ing themselves so they can make that threat more real.

CPA

13. The CPA is gradually strengthening itself. Bremer has found his feet, and he is open to our concerns when we articulate them. The arrival of key figures like Slocombe, Bearpark and Belka have improved the top team. Bearpark's first task is to build up the regional structure, especially CPA South which re-mains in a sorry state. The South is going to remain a UK responsibility, and we should not shed tears if the Dane, Olsen, opts to leave. Rather, we should seize the chance to put in a top quality Brit.

14. The other big gap is Communications Director. John Buck has done an ex-cellent job over the last month, but the White House have let Bremer down and failed to find a good quality candidate prepared to spend the next 8 months in Baghdad. This is a crucial problem: we cannot communicate easily with the Iraqi people and that remains a fundamental weakness of the Coalition. We need someone to tackle that problem.

CONCLUSION

15. It's three steps forward and two steps back. We have to carry on steadily building up the Coalitions and Iraqs capabilities, and putting out fires where they occur. We cannot allow those responsible for killing Coalition soldiers and destroying Iraq's infrastructure to think they can get away with it. Nor should we despair: it was always on the cards that security would get worse before it improved. We just have to make sure we have the right resources, people and level of effort to keep driving this forward, including through August when the West might be on holiday but the terrorists and saboteurs won't be.

SAWERS

YYYY

WSLNAN 9565

SUBJECT: IRAQ: POLITICAL CONSULTATIONS, 19 JUNE

SUMMARY

1. Iraqi and Coalition agreement on the need to establish a Political Council rapidly. Coalition more concerned than Iraqis to see a Constitutional Conference convened soon. Bremer concludes that he hopes both will be established by the end of July.

DETAIL

2. Ambassador Bremer and I held a second expanded political consultation with Iraqi representatives on 19 June. 24 Iraqis were present, including the seven political parties, Pachachl and Sherif Ali. Over half were Shia, and there was even balance (for the first time) of externals and internals. Four women were invited, though one failed to show.

3. Bremer opened the meeting with the Coalition objective: a free Iraq at peace with its neighbours and governed by a democratically elected government representative of all strands of society. Getting there would be a challenge, since Iraq was a complex country. The Coalition wanted to move quickly to establish the interim administration provided for by UNSCR 1483, with a Political Council (PC) and a Constitutional Conference (CC).

4. The PC, with 20–30 members, would have substantial executive authority and responsibility from the time it was created. It would have two immediate tasks: to propose men and women who could run the Ministries, and to advise the Coalition on long-term strategic issues which would determine the kind of society we had in Iraq, for example on regulation of political parties and educational and judicial reforms. Bremer said that he imagined that the PC would establish a series of commissions or councils of experts. The PC would consider the experts recommendations, and forward proposals to the Coalition for action or decision. The PCs actions would have an impact in Iraq long after the Coalition left.

5. Bremer continued that the 1970 interim constitution did not provide a basis for democratic elections. A new constitution would be needed. He envisaged a

Constitutional Conference of 100–200 representatives of all strands of Iraqi society. It would meet and select a drafting committee. The drafting of a new constitution would be by Iraqis for Iraqis. There should be a very intense dialogue between the drafters and the people: Bremer envisaged a series of meetings with town councils, governorate representatives and others. Once the constitution was agreed by the CC, there would be a referendum and an election. He could not say how long this would take: that was for Iraqis to decide. As soon as there were elections, a fully sovereign Iraqi government would be formed.

6. Bremer asked for input on the process, and for ideas for people to be on the PC and CC. He stressed that President Bush and the Prime Minister were in complete agreement on these issues.

Political Council

7. There appeared to be consensus on the need to establish the PC rapidly, many arguing that establishing the PC was essential to achieving security. None argued for more time. Dr Othman (Al-Khair Financial Investment Company) said that an interim administration should have been established by now, but Iraqis as well as the Coalition were to blame for the delay. Mehdi (SCIRI) said that the PC should be established within a few weeks, and urged Bremer to set a date, which Bremer said he would do.

8. Sheikh Qizwini (Hilla Religious University) raised the powers of the PC, arguing that the PC should have to approve all Interim Administration decisions. He also put forward ideas for the PCs own organisation and chairmanship; and urged the need for clear laws. Bremer replied that the 1969 Criminal Code was, by his order, in effect and being implemented. On 17 July he had ordered that the 1971 Criminal Procedure should apply, with three amendments (defendant to have the right to legal representation from the moment of appointment of an investigative judge; right to silence; torture outlawed). Iraqi laws were being applied in Iraqi courts. He said that the internal organisation of the PC would be for its members: he could envisage an elected Chair and Vice-Chair, or a rotating Chair, or a Standing Committee of 3–5 members to act as Chair. He undertook that, once the interim administration was established, the CPA would not take any major decisions without prior consultation of the PC.

Constitutional Conference

9. There was much less sense of urgency over the Constitution. Sheikh Qizwini said that the political process should focus on the PC for the time being: the CC came later. Drafting a constitution would take 2–3 years. Ibrahim Shaboot (Islamic Democratic Trend) Talabani (PUK) and Jaafari (Da-wa) also counselled patience. Nabil Musawi (INC) and Mukliss argued that a referendum on the kind of state (republic/monarchy) was necessary before calling a CC (there is a surprising degree of support for the constitutional monarchy among the politicians). Ibrahim Bahr al-Ulum, speaking on behalf of his father, argued for a directly elected CC, however long direct elections would take, a point echoed by SCIRI and Dawa.

10. I endorsed Bremers opening statement about the strength of President Bushs and the Prime Ministers agreement and desire for progress, and expressed concern at the implications of having a directly elected CC. Ideally, we would want elected representatives too. But an election would require a census, a register of electors and agreement on electoral boundaries. Did we really want to wait for 6–9 months before starting on the constitution. That could mean that elections were two years away. The alternative would be to bring together a CC representing all the main strands of opinion and traditions in Iraq, and ensure that it consulted widely and that the resulting constitution was put to a referendum for adoption.

Services

11. A few of those attending a political consultation for the first time argued that politics was not the key issue. Dr Othman said that Baghdad remained a paralysed city. Traffic, electricity, water, telephones, unemployment and salaries were most important. Iraqis should be addressing these; the US should stay in camps outside the cities. Bremer said that services and security were first priority. Baghdad was far better than when he arrived, 5 weeks ago. More than USD 500 million had been paid to the Iraqi people in the past 3 weeks alone. Petrol supplies were no longer a problem. 85,000 canisters of LPG for cooking were being distributed every day. He did not accept that the Coalition was not doing everything it could to improve services.

Conclusion

12. Bremer concluded that it was urgent to establish the PC, and important to establish the CC. He hoped both would be established by the end of July. He added that he was anxious to demonstrate that Iraqis were taking responsibility for Iraq. Recognising concerns expressed earlier by Dr Pachachi (IID), Bremer said he would be going to the World Economic Forum meeting in Amman this weekend with a party of Iraqis. He also said that there would be an Iraqi voting member on the Programme Review Board he had established to determine how to spend the Development Fund for Iraq (into which oil revenues would be paid), and that the International Advisory and Monitoring Board for the Fund would include Iraqis.

COMMENT

13. A polished performance from Bremer, and a constructive meeting, revealing a large measure of agreement on the Political Council. The discussions (reported separately) on the currency and payment to the ex-military, were also constructive.

14. I shall offer further comment on the direction of the political process over the weekend.

SAWERS

Decree that officially dissolved the Iraqi army

COALITION PROVISIONAL AUTHORITY ORDER NUMBER 2

DISSOLUTION OF ENTITIES

Pursuant to my authority as Administrator of the Coalition Provisional Authority (CPA), relevant U.N. Security Council resolutions, including Resolution 1483 (2003), and the laws and usages of war,

Reconfirming all of the provisions of General Franks' Freedom Message to the Iraqi People of April 16, 2003,

Recognizing that the prior Iraqi regime used certain government entities to oppress the Iraqi people and as instruments of torture, repression and corruption,

Reaffirming the Instructions to the Citizens of Iraq regarding Ministry of Youth and Sport of May 8, 2003,

I hereby promulgate the following:

Section 1
Dissolved Entities

The entities (the "Dissolved Entities") listed in the attached Annex are hereby dissolved. Additional entities may be added to this list in the future.

Section 2
Assets and Financial Obligations

1) All assets, including records and data, in whatever form maintained and wherever located, of the Dissolved Entities shall be held by the Administrator of the CPA ("the Administrator") on behalf of and for the benefit of the Iraqi people and shall be used to assist the Iraqi people and to support the recovery of Iraq.

2) All financial obligations of the Dissolved Entities are suspended. The Administrator of the CPA will establish procedures whereby persons claiming to be the beneficiaries of such obligations may apply for payment.

3) Persons in possession of assets of the Dissolved Entities shall preserve those assets, promptly inform local Coalition authorities, and immediately turn them over, as directed by those authorities. Continued possession, transfer, sale, use, conversion, or concealment of such assets following the date of this Order is prohibited and may be punished.

CPA/ORD/23 May 2003/02

Section 3
Employees and Service Members

1) Any military or other rank, title, or status granted to a former employee or functionary of a Dissolved Entity by the former Regime is hereby cancelled.

2) All conscripts are released from their service obligations. Conscription is suspended indefinitely, subject to decisions by future Iraq governments concerning whether a free Iraq should have conscription.

3) Any person employed by a Dissolved Entity in any form or capacity, is dismissed effective as of April 16, 2003. Any person employed by a Dissolved Entity, in any form or capacity, remains accountable for acts committed during such employment.

4) A termination payment in an amount to be determined by the Administrator will be paid to employees so dismissed, except those who are Senior Party Members as defined in the Administrator's May 16, 2003 Order of the Coalition Provisional Authority De-Baathification of Iraqi Society, CPA/ORD/2003/01 ("Senior Party Members") (See Section 3.6).

5) Pensions being paid by, or on account of service to, a Dissolved Entity before April 16, 2003 will continue to be paid, including to war widows and disabled veterans, provided that no pension payments will be made to any person who is a Senior Party Member (see Section 3.6) and that the power is reserved to the Administrator and to future Iraqi governments to revoke or reduce pensions as a penalty for past or future illegal conduct or to modify pension arrangements to eliminate improper privileges granted by the Baathist regime or for similar reasons.

6) Notwithstanding any provision of this Order, or any other Order, law, or regulation, and consistent with the Administrator's May 16, 2003 Order of the Coalition Provisional Authority De-Baathification of Iraqi Society, CPA/ORD/2003/01, no payment, including a termination or pension payment, will be made to any person who is or was a Senior Party Member. Any person holding the rank under the former regime of Colonel or above, or its equivalent, will be deemed a Senior Party Member, provided that such persons may seek, under procedures to be prescribed, to establish to the satisfaction of the Administrator, that they were not a Senior Party Member.

CPA/ORD/23 May 2003/02 2

Section 4
Information

The Administrator shall prescribe procedures for offering rewards to person who provide information leading to the recovery of assets of Dissolved Entities.

Section 5
New Iraqi Corps

The CPA plans to create in the near future a New Iraqi Corps, as the first step in forming a national self-defense capability for a free Iraq. Under civilian control, that Corps will be professional, non-political, militarily effective, and representative of all Iraqis. The CPA will promulgate procedures for participation in the New Iraqi Corps.

Section 6
Other Matters

1) The Administrator may delegate his powers and responsibilities with respect to this Order as he determines appropriate. References to the Administrator herein include such delegates.

2) The Administrator may grant exceptions any limitations in this Order at his discretion.

Section 7
Entry into Force

This Order shall enter into force on the date of signature.

L. Paul Bremer, Administrator
Coalition Provisional Authority

CPA/ORD/23 May 2003/02　　　　　　　　3

ANNEX

COALITION PROVISIONAL AUTHORITY ORDER NUMBER 2

DISSOLUTION OF ENTITIES

Institutions dissolved by the Order referenced (the "Dissolved Entities") are:

The Ministry of Defence
The Ministry of Information
The Ministry of State for Military Affairs
The Iraqi Intelligence Service
The National Security Bureau
The Directorate of National Security (Amn al-'Am)
The Special Security Organization

All entities affiliated with or comprising Saddam Hussein's bodyguards to include:
-Murafaqin (Companions)
-Himaya al Khasa (Special Guard)

The following military organizations:
-The Army, Air Force, Navy, the Air Defence Force, and other regular
military services
-The Republican Guard
-The Special Republican Guard
-The Directorate of Military Intelligence
-The Al Quds Force
-Emergency Forces (Quwat al Tawari)

The following paramilitaries:
-Saddam Fedayeen
-Ba'ath Party Militia
-Friends of Saddam
-Saddam's Lion Cubs (Ashbal Saddam)

Other Organizations:
-The Presidential Diwan
-The Presidential Secretariat
-The Revolutionary Command Council
-The National Assembly
-The Youth Organization (al-Futuwah)
-National Olympic Committee
-Revolutionary, Special and National Security Courts

CPA/ORD/23 May 2003/02   4

All organizations subordinate to the Dissolved Entities are also dissolved.

Additional organizations may be added to this list in the future.

Index

Page numbers in *italics* refer to maps.

A Note on the Type

The text of this book was set in Sabon, a typeface designed by Jan Tschichold (1902–1974), the well-known German typographer. Based loosely on the original designs by Claude Garamond (c. 1480–1561), Sabon is unique in that it was explicitly designed for hotmetal composition on both the Monotype and Linotype machines as well as for filmsetting. Designed in 1966 in Frankfurt, Sabon was named for the famous Lyons punch cutter Jacques Sabon, who is thought to have brought some of Garamond's matrices to Frankfurt.

Composed by Creative Graphics, Allentown, Pennsylvania
Printed and bound by Berryville Graphics, Berryville, Virginia
Designed by Wesley Gott